Military Secret

Robert David Graham

Las Colinas
Monument Press
1993

Published by
Monument Press
Las Colinas, Texas

Library of Congress Cataloging-in-Publication Data

Graham, Robert David, 1956-
Military secret / by Robert David Graham.
p. cm.
ISBN 0-930383-41-9 (pbk.) : $30.00
1. United States. Navy--Gays. 2. Graham, Robert David, 1956-
3. Seamen--United States--Biography. I. Title.
VB324.G38G37 1993
359'.008'6642--dc20
[B] 93-32602
CIP

For Sharon

Robert David Graham

Introduction

I joined the Navy in January, 1988. I was a writer, and like most of us, unemployed--or, shall I say, between projects. I had thought about the military several times since I first read Robb White's World War II novel *The Survivor*, and always wanted to be, or play act, a war hero.

I started college at age sixteen, two years ahead of my peers, and took Army ROTC at the University of Missouri-Columbia, while frat rats shot blanks at us during marching drills. I was going to be an airborne Ranger. My favorite song was Sgt. Barry Sadler's "Ballad of the Green Beret." I was barely too young for Vietnam, but talked a fellow karate kid into joining Navy Seals. He was older, and served in Cambodia when we "weren't there." A buddy of his got killed there months after Vietnam was officially over. As for me, this twelve year old blond kid named Billy told me not to go, and I obeyed him because I loved him so much. Then somehow I forgot about the military.

When I suddenly found myself 31 years old, I decided I owed it to myself as a writer, and to my audience if ever I got that chance, to trade in my happy gay lucky sex life, sans AIDS, and go "straight" for four years, behind our military lines.

I had a great time, even got my war, even got five medals and a hero's welcome home to San Diego. I served on *USS Ranger*, the night carrier in the Persian Gulf, flagship of Battle Group Echo, the ship that initiated Operation Desert Storm with the first air strike, and launched the very last load of extra special bombs on Saddam's bunkers.

I took part in the biggest military venture in modern US history. But I also found out more than I wanted to know about our military system. I found out how people could "smile and smile and be a villain," as Hamlet said. I experienced first hand the treachery and deceit of the buddies and chronies who made up the system, and most distressing of all, how problems faded away without resolution as you grew in the military. The worst part is at the bottom, and by the time you try to correct anything, you get promoted and preoccupied with a whole new set of problems. Those at the top can't help being out of touch.

By the time I was due to get out, I knew that the worst problem of all--blatant and rampant anti-homosexual bigotry of middle management--was just one more problem I would forget about as soon as my tour ended. So with eight weeks to go in my enlistment, I took action while I still gave a damn.

I wrote a letter to Dick Cheney, Secretary of Defense, in which I characterized myself as "a gay man in the military," and criticized the system for promoting sexual bigotry. Within two weeks I was tapped on the shoulder by my squadron's legal officer, and after three years, ten months and 22 days of a four-year contract, with shore duty pending, I was administratively discharged from the United States Navy with a certificate that reads, as the reason: "homosexuality--stated he is a homosexual."

During the last year, without knowing we would go to war, I began a journal. I was going to call it *The Missing Beach Diary* after Mission Beach, CA, where I lived in a beach pad for the time leading up to our war mission. The joke was that you could end up "missing" in Mission Beach, because it was a good place to gay bash.

Then I was going to call it *Sailor Boy*, using the slogan of the Philippine Island whores. But the right title finally came to mind.

Military Secret isn't just about being homosexual without your best friend knowing. The real secret is how the Navy system openly promoted sexual bigotry. In fact, you can't use the word "nigger" today without facing legal prosecution and fines in the Navy. But an acceptable replacement is the word "fag."

This book covers more than just the sexual bigotry. It is my war story. My sea story. And my life story. I don't smoke, and the Navy officially supported me to that end--but in reality, my chain of command consisted mostly of chain smokers. I had to share an office with virtually zero ventilation and a bunch of chain smoking khakis. I had a hell of a time accepting the facade between what was said and done. This is 20th century Navy life.

I never planned to make this my career, and if you ask me I succeeded in doing exactly what I set out to do. I had a great adventure. And I loved. But I might have stayed in, and I knew a few good men who could have done our country a great service by staying in. I watched them get out, and thought about why.

This book is my attempt to reflect how Navy people treated me as a person--and, sometimes, as a suspected homosexual. It's as honest and frank as I could be. Let's call it semi-fiction, and call the incriminating passages the fictional parts. I hope you'll keep in mind, this book was written under a great deal of stress--not the least of which was a combat zone.

There's some Navy lingo to wade through, and that makes it a world of its own. But every specialty has its own language--I remember when I didn't know what a stinger was and called myself a grip, in Hollywood. A stinger's an extension cord, and a grip is an electrician. Get somebody who's been there to tell you what I'm saying.

I've tried to catch the buzzwords and explain them as they come, but if you find you're lost, consider yourself wandering around on an aircraft carrier. The best thing to do is get lost, and find a new way out each time. After about twenty times, you'll never get lost again.

I've included a few original song lyrics in here. And some other text that may assault your eyes include messages, presented upper case like those mysterious voices on the 1MC, the *Ranger*'s public address system.

For the sailors, I called them by rate or by nickname. I fell in love with a beautiful man who was straight, so to protect him from the world, I've called him Sweet Pea, or Sweets in my book.

He was my Sailor Boy, I guess. And my military secret.

Robert D. Graham

Los Angeles 1992

ADMINISTRATIVE REMARKS
NAVPERS 1070/613 (Rev 3-91)
N 0106-LF-010-6990

E-32

SHIP OR STATION
CARRIER AIR WING TWO, FPO SAN FRANCISCO 96601-4401

OPERATION DESERT STORM

CARRIER AIR WING TWO

SERVING ABOARD

U.S.S. RANGER CV-61

On 2 August 1990, without provocation, the Iraqi army invaded and overran its peaceful neighbor Kuwait, quickly positioning itself for further incursion into Saudi Arabia. On 17 January 1991, following six months of unsuccessful negotiations, a coalition of twenty-six countries, under auspices of the United Nations, launched Operation Desert Storm to liberate Kuwait.

Let all who read this be informed that

PN2 ROBERT DAVID GRAHAM

was an active participant in Operation Desert Storm and served with great honor in the greatest military victory in modern history. He was an integral part of the United Nations Coalition Forces that defeated Iraq in a swift forty-three day offensive that returned the country of Kuwait to its rightful leadership.

CONGRATULATIONS ON A JOB WELL DONE!

J. A. Campbell,
Captain, U.S. Navy
Air Wing Commander

NAME (Last, First, Middle)	SSN	BRANCH AND CLASS
GRAHAM, ROBERT DAVID	493-62-1420	USN

13 10

Chapter One

Onboard *USS Ranger* 15 Jul 90

I've been ordered TAD (Temporary Additional Duty) from my shop, the Personnel Department of Fighter Squadron ONE (also known as VF-1, the world famous Fighting Wolfpack), to the Forward Galley onboard *USS Ranger* for ATA (Airwing Tactical Assessment) through the month of July.

This is our next to last exercise off SOCAL Ops (Southern California Operations) before deploying to the Western Pacific and Indian Oceans for six months; and comes as VF-1 just won the Admiral Joseph Clifton Award for being the best fighter squadron in the US Navy.

I am a PN3 (Personnelman Third Class, or Third Class Petty Officer), a rate and pay grade where the emphasis is intermittently bestowed on "petty" or "officer" depending on the situation. In my shop it was on "petty," so they sent me TAD to the mess decks where the emphasis now is on "officer."

I supervised an average of four NONPO's (nonpetty officers), which usually means kids about 18 to 21, in an operation about like McDonald's or Denney's.[1] The shift is 0800 to 2030 (8:00 a.m. to 8:30 p.m.) Monday through Sunday. If I had stayed in my shop, I'd be typing memos and service record entries and filing documents pertaining to the squadron's enlisted personnel, 0700 to 1930 Monday to Sunday.

I am in my rack in the 39-Man coop, about six feet under catapult one (of four). A few shipmates are sitting around the lounge under the TV talking about not being able to actually touch the toilet seat because of the nastiness of this naval vessel that is carrying the Navy's best F-14 squadron.

Above us, on the flight deck of this metal razorblade fodder of a ship, I hear the whir of a turbo-prop turning, and bootsteps of a blueshirt chock and chain gang preparing to park aircraft as the flight ops wind down.

Occasionally, more guys filter in and across the dim, red lit berthing area (coop) to racks like mine: three high, with a 2" mattress. In the coop each section has six racks bolted together as two sides of an aisle. The sheets are white and the paint is all pale yellow.

I'm better off with a top rack because I can sit up, although there's a girder five inches above my head now. I've learned not to raise up carelessly at reveille, since the light rack is deceptively unobtrusive. If I don't tuck my head to my shoulders, I catch the edge of my bald forehead on the light's knife-edge housing. You'd think a guy would only have to do that once. But

---

[1] A quick note about pronouncing Navy jargon: TAD is T-A-D and NONPO is NON-P-O. COMFIT and CAG are like they look. You sound them out by syllable most of the time, but COMFITAEWWINGPAC would be COMFIT-A-E-W-WINGPAC. Hours like 0800 are said like zero eight hundred or oh-eight hundred; 2000 is twenty hundred.

it's just like the knee-knockers (raised passageways): once you think you're used to it, lookout.[2]

My knee sticks into the aisle through the break in the blue cotton curtains. My boots are stored on top of the set of six shirt-sized, stacked lockers. My other knee grazes the metal sheet separating mine from another rack to my left as I face the neon light bar above my pillow. I have a clear view of the dozens of cables feeding power throughout the forward area of the 03 level of Ranger. There are worse places to sleep than six feet under a catapult. Like the arresting cables.

At least I hear a sort of warning, in the form of a growing crescendo, as metal slides on metal when the cat fires to hurl a jet off the bow. As it reaches a spot directly over my rack, the mechanism slams into a water brake, whatever that is, that shakes the entire forward section of the carrier and probably damages the fibers inside my ears. According to my latest hearing test, there was no substantial deterioration since last year. But they put me on a hearing conservation program then (which means, gave me a personal set of earplugs). After the slam-knock, I hear the quick drag of a chain as they retract the cat, followed by the gurgle of steam as it's charged for the next launch, or cat shot.

Now comes the vague, two-tone British cop siren indicating preparations for the recovery (trap) cycle, probably doing night quals, a cat-trap-cat dance for JO's (junior officers). It can be rough. Last time out, *Ranger* had a "rag" (training) squadron onboard. Some JO hit the deck so hard his jet knocked the vent system off the ceiling in the 81-Man coop (Wolfpack's largest berthing, located aft beneath the arresting wires). Boots (kids fresh out of bootcamp) back there get no warning, just: WHAM! Yaaannnkk, as the cable returns.

"One oh three on deck."

Boots have been known to jump out of their racks when they first hear a jet land on *Ranger*. After a while, though, you wonder if you'd sleep through a major conflagration, like the *USS Forrestal* in Vietnam, where bombs went off on deck.

I hear the tractors hauling jets to their parking spots on cat one, so they won't be shooting anymore above me tonight. Once I hear the chocks drop I'll nod off. (The blue shirts know I sleep down here, so they toss the heavy metal wheel stoppers, called chocks, hard as they can. It's a way of saying "hi.")

We have GQ (General Quarters, or Battle Stations) in the morning. My back is killing me so I took a Motrin a while ago. I screwed it up last night.

---

[2] A note about levels: the hangar deck is level 1. Going down they are 2, 3, etc. I think Ranger has 7 before you hit the hull. Going up it's 01, 02, 03, up to, I believe, 09. The mess decks are at level 2, and my normal shop, VF-1 Personnel, is on level 02. But there are guys who work on carriers for years who still get lost. So don't worry if you're confused.

At zero one hundred (1:00 a.m.), some dude passed through our lounge and flipped on the TV loud enough to wake me. I waited five minutes, then climbed down to investigate the noise. The lounge was empty except for an AT (Avionics Technician) who also woke up. "Some inconsiderate asshole," one of us said.

I flipped it off, and got two hours of sleep before the Line Shack supervisor's alarm went off. And he wasn't there. See, we had a power surge last night, and David was too tired to remember to cancel the alarm when his body clock woke him for work. So it kept beeping until it woke me, and I had to turn it off.

I stuck my head through my curtain, into the aisle to figure out whose alarm was beeping. I leaned down to the middle racks and determined the source across the aisle. I stretched across and down to his rack with only my feet still inside my curtains. Anything to avoid getting up again. I dug around and found his clock, flicked on his rack light and found the off switch. Now I had my head in his middle rack, my feet in my top rack, and my butt in the breeze, straddling the aisle. I reached an arm across and tried vainly to climb back up without getting down on the cold steel deck and nasty tiles in bare feet. I made it, but felt strange pains all through the vertebras in my neck, shoulders and lower back: Slept like a pretzel, woke like a knot. Above, the jet strains against its tie-down chains in the heave-ho of high winds and heavy seas, as the chock-and-chain gang drop chocks farther down amidships. I have my flash hood and gloves out with the Mark V gas mask, ready for GQ whenever it comes. So I'm going to sleep.

16 JUL 90. I got my first long look at the sky since pulling out six days ago. Here you check your watch to tell the day, not the time. I took a break at the starboard fantail between flight ops, and watched a helo practice SAR (Surface Air Rescue) a thousand yards abeam.

I missed the rack light, getting up this morning. But I hit the fucking girder. I made it to breakfast on the forward mess decks at zero seven thirty, and GQ went down at eight. For the next two hours the galley day check (day shift) sat at the aluminum mess tables in cotton flash hoods and gloves (to protect from spark flashes) with their bell bottom dungarees rolled inside their boots, trying to keep awake. In the real thing that would be no problem, but in a drill where these guys are excused from the hose teams, it would make sense to let them snooze, and have a guy on watch wake them up if necessary to simulate bracing for shock for inbound missiles. But common sense is foreign as military intelligence, in the chain of command--and as misappropriated. Put it this way: A girl on the edge of a multiple orgasm squeals "don't ... stop!" The intelligent officer interprets "don't" and before "stop" books the movers. And never looks back. But we're all volunteers, so who's to blame?

A guy told me a military secret tonight. He's been married for a while. Okay. For some reason, looking at the guy, I just had to ask what seems like the strangest question. "Is it to a girl, or a guy?"

"It's a guy," he whispered.

A-hah! He'll get no BAQ or VHA (Bachelor Allowance for Quarters and Variable Housing Allowance, provided to married sailors at sea). And if the Navy finds out, he's outa here. They hadn't even gone to a minister, naturally. "It would be too embarrassing."

Back in Hollywood I was best man in the marriage of my best friend to the girl I was living with and they had a gay minister. He paid her a thousand bucks for a green card, but the deal fell through right before the government granted him amnesty. What the hell, that's Hollywood. It's not the US Navy.

This boy wanted to show me a picture of his--husband, I guess--he's a skinny little effeminate type, so I guess he's the bitch. But some shipmates were milling around. "I'll show you later," he whispered.

Next there's the Puerto Rican working for me down at the forward mess decks. He looked at this other boy. "Your lips, man. I just want to feel them locked around me." He was full of sexual splendor, loud and bold.

"Yeah, I eat butt," the tough young dude boasted.

Several guys heard them, but nobody mentioned calling the captain, or confronted them or called them derogatory names like faggot or queer. Because they must be joking.

When we got to talking about Black's Beach, the famous nude beach ten minutes from Naval Air Station Miramar, where Wolfpack is homeported, I mentioned that it's also a famous gay beach. "I'd kill any faggot who got within five feet of me," said the guy who was just begging this other kid to blow him.

We all sign a contract upon enlisting that asks if we are homosexual or bisexual, or intend to engage in homosexual acts, which are defined as touching or other physical activity including anal intercourse engaged for the purpose of sexual gratification. In my three years as a Personnel Clerk, I've never seen anybody in the fleet who initialed a YES box on those questions. I believe this is why you'll never see two men embrace on a naval vessel, except in time of war or other life threatening, brutally honest moment when pride and dignity are unleashed and our pent up attraction is allowed free reign. The contract used to ask if you had ever been gay, but they dropped that clause a few years back. I wonder why, unless for the same reason they quit asking if you have ever done drugs: Nobody qualified. They say one out of four dudes gets a blow job from another dude by age eighteen.

I can tell a closet case by the way his three initials sway through the "NO" block on the question, "are you now." Kind of like a hurdling swerve, upward in the middle, like Jack jumping a candlestick. These kids grew up in a sexual revolution and came in with drug waivers but never experimented with bisexuality? If you ask me, the Navy breeds liars.

You wonder what happens when sailors play too much grab ass without relief, like on extended cruises. Like we're about to go on. Effeminate, or boyish, cute guys take an emotional taxing--if not physical beating--from brutes onboard. If two dudes really like each other, a brush of the wrist or a back pat makes your dick hard. But you only discuss it in boisterous jest, lest the ever present, ever media conscious chain of command sense the behavior and adjudge you "incompatible with military service." Still, you hear a guy returning from sea casually introduce his pal, one arm hugging around his neck. "This is my sea bitch." The way to be a faggot on the boat, then, is to be loud and explicit, then spice it with a jolt or two of fag bashing heterochismo.

I've got my tee-shirt and underwear, hand washed, drying on the curtain rail. And they're dropping chocks on my head on the flight deck. We have an unrep (underway replenishment) starting, so maybe tomorrow we'll have real milk again. We're using little plastic cartons now, the kind usually served on the Indian Ocean. I don't want to start thinking about that now. I promised this dude I would dream of him tonight.

2200 17 JUL 90. A female chaplain (chaplainette?) read us the evening prayer. She prayed about currents and temptations pulling us all directions, and asked for whatever it takes to make the right decisions. I always wonder what went on all day that gives them input for the evening prayer (nightly at 2155, five minutes before TAPS TAPS, LIGHTS OUT).

The boys in the lounge playing dominoes chafe at the bit for the return of Early Outs, contemplating fat joints in cozy rooms. And a CD plays, "Money-Money-Money-Money" and "The Back-stabbers." Above, they fire "no loads" on cats three and four, testing for a three a.m. strike exercise. Hopefully they won't use cat one, and I'll get to sleep until reveille.

The Navy Federal Credit Union sent me a notice that my rent check bounced on July 5th. I'm 200 miles out to sea. Should I send a money order or tell the landlady to resubmit the check? I don't have envelopes. I can get some tomorrow. My bank account is all fucked up because of car payments that I never had before. Here's how that happened. One night at Mission Beach I walked to Roberto's and got a burrito with Louie, my homeless pal from the Vietnam war. Something looked funny in my carport. "Didn't I park my Toyota there?"

It's odd walking the streets looking for a car that you know you parked in your garage. Evidently, some border town smugglers needed it more than me. It's a plain white station wagon sedan with a military base sticker that allows it to roll through the base and avoid the San Clemente border patrol checkpoint. A hot item for El Coyote. Tomorrow, tomorrow.

These guys are violating Navy policy, hanging around playing Dominoes after Taps. But violations of Navy policy will continue until this ship is razorblades; and anyway having some fun in the other room makes you feel like family, to the extent that one may belong. Especially one like me.

2130 18 JUL 90. Climbing into the top rack is an art. I come from the shower in bath towel and flip-flops--you never shower without shower shoes in the Navy, for obvious reasons if you've ever had a Navy shower: Scum city. I reach up from the aisle and grab the heavy metal curtain rails, one from each top rack in each hand, swing a foot up from a chair to the top of the stand-up lockers and slide my butt onto my mattress, all without losing my towel. Then close the curtains and I'm "home."

My rack light has a strange vibration. As I turn it on it emits this soft murmur which increases until suddenly I smack it, and remember why I didn't become a teacher.

That bounced $375 rent check: I prepared a check for $315 to an unnamed payee, and had $60 cash. The post office sells money orders but won't take personal checks. So, extending my lunch break, I walk from the post office amidships on the 02 level to 39-Man three decks up and half a football field forward to write a new check at my rack, then go back to the post office on the main deck and two more down to disbursing. At the cashier, I find out the daily check writing limit is $250. I don't have my checkbook with me, since after cashing the check and getting the money order I didn't want to walk around the ship all day carrying my checkbook. I go back up five decks and half a ship forward and write a new check for $250, then back down five decks to the cashier and cash the check for $250. Now I have to cash another check for $65 tomorrow, hopefully in time to get my letter out with the COD (also known as Miss Piggy). I assume we'll have a mail run tomorrow.

We had pizza tonight on the forward mess decks, so the place was jammed. The mess crank dude I call Broomstick described with enthusiastic details how he enjoyed anal sex with females. "She kept begging, 'get me in the ass, get me in the ass.' I call it my doggy style surprise."

"I prefer to go about it gently," I said.

"You don't know how to do it," he declared.

I didn't argue. Especially on the mess deck of a US Navy aircraft carrier with a long line of sailors hungry for pizza. "Why is it that women would enjoy a penis in the ass, and men wouldn't? Why should it be so different?"

"Because that's sick," he said without hesitation. "I can't imagine having a dick pokin' up my rectum. Wouldn't it hurt to have a penis poking into your ass?" I hesitated, and he immediately took several steps back and stared guardedly. It was all a joke, of course, in which I learned that men have a physical barrier--maybe a steel plate--which prevents an otherwise identical penetration.

I killed my rack light, and planned to drift to sleep while Clint and the boys took Grenada in the lounge. But soon the ugly waft of second hand cigarette smoke hovered over my nose. 39-Man is a small coop.

In January they began to implement a Smoke Free Navy program to enforce clean air on Naval vessels in support of nonsmokers. If one person in an office says the word, there can be no smoking in that office no matter who smokes or how many smokers share the space. And incorporated in the nightly order Taps is the phrase, "*The smoking lamp is out in all berthing areas.*" I pulled on my sweatpants and climbed out of my rack to see who was breaking the law. The coop cleaner was smoking, watching TV. I like the guy, which is even more important than the fact that I have a lot of respect for him, or even that he has rank over me. And there is the consideration that he is responsible for handing out--and not losing--my laundry. You don't want to fuck with a coop cleaner, no matter who he is. After all, he's the one guarding your rack when you're working. But once down, I felt obligated to explain why I got out of my rack in the first place. "Man, the cigarette smoke is hovering right over my rack and coming right into my nose."

"I'll put it out because it's after taps," he sighed, weary and reluctant. "But you're asking too much. If that's a problem you ought to get off this boat."

I don't know anybody who wants to be here, except Tomcat, our photo-nut lifer who loves to look at jets. Try sleeping on your belly in the bow of a rocking boat--now I know why that sailor in the seventies hit, "Brandy," sang, "my love, my lady, is the sea." Turning in can turn you on.

2200 19 JUL 90. Husbands begin to worry openly. "Tell a mo' fucker I'm goin' out to sea for a month, a'ight? Two days later he comes by the crib. Oh, he ain't home? I guess I missed him. Can I have a glass of water? Man, that's why I don't let nobody know the way to my house. Got to keep my wife off the prowler list."

Jets launch off cat one and I cover my ears as the rod hits the water brake, shaking my rack. Dominoes end at taps, residual awareness of the pointed scene last night. Now the TV is low for some lone, bleary-eyed sailor transiting work and sleep. Occasional flip-flops cross the coop. Distant roars bolt across the flight deck aft, and tie-down chains twist between pad-eyes and mainmounts directly overhead, holding jets down as we steam into the wind.

Finally got off the money order. If Phyllis back at the beach resubmitted my July rent check, and it cleared, she can use the m/o for August since I won't be back on the first. Otherwise I left the August rent check with That Guy.

Broomstick the butt humper straightened me out on his sexual preferences today. He once let a finger slip wiping, and it felt wonderful. He likes a broomstick. But perish the thought of a penis up there. Then he ran across the deck to wipe a table.

We're still getting newspapers from San Dog. Just read of the Baguio quake (in the Philippines). I should dig out some addresses when we get back, and write Ed in Olongapo to see if Jofferey survived. It already feels like Westpac.

1400 20 JUL 90. I've been getting an hour or so off in the afternoons to get away from the mess decks and rest. I usually hit my rack and doze.

At 0400 hours the rumble of dropping anchor woke me up. At 0700 they pulled it up again and we left our spot outside Coronado Island. A big tease that pissed us off.

Rumors fly about our date of return. One says some radar equipment is down, that we'll hit pierside for six hours and pull out again without liberty. Now, *that's* a tease. Another says the new non-skid on the flight deck is too rough, fraying cables when the jets land, causing the arresting wires to stretch and screwing up the mechanism; so we're pulling in early from ATA, the 26th vice August third. We'd all be happy to pull in. But everybody's getting the Westpac itch.

We must be doing twenty knots. I hear the cat steaming up and feel the rack vibrating. It reminds me of growing up in bunk beds with my big brother masturbating below: The bed frame would have this quiet but noticeable rock. At first I figured somebody was masturbating. But once I heard that distinctive squishy sound of someone definitely doing it, and saw that the rack was not rocking, I figured out that the boat has her own way with sailors. The trick is rocking against her. It's best turning into the wind before flight ops, listing and churning through waves, shaking to a throbbing vibration. In heavy seas wave upon wave slaps and churns at her framework. Ooh do I love flight ops.

1045 21 JUL 90. Last night at half past midnight I laid in bed as the sudden series of bell rings, followed by a single bell, indicated a fire up forward. "FIRE FIRE FIRE. *Fire on the flight deck*. Cat One." As the announcement repeated I wondered if an armed F-14 were burning six feet above me. It was worth investigating, rather than dozing off. As I climbed down, the boatswain's mate added, "R Division, man your high caps." High caps are emergency washdown controls reserved for a major fire on the flight deck. Two guys from a backup fire party standing by had already switched to channel nine on the lounge TV, and watched the live show on the roof in black and white from an infrared camera on the bridge. Steam billowed from the cat where a crowd of sailors in float coats (inflatable life vests) and crash suits surrounded the scene. I thought of the safety film "Fire On the Flight deck" about the *USS Forrestal* off Vietnam, where a show just like this added exploding bombs and fire parties flying in bits and pieces. But, after a tense minute, the boatswain's mate whistled again.

"FIRE ON CAT ONE IS OUT."

Now, about that other kind of fire. I was up in the 81-Man coop getting a jersey to complete my GQ outfit. See, VF-1 has a number of guys who look, if not effeminate, at least very sexy in their beauty and youth alone. One of these dudes was playing spades in nothing but a pair of Bermuda shorts. His smooth, slender back faced the corner where, strangely, PN1, my shop supervisor, sat unnoticed, eyes trained through glasses past a smoldering cigarette, like studying porn in some dark sleazy lounge, cigarette ash bending heavy. I thought wryly of his jokes at Miramar, and rubbing guys like frottage at the customer service counter as they came and went, and razzing me for some ability he thinks I have of attracting younger dudes. I wonder if he's a faggot in a contract marriage, hiding under his lady's apron strings. He wouldn't be the first.

1430 21 JUL 90. Once I was a customer. Now I manage the place. Once we deploy, I should hopefully be a customer again.

Last night in the RM (Radioman) lounge I flirted with a skinny dude who finally went to the head and to bed and left me in my US Navy Diver sweats on the couch. Then some other dude erupted with a rag about being called a customer in the mess. Since he didn't pay, he insisted, how was he a customer? This is the kind of stupid argument sailors kill for at sea. I explained that as a manager I'd consider him a customer simply because it was a useful term to distinguish him from the FSA's during training and briefing. I wondered, if I hadn't been there, how long would he have carried this resentment of his identity as a customer for its reminder of the life ashore, which in turn reminded him of being stuck on this bucket a tantalizing few miles off the coast turning donuts. He might have eventually grabbed a machine gun, gone berserk and shot us all. I may have saved numerous lives with my simple explanation in the midst of his rage, by allowing that as a manager I was his target and I had his answer. The truth came out then: He was scheduled to go TAD to the mess decks himself.

2215 21 JUL 90. Some sailors look so young they must have lied about their age to join the Navy. Then, for a select few, even that seems remote, since no recruiter would believe them. They only be considered stowaways; or in some wild guess maybe the Captain's son. Out of the five thousand men on this ship, I have found one or two who fit this description. And made it my business of knowing them. Most beautiful of all these boys, is my beloved young Sweet Pea. "I'm nineteen," he swears.

"Going on fourteen. Well, you're in uniform, and you have a rack, so I guess that's that." I have not seen him meet another sailor who didn't ask him his age, then refuse to believe it.

"Feed him a Coke and candy bar," his buddy Dean says, "and he'll spin like a top for the rest of the night. He bounces off the hangar bay, man. And if you take him to the beach and play Metallica, he'll puff out his chest like a goddamn peacock. If he gets too damn wild, just give him three beers. That knocks him on his ass."

"I like Dr. Pepper because it has the most sugar," he says.

"I wish you were twenty-one," I say. "I'd turn you on to Brave Bulls and get you shit-faced."

"What for?"

"I don't know," I lie. Because the human body is made to be licked and sucked and that's what you need, to quote my college drama teacher. But this is the Navy. And we don't say that.

Louie, the homeless vet, turned me on to the Brave Bull at Mission Beach. One shot tequila, one kalua. On the rocks. You swash it around in your mouth and climb over it, teeth first.

"Robocop" is the big TV movie. He shoots the crook in his nuts through the legs of a woman. Turn down the fires on this boat.

There are, as a matter of fact, several women aboard now. A cute blonde, always comes to the messdeck with a crypto-tech friend of mine, cute little Jimmy the bodybuilder with jet black hair and a few teen-age zits, and a voice that hasn't started to crack yet. I asked if he got lucky yet. He blushed and laughed. This other fine blonde showed up at the bug bar. (We call it bug bar and bug juice, why I have never found out.) She had on PT gear and got water with some stud, her workout partner. He was showing her the ropes, like breaking the rule against PT gear on the messdecks, at the expense of the other four thousand, nine hundred and ninety-eight shipmates who might also prefer to grab water here as go change first when they quit working out. For the good of all, in the interest of fairness, and to avoid a riot, I played the jerk. "You can't stop on the messdecks in PT gear."

"Well, we're not stopping."

"Hey, let it slide, bro," the big Puerto Rican advised.

Just as they sat at a closed table, the chief walked by.

"What's the policy?" He drilled me.

"No PT gear on the messdecks."

"That's right."

"Well, chief. Would you mind explaining it to them?"

I moved out of sight in case I ever ran into her in a bikini at Mission Beach. Still, I thought, that's one way to break the ice if I do.

"You kicked me off the messdecks on *Ranger*."

"That's right, baby. How 'bout a date?"

Sweet Pea came down for chow at 1920, ten minutes before V-3 had to muster in the hangar bay. They maintain that part of the ship, move jets around and run them up to the flight deck on huge elevators.

The nice thing about being a manager, or Red Shirt, is hooking up friends for chow. Like managing a theater and handing out free tickets to friends.

I pointed to a table. He got himself a glass of milk and I walked his tray through the line, got a chicken sandwich, fries and some ketchup. I sat with him, with Broomstick boy watching my deck--who kept poking me for attention--and let Sweet Pea leave his tray with me when he had to run. "The one thing I ask, is that whenever my friend in the blue shirt comes for chow, you let me take a break then and eat with him." I got the concession from my second class supervisor, a fat pig anyway, and didn't give a fuck if it raised an eyebrow.

"I know there's a second class on this deck," the chief told me. "But you're the one in charge."

I hit the gym for the first time since we sailed, rode the bike ten minutes and did sit-ups and leg-lifts. The trash had piled up at the fantail until it backed into the hangar bay by the gym equipment, even trapping some officers in a compartment. Ever the problem solver, I suggested to the Mess Specialist Chief-- who soon appeared--that the fantail watch could call the bridge when the fantail fills up, and tell them to call "*Hold all trash on station*" on the 1MC.

"That's a good suggestion," he said. "I'll pass it up the chain." We'll be in the I.O. (Indian Ocean) by the time it sees any action.

Sweet Pea was in the hangar as I walked from the gym. He was driving a tractor (multi-talented), moving an aircraft to El 4. They blew the whistle just as I passed, and chocked down the bird. So I stopped and stared at his face and made small talk. After twenty minutes I still didn't know what we talked about. But I had absorbed his curly hair, expressive lips and ruby eyes. Ohh, man. If my thought dreams could be seen.

I hope Red has my radio. He was still in jail when I left Mission Beach. He's another homeless bum, self-described "the most honest hippie you ever met." But he has no idea how many hippies I've met. I was 13 in '69. Why tell Red about my twenty thousand miles of hitchhiking, my past life as undercover narc for the DEA, my San Francisco life, or the murder charge in Hollywood? Why tell him that I killed a kid, either? He thinks I'm Steve McQueen, a little thin on top, straight from "The Sand Pebbles," which is a movie they could remake today and set in P.I. *How I met the hippies at Mission Beach*. Subtitled: *Never Let Go of Your Radio*.

I walked up to Ventura Place at Ocean Front Walk in the heart of Mission Beach by the break in the sea wall, where teen-age skateboarders ollie off palm tree planters as cops look away. Red the redheaded hippie in tie-dyed beachcombers wound up with a Dead tape in my deck that played well against the Dylan I'd spouted for the masses there, "My Back Pages" and other classics. So when I gave Lou a ride to his motel I let Red watch the box and play his power for the people. "They need to hear it," he pleaded. I agreed. But when we came back, the deck and Red were gone.

I hung out and met AWOL soldiers from the Canadian version of special forces who gave me an Army hat and a tent. They had arranged to surrender themselves the next day.

Red appeared on his beach bomber bike, holding my box. I was relieved. Then he rode up the boardwalk and the music faded to a long, empty silence. We went on a recon mission to beat his ass, and failed. The next day I came back to the sea wall and heard tunes as I spotted Red.

"Have you been sweating all day?"

"Nah, I knew you'd be here." Where else did he have to go?

I finally convinced myself that giving him the box was worth $85, to see Red extending my values. Even with a little Slayer, and speed metal for the cranksters. I had a back-up box at home if I really needed it. So I told him to take care of it while I went on this pre-deployment exercise. I'm such a generous fool.

2100 22 JUL 90. I chased a Marine off the deck at dinner. I watched him at a table with other jarheads until I decided he had settled in with PT gear on. After chasing that pretty girl off, it wasn't fair to let him slide.

"You have to get off the mess decks in your PT gear or I'll give you an MOR."

"Only sailors get MOR's," he pouted, leaving. An MOR is a Minor Offense Report, which you give one copy to the member and another to the

Ship Master-At-Arms (SMAA).

"What do Marines get, extra PT?" He didn't answer, but disappeared into the caged space in the middle of the main forward mess deck. We had a flood on the bug bar deck and the scullery deck as water backed up in the drains because somebody had screwed them down at GQ and forgot to re-open them. Water filled up the passageway until the guys in the berthing below called Damage Control Central and a guy from the Flying Squad showed up in a heartbeat. The Flying Squad are real good about responding to emergencies. Stationed all around the ship, if they're called by the 1MC, *"Away the flying squad, away. All hands stand clear of all decks, ladders and passageways,"* you better get out of their way or they'll knock you flat like a Marine, without a gun.

Smiles rolled across the mess decks when I showed the guys an article about Mrs. George Bush christening the *USS George Washington*. The bottom lines said the *USS Midway* is scheduled for retirement in 1991 and, "by that time the Navy is expected to have announced the accelerated retirement of two other carriers, with the San Diego-based *Ranger* a leading candidate for decommissioning." That means the *Ranger* will get dogged out on Westpac with no new gear, no new photocopier for Wolfpack Pers, no new pipes for the clogged up head drains, and continued dwindling supplies--like the *Iowa* with ancient powder enroute to the mothball fleet.

I just hope we're not caught in a pissing contest between Bush and the Persian Gulf as the ready carrier--aka expendable--on the *Ranger*'s last ride. Scuttlebutt says we have too many High Value Units aboard to be really expendable. I'm not sure if they mean F-14's or men, or classified material.

I have to talk about this other incident, while I'm touching on the news. This is about a San Diego hate crime. They called it "a particularly heinous crime" because "the victim was beaten just because he was Hispanic." Three guys mugged a Puerto Rican. One defendant got three years in the state pen. One got six years in the pen and the third got a year in county. They split the victim's medical bill, to fix his fractured leg. Compare that to Navy justice. Last April 15 a guy got set up by a "queerbait" from *Ranger*'s 1989 Westpac. The term comes from a scheme where a gang takes their cutest member and in some cases even cross dresses the dude in order to bait the fag around the corner for a bum rush. This guy sat on the beach off Ventura Place when his old buddy appeared to renew the acquaintance. They walked to his apartment where the victim gave his assailant a video of their last cruise and the buddy promised to give him $20 at the local nightclub later that night, after he and his bro's went back to *Ranger* to shower and change. They met for party buckets, got shit-faced, and split up. But when the dude crawled home, these four guys were all waiting at a picnic table in his yard. They followed him in and pounded him, broke his front tooth and scarred his forehead. "What did you mug me for?" he asked the dude on the ship a week later.

"Well, you said some things that weren't exactly straight."

Five assailants confessed to the NIS. They said the victim told all five of them to "fuck me hot." These were ugly dudes.

The San Diego Police Department said, "We're not gonna put them in jail, if that's what you want." The Navy gave these boys a counseling by their department heads, and that was that. Now the victim thinks about getting four other guys together with a set of pliers, and finding each assailant, beating him and wrenching out one tooth, and then confessing everything to get a counseling from his department head. The difference between the Navy and the San Diego Police Department regarding hate crimes and racial and sexual differences. Spics are bigger than fags.

2245 22 JUL 90. AO's (Aviation Ordnancemen) hang around the lounge with the lights on, forty-five minutes after Taps, arguing over Sparrows, Sidewinders, guidance systems and other classified items that should never be discussed outside their shop.

I think of Sweet Pea in the hangar bay. And Beanpole, the other dude who's always smiling, grinning and twinkling an eye on the night shift at the forward mess. Managers wear red shirts. The FSA's (Food Service Attendants) wear light blue teeshirts, not to be confused with hangar deck Blue Shirts like Sweet Pea or flight deck Blue Shirts like Rick. Those guys are Aviation Boatswain's Mates.

At 2015 Beanpole was talking with me and another Red Shirt. Some guy came striding by and grabbed Beanpole's left tit with a twist and a kissing mouth squeak. They flashed eyes and the dude disappeared. Beanpole kept talking to me without missing a beat. Just another example of blatant sexual contact between men that might appall civilians (or make them jealous), amounting to sexual harassment except between men. You could argue that the supervisor didn't grab the sweet baby's tit and squeeze it for sexual gratification: it was just a way of saying "howdy" among men. But what if, using learned behavior, the boy is later busted for the same thing as someone else freaks out? Say he grabs ass on a queerbait? Or suddenly on the rag a victim cries fag! Or he grabs too hard, squeezes too long. Or the petty MAA has it in for you nearby. Or the queerbait mugger narcs to the NIS that down on the messdecks you're playing with the boys. I wouldn't say take it personally. Except I was that dude who got mugged.

2330 22 JUL 90. I can't sleep, "Aliens" low on the lounge TV. The cat has launched her last bird, my thoughts drift back to Mission Beach, fond image of a Budweiser tall, in a brown bag at the sea wall, watching for cops. At 9:55 p.m. beer is legal. At 10:00 p.m. you may be arrested for doing nothing but leaning back, smelling the surf, and letting the time pass. Mission Beach is poised to explode with violence because it is the only remaining refuge for homeless bums at the end of the rainbow. As an experiment only, southern California beaches are closing to alcohol after certain hours.

"What are you doing?" I asked Lou as we met on the sea wall.

"Waitin' for six."

"What happens at six?"

"The bars open." The bars here, notably Johnny's Surf Club and the Coaster Saloon, close at zero two hundred, to re-open at six. But they ban booze on the beach from 2200 to 0600. My Toyota--before it was stolen--was not gouged by a drunken pedestrian.

Acid sales will simply go up. And if they get rid of the belligerent drunk knife wielders, it's ok by me.

A black dude, Afro-American, pulled out a bottle as a cop car cruised up the boardwalk toward the park. "Watch me," he said. And tipped the whiskey up in front of their car. They stopped and got out. Then he squeezed it. This was broad daylight and the bottle was plastic. He broke no laws, except the unwritten one that says cops are gods.

"Everyone vacate the area."

"Excuse me, officer." That Guy, my roommate, happened to be with me. We were drinking our first Buds of the night, totally sober and unintimidated. "I live here. I pay rent as a resident here and I'm not gonna move." I figured they would haul him to Detox for spite, the usual response--short of opening fire--to questioning authority of the San Diego Police. But this cop treated him with respect and charm.

"Well, it's not illegal to loiter at a public beach. But this is a problem area and we like to come by once in a while to move folks along so a problem doesn't arise."

"I find it offensive," I added now, "when you show up and harass these homeless people just because this is the end of the road and they're trying to sleep in the open to avoid being murdered."

Meanwhile, the cop's partner rousted Pappy and cuffed him. And a perfectly good patrol unit went out of action, to haul a harmless wino across town to dry out. Of course, the very next day Pappy was back, undaunted among the unrich of Mission Beach. Once they get rousted it usually has the opposite of the desired effect. Instead of moving on, bums huddle closer to business and housing structures, in the shadows right outside windows, alcoves and ladderwells, for protection.

2230 23 JUL 90. Rumors jet like an F-14. The best is still the nonskid cutting the arresting cables. Two have actually been replaced this month, compared to only one during Westpac '89. Rumor One has us pulling in 31 July. But ATA starts 31 July, so you tell me. And, this rumor has it, Rumor Two about the radar was supposedly bogus because it would be too expensive to pull in for just six hours, even to replace such a major piece of gear.

We're serving milk in Philippine Island packs, long shelf-life cartons I first encountered in '89. We only serve them at breakfast and midrats (midnight rations, lunch for nightcheck). At daycheck lunch and dinner, there's no milk at either galley, forward or aft. Good training for the budget crunch.

Sometimes a question boils out the very salt of a sailor, like what boiled the blood of a group that exited the squadron and the Navy recently. They formed it bluntly, and repeated it for emphasis: "Who runs this squadron? Who runs this squadron?"

"I run this squadron," our CO declared in response. But it has been clear for some time that VF-1 is run by the maintenance master chief, a fat fuck who repeatedly fails the PRT (Physical Readiness Test) for being obese. But the Navy looks the other way and only kicks out guys with less power. Wolfpack has won the Navy "E" award--for battle efficiency--two years in a row, and now the Clifton, best fighter squadron in the world, all attributed to that fat son of a bitch. I had to type his eval once. They called him a tenacious problem solver. Meanwhile, I needed him to solve a problem, verifying that a guy was notified that we were going to sea, so he didn't miss ship's movement. "I don't solve your fuckin' problems," he snapped, so very tenaciously.

1445 24 JUL 90. Another rumor broke this afternoon. Two guys from Weapons Department got caught having sex onboard this at-sea period. The ship's XO and CO (both Captains, as opposed to squadron CO and XO who are Commanders) know about the whole thing, but haven't acted. It will probably die quietly. "You can't tell by looking anymore," a Weapons guy told me. "Some of the toughest looking guys...." Do tell, girl.

My good buddy Muggerboy got bolder today. I have to live and work on this ship with him and his chronies. He walked up the port side chow line to get a glass of water. He stood aft of a hatch, drinking, as I stood on the forward side of it talking to a handsome young MS (Mess Specialist) who was monitoring the condiments bar, while the Weapons guys were handling ordnance. "They moved it to New Orleans. But it's going back to Saint Louis." He was talking about the riverboat I rode as a kid in Illinois. "They're gonna legalize gambling on the river and turn the *Admiral* into a casino. I wanta work there when I get out."

Muggerboy had a couple of drinks, then walked forward to the scullery. Since his office, the ship's DAPA (Drug and Alcohol Prevention Association--a misnomer for him, being a drunken hoodlum) is forward on the 03 level, four decks up, I didn't expect him to come back my way. But he passed with his right hand high as if to strike. He was holding an earplug in that hand, not twisting it into his ear or doing anything but holding it. This looked like an excuse to pass me with a raised fist and get away with it to freak me out, because he could do that. I dutifully ignored him. Later in the same meal period, two purple shirts (also known as Grapes, who work with fuel), tough looking Mexicans, loitered in the passageway between the bug bar and the main deck talking to a white sailor in dungarees, throwing glances my direction. "Bald headed faggot," one finally said. Another glance and they dispersed. Muggerboy probably set it up.

"Yo, that maricone I rat packed is the Red Shirt on the bomb elevator by the bar, if you want to see a faggot in the Navy." Why else would they come from the port side without trays, linger where everyone gets silverware and glasses, then leave on the starboard side without looking at the food?

Here's a classic Navy "hook up" if there is one: Muggerboy used to be the Duty Driver for the *Ranger* in port. He would get pizzas for the SMAA. Now imagine him being investigated by them for beating up a faggot. Not only that--he works in DAPA where everyone goes with their drug or drinking problem. Imagine the buddies to make in there, cutting slack for the problem children.

It's so safe to be a bully on a ship. Dare to be gentle and you become a target. And trigger fingers itch on Westpac, harder and harder as the days grow long, looking to stomp someone weak.

2150 24 JUL 90. I got off an hour early, true exception to shipboard life, haze gray underway. Not only that, they gave me the morning off until 1030. We have another GQ drill tomorrow. Zero eight to ten hundred. I'll have to be on station cowering with the kids on the forward mess decks. I guess if it were the real thing I'd be glad to be there, caring for those babes with my ancient age--most of them are eighteen, I'm 33. I would even hold them if they cry.

This tall lean, baby face crewcut kid I call Beanpole, who works in the deep sink of the forward galley, kept fooling with me all day. Throwing and pulling punches to make me flinch, and boxing the bill of my ballcap, knocking it to the deck. Finally, as another dude I'll call Cowboy described a bar fight, Beanpole came out of the deep pan room to listen. But as the cowboy talked, Beanpole kept rubbing his skinny, soft stomach against my arm. I moved away subtly. He stood up for a second, repositioned and leaned back again, discreetly coming closer and brushing me again, making me fucking horny. He had mail from a girl and acted so hetero. But he hasn't needed a shave since we went to sea, and still doesn't. He probably just wants affection and thinks I'm the man to give it. And I am.

I've never cared to draw a line between sex and affection, even though many societal influences seem to argue that there must be one now. I consider that our creation originates with the genitals. But society professes asexuality, like the stupid gold plate they shot to outer space to greet aliens a few years ago at a cost of millions of dollars: male and female figurines, *sans genitalia*, a colossal non-statement that appalls my sensibilities like modern circumcision--kids clean their dicks. Whether it's churches, book burners, motion picture raters, well meaning parents or teachers--or an older and wiser enemy nation--somebody's sold us an attitude of black, white or war, so that we revel macho, ignorant of nondisclosurists buying the carpet our grandkids would sleep on. We concern ourselves with sublime imagery and dialogue on film, while our substance--the land--is discreetly removed like stars that die as you still see light. Once we owned, now we rent, then we get evicted from the melting pot. Small Town America thinks only it's invaded by foreigners. They're all invaded. Nobody talks about it but the invaders themselves, still pleading for "equal time" on TV.

Cowboy's story of the bar brawl: A part time bouncer in a country bar when a rash came in the form of a biker gang that would sit down, light a marijuana joint and trash the place. The bouncers were getting the worst of it. "There's gonna be some trouble tonight," his bar-keep said. "I might need your help."

"You need help, whaddaya mean? I'm the bouncer."

A number of Cowboy's pals had been thrown out themselves.

"Tell ya what," he said. "If these friends of mine come and help, you give them free membership back in the club."

"It's a done deal."

When the bikers arrived, ten cowboy hats lined the bar, each with a beer and a head watching the door. They strutted over to a table in the middle of the bar, as the cowboys started picking their targets. "Come like lightnin' when you see me throw the first punch," Cowboy said. Then he let the bikers drink, and even light up the joint. After they put it out, he walked over. "Excuse me, but you and your friends are gonna have to leave."

"Ha! And just who is gonna make us--you?"

"That's right. Me."

"Now, how in the hell are you gonna do that, boy?" The lead biker stood, tall.

"I'm gonna pick you up off the floor and throw you over my shoulder and carry you. Then I'm gonna dump you in the street."

"No, I don't think so." The biker slung his bottle against the wall and yelled, "Let's get 'em, boys!"

"Oh yes I will," Cowboy still answered. In the same breath he cold cocked the biker as the nine other men at the bar doffed their hats like a chorus line and jumped in.

By the time it was done, Cowboy had busted three knees, got a demonstration of knee busting from one of his pals, and got all nine cowpokes a stack of free drink tickets.

"You boys are back in the bar," the bar-keep said. "Somebody call a couple amb'lances."

Cowboy had to admit being the official bouncer even though he was the smallest good guy and was only twenty, which made it a little more awkward. As the story ended, Beanpole snuck up and embraced me from behind, locking my arms to my sides and picking me up with a dry-humping motion that nearly made me hard before letting go. After that he kept making goofy eyes at me. I think he'll be all right after a cold shower. But imagine Westpac if it's this bad on a one month work-up. Later, as I monitored the main deck by a passageway on the starboard forward corner this bully from R Division sidled up and snatched my ballcap.

"What do you want?" I figured he was looking for pizza.

"That hat." He snagged it and kept walking.

"Give it back."

"If you want it, come get it," he disappeared down a ladder to his coop. I wouldn't dare follow him--a squadron puke in a ship's company coop is like a chick in a fox den. I'd get my ass beat.

What the hell, it only cost eight bucks. Ballcaps are an item that falls under, "may wear but not issued." The Navy will authorize you to wear it as part of your official uniform, but if you do wear it instead of the dog dish white hat they gave you in bootcamp (like who wouldn't), cough up the dough yourself.

I stood around moping and figured I'd write it off. He can have the fucking Wolfpack hat. What else could I do, cry to his department head? Whine to the ship's XO? Then, Cowboy was still around.

"I knew you wouldn't come after it." The burly dude came back and threw the ballcap at me. "You would have been instant monster mash."

He was a good guy after all, just trying to break the ice. In fact, Ice is his nickname. He's one of the most respected men in the Flying Squad, the kind who will end up saving somebody's life before he's out of the Navy.

Meanwhile, I had already mentioned it to Cowboy and watched him throw his shoulders back. "I'd a gone to another berthing right over there," he pointed to the Marines, "and got eight or nine guys and we'd a had a party. "Still, I'm pretty sure they could mug me on this boat and--once the slurs flew--I'd be on my own.

Chapter Two

2200 25 JUL 91. Beanpole finally cooled off a little with his green eyes. A kid from our squadron, Country Time, cut his finger on a can of tomato paste while preparing pizza last night. He got twelve stitches. I was there as it happened. It looked like he was fooling around, dancing across the galley, whooping and holding his finger. But the glob of paste on his middle finger was a much brighter red than the paste on the dough on the table. Then I saw the spatters on his face and realized he had a deep fucking gash.

He laughed today, telling us how we looked as we caught on, how our faces contorted from casual disbelief, to amusement, then sudden horror.

Just two nights ago another dude, from HS-14 (a helicopter squadron), cut off the top of his finger with a bread slicer and had to be medi-vac'd to Balboa Naval Hospital in San Dog. They immediately barred airedales from handling sharp instruments in the galleys. The MS's, if not thrilled, were relieved to know Country Time had cut his finger on the can, not the opener, since it meant they wouldn't get their asses chewed. I wondered which pizza got blood in the paste. I had a well done pepperoni.

Muggerboy pointed me out to another dude. That's about thirty guys now he's introduced from a distance in the past two weeks. Will they frag me on a ladder some night? Pull me into their coop off the soda deck? Beat me unconscious and haul me over the side? Whenever I work that deck I stick to the port side, just in case.

My LPO (Leading Petty Officer), a YN1 (Yeoman Petty Officer First Class), urged me to write to the CV By God CO about the slap on the wrist of the fag bashers onboard, and the ensuing menace.[1]

But like an SMAA said, "the dog that barks is sometimes the one that gets kicked." He meant, flagging a fagbasher flags a fag. What--me worried?

1315 27 JUL 90. We pulled in. Four hours pierside to fix the radar. And back to sea. Phone lines went up in the hangar bay until ten hundred, but I got no chance to call Phyllis. Now my check register is either up or down by $325 and I won't know until we pull in again. I'll just pretend I'm broke for the next two weeks. It's easy enough on an aircraft carrier. Free food, free house, free transportation.

With Air Show rehearsal this afternoon, the forward mess decks are secured while handling ordnance. It's an odd thrill wiping a table with your leg on a thousand pound bomb. It's not armed, of course--you can see the empty threaded hole for the detonator tip. But you never know what you don't know. I look at guys like Beanpole--except he's TAD--with mixed envy and awe, and excuse them. Ordies with goofy faces.

---

[1] A note about Ranger. Her hull number is CV-61, and her nickname CV "By God" 61 was christened by the ship's current XO.

We got another mandate this week. Whereas it used to be for E5's and above, now anyone in pay grade E4 and up testing positive for marijuana use will be separated from the Navy.[2]

I'm an E4, now vulnerable to separation for going home and firing up a fatty, whereas last week I might have pled insanity and been retained. I mention this only because the coop cleaner and a pal in the lounge this afternoon are discussing the pros and cons of naval service in the nineties, and the pot option came up as an early way out. It depends on what kind of job you want after this, whether you foresee ever working for the government again. At my age, I'd have a hard time getting a government job anyway. Too old to be a cop. Maybe I could be a mailman. I don't think I'd lose a Hollywood job because of a joint.

I don't know about this whole fucking drug thing. Take a kid from small-town USA and put him in a bootcamp urinal with a gruffy old bald-head staring at his dick, and make him pee. You got an exhibitionist in the making, bud! Wouldn't that be a kick, statistics show five years later that the Navy drug awareness program significantly contributed to the number of psychiatric discharges for voyeurism and exhibitionism? "Well, you know, Chaplain, I never thought I was odd until I joined the Navy. They had these pecker checkers, every time ya had a urine test? I couldn't pee, so I just stood there holdin' my penis. Then when I went to my rack, sir, it got to be a turn on. I liked havin' them look at me."

2300 27 JUL 90. Unless they change it in the Eight O'clock Report, GQ goes down at zero eight tomorrow, until ten hundred. (8 o'clock are nightly reports by the brass.) It sucks because tomorrow's my turn to sleep in until 0900.

They called Man Overboard as we steamed back out this morning. I hadn't notice what an ass pain it must be on the aft mess decks. We had already secured from chow forward. But since they weren't pleased with the time it took to account for every swinging dick (and the couple of women), they held another MOB at 1900--right in the middle of chow up forward.

This was the first time I've had to deal with clearing a hundred trays off abandoned tables, so the new--and long--line of customers could be accommodated afterward.[3] A lazy blueshirt, perched on a trash can, reasoned that most diners would return for their trays and get in the Seconds line. "So, genius, then what should I do with all these people standing around with full,

---

[2] A note about Navy enlisted pay grades: they go E1 to E9 with E1-E3 being nonpo's; E4-E6, petty officers 3rd, 2nd, and 1st; and E7-E9 chief petty officer, senior CPO, and Master CPO.

[3] A note about the help: How about if I say blueshirts for the FSA's, aka mess cranks on the mess decks; and Blue Shirts for the aviation boatswain's mates who work in the hangar bay and on the flight deck in REAL jobs.

hot trays lookin' for seats?"

"Go ahead then, and dump 'em." He sat on his ass.

I let my blueshirts skate too much. I guess it's because I resent the fact that this organization owns your body twenty-four hours a day, seven days a week, all year for as long as they want, or the term of your contract, which ever is shorter. Said contract is probably illegal and constitutionally unenforceable, except as alternative to conscription. We endorsed slavery, too.

I tried to watch Pacino, one of my favorite actors, in "Sea Of Love" on the lounge TV at 2100. But with the volume so low and the compartment shuttering from cat shots, instead of having to plug my ears I walked to the RM lounge, two knee-knockers aft.[4]

I sat on a couch in the back, unobtrusive. It gets touchy hanging out in anyone else's lounge, especially when seating gets scarce. I've actually seen somebody jerk a chair out from under his shipmate, callously abrupt, without warning and for real. I wrote the son-of-a-bitch up. Suddenly this dude I'll call Broomer--what is it with sailors and broomsticks--appeared in a chair to my right, a little in front of me. He seemed to be enthralled in the movie, until this big nigger playing Spades threw him a Pepsi from a poker game across the lounge. It hit the deck, and the nigger said something.

"What's his problem?" Broomer asked no one.

"He said you didn't get to play sports much as a child." I broke the ice.

He looked at me and smiled, tapping the can top.

"Let me know when you're gonna open it," I said leaning back.

"Someone told me if you do this it won't spray," he looked me in the eye again. He drank the soda and the Afro-American horny person of color threw him a Snickers. This was another frightening similarity between the Navy and L.A. County Jail. It had me wondering. The young white boy was a sexy babe.

"I don't know what his problem is," he bit the candy bar.

"I think he likes you."

"Oh no." He had a mock homophobic tone and got up and went forward over the kneeknocker. I couldn't see him, so I went back to Al on TV. In a minute, Broomer sat down again and started in on the broom. He put both feet on the brush, straddling it, and stretched his right hand up to the tip as he finished the candy bar. Next, he worked his hand down the shaft until he had it in both hands and started tweaking it with his fingers, eyes glazing over as if looking through the movie. Finally, he leaned his cheek into the handle and turned so his lips grazed the stick and I thought the broom would come. The movie ended and he let go.

"You did real good on that broom," I patted him on the head. But he

---

[4] A note about the knee-knocker: this is slang for the round, raised passageway doors made by cutting holes in the ship's frame. They are notorious for their grinding arrest of forward shin motion. Thus, they excel as shipboard landmarks.

jerked back as the pin fasteners inside his ballcap jammed into his forehead from the simple pat.

"Ow, man."

"Oh, sorry. You don't have your crow in your hat right." I showed him how to fix the pewter chevron that was centered on the front of his ballcap. "That happened to me until somebody showed me how to fix it. You get rid of those fasteners, man. They're FOD hazards anyway. Now, let me see your keys there. You take and bend these stems back so the crow stays on. And you don't need the brass things."

"You're a fuckin' genius."

"Let me know if you need another stick to handle." I went and took a cold *Ranger* shower.

I know I come off as rather curious in some passages of this book. But here's a real good one. The other night one of our guys took a dump and caught another dude peeping him from under the stall! You never hear the whole story, though, and seldom even hear both sides. Like, who knows if he was only crapping? But here we are a week from pierside and this shit happens? *Not on my watch. Not on my ship. Not in my navy.* Some guys would have stomped him. Imagine what Muggerboy would have done. "He said 'fuck me hot'."

This is the second case of homosexual behavior reported in three weeks. What'll happen in six months on the raging main?

I wrote my four-page letter to the CO about queerbaits. But thanks to this latest incident putting a whole persuasion in bad light, I don't think I'll show it around.

1100 28 JUL 90. GQ went down at 0800 and secured at ten. I got to help with a Red Devil Blower, carrying a vent hose to the hangar bay, and actually worked up a sweat. One end of the hose was bent and wouldn't connect. After fighting it, I finally had to discard the section for another because there was no tape to make it work. In a real fire it would have cost ten minutes, and maybe a life. But when I notified the R Division DCPO (damage control petty officer) he already knew about it and didn't care because he'd have an OBA (oxygen breathing apparatus) himself. That made me wonder how fast this crew would abandon ship in a real conflagration. Hopefully, if real courage is called for they'll be heroes.

I had to take this dude I'll call Boxer down to the SMAA after GQ. They had announced, "Relax battle dress, restow all gear." So I told the blueshirts to grab a swab, since the fire party hose teams had charged hoses and soaked the mess decks in saltwater. "Could I go restow my gear first so it don't get stolen?"

"Every time you go somewhere you don't come back for half an hour."

"So in other words, no."

"That's right. Grab a swab."

"Man I ain't doin' nothin' you say."

"Look, this is a fuckin' mess here and we've gotta clean it up. Now I want you and three other guys to grab some fuckin' swabs and rinse buckets and get at it."

"Get your hands outa my face."

"Did I touch you?"

"Why you yellin' and puttin' your hands in my face?"

"Just get the fuckin' swab."

"Okay, man. You an' me are gonna have our own smoker. You just signed up."

"All right that's it. Man, I hate to do this. Let's go see the chief."

He followed me aft to the S-5 office. He had disobeyed a lawful order and communicated a threat, and more importantly been a shitheal from day one talking back, acting disruptive and unmanageable, embarrassing me in giving the impression that I couldn't manage. It would only get worse unless I cracked down.

"He communicated a threat?" The chief didn't even look up. "Take him to the master-at-arms."

They let him stew at parade rest on a huge hatch in the middle of the wide passageway, on display, and took me into a small office.

"You know, we've had a lot of this kind of problem today. Because we've been at sea for a while and we had that teaser yesterday, pulling in but not getting liberty."

"Yeah, I see what you mean." I'm an easy melt.

"I tell ya what, you can fill out this blue card. It goes on file--it's more than a warning--so if anything else happens, we still have this complaint and we can file it then. If you want, we can go ahead with your complaint right now."

"Nah, I'll back off. Just give me the card."

"I'll let him chill for a while out there, then give him a stern warning."

I got mail this afternoon. Not the heated love letters that younger dudes and married men receive. Me, I got license plates. And a notice to pay the bank on my cash reserve--which I sent yesterday. And, a letter from the squadron Legal Officer: I told Ship's Legal about the incident and they were not aware of it. The five report chits have been handled and all members were counseled at Department Head level. Ship's legal is checking into (Muggerboy)'s second incident, but I wouldn't hold my breath. If there are any problems, give me a call. X7145

One of the guys TAD to the mess decks from the SMAA division had asked Muggerboy about this second incident, and I overheard. I had told my Legal Officer, thus the note back. Supposedly some dude in the shower told him he had a nice ass and he pounded the guy. I don't know if it was a variation on "fuck me hot" or a separate incident. But he's got no great ass, and being a sucker for a pretty face, he sure didn't turn my head--like he'd have the Navy think. Still, if he's a queerbait fagbasher I thought Legal should know. Not that they'd really give a fuck, with this being such a man's world.

I pulled off a good coup, in Pers. I sold my refrigerator out from under those assholes. Ha hah. I had bought it from my last PN1 (Personnelman First Class, my boss) when he transferred. Now these suckers, my chain of command, conned me into carrying the thing up the brow and all the way to the office (with the help of YN1, who's a cool black dude who should have made chief long ago). And they got me to chip in two bucks to join a soda mess--which they'd keep cool in my refrigerator--and pay for my own sodas. I bought one before they ran out, and they never did restock. All they did was use my fucking refrigerator while I went TAD. So I sold the bitch for eighty bucks and had the buyers pick it up themselves. And I felt great.

2245 29 JUL 90. I got the day off, but had to keep it a secret because such a thing is unthinkable on a Naval vessel. It would upset too many jealous and childish men. It wasn't like I could hop in my car and go. I slept until noon, six hours over normal. I had to sleep with an earplug in whichever ear I didn't bury in my pillow, to block the lounge noises and the flight deck maintenance.

I went up to the flight deck and discovered the Coronado Bay Bridge. I could nearly see Louie on the sea wall and the Coaster Saloon. What a thrill, what a tease.

The catapult crew had the deck plates up, greasing cables on cat one. At the starboard bow they had a huge African briefcase tuned to KGB, ironic call letters for the most popular Navy town radio station. Boats sailed by with women flashing tits. And a jet ski rode through our wake close enough to turn my stomach at the thought of him churning through the screws.

I worked out at the *Ranger* gym for an hour: legs, butt, gut and back. Then rode the exercycle a boring five miles.

Jack, a YN3 from Admin, sat with me at lunch. "Man, they want my head on a silver platter at the office."

"What for?"

"For gettin' rid of that refrigerator for ya."

"Hah hah hah."

"They ain't got no real complaint, 'cause it's yours."

"Hey, fuck 'em. They're just takin' advantage of me. I'm sick of it, man."

"It weren't doin' you no good, you're TAD."

"Besides, I can use the money to party next week."

We had an Ice Cream Social from 2000 to 2200, and TV Ranger Bingo. Just before it, they called Man Overboard for maneuvering purposes only, which meant no muster was required. And they had pizza forward, where I hooked up Sweet Pea and a couple of guys who worked with him.

At the Social, I took my head of the line privilege as a Red Shirt and got two cups of ice cream. I took one for me and one for Sweet Pea, and went up to Conflag One where he stood watch. I sat up there and stared at him for two hours.

2200 30 JUL 90. We've anchored off and on, had GQ and shot a flare with a missile from an F-14 today. We're close enough to San Diego to get shore TV. "Alien Nation" and "Star Trek" were the favorites.

I got off at 1730 and went to the fantail to watch the missile shoot--they're practicing for Dependent's Day Cruise. Then I stared at the wake churning under the four giant screws thirty feet below, and watched the F-14s fly the ball twenty feet overhead. A slight mistake, or malfunction and I'd chew the cockpit--or an intake would chew me--until it burst into flames. The fantail is closed during flight ops, but sometimes guys have a look anyway.

At GQ we sat on the mess decks bored silly while hose teams worked around us. A dude asked me to play Spades. Then a DCET guy came through. (DCET is roughly Damage Control Evaluation and Training.) "No one is playing cards in here, are they?" He boomed. "Because I take General Quarters very seriously." He should take the Navy's body fat standards seriously. He looked like 50% body fat. It made him seem larger than life.

I respected his seriousness and was eager to play along. But just to sit and stay awake doing nothing for two hours in hot long sleeves and hoods and gloves with stupid bell bottom pants tucked in boots was too much bullshit. Finally they put us on a hose team, and it was a clusterfuck. Better now, though, than in a real fire. Now comes a sudden rumble, vibrant, deafening, as we drop anchor. I hope we don't do this all night. Besides cat shots jolting our coop, since we are directly over the forecastle the anchor rattles us crazy. Each link is as long as my arm, and it makes a helluva clunk slipping through the hole in the bow. When the sea tugs against the ship and the links start to slide, they clop like a stethoscope up a zipper.

This lean pup, Jeffery in the bake shop, swears he won't be able to walk this Sunday after spending a night with his girl. She's promised him a big surprise and said in her letter she's going to get "exactly what I want."

Two guys in the berthing have been lisping and swishing lately. Pretty weird. One of them isn't in VF-1 and the other has never acted that way before. I thought I was special when they announced me with fanfare, thought they were singling me out with ridicule. I played it off, responding in laughter, then sat down and watched them do it to everyone who entered; even to the Television. "Isn't that special," they'd say over and over, giddy. That phrase came and went a year ago, and was stupid then. Finally somebody threatened to beat ass and everybody capped on them. "I'm beginnin' to wonder about you two guys, if you really mean it when you act that way, like if that's your real nature and you've been hidin' out or somethin'. And I might oughta have to beat your ass."

"Yeah, man. Come here bitch. Gimme a blow job. Get up on this."

"I think you boys need to see the doctor."

"Somebody take 'em down to the chaplain."

"Hell, I heard he's gay, too."

"Talkin' like that's enough to make me sick."

We've only been at sea for a month.

Another guy actually did come out to me tonight. I never wonder about the sexuality of a dude I don't want, so I was surprised, and even curious why he confided in me. But I played it off like what the hell. He has discharge papers in his rack, and as soon as we return he'll start bartending in Hillcrest (San Diego's gay community). "Oh, come on. Haven't you ever been to the Peacock, or WW?"

I had never heard of them. I guess I'm deep in the closet. I'm even from San Francisco's East Bay--but it's not like being from San Francisco by a long shot. Suburbs have a large redneck anti-gay majority. In fact, nigger and fag are synonymous in my county. Anyway, this dude was tired of being called "home" by the guys in his shop, tired of being asked if he knew the guy who peeped the Ordy in the toilet stall. Meanwhile, the chiefs concocted a story that he's getting out for some "legitimate" reason like "didn't get the orders he'd requested." They are concerned he could be thrown overboard for being a fag, if anybody finds out the truth behind his discharge.

Sweet Pea goes home on leave Saturday. I want to take him to the San Diego airport, and maybe get a farewell hug although I must be dreaming. It's up in the air if I have to work Saturday, since the forward mess decks will be secured for that Dependent's Day Cruise.

I'll arrange my life around meeting his needs, if possible. I don't have a girlfriend, so it's at least heartwarming to have some friend in my life whom I'm desperate to please, or help rescue, or serve. He was gonna take a cab.

Even with the apparent threats of Muggerboy and company, and the myriad frustrations that come with serving the Navy, I feel invigorated from this at-sea period, for having been around all the affection. For that, I am rich.

2230 31 JUL 90. Day One, ATA. (I thought it was Advanced Training Assessment; it's Airwing Tactical Assessment.) Two MOBs and two GQs. This time instead of playing cards I entertained my boys on the mess decks with a wadded napkin under one of three bowls, using sleight of hand. I actually fooled them a couple of times.

This afternoon's MOB was a good one. We have a couple of boatswain's mates TAD as blueshirts, and they tipped me off that their division was standing by in the forecastle with Oscar, the dummy, to throw him overboard at the Captain's signal. But the time approached, arrived, and passed. "How good is your gouge?"

"My what?"

"Your gouge--your info." I shouldn't use pilot lingo on a blackshoe.

"I'll call them again."

He came back with the same line, "any time within the next five or ten minutes."

I wanted to get as many shipmates as possible involved in clearing, rather than abandoning, their trays at MOB. Because when the drill is called away, they all jump and leave their trays as they run to muster at their shops.

"GQ in five minutes," I repeated quietly as I walked from table to table.

Most guys responded by hurrying up and getting their trays to the scullery, exactly as I wanted.

At 1531 a blueshirt grinned, "They're exactly a minute late."

"BMC ALFARO, EXECUTE." *Ranger* XO's voice was unmistakable on the 1MC, but nobody knew what the hell he meant. Except me and the boatswain's mates. Guys on the deck who hadn't heard my warning looked up quizzically, then went on eating.

At 1540 nothing had happened yet. I was about to feel embarrassed for warning so many people earlier and sending them on to their shops in the middle of a meal.

"*Man overboard, man overboard! Starboard side. Make ready the lifeboat, man up all rescue and assistance stations. All hands stand clear of all decks, ladders and passageways. Submit reports to the officer of the deck in six minutes.*"

Suddenly it was called away, something like that on the 1MC, by the boatswain on the bridge. As I started aft to muster with the Supply department on the main galley deck, I saw my gouge master.

"What took 'em so long?"

"I just got off the phone with the boatswain's mate on the bridge," he said, following me down the crowded passageway. "I asked if they'd thrown Oscar in the water. He said yeah. So I asked him, well, didn't the buoy watch see him? Then he went 'ah shit, man overboard,' and called it away. I'd hate to be that fantail watch. He was prob'ly asleep. He's gonna get his ass chewed."

Oscar had been tossed on XO's order, and was in the water nine minutes before anybody called MOB. Nine minutes later he was picked up by helo. In all, eighteen minutes, three minutes longer than the normal life expectancy for SOCAL OPS.

2330 1 AUG 90. Another MOB and two GQ's, graded this time. On the forward mess decks we have one giant watertight door that has to be slammed, and scrapes between the deck and the underside of the ceiling mounted vent pipe where the asbestos lagging is torn away. Mild carcinogenicity, to be sure. The adjacent head deck drains are supposed to be screwed down in setting Zebra (a material condition of readiness where all watertight fittings are secured). But the threads are stripped and the drains are popped open so that in real flooding the water would back up onto the mess decks. Oh well, it's an old boat.

The scullery is down from 98 degrees to a mere 94, with a large standing fan in the side passageway. One of the two vents is operating half-power and can't be fixed until we return to San Diego. So I've been keeping the guys on a ten minute rotation, alternating the scullery job with wiping down tables.

The Weapons guys had us secure the main deck in the middle of dinner. Everybody had to get up and move so they could haul fifty missiles from the flight deck to the magazines. They come down an elevator by the bug bar and traverse across the mess deck to another elevator. One of the guys told me that on last Westpac saltwater had leaked in where they stored saltwater activated ordnance. Now they had live missiles on the main mess deck during GQ and were running charged saltwater hoses from starboard to port, with a leaky connecting joint twenty feet from a missile. The gunners had ordered the hose team not to charge the hose during this drill, but since the evolution was being graded they couldn't simulate charging the hose. So they charged it and a stream of saltwater sprayed ten feet in the air, from the coupler, causing a stream heading straight for the missile. I grabbed a swab as someone else got a rinse bucket around the coupler. These were not saltwater activated missiles. But they might have been.

One of Muggerboy's pals works in Repair Locker Two-Bravo, and I saw him stowing his gear and debriefing. Somebody called him by name so I looked and read it on his dungaree pants over the right rear pocket. I remembered his leering face raising the chair in my apartment just before the lights went out in Mission Beach. He's tall, maybe six-two, lean, maybe twenty-one. It will be grand working around him all cruise. "Secure from General Quarters," said the omnipotent voice on the 1MC, after a long, shrill roller coaster whistle. "On deck set the normal underway watch. Officer Section Four, Enlisted Section Two."

My blueshirt gouge master came back and wanted to smuggle some coffee to the forecastle. He blushed when I caught him, but I didn't care. We're in the same boat, and what difference does it make if you get coffee from the coffee issue or the galley. It's easy for us to pick up, but shops have to wait until they schedule a break-out. I walked up to the forecastle with them, just to ask about this mugger bud from Two-Bravo. "Did he ever tell you about beating up some fag in Mission Beach?"

"Yeah, he was out there."

"Well, I'm the guy he mugged in my apartment with four other guys."

"Oh, man. I can't believe he was involved. He's about the unlikeliest guy to fight that I've ever known."

"What about these other two guys," I named off. It turned out they knew them all.

"Only the one dude. That guy's in the brig right now. He's getting a Big Chicken Dinner for lying to some officer."

"He was always an instigator," another said. "He's really a pussy, unless he has other guys around to make him feel tough."

"Well, I guess he got what he deserved, anyway. Just tell what's his name, as far as I'm concerned it's over. I don't want to have to watch my back all cruise, or him either."

"We'll tell him."

We have another unrep tonight, a tender coming alongside with goods. The boatswain's mates are already dog-tired from the drills, and now they'll be working hard in the dark with knives and heavy lines along the edges of the carrier.

"Go to your stations, all the underway replenishment detail. Man all starboard refueling stations."

A Defense Department security brief airs on KRAN (the call letters of *Ranger*'s onboard TV station). "Do not play James Bond to the Russians who are visiting San Diego. If you obtain a method of re-contact, identify a Soviet intelligence specialist, or get too personal questions, even attempts at sexual contact or home visits, let the NIS know." (The NIS is the infamous Naval Intelligence Service.)

I got tomorrow off. Man, I've been skating all month. (I don't know where they got this term either, but to skate is to have it easy.) No drills tomorrow either. Maybe I'll hide in bed from all the uptight, anxious sailors chafing with matchstick tempers and avoid the fights. If I don't get tossed overboard by the boatswain's mates, now that I have confronted them about the Mission Beach mugging. Maybe I'll even reconcile with Muggerboy himself tomorrow. Nah, let the sleeping dog lie to himself. If I catch any of them at my home again I will still shoot them.

At least puppy in the bake shop won't suffer alone. We both have to come back and work after the *Ranger* pulls in. Our whole squadron gets off, but we're TAD to the ship and the ship will fuck us before fucking ship's company. That's the main reason for having TAD support from the air wing. When he comes back in Saturday, weak, wasted, and worn out in the loins, I'll be there grinning. He can tell me his glory of fucking her silly. He'll probably marry her, and raise hellions for kids.

AFTERNOON 2 AUG 90. On the mess decks on my day off. Using my red shirt for the benefit of early chow, eating with the boys. Today the pork-n-beans taste funny. How can you screw up beans when they come right from the can? I think they burned them.

Broomstick sets a Pepsi on the table, unexpected but not surprising. I slug the coffee and convert to the new generation.

"Just think, Graham. Pretty soon I'll be handing you a beer."

Pup walks by, headed for the bake shop.

"They want my liberty card." He's a nonpo. Petty officers don't carry liberty cards. If you're E3 or below (a nonpo), you can't get off the brow without your liberty card. This guy has been itching to fuck this whole chapter.

"Wanna see Rambo go crazy on the mess decks? I'm gonna steal a Marine's M-16 and go shoot that MS who wanted my liberty card. They won't be able to count the holes. They'll have to count the clips."

A guy from Whidby Island raves about how much nicer *Ranger* is than *Enterprise*. He says *Enterprise* is 24 years old. *Ranger* is 33, same age as me. I wonder if my plumbing is so bad. He talks to me for ten minutes and I get no solid example of what he is comparing. All I can think of is the stream from my shower faucet last night. And the puddles around the crapper stalls, brown and gray.

A first class Red Shirt stops by. The dude always gives me sweet tarts.

He's too fat, sent TAD by his squadron, probably about to be kicked out for body fat standards because he's not a maintenance chief or a fire marshal. At least he goes home this Friday. "The dragon's down," he says. The dragon is a nickname for the dish washer. "Some rubber gasket ripped out and another one just like it popped out. I guess it has something to do with a shock absorber between where the trays go through and the motor."

"So what are they doing?"

"I guess they're tryin' to fix it."

A guy in blue coveralls moseys up. "We had to discharge a hose up there, so there's water all over the deck. I'd get it cleaned up but I've got to go to a DC meeting."

"That's okay, we'll take care of it." The PO1 (first class petty officer) goes off to find a blueshirt.

The Weapons guys haul Phoenix and Sidewinder missiles across the mess decks and nobody secures the chow line. But it is slow, probably no need. Pup goes skating off to the game room, playing videos, then to have a smoke on the fantail. "*The fantail is closed. Hold all trash and garbage on station. That is, the fantail is closed*," getting ready for flight ops. I never have figured out the difference between garbage and trash.

Ranger tilts as we turn into the wind to get twenty-five knots across the flight deck, enough to get a young boy slightly airborne as he opens his coat and leans forward at the bow like a new airedale on FOD walkdown. (FOD means Foreign Object Debris like screws, pens, tools or anything that a jet engine can suck.)

Broomstick comes back from wiping down tables at 1630. Chow secured at six, and they're still shuffling bombs in preparation for tomorrow's air show. "Don't forget to check the napkin holders."

He cocks his head as if to say, "fuck you, you're on your day off." But later I see him stuffing napkins.

I can be had. I bought into the mooring pool. Also known as the anchor pool. At twenty bucks a box, you buy one of the sixty boxes allocated to represent your guess of what minute within whatever hour the ship will moor, as called away on the 1MC and logged in the Quartermaster's logbook.

Here's how they explained it. You have a sheet of paper with sixty blocks, numbered randomly from one to sixty. Over that you have a carbon paper, and over the carbon is a sheet of unnumbered blocks. Sixty blocks at $20 makes a hefty $1200 pot.

Man, was I suckered. The tough Puerto Rican fag killer (the one who wanted the skinny boy's lips?) presented this scam. He'd already bought two boxes, but wanted to increase his odds by hooking partners at $10 a box. I put in $40, my beer money for Saturday night after the Dependent's Day Cruise. Half my cash from selling the fridge. I'd take $600, half the winnings, if any of my four half-boxes hit. Something kept telling me, this dude has been around. But I find that even when I know I'm being suckered, I just step right on down that drain. It's masochism.

Broomstick, who was gonna hand me that beer instead of a Pepsi Saturday, handed the conman $50. We talked about having a helluva party, eh. Sailors are stupid with money.

1930 2 AUG 90. Sweet Pea looked me up at dinner, wearing his green fatigues ("greens"), blue hangar deck jersey, and float coat. I was already eating, just a ham and cheese sandwich and a glass of milk. As usual, he had only ten minutes to eat before mustering with his division in the hangar bay.

This could have been our last meal together for a while, since everything goes crazy when the ship pulls in. It's like high school graduation, everybody goes his separate way. When he got in line I was going to get a tray for him. But the line was short so I came back to my table and waited. It seemed like forever before he came over with two hot dogs, fries and apple juice. Then as soon as he sat, a voice called from the table by the Weapons' shack. "Ah shit. I've got to go see what my supervisor wants." All the Yellow Shirt (a hangar deck director) wanted was to sit with the kid, to joke with and tease him like everybody else who falls under the spell of Sweet Pea. "Let me just go see what he wants and I'll be right back."

He took his tray so I knew that was it. I finished my sandwich slowly, stalling, then finally gulped down the half glass of milk and walked to the scullery without looking back, dumped the tray and headed for the ladder.

"Hey, would ya help me with this table?" It was a blueshirt who was always flipping my hat and trying to order Broomstick around.

"This is my day off," I kept going.

"Then get outa here."

I didn't get to make any arrangements with Sweet Pea to see him Friday night. He was getting off the ship at around two, and I get off at 2030. Since I have to be back at 0600 Saturday I don't plan to go back to Mission Beach yet. I'll just sleep on the damn boat. At least I'd like to go to the Mexican Village as a treat, if I can find somebody to go with me.

My boss, in Pers back at the squadron, smugly announced to me that I've got offload Tuesday. I knew that would happen, soon as I sold the fridge.

"Oh, thanks for the favor," I said.

He cracked a glib smile and had to turn his head. If some other Flip had been there have broken into Tagolog.[5]

---

[5] A note on languages: Tagolog is pronounced tuh-GAH-loge. Speaking foreign languages in the work environment is technically illegal, or against Navy policy; and this has been the subject of numerous complaints. But the rule is ignored or abused whenever two Filipinos eat chow, or a Filipino is pissed at an American, or if Filipinos don't want you to know what's going on. To be fair, it's also natural to communicate in your native language. Still, when one finds foreigners in supervisory positions in the Personnel Department handling sensitive items such as cyclical performance evaluation reporting, and ongoing performance test verification, as well as annual

I could pack now, work all day tomorrow, pick up my bags from the Ready Room or Pers or wherever else they let us stow our bags all day; then take my stuff home tomorrow night instead of going to dinner. It would be nice to come home Saturday night and already have my stuff put away. But then I'd have to either sleep in a Ready Room chair Friday night, or fight early morning traffic to the *Ranger* Saturday to muster on time. And with two thousand civilian guests coming on the Dependent's Day Cruise, I could have trouble getting over the brow.

All VF-1 coops are turning over to Ship's Company tomorrow at noon, so everyone has to be out then. However, TAD personnel such as myself, remaining onboard to assist the D-Day cruise, may berth here tonight, moving from the other berthings by 1300. Screw it. I'm going to pack tonight, haul my sea bag and garment bag to my shop at the other end of the boat before I go to work tomorrow morning, retrieve it at 2030 tomorrow night when I get off, haul it home, and fight the traffic Saturday morning. I'm packing now.

2230 3 AUG 90. Back on the beach! My roommate, That Guy, although out for the evening, had his Mustang GT parked safely in the carport--so I had to park my brand new 1990 GEO Metro on the street. Fortunately, I found a spot right out front. My Toyota--shortly before it was stolen--got the front bumper ripped out at nearly the same spot where the cops shot to death a bat wielding attorney smashing his girlfriend's car windows.

I found some mail on my bed. Two notices about the Toyota. First a towing company announced its imminent sale, 3 August. That was today--tonight now. Second, a notice from the Orange County Sheriff advising me that it was found on a road in San Juan Capistrano and towed at 1500 21 July. So while I served my country, ordered to sea in the US Navy, my car was recovered by the cops and sold by the tow yard. What a racket.

I walked up to the sea wall looking for Lou. Rounding Roberto's I saw the Roller Coaster finally running, and two cops talking to a civilian on the sidewalk. I knew I was home. Red was out of jail and had my radio in good hands. Nobody had seen Lou all day.

My teen-age buddy Louis, half Indian, half Mexican, came by the wall and hung out with some girls from the burbs; then came to my place to borrow my boogie board. He showed me how the one he'd been using was scraping his nipples. It wasn't long before we snuggled on the couch and you know the rest.

Only a few weeks before the six-month deployment we call Westpac. And,

---

advancement qualification; and in the Disbursing Department handling pay records that fluctuate like the stock market, the pure American sailor faces real danger of becoming terminally disenfranchised by a subtle sort of coup. The 39-Man coop cleaner is a PO2 in the First Lieutenant division--which in the Navy means the janitor department. He announced that the berthing is to be vacated by ten hundred except for persons staying onboard overnight.

we could get sent to the Persian Gulf on emergency recall, since we're the "ready carrier."

I have to get up at 0430 to have a clean shave, get out the door, down I-5 and on the boat by 0600.

SOMETIME SUNDAY AFTERNOON. I don't know what happened to my watch. I have my boogie box, beach towel, beach chair, beach bag and no less than the beach itself. They can turn Iraq into glass with some other carrier. I'm catching rays.

Roadrunner came over, from the ship. Right now he's boogie boarding with Louis.[6] Roadrunner looks nearly as young as Sweet Pea, but with straw blond hair, and a tattoo in a strange place.

I can see inimitable JayCee and undauntable Dave, boardwalk ambassadors. Dave shakes hands with a tourist, about to hit him up for a smoke or beer money. He's got the stance of a man who's already been executed, faced God and been sent back to haunt us. He must have been a gunslinger in his past life. His eyes disarm you and you don't know, until he speaks, he's drunk off his ass.

South of the checkered flag, Roadrunner and Louis go back to the water. Roadie brought his own board. Louis rides mine. The radio has died, and I'm out of sunblock. I'll enjoy the laughing shrieks of children, and the gulls and passing jets (commercial, that is). And play in the sun as it burns through sparse haze. My $90 Ray Bans cut most of the glare, and the sun is still high enough so that the bikini G-strings are more than silhouettes- ah, much more.

I haven't been with a girl since Amy dropped me like an egg and I splattered into the Navy. That Guy came in this morning with claw marks at 0800 and left before noon to his part time gig as a runway model. He's in the fast lane. Me, I'm over thirty.

I almost married a couple of times. Cinda, from Wellfleet on Cape Cod, thirteen long years ago. She made love to me once. I loved her for three years, the last of which she lived with a dude I never met.

Then Amy. Heiress to Western Temporary Services, card carrying member of the Malcolm Forbes yacht club with standing front row seats to Billy Graham. I lived with her for two years and spent Christmas at Denney's alone the first year. The second year Denney's was closed.

Then I broke up with her and joined this fucking military bullshit. It got me out of town, which is what I wanted. I couldn't stand passing our milkshake cafe down on Main street. The only female I've been with since was a whore in a Thai massage parlor, SabaiLand in Pattaya Beach, whom I met on the bleachers behind a glass window. Number 120. I'll never forget. Low cut evening gown, large round pin with the number, clipped my nails badly,

---

[6] A note on the Lou's: Louis is the 16-year old, Lou or Louie is the Vietnam vet, and Louis/Louie is a PN2 supervisor I have at the squadron. Get that?

bathed me nude, put me on a warm, soapy air mattress and sponged me with her cunt. It was a cheap thrill to deny her my come. She whispered "*bac lat*"-- Asian for "fag." I had told her I was saving it for my tour guide outside.

The seaward side of the sea wall is lined with brown bags which hide cases, twelve-packs and six-packs. Underage drinkers smuggle the canned contents into plastic or paper cups and sip beers like sodas from straws, while drug dealers wander up and back from trios to points of contact peddling twenty dollar dime bags of grass and sheets of acid, pieces of paper people chew to get illucid perceptions onboard roller coaster Earth. Here comes Roadrunner to sip plastic.

2300 5 AUG 90. They have not yet sold my car. I called the tow yard in San Juan Capistrano. They said for $224 I could come get it. Roadrunner stayed with me, even after I slowly tickled his toes and massaged his foot and gently grabbed his leg last night. He slept on the couch, like I slept in the spare bedroom at Travis Clark's house shortly before he created the TV series, "Tour Of Duty." Sometimes you know what they want and they don't force you into things and nothing happens, nothing at all. Not even your career. At least Roadrunner drove the Metro for me and I got my old Toyota back. I sold it to That Guy for $650, $75 down. Wish me luck.

We offload in the morning. Wolfpack got Monday off, along with the weekend. Do I get Tuesday off in comp time? Nope. I got offload Tuesday, remember? Wah. I feel my boss smiling.

Lou the vet is living downtown in a motel. Registered for only a day, sleeping there all week, able to pay whenever they discover the oversight. That sounds like a disaster of wishful thinking if I ever heard one. Especially if his habit gets out of hand.

I went into my bathroom and found red dots splattered all over the wall. Louie confessed it was his blood. Now I know why he takes so long when he uses my bathroom. He's shooting up. Why didn't it occur to me? I knew he was the busiest acid dealer on the beach, and knew he had a wound in his back from shrapnel, causing pain. I knew that as a street bum he could forget medicine. He was self-medicating with heroin to kill 20 years of pain.

2355 8 AUG 90. Just came back from Palm Liquor on Mission Boulevard at Palm Avenue. Twice in half an hour, Lou talked me into driving up there and charging a bottle of Jack on my credit card. The first bottle slipped out of the bag as he pulled it out of his jacket getting out of the car. He is out of control.

He insisted on returning the shards as sold in a defective bag. But they whined that the distributor wouldn't give a fuck about them, so why should they give a fuck about us.

Today Scrapper, the airman striker (wanna be a PN) in our shop announced he no longer wants to be a PN (Personnelman). He put in his request to go back to the Line Shack. PN1 approved without blinking, then blamed me for influencing him with my bad attitude. Meanwhile, I requested a transfer to First Lieutenant. Of course I was denied. My request would reduce manning by more than 30 percent. At least all this brought attention to the fact that Pers is fucked up. Nobody wants to work for my boss.

The YNCS, our LCPO, hauled PN1 and me into the skipper's office for a knock down drag out chat.[7] The skipper was gone and there was a big Raggedy Andy in his chair with a hand on a coffee cup labeled STRESS. A perfect set for the drama to unfold. Senior said the CO had been losing it lately and because of that one of the maintenance chiefs had just quit. He's gone back to a less responsible job. "This guy's responsible for the tone in our office, and he's the one who's got me ready to get out." My thousand yard stare scared Senior as I went off on PN1.

"I can see murder in your eyes," Senior said. "You look like you're about to jump out of your chair and strangle PN1. That scares me, and I don't want to see it again."

He knew I had been charged with murder up in Hollywood in 1985. That's supposedly why I'll never get a security clearance, even though I was acquitted. Everybody in Admin and Pers finds out, sooner or later. "I'm not gonna kill my supervisor," I said. "I just want him to quit speaking Tagolog when he's talking business on the phone, because I don't learn anything. And to quit smoking in the office, and quit bullying us around like Hitler. That's all I ask."

"Well," PN1 said. "I don't want you to have any work in your pending basket at the end of the day. And do I talk to you in Tagolog?"

"What a stupid fucking question!" I looked at the senior chief and got no support. Right, the man had rank over me so whatever he said--no matter how inane--was good as gold and beyond reproach. This is the Navy. I wasn't dealing with guys who had a full deck. They have bluff and power, and government pay. That's all they need.

I put on my dive trunks, walked to the beach, and practiced karate for the first time in fifteen years--with the exception of a couple of moves that saved my ass in Hollywood. I jogged to the jetty and back to the palm tree park where I found Louie.

I don't know why, but it occurred to me that if I shot myself with my .44, I'd probably do it through the heart, and do it on the beach at night. I promised Lou I'd tell him, so when he heard the shot he could direct the cops to the shoreline before some kid found my body and screamed.

1730 9 AUG 90. I came around the Jack-in-the-Box and looked to see if That Guy's Toyota was parked in my stall. It was. So I parked in front of a new rollerblade shop on Mission Boulevard and walked across the street with

---

[7] A note on terms: YNCS is the Yeoman Senior Chief, or Senior Chief, or Senior; and he's the Leading Chief Petty Officer in the purely military view. Kind of like a department head, but with more power and less authority.

my cover off. I would rather burn my bald head than wear that fucking dog bowl the Navy calls a hat. Only the perkless enlisted must wear it, of course.

I checked the mail after changing into knee torn jeans and putting on the black Spanish leather shoes that Dad gave me last time I as home. No new returned check notices, that's good. I turned on CSPAN and caught a Q-and-A on Iraq with the State Department. The news is starting to get my attention. They had some local crap about forming a citizen's committee to review a racial shooting, but as the blurb belched on, it became a political media event; and my mind drifted back to the *Ranger.*

I have to (get to) pick up Sweet Pea on the 19th. I miss him. I'd marry him if I were a girl, or adopt him if I could. He's had no dad since he was six. The dad left his wife flat. No child support, nothing. I want to be Sweet Pea's hero. So, I'll leave him alone until the Iraqis hit *Ranger* with chemical weapons. Then run to the hangar to find him and die in his arms. I like several men on *Ranger*, but there's no one I'd want to be with more in the dying, agonizing moments at the end. I wish I could say, "let's not and say we did." But the Battle Groups are moving, and the rumor is we're moving Westpac up six weeks. We're on 96-hour alert from now on, which means if they give the word, 96 hours later we'll pull out. Even with the leaky boat and the creepy squids, if I have to play war at least I'm proud to play with Wolfpack onboard *Ranger*, Top Gun of the Pacific Fleet. I had to buy another ribbon today.[8]

While we were out off Mexico all month, we were told that *Ranger* and Air Wing TWO got a Meritorious Unit Commendation for the last deployment. Sometimes it takes years to get awards for what you've done. So now I've got the MUC, a Sea Service ribbon for being at sea more than 90 days (no small achievement itself) from last Westpac, and the Navy "E" ribbon--with two E's--for best fighter squadron on the west coast in 1988 and 1989. Everybody in the squadron is ready to kick ass, too. We're already fussing and fighting. WE WANT WAR! WE WANT WAR! It's like a chant going around. You can smell it.

"Not me," Doc Robson calls himself an exception. "I want a nice, boring, relaxing deployment full of friendly ports of call, sunny beaches and a good time."

Right now it could go either way. But we won't have any of that Vietnam half-baked bullshit, I know that.

2200 9 AUG 90. There's even violence at Mission Beach.

---

[8] A note about dress: Ashore in summer we wear white uniforms called summer tropical whites. On the boat we get away with white cotton turtleneck jerseys and green fatigues, or, if they insist, a blue denim shirt and pants outfit they call dungarees. Admin and Pers mainly wear whites in summer at Miramar, while the line rats and maintenance guys wear blue coveralls or dungarees.

"You don't talk to a kid that way!"

"I understand, sir."

WHOP! POP! Two socks in the face. I knew this guy was weird when he told me he could access my files through the FBI. I'd never seen him before or told him my name. But he said some words to a pretty little boy on a skateboard, and the kid's dad happened to be riding around making dope deals in the area and the shit hit the fan. I wonder what he said, wonder if I might have wanted to say the same thing, and wonder if the FBI type dude will come back as a rooftop sniper. "I just hope he recognizes me in the crosshairs," said Chuck, the man behind the man behind the acid on Mission Beach. "Because I've always been good to him."

"I hope he doesn't see me in his crosshairs," I said. These are the nineties and I've lived in Hollywood. That's enough to ruin anybody. I've had neighbors who were males with real female breasts--transbreastuals. They didn't have cunts and they had real dicks. They just had real tits also. I've had a few sympathy fucks, like the hot skinny blond male go-go dancer from the fire escape of a hotel overlooking Hollywood Boulevard. I wasn't his type--he did me a favor. I want someone to worship me, to put a silver chain around my neck and swear "I love you" and not be kidding. Someone to live for. I just need a boy who needs a hero. I think I was Shane in my past life. From the gunfighter book.

How did my English professor put it ten years ago, as I was graduating from college: "The warfare between ideal love and new selfhood, and perverted (though appealing) love, could be a theme of major importance in the eighties." Well, it is now.

See, I grew up with this problem named Billy. Straw blond hair, bright eyes (I've forgotten if they're blue or they're green), bright thin-lipped smile, bright brains, the kind of kid who ends up fucking four girls a night by the time he's out of high school. An angel like that is bound to attract one or two dudes, too, don't you think?

By the time I hit college and get in this English class, it's over with Billy and I've been writing him for a couple of years anyway, stoking the dead ashes. So there I am in New Testament Greek and my English professor's kid outside playing frisbee on the Whitworth College campus looks just like Billy.

I walk across campus to my dorm after class in some deep emotional tailspin, write poetry and forget all about my next class, which is a fucking poetry class in fact. Rod Stewart was right--the first cut is the deepest.

Outside my apartment, the brakes and whir and shrieks and laughs of a carnival Thursday night. Let's kill. Let's love.

Red talks me into buying a Grateful Dead butterfly button that I pin to my gaudy green and red and black Thai shirt. I watch him argue with the cops over ticketing a young kid for doing an ollie off the planter by the lifeguard station.

The San Diego City Council orders the cops to ticket young kids $60 for allegedly filing down the concrete like hands that rub the brass off Abe Lincoln's nose when little kids tour the capitol of Illinois. City Council makes money off my military salary, but what would they think if they knew our rate training manuals, at 45 pounds per box, were sent by the dozens of boxes to *Ranger* at sea, air lifted, and didn't get to us anyway until right as we got back, so we could have picked them up at Miramar, and in fact we already had the manuals at the beach so now we're tossing all the extras? What would the city think about that, huh? Nothing. Maybe the federal government. Nah, they're in D.C. Nobody gives a fuck about decentralized waste. So get your money from kids on skateboards; maybe they have rich parents. Still, I hate the perpetuity of social falsehood and the cultural schism fostered by a Board unwilling to accept it that eight years from now--maybe--today's skateboarding at Mission Beach will result in minor maintenance. They have cops insisting that fining kids pays the upkeep of the concrete boxes, which at worst are rounded enough to sit on in comfort. *Thanks* to those kids on their skateboards. They skate for hours, hit no girl, rob no store. Suddenly cops. Stop, mill about, act natural. Cops go. Now skate again, heroic, brave; continue daring art--systematic wearing down and rounding corners of palm tree planters so that I, local tenant, feel smooth edged boy-made bench, realize beautiful flying dream hammered real before mesmerized gaze. See cop slogans "America's Finest" and "To protect and serve." See big lies. In this case. I toast the daring young men in gratitude and donate my radio to Red, may he boogie on as I deploy to protect and serve you on high seas, keep you safe from all enemies, foreign and domestic.

0400 11 AUG 90. Carlos, a freaky looking longhaired white boy who parties with That Guy, knocks on the double bolted door until I answer with my .44 and find That Guy letting him in.

"Let me in." He is frazzled and drenched. "Please. I'm sorry, I'm sorry. Just listen to me, will you just listen to me, all right?"

I stand in the hall in a teeshirt, my dick hanging out and my gun in one hand, tugging down the shirt with my other.

"I was at my friend's house. They all started to do drugs. I don't do drugs. So I walked home. I was coming across the bridge on West Mission Bay drive. All the sudden this bunch of black guys, they stopped me at the top of the bridge. Three cars. They jumped out and pounded the shit out of me and threw me in the water. I thought I was gonna die. My god. I'm not prejudiced but these fuckin' eight niggers. I've never been prejudiced but I am now. They threw me off the bridge. Look at me--I'm soaking wet." He uses the phone to call his brother to pick him up at Jack-in-the- Box across the street. I call 911 to report it, in case the niggers are still out there playing.

"Can I talk to him?"

"Sure."

I tell Carlos the dispatcher has some questions, and hear his rapid fire answers.

"You'll never catch them because I couldn't identify them or the cars. Three cars and six or eight fuckin' niggers. Excuse me, I'm not prejudiced but they were fuckin' niggers. They just beat me up and said 'fuck you' and threw me off the bridge. I thought I was gonna die. I should be dead right now."

"Hey, I know it's a traumatic thing you just went through. But I've gotta work in two-and-a-half hours and I need to sleep."

"Okay. I won't shout. I'm sorry."

That Guy turns the TV down. I had turned it on to create some kind of comfort zone for the poor dude.

Add anti-white terrorism to anti-gay terrorism and Iraqi terrorism that could strike San Diego, and I feel compelled to carry my Bulldog at all times. I must be getting paranoid.

Chapter Three

2330 11 AUG 91. What if it's a holy war? And if Saddam sends a commercial airliner over the *Ranger*? Would Iraq provoke the nuking of the Holy Land on some hunch that it could never happen? Given people's capacity for frenzy in the modern world, why not? What makes the Holy Land holy, except that it's designated? Can't they destroy it and believe thereafter that God designated some other place holy?

Louie hasn't slept since they evicted him from that hotel without his belongings--ironic term for a homeless vet--including my nonmilitary Captain's hat. Tonight "to ease the pain" he talked me into driving him downtown to buy a balloon. It was squashed with brown junk inside, which he warmed in a spoonful of water using the last four matches from the only matchbook in this apartment. He tore off the head of a Q-Tip and dropped it in the spoon, stuck a $3 rig, freshly soaked in bleach, into it and drew his solution into the syringe. That done, he tied a belt around his upper arm and--while I cringed--jabbed at the muscle on the far side of a vein. He pulled it back, but couldn't get the blood to flow. He took it out and jabbed, again and again, playing darts until his blood pooled on the arm. I ran to my bed and pulled a pillow over my head.

"God fucking dammit," he murmured from the bathroom. He came out and sat in the living room chair, and never came on.

"We could have bought Brave Bulls."

"I know."

He conned me out of my last ten at Johnny's Surf Club where Greg, the bartender, poured smaller glasses than Walt.

"Walt gives away too much," Greg said.

"Lazarus got busted," Lou said. Lazarus is a beach bum who sings and plays a sweet guitar. "And he told the cop, 'let me kiss my wife goodbye.' And that little kid Mike came up and kissed him on the lips."

"I'd like to sing 'Child Of the Street' to that little homo."

I knew the hyper little green eyed twelve year old blond he was talking about, who went by Mike, a recent runaway who hung at the beach with some local thieves. He was real cute but obvious trouble.

Lou just laughed and shook, exhausted.

1830 12 AUG 90. He called himself Mike Tate, looked 13 but claimed to be 15. Came up with young Louis and passed the hours at my beach towel, telling me about himself. Was his sob story true, half-true, untrue? His parents were druggies. Two weeks ago they brought him to the beach on a family outing and told him to wait on the corner while they parked the car, then left him in his beach attire waiting, waiting, and never came back.

Ray is the social worker living upstairs. Grilling burgers in our barbecue pit, he knocked on my door right after I closed it with Mike inside.

"Hi, Ray."

"What's up with the kid inside?"

"I think he's an abandoned child."

"And you're gonna help him."

"I guess so, why?"

"Because I work with kids. I'm a social worker."

"Maybe you should talk to him. If you want to come in?"

"Well, outside."

"Hey Mike."

He stared at Ray from the couch.

"Where do you live?"

"I used to live in Spring Valley."

"Where do you live now?" The white-haired, ruddy old retired sailor let his burgers burn a little as he stared at those little green eyes.

"Out here. Sometimes with my uncle."

"Well, you know what we've gotta do, don't ya?"

"What?"

"Call the cops."

Ray went back to flip his burgers. When he returned Mike had his sweatshirt on and was pulling on his socks and shoes. "What are you gonna do? Live on the beach and sell your ass?"

"I'm not goin' to a foster home. I hate foster parents."

"Hey, I'm not gonna chase ya."

Ray was planning to let me feed the boy, then have the cops or a social worker pick him up in a couple of hours.

"Thanks for the dinner offer." The little dude vanished out the gate and up the walk, headed for the boardwalk like his legs were stinging.

Ray and I looked each other over. He meant well and had age and experience on me. Maybe he had saved me from myself.

"You don't bring boys into your home alone," he said. "The first time he rips you off, then you'll tell him it's over and he'll tell everybody that you tried to fuck him. He knows the language that you don't know. And you were letting yourself in for a lot more than you'd be able to deal with. You don't need those kinds of accusations, true or false."

"Some guy," Mike had told me this afternoon, "asked me to go in the bathroom and play with myself for ten minutes. I asked him why and he said he just wanted to see how big my dick would get. I told him that was sick. Guys like that should be in jail."

"I know what it looks like," I told Ray. Like Frankie who slept in my arms at my parents' house one Christmas, my brother's second wife's pre-teen kid. It wasn't my idea he slept with me. They put us together because we had played all day and someone had to double up. I was glad. He was priceless.

"I'm sure gonna miss Uncle Bob." He started to cry as they drove off that morning. Suddenly his paranoid wife instilled the notion of pederasty and drew a straw that broke the back of their marriage, so I heard. Later Frankie admitted that he'd lied when she asked if I touched his privates. He told her what she wanted to hear.

"Well," I told Ray, "you accomplished one thing. Mike didn't get chicken."

"Maybe he'll come back. If he does, let me know."

"Sure." I put the chicken back in the fridge.

It's foggy; it will be cold on the beach tonight. I wonder where throwaway Mike will sleep, where he'll get food. Piece of ass for pizza.

I hitchhiked over 20,000 miles. When I was 13 I went 400 miles without getting molested. I guess, like Mike, I was so small and vulnerable they took joy in being my protector. But if I hadn't gone back home to my good parents right away, I might have met the same men I met when I went back out at 17. I was lucky even then, considering the decrepit white house, front porch crammed with rusting bedsprings in some Oklahoma town, a five-thirty pickup from a guy out "chasing pussy."

Several miles down the road he added that he'd give me the best blow job of my entire life. It still rates up there, fifteen years later. But he might have blown my head off, or took me to a soundproof room with a chainsaw.

Meals were sometimes good, but I had sardines from an empty house for sale. Mainly it's sleep that you trade for places to sleep. You don't ride with them to a trysting place to tryst. You ride to drop off safe from the possibility of murder; yet invite it by going, as much as by staying on the road overnight. Like it would be better to be murdered in a warm, dry place. And you have to stay awake to please them, even if it only means to let them please your flesh, which is often all they desire. Men who give you rides usually give you head if they have sexual designs picking you up. But they might thrill at turning you out by sliding a hot, wet finger in your ass as you spurt on their tongue. That you can't retreat from.

2300 12 AUG 90. I turn in lonely. My lot in life is to broach sensitive subjects with men who would kick my ass, and avoid getting slapped. Not that a woman wouldn't kick my ass, too. I'm just voicing the astute observation of my roommate, you know, That Guy.

I wonder if it's possible for society to ease me out of this gracefully. Who wants to be an old queen? You can sap the strength of youth for only so long; then feel foolish. Assume there is a Miss Right. A rehabilitated lesbian? Gorgeous, of course. Elegant, tough, vulnerable.

If Mike scratches at my screen tonight will I shoo him off? If he sleeps here will anyone see, like the NIS or SDPD or RAY? If only God saw, how would we behave? Explode with lust? Then, could I roust him out when I went to work at six? Could I leave him sleeping here to face Phyllis and RAY in the morning? Would he steal my things? He hangs with thieves, knows guys with bolt cutters, smokes marijuana, eats magic mushrooms, and smokes cigarettes when drunk. Age 13-15.

Okay, forget Mike. What will Ray say about Sweet Pea? The sailor who's 19 turning 15. Don't have boys in your house with the door closed. Okay Ray, now mind your own fucking business.

"Just like the Navy," Ray said. "You go from a good to a bad command and eventually you hit a good one again. He'll find a good foster home."

Only this isn't a good time for drawing comparisons. I'm in FITRON ONE (aka, FUCKTRON ONE; Wolfpack, aka Workpack). And I work in Personnel. Everyman is canceling his inoperative extension and getting out.

Such as Five Day Wonder, the gay guy who gets out tomorrow, a "convenience of the government" honorable discharge entitling him to the GI bill and veteran's assistance, and no service in the Gulf. Living proof that--if I wanted--I could avoid our looming confrontation. If I truly didn't want to serve my country and be with Sweet Pea in the hangar bay dying of chemical rain. One breath, three simple words. "I am ---." Then sit in the states and worry for Sweet Pea.

I wonder whose cozy apartment Mike will find now, if he'll be crying in the palms where the tourists buy their drugs. Fuck Ray and his God Squad witch hunting clan killing children on the lamb. Why not sell your ass? You might get lucky and find some man who will take care of you, buy you pants and a shirt and give you hugs AND drugs. Or educate you like a Roman. How is Foster Care the only way out--and what did they do before? I was thawing a chicken, until a nosy neighbor protected us from potentially exploiting each other. Now on the beach out there, somebody else may be staring at Mike. Thawing a chicken.

2315 13 AUG 90. The PN1 is gone all week. I want to wear dungarees instead of whites, ballcap instead of the dog bowl. But in respect for PN2, who always wears whites at Miramar, I keep in step. Scrapper, the striker, wears his dungarees, as he has ever since he came topside from the Line shack.

I called the county adoption agency from work. At least with PN1 gone I can use the phone without having my ass chewed or put on report or court martialed or fucking shot. The oldest boy they have is eight unless they check nationwide. Usually older boys are considered unadoptable. Doomed as too tall weeds.

The lady said I should go find Mike, get the truth out of him as to the name of his foster home and social worker, and they would assist in legally hooking us up to be together. The government, according to this understanding woman on the phone, would be only too happy to find the child a foster parent who takes a specific interest in him, rather than some artificial match that frequently fails.

I found him on the boardwalk. Same sweatshirt, trunks, tennis shoes and socks he's worn all week. But thanks to our concerned social worker, Ray, he spooked off in the company of thieves. Another boardwalk John, named John coincidentally, took a shine to Mike. I suggested he become his foster parent. What the hell. He was giving Mike money already, and making him spend it on food. I pointed out that redheaded strangers were ogling and taking our Mike down the strandway. He didn't like that, and went after them. I stopped at home and got my gun, thinking I was the Lone fucking Ranger. An hour later Mike followed John back to the wall. The redheads had employed him to burgle. Better than selling your ass, I suppose. "Do me a favor," John whined. "He won't come and talk to me if you're standing here. So just go away for a little while so I can talk to him. All right?"

Jilted off the wall. I walked over to Johnny's and found Walt.

"The usual."

He pours a bigger Brave Bull than Greg, and was glad to see me. I said Lou's on a thin limb.

"Yeah. That guy can hold it pretty good, but he had to be eased out of here a couple a nights ago. And he owes Gary twenty bucks."

He owes me thirty-five, but I didn't tell Walt. Lou will settle up when his disability check comes.

I watched Mike and John walk down Ventura together. Mike knew I was in Johnny's, and looked over as they passed on the other side of the street. Is that John getting in his ass? A boy has to work who he can find out here. Maybe they'll pair off famously, until Mike moves on.

2145 14 AUG 90. The skipper wants a list of every swinging dick on leave outside the county. From now on, final approval can only be granted by him, vice Department Head. And suddenly we have Quarters at 0730 in the hangar tomorrow. The world gets nervous. "You know where I'll be at 0730?"

"At Quarters," Senior said.

"No--picking up the paychecks."

"That's okay."

"What, pick them up later?"

"No, pick 'em up at seven thirty. We can pass down to you whatever is put out at Quarters." Picking up pay checks is one of few things more important than listening to your CO.

I got thrown the household goods potato. That's okay, I'm worried about my own. One Exocet could send us out post-haste. I dug through the archives to Westpac '89 and patterned a memo after what was done before. Names, rates and social security numbers.

I bought a Will Writing Kit from a stationer store and ran off some copies for the Legal Officer, then ran a note in the POD (Plan Of the Day, all hands required reading). I put my brother and my dad as executors. Who will I give all my stuff to, and what do I have? Five thousand guys onboard *Ranger* will ask this question. Two hundred guys in Wolfpack.

Two hours on the phone dropped my car insurance bill a hundred bucks. Good thing PN1 wasn't around. He'd have bitched me out for making personal calls.

I worked until 1900 protecting my country from all enemies, foreign and domestic. So what do I do when I find out the jokers who stole my Toyota were smuggling illegal aliens?

A recap on my car: The Toyota got ripped off from my Mission Beach carport, so I got a loan and bought a brand new GEO Metro. Then it got recovered and since I had the new car I sold the Toyota to That Guy for $650. He put $75 down.

That Guy found the birth certificates of two boys from Michuacan beneath a seat. I photocopied them and sent the originals with a letter from the Admin Officer via the Legal Officer to the Director of the INS. Some idiot had left the business card of the Spanish/English notary public on the front seat of the car when they abandoned it--probably thinking they had blown the engine because the radiator hose broke. Of course, since I'd bought the car from a master chief who kept back-ups for everything under the seat, when I went up there with Roadrunner all I had to do was replace the hose, add water and drive it home. Now I hope the director of the INS isn't a coyote, corrupt smuggler on the side.

Here in the modern world, it could happen that the US is being invaded by Cuban Hispanic loyalists coming through Mexico, assisting Spain to conquer whatever they thought they once may have had. In prudence, I sent a copy to my long-time attorney. I just hope they don't rip off that car again before That Guy pays in full.

1115 15 AUG 90. I don't know whether to wear my raincoat or sunglasses. Lunch time at the galley. The big passdown: *Ranger* is now on 72-hour alert. If the President sends another carrier to the Gulf it will be us. I work my ass off to get storage arranged for cars and household goods.

1930 15 AUG 90. Pastel sunset, matching afterburners up the Miramar flightline, over hangars two and three. Flashing red and green tail lights glide Wolf emblems left and right, practicing. I should bring Mike up to the base to watch. Introduce him as my wife.

"Are you ready to take us to the Gulf and kick some butt?" I meet the skipper in the hangar passageway with a patriotic show.

"If they want us to, we'll do it." He doesn't flinch. I don't blame him for blowing up last week--we're all on edge. We're the best. TOP GUN not the movie.

My baby blue GEO beebops toward the beaches, over the hill to West Mission Bay Drive. The sun burns a hole through aluminum siding clouds, an orange kissing goodnight. Days are short. And work, long. Yesterday the sun beamed through the roller coaster structure, silhouetting hippies at the sea wall.

Today a member reenlisted, four years. His ID application had five extra months, and with his wife standing there I had to explain that he had to obligate extra service to accept the orders he just got. Or get out with an RE-4, not recommended for reenlistment--ever. But down the road, if he plans to be a lifer, he can reenlist again. That will override the extension. He cooled, though technically he'd been had. Two hours later I got word to type up emergency leave papers for him. His sister died.

We shuffle carport spaces at the pad, and tonight wasn't my night. So I made a run up the block and back, then up the alley past the carport. It looked odd at first--That Guy had Fran's spot, she had ours, and both cars had on car covers.

I made a left on Strandway and came out over the body sketch somebody painted by Hamel's Rollerblades--where trends begin. I don't know if anybody died there; but it embodies Mission Beach.

I turned down Ventura, from the sea, and eyed the lot by the coaster, down by Mission Boulevard. There was Danny in a 4x4. Dashing blond, he knows I've got the hots. But he don't swing. At least, to me. He actually spoke to me in the Enlisted Club at Miramar last week. He must have been drunk. He let me talk him out of smoking a joint with some bitches on the shoreline here one night, pissing off the girls.

"Well, what does he do that's wrong?" There had to be something.

He hesitated. "Well, he's a sex fiend."

He's looking for acid. I could get it free, but he prefers to think I don't know.

Acid, the sailor's drug of choice, can't be observed in a whiz quiz. But you sure wouldn't want to be caught dealing.

Rounding Roberto's, I saw Lou. He looked like hell and flagged me down. I whipped into Jack-in-the-Box.

"I just got the shit beat out of me," he whimpered. He could barely breathe. "Can you help me?"

"I knew this was coming."

"That fuckin' Chris. He threw me into that street sign at the top of Ventura. You know, the one JayCee is always kicking? I think my ribs are cracked."

"Your cheek is cut. It looks like somebody hit you with their knuckle. What do you want me to do?"

"Take me to your place and I'll call my daughter."

I rolled a joint for him while he cleaned up in the bathroom and waited for his daughter. I wonder if rolling a joint for someone with their own pot is as bad as allowing someone to drink in their own car while you're driving. "Lou, why don't you just take a menial job?"

"I try but they won't let me. I'm overqualified."

"Play dumb."

"I know. I should tell them I have a third grade education."

"And that you're a vet."

I don't condone smoking anything. But I can appreciate the sedation of a stoned stupor for a guy who just had his ass beat. He's the second guy over forty who's brawled on this beach in a week. What are we teaching our young?

His daughter and her boyfriend took him to the VA where they hoped he'd be admitted. I hope they keep him for a few days so he can sleep. He hasn't since I went to sea. I was putting him up on my couch through the weekends. The rest of the week he was out in the cold. Now he's been outside all month where it isn't safe at night and it's too noisy to sleep in the day. People who are not homeless don't know, and don't give a fuck about this.

Tomorrow--if he's not in the hospital--he plans to get a place downtown at $400 a month with a guy named Tim. Lou gets $560, Tim gets $650--both on disability, shot up in Vietnam. They can support me when I come back twisted from the Gulf, or kicked out for being all I can be.

1200 16 AUG 90. At lunch, returning my pager to the San Diego Paging company, I found myself in some streak of pride donning my dog bowl and crossing the lot. I had lunch at McDonald's, the only man in a military uniform.

Across from their mother, twin girls looked. "Daddy."

"That's not Daddy. Maybe someone's daddy."

I said my mom was a twin. Then half out of warning, half out of sad self-indulgence, added that they had died six months apart, of cancer in 1986. I didn't throw in the part about Mother's Day; it would have been maudlin. I used to joke that faggots have a lisp. Lithp, that is. But since my night with Muggerboy, when they broke the top off my left front tooth, I sound like Humphrey Bogart. I bet he had a capped tooth. I don't imagine he was a fag.

0500 SATURDAY 90. I have to (get to) pick up Sweet Pea tomorrow night. Up all night watching some woman save a gook community on the Texas side of the Gulf of Mexico. Made for TV movie.

I went back to the sea wall for my radio. Not Red's, mine. Tonight was one of those nights you had to take care which way you turned; and I had let some kid who's leaving town tomorrow keep an eye on my radio.

Two bum thugs wheeled behind me on the boardwalk and I went down to the park where it was better lit. This is America. What a bunch of fools watching TV and laughing in the suburbs. They could be here with a real live person crashed out across the sidewalk where a beat up van is parked with its door open and a price tag of seven hundred bucks.

Lou is in the hospital. He went to Scripps until they saw he was a bum; then the VA. At least Scripps gave a proper diagnosis: Two broken ribs.

Mike is staying with a fag. He gets clean clothes and looks well fed. But later on the dude was asking, "have you seen Mike, has anybody seen Mike?" And implied I might have fucked him.

All evening Mike was on the boardwalk lifting his teeshirt, putting his crotch against somebody's knee. In the fast lane. He'll be a great sex machine--then what.

"The first time he rips you off," Ray said.

"Ray who?"

SATURDAY AFTERNOON 90. For the first time since the boat det, I do not feel pre-occupied with the Navy. I feel like a beach bum. No watches to stand; no zero seven hundred muster; not even the beeper anymore. Some guy called, not even in my line of work, he must have been high. He wanted to pay me to take over his barracks fire watch tonight, 1600 - 2400. Last thing I want to do is baby-sit over there.

Louis has my boogie board. It's muggy. A guy next to me reads, *Bonfire Of the Vanities*. A few years back I would have leaped into that. In my hippie days. Now maybe I'll see the movie, if I'm in the states when it plays.

"Have you lost your mind?" Red asked me.

"How was your night?" Chuck grinned.

"I don't know. It must have been pretty good."

"Yeah," Chuck said. "I was sittin' here at three-thirty and decided, well, I guess Bob isn't comin' back."

I had finally attained such a position of grace and respect that the beach bums looked after my radio once they got me high. I was only going to the store to get a beer and come right back. But a half block is a new world under mysterious influence.

"The waves are huge, dude." Louis came up to pull off his wetsuit. "Massive." A girl in lime green bikini dragged her boogie board across the sand. "Well, I guess I'm goin' back in."

I don't know. He comes to my house for handjobs, likes me to hug him and reach around. But he displays that regular macho teenager attitude toward women. Sex is sex. I guess he's bisex.

"Don't have boys in your house alone," Ray said.

But what a butt. I met him at sunset on the sea wall, wondering if he spoke English. I had seen him a couple of times, then he positioned himself near me and I walked over beside him. That's how it happens--like chess. After five or ten minutes of pretending to be there by accident, I finally broke the ice. "La luz," I said.

"What?"

"You're gonna miss the sunset."

"Oh, yeah."

The second time I saw him I was getting a beer from the liquor store as he went into Luigi's, an Italian giant slice pizza place just up Mission Boulevard from the roller coaster, across the alley from my apartment. I suddenly got two beers, each in its own single bag. His motorcycle was idling in the alley, so as I passed I set a beer on the seat.

He came back out and although we met eyes, I didn't turn back.

"Thanks a lot!" I heard from behind me.

I spun and gave a thumbs up and went on without breaking stride. I believed I would see him again.

Louis told me he had walked out of his house last year and never gone back, never will go back. It was Joe's Harley. He lives with Joe, a waiter at Luigi's. Joe found him asleep on a downtown sidewalk.

Louis tried to show me some Zeppelin riffs on my Strat. But if I hadn't learned in twenty years of strumming, I wasn't going to now. I played a mini-concert for him in my living room, with a neckbrace harmonica. I played

"Just Like Tom Thumb's Blues," by Dylan. Then rocked him to sleep with my ballad, "Made By You," about Danny Robling, a beautiful young man from Concord, California, who drank himself into oblivion, and passed out on the subdivision sidewalk beside his jet black Mustang.

If you were a gay version of Dylan what were you, if not a folk singer? I might have made it big if I'd moved to Boston where the new folkies like Tracy Chapman and Suzanne Vega came from. But not California, not Los Angeles. And certainly not Polk Street.

I came from the Show Me state to San Francisco, fag capitol of the world, where they don't separate the men from the boys. Why shouldn't I cover gay topics? That's what I saw, my portrait of the world as an abstract chronicler of the times. But nobody would sell it. So no one could buy it. Since no one bought it, nobody would sell it. You have to read between the lines, where the advertisers hide from consumers. These people determine what others think.

I sent songs to a guy in New York, Bob Esposito, who claimed to have taken "Mandy" to Barry Manilow, and "Close to You" to the Carpenters. He loved the R&B riff of "Hustlin' Business," my definitive tune about San Francisco's famous Polk Street, where the boys are--but couldn't take the lyrics. Finally, I packed a box of bubblegum flavored Chicalets in a cassette box and mailed them off. "If you want bubblegum," I said, "here's bubblegum."

SUNDAY AFTERNOON 90. Clouds recede. Lovely on the beach, odor of sunblock. Mega people. Louis brought a Megadeth tape.

He's in the water chasing the girl in the green bikini from yesterday. While he boogies, I tune in KGB fm.

The Navy would give me $1000 cash incentive to adopt a kid. Louis--not Mike. And $300 extra each month on top of the $350 extra they give me to live off base because the barracks are inadequate. And another $60 each month as "Family Separation Allowance" when we deploy. That Guy could watch him--not that he needs watching. He could still sleep with Joe if he wants. "I could go back to school," he said.

2000 19 AUG 90. I pick up Sweet Pea--aka Sweets--in two hours. At this time in my life he is my Prince of Peace.

Like my English professors all said, you write about what you can't say. That's why you've never read an autobiography on faggots in the Navy. You can't even say you like dudes without facing a discharge. You don't even have to be gay, just say you are, and if they can't prove otherwise you're out in five days with an honorable discharge. And they won't try to prove that you're not. Me, though, I've got one year left. One last Westpac. And by the time this thing is over and I get out, I'll publish my book and then you'll know what it was like to live in a system that treats you like scum and encourages it among your shipmates.

I have not longed to embrace a man as much as Sweets, since Billy in 1977. The only other boy I've called Prince of Peace.

What makes me long to serve, wait on, accompany, eat with, pick up at the airport, embrace and even love Sweet Pea? I'm not the only dude who gawks at him. So is it us? Or is it him? Is it his body? He's full of defects: A mole under the right leg. Scars from moles removed. Fluctuating weight, sometimes skinny as a skeleton. Chicken legs. I watched him in his underwear, ironing his pink Hot Tuna tee-shirt the night I took him to the airport. All right, he's got a great ass. And his face is deeply gorgeous, especially his eyes. You want to cup his cheeks and behold his face in your hands. Add to this a high cracking voice, zest and charm, and endearing vulnerability. He'll be tired. He has to work tomorrow, too. I'll have to deliver him straight to *Ranger*, then drive home alone to my big bed, with sleepy thanks, and a "see ya soon" that he'll renege. Maybe after dropping him I'll grab a drink at Johnny's. Naturally, a Brave Bull. Lou is still at the VA, coughing up blood. Beach bars aren't the same without him. Chuck will be at the sea wall, fighting the cold or high on the acid he's selling, grinning. Nah, I'll just pull into the carport sober. And tomorrow be sad. I won't fight with my boss, won't dog out my striker. When they ask what's wrong I won't say I'm in love. I'll act cheerful and upbeat, and hide the hurt. I want to breathe on his eyelid, kiss his brow, nibble the top of his ear with my lips, slowly slide my fingers through his black and wavy hair and down his neck, tickle him collar to chin, and hold his graceful fingers lightly in my hands. But I can't. So this will simply seethe, while I concentrate with all my heart on a brief macho handshake we'll have, trying not to give my love away.

After Billy spent the summer in France--many years ago--I picked him up for a movie, met him on the manicured lawn of his house while his sister looked from the foyer's picture window. He was twelve, I was seventeen. I jumped from the car, ran to embrace him. He struggled free and yelled, "Fag!"

At the movie we shared a straw and he rested his small legs on my knee. But I never tried to embrace him again.

2120 20 AUG 90. I stood at the gate waiting as the plane emptied. Families reunited, hugged and kissed. Finally, a stewardess came out.

"Is that it?"

She shook her head in empathy. "Are you going to ask the agent?"

"I'll just go to the ticket counter." I walked back through the airport.

"We're all closed up here."

Wonderful.

"But here's an eight hundred number you can call for flight information." I went to a pay phone, dialed, and endured recording after recording, put on hold between. Finally a person spoke. "We're not allowed to give out passenger information."

"But I'm here to pick him up and he wasn't on the plane."

Finally the man said Sweet Pea's flight had been delayed on take off, causing him to misconnect. If he caught the next flight he would arrive here at two fifty-three.

I went back to my apartment, plopped on the bed and set the alarm for

0230. I had to be at work at 0700. So what. At 0230 I got in my car and went back to the airport.

"I can't believe you waited," he said. "Nobody else would have." But he still didn't get it. His face was lit up, and he wore his pink teeshirt again. I think he always does that just for me. I mean, when adult males wear pink aren't they trying to tell you something? Maybe I just don't get it.

He called his mom while I stood by. It was after six in Connecticut. Finally I heard him say, "I love you, too."

I carried his sea bag to my car. He was hungry but at 0330 I couldn't find the Denney's that was supposedly on Harbor Drive and we happened onto the entrance of the San Diego Bay Bridge, so we headed to North Island, where the *Ranger* sat in front of the *Nimitz*.

Sweet Pea got out. I gave him his bag and he promised to see me soon--maybe--at my place in Mission Beach.

Lou called me from the hospital. He's been getting three squares a day and plenty of rest. And Percodans for his cracked ribs. First he told them he was a suicidal maniac drinking eight cases of beer a day; but they wouldn't take him. Then they determined he had pneumonia, so they changed their mind and said come right in.

He says he's not going back to the "dead end beach scene." He only hung there because of me, Chuck, and maybe Keith. But Keith disappeared since the last drug sweep, probably extradited. Chuck says he's going back to the studio apartment he's always had in La Mesa--he likes people to think he's a bum. And I'm going to the Gulf anywhere between 96 hours and November. The VA's hooking Lou up with Saint Vincent de Paul, a shelter mission.

Phyllis, my landlady, cashed my August check for August, resubmitted my July check and it went through for July, and cashed my money order for August. So the August check bounced. Then she got mad that two checks have bounced in six months. The August bounce cost her two dollars, which she demanded Sunday. The July bounce cost another two dollars. But she shared the blame for August and gave me back two dollars. Because she cashed both the July and August checks and the money order, I had four checks bounce in six weeks for penalties of $8.50 each.

2100 22 AUG 90. You know you're getting close to deployment when guys start disappearing. Two guys went UA (unauthorized absent) last week but just came back. One is now in 1st LT on hold for court martial. The other's in the brig, pre-trial confinement. No word on two wallets that disappeared the same day, or the $400 cash one idiot had in his.

Tomorrow I provide my tape recorder and microphones to the Legal Officer for an Administrative Discharge board. Since I work in Personnel I can't help knowing a lot about what's going on in terms of charges--and discharges. But since I don't have a clearance I make it a point to keep my nose out of things I'm not directly involved in. Like I know this guy's got a board tomorrow, but don't know what he did. He talks to me like of course

I know.

I did stumble across the fact that one of my favorite LT's is getting an involuntary discharge. The YNCS was typing it up this afternoon. "Meet me in the Ready Room tomorrow and we'll get it done," he told the officer. I stood in the doorway at that brief, sad moment. He was a fun guy if you didn't work for him and weren't affected by his incompetence. But we're the Navy's best F-14 fighter squadron. And Wolfpack's preparing for war.

My English professor, teaching British Literature in 1980, pointed out that every time a major world power fell on hard times at home, they embroiled themselves in wars on foreign turf. With this in mind I wonder about our saber rattling Bush. Who's zooming who?

Consider the economic advantages of a war in the Gulf. America made billions selling weapons to Iraq; glutted the market with arms; now has to destroy them to create another market for more arms. We must expend (destroy) billions in good guy and bad guy--mostly bad guy--hardware to bolster defense jobs worldwide. We destroy the consumed goods, create another marketplace, and meanwhile divert attention from troubles at home and justify emergency austerity like high taxes and gas. Not to mention the Keating Five or George's son. Convince me that the world powers didn't close their doors and say, "we need a world war." Or that Bush didn't cut a deal for Hussein to play the bad guy, to put him in a safe house while we trim his population and leave his ass in power in the end. Why is war considered the intelligent method of trimming a population, rather than homosexuality? God said, "be fruitful and multiply." Mission accomplished. Now we should consider outliving life's textbook.

I don't remember a mandate to overpopulate and deplete our resources. But if homosexuality is the intelligent method for curbing population, war is the civilized cure for overpopulation.

Too many intellectual civilians bear arms in America to have a population trimming exercise on our turf. But when the day comes that only cops and armies carry guns, you should expect war on American soil. We have it now in the guise of AIDS. Tell me AIDS is not germ warfare. Why was AIDS traced to 1981 when, coincidentally, the Neutron Bomb, until then ballyhooed as the ultimate new germ warfare weapon that could wipe out entire civilizations without harming a single structure, suddenly disappeared from the face of the press? Just as "reclassified" became the buzzword of choice. Where would you test a plague bomb, if not among human-like ape tribes in their natural, otherwise undisturbed habitat, like in deepest darkest Africa, where they tell us AIDS originated? The LOI is out for READI-EX (Letter Of Instruction for the last work-up, Readiness Exercise). We're supposed to pack for this as if we won't come back. So as of 1 October, adios, Mission Beach. Phyllis has my notice.

If we do come back for the month of October I'll tough it out in the barracks--ugh--or figure something out. But I have to get my belongings stored before this next detachment. Gouge is we'll leave 8 November. A month early. "Petty Officer Graham," one of the pilots comes up. "Do you have any extra screenplays? I want to write a script on cruise."

"You can go," I cut my striker loose and think about this request.

Who the fuck does this LT he think he is? I bust my ass in L.A. for two years; get wrapped up in a murder and fight that charge for a year while my sexual history goes public--which nearly keeps me out of the Navy; ultimately turn it into a movie script, and come this close to a sale to Columbia Pictures. Now this dude is tapping me for advice to make a killing because everybody likes that Naval aviator stuff. Screw him. I'll write my own script about the cruise--from the enlisted point of view. Why help him? He's got a fucking laptop and a stateroom. What have I got--a legal pad and a coffin rack. "I tell ya what, sir. I've got a book you can borrow on script writing." I wasn't gonna show him my screenplay about Los Angeles, that had my own public defender calling me gay.

2300 23 AUG 90. I pick up Lou at the VA hospital, and take him for a drink at Michael's, a dark bar in the new La Jolla Hyatt, where That Guy has a part time parking cars. We get a $7 valet hookup and a space by the door. But four Brave Bulls cost $25. Never run a credit card tab.

Back at the beach I see a kid melting into a palm tree planter, another cementing himself to a car hood. Chuck says everyone is on acid tonight. Mike the queerbait looks sober and asks for a buck. I don't give it so he stops flirting. He has new clothes.

I have a court appearance in the morning. And the day off. I will plead not guilty and demand a jury. Never go before a judge in a bench trial against a cop. The judge will naturally believe the cop. I'll put you, the jury, in my shoes on the fourth of July drinking legally at a public park as this blonde little bitch chugs my beer because my back is turned for thirty seconds and my hot hand isn't nailing it down. Since we're leaving, I'll waive time and probably die defending my country before the stupid trial is settled. "Darling," I say under my breath as a young boy catches my eye, passing me on Mission Boulevard. But I don't look back right away. When I do, I see him throw his arms up in despair and continue on around the corner toward the beach.

I was a little faster in Tijuana, and saw the boy look back. That time I turned and saw him walk into a video arcade. I went back and played a game beside him, started talking, and let him lead me two miles down the border canal where I sucked his dick and licked his butt in the starlight until he came. We left just as two crouched men in cammies scurried over the black field toward us from the US. We got halfway through a neighborhood and I stopped him. "Mira," I rolled the 'r'. And spurted in his shadow.

0815 24 AUG 90. Downtown San Diego greasy spoon with coffee and massive headlines on Kuwaiting. "You're here on embezzlement? Somebody put the wrong first name in the Graham folder. That sent me to the bottom of the slush pile. "I'll have to finish with the rest of the names I called. Then

I'll go back inside and have them get the right file."

I work in Personnel, a paper intensive bureaucratic division of the military, so I have a high tolerance for inept and stupid bungling.

"It's a conspiracy between the cops and the courts and the meter maids," some guy observed. "They know most people are gonna be here beyond two hours. So they put a two hour limit on the meters. Who's gonna walk six blocks to feed the meter?"

"Not to mention leave the courtroom long enough to walk that far?"

"Yeah, for fear they'll miss their call and get shoved to the bottom for another two hours."

"And have to walk back to feed the meter again."

"You've been charged with Minor in Possession of Alcohol, on Ocean Front Walk." The public defender explained the way of the court to a juvenile. "That's a fifty dollar fine for no contest today. Or if proven guilty, two hundred and fifty. They take VISA." Maybe his daddy's VISA.

I went to the Revenue and Collection lady to determine if I qualified for a public defender. As I hoped and feared, I did. I make ten bucks a month net profit as a third class Navy petty officer. I still have to pay the undetermined public defender's cost--even if only $15 monthly. Innocent or not! Now that's a scam. What motivation does San Diego have to curb false arrests, when they profit from court appearances regardless of the verdict?

1830 24 AUG 90. Jonesing for Sweet Pea. What will he want to do his first weekend back onboard *Ranger*? Get out to Mission Beach and play Metallica up and down the boardwalk and chase girls but keep them at arm's length by not realizing they think he is gorgeous--like the last time I walked there with him and his pals. He'd make eyes at one, then turn his head before she turned hers. He's too shy to see the titillated girls ogling him who are too shy to grab his butt.

If I could afford the range time I'd take Louie shooting. I have bullets. I feel like popping cans with my little Bulldog 44 Special, sucking the sharp, sweet kick into my palm as it barks with spitting fire. But I ain't got the dough.

The cops took two kids' skateboards at Belmont Park for skating in the lifeguards' parking lot. And ticketed them. A kid in court today was fined $30 for skating in the wrong place.

My public defender is blonde, trim and pretty, smart, and a die hard crusader. Perfect for a bogus misdemeanor. I can even have a jury without showing up myself. "We'll just put your hat in the chair," she said. This is one time I might be pleased with the dog bowl. "And just ask the jurors if it bothers them that you're not present in courtroom because you're in the Persian Gulf defending the country."

Loneliness washes over me like a wave of saltwater, seeking out the freshest wound. I get self-esteem from big plans of fame and fortune, none solid. I take this stupid job as a clerk for Uncle Sam and cling to it like life, when it's nothing but escape from Amy's rejection, a chill until the street cools enough to let me back in Hollywood without a war. Now I have to maintain good graces with sexual bigots who don't, hoping they won't devour me for being all I can be, or kick me out before I'm done.

1100 25 AUG 90. The base theater as NAS Miramar bustles with a crowd who've shown up for the pre-deployment brief. Puppy is here with his new fiance, hat turned back cholo style. Others and their wives. And AO1--the guy who got peeped by the fag in the head onboard *Ranger*--arrives with his wife and two daughters. Pup's girl pats her hand on his torn jean kneecap as his foot rests on a seat in front of them. Skipper walks on stage. "Let's all move down," he gripes, wry. "They have enough carriers out there to do the job, if anything needs to be done."

We could deploy right before or after Christmas, and if so we'll have to go out twice between now and then to keep the air crew qualified. Single BAQ and VHA stop 30 days into deployment. COMRATS stop the day we leave. If your vehicle pass is going to expire, get it renewed before we deploy. Wills are probably not necessary if you're single and have no children. There could be up to three weeks between mail going out and getting to the ship. Send good news only, or complete letters resolving worrisome news. If you move, please let your husband know. And realize that telegrams are not private. They might stand in line for hours to call home from a port, and you might not be home. Just hang in there. The Chaplain speaks. His shirt reads, "Burke's Tavern." Why do Navy Chaplains unfailingly project irreverence? He talks about anchors away, when you set the sea and anchor detail. Anger, frustration, loneliness, riding a roller coaster of mood swings, wanting to cling to and push away a thousand words unsaid until the day of departure, numb ride to the ship, exile of ordered necessity, day feared until reunion, "goodbye." Why do we fight the last few days before we deploy? Isn't it easier to say goodbye to someone we don't like, someone we're mad at?

Now I'm ready for the keg.

At the park this afternoon, the Wolfpack banner ruffles in the breeze. Officers play the enlisted, an impromptu softball tournament. The second of three kegs runs dry as the soda barrel is refilled. Wives and children acquaint themselves. The crack of an F-14 in the brake reminds us it isn't a city park, it's a Naval base, and a tough job lies ahead. For now it's hamburgers, hot dogs, and chicken on the grill. One down, play's at first. Easy out, nice play. Hum around the infield. These are the families and friends of the world's finest fighters. Lieutenant Gram plays center field. At the end of the Tiger Cruise on Westpac 89, he stood on the LSO platform holding the pickle, guiding and grading traps. It was real Combat Air Patrol, and real Migs showing their bellies, with weapons off the coast of Vietnam. But that was so much a facade, pretended gamesmanship in a climate of political warmth. Nobody had to think too much of ejecting over land, or being eaten by captors like this freak Hussein has promised. Skipper hits the last out, takes the mound, and catches the last out. A lot of guys made Westpac 89, and didn't make the brief, but showed up for the picnic, probably the last time we'll have to relax before deployment. Even Freddie, who's always in L.A. on Saturdays. And wives with babies six weeks old. "There's no Filipinos here," says DK2 (our Disbursing Clerk). I look around. I should see PN2 and PNC (we call him that since he got selected, but he's still a PN1). And several guys in Maintenance are Filipinos. None are here but DK2. He came because we sent a letter from the CO recalling him from TAD for the 25th. His mother flew over from P.I. to stay with his wife and infant while we're deployed. The morning brief was important to them, but the picnic is awkward.

Most of the members see me for answers to their pay questions, even though DK2 does pay. They have no patience for the language barrier. So they don't know him. Since I was playing softball, he and his family had some burgers and left.

I played five innings with a boy at my side. AT1's kid. They didn't want to let him play and refused to let him bat. We still lost, and the boy missed an ego boost those men might have given.

My radio is on the sea wall with Louis, who saw me this morning. I told him I'd get back around two, and it's 1600.

2400 25 AUG 90. I watched Farm Aid between trying to get news on CNN Headline News instead of commercials and 30-minute reminders on CNN Headline News that they were broadcasting news on CNN Headline News. I glimpsed Jackson Browne on another channel, and it inspired me to carry my radio back up to Ventura Avenue and Ocean Front Walk, to play his tape for the hippies.

Turtle was carrying a thousand sheets of LSD. I think a sheet has fifty hits, or a hundred. Either way that's a lot of hallucinogenic drugs to be floating around with, and ultimately a lot of cash, at four bucks a hit.

Everyone at the sea wall was on LSD being calm, unobtrusive, polite, friendly, and stylishly dressed in black or late sixties tie-dye. Someone played a Dead tape, naturally. And most of them, if under twenty-one, had a beer they hid from the cops. The cops were busy, too, even ignoring the skateboarding boys for a while. Earlier, they had a race riot with blacks and whites drawing blood. So for a while the cops earned their pay.

0900 26 AUG 90. Soft tapping stirs me from light sleep. I find my white jeans and scramble to the door as Louis leaves the patio.

"I tried not to wake you."

"No, it's nine o'clock. I should be up."

"I got a new Zeppelin tape."

The sun is starburst in a rich blue sky.

"It's gonna get real hot."

1200 27 AUG 90. Unscheduled day off, eating a cheeseburger. I look around from Luigi's patio, across the alley from my carport. I don't see That Guy's Toyota. If I were living on edges before, now the rubberband snapped.

For the second time in my life, I have rolled over twice inside a vehicle and walked away. Only a few bruised ribs, my left side near the sternum. Keeping up with Lou.

I got an ambulance ride to Balboa Naval Hospital with my bald forehead taped to a board last night. It hurts to get into cars, but that won't be a problem with my Metro anymore. Wiped it out.

Dylan's "Rainy Day Women" plays on Luigi's FM as I chew on my burger, wash down narcotics, and pleasantly droop through the blue summer sky, as cars go by. I wonder if dear Vic got the message to his Coyote pals: Stop stealing the white Toyota from Mission Beach.

Lou told me brandishing a firearm in a bar is a felony. Good thing I didn't. "Maybe you should write a note to Vic," the bartender stood explained at attention, next door to the bilingual notary's shady place of business.

"Dear Vic," wrote Lou in Spanish-English. "Please tell your friends to bring the car back that they stole from Mission Beach. No questions asked. Understand?"

I try to recall the wording on defense of property from my first degree murder trial. How far can you legally go to get your car back? When does righteous protection of property commute to murder?

If I empty my guns and lock the clips and speedloader into my briefcase like they had me do to get range qualified at the sheriff's indoor range, and go stake out my suspect with every intention of calling the cops, but with another intention to protect myself if detected between the time I spot the car and the cops arrive, is there any culpability for conspiracy to do anything but defend myself?

I drove Louie back to Saint Vinnie's shelter (where he went after the VA) and took myself home. But that Guy's gun wasn't in the glove box. I scrounged under the seat and through my briefcase. We had packed both legally, with the 22 clip and the 44 gun and my rounds in the briefcase, and the 22 itself in the glove box unloaded. But the 22 was missing as I loaded my 44 to walk from the carport late at night, which is understandable when guys get blown away and hang out of windows next door, dead in broad daylight. And That Guy, the roommate, had just greeted me, walking up the sidewalk from Roberto's as I parked. Not to lose face, I zoomed back over to the shelter to see if Lou still had the gun.

Time was tight at 2140, but at most it was fifteen minutes to Imperial Avenue via I-5 south. I pulled out without telling That Guy, and as I realized later, without unloading my gun and locking it back in the briefcase.

The last drinks we had were at San Juan Capistrano, some gangster hide-out a good hour north. Then I dropped off Lou and came back to Mission Beach. I had one drink in Anaheim before that, just before pulling my gun--I mean, just before talking to the bartender about getting my car back. I was virtually sober by the time I got to, and left my carport.

At Imperial, one block and ten minutes to go, some idiot pulled onto the freeway at 40 mph. On my left, another car was pacing me at 75 as I downshifted. My speedometer read 56 as I locked up the brakes and veered over the shoulder to the right. I missed the ass of what appeared to be a Pinto, which probably would have blown up, then skidded along the dirt, tar, mud and grass, on and on, appeared to flatten a sign but in reality got flung by said sign, swung sideways, rolled twice, blew all four tires and exploded the passenger window, and finally stopped on a southbound ramp, facing north. I got out right away in case it burned. But it stabilized, still idling, so I got back in and turned it off.

"Stay there," a man said. "Just relax. Don't move. An ambulance is coming." They lifted me out and placed me on a spineboard where they taped down my forehead. "Where do you want to go," the ambulance crew asked.

"I'm active duty Navy."

"Balboa, then."

First a doctor waved his fingers in front of my upward gaze. Then a guy in khakis appeared. I thought the CHP was assisting with an assessment of possible nerve damage, but later realized I had passed a field sobriety test.

"We recovered your weapon."

"The twenty-two?"

"No, the forty-four."

"Oh, that was supposed to be locked in a briefcase."

"Well, I'm not citing you for that."

I gradually realized I had rolled with a loaded revolver that a hard knock might have triggered. They wanted me to whiz in a bottle. Of course, I was afraid of the booze showing up. So I feigned I couldn't pee in front of them, didn't need to pee, hurt too bad to walk to the bathroom to pee, couldn't lean over to pee. "You're not leaving until we get a urin sample." She was a wicked, man-hating bitch bull dyke nurse of a Navy Lieutenant if ever I saw one. I was already hooked up with a sodium I.V., and she cranked three more bottles into my veins, bloating my system. Four hours later I pissed like a Clydesdale. It tested Point One One. But the CHP had written, "had been drinking, not under influence." I officially held my liquor.

The Navy's medical and safety representatives tried to stick anything they could, tried to characterize the wreck as alcohol related. The Safety Petty Officer even tried to send a general info safety message around the military world. "Why were you at that exit ramp?" He asked like it had to do with why a car pulled in front of me going 35. What could I say, "getting my roommate's gun back from a derelict who helped me strong arm a bartender who knew the dude who stole my car"?

The skipper shot it down. I didn't have to lie for the record that I planned to go shooting at San Diego Indoor Range when my bud Lou talked me into having a Brave Bull at Johnny's Surf Club instead, that the guns were locked up in a briefcase in the car, and that I took him home to find That Guy's gun missing and hurried back to get it when the car pulled in front of me.

"I left it in your car," Lou said two days later.

Either it actually is on the freeway at Imperial, or it's in the hands of someone else at Vinnie's where Lou sold it for a fix. I don't want to think he's too hooked on junk. The clip was recovered, and I thought it was in the briefcase. So the gun may be there as Louie says.

This is the third major car wreck in my life, second time I've rolled, second wreck over 70 mph. I keep walking away. I have a reason to be here. This time I rolled twice, didn't hit another car, didn't get a DWI, didn't get a ticket for (or shot by) the loaded gun. And the car was fully insured. In fact, the ink wasn't dry on the policy. They'll be pissed.

Chapter Four

2030 30 AUG 90. I came in the house to my roommate's slop. I couldn't find a ride from Miramar, so took the bus. And they cut me off the pain pills because they're addictive. Quarters was at 1730 and you couldn't hear a third of what the skipper said. It was just an exercise: fall in down in the hangar bay, listen to feedback bouncing off the metal walls and plug your ears when the jets roar by, if you dare move at attention.

At the beach hippies are frying as usual. Keith is out of jail. Lou is out shooting junk on the $40 he got for That Guy's gun, or whining about his slick thieving Saint Vinnie's roommate.

Nobody loves me. Who in the Navy sticks their neck out for me, just to be kind? None seem committed to helping me feel like this world is a good place to live. The nicest thing anyone here has done lately is not call me fag or whip my ass. The bus isn't that bad. It's just these bruised ribs.

I stood at the sea wall in a black shirt, Navy blue Wolfpack ballcap with silhouetted F-14 over the bill, and patched Levi 501 button downs from the gay days of San Francisco. Chuck rode his little stunt bike he got for ten bucks, worth $200. I said I'd trade him for the rusty beach bomber somebody sold me for $20 when it rolled off a ship from Hawaii. His needs a bearing.

A couple of drunks started arguing, so Chuck peddled off to another spot along the wall. I stayed until I began to become their negotiating table, then split across the boardwalk as Red rode over on his bike.

"Did you hear about my car?"

He squinted toward the moon, feigned concern. But in a minute he was on the wall handing out the Beast (Milwaukee's Best) to his clan of hippie children, and again I stood alone.

I stared across Ventura several times at a short young skater who looked back and seemed to talk about me to his freaky hippie pal that I scoped on yesterday. They made a sexy pair. I left before I became suicidal.

Now I'm in a dangerous place--home--gathering the forces of esteem and ego. I am hungry (funny how that works). My cupboard is bare. I can either go hungry and take more of my remaining pain pills, or grab another beer and take more of my remaining pain pills, or go back out to the madding crows and buy a burger and face the loneliness of being ignored, superficially treated, and reminded of the lack of love permeating my life. And take a few more of my remaining pain pills.

The Public Defender called me today. It's when you're up for murder that you have to call them.

"Was there anything on the back of the ticket, like the girl's name or anything?"

"Just furnishing alcohol to a minor, a twelve ounce Bud."

"They might dismiss it."

"I want the officer reprimanded. The same cops that are shooting too many people are writing too many tickets."

"Well, it goes into city funds. That's why they won't investigate it."

Out of the blue, a guy named Dave called to offer assistance about my accident, talk to the cops or the Navy if I got charged with anything. "Your roommate answered when I called earlier. It sounded like he ran to the phone."

"He was having sex. He put her on pause."

"You were in the far right lane, trying to exit onto Imperial when the guy cut you off. Did you see what kind of car it was?"

"I think it was a Pinto."

"Anyway, you didn't have a chance. Were you wearing your seatbelt?"

"Yeah."

"That's probably what saved you."

"How bad was my car? Did you get a look at it?"

"I didn't want to tell you at the accident. All four tires were flat and the right side was wiped out. The worst part was the front end. It was all crinkled up. It'll never able the same, I can guarantee that. I'm glad you're all right."

"Just some bruised ribs."

In the Navy, if you have no middle name you are assigned the middle initials NMN. Which stand for "no middle name." If you sign your basic contract like most people sign their paychecks, abbreviating the middle name, for instance, "D", from then on your record will reflect your middle initial in quotes. If, at some point, two or three duty stations down the road, some Personnelman discovers you have a middle name, they will ask if it were your intention to change your name to John "D" Doe. You ask, "what the fuck?" And all of your service record pages will be corrected to reflect the unprinted letters. This stupidity, promulgated by Naval intelligence, happened to me, too.

2020 31 AUG 90. Brakes sneeze. Motor grinds. The 81 South rolls down toward Roberto's. It makes a left in front of the Big Dipper roller coaster, passes the bus stop with the mail drop where the plexiglass has a hole punched through, and drops off another sucker.

Welcome to Friday night at Mission Beach, California, where the cops will taunt you 'til the meth heads roll you and the old hobos panhandle you bleeding in the sand, and if you make it out alive you'll win two free tickets to come back with a friend.

There's gonna be blood spilt, no kidding. But you can hope it's not yours. There will be sexy women in tight, black, short leather skirts, a biker's paradise of choice motorcycle parking out front of the Coaster where Brave Bulls are $2.75, unlike the Red Onion, San Diego's hottest nightclub, across the parking lot where tourists stand in line to get out and the Bulls are $4.50.

Meet Carl, in blond locks with a six gun, wild wild west, high noon cowboy stance. If anyone looks like a gunslinger, he does. He slouched over a guy's bicycle last night in front of Roberto's. Just draped himself over like a corpse in a saddle, until the owner propped him back on his boots, and he staggered to the liquor store. Hand him a Marlboro.

Those two blond boys may talk funny and take acid but they won't take yours, so don't presume to be coy. Just shut up and let me show ya 'round. Keep your eyes wide open, head down, and your big mouth shut. The little white sheets changing hands with green bills? You don't want to know. But here. Chew this. Put it under your tongue and don't swallow it. And keep your mouth shut. Okay now, come on.

"Nobody move!"

Ignore that guy, he's not a cop. He's just another sailor, an acid head on sabbatical, laying his Naval career on the line to examine the psychology of the dichotomy of anti-war activists faced with hero worship. Contracted four active years, behind enemy lines, he thinks he'll bring back the same heart he took in.

Two sailor boys approach as I lean on the sea wall with the Boss Acid Head of Mission Beach. I know one of them, in fact I have the hots for him. He dutifully ignores me. He looks for LSD and doesn't want me to know, fears I may report him. He and his shipmate wait beside a palm tree after handing over some dough to a young girl hippie who takes a few steps and talks to a boy hippie.

The hippies walk off to hand over dough in the shadows. A few minutes later he walks back to speak with another hippie and hands over dough. This hippie steps up beside me to get a strip of six 1/8" squares of white blotter paper, and hands over six dollars to my friend who bought them for about 25 cents each. This hippie walks back to that hippie who walks back to the girl hippie who sits by the pretty sailor boy and his closeted macho image wearing fag bottom buddy who paid thirty bucks to keep me from knowing they bought acid. Meanwhile, the retired Navy Seal sitting here offers me all the acid I want for free.

I work in the Personnel Department. I carry a green card I could sell for two thousand dollars and say I lost and type up a new application and have another one in forty-five minutes.

In 1984 Hollywood I am starving, then enjoying tortillas con carne with undocumented workers, at a stove in a room full of roaches. We drink beers. "Take a look at my son," he says in broken English. "He's about your age. Don't you think you would like to give to him the certificate of where you were born? I give you good dinner?"

Now back to 1990, calling the INS to report the papers That Guy found in my Toyota that's been recovered after being stolen. The birth certificates of two teenage boys from Mechuacan. They put me on hold for nearly an hour. I wait. Finally the Mexican woman comes on the line.

"They might have been dropped in your car some other time."

The last words my mother said were, "aarrackk," which we thought was "heart attack," since she'd kept a dehydrated finger on her carotid artery all week. But maybe she said, "Iraq."

A jet black Stratocaster drapes across my bare ankle, over the black patent leather shoes my father bought in Madrid for himself, but they didn't fit. I scraped the top of one on a knee-knocker on *USS Ranger*, CV "by God" 61, Top Gun of the Pacific Fleet.

My harmonica holder lays on the couch with a G clipped in, atop the crinkled copy of *Beach & Bay Press*. The big headline, "Residents Refuse to Compromise." I'm lousy with grammar, spelling and basics of the English language. Because I was too good at sixteen, entering University of Missouri, Columbia, I tested out of Composition, went straight into Exposition and have shot off at the mouth ever since. Louie calls me "loose cannon" and gives me hell--a jobless CPA bum who thinks he's an English professor living at Saint Vinnie's because he prefers to. "I don't want to live in a neighborhood of locksmiths and gardeners," he'd say.

The Fender neck lays across my arm, in case I am found that way. Who knows if the coyotes up in Anaheim were hooked up with the INS? They found the cholo in the Hollywood apartment with a baseball bat laying in the crook of his arm. Then drew him face down and charged me with murder, when the bat would have rolled off his arm if he'd been face down. The cop forgot to draw the eyes in.

"I'll shoot him." Some determined youth passes by the court out front.

"Yeah," says a girl by his side.

Shrieks and profane, deep masculine yelps echo over the din of late night weekend traffic pouring into the heart of Mission Beach, right where I live. Now a car blaring Dylan via Guns and Roses. Let them meet Jesus, the beach bum up there pounding his fists right now on the boardwalk at the end of Ventura Avenue. It really doesn't hurt much to just sit here. It's not even getting up that kills me. It's the initial engagement of muscle to bone tissue and the instantaneous gnarling-jabbing-twisting-grating-biting pain from somewhere inside my chest that hurts. You've never really felt pain until you've felt it in the ribs. It's barely ten-thirty. Sidewalks sing with the rhythm of skateboards. A wild man yells from a truck at some broad.

"I like that hat."

No response.

"Nice hat."

Nothing.

"I like that hat you have on."

Traffic goes again, he's losing her.

"Nice hat!"

"Go on," she finally says.

"You gotta fuckin' problem?" He screams from his gut, but is soon drowned out by sirens and motors and engines and brakes.

I am a washed up has been. I wanted to bring back Dylan but never got it together. They threw joints at me from the balcony of Odyssey Pub in Berkeley, on San Pablo Avenue with its dull yellow bulb in the doorway and the rumble inside.

Fifteen years ago I was eighteen, estranged from righteous calling as an undercover narcotics informant slash DEA agent, hated in my hometown, half gay already from a too brutal sister and too gentle boyhood friends, thrust to San Francisco from the Show Me state one year after Viet Nam. I loved to be cuddled but wasn't a kid, loved to cuddle but lost all my baby faced friends. I wrote gender nonspecific, but occasionally explicit, dirges for the loss of those babies who sheltered me through adolescence by letting me nurture them to the teen age.

My writings piled up and fell out of the closet, so I put them in a huge trash can that got carted off to the Acme Landfill in Martinez, California. Even my journal of Hollywood is there. My self-actualization counselor said I threw out the wrong files.

I smoked pot, had gay sex, and of course lied about all of it to join the Navy. I'd never done anything that I hadn't been busted for. Just like they put it in our Plan Of the Day that we have the right to remain silent with the media, about the events brewing in the Gulf.

We're on 96-hour alert. Reservists are over there now. One Exocet and we're at war. It's a matchbook planet, and the Middle East is the match-head, scraping against military satellites.

God, if only Sweet Pea would quit the Navy and move with me to San Francisco. He's pre-occupied with murdering his father for leaving him at six. Now he looks fourteen but he's going on twenty. I should have got married and had kids. Then I might understand these feelings.

Another slut calls my roommate. He's either parking cars or banging chicks or slaving over memos at Top Gun, the famous Navy Fighter Weapons School. "Call me no matter what time you get in," bitch drools into the answering machine.

SATURDAY MORNING 1 SEP 90. Louis has my boogie board. It's barely 0900, already scorching at the beach. Three-foot waves. "Waves fuckin' suck. Water's freezing, too."

"Do you want the towel?"

"No. I'm goin' back out again in a minute." Goosebumps rise on his light brown skin.

Today we're north of the checkered flag, scoping a lime green bikini. Nice tits. Nice legs.

The Grand Opening of the Big Dipper roller coaster ride is scheduled for this weekend, according to Joe. It's a bona fide Historic National Landmark. They expect 300,000 men, women and children. And 200 cops at Mission Beach.

2230 1 SEP 90. Louie the vet showed up. We took a two hour bus ride to the scene of my car crash, and walked down the ramp. I found the hubcaps and scrapes of blue paint. The entrance ramp juts sharply into the freeway, as the southbound lanes curve around to the right on a downhill slope. I never had a chance.

The tow yard was closed, but a driver there helped anyway. "I just want to get my house keys and personal effects."

"It ain't here no more. Didn't your insurance company tell you? It was totaled, and they hauled it off to the County Auto Pool for auction. They took it yesterday. And I didn't take nothin' out of it." He'd towed six GEO Metros and all were totaled. One was a convertible whose driver was beheaded. "We call 'em coffin cars."

Lou cashed his check and repaid the fifty bucks he owed me, plus another $75 for That Guy's gun. I knew That Guy would renege on the September car payment. He lied about changing the Base Sticker, lied about buying more toilet paper and laundry soap as he used the last of mine, and basically just habitually says whatever you want to hear and then pleases himself. So I took the $75 from Lou off the $500 balance owing from That Guy.

1330 3 SEP 90. Labor Day, duty day. Somehow Lou got around to asking the big question. "Why did you join the Navy?" Then he added, "I could never be in the Navy because it's so restricting on your life." He was a sniper in Viet Nam. "Well, you get to travel to a lot of the world." My oldest brother ran away to join the Navy at seventeen, and stayed eight years. My next oldest brother joined the Army's Old Guard for three years, and shined brass for funeral marches instead of getting drafted. One of my other brothers, the one born on the fifth of July, spent eight years in the Navy, then became a lawyer, then took a commission in the Naval Reserves. Lots of guys talk about becoming an officer specifically to come back and make some bastard chief salute them.

"The last real day of summer," some passing voice says as I walk up to the beach. An old green Army airplane hauls a white banner ad across the sky. Loud fast music blares from boardwalk apartments. The sand and sea wall are packed as ever. A hundred sailboats dodge each other in the hot breeze. Two college guys play paddle ball, one with a beer in hand. Volleyball starts next to them. "We'll have to jump a fence back to the base tonight," one Sailor says to another.

Stevie Ray Vaughn is dead. And so is Johnny "Rocko". Johnny Rocko was a local strongarm. He'd ripped off Chuck at Hippie Hill in Belmont Park. And may have been the one who robbed and kicked Jeremy and put him in the hospital so bad his mother came here from Washington state and took him home, after originally kicking him out of the house for his own good.

Johnny finally pulled his arrogant crap on the wrong dude, and Steve shot him six times in the back in self-defense. Which sounds iffy. The guy was in Steve's apartment. Actually, he was hanging limp, half out the window. A stream of blood stained the shingles of a liquor store, and sidewalk down below. I'd heard the shots like firecrackers, from the carport across the alley as I fixed the Toyota's ignition. They say Johnny could hug you or hit you and you never knew which to expect. Poetic rumor has it he was gonna hug Steve.

My little white wagon has been stolen and recovered, stolen again, and re-recovered. Lou and I wonder if our brief trip to Anaheim had anything to do with the prompt recovery this time. We visited on Sunday, and the cops found the car unscathed in San Diego the following Friday.

That Guy finally bought the Club. And it looks like he'll continue his payments. But the landlady just complained to me that he hasn't pay his September rent. And, he never gave his former roommate her utensils back. Once he moves out in October, and I go to sea, will he still make his payments? "Yo," I yelled. "Phyllis says you haven't paid your rent."

"Tell her I'll give her check in a half hour."

"We've gotta get some more toilet paper," I told him.

"I've got toilet paper," he miraculously volunteered.

I didn't mention the roll stashed under my bed.

2245 3 SEP 90. Phyllis has hung out her shingle. That Guy has his deal--a date back in suburbia September 29. He seems to have tired of all the drunks and the drugs and the fights and the shootings and the helicopters. And doesn't want to stick around long enough to have his car ripped off again.

Christa, owner of Christa's laundromat across the alley, had her van parked in Phyllis' stall when That Guy and I drove back from the impound lot with the Toyota. He recognized the van, and asked her to move it or allow him to park in the space in front of her laundry. She wouldn't agree to either, and went crying to Phyllis about leaving her van alone. "I don't charge you rent for that space," Phyllis said.

"But I offered to pay rent and you declined when you told me to work it out with Fran."

"That's all right, I'll move it."

"No, Christa. Is your car still in the space? Don't move it."

"No no, I'll move." Off she went.

"I owe her an awful lot," Phyllis wheezed through a plastic hose in her nose. "That space is not to be used for storage."

"The car runs."

"That's not the point. It isn't to be used for storage."

I wonder why I'm in this conversation instead of That Guy.

"Well, whatever he does with it is up to him."

"It's not up to him. It's not to be stored there."

She never said anything to That Guy. He's moving in three weeks anyway.

If I move, it's back to Miramar. Ugh. I could get another apartment but I'd need a truck to move my stuff and my ribs still hurt.

Tomorrow I have to make a call from work, which will piss off my boss, to chew out my insurance agent for not telling me that my car was totaled, and for sending it to the auction lot with my stuff still inside. Then if I can get the facts of how much they'll settle for, I'll get a new loan and maybe get a Ford Ranger. Why not, since I'm attached to the *Ranger*?

If Phyllis accepts Joe's application, I'll stick it out here to December. Then

Joe and Louis can shoulder the rent (meaning Joe, since Louis is like 15)--which Phyllis intends to jack up to $800--until next June when I come back from Westpac. But who knows what could happen in six months. Luigi's could burn, Joe could wreck his cycle, Phyllis could have a heart attack and her family could jack the rent and force Joe out. And Ranger could get hit by a Silkworm missile.

2230 4 SEP 90. The CMC had assured me that since all such messages had to go through him, there would be no traffic to Washington about my accident. "The message will go out," he said today.

"Does it say alcohol related?"

"Yes. But there's nothing legal involved. It's only for safety statistics, and doesn't carry any legal weight at all."

I asked who would release it, but he didn't hear. I was trapped in a head full of urinalysis testees, labeling bottles of piss water for the unit sweep. We're supposed to use individual tamper resistant red seals, but we don't. Somebody forgot to pick them up at SERVMART (the Navy supply store).

"I took a ten milligram Valium Saturday," I told Doc Rob. "Will it show up?"

"It might. But they'll come back with all this other stuff you're taking for your injury and that will be it. I wouldn't worry."

"I should have smoked some dope."

It sounded like Phyllis' smoke alarm. She's very old and has emphysema, so she walks around leashed to an oxygen bottle. I went to investigate. From the patio it sounded more like the neighbor lady's smoke alarm. Then it hit me, it also sounded a lot like the door ajar buzzer on the Toyota. I went back to my bedroom and got the Bulldog and walked outside and around the building down Mission Boulevard to the carport in the alley across from Christa's, where I saw Tim waiting on his bedroll in the dryer. I saw some Mexican women with a baby carriage across the street. I had the Bulldog under my tee shirt on the waistband clip inside my pants. I intended to ask Tim if he'd seen anyone messing around in the carport, but forgot all about it as we started talking. "I've been tryin' to get ahold of Louie," he slurred through a high gravel voice. Like most of the sane, gentle homeless men, he drank heavily to keep a shield of painlessness between himself and sudden brutality, should it spring on him as others.

We talked about who shot Johnny Rocko, and why. And it came back to Louie and me and if we'd like to get a place with Tim. "I'd worry about coming home to the strangers you'd let in."

"Oh, no. I, I, I like my privacy. I really love it."

"You guys would have to shoulder the rent after December, while I'm at sea for six months. But then I'll be back." I couldn't believe I heard myself say that, like Louie, I need to move away from the beach even if I don't want to.

The beach is just a crazy place for surfers and runaways. Only the homeless and helplessly hopeless have a right to exist in this fantasy--and do at their peril, which they don't seem to mind so long as they refuse to hope. But a guy like me, with a job and a shelter and sometimes a car, comes along and rattles them with ideas about getting something going again. It must shock and disturb, distress and depress them. They start letting on that deep beneath the alcohol glow, they can't take this scene another minute.

"I just want to get off this fucking planet!" The war cry of a Mexican one early morning as I arrived at Mission Beach. Lou repeated it, but not since Vinnie's. And it reminded me of Hollywood, my alcoholic Puerto Rican host tipping back some Vodka and holding his kidney. "I don't care nothing but drink until I die!"

Death would come too easy. Like with his fresh Disability check Lou wined me and dined me at Croce's downtown, famous bar and restaurant of Ingrid Croce, wife of Sunday Morning Mission, Box Number Ten, sleeping in a hotel doorway Jim Croce, 1970's folk and blues guitar hero whose concert I had tickets to the night his plane hit the Midwest mud.

Louie insisted on getting off the trolley a little early, and took me on a quick detour to a dark neighborhood near that tow yard where he walked through the gate of a house and bought a balloon to pop and chew. "Only because of my broken ribs, to ease the pain." He has broken ribs and chews junk. I have bruised ribs and prescription drugs.

1230 6 SEP 90. A brief meeting with my Public Defender. She has received some new discovery. A statement on an addendum to the ticket: "I was walking up behind Graham when he handed a can of Budweiser to (the girl) who said she was 14. (She) took a drink from the beer and handed it back to Graham."

I can't find anyone in the phone book with her same last name and street address. My PD will ask for a continuance to find the mystery girl and obtain her version of the fourth of July. So far I'm into the county for about $131 but she's not sure. The Revenue and Collection folks will see me when it's over. If and when I have a jury trial, it will accrue at $300 per day, win lose or draw. So any cop in San Diego can arrest any civilian and make trial money for the city coffers to pay the judge and bailiff and public defenders and prosecutors no matter if the arrest is totally bogus. What a racket.

My PD encouraged me to file a complaint against the cop--but it has to be filed through the cop's own department. Supposedly it will put "a black mark in his record" whether or not anything is ever proved against him. I wonder if I can sue that little bitch and her parents for court costs.

They tried to get me to cop a plea--shades of Hollywood. I could pay a small fine for being the victim of this young girl stealing my beer as my back was turned. And then go to Mast with my CO for committing an infraction off base. That means packing a full seabag, seeing the Legal Officer, standing at attention in the passageway outside Admin before seeing the XO--embarrassing. Then telling him why I pled guilty. Right on top of the Safety Petty Officer's message concerning my alcohol related car wreck.

1800 6 SEP 90. On the sea wall Carl Gunslinger staggers kindly with a plastic bag full of cans. "Say brother," head down, eyes in dirt. "Could you possibly loan me fifty-five cents for a beer?" He performs like John Wayne. The tourists are back in school and everybody here knows him too well. But he finagles a young hippie out of a cigarette.

Black Marlin strums and finger picks a 12-string with six strings, D C and G chords against the steady break of waves, smells of salt, wet sand, trash can garbage and sea weed awash along the shoreline. Stony Tony hangs with Marlin. Last night Marlin passed me at a phone booth where baby faced Beanpole from *Ranger* called up some girls and didn't get lucky. He could have walked to my house for some fun.

"I need some money," Marlin whispered as he hurried toward the wooden deck of a taco shop. I shoved into his hand a $5 bill I'd found a half hour before in the pocket of my leather jacket. He put down his guitar to eat, and I borrowed it to play.

"That one song," Beanpole said later. "Whose was it?"

"Mine."

The sun set twenty minutes ago. No loud tunes, only vague tapes. Fifty feet or fifty decibels, the law at Mission Beach. A few screams in harmony announce the roller coaster. I have yet to ride. "I'm not going to rent to your friend. Because I want to see if I can find someone to move in who will help take care of me." Politely exacting revenge for Christa.

Right now I could move on base, store my stuff, get my $375 deposit back, not need a car, and take the money on Westpac. But we won't be hitting ports. Just Hawaii, the Philippines, and the Indian Ocean enroute to the Gulf.

I get out in January, '92. Eight months after Westpac. If I stay in, it will be for orders to a tropical island. What else can you get out of the Navy?

0030 8 SEP 90. The sound and smell of a 12-ounce Bud. It could be more chilled. Jackson Browne sings, "Jamaica Say You Will." Lampshade cocked for better light. Two knit bags of laundry on the floor, whites and colors, stuck together with a big safety pin. Ribs sore--a week after the accident.

I've been up at the sea wall gazing at two boys for several hours. One is short with crewcut bleached blond hair and heavy black brows. He stands at the edge of Strandway and four friends group around him obliviously gazing while he obliviously performs the art of being pretty. None but me says he is a beautiful boy. The other, tall, long pony tail and sunburst oversized shirt, acid-grin cheeks on a baby face, hugs girls: one here, two, four more. He has a strange accent. Neither boy allows me to exist beyond my plain balding shell, whispering along the beach.

I have never seen so many foot patrols around the palm tree park with black flashlights. The Internal Affairs Department must have cracked down on false arrests. Now the cops are lashing back to drum up a good bust. People here want to buy the cops a cup of coffee and lace it with LSD. Or gram of Meth and call the IAD. But others want to kill them for harassment.

Red finally got the Sony snaked. I told Chuck I guess it was homesteaded by now. Red fed me a good yarn but I didn't really listen. I didn't really hear Chuck either, and didn't exactly pay attention to where I was walking and hit a sign. I'm not on drugs. It's my quarterly depression creeping in. The gun is loaded six feet from my temple at the head of this bed in this stuffy, muggy humid little, bedroom dead room. Except I would do it at the seashore, even if it wasn't through the heart. A hollowpoint would blow my bald head off. Maybe it wouldn't be such a bad thing: when you're dead you're dead and there's no more pain of trees uprooting in a lively forest. "And the sun may find him sleeping in the dust of some ruin far away." I am the character in that Jackson Browne song. We were all a little wrong, but I got left behind.

That Guy, my roommate, said he was going to work on his Toyota today. So I couldn't borrow it to drive to work. I let him have it for $75 down when I had three other offers.

I spent about $50 on calls to Los Angeles today trying to hook up my director friend, Khaled Siddick of Kuwait, who is now in L.A. with frozen credit cards and about seven thousand U.S. dollars until Saddam Hussein backs the fuck out. I tried to get him in contact with the Hollywood producer Jim Abrahams (now making a spoof on Navy pilots called "Hot Shots"). Or with writer Don Stewart (writer of "Missing" and "Hunt For Red October"). Jim was in a meeting, Don was out of town.

SATURDAY 1330 8 SEP 90. *Once again, surfers, don't take right into the swimming area. Don't take right into the swimming area.* Seems like that was twice again. It is more packed than ever by the checkered flag. The tide seems to be in all day and the surf is great. But the water's cold.

Scrapper, my Airman striker, is probably diving today.

Visibility in southern California is never better than fifteen feet, so I'll wait until Westpac and maybe dive Hawaii again. It's fun pushing buttons underwater, inflating and deflating the BCD, breathing through the regulator and spinning weightless circles with a blue water view and fish.

Chuck arrives to buy my beach bike. "Hey, come on in, Chuck. Want some coffee?"

"Just black. I've been up all night." He doesn't do heroin but he sells acid, recycles the profit, and stocks up on sheets while the Berkeley hippies are here. After they leave he's the main connect, and makes his bank.

"Bob, come in here for a second." That Guy has awakened to a phone call, now notices my friend Chuck drinking coffee. "Hold on Dave. Bob, that guy's a bum. I hate bums and I don't want him drinking my coffee or drinking out of my cup or touching any of my stuff. I'm not saying you have poor judgment in choosing your friends. But the people you bring over here--you have to admit there's a pattern of problems that grew out of Mission Beach."

"Look, man. I rolled my car because I went to get your car back." I should have added, Because I knew you would otherwise renege on the payments. I am reassured, however, that I'd better get him to sign the lien agreement before we move. He's the dude he keeps warning me about.

"I'll match bankrolls with him any day," Chuck confides. "When he's got a house in his own name, and makes two thousand dollars a month, then he can call me a bum. I live out here by choice. But I own a house in La Mesa."

"Yeah, well. He's got a lot to learn about life."

Chuck leaves. He's paid me for the bike, advised me on used cars and tipped me on a cherry Camaro with a new engine, black leather cherry interior, black vinyl top. His sister's.

"Hey, I'd like to use the Toyota to get my keys from the tow yard."

"No. I'm resolving all my problems and that car isn't registered yet. I don't want anymore problems." It hasn't moved from the stall since Phyllis insisted that the stall not be used for storage.

1800 8 SEP 90. This is one of those more incredulous Mission Beach nights. The police have dogs and feel awkward. The glowing sun casts a red tone on the face of a young Princess yawning. Carl shades his tall Bud. A long-blond headed, dark sunglassed dude passes with a pot bud tattooed on an arm. A cop cruises past on a quiet scooter. Everybody knows what was going on: both had blood on 'em, so I guess that was fair. This guy beside me keeps offering me sixty bucks for my boogie board--but he only wants it to drown that crazy nigger slave boy Carl. The old fart talks through some crazy amplifier, a voice vibrator stuck to his throat, and smokes a cigar. He shows me his military ID, a retired senior chief. Three years in Seals, five in subs, ten on tin cans. He points the cigar stub at his bullet scars. "Nine fuckin' times," he vibrates. "Nine fuckin' times." Now he sells acid to the hippies around Mission Beach. And to sailors.

All I can think is that skateboard crewcut dyed out blond head bombshell in dark eyes on this dark beach and Rock Lobster, dance of death so hot, nose guard and butter. My roommate turns MTV to a commercial. Promotion of life and death, attention to campfires. Land. Some warm sleepy friend comforting, "sign here would ya?" Phone shatters, music dies, human voice. Something happened to someone important to you. Drop everything and change your entire life, start a new journey, turn the music up louder!

Progressive black music in America is where it's at. Hot Woman Beat can only survive blackness in a big way (try me?). She looked good and white over the cresting orange bowl. I paused and took it in: Mission Beach, California! Day or night. On the phone or the boardwalk. Trust me. Or was it, Try me?

He should have changed the channel, but the music is back and we can forget about the dude in dark glasses who believed in the Mexican tattoo and the land war, who's gonna take it by grenade while you're dancing.

Like the fart with the cigar and vibrator and retired ID.

Harlem Brown. What a name. Some spots up in Harlem where they say it's sudden death. Sweet girl and a hit record. The black man, when he talks directly to a girl, better be love because if you lose you're out of the club on your ass with buns in the dark and the cold sand and grit, grinding fucking beat baby you will dance with me. Fade out cut to bust fresh!

2000 9 SEP 90. Take your time, Bobby. Pretend you hold the heart of the world. Earphones, high riffs on Les Paul with back beat and driving bass. That Guy dressed like a stiletto heads to a movie with someone. Who, Miss Summerend? "You left your keys in the door," he rousts me from deep in the headphones. "The door is open," I say.

2130 18 SEP 90. Where was I? Mission Beach. Stiff ribs. Bleached blond skateboarder dodging black and white units who arrive at the boardwalk to protect and serve, long after the great orange fireball glows above the isthmus filled with sail masts and the structure of our landmark rollercoaster.

Screaming riders frame late night radio. Barry Manilow, of all stars, sings, "When will I hold you again," followed by "Here Comes the Sun." And I say, it's all right. He skates past me repeatedly, in giant tee-shirt and knee- length shorts, to the edge of the lifeguard parking lot to Ollie off the planter and hop the cement light pole base. Each time he skates around I turn my head and shoulders, locked on and obvious and carrying my bulldog in my waist, in the even some third party comes prying in between us with a crowbar. He has a group of friends that include a couple of girls and it is enough to keep me guessing about his preferences. "I love you," I whisper as he passes. I think he hears, but he's only 18. It's too much, too new, balding man in cholo rags and string-cuffed green fatigues with leather jacket and black Spanish leather shoes straight from Madrid, subtly coming on.

He gives repeated indifferent returns, not curious or angry, and if longing, too well concealed. Under a watchful status quo. "Later," I whisper yearning by a car on the Avenue sidewalk.

I was up there drinking with Dave. By the time I got out of my uniform the sun was down. But since "Miami Vice" was off the air, nothing could keep me form the sea wall and ions of surf. Unshaven Dave was leaning on the liquor store.

"What are you doin'?"

"Aw, just tryin' to hustle up a beer."

"I'll buy you a beer. What kind ya want?"

"Oh, Milwaukee's Best would be fine." I bought two and we walked up and I saw Blondy and knew I'd be stuck for a while.

"You got any chump change," Red asked. "I've almost got enough for a 12-pack."

Red was at The Front, as he calls the corner of Ventura and Ocean Front. I gave him seventy-five cents and got another beer out of it. This twisted closet fag type dude named Rusty came up and had to tell me something. "I remember what you told me about talking to my old man," he said. I didn't know what he was talking about, but something vague was there.

"I asked him what was up. Did he trust me. Now I got the keys to the marina and the yacht. I'm livin' on the yacht."

"I love it," I told Dave, "when people tell me something I told them had meaning."

What's Blondy's name, where does he live, how can I become his friend?

"Cop!" Blondy's buddy was zooming toward the lamp post as I saw the unit turn into the lot. The skater hopped off subtly, so they ha-hah couldn't tell he was skating. He stood still, then kicked the board up to his hand. "Thanks," he said.

I wanted to tell him his lover sends me. But of course I could not.

0900 23 SEP 90. This is Sunday. Why am I still writing in military time? Blondy came out with black hair for one night, next day in a green sheen that glows in the dusk.

Louis' missing. It's the eighth day since he vanished without a trace. He's 15, long brown hair, funky teeth neglected of braces, Indian Mexican skin, and a skateboard. Last seen at Joe's hotel room downtown. Didn't want to go with Joe to the beach like normal Saturdays. Joe got off early, went home at 11, and found Louis gone. He only took his skateboard and flannel shirt. The one he wore unbuttoned as I gave a reach around. He left his wetsuit and boogie board and bass guitar and rock tee-shirts. It looked like he was headed out to Mission Beach via the trolley and buses. The manager said he left alone.

Joe checked with the cops, juvenile hall, child protective services, and the runaway shelters. He even got the boy's mom's telephone number. She hadn't seen him in two years, and seemed vaguely indifferent--strange, considering she's a social worker.

2315 24 SEP 90. At sunset yesterday as I sat Indian style on the sea wall, my back to the heat, two niggers rode up surly in a surrey talking shit. I ignored them and they moved next to a Frank Serpico looking dude who never talks, who is actually a cab driver from the middle east. They got a word out of him and slapped him. A third nigger took me by the leather and swung me in circles, dipping me back so I pulled my feet out and dropped to the sand. He grinned. "God damn," I grinned.

Today's *Metro News* told of the gang of blacks attacking white beachgoers on the boardwalk by the roller coaster last night, who got jailed on fifty thousand dollars' bond. Lucky I wasn't packing my bulldog. And I didn't get thrown to the concrete for being white.

2030 25 SEP 90. The sea wall chills while autumn sneaks around. Carl stands tall feigning comfort in his shirt. Pappy snuggles in a corner by trash cans without blankets, blocking the sea breeze with the concrete sea wall. He's been a happy drunk all day. He walked up to me miming a microphone, singing like a wino. Chuck rode up on his latest bike watching the sun set off the horizon full of clouds. Then "closing up the store," he said buttoning his jacket.

I saw Sweet Pea finally. He was in a working party on the hangar deck as I came aboard with the computers. I tapped on his shoulder and he motioned me aside where he raved about calling me back. "I got this number on this note that said 'call Bob.' And I thought, who is Bob? Then I said 'wait a minute, that's Graham.' And I transcribed the numbers and I got ITVKLAP and I knew it was you so I called."

"I never got the message."

"I called a bunch of times. I always got a message saying that you weren't home. What am I gonna do, leave a message, 'call me at what number?'"

"You could've said what time you'd call back and I would stick around."

"I wanted to come out there, too. I was bored with nothin' to do and you were gone all the time."

"I thought you just didn't like me and forgot about me."

"We definitely need to talk."

2130 27 SEP 90. The cats have stopped exploding. The squadron came out for touch and go, trap-cat-diverts between the *Ranger* and NAS Miramar. It's so slow, a Line Rat checked out a book from the library this morning. I was there looking for a newspaper and not finding one. Cut off from the daily build-up again, focused on managing mess decks, waiting to be surprised to find myself home or in the Gulf.

The birds are scheduled to fly-on Sunday night. And the beach det will COD aboard soon after.[1] A tie-down chain creaks, twisting in the wind between a jet and a pad eye six feet over my head as we list to port, turning after flight ops. Or back into the wind for the next event. I can't tell how late we're flying, since they're diverting to Miramar. Normal blue water ops have them on deck by 2230. At any rate, we're crossing a current and cutting waves above it. While not so big as to hear, they're strong enough to make the hull vibrate. Or else a dude is jacking off in the rack beside me. Maybe both.

It's a new set of faces on the mess decks. No real baby faces this time. They're all gone to normal billets. Cowboy is a gunner now, in a red jersey. Roadrunner wears dungarees of his helo squadron. And that little broomstick lover is a green shirt for Damage Control. But, they all still eat, and now they ask me for their hookups.

Taps Taps, Lights out. All hands turn in. Maintain silence about the deck. The smoking lamp is out in all berthing areas. Now Taps. After months at sea with a nightly announcement every swinging dick onboard can recite it by rote. On Westpac 89 the Marines convinced the OOD to announce *via* trumpet recordings, until they wore out the tape and it warbled like a warped album, and the 1MC finally gobbled it up.

I was wrong about the turn. We're in the wind at 25 knots, launching six birds after the Chaplain's Evening Prayer. Steam, dull roar, scrape, slam, wind, gurgle, sudden silence. Unless you're asleep you always plug your ears before the slam. Sweet Pea stood beside me on the ramp to the bomb elevator at the bug bar deck for what seemed like ten minutes. I am love sick

---

[1] Jargon: COD means Carrier Onboard Delivery, a fat turbo-prop plane that takes equipment mail, and people to and from an aircraft carrier. Usually in that order.

for him as I have never been for a man in all my born days. But I can tell no one, least of all him.

"Sweet, Sweet, Sweet, Sweet, Sweets," I whispered his name into his ear. He looked at me with halfclosed eyelids, bedroom eyes if it were a girl's look. But we are men.

"Are you doing that gorgeous Public Defender?"

He aches, just like a woman, and he fakes, just like a woman, and he makes love just like a woman, but he breaks just like a shy little boy. He and his buddies saw me at her car on the pier the night she drove me to the ship after dinner at the Mexican Village on Coronado Island. She'd told me of her jealous boyfriend deputy sheriff packing a piece and a violent temper. Not my idea of a challenge. "You know women," I said.

"Yeah, I know. I just had to ask to be sure." I don't know what he meant, and I have no idea whether, or how well, he knows women. But men have this thing about "us" and "them" that works.

He went back to his job as an Elevator Operator, bringing some Intruders down from the flight deck to the hangar bay.

"One two three four, we don't want your fuckin' war." Tom Cruise, ex-Top Gun, chants now in "Born On the Fourth Of July." My brother Tim, 15 months older than me, a lawyer in St. Louis, eight years in the Navy, born on the fifth of July, 1955, just missed Vietnam.

Our once bright and shining port schedule has been revised to possibly 4 days in P.I.--after steaming 2 weeks--and 100 days in the Indian Ocean or the Persian Gulf itself--after steaming another 2 weeks--then a 4 week return trip to Sand Dog. Which totals 6 months to someone versed in higher math.

I worry that the *Independence*, whom we replace, is sitting like a duck in a shooting gallery in the Gulf. What if they sink her? What if she gives them the idea, and they sink us once we relieve her? What if Israel deploys nuclear weapons against Iraq and it somehow ignites half the world's oil, and pollutes the country for years? They'll have to space shuttle the diplomats to the middle east. Hopefully, *Ranger* won't be melted to the bottom of the gulf.

2200 29 SEP 90. Other guys read letters from their lovers. I get a bank statement and a past due notice from Visa postmarked two weeks ago. It says my balance owing is $800, but just before we left I put $500 of my car crash cash there knocking it down to $380. Best car crash I ever had: the ink wasn't dry on the new insurance contract when I rolled; 2900 miles on the car; they paid it off, so I didn't have to worry about the fender I bent backing out of the carport; and I walked with a check for $850.

Some stranger put his blanket in the bottom rack, and his bald head makes me look like Paul McCartney. He checked into the AE shop Wednesday. His name is Bob, too. Greg used to live in that rack, but moved to AK1's rack as AK1 moved to the Rain Locker (so called because of condensation from its location beneath the vegetable preparation room off the aft mess deck). The condensation will keep them cool in the tropics, and the depth inside the hull will dull the chock-drop clatter and cat water brakes that are hellish on my ears up here. "Well, I'm gonna smoke a cigarette and go to bed," Bob says. He goes to sit by the lounge TV. I don't bother reading him the riot act on smoking here. Beave, our coop cleaner, may have noticed and may think it's a white thing. Am I prejudiced, or have I lightened up since he told me that I needed to get off this boat?

Notes from a televised Captain's brief with the Admiral: We are part of Central Command in Desert Shield. We will maintain interception. We could go into the Persian Gulf per President or Secretary of Defense. Above ten degrees north latitude we will get an extra $110 per month called Imminent Danger Pay. Will we still hit ten ports? "No, we'll find ourselves on station."

Ninety days on station flying CAP (combat air patrol) and supporting sanctions. Sixty out of sixty-one participants supported UN Resolution 661. Other airwings aren't as capable as Battle Group ECHO to reach out at night. We'll have chemical weapons suits. "We have a real mission."

Our mission is to play a part of CENTCOM in Operation Desert Shield, as well as provide for maritime interception. Resolution 661 is supported by 60 of 61 to be enforced by CV 61. A numbers game after all. We may be the first, instead of the *Independence*, to enter the Persian Gulf. For as long as we float above ten degrees north latitude we'll get IDP. Back in L.A., in 1984, imminent danger was the argument that won my case against a first degree murder charge. I killed a 17-year-old kid, god rest his soul, whose actions put my life in imminent danger for a few minutes. Now I'll be placed in imminent danger for days, maybe months. But not alone.

Sweet Pea came down for the fried chicken tonight. "Go! Hurry up! I don't have time to wait and I'm hungry." He snapped his fingers like a spoiled rotten Prince.

I made sure the line attendant gave me white meat, made him take back a leg; and I stopped for lettuce, tomatoes, grapes, an apple and two kinds of juice. He wouldn't eat the salad, grapes or apple, but he gobbled the breasts and sucked that cherry juice. Hmmm. I drank the other juice and sat with him and one of his million ever-present friends, while others came by and tweeked his ear or said hello, depending on how bold they were. (How can cute young men stand the affection they get onboard Navy vessels? Sweet Pea seems to have a matching need, though, that makes it magic.)

I called a truce with Muggerboy, what the hell. He passed the bug bar and caught my eye so I called out. "I found out the story," I said. "I guess that other dude was the mean one."

"He got a bad conduct discharge."

"I guess you just got sucked in."

"It's gonna be a long 'pac. No sense holding grudges."

I felt a pain in my spine as we shook hands.

2130 30 SEP 90. My bounced checks come back to haunt me. PNC arrives on the mess deck to call me back to Pers. "Senior Chief wants to see you," he barks.

I am shown a memo on *Ranger* letterhead from the Disbursing Officer attached to a copy of a check I wrote to a shipmate. At 1600 I'm instructed to introduce myself to our new Admin Officer in the Ready Room, to explain this memo. Nice first impression. "I gave the landlady a money order in case the July check bounced again. But if it cleared she could use it for August instead of the check I left her for August. She resubmitted the July check and it cleared. Then she cashed the money order for the August rent, but she also cashed the check I left for August. And I had four checks bounce because of that." I don't mention Phyllis is 80 years old walking around with oxygen on a leash. "Let's say that by close of business tomorrow you have this resolved." Young officers are wonderfully direct and tactful.

"Welcome aboard, anyway," I say.

At 2100 I find my shipmate, an MS1 who works in the officer galley up forward. Nobody told him anything about my bad check even though I wrote it to him. See, he was standing in front of the line at Disbursing when I came by during all that running around to cover my ass with the rent Money Order, and rather than go to the back of the line like I was supposed to, I selfishly asked if he'd let me make it out to him so he could cash it for me now. He agreed and the cash went from the DO to him and right to me. And bounced. And Ranger sent a letter to Wolfpack. So I have to go back to Disbursing tomorrow to see if they have this returned check for which I owe them $250. The funniest thing is, if I do still owe them $250, will they take a check?

2100 2 OCT 90. Pizza night! On Westpac we'd have pizza once a week, which is how you knew it was Friday. But this is Tuesday. "Major Dad" plays the lounge on TV. I'm in my rack. The pizza was lousy, especially since Sweets said it sucked.

Typical military intelligence: I paid off my bad check with a check.

2300 3 OCT 90. Even pizza doesn't bring a crowd like fried chicken! We served 3,000 men on the forward mess decks between 1600 and 1930.

I waited for Sweet Pea until they ran out of fried chicken and switched to baked. At 1925 he appeared with Cup-O-Soup and Nachos' Cool Ranch chips, as my guys swept and swabbed the main deck. I gave him a plastic fork and let him sit with some other buddy of his, talking about the hangar deck madness in the high seas we've just hit. I got to join them for a whole five minutes, before this second class petty officer I work for crashed our party. Three blue shirts got sea sick including one who yakked on his uniform. Another collapsed in the scullery and the medics had to take him to sick bay. The third came to me just in time and I sent him to Medical, about a hundred feet aft.

The guys of Fly One are chocking and chaining a bird on the flight deck over me now. I hear the engines winding down and off, then only chains, twisting against the pull of the carrier. The hated smell of JP-5 jet fuel wafts into our berthing. Boots clomp around on the flight deck nonskid above.

Meanwhile, shots ring out in "A Fist Full Of Dollars." Eastwood night on *Ranger*.

I am assistant manager of a buffet restaurant serving 3,000 to 5,000 ruffians per meal, three meals a day. I supervise 20 men. I could get a job as a restaurant manager on the outside.

Today as the decks were packed with chicken lovers, they called away Man Overboard (MOB). Eighty half-empty trays cooled on the main deck tables, forty more on the bug bar deck, thirty on the scullery deck. The soda deck was secured for rehab work on a bomb elevator. After MOB secured we had all those trays to clear in front of a new mob of hungry chicken lovers.

We have this leak in one spot along the serving line, so that every time the ship turns left--and leans right since she's top heavy--a wide stream flows across the main mess deck under tables and grimy boots. An extraordinary challenge to maintain clean decks when combined with MOB.

We hear the *Indie*'s in the Persian Gulf. I wonder what it would be like to see a missile burst into your berthing or your space on the ship, and feel the intense heat just as you shrivel and your burnt skull pops like corn.

Line hopping. We have two serving lines forward, one port and one starboard, with the galley between. Port serves hot dogs and burgers ("sliders") and fries or pork-n-beans. Starboard faces the main deck and serves entres like chicken and pizza. Sometimes a skatemaster takes a tray through a short line on the port side just to soil it, then jumps in the "seconds" line on the starboard side to beat the crowd. It amounts to "head of the line privileges," and pisses people off. Unless I'm doing it in my Red Shirt capacity, which probably pisses some people off. But I don't give a fuck because I'm the manager. Tonight some dude did it and a First Class nailed him, and brought him to a Red Shirt who works for me. But that Red Shirt had let the dude, which pissed off the PO1 who couldn't drop it and wanted blood. Instead of eating he used his mealtime to find our LPO (Leading Petty Officer), another PO1. Our PO1 came up and read the riot act to the Red Shirt. That satisfied the other PO1 more than a meal. Kind of a religious thing I guess. Next, a shitheel in blue coveralls grabbed a mess crank hat off the galley door and feigned throwing it. Last thing I needed was a food fight. He tossed it into a filthy mop bucket as I walked up. "How would you like someone to shit on your face?"

"Huh?"

"We have to work in that and pull that out. In fact, you pull it out now and throw it in the trash."

"Fuck that. I'm not diggin' in that water."

"I'm holding up this entire line until you do it. Unless you want to walk with me down to the Master-At-Arms shack."

Two hundred people began threading around us in the serving line. The dude grumbled, then fished it out and threw it into a trash can. An Ordie behind him filled me in. "That guy's been causin' trouble the whole way through this line. When we were in the passageway he was blockin' it. And some First Class came walkin' past, tryin' to get through. And the First Class told him to move and he just stood there. Man, if I'd have been that First Class I would have nailed him."

The ship stopped shaking and tumbling for a couple of hours after dinner--as if letting us digest. But I guess the OOD has decided to rock the CO to sleep now, because she's heaving again. Woah, ride 'em cowboy! On the flight deck I can hear the integrity watch adding extra tie-down chains to lash the jets to the carrier. I hear them spinning the nuts, tightening them up.

I have no idea what it's like outside, except that Sweet Pea was talking earlier about the hangar getting soaked. The motion of the waves sickens some, and comforts others.

0400 6 OCT 90. In port San Diego. I barely made it across the brow. I have to be at work by 0800. But then, half a day and I'll have a weekend off--Saturday night, Sunday and Monday. We pull out Tuesday for another two weeks. I walked across the hangar bay looking at San Diego, all so neat and clean, and lit up in the night.

I took a motorpsycho nightmare out of North Island with a dude called Cuz from the Wolfpack. He wanted me to get him some acid but his gas key was at Miramar. Mission Beach was on the way, so we went there anyway and found Marlin on the boardwalk strumming the six remaining strings on his twelve-string guitar, loaded with sheets of LSD.

We went back to my place where Cuz packaged his deal for his chums. He showed me a cool dive with the cover of a pizza place where three of his buddies played in a band. I started smoking. When we went to leave, his band buddy coaxed him into snorting a line of crystal meth. I couldn't believe it. Man, acid is one thing the Navy can't test for. But they can catch you snorting meth. It shows up in a piss test for several days, and you never know when they'll have one. He said he was good at evading the whole whiz quiz scene, and liked playing roulette.

Riding up to Miramar, things got warped. Like the gas tank. I began to realize how big I-15 was, walking north out of gas, with no gas key. First we abandoned his cycle. Then we turned back, and he actually got it started again. We laughed. Then it stalled again and he pushed it. I watched for cops.

He got it going a third time. It was years since I'd rode on the back of a bike. It kept lurching as we plodded onward. I thought sure he'd wreck, and just wanted to get off that bucking bronco. Much later, he explained that he was lunging the bike to the left and right to swash any bit of gas still in there into the carburetor. Miraculously we got all the way to the main gate. I hopped off and ran up the embankment of the exit ramp to Miramar and expected to find him at the top. But I looked down the hill at the gate and saw him way down there, walking toward me, his bike parked at the edge of the shadows near the Pass and Decal turn-in behind him. He was afraid to face the gate guard, sure they'd bust him and test him.

"Say nothing, act natural."

"As long as you're walkin' I don't care if he's drunk." The gate guard was very understanding.

"Where can I park my bike?"

"Well, you got that great big parking lot right there."

We had military ID cards and walked through the gate. No one out there could touch us, and the guard was cool. We were home free. We walked across the base to a barracks where a bunch of his acid head buddies were spacing out and getting ready for tomorrow's zone inspection. It was surreal, visiting a drugged out Navy barracks, with a guy running a buffer in the middle of the night, after weeks of preparing for war.

2230 8 OCT 90. Safely back aboard *Ranger*, after a weekend at Mission Beach. Louis came back. He'd bailed the beach scene and gone home. He's back in school. My rap about self-educating must have scared him. "Stop rubbin' up against me or I'll beat your ass."

I was following Sweets when he stopped abrupt. "Well, excuse me."

Later on he passed through the mess deck.

"I didn't rub against you on purpose."

"I know that."

He spent a day with me at Mission. In my apartment with the door closed. But hardly like Louis. He took the 901 bus to the courthouse, changed over to the 34A to the Giant Dipper (the name of our famous roller coaster), and walked up to my place to learn how to hold a guitar. I sat too close on the couch and finally took his cheeks in my hands and pressed my forehead to his for a blissful second, as my hopes and dreams began to build. "Will ya stop grabbin' my foot for Chrissakes?" Like needling a balloon.

The girl admitted stealing my beer. My public defender got me dismissed while I was at sea. I told the Internal Affairs detective I wouldn't sue for false arrest. I made one last call to my public defender. "Now that the case is behind us, I probably won't be talking with you anymore. Unless you want me to call."

"That would be good," she said. "I have your number and you've got mine."

"Is that an indication that you want me to call?"

"Sure."

"Well, in a couple of weeks when I get back from sea, I'll call you and see if you'd like to have dinner again."

2245 9 OCT 90. Back on the boat for the rest of our sea trials. I'm arranging my rack for General Quarters. It came suddenly this afternoon, in the middle of chow, so just like MOB we had hundreds of trays full of burgers and fries left sitting. Once GQ secured we had five minutes to re-open for dinner. Now rumor control says we'll have another GQ at 0300. If I am sound asleep I want to be prepared to jolt up without hitting the rack light, get off my sweats and pull on my underwear, socks and dungarees, snatch my gas mask and boots, and run to the second deck (three down from here), all within five minutes of the alarm, before they set Zebra.[2]

If I don't make it I will have to stand and fight the ship from wherever I end up, which would probably be the hangar bay. I wouldn't mind being stuck out there with Sweet Pea--who, by the way, told me he was blown off the ship in this afternoon's drill. Not literally, but according to the casualty scenario. He would have floated around with the sharks while we took hits.

I laid my pants over the rack curtain, underwear beside them, socks inside my flight deck boots which hang from a brace that keeps electrical cables off my rack. I wedged my gas mask in its canvas bag between those cables. I can get into my boots in a heartbeat with one pull on a shoelace. The point is not so much to be ready for a surprise tonight, as to be configured for sleeping in the Persian Gulf.

---

[2] A note on Zebra: it's a material condition of readiness where all watertight hatches are sealed, and if you haven't got through, too bad.

Chapter Five

2145 11 OCT 90. Wrestling noises from our lounge. "All right, fag!"

Out of water in the showers. I went to the Radioman's head.

Tonight the Chaplain prays, "focus on the job."

One of my miscreants used religion to get off work tonight. When he returned I gave him to the nightcheck PO to make up the time. Am I cruel? This is a warship and religious endeavors don't justify time off. You must make up the time. So I don't go to church.

Dinner closed on the forward mess at 1930. Rumors of GQ went all day long. By 1910 I secured the scullery deck, the soda deck, and some tables on the bug bar and main decks. Right then a line of guys just off daycheck arrived and needed seats. I had briefed the blueshirts about possibly having to unsecure tables. One tired miscreant caught a customer seated at a secured table and told him to move. They were already yelling when I got there from the other side of the bomb elevator. One of my Red Shirts had just got there and was trying to handle it. "I asked this guy to leave and he won't leave a secured table," the blueshirt whined.

The customer was moving now, but I had to say something so he wouldn't go away mad and forget a flashlight in a jet intake. "Just so you know the way it works around here," I began.

"Yeah, how does it work around here?"

It was the LPO of Wolfpack's Line shack. He runs an outfit similar to mine--boots at the bottom of the barrel, new to taking orders, whiners and moaners who don't want to be here. "Well," I said evenly. "If the condiments are on the chair that means the table is secured."

"You secure the tables when you're still open?"

"Some of them, so we can get the job done by turnover."

"Tables are here for people. Not just to be cleaned and looked at." He was yelling now, obviously stressed out beyond all reason, and taking it out on me in front of my subordinates.

"You know better than talk to me like that," I said twice.

2245 12 OCT 90. Tension begins to peak on the ship and the mess decks. A guy from the galley came behind the bug bar with a knife arguing with our local skinhead who pulled a butter knife in retaliation. Luckily, two SMAA (cops) sat nearby. I enlisted their opinion if the galley dude was authorized to have a knife. "Do you have a knife chit?"

"No."

"You escort him to his locker to put it away," one ship cop said to me. "And you, run a chit through your Division Officer if you want to be authorized to carry the knife."

We got as far as the Galley Watch Captain who took charge of the knife and probably gave it back when I left. He hasn't come behind the bug bar since.

Sweat Pea is a Sea World freak. Next Friday afternoon is *Ranger* Night at Sea World. I gave him a Sea World pin that I got from a third class who's working with us. Hopefully, he says, Sweet Pea and DeeJay, one of his million buddies whom I met at pizza night, and I'll all go to Sea World together. Then Sweet Pea's going to Huntington Beach for the weekend to be fitted for a tux. He'll be in a wedding party, no doubt mistaken for an altar boy.

"How did you get so cultured?" I had to ask, watching him eat. "You must be the son of a great monarch." He pushed me back with a hand on my bald forehead. Maybe I should have remembered that his father left him and his brother and mother in a lurch when he was six.

2345 13 OCT 90. I fired a Red Shirt and stuck him in the deep pan room as a blueshirt. I had caught him too many times bullshitting with trash at his feet. And with a foot on a table shooting the shit with buds instead of working. I was tired of picking up the litter and the soda cans and a tray of dried beans and the full trash can that should have been emptied, and finally went into a rage. Once he drifted behind the bug bar that was it. He kept on bullshitting with the bug boys who consequently forgot about the juice and milk containers while the customers got pissed. "If you want this station I'll let you bullshit here from the bomb elevator, outside the bar where you can see what's going on and what's running out." He was a fence post. I gave him five face-saving minutes and came back. He was still behind the bar. "They need ice here." He got off his ass, but that was too late. He'll be in the deep pan room tomorrow.

Next this Catholic fruitcake came crying. He was working the bug deck with a black guy who was slouching. The skinhead told him, "why don't you have that nigger do that?"

"I hate working with prejudice people."

At 2200 I had to find him and deliver him to the MAA shack to fill out a voluntary statement charging the skinhead with a racial slur. Ship's Investigations and the NIS got involved.

2300 14 OCT 90. Rocking and rolling in heavy seas. The rack light vibe creeps up until I slap it.

I've been talking management style with the coop cleaner. We just watched "Glory" together. He's black, I'm white. "How did it go with your new Red Shirt?"

"He's doing great. Just like I knew he would. He came up and volunteered to work a couple of extra hours tonight to finish stripping the scullery deck." I told him about the racial slur, and explained that I solved it by making the skinhead and the "nigger" work in the deep pan room together.

"It might have been love at first sight," Beave offered.

"They get along fine, now." At first the skinhead insisted that in "no fucking way" he'd work with the black. Then he realized that if they both worked hard and took turns knocking out the job, they got the longest breaks on the mess decks.

I gave them two guarantees to make it worth working in the deep pan room. First, if you get the work done you set your own breaks. Second, you will get relieved by nightcheck at 2030. We mustered at 2020 on the main mess deck and the nightcheck deep pan guys were not on station. "Huddle up, guys. I don't want the galley Watch Captain to hear this." We gathered near the bomb elevator on the main mess deck. "I don't have anything to put out, but I don't want the galley crew to hear this. Look, if I cut you loose the deep pan guys are gonna have to go back in there 'til the nightcheckers get down here and take over. None of you would want to stay after the rest of the daycheck secures. I'm holding the whole crew 'til the deep pan guys are relieved. I'd rather have 'em mustering here with us than in there working past 2030."

The nightcheck supervisors, a PO2 and a PO1 walked up. "I'm holding my entire crew until I get two replacements from your crew in the deep pan room. And it's either gonna be the nightcheck deep pan guys or the nightcheck supervisors, but I want two bodies in there now."

Being a third class, I was a little bold addressing second class and first class petty officers like that. But I've earned their respect by running the daycheck myself, in spite of the no load fat second class who only gets in the way. They looked around and found two nightcheck blueshirts and stuck them in the deep pan room, and I cut my guys loose.

Now I hear the turning nuts on the tie-down chains, and the links dragging over the flightdeck as the Blue Shirts of Fly ONE (on the forward section) add extra chains due to the heavy seas we're plowing through.

Sweet Pea showed me an article in *Ranger*'s *Top Gun Gazette* about the hangar crew passing 3500 "crunch-free" moves. Then he laughed. "Guess what happened last night, as the paper was being printed. I'm glad I'm going to bed. I wouldn't have liked working for the chief all night."

0445 15 OCT 90. The voice on the 1MC was almost soothing, vaguely stirring me from sleep. "*Man overboard. Man overboard. Port side. All hands stand clear of all decks, ladders and passageways.*" Suddenly the berthing sprang to life with men jerking open rack curtains to wake everyone. It wasn't followed by the customary aside, "*This is a drill.*" I threw on my sweats and ran down four decks and aft to the after mess deck where my crew was already mustered. "This is a more updated muster sheet," someone in khakis shoved the paper into my hand. "Remuster." I went down the list bleary eyed as the skinhead laughed at the stupidity of remustering. "On *Ranger*, this is the Captain. We've had something the size of a man hit the water on the port side. And all reports indicate that this is enough information we have to consider that a shipmate may have gone overboard. So it's real important that we get this muster accurate and as fast as possible. We're turning around and backtracking about five minutes and manning up the duty lifeboats."

0515 15 OCT 90. I walk past an open hatch where the waves below slap the port bow, and think of the conversation I heard yesterday afternoon on the mess decks. "They're gonna COD him off in the morning for his own protection. They better station him inside a nuclear shelter, brother, or they'll get him. 'Cause he took a lot of people down with him--first class petty officers who got a lotta years in, and families, bro'."

"A lot of people were breaking the law and he dropped a dime on them."

"I knew about it, too. The NIS is bringing me up on seventeen charges with a General Courts Martial. But the only thing they can stick me on is conspiracy 'cause I knew about it." He was the big Puerto Rican who wanted that other boy to suck his dick, but also said he'd kill any faggot who came near. Now he's up on two major crimes. First, conspiracy to steal two laptop computers from the Operations Department that happened to contain our Battle Group's highest technological capability for computer data link of radar systems for offensive-defensive battle coordination, top secret equipment that was found a few days later in two plastic bags at the bottom of a ladder. If we went to war with Iraq and they had this equipment, we'd be sitting ducks. Second, this dude was allegedly assisting a phony marriage certificate ring through which a lot of people had illegally collected Married VHA (Variable Housing Allowance) and Bachelor Allowance for Quarters (BAQ) at the "with Dependent" rate, which provided each customer with around five hundred dollars a month for the rest of his career. For each certificate the guy running it had been charging the member's first three thousand dollars of VHA and BAQ benefits. One dude got antsy, and took a certificate that wasn't quite ready. He got caught, and rolled over on the whole ring. They were exposed now, and soon to be ruined. He was the only one in jail--for his own protection--and they were discussing how to throw him over before he could be flown off.

2215 15 OCT 90. I have to check my own six. The Catholic fruitcake who cried about the skinhead was flirting with me now. I came back with a kinky gesture. "Man, I'm gonna take you out to the beach, tie you up and whip you."

"Petty Officer Graham invited me to his house and wanted to tie me up."

Earlier, he called me a penis head.

"That's better than a felcher," I said back.

"What's a felcher?"

"Somebody who likes to eat shit out of someone's ass."

"Petty Officer Graham said he wishes he was a doctor so he could lick the shit off of people's bodies."

You have to watch what you say around certain people.

No-load, the Second Class PO, comes up to me. "You and me need to sit down and talk about somethin' after dinner." But he never did.

"I ain't no faggot," the fruit said under his breath.

The nightcheck supervisor took me up to the hangar deck for a private talk. "Bob, I don't know if you are, and you don't have to tell me. But if you're gay, I want to warn you that the NIS is just waiting for you to lick someone's ear."

"Well, they have a whole file on me already from when I was mugged by some guys off this ship."

"We pray especially for the Supply Department tonight," the Chaplain said, "going through a major inspection. Please let them know they are deeply respected and appreciated."

0415 SATURDAY, MID-OCTOBER 90. Mission Beach. FM radio. Lou has a woman on the boardwalk trying to keep warm with him as I sit in this empty apartment.

Tonight I got arrested for dialing 911. Five cop cars had stacked up in the lifeguard parking lot and vacated the park full of hippies like a knee-jerk reaction. It reminded me of Steve in Venice Beach telling me of his trip to El Salvador and meeting up with the Death Squad. Only this was San Diego and they were just an anti-gang unit coming off shift, loitering at the beach at the expense of the locals who split. I wanted to complain. I saw the pay phone, walked over, and didn't have change. So I dialed 911.

"Police and fire emergency."

"I wanna know why five cop cars and ten cops are hanging out at the Mission Beach lifeguard station instead of patrolling."

"What's the nature of the emergency, sir?"

"I just wanna know why these cops haven't turned in their cars."

"What's the nature of the emergency, sir?"

"Fuck this." I slammed the phone and walked up to the cops. "I wanna speak to the supervisor here."

"He's the supervisor."

"Yeah, whaddaya want?" A sergeant said.

"I just called 911 and it took seven rings for the lady to answer and they're supposedly busy all over San Diego and you guys are loitering here with your cars and I wanna know why."

"You called 911 to ask that? Ha-hah, you're outa here."

He cuffed me.

"So, you handcuff me for asking a simple question?"

"You work a long day and you wanna shoot the shit afterward with some of your buddies about what a bad day you had, and you don't wanna give us that right?" A cop leaning on one of the cars admitted the truth. The sergeant choked me inside his elbow and led me to the cage inside the lifeguard station. "Kelly," I read his name tag over my shoulder. "Your name is R. Kelly, and you're twisting the cuffs up into my back." He let off. "And you're shoving my face against the wall and jamming my knees into the bench." He put me in the cage.

"This guy's wah," he said to another officer, cocking his head sideways.

"Are you taking any prescription medication?"

"No."

"Are you under the care of a physician for any psychiatric disorders?"

"No, and I resent the line of questioning. I have a right to do what I did.

I still wanna know what the fuckin' cops are doing hanging out here with taxpayer equipment."

"Close your eyes," he said, inspecting my nostrils with his flashlight. He was looking for methamphetamine, which is what all the tweekers and violent femmes use at Mission Beach. "We're gonna turn out the lights and check your pupils," another cop said. "It helps if you squint real hard."

Helps what, I thought. I didn't listen to their bullshit, but looked past the guy's tracing fingers at his eyes.

"You're having a hard time following my finger."

"That's right, I'm pissed off." I didn't mention the acid.

"He's Navy."

"Do you want a courtesy turnover to the Navy Shore Patrol? Or would you rather go downtown?"

"Just give me to the Navy."

"Well," a female cop finally spoke. "To answer your question, sir. The officers outside are from an anti-gang unit stationed nearby."

Shore Patrol hauled me to the wrong Naval Station--32nd Street--then back to NAS Miramar where they turned me over to Base Security who called the squadron and turned me over to the duty driver who brought me to the SDO desk and got me on the phone to the SDO at the BOQ who told the driver to take me home. Instead of fireworks on the 4th of July, I had a fucking circus.

I found Louie on the green tweed couch at my apartment. That Guy had let him in and gone to bed. "I got arrested."

"Me, too."

"So what did you do with the girl? Did you lose her? Get rid of her?"

"Finished her." He knocked the ash into his empty cigarette pack. "How were two?"

"Well, I'm still up."

0930 SUNDAY 90. The beach has a blue roof and winter breeze just like yesterday. I'll make coffee in a minute and loiter out on the patio as skateboarders, surfers and lesbians pass by, and the traffick backs up Mission Boulevard north of the coaster and Joe waits on tables at Luigi's and Christa washes clothes across the alley. I took the bus to Lucky's with Louie last night and got some food. He limped around on his war wound without whining, and followed me from aisle to aisle as I spent sixty bucks.

We stopped first at the ATM by Pacific Eyes and Tee's. "My checkbook says $850. What do you think my ATM'll say?" It said $730. I subtracted the difference, since banks are always right, and bankers never embezzle.

I made a salad last night in memory of Amy. I can't recall the name of the lettuce but it's dark green with stalks instead of a light green round ball.

She must be done with art school, in Pasadena. I was "the one" for a time. My mom died feeling comfortable that I was set with Amy, a new woman to nurture me. And wasn't gay after all.

I hung onto straight little Billy for so many years. I had known him since I was fifteen, and he was a beautiful tiny nine year old blond who couldn't make the after school softball team on a gravel playground at the University of Missouri Lab School, in Columbia. I felt sorry for him and we sat on the sidelines covering each other's legs with gravel. I started brothering, then bothering him. I couldn't compete with the girls--he had three a night. I was Puff, the Magic Dragon. And he grew up.

"Billy," I called him on February 24, 1985.

"Yeah?"

"I told God, if I got acquitted I would want to see you."

I heard a munch, then the phone sliding down his shirt.

"Sounds like you're eating celery," I lightened up.

The phone went dead.

"Hello?"

Then a dial tone. I thought we got disconnected. His phone was busy as I dialed back. I finally gave up, and when I tried it a few days later it was unlisted. I finally got the hint.

I guess my Sweet Pea fantasy is over, too. He and Dean were supposed to come over after Ranger Night at Sea World. "Reveille at 1100," he said. They'd catch the bus by 1300, drink wine coolers with me until four, and take the Navy bus back to the ship at the end of the night. At 1900 I lit the fireplace and burned my lousy ticket. I knew I'd be stood up ever since he insisted that I buy my own ticket rather than let him buy mine or me buy his. He's just using me for head of the line privileges in the forward mess.

1850 22 OCT 90. Heating lentil soup with jazz and a good book, *The Main*. Reading in a chair by the living room lamp. Sudden flashback to Venice Beach, Paloma Court and Ocean Front Walk. Life atop the Figtree's Cafe, third floor window over the boardwalk, tourists throwing quarters at me singing in my window. Walking north on Santa Monica Boulevard, stopping to shop at the health food bazaar on a warm winter evening while the rest of the USA is on ice. Working in the film business. Unknown. Rewriting a movie script for Khaled Siddick, a director from Kuwait. Doing a job worth $14,000 for $1000 as a nonmember of the Writer's Guild. I had asked $200,000 and a principle role. The movie never got made, and I barely paid my rent those two fun months. I got my first professional check in the entertainment business, got my flat on the boardwalk, and got acquitted of first degree murder, all in the same week. On top of my bittersweet world. I had a job at a law firm as a paralegal, and took a two week vacation "to film on location in Atlanta with Khaled," but really to stand trial in the L.A. County courthouse in front of 75 potential jurors who got whittled down to twelve and two alternates. Then sat before them as the trial went on with bloody pictures of a dying cholito with a tiny body and a huge swollen head, a lying detective and a closet homosexual anti-gay biased judge and a bumpkin county prosecutor. Represented by the best public defender in L.A., James Bisnow.

Then hired by slick ad agency k/d/p in West L.A. because, as the gestapo personnel manager said, "you had a personality and a presence that convinced us you'd be calmer under pressure than the applicants with MBA's." We brought in the Suzuki Samurai.

2300 24 OCT 90. Shirley read me the Penal Code, laughing about this second arrest by the Mission Beach police. I was no competition for her gun carrying jealous deputy marshal lover. She was a Sweet Pea distraction, a fast fading fantasy of comfort and safety in the fag bashing world. We'd have looked right. But nobody desires a bald head, especially one that stood trial for murder. There's always that question, "did he do it?" CA Penal Code 148.3(c) calls it a violation when calling 911 would result in a reasonable expectation that emergency services would be dispatched to the scene of a non-emergency.

"Why are these cops hanging out?"

"You called 911 to ask that? You're under arrest." In San Diego County, the arrested pays for the court costs, win, lose or draw. More arrests, more county court job security.

I got the sudden word, That Guy and I are vacating the first of November. I thought I'd clarified with Phyllis that it would be 1 December. But I'm good at moving in a hurry. I left Venice that way on the night I got mugged by the dude who had burgled my apartment the week before, then caught me on the street. I saw him on his bike in the alley, called the cops, had him arrested, then packed and split in the wee hours before he made bail.

In Tucson when Stella's sister called me a fag, I left her and her family in a couple of hours while the juvenile department encouraged me to stay. They were probably trying to stall until they could find some evidence of child abuse. I had spanked her little six year old with a belt. And her sixteen year old was an attractive young man. I'd gone as far as massaging his back, and he'd massaged my scalp with aloe plant juice from the desert. But he didn't respect me as a father figure, and I wasn't skilled enough to work it out, and I didn't want to fulfill a prophecy. She had put me up in Hollywood before the cholo killing, and had four boys. They all liked me, but were so sexy and pubescent and affectionate and horny, and I was too bisexually inclined and immature to say no and would've gotten us in trouble if I stayed. I made the mistake of following her to Arizona after the trial, and had to leave after giving her about $2000 to get her family situated. Back in San Francisco I made another mistake of trying to explain all that to Amy, and lost her. She felt I was morally bankrupt and would molest our children if we had them. Now Lou showed up. "Hey Bob how are you?"

"Lou, come in. Just discussing an accounting problem."

"Well, when everything is going whoosh, don't follow the first little man that you see." Sage wisdom from an acid head. He took me out of the kitchen up to Johnny's for some Bulls and Blondy was skating across the street. When we left, Blondy was standing right outside the bar with a buddy on the pay phone across the doorway. "If you can't bite don't growl," his tee-shirt read.

"Grrrr," I said, looking him in the eye as we left.

"He looks so sad," Lou said.

"He's beautiful."

He stared at me as if wanting to speak. But he could have been a queerbait. You know, a fagbash disaster. So two ships passed in the night. Just like any other summer, only more so.

1700 25 OCT 90. Waiting at Fashion Valley for the 81 South to Mission Beach. Even though he's still my roommate for a few more days, I mailed That Guy a certified letter requesting his earliest return of my car and keys, for nonpayment of $50 due October 15. "We can work out the car problem after we move out." Fat chance. I mailed it to his job.

We both wonder if Phyllis will return our $375 deposits. "I've never had so much trouble in all my life," she said. I had cleared up the move out date with her. But she was on her Oxygen leash. Maybe she gauged it too thin.

I left a message with the Air Department of CV-61 for Sweet Pea to call me this evening. It's Thursday, so he gets off at three. My last weekend at Missing Beach. Will the message get delivered? Will the duty section cut me some slack, will we make it? Or will we end up toughened by the boat for six more months, then fade away? Will he get blown off El Four in the Gulf? Will I burn up in a sea of JP5 washing down off the flight deck? Will we both abandon ship and wind up in Oman, Bahrain or Kuwait City?

0300 27 OCT 90. Fog hits Mission Beach. In a note to all bartenders, Johnny of Johnny's Surf Club writes, "this is no reminder: no street people." I think it's a rights violation.

The San Diego Union has a Wednesday feature article entitled, "Tides of Trouble." It reports on the homeless drunks at Mission Beach, shirtless, barefoot and beer bellied, guzzling Milwaukee's Best. Hamel's Rollerblade storefront in the background flies the banner, "Mission Beach is for children, not drugs, drunks or derelicts." Pappy sleeps on a sheet spread over sand with two teenage boys, a makeshift hobo camp. A second picture's captioned: "At Mission Beach, residents say the beaches are becoming a haven for the homeless." It must be a crime.

Lou played me real slick. He became my buddy two or three days before I realized he was homeless. "So, you live around here, too?"

"Oh yeah, just up the way a few blocks," he nodded.

The extremely good wordsmith put my English BA to shame.

"If I were--not if I was," he'd say.

He said he was a CPA before Post Traumatic Stress Disorder from being a Vietnam sniper snuck up. So every weekend all year I've put him up on my living room couch. That Guy hated it, but learned to like the bum and didn't complain. He never stole or broke anything, and kept me from killing myself more than once.

0300 28 OCT 90. Sweet Pea came over last weekend--for the day, not the night--and I wrestled him to my bed for all of five minutes. "Get off me. Now look what you did." A wart on his back, just over his beltline, was bleeding. "I gotta get that taken off."

He sang "Knockin' On Heaven's Door" with me. The kid has a beautiful voice. Alas, the messages I left all this week went unanswered.

"Don't growl he's here," Lou observed from the sea wall.

"I know." All weekend I stared into Blondy's brown eyes, watching him skate. He was never alone until tonight, when they left together and he came back. He sat on a palm tree planter. I gathered my courage and walked over, eyeing him as he watched me. But I couldn't bear to come right up so I choked, stopping at a planter nearby. "I love you," my lips moved in silence. He suddenly skated off toward the Red Onion, a world behind questioning eyes left unexplored, unanswered. I never asked his name or age, hardly heard him talk. The hair on his legs contrasted his baby face. I can't remember if he smoked. He came back one last time with a guy and a girl, and caught my eye and whispered, made friendly and innocent statements with body language. I probably stayed away unnecessarily.

2200 28 OCT 90. Big band jazz on the little clock radio. Yellow pink red rust lamp light. That Guy in the living room in dim blue TV light. He sold his Japanese fighting fish to Dianne tonight, but wanted to watch them mangle each other.

Red Cheeks up at the front had the real name Paul. He was frying on acid, looking for a cigarette. I bummed one off Lou and threw it so it dropped out of the blue. A cute move for a baldheaded faggot in a black leather jacket under roller coaster lights. It melted the ice, but didn't break it. I started smoking that night.

Lou finally headed for Hobo Hilton, a row of moon shaded, overturned sailboats on Bayside across Mission Boulevard. "I'll walk ya to the corner."

"You know where it says, at Harry's, no ID no beer?"

"What about it?" I walked in and bought cigarettes.

"We are everywhere." So that was it. The main LSD manufacturer of Mission Beach was wrapped up in a lawsuit over his house burning down, and all the acid was coming from Berkeley now by PSA via weekend jaunts.

I stood by a DO NOT ENTER sign with a cigarette staring down Ventura Avenue at the coaster's slow blinking lights. It felt winter cold in the fog. I was chain smoking and I didn't even smoke. I didn't inhale, just flicked ashes like a pro. I had learned to fake it as a chain-smoking Doctor Spivey in the long running Contra Costa Community Theatre box office hit "One Flew Over the Cuckoo's Nest" before I'd gone to Hollywood.

Red had a different boogie box now, but promised mine would be here after the war. And he said I could will it to him.

Cops had the decency to stay away from me tonight.

2230 29 OCT 90. That Guy dropped me off at Household Goods at Naval Station 32nd Street at 0700. I took care of business and caught a bus to

Miramar. People keep asking me why I'm on the bus when That Guy owes me $350 for my car and drives it. I am trying to let him use it until he gets his Mustang out of the shop. But he's waiting on a check from a girl who hit him with no insurance. He says he'll get the check any day now. But he's moving out any day now, too. In fact, day after tomorrow. "I need to be at work by 0700 tomorrow."

"So take the bus."

"I need a ride because I'm taking my 4-track so the Legal Officer can tape an Admin Board."

"Well, if I get up I'll take you."

"No, I have to have a ride and I have to be at work by 0700 because I don't want to carry all that shit on the bus and my boss gave me hell today for coming in at 0730 every day since I totaled my GEO."

"Well, I don't see no problem."

"I just need to make sure you get up."

"What did I just say?"

"You said you don't see any problem." He looked like he'd throw me out of his room. He's planning to steal my car.

2400 31 OCT 90. That Guy's gone. I got my car back. I'm lying on my Westpac comforter with Jazz San Diego Style and a couple of sea bags. The movers picked up my six hundred pounds for deployment storage at 1630. That Guy left the plunger in his bathroom sink. I cleaned the refrigerator, stove, oven, cabinets and kitchen shelves. He left his empty drawers stacked atop his chest-of-drawers. And left an extension cord I'll use six months from December 18, when I return to San Diego and move off base to another flat along the beach.

Blondy wasn't skating tonight. But I found out his name is Matt. I guess he's drunk at some Halloween party tonight, being 20 and looking like 15.

America's Finest rolled up Ventura Avenue past Johnny's with a pumpkin on a spotlight. Even cops have some humor tonight. It was after ten, so they stopped every 15 feet along the boardwalk to hassle the drinkers. Tomorrow Lou will drive with me to Miramar. I'll get out at the flight line parking lot at 0655. He'll drive my Westpac gear to his daughter's garage, and register his new used Toyota at the DMV without having to re-smog. It's been stolen once, recovered once, sold once, stolen again, recovered again, repossessed, and sold again, since I bought it from Master Chief Hurst. But Lou needs a leg up, a way to get to a job. I'll be at sea onboard *Ranger*. He can sleep in the car. Tomorrow we'll get a hotel for a week. Better than living in the barracks with brats. Better than sleeping under boats.

2030 4 NOV 90. If I had moved back to the barracks I'd have lost my BAQ and VHA, $350 per month. I'm on the ship this month from the 7th to the 15th, then going home on leave from the 16th to the 25th. I may as well forget to update my VHA certificate, and use it for one week in a hotel vice a month in an apartment. I'll keep my receipts, just in case.

We got a roach hotel down by Balboa Park with jets landing almost on our roof, so loud it reminds me of bootcamp at RTC San Diego (a few blocks from here), when the Company Commander would bark, "if you don't..." and the rest would be drowned out by the noise of a jet landing until he'd finish with, "...you're going to a marching party! Do you understand!" "Sir, yes, sir!"

2245 6 NOV 90. Lou took me to Nite Life, a titie bar on El Cajon where the doorman owed him thirty bucks. He'd been hitting a bottle of Vodka since mid-afternoon and got depressed. I found a balloon in the toilet. But he swore he hadn't done junk in two months--as he tore thirty dollars out of my hand and threw me out of my car. I hope he's back in time to get me to work tomorrow morning. I'm trusting him with my valuables while I go on leave?

0005 12 NOV 90. "*Now set INCOMM condition hero eight modified for lines 8, 12 and 14 to read echo. Make reports to INCOMM control at extension 7221.*" What the hell does that mean?

War is at hand. Separation is the order of the day. Louie, our PN2, just informed us he's getting out at his EAOS (End of Active Obligated Service) in January. Which is too late for us to get a replacement before we cruise, so PNC and I will have to carry the ball alone together for the next six months in a war zone. Chief's trying to talk Louie out of it. Until now he's done nothing but harass the shit out of the guy, so I doubt if Louie's gonna change his mind and join us in that tiny office on the ship for six more months. Besides, Louie's only been married for a year. And he's been up for PN1 so many times he's given up trying to advance in the Navy. He's moving out, not up. Still, we changed his mind and got him to take the advancement exam one more time.

Chief is no longer capable of hiding the truth that he's a motherfucking son of a bitch to work for. How he ever got into Personnel--a customer service rating--boggles my mind. He insisted I use myself for the data in a prototype DD Form 214--discharge certificate--that I was creating on the computer. "What kind of discharge," I asked.

"Put down dishonorable," he barked.

"Thanks a lot, Chief. What reason?"

"Homosexual."

"I'm not putting that down." I put down Honorable as the type, and Expiration of Active Obligated Service as the reason.

I walk around Ranger imagining bent wreckage, twisted steal, flooded passageways and gritty smoke, rocking, deafening bombs going off, and flying corpses. I worry about Sweet Pea, and Roadrunner.

"This ain't right," Roadrunner said at his barracks inside the locked door at North Island. Then shot salty hot jism down the back of my throat.

Cable News Network said that *Ranger* deployed for the Gulf. Some guys who parked their cars in the 20-day lot on the pier had a nervous little laugh. We had been told to pack for this last work-up like we might not return. I stare at my Last Will and Testament. I have a computer, electric guitar, and amplifier. And a pick-up truck in Stockton in my brother Ken's garage.

2200 12 NOV 90. In the rack by TAPS. They're hunting "Red October" in the lounge.

One of the Shooters calls me Tender Loins. A polite way of calling me a fag. The dude I call Clark Gable was in their shop, right outside Personnel. I touched his hair as I left.

"*Ranger* is commencing her approach on *USS Kansas City*." Taking on fuel and stores.

Another rumor drifting up from the mess decks has us pulling in early. Wednesday or Thursday. Lou, whom I can't reach, is riding around and sleeping in my car, planning to meet me at the NAS North Island visitor lot at the main gate at 1400 Friday.

2300 13 NOV 90. War starts in one hour. Battle Group Evaluation. Of all movies to show on a warship, tonight is "Imagine," a documentary of John Lennon protesting for peace before he got murdered.

Midnight begins our 60-hour war. Someone fucks with us and we blow them off. They persist until IT'S WAR. I wonder when they'll call GQ. I'll have five minutes to be dressed and down to the opposite end of the carrier before they dog Zebra.

"Imagine no possessions." Lou sleeps in my car, a sniper from the Vietnam war on disability using heroin because the VA won't prescribe drugs for the pain of his 5 cracked ribs from the fight against Chris who owed him money from a drug deal to survive because he can't hold a job since he was alone in the jungle too long and flown back here too quick and experienced too much of a shock to assimilate appropriate behavior for the past 20 years.

All leave has been canceled so we can keep eleven jets up. We get November 21-25 off. A letter from the Legal Officer requests consideration of creditors for "No Refund No Exchange" airline tickets such as mine.

PNC says he'll let me go provided I go during the four days off and keep my mouth shut. Which is no break, because it means changing the dates on my ticket, which won't happen. Ass.

Ringaling, ding. "SMOKE SMOKE SMOKE *in compartment 03 tack 79 tack oh tack lima. Away the flying squad, away. All hands stand clear of all decks, ladderwells and passageways.*" That's close to 39-Man and my rack. I hope it's just burnt toast from the Officer's Galley.

The miracle of military brevity. The bell ring immediately signifies an emergency, typically a threat of fire or flooding. Beginning with the rapid ding-ding-ding-ding-ding-ding, it's followed by one, two, or three distinct dings. One ding on the end of it means that whatever the threat is, it's up forward. Two means amidships, three means aft. This code gets the Flying Squad--an all purpose emergency response team--running in the direction of the threat even before the specific location is announced. A flood on any ship, or fire on a warship full of ammo, can mean instant disaster. In two seconds this emergency response team knows there's a crisis up forward. Already running, in the first word of the Boatswain on the 1MC they know it's a possible fire, still in the smoke stage. Next they hear the compartment: first, the level is 03. That means the third deck above the hangar deck. So if the guy on the team isn't already on that deck, he starts looking for a ladder to go up as he's running toward the bow. In the next words, "tack seven nine," he's told that the crisis is at the ship's frame 79. Since the frames--main structures--of the ship are numbered from the front to the back, he knows how far forward he needs to run before he'll reach the crisis once he gets on the right deck. That way he doesn't run too far forward before cutting up a ladder. The next part, "tack oh," tells him which side of the ship the crisis is on. In this case, it's in the middle of the deck. If it were to one side or the other it would be "tack oh one" or "tack oh two" moving outward, with odd numbers on the port side and even numbers to starboard. Finally, the last part, "tack lima," pinpoints the exact compartment number. Every compartment on a Navy ship, no matter how big or small, has a precise identification assigned by number and letter. By the time this sequence could be explained, almost anybody on the Flying Squad would have gotten to the scene. "*Fire in compartment oh three tack seven nine tack oh tack lima is out.*"

I had XOI (Executive Officer's Inquiry) tonight with VF-2, our sister squadron. This was over a dude who walked out of ranks during muster on the mess decks last time at sea. That means he walked off instead of standing at attention in formation with the rest of the staff as I was passing instructions. He's a real Jesus Freak whose savior seems to intercede between him and his job most of the time. Not a guy to keep on the flight deck. "Why did you disobey Petty Officer Graham's order?"

"Well, sir, because I was having a bad day."

"You were having a bad day? Well, how about if I have a bad day and start raining down on your head?" The XO recommended the case be forwarded to Captain's Mast.

I remember being born again a couple of times. What a relief, turning your trials over to Jesus. However, eventually one must toil for a living. Anyway, some things are hard to reconcile, like the Bible saying "a bruised reed he shall not break" and the Bible saying "he cursed the figtree and it soon withered." I took it for what it was worth. And I'm convinced, we already had the Second Coming and the joke's on you who yet stand looking. I'll show you that in a movie script later.

2200 14 NOV 90. Ten days and a wake up to age 34. Thirty-three was the Christian year to my mind, the year of the mission. I heard that Jesus Christ was that age when he died.

At 13 I prayed constantly for a heart attack or a car to hit me. I played one round of Russian Roulette, depressed about the persecution of fanatical know-it-alls who said that I could not be 16 and love a nine year old boy with the passion of marriage. When Matt sat on my lap, age nine, and whispered, "If you're gay, I'm gay," I sat there, held him and couldn't speak up.

I was too young for Nam, nearly too old for now. But I just made it and they sent me to the Navy's finest fighter squadron in direct support of Operation Desert Shield, heading so far west it's east, in the middle of a 60-hour mock war, at MOP Level Two with a gasmask on my hip, while in the hangar bay men open crates of chemical weapon protection suits.

If I die it will be for America's values, America's way of life. And what a life it is, eh. Rampant killings and corrupt cops, electronic ballot counters made by strangers, undisclosed foreign purchases of land and corporations, bankrupt loans, mad starving farmers, illiterate educators, militant separatists of every race, insurance rip-offs and embezzlers.

We're going to kill the bad guy of the world and his family and army so our country will have gas and not solar energy for twenty more years until the grandkids of the gas barons retire. But they won't die, they'll multiply. And Saddam is a pawn in their game.

0850 17 NOV 90. Rising over *Ranger* like the morning sun, on PSA. She's the only carrier in San Diego harbor, as I head home on leave. Thanksgiving in San Francisco, but I'll still miss my birthday. I have to go back to Sand Dog the day before. I will drink with Lou, and hide from cops. "Don't disapprove my leave and have it approved over your head," I said to Chief.

"You know it's not going to be approved. I think you just want the CO's autograph. Why don't you just go ask him. Ask him for his autograph."

He argued the command policy as published in our POD that no old chits would be approved with previous dates. But working in Pers I'd seen more than one such chit already and put the control numbers on that we don't put on unless it's been approved. Plus, the Maintenance Officer's wife--a San Diego travel agent--was the one who arranged my flight. You think it would get turned down? "You got your chit approved. Why didn't you tell me?"

"I thought you knew. Senior Chief said he'd tell you." He had stumbled across my number in the Leave Control Logbook.

We have a black kid, Kelly, who's a fag Mess Specialist in the Admiral's Wardroom. He sings like Keith Sweat and made the callbacks for the Apollo Theatre's regional auditions, which are being held in San Diego on Friday--the day we pull in. He came to us for a Special Request to be flown off the ship on Thursday. "Don't run the chit," Chief said. "It's not going to be approved."

The Captain of *Ranger* personally approved Kelly's chit, and PNC looked like a mean man again.

2200 17 NOV 90. Driving our boulevard of broken dreams to pick up my stepsister at Chuck E. Cheese Pizza Time Theatre. I drove through the neighborhood where Amy chased me in her white VW Bug one of the many times I left her. Each time I come back to Walnut Creek I feel those changes I confronted with her. It was my town until she came here. I was already grown up, eighteen, when I left the Show Me state for the San Francisco Bay. Billy had ruined me for girls, even Amy. Now she's ruined me for boys, too. I'm just ruined, period. I'm a nomosexual--no more sexual.

I had cheated on Amy with Chris, a fifteen-year old pothead boy next door, down in the spa while she washed dinner dishes. He looked like the son on "Married ... With Children." Nothing really happened with him beyond a circle jerk type of reliving puberty. He sat on my cock in the unlit sauna, but we didn't force it in. He confessed he did like fingers up his ass. Then I stroked myself off, looking him in the eye, with two fingers up my ass. He got hot as I came, and made me an offer. "I bet you'd like me to fuck you," he said. But we men are so typical. Once we've come, we're gone. "Don't ever make that mistake," I said. What good it did to tell him that, I'll never know.

Lou told me JayCee was off the beach. He'd made the *San Diego Union* as a homeless bum, and was quoted saying he "didn't care" about people's feelings toward him bumming around. So the cops picked him up every day for a month, and once he'd racked up 28 failures to appear they booked him into jail for three months. Chuck jumped off the wall and cold cocked Dino, but Dino had wronged Chuck and eventually apologized and made peace. Dino can never come into Johnny's again. And Chuck won't. Keith's out of jail again. I'm sure glad I'm off that crazy beach.

2130 18 NOV 90. I woke up dreaming of Sweet Pea. He wore a yellow sweatshirt, oversized with deep blue college football letters across the front. I can't see the name of the school. He was walking in on me in the bathroom at my dad's new house in Walnut Creek. I wrote him a letter this morning, not detailing but mentioning the dream, and said I would tell the church how young the brave kids are on *Ranger*. I wanted to tell him to get that wart removed from his lower back. It's ugly and bleeds and bothers him, and JP5 and elevator grease infect it. But I just gave him my Miramar number and said something macho like "see ya when I get back," in case the NIS steams it open, or a shipmate reads it over his shoulder. He doesn't know what he means to me in a world of increasing hate crimes of assault, even murder committed against people for not dressing the same, behaving the same, or having the same mom. Soon people will be shot for even stupider crimes: blacks will shoot blacks over whether to eat pussy. Whites will shoot whites over long hair and ear rings. Mexicans and Japs will shoot each other over cock size--human cock fights. When the smoke clears, Tieneman Square will look like a tea party.

Where in this crazy world will Sweet Pea and I be? Strained through the psyche psychotic uniquely American homophobic barrier of modern maturity to gaze at each other. When he was born and I was 15, it would have been normal to hold him in my arms and rock him all night long. The world would have applauded. It would've been normal caring and nurturing. The queerbaits and fag bashers would've been murdering defective adults, and would've come home, smiling at me, "what a sweet boy with the baby," expecting me to goad him into bigotry.

0035 22 NOV 90. The father of our country was a pothead. His diary in the library has him lamenting the late separation of male and female hemp plants. Since this makes no difference in its use for rope or paper, it means George Washington knew what a big difference it made in the quality of smoke. And, until the cotton gin was created, our flag was made from hemp. Then drug manufacturing companies evolved with cures replacing herbs and changed our laws. Suddenly valiums were in, joints were out.

George Bush is in Saudi Arabia for Thanksgiving Day. He is likely to cry WAR within five days because on November 30 we turn our leadership of the UN over to Yemen who reportedly is least likely to support "US aggression in the Middle East." Margaret Thatcher is nearly ousted from Britain, awaiting another round of votes next week. Imagine Margaret out and George assassinated. Quayle runs America, and Yemen at the UN is somebody's puppet. I imagine rockets' red glare and bombs bursting in air over the hot tub in Walnut Creek. "You're painting an awfully scary scenario," Dad says. At that, a star slips through the atmosphere with a hot red tail. Maybe God is confirming my fears. Or an angel. Or maybe Mom watching over us.

THE SECRETARY OF THE NAVY
WASHINGTON

The Secretary of the Navy takes pleasure in presenting the NAVY UNIT COMMENDATION to

ARABIAN GULF BATTLE FORCE

for service as set forth in the following

CITATION:

For exceptionally meritorious service in action during Operation DESERT STORM from 17 January 1991 to 7 February 1991. The units of Arabian Gulf Battle Force performed superbly in combat and provided extraordinary logistics support for coalition ships, significant air strike capability, close air support, and Naval gunfire support for ground and sea forces. Often operating in mine filled waters and under continued threat of shore and air launched cruise missiles, their endurance and perseverance provided the necessary sustainment, ensuring a swift and successful campaign. The units of the Arabian Gulf Battle Force combined air and surface warfare to eliminate the Iraqi Navy as a potential threat. Their personal bravery, bold initiative, and resolute determination helped set the stage and execute the stunning coalition victory.

By their superior resourcefulness, indomitable fighting spirit, and courageous dedication to duty, the officers and enlisted personnel of the Arabian Gulf Battle Force reflected great credit upon themselves and upheld the highest traditions of the United States Naval Service.

Secretary of the Navy

Chapter Six

1230 22 NOV 90. Finally composing on a lap-top. Just the thing for my rack onboard *Ranger*. Hopefully SMAA won't arrest me any for bringing it onboard, or call it a safety violation.

Home (!) on leave, I watch the Pontiac Silverdome football game and broadcasts between American families and their children stationed in Saudi Arabia. A girl in the Army has a family in Pleasant Hill, California, three miles from this television set at my dad's house in Walnut Creek. O. J. Simpson watches with them. It's midnight in the desert. "We don't talk politics over here, we just enforce it," one soldier says. Playing the patriot game.

"How's everybody doin'?" The soldier girl asks Mom.

"Oh, everybody's fine."

In the background as the picture fades, an Army man yells. "Don't volunteer!"

2000 22 NOV 90. Drunk on wine in Walnut Creek, about to slide into Dad's new hot tub. Thanksgiving dinner with friends of my Dad and stepmother, staring up the skirt of a 14-year old basketball player. Not staring, only glancing, punching up my blood pressure and watching her blush. She knew I was a sailor.

A message from Duane on my Dad's answering machine. Duane is a fire fighter in Sacramento, down at his parents' house for Thanksgiving. He's got to be back at work by 0800 tomorrow.

Duane and I were next door neighbors when the Graham's moved from the Show Me state to the San Francisco Bay. We've been best friends ten years, and always will be I suppose. Unless he sees my book, re-evaluates, and hates me as a fag. He never thought of me as a fag, and still gives me strength in my fantasy of winning with a woman--such as Amy, whom I'll try to explain later. We don't discuss certain items like Sweet Pea.

Dad's hot tub was a little too cool. He and Ruth had used it earlier, and honored my request to leave it uncovered for me and Duane.

They just completed building this half-million dollar house, started after Mother died on Mother's Day in 1986 at 11:37 p.m. in his master bedroom. He and Ruth, his former secretary of ten years (endorsed by dying Mom), get on famously.

"What do you think is really goin' on over there?"

"Well, I'll tell you...." I knew more than I could say, and still said more than I knew. I had read in the paper that we'll have, in January by the time we get on station, one quarter of America's military might committed in the Gulf. Meanwhile, right wing Russian hard-liners are giving Gorby thirty days to put up or shut up. So now blossoms Kruchev's forty year plan. We clamor to embrace Peristroika; but they commit no forces to the Gulf. Arab loyalists, including Syrians, surround our Marines. (The same guys who drove a truck of TNT into a Marine barracks.) What if these Syrian, Saddam loyal, neo-Kamikazis turn their barrels on our boys? We'll croak with a look of shock. Meanwhile, Russia dismisses Gorby, returning to martial law. Prime opportunity to finish America, young and impudent compared to their grand continent. Soviet hard-liners time it so Gorby is sitting in the White House like the Jap ambassadors talking peace with our President until bombs fell on Pearl Harbor. Last cruise, one guy told me, a Jap tourist asked him where was the USS Arizona? "Right where you left it," he said.

Gorby's the sacrificial pawn in their game. Mother Russia can build a monument to his facade, the dead hero super spy who brought America down. Bombs over the White House. His denials fade to black. In the Gulf aboard the *Ranger*, CV "By God" 61, we will hear sound bites of black news from home, and feel like the submariners of "On the Beach." Arab nations will reunite with Saddam against the West, in a chemical rain dance. They'll surround us, pick us off like ducks in the gallery of Ramadan, a funny thing happening on the way to a storm. But the boys who read our fable will be Arabs. They'll call it, "A Mouse That Roared."

I ran out of breath. Duane went away shaking his head, a long drive back to Sacramento, to work in the morning. I meant to ask him how he felt about the Vietnamese journalist immolating himself last week in front of the White House.

2230 23 NOV 90. Sweet Pea's birthday's December 14th. He's a Cupid Zodiac (Saj) like me. I doubt I'll lick his ear or kiss his neck, much as I want. I bought him a shirt, dark blue with wide magenta stripes, to match his ruby eyes and his black curly hair. This is his Christmas present, too. We'll have Christmas in the Philippines, where nobody wants us.

I didn't think I was racist until I joined the Navy. And I don't know if it's racism or self-preservation, but my feelings grow strong. When the American Navy pulls out of the Philippine Islands, we should phase Flips out of the Navy. In my experience, nobody can screw up a sailor's career like a Filipino. Since they can't get a security clearance, the Navy assigns them to handle pay and service records instead. In this capacity, through misunderstandings and misapplications of minute details of policies and regulations tied to subtle aspects of the English language, lacking any philosophy of the American way, our foreign helpers overpay, underpay, and erroneously complicate the enlistments of voluntary members. They're taking over this country. Drive through San Diego tuned to channel 19 on your old CB and tell me you don't think you're in a foreign land. That would be P.I. I wonder if they will try a coup in San Diego, set up auxiliary communications like Mexicans have supply lines in L.A. The CB is overrun with Tagalog (not TAG-uh-LOG, but tuh-GOL-ig), the native language of Olongapo City--where the girls are so tough and the boys are all pretty--and the majority are bisexual (which I think is natural).

Leftover turkey sandwiches. I saw my oldest brother, Dee, in San Leandro. He is an AK1 (Aviation Storekeeper First Class Petty Officer) up for Chief for the second time. The Navy asked his unit for volunteers. No one raised a hand yet. If they're called to active duty, he'll most likely go to Diego Garcia. In the British Indian Ocean Territories (BIOT), this island oasis serves as an American military communications outpost but looks more like Gilligan's Island, a small dot in the middle of several thousand wet miles, where we keep the B-52's that hopefully soon will rain hellacious weaponry down on Saddam's insane head.

It takes a lot of soul searching to fathom how we can bilk our economy out of a future for the sake of our nation's defense, in terms of nuclear weaponry, then send half our youth to join the foreign legion, when we could shoot that missile from Idaho and finish the job without spilling a drop of American blood.

When it comes to that one American who must die--if that one is you--how important is protracted warfare? Wouldn't you prefer that thousands of weak, incompetent rebels across the globe meet death in the elimination of their tyrant, than you? Still, we've got to save that oil. We can't be blowing up the world, we'll run out of gas. And besides, who are we to bombrush Baghdad?

1400 24 NOV 90. If you take the snack flight, don't take the snack if you want to write. Plus, I think next time around I would buy a notebook instead of a lap-top. There's barely enough room in coach to tilt the screen against the seat back of the kid in front of me. Dust shows up great in the ozone free sunlight. The LCD screen is a challenge. Get a screen that makes its own light. Oh well, this was only five hundred bucks.

I hope Louie's at the airport with my car. I should be rid of these jitters by now. But finding balloons in the toilet will burst any bubble of confidence. He may be in jail for possession of heroin, or for sleeping in a car in a civilized community. My Toyota could be towed, collecting impound charges. I could have to get a cab, and have no cash. I just hope he is there, and keeps on until *Ranger* rides again.

Up half the night last night thinking about Sweet Pea. I wrote a homo-erotic free verse love poem and dared to print it on my dad's laser printer this morning. My folks offered to print my material, if I slip them a disk from the Gulf. But I'd be too embarrassed. I write secret words and can't get a clearance. My military career is a farce. I entrust my sis-in-law with typing the handwritten draft.

There's no reason for limited conflict, eh. My book comes out with a bang, I get discharged. But after I've passed up my chance to avoid the Gulf War. And proved that anyone with guts can put his life at stake for America. Even one whom a redneck may scorn.

0030 29 Nov 90. The news overwhelms everybody, just as it was designed to do between the commercials lulling consumers to sleep while the world plots against us. January 15 the deadline, thousands of body bags are loaded onboard. We leave in nine days.

What if the Mexican immigrants of the past six years were all soldiers financed by Castro and Gorbachev, in the spirit of Nikita? Moscow's forty year plan, assault rifles previously accessible to illegal aliens are now snatched off store shelves by "discerning politicians". America's militia, unable to defend us from an onslaught of illegals, sleeps, or watches Letterman as Russians storm the door.

2100 1 DEC 90. Renting a dive called the Budget on Highway 8 at US 163, dining beside two motorcycle CHiPs and four nuns at the Pen & Pun 24-hour coffee shop. My Variable Housing Allowance and Bachelor Allowance for Quarters total about $350 a month, but I'm out of my apartment. So in 1 hotel week I blow the same as a month's apartment rent.

Lou raises the question. "If you enjoyed having sex with Amy, then do you believe in commitment? I mean, if you enjoy either sex, sexually, why can't you choose one or the other and make a commitment to Amy? I can't understand why you couldn't make a commitment."

"Pedomania. Is what psychologists would propose."

"I think you're an emotionally disturbed adolescent."

I'm thirty-four. Perhaps I'm suffering from terminal adolescence.

Gay dudes in the Navy tend to be male secretaries. The guy I replaced at the Wolfpack had AIDS. Fags can eke out a Naval career if they don't make waves or--God forbid--complain about sexual harassment. True, they can forget being a journalist or photographer or intelligence specialist or anything requiring a security clearance. The military establishment is firm in its certainty that the homosexual/bisexual is incapable of keeping a military secret. Or if nothing else, their lover couldn't keep it. A fag could be a Mess management Specialist, but more likely would be found out pushing a pencil.

1400 2 DEC 90. A week at the Budget, on 163, with Louie unable to sleep on the floor. It's like the boat, cooped up in a little room with him at night. I wonder what he does all day, if he sleeps at all. He's restless when I'm here, and comes in late after driving back to Mission Beach, bringing in strangers to shoot up crystal meth in the bathroom while the light streams under the crack, and they turn on the fan to muffle their words.

He got sleep last night. I got sleep. We're both hungover and he's pissed that he didn't win thirty million dollars on the Lotto. At Johnny's Surf Club in Mission Beach we were Lou, from Seal Team Eight just back from the Persian Gulf, and Bob, of Seal Team Six prepared to embark. Didn't get laid, but Lou met a cute brunette.

At the sea wall Chuck read paraphrased the paper, "thirteen thousand potential Mission Beach customers are heading out to the Persian Gulf. Bush is fucking up our Christmas!"

Johnny's was closing as this baby-faced little dude came in, and I told Greg behind the bar, "I want that striped shirt." I wound up in his car with my arm around his neck, and under cover of the fog, we kissed.

"So, you got a big dick in there?" He grabbed my crotch and I went from a wild fantasy to wild reality so much quicker than I dreamed, I felt like in shock.

Lou had already gone back to the room in my car, so little Stripe-Shirt drove me home. Lou kindly removed himself to sleep for a couple of hours in the car in the hotel parking lot, amazed as I was that this pretty boy had me. It was rich. And I was in shock for a while. But now it's, "next." I wonder if that would happen with Sweet Pea.

"The chase and the loss are the two things that count." Did I make that up, or Lou, or did I read it somewhere?

2115 10 DEC 90. Deployed onboard *USS Ranger*. Heading west. Back in 39-Man again, another home away from world. "No Way Out" plays our TV lounge. Now they call me PN2. I've made it to the rank of second class petty officer, in the Personnelman rating. I made my goal, advancing to PN2 (pay grade E5) in less than three years. "Yeah, abut you cheated," Sweet Pea says. I came in E3. "But I did my time in college."

Our other PN2--not Lou the Vietnam veteran hobo from Mission Beach, or Louis the Mexican-Indian teenager sex partner from my dreams--but Louie my quiet, soft spoken, friendly Filipino former supervisor, made PN1 this exam cycle. And missed the boat. You heard right. He made Personnelman First Class, and didn't come aboard when we pulled out. He's UA. I can't believe it myself. I bet he had an argument with his wife. He was considering getting out in February in the Philippines. He was due to reach the end of his active obligated service, including his two month extension. But his US citizen wife hadn't completed her petition for his immigration, so the Navy would have had to drop him off in P.I. And the Republic of the Philippines might not have let him return to the US. And if he stuck around long enough to be noticed, radicals might have shot him as an ex-U.S. military. So there I was onboard *USS Ranger* expecting Louie to do the morning muster report for VF-1 on 8 December 1990, with CAG (Commander, Carrier Air Wing TWO, our boss) breathing down my neck, two hours late culling numbers from the data bank. CAG was actually breathing down PNC's neck (by phone). PNC was standing over my shoulder at the computer. At that point our dedicated maintenance chief walked in. "Why aren't you manning the rails?" He was in charge of the *Ranger*'s flight deck parade leaving San Diego.

"I can't. I've got too much work to do." Besides, there were plenty of sailors up there.

"Go," PNC caved in.

I left him finishing the numbers game and walked to the bow on the 03 level, donned my dress blues, walked back through the knee knockers to about frame 215 somewhere above the fantail, and stepped out into the bright morning sun on the flightdeck. When we left for Westpac '89, a relative non-event, there had to be a dozen women and children at the pier. Today thousands of wives and kids lined the pier for the send off. They must have felt this was different. It's perhaps the most frightening send off since Vietnam. We're due to arrive in the Gulf around 15 January, just as the UN Resolution calls it curtains for Hussein. If he hasn't pulled out, *Ranger* will send F-14's and bombers for surgical strikes and ground support.

We're the major threat off his coast, a likely target for chemical attack. That's why, two days into the cruise, we're already practicing General Quarters drills with NCBR (Nuclear, Chemical, Biological, Radioactive) protective gear. Everyone agrees our masks are infinitely more comfortable than the old Mark V. These even have a feeding tube for liquids, in case we have to wear the suits a long time. But since they have a finite lifespan that can be measured in hours, we won't drill in the actual suit--at least not until we're in the war zone.

I'm given to horrible imagining. I keep seeing my chief dangling from a hole in the side of our office, seas roaring below. I'm grabbing for his arms to pull him in, after a missile hit. His skin rots off and he falls, like that classic Hitchcock jacket scene.

Louie, Louie, Louie. I still can't believe he went over the hill. Maybe he got sandwiched between two other sailors driving tearfully, and we'll hear he's in a hospital. Except his service record is missing, and his medical record. Did he plan the whole thing? He hated PNC; but at least they were both Filipino. I talked to him last Friday night, the night before we set sail (set steam?). He never hinted that he might jump ship. He was considering making a twenty-year career of the Navy since he had finally made First. Maybe his wife didn't want him to leave and be exposed to the lifer dogs without her influence. In two months he might get off the boat in P.I., just to call and tell her he's reenlisted. Or extended for cruise.

Not only Louie. A dude named Lucky got himself left behind, by slashing his wrist at the last minute. Of course, he did it wrong, a telltale sign that he only wanted out. He cut himself across the vein, rather than lengthwise.

I took his medical, dental, pay and service records to Balboa Naval Hospital in the duty truck, at midnight Thursday night. It wasn't even my duty day. They told me he checked out at 1300, as "the squadron authorized him to be picked up by his girlfriend." However, I reached him at his wife's phone number as listed on his emergency data (Page Two in his service record), and she answered from the bed and handed him the phone. He said he was coming in to talk to the skipper Friday to decide what would happen. I took the records back to the ship, and, since Lucky was in charge of sheets and blankets, slept on my comforter.

So much has happened, and is still going on, it frustrates me as a writer to be so exhausted I become incapable of writing it down. I haven't even covered how Louie the beach bum punched me in the nose.

We spent the last couple of nights at the Hanalei hotel, a plush Hawaiian place across 163 from Budget. I got off work at Miramar and for the first time went straight to the lounge instead of the room. I ordered a gin and tonic, drank it down and called the room. Lou was there, but something was wrong. He dropped the phone, and couldn't understand that I was inviting him down as I gave him directions to the bar. When he did come, he walked up and grabbed my jacket and twisted it upward. "I'm gonna kill you--but you've got nothing to worry about." He was totally schizophrenic, half mad about me taking my car (what do you mean, your car--your lien car) to work while he snoozed in the luxurious queen-size bed in the beautiful room charged to my credit card.

"Let's get outa here. It's damn near your last night in the world, and you need to get fucked up."

"Where are we going?"

"Wherever you wanna go, bro."

I drove us to Johnny's. On the way, Lou pulled the parking brake up. Headlights nearly crashed into my rear view mirror as I veered to the curb. He shifted down and up for me when I was not in need (it's an automatic). But at least he didn't kick it into reverse.

"Fuck off and die, mother fucker."

He didn't know the three gentlemen at the next table--least of all, the one he addressed. So I moseyed across the bar to the pool table, and Greg walked up to settle the problem. "I'm sorry, let's shake hands."

"That's okay but I don't want to shake. Just go your way."

"No, mother fucker, you shake my hand or I'll beat the fuck out of you."

Lou finally turned to the bar, and I went to see how he was.

"Gimme my car keys," he demanded, towering over me.

"I don't think so. I've got to make sure I get to work tomorrow (I had onload)."

He socked me in the nose in front of the bar flies and Greg. I went down, like I did when the other asshole who was fighting his wife shoved me last week in Johnny's. This time I got up and got in the car. Lou bent the radio antenna like putty in his big hands. I backed away locking the door, then squealed tires back to Hanalei, and checked out. I was sure I'd lose everything he'd conned me into leaving at his daughter's house, convinced that was his plan all along. Three thousand bucks in audio/video equipment, and my Stratocaster electric guitar. But there comes a sense of relief in sudden desolation. I drove to North Island, parked in the 20-day lot, and slept in my rack. I got up the next morning and drove to Miramar. Around ten, he called.

"Are you all right?" I asked him, knowing it ought to be the other way around.

"Fine. Are you?"

We got back together and I charged dinner and drinks at the Mexican Village as our last supper. He helped me get my stuff from his daughter's house, carried half of it up the gangplank and all the way to Personnel. He threw up in a trash can outside the door. We made five trips from the pier, and I walked him back to the car at the pay phones by the ship. I scraped my base sticker, and he drove away.

"Bob who?" He called back out the window.

Dean, Sweet Pea's best friend, was on watch as Elevator Operator in the hangar bay. He was starving. He couldn't believe it when I volunteered to walk across the Naval Air Station to Del Taco to get his dinner. But I wasn't tired and he was Sweet Pea's buddy. We talked about Sweets and I finally told Dean, "I wouldn't do it for just anybody."

In the morning I woke up dreaming that Sweet Pea was coming in my face and I was instantly licking the sperm off his naked chest. I wondered how that dream came to me, if he was sending it from his rack at 0600. He has a phrase, "fuckin' Graham." I got real drunk Friday night with Dean and told him if I were a girl I'd marry Sweet Pea.

"That's the thing about him, you know? He always tries to get me to date his girls."

"Maybe he doesn't like girls." I could have been praying.

I imagine walking through the hangar bay looking for him in the rubble of war, and finding his dismembered head. We invest our lives in lives of others, and death becomes proportionately disturbing.

2200 20 DEC 90. Last night as I flicked off the rack light that voice, mysteriously omnipresence on the One MC (and one hell of an MC), squawked. "*Now advance all clocks 24 hours to conform with time zone* (etc)." We lost 19 December and a few birthdays.

At least one man on this boat had a pretty good birthday. Sweet Pea did. 14 December was his last birthday as a teenager, a precarious entry into the bar scene. Twelve months in limbo, neither teen-aged, nor 21. He only drinks wine coolers anyway.

I did up his rack unbelievably. While I was home on leave I went with my little brother, Mike, to work up in Stockton, and got some balloons from a girl who hadn't used them for an office party. Pink, green, yellow, orange, and baby blue balloons, and party hats. And I bought tons of candy. I stuffed his rack so full he couldn't get in.

"Petty officer Graham." He called, next day at lunchtime.

"Who's this?"

"You don't recognize the voice?"

"Oh. I know who this is. How was your birthday?"

"I--my god, I'm still, I can't get over it. It took me half an hour to clean up my rack." He raved. He had asked but nobody knew who did it. He has a top rack like mine. Dean got pictures of the whole thing.

Sweet Pea didn't go to his rack until 0300 because, when they told him his rack had been decorated with blue crepe paper and balloons, he thought they were setting him up for a birthday batting (spanking him with such ingenious articles as the elbow pad of a chair). In fact, they were planning to get him. But he outlasted them and got away without an ass whipping. "You didn't have to get me all that stuff," he said. The list included a shirt; a flashlight with colored filters and an extra bulb, with a belt pouch; a Wolfpack coffee mug; and candy. His mom couldn't have treated him better. It was great, but now he has to worry about having a guy onboard liking him enough to do that. What will the homophobes say? It might embarrass him a little, make him feel he's gotten too close or allowed me in too far. He's a Sagittarius like me, and we're independent.

We had a guy, poor Marty, who got an AMCROSS (American Red Cross message) that his wife had been in a car wreck and his six month old baby had been killed. She was in the hospital. They brought him to the Admin office where the skipper and the Chaplain were waiting. I couldn't hear for the shop noises, but I saw him break up. We had to write funded emergency leave TAD orders and get him a COD flight the next day. He's supposed to come back, but his life must be shattered. We're all afraid he may walk into an intake. As long as his wife survives, he'll hang tough, I guess.

Our Admin officer's dad died, and he took emergency leave. Two men out in our first two weeks--not a good cruise omen. We had some instant training sessions and I put together a standard emergency leave TAD order form for OUTUS (outside US) to CONUS (continental US) travel, two versions--one for expected return, another for PCS (permanent change of station) if we don't expect him back.

We've been working around the clock, my mean chief and me. We finally got our striker back from TAD to Ship's Dry Cleaners (yesterday), so I found time to make a diary entry. I had to do a "diary message report" on Louie my 2nd Class supervisor who's now considered a deserter. What the hell came over him--did he get pussy whipped? I'm learning his job, diary messages to EPMAC (Enlisted Personnel Management Accounting Center or something like that), New Orleans, LA. Today I started handling transfers, figuring out how far in advance we need a member's Transfer Information Sheet in order to process him. As usual, the PNC just let me flounder and find my own way. Also, we had E6 Evals (enlisted performance evaluations for first class petty officers) due November 30. And all the paper work attached to advancements. I made second class, and Louie made first. We had to write the Naval Education and Training people in Florida today to stop his advancement. I had to do about forty letters from the skipper congratulating the frockees, forty Page 13's (administrative remarks pages for their service records which they must sign in agreement that they will pay for their uniform adjustments, i.e., buy their own crows, while in a frocked status--which means they have the crow on their arms and the responsibility of the next higher pay grade, but not the pay), and 40 ID applications. They all need new ID cards to reflect their new rates.

I don't know what all I've been doing but I've been leaving the office at about 0200 and arriving at about 0700, maybe 0800, for the past two weeks. I got nominated for Sailor of the Month, whoopee, but a couple of chiefs despise me, and I didn't win. It doesn't bug me too much because there's always been someone somewhere who hated me and I'd probably feel ill if everybody liked me.

The waves are crashing into the ship rather hard. We're not too far, about a week out of PI, and there's a typhoon "Russ" between us and the Philippines. We plan to outrun it at the crossroads, but there's a good chance we'll plow right through it. If so, it'll rock us like a small boy.

Two Westpacs ago, I'm told, *Ranger* plowed through a typhoon that bent the sponsons and broke off some life raft canisters. Those waves crashed down on the flight deck so hard that planes with 12 tie-down chains were popping loose. They flattened the tires to keep the jets from bouncing. Now we're heading into battle with Iraq and we're at risk of losing jets in a typhoon before we get there.

I'm extremely tired. I moved down to the 81-Man berthing, all the way aft past our Wolfpack Ready Room. On the same deck, 81-Man (like the name indicates) has more than twice the men as 39-Man. I spent Westpac 89 forward, so for comparison it might be interesting to live here on this Westpac. The thing is, on the *USS Forrestal* during the Vietnam war, when they had their infamous "fire on the flight deck," and all the bombs cooked off, most of the people who were killed were in their berthing beneath the aft, port side of the flight deck. Now I sleep beneath the aft, port side of the flight deck, a few feet under the arresting cables. If a plane has to catch a barricade and comes in low, it might smash right into this berthing.

Operation Dear Abbey, America Remembers *USS Ranger*, is a program where grade school kids write to "Dear Sailor," tell us about themselves and assure us that they hold us in their hearts and minds. We got some cute cards and a banner from Room 26 of some school in Auburn, California. And they sent us comics, and they can't figure out how we keep ourselves busy when we're out at sea. I can't either.

One of the arresting gear crew, a Green Shirt, was so hungry the other night he slipped a sandwich from the mess decks up to his work center. As he was eating, a second class petty officer snatched it out of his hands and threw it in the trash. The kid went all the way to the Division Officer, and the PO2 got chewed out, so there was some satisfaction. But the kid is getting out of the Navy and you'll never change his mind. It's a volunteer force. And some people in here are crazy.

Our next expected mail call is 24 December. A COD came onboard today with mail, but for the small boys. Several dudes came by Personnel hopeful, and went away sad. I had the ones who were frockees sign their Page 13's and 1172's. Page 13 is a Service Record page used for Administrative Remarks, such as that agreement that they have to pay for their own uniform insignias. 1172 is the ID card application. Forms are usually referred to by number vice name because it's quicker and easier to communicate--once you know the language.

I've got my striker doing non-OCR Page Two's. I'm doing the OCR's. (The Page Two details who gets your money if you croak or get captured. OCR copies are used when the member's number of dependents changes--such as marriage, kids, etc.).

Chief is updating the EDVR (Enlisted Distribution and Verification Report, a monthly status report on who we have and who we're gaining or losing). Across the room our Command Master Chief (CMC) is watching porno flicks nonstop with a long-ash cigarette drooping out of his mouth. YN2 Jax is short (short isn't a height measurement in the military, it means he's leaving soon), so he's doing very little work now, deservedly so. He's about to go to Meridian, Mississippi to skate out the rest of his current enlistment. YN3 Black Thing is fumbling around with our dying shredder.

The fantail finally opened after flight ops ended, and I jumped in there with a bag of sinkable nonplastic trash. Good old Monty was lifting weights on the hangar deck by the fantail, buffing to beat up a faggot ass, no doubt. But he's a nice guy.

0030 22 DEC 90. Billy's birthday was yesterday. If he's alive he's 28. When I last saw him he was 15, as he and his big brother dropped me off on the Arlington Beltway, in his brother's Camaro, and I hitchhiked back to San Francisco. I last heard his voice in 1985. That call from Venice Beach, as I got acquitted. Now I love Sweet Pea, twenty on 14 December, another Archer, another cupid.

Liberty regulations change as we approach the Philippines. First it was the gates were closed. Then they were open with a 2200 curfew. Today it became possible to go on leave and have overnight liberty outside the Subic Bay naval base. But tonight it changed again, a re-interpretation of the message so that only people stationed at P.I. can have such luxury and freedom. My Filipino boss swung from frustrated and sad to elated and relieved, back to quiet desperation and a threat, "get my report chit ready." What if he goes UA? That'll be two lost from our department.

We got a strange pain in the ass request from CAG yesterday, I think I'm finally getting an idea now what it's about. They want a list of all personnel who can read, write or speak a foreign language, and whether they are poor, fair or good at it. I believe they were tasked by higher authority. If we do go to war, which we now generally think we will, we may be called to assist in evacuating wounded civilians from Kuwait or neighboring battle zones. Maybe there are Kuwaitis who speak Spanish and Hispanics who can translate that to English, or English speaking people who can translate halfway to some other translator. And *Ranger* may become a conduit for evacuees, like we airlifted the Vietnamese refugees on Westpac 89.

I got the office going this afternoon when the striker put some batteries in my Casio sampler. I hooked it up to my amp and sampled the phrases, "fuck you" and "you're an asshole." It got the YNCS and the PNC, even the CMC laughing and playing with it. Master Chief would just look at someone and flick the key, "FUCK YOU. FUCKYOUFUCKYOUFUCKYOU. YOU'RE AN ASSHOLE." YNCS suggested the line, "There's no fucking mail." I added, "We don't have any." And YNCS added, "Go see the skipper about it."

We turned south today, rethinking our position and hoping to avoid Typhoon Russ by slipping in behind it. Right now *Ranger* is rocking pretty good, slapping doors around like a haunted ship. If the vents and motors were off it'd sound like a poltergeist.

I got my new white uniform jerseys stenciled with Wolfpack emblems, and put one on with its third class crow, then wore it down to the mess decks where I ran into Sweet Pea and his pals. "There she is," he said. I seized him around the neck at his table and enjoyed the hell out of pretending not to hug him. It was over too soon.

One of my squadronmates is the nephew of Dick Gordon, Mayor of Olongapo City, Republic of the Philippines. But he doesn't know my buddy Ed, or Ed's sexy little cousin Geoffrey.

I hope Geoffrey wasn't killed in the Baguio quake. He was 17 on Westpac 89 when I stayed at the White Rock resort hotel and took two trips to Manila and ate a bahloot with him and Ed. We had some good times in a couple of motel rooms. He wore braces, and wanted to join our Navy to become a dental technician. His dreams are probably fading now that the P.I. wants American bases out, and we're phasing out Filipino enlistments.

Haircut appointment with the ship's barber shop tomorrow morning. I don't have a haircut hookup anymore, and don't care to try to get one. A crowd of whiteboy Wolfies got skinhead cuts since we pulled out. They're saying it's because girls won't be looking at them, and it's much easier to maintain. But I really think it's a secret, preemptive move against black antagonism they suffered on the last Westpac, out and out gang activity in our own squadron--particularly in the Line Division--where the blacks organized to treat the whites like slaves.

Last cruise, and over the last couple of dets, blacks maintained a dominant presence, loud and into rap. But it quieted down after a large number of tough whites dudes shaved their heads. Maybe it's a coincidence.

I don't think I'll shave my head, because I'm bald enough and afraid it won't grow back. Maybe I should do it to get used to what I'm eventually gonna look like. Will Sweet Pea hate me bald? Will he like it? Will I look younger, or older? Forget it, I'm not doing it. But I will get the sides and neck cut short. It is impossible to say just what I mean, to quote a phrase. Boat, rock me to sleep.

I'm switching to nights tomorrow. Naturally, since Navy life is always a SNAFU, I have this haircut appointment at 0815. I could blow it off since I won't be on days. I don't even know when I'm supposed to come in, but I think it should be 1900 to 0700 or right around that.

Sweet Pea, it just so happens, told me he was probably going to nights soon. His shift is 0730 to 1930 at sea. So his night check would be 1930 to 0730 I guess. I didn't plan to coincide with his change, my boss dictated it. But it's cool with me.

I have to climb down out of my rack and put this lap-top back in its case and lock it in the coffin I sleep on.

I told Sweet Pea I was worried that he'd be operating the elevator (he's an EO) as a missile came into the hangar bay. We joked about it, how neat it would be. Especially if it went on, through the doors on the other side, without hitting anything.

1000 25 DEC 90. And so this is Christmas, another new year. Let's hope it's a good one, without any tears. Christmas of 1987 was worse than this going to work at 1900 and getting off at 0930 Christmas day. Worse than sleeping through the squadron party in Ready Room Eight. Worse than those guys kicking it on the flight deck (which is open for jogging) as we putt ahead one third.

Christmas in 1987 was dining alone at Denney's. And it being over with Amy, who had not invited me for Christmas dinner. Instead, she had some politically correct phony girlfriend over and hated it. But she was accepted by Daddy, and that mattered.

I wonder what kind of husband I'd have made anyway, with my sweet tooth for Sweet Pea. I don't seem capable of commitment, even to him. So I couldn't ask the same of him. For one brief instant, when I gave him the rack party and he did lunch with me, he seemed to have approached the subject of commitment. "When we pull in, where do you plan on living?"

"Where do you wanna live?"

"I'll probably just live on the boat." Then he must have seen the hurt in my eyes. "It'd have to be someplace near the boat, so I could get to work."

I wondered if he was interested in being with me, or if he was merely thinking of coming to see me some Saturday afternoon for a couple of hours and maybe a wine cooler.

I have the sad feeling that the best thing I could do, the best Christmas present for Sweet Pea out here, is if I stay away from him, put some time and distance between us. He would be relieved from the awkward series of meetings in the hangar bay. "What brings you to the hangar bay?"

"Just getting some sunlight, and dropping by to see you."

My heart sinks into my gut and both arms tingle as I let go of him. That's how it is. I can go look around for some other Chesterite; there's another kid showing his belly to me. I am so tired of the sting of doing something wrong. If I'd quit looking my pain would go. Buddha said, happiness is absence of desire.

If I didn't expect Amy to get married at 25, it's ludicrous to expect Sweet Pea, at 20, to not go back to Connecticut when his EAOS comes up after cruise, and to live with an old baldhead for the rest of his life. I'm sad that he won't, and I'd be sad for him if he did because I know he'd feel trapped. He's got a long way to go before he even allows that he could be gay, and he's still got a chance to have kids of his own because he still talks of women, and one may capture him. They might divorce, but he could bear some children. If only I could convince him to attend UCLA. I'd go there for my masters while he got his BA. We'd room together and I'd make him a star. But some director would steal him from me. He is a living doll, nobody has any question about that. Not me or anybody. They'd go crazy in West Hollywood. I want to buy him his first drink and watch everyone call him the paperboy, right out of Carson McCuller's, *A Tree, A Rock, A Cloud*. Then take him home. I want to. But I should leave him be.

0900 28 DEC 90. The Captain just got off the 1MC telling us we're entering the Molacca Straits. It's a stormy, cloudy day, he said. And it should keep looking better as we cross into the South China Sea by this evening.

I wonder again about Ed and Geoffrey. I quit writing back to Ed after he kept asking for money and telling me his parents were planning to divorce. He's probably still there, but I don't feel like being called a bac'latt, boc lott, backlot, or whatever it was his female entertainer prostitute next door neighbors were calling me before. It's same as maricone. You know, faggot.

I wonder if Ed is still wearing the cammies I gave him last time. Has he taken part in any of the coup attempts against Aquino? Probably, since his brother had that banned book on Marcos at their house.

I sit in the rack, nude in a sweat, writing, pulling at a gray hair on my chest. Bos'n whistle: "NOW SET THE NAVIGATION DETAIL."

We were turning like mad for ten minutes this morning, and I wondered if we were avoiding a collision. I figured we must be near the Straits. The Quartermaster, a buddy of mine from last Westpac, told me last week I should come up to the bridge around the 27th and have a look, that we'd be where we could see some land and lights. I've just been too busy.

We had sorties at 0300 and 0400 today, and since our Ops Yeoman hit the rack at 0200 I got the honors on the 2JG phones in the Ready Room. It was a worthless task, since all the aircraft are plotted on a televised module and there's no question which bird is landing when. I went up twice, sat in a chair and held the phones to one ear, listened in on the bullshit conversations between Air Ops and Primary, heard a naive phone talker from our sisters at Ready Nine (VF-2, the Bullets) get ignored by asking stupid questions, and performed one perfunctory phone check.

"Air Ops, Ready Eight."

"Ready Six?"

I waited to determine whether he thought I was Six or if he were trying to call them at the same time by coincidence. After a silence I called again, and finally got my phone check. I had a highlight, though, when the SDO wanted to know where 101 was so he could tell if he had time to put the VCR in playback and show one of the pilots how his trap looked.

"Air Ops, Ready Eight."

"Air Ops."

"Yeah, could you tell me where is One-Oh-One?"

"Flyin' around."

"One-Oh-One is flying around, sir."

"--Roger."

I'd not told him a hell of a lot. But by then he could see on one of the TVs where the hands under the camera had positioned 101, up in the top left of the screen indicating she was in the pattern, turning downwind heading aft, a long way from the brake. He played back the other trap and the guy swore to the XO that he didn't have his nose down when he applied power, so there was no explanation why all the sparks flew as he hit the deck.

"Jesus fucking Christ," XO swore. Obviously, the officers were as tired as everyone else on this piece of metal at 0400 the day before Liberty Call.

Sweet Pea had breakfast with me yesterday. Eight other guys are pulling him eight other directions, wanting him to spend his liberty with them. I've got three tickets to the base New Year's Eve party, exchanged for the two unused tickets I had for *Ranger* Night at the US Grant hotel in San Diego.

"Well, I'm not gonna compete with eight other guys," I said resigning. "You can call me if you want. You have my number."

I get through the at-sea periods by dreaming and fantasizing how when we hit port I'm going to finally escape this maddening crowd and get alone together with Sweets. Then when we hit port, just like last Westpac, it turns out he's completely ripped apart by contestants for his attention. So I never get to see him away from the ship. Maybe it works out best that way, because I never have a chance to ruin our relationship. But I hate it. All my life I've been wrapped up in similar situations. Don't touch me, I'm yours. I guess I'm a glutton for masochism.

"Now muster the 15-man Project Handclasp working party in the library with the petty officer in charge." They'll distribute food, and provide services like building shelters for impoverished and underprivileged Filipino residents around Olongapo. It's like a condensed version of the Peace Corps. Funny, though, I just read in the Navy's *Enlisted Transfer Manual*, among other qualifications for overseas duty, you must have not worked in the Peace Corps. Put that together.

Sweets, Sweets, Sweet Pea. He ate like a bird yesterday, a half bowl of cereal. He could barely hold his eyes open because he'd played cards until 0100 or so. New hand at Spades, he loves it. Spades must be the standard Navy shipboard card game, other than poker. But you only play poker for money, so less people play it. Our Ops yeoman has won about twelve hundred dollars in the past two weeks at poker.

I got a Letter of Appreciation from *Ranger*'s Supply Officer, Captain Archer, at quarters today. Our CO tried to summarize it but I could tell, standing there, that he barely had an inkling.

"This is for all that stuff you did down on the mess decks."

"I read it."

Then I got to see him again for my frocking.

"PN2 Graham. You've come a long way."

Right. You never unload on your skipper. I've been here a long time, I felt like saying. And still don't have a security clearance--how about giving me that? Then I'd have a long way to go, maybe even a career in the Navy, be all I can be, get into the journalism or photography rating where I'm better suited and I'd have fun.

I have a year to go, come January 25. Also, I can get out with an Honorable Discharge as a pinko fag after this January and still get my GI Bill and go back to school for a Master of Fine Arts degree in Screenwriting at UCLA, USC or the American Film Institute. As long as I don't fuck with Sweet Pea or any other sailor, or a hustler under sixteen. On the other hand, so long as I mind my manners, watch my P's and Q's, keep my hands to myself and otherwise behave, and so long as nobody knows I'm a stark raving fag, then I could go on and extend for a year to live on the remote, tropical island Diego Garcia, lift weights, save thousands of bucks, get tanned and sing along with Jimmy Buffet tapes. After a year at Dago, I could exercise a coast swapping option and wind up in Virginia Beach, looking for Billy. God what a thought. Fifteen years since I saw him there, and swore I'd never dance with another. Well, if I had one goal to make in this man's Navy I did that. I made it to Petty Officer Second Class. That's the skate rate that a lot of guys enjoy because you don't have the heat of a first but you have a lot more clout than a third. Airmen and seamen get out of your way, and some chiefs even begin to respect you. You appear career oriented.

I came in at E3, six months later made Petty Officer (E4), and now I've reached E5 in less than three years. But I have to have 36 months at E5 to even test for E6. I can get two extra points on the beginning multiple of my score for the Navywide advancement exam if I earn Enlisted Aviation Warfare Specialist (EAWS) wings during cruise. I plan on it, just in case through some god-awful event I'm still in. Also, the EAWS program can keep me out of trouble (if that were possible), and might even prepare me for Iraq. Everybody thinks it should be a quick and dirty war. I'm afraid the US won't fight like a street fighter, and Sodomite Who's Sane will. We could lose a couple of carriers in 75-mile by 3-mile strips of chemical cloud before we nuke the Middle East. Meanwhile, what about Russia and China? Will they invade New York while we're off fighting in the Gulf? And will they mine this boat in Subic Bay? And will they toss grenades into the bars along Mag Sai Sai while we're there? I just hope Sweets and I survive.

1000 3 JAN 91. Steaming out of Subic Bay, big news about a fire. I haven't called or written home to tell my dad it wasn't me from Wolfpack who was killed. It was Buck.

I had duty the second day in, came onboard half an hour late, and walked past a group standing at attention in the hangar bay. I realized it was our duty section, and waved at the LT. "Well, I'm here."

I went straight to the office and learned that the ship's XO had Buck's ID card. That was a bad omen, finding an ID without the guy who owned it. There had been a fire at the Royal hotel in Olongapo City after midnight. Some of my friends had seen it, and later took me to the ruins.

Our first thought is that somebody torched the place when they found out servicemen were sleeping there. I've already been worrying whether a group of loyalist Hussein mercenaries could be mining Subic Bay.

Buck had been drinking heavily and took a bar girl to the hotel. They found remains of two Americans and a Filipina. XO took Buck's dental records into town, since the bodies were all burnt to hell. I began a pessimistic head start on the Casualty Report (CASREP) in case it did turn out to be Buck.

I didn't leave the Pers office for the next 16 hours. I spent all day researching two pages worth of Info Addressees for the message. His Page Two listed his mother and a stepfather as Primary and Secondary next of kin. Late in the afternoon they confirmed that he was one of the victims, and we sent out the message stating that his PNOK and SNOK had not yet been notified. When it hit the news, it only said "a member of *USS Ranger*," name withheld pending notification of next of kin.

Now I look at his empty rack across from mine. A couple of his buddies popped the locks on his rack and locker and boxed up his personal effects, and mailed them home yesterday. I didn't know Buck personally, didn't party with him and didn't know much about him at all--before he died. What shook me up most was not doing the CASREP all day, but when I got done and started thinking about where we're heading, and how many more I could have to do if we do have a war, and if I survive. Other than that, I had a good time in P.I.

We berthed at Cubi Point, across Subic Bay from Olongapo City, and took buses to the other side. Coming out the main gate at Subic I changed $40 into six hundred pesos, walked across Shit River and borrowed a phone in a little shop on Magsaysay (for a fee). Ed (aka Jong) was in the Province. His father invited me over anyway, and when I showed up Geoffrey was there. We still had a thing.

Geoffrey split for a while and I checked out Apple Bar with Ed's father. Ed senior and his wife seem to have worked out some kind of relationship. Little has changed but at least they still live together. Ed senior can cheat. Not that he can score.

I had a list, a full page of bars off limits to Navy. I don't think Apple was on it, but I didn't get the actual street address. Ignorance is bliss, so I went along with Ed Sr. to look for a girl. Apple was dark and loud. Jarheads groped, barfines were 680 pesos per overnight ($45), duration of time after 1900, please pay your barfine at the counter.

"Hello, I'm Mamasan. You don't see any girls you like?"

"No." They were all pudgy.

The bathroom urinal was a tile wall over a trough that you pissed into and it rolled away. A good place not to be during the standard rolling blackout, at 1800. Ed never found his girl. She was out on her barfine, paid by an American sailor, no doubt.

Geoffrey had been at the Hyatt in Baguio the morning of the quake, hours before it hit. It was worse than the San Francisco quake. We didn't get together like before. He has a girl now. But they introduced me to Totoy, real name Eduardo, 18 going on 16, pretty, smooth, kind, wanton. He had a tank top on with his shoulder under Edwin's arm. Edwin (pronounced Edween) wanted me and I wanted him last year but our schedules prevented trysting. Edwin went back to the province that night, but Totoy was my toy. We spent the pre-dawn hours in Jong's bed while everyone waited, and waited, and waited. Rumor has it that Geoffrey was peeking through the keyhole as I ate out Totoy's ass. When we came out, the one true fact was that Totoy was very relaxed.

We took the Air Con (air conditioned bus) to the Province of Edwin, as Geoffrey calls it. It was a long ride, to the Province of San Filipe in Zambales. We sat in a grass hut and drank San Miguel beers poured into a pitcher with ice blocks while Geoffrey fucked his girlfriend on a bamboo bed. A young guy we called The Gunner did the pouring until he couldn't keep track who was next. We walked to Bye Bye Beach, named for its beautiful sunset, and watched it sink while cooking a tuna in a small sand fire. The beach was all course sand and had dozens of small fishing boats with pontoons on the sides and little inboard motors. Some puttered by as men stood in them alone, silhouetted in the sun.

It stayed warm after the sun went down. We walked through the dark along shadowy roads, that reminded me of Mississippi, to the house of the family who sold us the cases of beer. They cooked more food and we ate until we couldn't eat anymore, and then some, and drank until our eyelids were too heavy to keep open. They had a strange movie on the VCR, that must have been duplicated hundreds of times before it reached the Province of Zambales, hardly more than streaks of color, blurry pastels, and muffled dialogue. It wasn't even porno. It was an old fashioned semi-Shakespearian romance. It was all they could get besides AFRTS (pronounced A-Farts, Armed Forces Radio and Television).

I slept with Jong in a guest room, and the family slept outside in the hut. I never had a thing for Jong, so nothing crazy carried on. Talk about old fashioned hospitality. Jong said the next day that Edwin had wanted to sleep with me but his mother wouldn't let him because it wasn't proper for the host to sleep with the guest. He slept with his cousin Bu Boy. Oh well. Edwin is beautiful to look at. He has dark skin, almost negro, but his parents are not black. He's skinny with health, and hospitable without flaming like a faggot. Shy and reserved.

I found out later that in the Province if you squeeze a woman's hand you mean to marry her. That explained why they put Edwin's grandmother between me and his mother when we said hello and goodbye. She was already married to a sailor who was once in the US Navy. Now he's a merchant sailor in Portugal.

We went to Grande Island yesterday. Me, Bu Boy, Jong and the Gunner. We had a couple of six-packs and some cheeseburgers. It didn't compare with Bu Boy and Jong eating eyes of a tuna, but we did eat some fresh clams Bu Boy gathered. "Survival," he liked to say.

I found out my friends were all members of the NPA. But it wasn't the New People's Army. "No Permanent Address," Jong laughed.

They all slept here and there, trying to avoid wearing out welcomes wherever. None had steady work, victims of a depressed economy. Bu Boy had worked at White Rock part time, that was it.

I was happy enough paying for everything, from cigarettes to air con rides, to food and beer. It was a vacation that cost me less than $100 complete with Jong's tour and Totoy's sexy ass. I gave my $90 Ray Ban's to Geoffrey, since he asked for them. In the long run he never did anything with me that Totoy didn't do, and I wish I had given Toy something. I did give him 200 pesos for spending money. A whopping thirteen US dollars for his love. And none of the diseases of a bar girl.

Onboard PNC asked me, "what did you do in Olongapo?" He said I should have called him, "we could have gone out. But I bet you had a boyfriend. Did you get a boyfriend?"

"Fuck you," I said.

1745 8 JAN 91. It's really still 1845, but at 1900 clocks retard one hour to conform with time zone "Six Foxtrot." F is the sixth letter in the alphabet so I guess it's redundant, but it makes things clearer when you say it two ways, and if you do it briefly they can take it.

We went to Tee-Shirts (and pants, in case you wondered) once we hit the Indian Ocean. Crows are optional now, and I prefer to let people think I'm a baldheaded airman. It gives me a sense of hidden, quiet power, sort of character enhancing.

I just put twelve tee-shirts in the laundry, and may never get any back because a guy in First Louie keeps bitching how he hates his job, hates his ship, hates his navy. He's been busted three times since the Navy paid $75,000 for his technical school (Aviation Fire Control Technician). One bust was for walking off a watch. If Congress declares war in the Gulf and he does it again, I suppose legally he could be shot. Some other guys might wake up then. He constantly slams the door going in and out of the berthing. I want to yell, since that door is beside my rack. But he does pick up the laundry. And my name is on each shirt I sent down. I keep my rage to myself, while he vents his. So he doesn't vent his on me and my tee-shirts.

PNC didn't want to recommend our striker for advancement to PN3.

Scrapper (his nickname) finally admitted to me that he had only done the first three (of ten) lessons in the course book for advancement. I ordered him to bring his book to the office, then looked it over. He least did those three right.

"NOW RETARD ALL CLOCKS ONE HOUR TO CONFORM WITH TIME SIX FOXTROT. THE TIME IS, 1800."

Ranger's Captain is on the 1MC telling us about the heroes of the day. The COD crew got up at 0130 this morning and zipped off to Singapore to bring back our mail. We've had two mail calls today already, and she's landing again in a few minutes as *Ranger* turns to the wind and shakes. When that gets sorted we'll have a third mail call. I wonder if I got my J C Penney's bill. Much less a personal letter.

Sweet Pea.... I rang him up. He's doing just as I thought, hanging out in Hangar Deck Control with his feet curled up in his chief's big barber chair overlooking a table model of the hangar, where parked aircraft are positioned as little icons. He drinks cokes, makes coffee, and bitches at Dean for smoking. "I'll call you later for chow and we'll eat midrats, or breakfast."

Midrats came and went. So did breakfast. Sweets was only being sweet. Hangar Control is right above the NIS office, and I wonder if Beach Bum Louie had it right: the kid works for them and I'll get busted on a fag charge. Not really. But why do I feel Sweets would not be happy in the San Francisco Tenderloin?

I caught Dean at dinner and told him I missed Sweet Pea.

"Let's go up there." He filled me in on what Sweets did at Subic Bay.

"I know he didn't get laid," I said.

Dean laughed hard. I don't know why it was funny but I knew Sweet Pea aka Cherry Boy would never get laid by a hooker, and I still wonder if he'll get laid by man or woman, if at all. Maybe never. I'll have to ask him if he goes to church.

I sweat in my rack doing nothing but typing on this lap-top. Sunset on the flight deck, but you have to be in full flightdeck gear--floatcoat with gloves and a cranial--because they're doing flight operations. So forget it.

Yesterday was our first Steel Beach, a picnic on the flight deck. They held a smoker (boxing match) I heard was fabulous. And a band I heard nothing of. Working nights, I slept through the entire affair. I knew what it would be like, knew all the guys would get sunburns. And I was afraid of running into Sweet Pea. I've decided to leave him alone, and he may fade from this diary by the end of Westpac. But God, he was a good inspiration for my dreams of love and youth.

We qualified for Imminent Danger Pay for January. We were nine degrees north latitude when I checked last night. Anything above ten degrees north qualifies now. So I guess I should be near my gas mask, and wary of a silkworm's rude awakening.

Yesterday I had to give them a list of all VF-1 enlisted personnel with name and social security numbers, for Medical to use in giving us inoculations against biological attack. We're supposed to get a shot in the ass pretty soon.

For some reason, my boss put my body fat down as 17 percent on my close-out performance evaluation for E3. I may be a little flabby, but not that bad. I had our corpsman remeasure me. I'm actually 12 percent, same as my last eval. Sometimes I wonder about my chief, if he's attacking my self-esteem or something.

I typed it smooth and sent it to the PERS 'O', and the chief got really upset. Which was really confusing. "You're not supposed to send it. I'm supposed to send it." Going on cruise puts a lot of twists in your personality, and brings out some really weird behavior. You begin to go off on people over nothing, and make assumptions that you would never think of under normal circumstances. He must be missing his wife and kids, because he gives out these sensual looks and sighs, and holds still when he bumps you and leans up against you and does all kinds of bullshit I wouldn't even do to Sweet Pea no matter how bad I wanted him. It almost seems like sexual harassment, but since we're both guys, I don't know what to call it. But it does seem to reflect some kind of lack of respect.

Chapter Seven

1000 10 JAN 91. YNCS (Senior Chief) came into Admin with Channel Fever at 0430, as I was viewing my tapes of Westpac 89. I had my Sony Video 8 on my desk with a cable running through the overhead to the TV on a filing cabinet. "You've got tapes of coming home from last cruise? Put 'em on." He kicked back in his chair through the doorway to Admin. As he began to relax, he opened up. "Man, I just can't get into this cruise. I wasn't ready for it when we left and I'm still not ready." Now I know why he's been going rounds with PNC. At GQ he flipped the lights off to cool things down, while PNC was in the middle of a letter to his youngest kid. PNC said he was losing his patience.

"*Fifth Marine Expeditionary Force*, arriving." Another six bells. "*Amphibious Group Three, arriving*." I guess those guys up in the Captain's cabin are getting ready. We are five days from, what--D-Day? VE-Day? Kuwait invasion day? UN-sanctioned Death Charge Day? Whatever it is, we have sandbags around the gun mounts, unlike Westpac 89.

We have at least four sea-whiz gattling guns, one near each corner of the carrier. Several missile stations. And gun mounts all along the gunwhales, for marines and gunner's mates. They can put up a firestorm, as they showed us the other night after dark. They called it a demonstration of the United States Marine Corps' ability to "reach out and touch someone." The night sky flickered with tracers blazing off the black sea.

The 8 O'clock reported a pool that lent some comedy to this war. For $1 you could pick a fifteen minute time slot during which the first *USS Ranger* weapon might hit an Iraqi target. The winning prize is $658. I can imagine the RIO having missile lock on a target, and the pilot's in the pool. "Good tone!"

"Not yet! I've got forty bucks riding on the next fifteen minute slot. My time doesn't come up for another minute. Don't lose him but don't shoot yet!"

I called Sweet Pea again. I wasn't gonna do that. But I was in the Airframes shop and there was a conflag watch (Con 3 shares the space), a Blue Shirt from the hangar deck, sitting there overlooking the hangar in a little alcove. I walked over to him after bullshitting with the AE's.

"Aren't you supposed to call in all secure?"

"Yeah."

"Call up Sweet Pea."

He did. Then I got on.

"You never called me for breakfast."

"Oh yeah, we've been real busy. We've had a lot of traffic."

Right. I suppose so.

"I'll call you later for breakfast."

"Okay. I just called because I was in Conflag Three and the Blue Shirt made me think of you. Is Dean doggin' you out?"

"He doesn't know how."

I was still there when the watch called Hangar Control again and got

Dean on. "Hey Dean, Sweet Pea says you don't know how to dog him."

"I just got done."

"You just got done doggin' him?"

"Yeah, I made him strip the passageway by himself."

"Well, he never called me for breakfast."

"He didn't? Well, he's gonna go early this morning. I'm gonna send him around four or five because I got another guy who hasn't eaten all day."

"Send him to get me for breakfast."

"All right."

I saw Dean at chow.

"Sweets didn't get you?"

"Never saw him."

"I don't know what's wrong with that guy."

"Lack of sexual contact," a friend of Dean said first.

YNCS buckled about our greens, last night at GQ. I went on about the Ops Yeoman wearing them and finally he snapped and said, "go put your fucking greens on." Then he sighed. "It was only because of the old Maintenance Master Chief anyway. He didn't like us Admin types wearing a working uniform."

I actually have only one pair of greens onboard, and they were in my sea bag in the void (the cable trunk for the bomb elevator). I dug them out and wore them tonight. They reminded me of Mission Beach because greens are my favorite outfit around the beach. I only wish I could have known the policy would relax before we came aboard. I would have brought the ones I put in storage. It's hell to try to get them from Maintenance. They don't have greens for the six men expected to arrive this month.

During GQ a couple of nights ago one of my buddies, the guy who helped me with his truck when I moved from the barracks to my pad at Mission Beach, got hit by a piece of equipment on the flight deck. It put him in the hospital ward with a hairline ankle fracture. A tractor driver rigging the barricade was too enthusiastic, speeding, and let the tractor crash against a tow bar connected to an F-14. The tow bar snapped loose and slammed this guy down, then dragged him several feet in the barricade.

I tried to jog on the flight deck after I got off work yesterday. It was beautiful outside, deep blue water and sky all around. I hadn't seen daylight since the Philippines, and needed exercise. But after two laps around the flight deck my left knee starting giving. I walked for a while, then shot the shit with a Blue Shirt. (Flight deck Blue Shirts are the ship's company counterpart to squadron Line Rats, and basically paint the deck and park the birds.) One of the Blue Shirts he was with was hanging over the round down above the fantail with a caliper measuring the thickness of the wire mesh safety net. The true life of an aviation boatswain's mate. The net would be a perfect spot for sunbathing but they won't let us. The measuring dude was a friend of mine so I hassled him. While I was there he found a cartridge, which could FOD an engine if bad weather blew it back up on the deck. But it might have been there for months.

Six bells, the ship turns into the wind, we begin to shake. "*Carrier Group Seven, departing.*" Right after that, "*Now launch two alert five fighters. Now launch the Alert E-2.*" I wonder if it's routine, if CARGRU SEVEN is in the E-2, or if they're flying cover for the COD he's on. Or if, coincidentally, there is maybe something out there.

I have the old Mark V gas mask that we were supposed to turn in after our last at-sea period. I keep it above my head here on my rack. My modern mask, with its charcoal lined suit, waits on station in the Personnel Department--not far, since I moved back aft. But if they get blown up before we go to General Quarters, I'll have this old one. I don't know why they haven't set us all up that way; but they want the modern outfits to remain at the shops (thus, at our GQ stations). What if you can't get to your shop when we're really attacked, because say a Silkworm explodes between you and there? This should sound like nonsense, because we ought to be at GQ by the time there is any indication that we might be under attack. But it doesn't sound like nonsense to me.

Six bells. "*Fifth Marine Ex Brigade departing.*" Six more. "*Amphibious Group Three, departing.*" Maybe they were only here to get in on the pool.

0830 12 JAN 91. My phone rang at 0430. "VF-1 Admin-Pers, non-secure line, Petty Officer Graham, may I help you?"

"Petty Officer Graham? Is that like in Gray-hamm?" It was hard to tell his voice with all the ship noises. But who else would be calling me?

"Oh, it's my friend."

"So what's up man? You hungry?"

"Yeah, I guess so." I was not hungry at all. But it was Sweet Pea.

"You wanna come get me?"

"Well, do you want to come by here?" I don't know what I was thinking except it still hurt from him not calling all week. By the time I had opened my mouth it was too late to backtrack.

"I don't know. Since you're closer, I guess I can just meet you."

"Where could we meet?"

"Over by the milk machines, I don't know. You'll find me."

I saw him crossing the aft galley deck looking for cereal as I stood in the starboard line, and he and Dean came up on me. "There's that bald headed squadron fuck," Dean said. He was feeling frisky. Probably had too much coffee all night. He's a skinny guy like Sweet Pea, except he has a bit of hair on his chest, and one eye looks off a bit. In fact, if you wanted to exaggerate, you'd call him Gumby.

"Congratulations on your military leadership exam."

"What? I made it? Great!" Sweet Pea perked up like an over-excited kid, and even made the litany of what he had to do yet sound exciting. He'd gotten his PARS (personal advancement requirements) signed off in twenty minutes.

He was so happy that people stared. It amazes me how he can get so excited over such a routine thing for everybody else. But I'm proud of him. He's no lifer dog (careerist), and I wouldn't want him to be. He's the kind of man who's meant to go through this time in his life in the Navy, to become worldly, have some exotic experiences to always remember, then go home to college and probably become a writer. Or a movie star, since he's got the beauty, charm and charisma.

For ten minutes I've been listening to that asshole again, clear down at the other end of 81-Man, down a row of curtained racks that nearly spans the breadth of the flight deck, yelling in his high, whining voice. I finally climbed out of the rack, pulled on my greens and walked down there. "Shut the fuck up."

I'm glad he didn't stand up because he's a tall, imposing individual. I probably sacrificed my laundry.

"Hold on, Graham. You got no right tellin' me to shut the fuck up. You can ask me nicely, 'could you please be quiet."

"Did I insult you by telling you to shut the fuck up?"

"Hell, yeah! And you can kiss my ass."

"And did you insult me by all that yelling?"

"Yeah."

"All right then, you can kiss my ass. We'll both kiss each other's asses and everything'll be fine. Thanks a lot."

"We'll be quiet, Graham." Another black dude, but a second class petty officer, threw that in. I know he'll try to control his ignorant shipmate.

I heard my name a couple of times in the muffled whining as I climbed back up here, but didn't give a shit. That dude needs to be sent back to the states and good luck as a mugger. And if anybody has to buy it out here, let it be an asshole.

Speaking of, I saw on the TV screen teletype from Associated Press that Baker's talks failed, Saddam didn't get Bush's letter, and Congress gave its blessing to the war. The House concurred, and we're now two days from D-Day. Bush is supposed to give a news conference sometime today, whatever time it is back in the states. We're in time zone minus four delta, while San Diego as I recall is plus eight--except you have to add or subtract 24 hours since we're across the International Date Line, too.

You know the time of day here by the bells on the 1MC, eight bells every four hours, one less bell per half hour less. If you know it's mid-morning, or mid-afternoon, you're in the ballpark. Then you know that one bell is zero eight-thirty, or five bells is six-thirty, respectively. The day of the week is what you'll never know without a watch.

One thing I can count on: the Captain will get on the 1MC tonight and relate whatever Bush said while I was sleeping, then we'll go to General Quarters. It's looking more like we'll be ordered into combat than this thing will be resolved in peace.

According to a message this morning, one guy who got out of the Navy six months ago, and served on last cruise with Wolfpack, is coming back to us because they recalled him to active duty. I told him when he left, they would. He'll be one unhappy camper stepping back onto the flight deck. He's an Ordie. We also have a PN3 coming from the reserves. I don't know who he is. A PR says he knows the guy's wife, but none of that.

YNCS told us we've been volunteered to help Maintenance with such mundane tasks as pushing carts around the hangar deck and holding equipment for technicians, if need be. "Does anybody have any problem with that?"

"It sounds like fun." I secretly hoped it would allow me to run into Sweet Pea, maybe even be with him when the shit hits the fan, if we get hit.

I got my camcorder out after work yesterday morning. I was gonna jog on the flight deck but as I came onto the sponson I heard the splat of a garbage bag hitting the sea, and it made an artsy picture looking through the iron grating down five decks to where the bags were being tossed off. I wanted to document our violence against nature, floating soda cans that may eventually work their way across the seven seas to end up on Galveston Beach in the Gulf of Mexico. At least we've stopped dumping plastic. We only dump "sinkable nonplastic trash and garbage." Shark fodder and compost. A trail behind our wake that only worries us for its classification, whether anybody is letting written words leak out in bags that might be salvaged by Russian trollers or some enemy Iraqis who might still not know our whereabouts, and our plans, except by a letter in the garbage. I'll tell you what: If they don't know we're coming by now--well, they must know. Still, I'm using the shredder.

I wonder if my letter ever made it into *Forum*. I wrote of Sweet Pea, a little fantasy I had. They sell it on the boat and I've been waiting to hear about anything remotely related. But he probably doesn't read it. I'm sure, he probably doesn't even masturbate. His mom raised him and by the way he does everything he doesn't seem to know he has a dick. Maybe that's a blessing. He could be a horny little fucker in disguise, though.

0930 14 JAN 91. All day we've been in a state of readiness called Material Condition One, which is like Duty Section General Quarters, where some people are already at their Battle Stations, and the rest of us function normally with the exception that we're geared to go to GQ with a moment's notice. From now on, this isn't a drill.

Supposedly the *Ranger* is designed to withstand four of the largest conventional mines on each side and still maintain flight operations. We'd be four feet lower in the water. But how can we steam at 25 knots with eight holes in our hull? I don't want to know.

Sweet, Sweet Pea. I had the guts to call Hangar Control at 0400 and ask for Dean, not Sweets, just to keep people guessing, and told Dean to call me for breakfast.

"VF-1 Admin/Pers, petty officer Graham."

"Graham, Sweets."

"Dude! You called!"

"You ready to come get us so we can go eat?"

"I'll be right there."

Sweet Pea had a plain tortilla, with two flapjacks (as Dean, being a fucking hillbilly straight out of the Appalachians, had to call them) and syrup. And a bowl of frosted flakes that I got for him when they brought a new carton of cereals onto the line. I had a refried beans & cheese burrito, a bowl of frosted flakes, a glass of orange juice (with ice!) and a proverbial cup of java.

"Bald headed old man with your coffee."

"If you ever go bald I'm never gonna let you live it down," I told Sweets, going down a ladder on the way to the galley. I tousled his hair twice and he slapped my chroming dome.

"Ranger *is commencing her approach on the* USS Kansas City (again)." We just had an emergency breakaway that was not a drill. I don't know how the seas are but we're not rocking and rolling inside. Maybe they just took a bad tack the first time.

We'll enter the straits of Hormuz sometime today, and might go to GQ throughout our passage. I should sleep while I can, but I don't feel tired. There was nothing to do last night in the shop, just pluck my guitar. I tried writing a doom dirge about a sleeping giant lulled by Gorby and suckered to a shooting gallery while he masses his forces under guises of rebellious republics. But I shredded it as I came out of Pers. There won't be any time to play it between now and whenever what finally happens.

I traded my new gas mask satchel for my Missing Beach bag and put my mask, top, trousers, and shoes inside. It wasn't going to work hanging and dangling from the government case. The PR's are making bags for the guys on the flight deck but they told Pers in so many words to fuck off.

"You guys just sit in your office."

I didn't argue that we've been volunteered to assist in the hangar bay; it would have brought a laugh. Besides, I can fit more in my beach bag. In fact, it's becoming a survival kit, in hopes that at worst I still land on some Gilligan's Island.

My personal survival list:

(1) Navy issue sunglasses
(1) Navy issue miniature toothbrush
(1) Locking thumbcuffs
(1) Large laundry pin
(1) Cherry ChapStick
(1) Sunblock
(2) Web belts
(1) Bottle of Penicillin

(1) Shampoo, 1 fluid ounce
(1) Flashlight
(1) Zippo lighter
(1) Strobe light
(1) Strip of twine
(1) Sewing kit
(1) Manicure set
(1) Ballcap
(1) Large knit mesh laundry bag
(1) Navy issue swimming trunks
(1) Navy issue towel
(1) Navy issue white hat
(1) Navy dog tags

How in the world is all this going to cram into that bag? Oh yeah, since I have it, also a small New Testament Bible including the Psalms and Proverbs. And some anti-fungal cream. I wish I could fit my new Jordache tennis shoes but they're out of the question. Same with my shaving kit, and my one pair of greens. Hopefully I'll have the greens on if I go over. What about my lap-top, my disk, my book? I'm sending home excerpts every few days from now until it's over, or we're at least out of harm's way again. That way, even if I don't make it, whoever's in my will can get something out of this war.

As we round the corner and start heading into southwest into the Gulf itself, we'll enter out of the Silkworm threat, and yet remain in the condition that I talked about earlier today, that Readiness Condition One.

We received on board a message here not too long ago, which placed this particular area of the world, by the President, CENTCOMM, under what is called Defense Condition Two. It is meaning that hostilities, if not imminent are probably imminent. I don't know if that's a very good definition for you, but we normally exist in Defcon Four worldwide, and worldwide the US is still in Defcon Four. This area of the world is in Defcon Two. And it is gone to Defcon Two in preparation for hostilities as a result of our impending meeting the deadline that was imposed by the UN Resolution.

It would be anticipated that as we reach hostilities we would slide into what is called Defcon One. So, when I told you last night that we would not be calling GQ's away very often saying "this is a drill, this is a drill," I did say that we would call them away for real. And when I tell you that we're in Defcon Two, here in this area, this is for real. I'll let you know as things transpire, you probably know, if you're able to see the flashes on TV on channel six on CNN News, and we're still workin' to get that darn satellite workin' right, you've probably have maintained as much of an up to date picture of what's going on as I have--this morning I picked up, turned on channel six on CNN and found out that the *Ranger* was in the North Arabian Sea. So the CNN network, the intelligence network is alive and well.

If you have a chance to get up on the flight deck and look around, if the visibility improves, love to have ya out there and see a little bit of history out here. We'll be rounding the corner here in a couple, in an hour, an hour and a half or so, and then headin' southwest towards our Modloc, our Modified Location for Operations for the next few weeks.

I'll talk to ya again a little bit this afternoon when we clear the area, for the time being though that's all.

1200 15 JAN 91. Mid-day, D-Day. Today one of the Ordies told me I should videotape them loading, but said later that the Gunner said I couldn't. I wouldn't want to be in Saddam's shoes, or in his city after midnight tonight.

We're at Modified Condition Zebra, where most of the hatches are dogged shut and especially around the hangar deck you have to crawl or climb through scuttles to get up or down a ladder. It's one step away from General Quarters. This whole area has been recently designated as Defcon Two by the President. The rest of the world is at Defcon four. I've been looking for a baggie to keep my computer disk in, if I lose my lap-top in the raging sea.

Turner Broadcasting Service flew by the *Ranger* a couple of hours ago, and the Captain came on the 1MC as I was on the flight deck with my camcorder, and told us to look at the escorted plane off the starboard bow. We were on Cable News Network and he was watching it on his TV via satellite.

The sky is overcast out there, and I feel better because of it. If they hit us with aerosol, we could use a good rainstorm. I'm praying for rain, a rain water wash down to protect us from chemical weapons that the Butcher of Baghdad will certainly use. We've passed the Straits of Hormuz. I got some shots on tape of the land on both sides, infamous Iran to the east, Saudi Arabia to the west. We're heading northwesterly, so if I go over I want it to be the port side. And snag a lifeboat headed west. We passed an Omani missile gunboat, the kind I'd like to be stationed aboard if I did another tour of sea duty in my career. She gave us a wide berth. On the news last night I heard about a major protest in their country. We expect a COD with three tri-walls of mail this afternoon. The Captain told us he'd received 14 phone calls asking what's a tri-wall. "It's a box measuring one cubit by one cubit."

I called his number and my buddy Dave answered. He's the CO's Orderly this quarter. "Dave, don't tell him who called. But ask him what's a cubit."

"He doesn't know. But he's coming back on the 1MC."

"Okay, bye." I got off quickly.

"All right, no more phone calls. A tri-wall is a cardboard container four feet by four feet by four feet. That's all."

Since we had a Bible handy, I looked up cubit in the back. Then I had to call again. "Hey Dave, we have a Bible down here and I looked up cubit. Just so he knows, a cubit is a measure of 18 inches." I gave the Captain one last chuckle. And hope it encouraged him that others, besides Chaplain, also had a Bible handy.

Sweet Pea and I are an item again. I called Dean last night to get together. He was reading, and I heard heavy metal music in the background that he attributed to Sweets. I told him to call me for breakfast, since he wasn't going for midrats, and he agreed. But when I got to the forward mess deck and was almost done eating, Sweet Pea showed up. I was just moving to a table with a couple of guys from the AT shop when he walked in. I suddenly veered over and landed at his table. You don't care what it looks like when you follow your heart.

"I want to see you at every meal until this thing is over."

"Why?"

I glanced around, and looked at his doll face.

Because I love you, I wanted to say. But someone else might hear, and he might not want to hear it. It could alienate him.

"Do you think we're gonna die? We're not gonna die." His whole body raised out of the chair to hover above me from across the table, exaggerating. Being funny as always. And charming.

"I've got just enough time for a soda and a video game," he said as we dumped our trays in the scullery line. But once we got to the game room he checked his wallet. "Hmm. I don't have enough money for both. A soda is more important to me right now that a video game. So I'll just buy one."

He got a Pepsi. I followed him up through the hangar to the companionway leading to Hangar Control. He put his hand out. I shook it thoroughly, as always.

"You better fucking survive," I said.

"I'll be fine. They're not even gonna get through to us."

"Call me." I said.

"For chows."

Ranger's Commanding Officer: "I'll let you know if anything changes. As you all know, there's something in the air. That something in the air means that all the talks have stopped. We're loading real ordnance, guys, and we're preparing for whatever eventualities may come up. And, the answer is to be ready now, because it could happen on a right now basis, within the hour, within ten hours, within the day or within the next few days. So be ready, be sharp, keep doin' what you're doin'. You're doin' it great and you're lookin' good down there. That's all."

Five hours later the phone rang.

"Get your butt over here." It was Dean.

Five minutes later I was hanging out with Dean and Sweets and Steve, a Yellow Shirt (hangar traffic director) from V-3. Dean dropped some stuff at their Division Office and we slipped through a couple of scuttles. Soon we were eating cereal and flapjacks on the aft mess. They called away Condition One at six, instead of seven, which caught us below without our masks. This is what I live for.

Admiral Zlatoper (COMCARGRU SEVEN): "Combat is likely. Few of us have been there. Perhaps your CO, me, the Chief of Staff, or the older folks, if you will. Most have not. There are tensions associated with it, and you can probably feel it on your ship. Please. Take a breath, breathe calmly, and take care of each other.

"There's a guy named Klausvitz, who wrote a great book about a hundred years ago on principals of war fighting. In it he talked about, quote, the Fog of War, end quote. Basically, it says that in a war time environment, in a hostile environment, nothing goes exactly as we planned it. Given that, we need your thoughtful good sense to do the right thing, no matter what comes along. We don't want you frantic, we want you focused. We don't want you laid back, but I certainly want to make sure you're calm and in control of all your actions. We want you attentive, but not trigger happy. We can win if we do that. We need to set a tone here in this Battle Group, now Battle Force, of cooperative teamwork. We're a team, we've worked together, we've impressed everybody we've been with thus far, with our teamwork. Now let's put it together for real. Let's do things correctly. That's even more important in a conflict than it is in peacetime.

"I'll give you an example. The Vietnam war ran almost in excess of eight years. Those of us that were in it are aware that there were four major conflagrations on aircraft carriers: one on Forrestal, which I was aboard her for, one on Ariskine, one on Coral Sea, one on Enterprise. Terrible fires. Not one of those were caused by enemy action. All were caused by well meaning sailors, who just rushed through and did improper things, in the fog of war, in their hurry to do something. We've gotta do it right.

"We started training for this deployment last February, most of us, over twelve months ago. We started training specifically for where we are right now last August. Six months ago. We know how to do things the right way. We've shown every inspector from San Diego all the way through Subic. Now we just have to do it.

"We're probably going to find ourselves under a considerable amount of strain (laughs) over the next few weeks, to say the least. I can't over-emphasize the words I've already heard so many times on your 1MC. From your CO, from your XO, from your Engineer. That is, Safety Must Come First.

"Each of us is going to be tempted to cut corners, to get something done in the heat of the moment, and that's when the serious injuries start happening. Having said that, the ordnance we have on board is for use against the enemy. Let's get it off the ship safely, and onto them: on target.

"We will cut no corners. The safety standards we have set up are based on the many lessons that we've learned over a long period of time. Both in combat and in peacetime. We simply can't afford to lose one of you, or one of your shipmates, or an aircraft, or a piece of equipment, due to improper application of basic procedures.

"Others have learned the lessons the hard way: in blood. Let us learn them the easy way: from their lessons. Look out for your shipmate over the next few weeks. Take care of each other. Regardless of his rate or his assignment. We're fighting for him or her, as well as for our country, for our family, and for an unprecedented number of nations that have banded together in a United Nations Charter against one country right now, and I should say more specifically against one dictator.

"The standards that your ship has set will help each one of us survive the taskings that are going to come our way. All we need to do is observe those standards. We're going to have an opportunity to relax when these future events are overcome. And our jobs are done.

"I'll represent each of you for our mutual interests (laughs again) at that time when Westpac liberty comes up, and we'll do it right on the way home, too.

"You're on the right side on this, folks. Morally, politically, militarily, economically, by any measure. An unprecedented number of nations have joined together now, to condone the actions that we are about to undertake, and to condemn those of a dictator who has killed his own people with chemicals, and has overtaken and destroyed an independent nation.

"There are times in life when we confront values that are worth fighting for. This is one such time. That said, I know there are a lot of tensions out there, I've seen it here on the Flagship. We need to take care of each other, to calm down, to breathe if you will, to do it right, and to realize that those tensions are to be directed against the potential enemy--not against each other.

"Let's stay the close knit team that we've shown ourselves to be over these last

> six months. Let's get on with our business here. Let's do it with the style, the class, and the aplomb that you've become known for throughout the fleet. Stay calm, think through your actions, and just do it right.
>
> "I'll certainly keep you informed as things evolve. We'll let you know the first things when we get a real go time. That said, we're all a team. God bless you, and I look forward to serving with you here in the next month or so."

0900 16 JAN 91. "*The smoking lamp is out between frames 29 to 89 while handling ordnance.*" I awaken to it, and doze off to this announcement. Practically the entire mess deck is packed with cluster bombs, each holding 906 large grenades. In the Ready Room the aircrew now pack sidearms, little .38 Special, five-shot revolvers without hollow points. LT Davis was the SDO (Squadron Duty Officer) as I manned the 2JG phones to call the line up for event One Alpha One.

"I should have let you bring my .44 Special after all."

"Yeah, I was thinkin' about that," he said. "I wish I had."

My Bulldog is safely stored in San Diego with my household goods, doing nobody good. I wish I had it in my survival kit. But they only authorize weapons for men in Gunnery billets, the Master-At-Arms, Shore Patrol and aircrew types. And of course the Marine Detachment (MARDET). Normal sailors don't need them.

Sweet Pea had a watch in Conflag Three, and caught midrats at the last minute so he didn't try to call. But since Con 3 is in Wolfpack's Airframes shop, when Dean told me where he was I went up to be a bother. I had twenty minutes to kill before I had to be in the Ready Room. About ten people were in Airframes watching "Gremlins Two" and I almost felt awkward coming to see my ship's company friend.

"Hey, Graham. What can we do you out of?"

"I just came in to see my buddy on watch."

Nobody cared, nobody called us boyfriends. A couple of guys did ask personnel type questions. Sweet Pea was bored, restless at his window overlooking the hangar bay, tapping his fingers to the too easy beat of the movie soundtrack.

"Are you gonna make it to breakfast?"

"Oh, I don't know. I have this disgusting watch until seven. Then I gotta do FOD walkdown at seven-thirty."

"Chow doesn't close until eight, does it?"

"I don't know, maybe seven, maybe seven-thirty. I'm not sure. I'll probably just go take a shower and go to bed."

When I left for Ready Eight I found the YN3 already had it covered, and they didn't need me for the 0400 launch.

"Just be here for the line-up at five-fifteen," Rod said. "And if you'll take the 0600 launch, you can have YN1 tell Jax he's got the 0730 recovery." I went to chow.

An engineering friend (a rarity if I may say so, a snipe and an airedale as friends) gave me two boxes of Nut & Honey cereal. I already had a ham and cheese omelet with toast and OJ and coffee, and didn't need them. But Nut & Honey made me think of me and Sweet Pea. I stashed them in the green bag with my gas mask, and took them up to Conflag 3.

I came in the doorway and caught his eye, and threw the boxes across the shop to him.

"Hey! You bring him cereal and forget about us? What's the deal, man?" Half the shop raised hell.

"Well, he's on watch."

Sweet Pea played it off about me treating ship's company better than my own buddy squadron pukes, and I felt that he was just covering the spectacle of me caring for him. Nobody made anything of it. AMH2 Russell asked about some line I'd borrowed to tie everything down in my shop, and came back with me for it.

Pers looks like a spider web. Lines cross over the photo copier, the computer, and the TV; both coffee pots are wired to the bulkhead. Filing racks are tied to desks; the typewriter is even roped down.

My Tascam, a four-track audio mixer/recorder, and lavaliere mikes are wired up to the TV speaker and the 1MC, with the levels set so that anyone can flip the record button and catch any news the Captain or higher might impart while I'm in the rack.

We heard the Admiral and Dan Quayle last night. The Admiral told us we (Battle Group Echo) have joined up with another group to become Task Force Zulu, aka Zulu Warriors. I suppose it's based on the Zulu of Greenwich Mean time, midnight January 15, which in the US will be this evening. YN3 told me they have a voluminous battle plan laid out, and we're just waiting. But it's classified, so he can't tell me anything about it. We'll know when we have a need, as it goes down, or after it's over.

The Vice President's speech was a couple of days old, dealing with the hopefulness of Baker's trip to Geneva that we already know has failed. He was asking Congress to endorse war, and it was good to hear it even though I already knew from Armed Forces Radio that they had given Bush a green light. It was a sort of pep talk, and a measured call to reason, if in the end our point of view is correct. I don't have heartburn fighting over the price of oil and the future of nuclear weaponry, and I don't mind killing a dictator who used chemical weapons on his own people. And who's trying to get nukes, who's "never owned a weapon that he didn't use."

"*Now launch the Alert Five Fighter. That is, Now launch the Alert Five Fighter.*" I've heard that phrase probably one hundred times in the past two years, maybe more. But there was no overly dramatic, or hammy tone as I've always noted before, no matter how subtle. This is not a drill, by god. This is all business. Urgency seethes through the announcer's attempt at a measured and safety minded directive. Everyone on this boat is operating with high adrenaline.

The squadron's regular cyclical events are BARCAP, Barrier Combat Air

Patrol. We have drawn a line in the Persian Gulf a couple of hundred miles northwest of our position that we intend to keep the Iraqis behind. We've seen some Iraqi gunboats out there, according to the Captain this morning.

I debated taking my gas mask with me to the shower, and opted for a closer, messier shower room instead. The one Sweet Pea uses seems too far to run from, back here if they call General Quarters. I guess I'll forego my chances of rubbing his lithe sexy body, wet, warm and naked, between now and the end of our third world war.

0200 17 JAN 91.

> Ranger Commanding Officer: "You remember in August of this past year, Iraq invaded and dismantled a country, Kuwait. That country has virtually ceased to exist in the last six months. At the present time Iraqi armed forces now occupy Kuwait, and our best guess is that five hundred thirty thousand men and forty-one divisions presently occupy the KTO.
>
> "In October the UN resolved that if Iraq did not withdraw from Kuwait by fifteen January, force would be authorized. That time, fifteen January, has passed. Two days ago, the NCA, the National Command Authority, declared Defcon Two in the theater, that hostilities would be imminent.
>
> "A few minutes ago I was informed by COMCARGRU Seven that we have a Tomahawk in the air, strikes are underway, the execution order has been given, and we will commence hostilities against Iraq. Guys, I think there's very few men in the United States who are privileged to stand up and be counted. We have been given the honor of being able to stand up and be counted. We're here at a moment in history.
>
> "We volunteered for the Navy, we volunteered for this day, we've been trained over the last year. And we're ready for the day. For your information at 0400 this morning Ranger will launch, and Air Wing Two will strike targets in Iraq.
>
> "There is no doubt in my mind that we will make Ranger's presence felt, here in this part of the world. No doubt that we'll make a measurable difference. I don't know how long this will last, but there's no doubt in my mind that what we do is right. We do it for all of the right reasons. And then for those of us who steam, feed, fuel and build-up, for those of us who are not fortunate enough to fly, for those of us who do fly, we are greatly counted on at this present time by our country.
>
> "For the aircrew who are gonna be flying the missions, God bless ya, God speed, good huntin'. As we always say, keep your powder dry. We're gonna be back here, puttin' it together. So for all of us, for Air Wing Two, for Ranger, for the staffs that are aboard, let's go get 'em guys."

On our TV the A6 Intruders loaded with cluster bombs and anti-tank weapons and radar jammers line up on and behind the catapults. The bombs have been autographed, by guys walking through or working in the hangar bay, with grease pencil slogans like "wake up and go to sleep," "ride this camel," "love from Dad," "America remembers Iraq," and more American wit.

For the next two days young Sweet Pea will man the elevators until he drops, and try to sleep in his blue shirt and greens, maybe even in his floatcoat. I hope he'll be careful, and those around him will take care, and take care of him. God protect the hangar deck from missiles. May our planes all come back, without bombs.

YN1 just mentioned, we'll have to wait until 0700 to do the daily muster report, rather than turning it in early anymore.

We have the unusual and phenomenal experience--belay that. We *had*

CNN live via satellite--until reporter Bernard Shaw in Baghdad was cut-off. And we heard anti-aircraft sirens in the background. He said, "Iraqi officials have informed us--."

It's rather amazing to hear the news, thirty-five minutes after launch, as things fall silent on the flight deck of the *Ranger*, and John Holliman reports from the Al Rashid hotel near Baghdad that tracers now shoot into the air.

Our planes, "if there is an attack," are attacking near Saddam International airport, although the reporters have no signs of actual aircraft. We hear gunfire on TV, anti-aircraft guns, twenty minutes to three in the morning, same time zone as *Ranger*. We hear planes launch from the carrier, and hear guns fill the night sky with a hail of bullets.

> ... Off in the distance loud reports and you can feel the building of this well built hotel shaking. Baghdad is still not blacked out.

They hang the microphone outside the hotel window for us, and I wonder if they'll become martyrs for CNN.

> If in fact this is the real thing ... stepped up activity in the Pentagon. ... one bus on the street, Al Rashid ... no firing, no signs of any tracers ... still lights on ... some tracer rounds over this capital city of four million people ... all right, Baghdad is beginning to be blacked out now, large sections of the city losing their lights ... a large oil refinery visible from our vantage point in the hotel ... no signs at all of burning ... bombs about 10 or 15 miles from the hotel at the airport....

Microphone in the window again. Rapid gunfire bursts.

Back at the White House, Fitzwater in his office watching the same reports, emerging for the Oval Office. "*I'll tell you as soon as I can.*"

No explanation of what's going on in Baghdad.

The Pentagon. Indications that if this is the real thing it's part of a US game-plan, not to begin on the holy day Friday.

Communications restored between Al Rashid hotel and CNN. What's happened in the past fifteen to twenty minutes. Static increases on our TV as they summarize:

> Two hundred guns firing in the sky, alarms, loud explosions in parts of the city ... the airport. A bus went by. Sky filled with tracer bullets. Now a big portion of the city blacked out. Lost electricity. To the south more tracer rounds over the main downtown buildings in the direction of the Presidential Palace. The hotel has not been hit as far as we can tell.
>
> "Holy cow, a large air burst. If you're still with us you can hear bombs, in the center of the city.... We're crouched behind a window, about three miles from where the center of activity is, I guess planes coming back for more targets.... A main communications link to the outside world hit with a bomb.... Two major explosions, one at the Comm Center, one somewhere else ... sky continues to be filled with tracers, started about 0230 Baghdad time, thirty five minutes ago ... no sign that any allied aircraft have been hit.
>
> "No swooping attacks, more of a strategic approach ... we've no idea what the extent of this raid will be ... nothing has landed near the hotel.

Marlin Fitzwater is about to hold a press conference. About to make history.

> I have a statement from the President of the United States. The liberation of Kuwait has begun, under the code name Operation Desert Storm.... President Bush will address the nation from the Oval Office at nine o'clock, little less than two hours from now [in the US].

So it's 7 p.m.--on the 15th, I think. And 0310 in Baghdad.

> The entire city is blacked out now. There was a bomb that came down near our hotel, let's get that one light out that we have. There's a very bright flash at a refinery, five or so miles away. Eight to ten sharp white explosions. It's not on fire. Now there's a fire.

Lost signal. Regained.

> Directly in front of us. .... We can hear the sound of the incoming bombs in the early morning ... no way to keep score on how many of these bombs have come down ... the entire city has now gone black, except the emergency power at our hotel.... It appears there have been at least three waves of bombings so far.... The anti-aircraft fire has stopped.

Onboard *Ranger* they're playing our song, the William Tell Overture on the 1MC at 0320. Countless A6 Intruders loaded to the gills with death. Hit the Palace, not the hotel. We are presently stationed at 26 North, 52 East. The news crew on CNN are being told to get inside and are getting their gas masks out.

0355 17 JAN 91. Ready Room Eight. The brief just finished for the 0500 launch. LT Chris (Chill) Hill, the pilot kid, LCDR William (Whiskey) Bond, our ex Pers-O, LT Doug Ross the harmonica player, and LT Barry (Ranch) Davis, ex Legal Officer. They look uptight, strained. They know the air will be hot and heavy, no surprise advantage, mustered enemy forces, all the anti-aircraft fire we heard on CNN. Right now our current Pers-O, LT Malynn, is flying BARCAP at Whiskey I with the Admin Officer. Our Admin Officer and Personnel Officer in the same jet.

The CDR Ron (Bongo) McElraft, our CO, bites his lip, arms crossed. He orders the SDO to get CNN on the TV and kill the movie on the VCR. He tucks his hands inside his flight gear straps, on his hips, and walks into Maintenance.

"One Twelve Airborne, One Twelve Airborne." On the 2JG. LCDR John (Deacon) DuGene, and LCDR (Spike) Riker have Nuts (100), and LT (Waylon) Jennings and LT Zimberoff in 112, already manned up for the 0400 launch, Strike Escort. I wonder how long it will take to appear on CNN.

"The anti-aircraft fire is again going up. Another wave, a lot of fire, the night sky lit up, by the time the guns respond, it's too late--woah, that was a bright light, everybody get down."

On TV another A6 launches, followed by 210, a Bullet F-14.

"An enormous explosion, one after the other."

Bright tail lights of 105, controlled rockets burning out the aft end. CAG has the lead for the Strike Escort.

CNN called it massive. Now they call it mammoth. Air raid sirens go off in Saudi Arabia, they don't know if it's a drill.

Deacon and Spike taxied out to the cat and hit the thing with their main mount and blew a tire. Now Deacon sits in the front row watching CNN. Pissed. He missed the strike escort.

Coming up to the 0500 CAP launch, calling "*Launch complete*" for the 0400 strike. The President is about to speak from Washington, as the Baghdad hotel hears a crack and sees a large flash through their window. The reporters hide under beds as the Iraqis knock at their door, avoiding having to hunker into a bomb shelter. Who knows if they won't be shot as spotters? Although, on the other hand, Iraqis might feel safer with them in their hotel--another human shield. We go now to the White House. A live 12 minute address.

"I don't want to hear the rhetoric. I want to hear that Iraq is launching their jets." The SDO wants to fight.

"*Ready eight strike.*" On the bitch box Strike says Opus, our pilot in 105, is coming back single engine. They were on Strike Escort. Strike wants a Rep in Cag Ops. Hopefully it's not from being hit. Reportedly no lost planes, Saudi or US, on the first raid.

0830 18 JAN 91. Two raids later. We've heard via CNN (we do it here, it comes out there), one US F-18 and a couple of allied jets didn't make it back. Our guys are still unscathed, but we're only flying BARCAP. The Pers-O saw some fireworks, but never got in the thick of it.

This morning's raid was electrical, meant to knock out power grids and phones. We have another raid at 1700, strike escort. We've seen the news that Insane (Hussein) attacked with his portable SCUD missiles, damaging Haifa and Tel Aviv. Israel may respond in righteous anger. I hope she does. Then the Arabs and Israelis will hit the fan with the shit, and we'll have world war three. Go baby go baby gobabygo!! Kill 'em all! Nuke Iraq! If Iran jumps in, nuke 'em! If Syria, nuke 'em! NUKE 'EM ALL!!!

I wonder if John Holliman and company were shot and killed after they disconnected from the Baghdad hotel. I can imagine Sodomite Insane in his whimsy, "take the news media out of the hotel and shoot them." Except he'd probably butcher them on TV.

Everybody in 81-Man is walking through yelling "kill them all!" and "nuke 'em!" More bombs have been autographed on the hangar deck and flight deck. I privately worry that we haven't dug deep enough into their craters, and that sand is a very good shock absorber, and that Iraqi soldiers are hiding under civilian skirts in suburbs, and that soon, suddenly, all hell will really cut loose.

"There she is."

"Uh oh, he found us."

"Oh, well, I'll just walk on by and pretend I didn't see you."

I hadn't call, wasn't called. And didn't want to throw any more dirt on Sweet's reputation, like, "your butt buddy called," or "your woman's on the phone." Maybe he already gets that, I don't know. If somebody from another division keeps calling a guy in your division, and if you're the type who likes to razz and looks for reasons to razz, you'll end up making them both out to be fags. He's so well liked, that probably won't happen. But I don't want to embarrass him, so I don't like to call. But I do want him to call me if he really wants to call. But he may not want to be heard calling me every meal.... It was so easy to get together when I was a Mess Deck Master-At-Arms.

I don't know why he started calling me "she." The first time was when I donned my white Pers Department jersey. That time he announced "there she is" and I rubbed his head. But he says it all the time, now, and I don't know if it makes him feel macho, or if it's his secret desire to come cuddle with me and my soft, hairy chest with my slender arms around him. Or if it's a quirky to fend me off. I don't want to know.

I really said what I felt this time. Their joke hurt. I'd seen Sweet Pea befriend another guy who lingered around him, and when the guy left Sweets would talk like he really disliked the guy. I just hope to God that isn't how he really feels with me. I ended up eating with him and Steve (the Yellow Shirt). They had fun with me, were kind, and didn't make me feel like the object of an inside joke; but they taught me how they did joke on others in front of their faces. "I've been talked about behind my back in front of my face, too."

They call the guns in the ready room capguns. They're .38 Specials, small enough to fit in their flight bags if they pull out their water bottles.

At 1645, tired as shit, I heard a familiar voice calling a familiar name in my ear. "Graham. Graham." It was YN3 Black Thing. I pulled the curtain open. He had already disturbed the guy below me, and was telling him they needed me. "Graham--they need you down in Admin to do a piss test. They need a printout."

"What?" I could scarcely imagine having to take a piss test in the middle of a war. Then I thought, well, some people might take advantage of the improbability of a whiz quiz out here.

"Yeah, man. A piss test. They need you to print a list of everybody with a social ending in 2, 3 or 8."

"Two, three or eight. Okay." I had not turned on my light.

"I'm not leavin' 'til I see some movement."

"Oh, yeah." I thought I was dreaming for a moment. I hit the light and started digging around for my greens.

"That's better." He left and I followed soon after. I got down to Pers and printed the list. YNCS was mad as hell, pissed at having to piss again.

"I wish they'd catch that son of a bitch. This is the third time in a row for me and it's not random. Somebody they're tryin' to catch has the same last digit as mine. Take me off the list."

"Well, I wouldn't want to get my ass chewed when they start wondering if I did that for anybody else, Senor." I figured he wasn't on drugs and I felt sorry for him. But if I played around with the numbers I'd have my own ass in a sling. Actually, last time, I made a typo that made a guy have to piss who shouldn't have. Better that than the other way, I reasoned. I didn't tell him.

"What time do they have to test?" PNC asked me.

"Between 1700 and 2000." It was already 1730.

I made two copies of a list of about forty guys with 2, 3, or 8 as the last digit of their SSN. I sorted the list by alpha order, and made another by shop, to facilitate phone calling. We had to locate all TAD guys and if necessary get them out of their racks and down to the MAA shack. About 1830, after most of the TAD guys had been notified, the ATC (Avionics Technician Chief) called, bitching about the realities of war. Meanwhile, one of our guys TAD to the MAA's came up with the memo, and YNCS gleefully pointed out the phrase, "unit sweep." "If I have to pee, we all have to pee." It was from the XO of the *Ranger*, and it did say "unit sweep."

I called the SDO in Ready Eight. "Sir, we have a memo here from the Master-At-Arms shack that says this is supposed to be a unit sweep. Did you realize that?"

"They must be kidding. There's no way. I'll call 'em. But you better call everybody back." Now I had to print out another list of the entire squadron.

Meanwhile, our man TAD to the MAA started asking questions and bringing up points. "Usually all they want is a random sampling. There's no way they'd get the entire squadron down there before eight o'clock anyway. Here, give me the phone." Sure enough, as he hung up he informed us. "Just the numbers that the SDO came up with will be fine."

I called again to the people I could reach, and told them. Then my phone rang. "VF-1 Admin/Pers, PN2 Graham, may I help you?"

"Yeah, Petty Officer Graham, this is Lieutenant Sieck again. The urinalysis is canceled."

It was too late to go back to my rack in Iraq. In fact, it was 5 a.m. before I could shave. I had to man the phones, get a PN2 job survey completed, sort out the January flight deck pay, help YN1 fix his computer, and fight a virus in our hard drive's partition, which I didn't beat yet. Who knows what else I did all night. But I watched CNN live and recorded much of it on my 4-track. Maybe if we live through all this and come out victorious and I get back together with my famous European film director, Khaled Siddik of Kuwait, he'll need this stuff to help him make a movie on the war.

I'm hoping I don't get awakened by GQ. We have growing anxiety all around that if Hussein is ever going to come out, the B-52 carpet bombing from Diego Garcia that is penetrating any bunkers he could conceivably be hiding in, is going to shake him loose by tonight, and his troops will prefer dying in combat to dying in rat traps.

The Captain has spoken. According to him, there are 16,000 pounds of mail backlogged in the Philippines, waiting to get to *Ranger* whenever we can get it here. I wonder if my JC Penney and VISA bills are in it. I suppose the book club will have assumed by now that I wanted the selection of the month.

Chapter Eight

0600 19 JAN 91. The boatswain's whistle blows, a dude calls over the 1MC. "*Reveille, reveille. All hands heave out and trice up. The smoking lamp is lighted in authorized spaces. Now reveille.*" Ready Room Eight rattles under the roar of Bullet 202 in full burn on cat four ... airborne! The Squadron Duty Officer (SDO) asks a pilot to turn up the TV volume on CVIC, and crank it down on CNN. One screen sits on top of the other on a customized shelf in the corner near the mission board. The two screens at times look identical: Forward Looking Infrared Reconnaissance (FLIR, pronounced fleer) video of targets exploding on *Ranger*'s in-house productions, smart bombs exploding on satellite news. A khakis clad guy briefing the press on CNN, a green flight jacketed Spy from Intel briefing ready rooms on the upper monitor.

"Ready Eight, Air Ops."

"Ready Eight." I squeeze the little metal button on top of the black rubber mouthpiece of this clumsy, greasy headset, and let up after responding.

"Could you give me your line up for Seven Alpha One?"

I cock my head past the red backed barber chair craning to read the wipe board beside the SDO. "We don't have the birds but I'll give you the names."

"Go ahead."

"Okay. Jennings, Jones and Gassie."

"Jennings, Jones and Jackson?"

"Jennings, Jones and Gassie. Like gassing up your car."

"Oh, Gassie. Okay, I got it."

You're lucky if you hear anything but a vibration inside sound powered phones. Somehow the Navy came up with a glorified version of sticking a couple of cans on either end of a string, and calling it an intercom. It's worse than a phone call from southern Somalia to Honduras, except there's no echo.

"On three, one oh seven!" The kid sounds so excited with a roar seeping through his headset as the aircrew flips the channel from CVIC to the PLAT (flight deck camera) and I see afterburners lighting. The digital clock ticks off at the top of the screen, 06:14:57, 58, 59--. "One oh seven airborne!"

"One oh seven airborne," I relay the call to the SDO, turning to see him watching the small TV monitor on his desk. Just doing my job, who knows when he may be distracted.

"Roger." He is polishing his boots, in fact. But he turns and draws the upslant half of an inverted "v" across from number 107 on the event board in red, and writes the exact time over the slant in tiny blue numbers. Seconds later 101 goes airborne off cat four. I wonder if some new blue shirt was laid out between the roaring afterburners with knuckles white, grabbing pad eyes, his dick bouncing off the vibrating flight deck. They do that sometimes because, they can. Earlier this evening, about 0040, the phone rang. I picked it up and hesitated to say anything.

"VF-1 Admin Pers, Petty Officer Graham." I was tired.

"Alpha Strike!" It was Sweets.

"Hey dude!" I was suddenly awake, enthusiastic, happy, had a reason for living and felt alive, loved, wanted, wonderful and healthy. All my troubles and frustrations disappeared. I forgot the war and the killing and the missing aircrewmen from the *Intruder* that went down a few hours ago from *Ranger*. All I could think was to get down the passageway and stare at his sweet face.

"You ready to go eat?"

"I'm gone. You want me to come by your shop?"

"Yeah."

"I'll be right there."

Standing in line he stretched his arms on an overhead pipe, his slender back and skinny waist aching for my arms to surround him. But I couldn't express that kind of affection. There was an Ordie from VF-1 right behind me. "Where are you gonna be when we pull in?" Sweet Pea asked again. "You won't have any place to live. Will they let you stay in the barracks?"

"Oh yeah, I'll stay in the barracks until I get an apartment and a car."

I wanted him to buy a car and I'd take the bus and we could get a place on the bus line. Or I would buy my dad's Buick, that used to belong to my mom. I could get it for a couple of grand, maybe $1500. But would Sweet Pea live with me if he didn't have a car? He's lived on *Ranger* ever since he arrived, and doesn't know anything but home, bootcamp and this ship. He's never had to budget groceries, cook his own food, do his laundry in town. Well, he did his own laundry in every port last Westpac, and this last time in the Philippines. And he did take a lot of cash home when I took him to the airport. He's "shorter" than me. When we pull in, he'll have barely three months left in the Navy. I'll have seven. What's in San Diego for him? Once he goes home to Connecticut, I might as well forget about him. Because I will never see him again, just like the long list of loving and beautiful children I grew up with and didn't grow up with and lost and will never see again. What the hell, what the hell. "Are you ready?" He was done eating whatever we had.

"To say goodbye?" Sometimes I can't believe the words that come out of my mouth. But right then I had him to myself, and couldn't afford to dress up my feelings.

0845 19 JAN 91. I dared a gas death and took a shower without taking my mask down the passageway forward of our Line Shack, to V-3's shower room. The slogan on their berthing door nearby reads, "we like it tight," and sports a drawing of three A-6 Intruders stacked wingtip to wingtip, the middle one facing the opposite direction. V-3 is Sweet Pea's division.

I must be trying to catch Sweet Pea naked. Why shouldn't I be thrilled if I did? I think he mysteriously gets clean without taking showers. I have seen him with a towel around his waist in the V-3 head before. But I was only passing by. He was on day check and this was in the evening. Now he gets off after FOD walkdown in the hangar bay at 0730. I haven't seen him in the shower, although I've been there at 0800, 0900, 0950, and 1100 (on different days!). The V-3 head is secured between 1000 and 1100 for cleaning.

He was hoping to watch a comedy after work today, so maybe he was in the berthing. I found the shower room occupied by this big black man (a Yellow Shirt), playing extremely loud soul music on a boogie box, picking his teeth. He's a cool guy, and it was something like Keith Sweat he had on, which reminded me of Kelly, the skinny little soul singer who I can now say was that MS dude from 39-Man coop who married his butt buddy sweetheart from grade school. He got out of the Navy with an Honorable Discharge, four years of undetected crime. If they knew, they left him alone, since he was such a nice guy. I was told the senior medical officer on board is a closet case.

Once in a while Kelly would tell me about some jerk that he'd confided in, later mad at him, spreading gossip about his "business." But you had to have seen the whites of his hazel eyes light, whenever a big, black hunk with a ten-inch cock would strip in the head. He'd go weak at the knees, clutch at the sink and turn toward me to hide a locked open jaw. I got a good laugh since it didn't attract me.

I'll never understand the perverse double standard the Navy breeds, where a thirty year careerist E-9 Command Master Chief can run 24-hour porno flicks like a masked man eating feces off a dinner plate--after his woman shits it there in close up--with an office full of military heroes watching in awe. But a homosexual gets kicked out in five working days for merely stating that he's gay, without committing even a bisexual act to prove it.

Before turning in, I've got to mention this problem of smoking. The Navy has instituted a "smoke free Navy" program, particularly for ships. They frequently show safety films on topics like the hazards of second hand smoke. But what happens if your entire chain of command are chain smokers? My chief, PNC, is a chimney. He averages a fourteen hour day, half with a burning cigarette. His boss, the senior chief (YNCS), is worse. There won't be a day on cruise without two empty packs in his trash can (from him). I'd say he smokes fifty cigarettes in ten hours, five an hour, one every twelve minutes, about eight minutes each, four minutes between. That's an average, between the two of them, of zero smoke free minutes in an average day at the office for the rest of us. One cigarette burning solidly through the entire workday like a stick of incense might not be too bad in a war zone and all that. But these two guys are only half the problem. Our Command Career Counselor works 1200 to 2400, then hangs around until 0200 or more. And seldom forgets to light his next cigarette off the last. NC1 is the poster boy of chain smoking. His desk is right beside mine, and I've yet to come to work when he was not sucking a fag. Next is our Command Master Chief, aka Porno King. He can't watch those fuck flicks without sucking something. So he's glued to the screen, always puffing away (or hanging ash). Four chain smokers: my boss, his boss, his boss's boss, and NC1. I haven't mentioned the Pers-O. Last night as I drafted a letter to the ship's XO about the petty problem of not having anyone in my squadron to complain to about the smoking problem in my shop, the Pers-O came down from the Ready Room (where he can't smoke), and asked me the ironic question. "Say, do you mind if I smoke?" I buckled.

All of these guys seem basically nice, with the possible exception of PNC who strikes me as just mean by nature. None of them care about my health, though, much less their own. They lie to themselves about quitting, cry to me about intending to quit, and eventually turn on me as the enemy and look for faults in me to make them better. They retaliate. I'm under constant pressure and doing the best job I can, so they don't have performance evaluation bullets to sink me with in rages, as I win all the arguments against hazing our office with smoke.

The XO is a cigar smoker. The skipper I'm not sure about, but he's due for a change of command. Like everyone else, he's on Ophold for Desert Shield/Storm; and I'm not gonna bother him with my petty office while we're fighting. I'd be proud to die serving my country. But not from second hand smoke I had to live with in your Navy. Sweet Pea is a nonsmoker, thank God. And he's so clean and neat it makes me sick to know I'll lose him next September. What a lover--I mean, what a roommate--he would make.

He and I had midrats. Nothing to eat was good. Ordnance was strewn all over the forward mess decks with nowhere to sit. But there was no line and even though he had very little time we were able to talk. "I'm already thinking about how I'm gonna be missing you."

"You won't miss me. You'll be up there with a best seller and a house in Beverly Hills and you'll be involved in show business."

"I'll probably move up there with a buddy who lives in a poor section of LA, and I'll be working temporary jobs, hopefully working for studios, probably at glamorous places but not doing glamorous jobs. What about you?"

"I don't know what I'm going to do."

"Live at home?"

"Probably, until I get my own apartment."

All the years I wanted to fly back east to see Billy in Virginia Beach crept into my head. But I didn't let it upset me, and didn't pretend I would find myself in sandals on the Cape Cod Highway, hitchhiking with guitar and backpack again, sleeping in the bushes of a stranger's yard up a road since his best friend's older sister's parents didn't want me to crash at their Wellfleet beach house on the spiral staircased deck overlooking a sailboat.

My hookup, Johnny, is the nightcheck supervisor in Wardroom Two, the main officer's mess. Johnny is the only Wolfie ever to win Junior Sailor of the Month while TAD. He'll probably become an officer, or at least make Master Chief in his career. Last night I hooked him up with Wolfie stencils, came down and sprayed them on his jerseys. He fed me real ice cream in return, and asked at the end, "how much do I owe ya?"

"Come on, Johnny. You don't owe me nothin'."

"Well, if you ever need anything you know where I'm at."

Walking back from the forward messdecks after chow, Sweet Pea and I passed Wardroom Two. "If you ever want anything from the wardroom, like some ice cream, I have a hookup."

"You can get ice cream?"

"Yeah--right now. You want some?"

"Heck yeah!" He lit up like a Sea Whiz.

"Well, we'll have to cut across to the other side." The deck was roped off with ordnance, ugly green 2000 pound bombs destined for the desert.

"Then let's cut across." We walked right by the bombs.

I brought him into the wardroom and Johnny looked him over. He knew I liked Sweet Pea a lot. At one of our Battle E parties in back of the Miramar Enlisted Club, Johnny asked if I sucked. "I guess I'm a sucker for a pretty face," I told him. Now he looked to see what I saw in my friend. Sweet Pea has the most beautiful face and his body goes with it. Johnny didn't give any indication of anything derogatory, didn't make any special faces or in any way seem freaked out about the relationship.

I followed Sweets up to the 0-3 level by his coop where we parted.

"You could bring your ice cream down to my shop."

"I'll just take it down to the hangar and eat it right there by the elevator."

"Even if I do sell that book and buy that house in Beverly Hills, I'll be missing you." Twenty minutes later the phone rang in Pers.

"What's the idea of sending him up here with ice cream?"

"Who is this?"

"It don't matter who this is. Do you have any idea how many people you pissed off?"

"I know who this is." It was Dean. I recognized his drawl.

"That don't matter. You got a whole room full of pissed off people 'cause you sent him up here eatin' ice cream. Out here that's like eatin' pussy." Still eating my own, I couldn't help laughing and grinning as I tried to talk. I was so pleased to give Sweet Pea something special that made them all jealous. It was better than sex, and it *was* like eating pussy. It nearly gave me a hard-on, imagining them bitching, him laughing and defending himself between bites.

Dean thought hard how to persuade me to come up with a five gallon barrel for their shop. But there was no way I'd strain my hookup for a third party. "Who's your hookup?"

"Aw, come on, Dean. You wouldn't ask a guy for the name of his hookup, would ya?"

"Well, try to get us a five gallon can. If you can get it, I'll send Sweet Pea back down there to get it. And he'll be there in a heartbeat."

"If I get to see him again for five minutes, I'll do the best I can."

"What?"

I had failed to screen my affection with the mental elbow room needed to maintain a macho image. But Dean knows I love Sweet Pea, so I repeated myself. "I said, if it means I'll get to see Sweet Pea for another five minutes

I'll do the best I can."

"Well call me back if you can, or if you can't. But let me know either way. I'll be right here by the phone waitin'."

Ice cream is serious business for the hangar controllers. But I didn't want to use Johnny for anything but Sweet Pea, I'd already decided. Unless Dean was along with us. I made a mental note to tell Sweet Pea, from now on if we get ice cream, not to tell anyone else and not to take it back to the shop. We can eat it in my shop where nobody will bother us. I was so tickled that my baby got so envied.

"*Ranger* is commencing her approach on the *USS Kansas City*." We're beginning a vertrep (vertical replenishment), helicopter onloads of lettuce and bombs "and some other goodies" as the Captain said today. I don't know if he meant special stores or special weapons. I hope he meant weapons because I want to kill that crazy dictator. If we don't, he'll come back to haunt us.

I found out that during the emergency breakaway we had last week, another ship on the other side of the *Kansas City* actually hit them. I don't know that anyone got hurt, but they did hit. On the PLAT (I don't know what PLAT stands for but it's the on-deck TV camera) the chopper, a two-bladed, large, Sikorski I believe (I don't know a damn thing about helicopters either), hovers over the flightdeck with strobe lights exploding on the black and white screen. It dangles a rectangular case, squats low, and with its cargo finally stable, eases down until the cables fall slack and the box comes to rest on the flight deck. In seconds it is up and away, and a team of guys in floatcoats and cranials runs up to pull the cables off and forklift it away. They get the cargo moved just as a second helo positions herself with another crate. Usually two helicopters perform a vertrep, sometimes four.

"*At this point we have delivered on the enemy 100 tons of ordnance.*"

Back home, as they get our day-by-day play-by-play, we get the word about protesters in San Francisco. And in the streets of Washington, D.C., protesters across from the White House. I wonder if they'll spit on American sailors and soldiers when Johnny comes marching home, or if they'll accept it that we had the watch when the shit hit the fan and bless us for killing so they could live to regret. Who do they think we are fighting, and why do they think we're operating in the Persian Gulf? Blood for oil? Or to reverse a situation where a madman has gone mad?

Maybe Saddam should raise gas to fifteen dollars a gallon, or thirty dollars a gallon, so that the average citizen of his country will have equal status among the billionaires in Beverly Hills. What if it took the blood of our loins to get back and forth to work each day? Like it does in other countries. Perhaps in Manilla, where an Iraqi just blew himself up in an attempt to bomb a target of opportunity, Mrs. Aquino should raise the price of real estate by twice, thrice what we pay, and let us lease the bases. Perhaps their protesters won't complain anymore. And instead of twenty-three pesos to a dollar, make it one to one. Then all our multi-national corporations developing the third world as much as it is will pay US citizens a fair wage on global terms, about what we earned in the dust bowl era. When somebody slaps you, be a masochist and offer them your other cheek. Then if they drink and laugh and shoot you in the other, die a martyr. Unilaterally disarm. Become a blissful isle of peace overrun by tyrants on a nuclear whim. They'll remember you a byword, won't burn your flag; they'll forget you had one.

0530 21 JAN 91. Larry King live on CNN with John Holliman and Bernie Shaw. Those guys are heroes. I should have been a war correspondent. That's what they call me down here in the shop anyway. I would have been Holliman. Or that dude in Riyahd, Charles Janko. Or Peter Arnett. I look like Charles. He probably wishes he was Peter. Where the action is.

I listened to Iraq's Ambassador; he's sad for his country, sad for this war. Maybe in the quiet pre-dawn it's all right to forget that Saddam invaded Kuwait City and raped families. I can pretend America is wrong to pound the living shit out of a crazy motherfucker. The word *scud* takes the place of *scum*.

Ready Room Eight came alive this evening, or rather this morning. The jet jocks came back from Strike Escort elated. Triple A fire had lit up the clouds beneath their F-14A's. LT Gram was most excited, around 25, young and lean, high tenor voice. "Was that a HARM or SAM? It scared the livin' fuckin' shit out of me. I didn't know they go ballistic."

"Never CAP over SAM sites on top of cloud cover," somebody else tried telling him, walking off.

"Man, we need to talk to them," Gram's RIO said. "We're not stupid." We've heard POW's reciting speeches in front of the Iraqi captors, decrying war and in particular American aggression against peaceful Iraq. Give me a fucking break. I guess Saddam never watched any Vietnam tapes. At least he hasn't butchered any of them yet. He probably will as the bombing goes on. So far, Fighter Squadron ONE has not had to fire a single missile or take a bullet. But *Ranger* lost an A-6 Intruder, with both aircrew down on the ground somewhere around the border of Iraq and Kuwait.

We operate in tandem with two other carriers, the *Teddy Roosevelt* and the *Midway*. We steam up to the edge of the area and perform flight operations for twelve hours, then fall back and replenish as another's ordered back to the front. I don't know who's in the Med. Maybe the *Kennedy* and *America* or *Nimitz*. I know the *Forrestal* is headed for the Gulf. I saw it on CNN. The famous carrier that taught us about Fire On the Flight Deck.

I prayed for rain last week so if we got hit by chemicals we'd have a natural washdown already going. But it seems the clouds are giving too much cover to Iraq to confirm targets. I'll pray for the skies to clear, so we can do our worst better. "Be careful what you pray for, you may get it," YN1 said.

I copied and reduced instructions, *Self Treatment for Nerve Agents*, taped it to cardboard, punched a hole in that and plastic tie strapped it to my gas mask bag. I hope I can read it when the time comes, if I'm breathing fast and hard and sweating under the mask. Main thing to remember is: little shot,

BIG SHOT, little shot, BIG SHOT, little shot. After that get to deep shelter and find a corpsman.

I woke up dreaming of Sweets. I could clearly see his small, soft white, smooth muscled flesh on his arms, shoulders and legs. I think he was nude and we might have had sex. His eyes were looking into mine and we were talking quietly, intimately, about something trivial and domestic, or social. There was no stress. I did not want to get up from that dream, but it was fifteen minutes to seven.

After I rode Scrapper everyday for being late, today he finally showed up on time and I was late.

0800 21 JAN 91. We spent an hour last night opening a can of coffee. Not your ordinary consumer variety, of course. This was the Navy issue 20-gallon container. These cans are supposed to go to the mess decks--but, like the ice cream, a few things here and there get hooked up. I don't know how it got to our shop. It just appeared in a large brown trash bag when I walked in.

We tried the can-opener from my survival FOD pouch first, but that bent. CMC tried his, concentrating sternly as if he were watching a porno. NC1 tried his Vietnam vintage P-38 C-ration special. Nothing worked. CMC ended up using a screwdriver, pocket knife, hammer, and channel locks. We wanted that coffee! We cut two fingers before it was over. But once we had filled the Folgers can and perked a pot, everything was groovy. It wasn't Folgers, but it got us going.

"I'm goin' to chow," I told Woody (YN1). I had watched the clock until about 0650, waiting by the phone. I know it's stupid to romanticize over a Blue Shirt from the hangar deck who doesn't even realize what's in my head, sweet dreams of Sweet Pea.

I'm treading on my contract with the Navy. But I'm here, and telling my story. I am what I am in the role I must play. Amy will hate it. Sweets may, too. They say you hurt the one you love.

He was challenging Steve, the Yellow Shirt, to how many bowls of cereal they could eat today. Steve set a record of shoving five Frosted Mini Wheats into one mouthful. They come six packages to a variety carton, and Steve had seven. Sweet Pea was having Frosted Flakes, his usual favorite, with french toast, bacon, and crackers with salsa. It looked like he had on the same blue jersey he spilt syrup on yesterday. "Or did you just spill it in the same place?"

"You guessed it." He rubbed it and I saw it was fresh.

"Hey," Steve jumped in. "You've no idea how often we get clean laundry."

"These are the same greens I've had on since we left P.I," Sweet Pea said.

"What do you do, stand them up beside your rack when you go to bed?"

"We sleep in 'em," Steve said. "*He* keeps 'em clean. He showers in 'em."

Sweets read the sports page of the *Ranger Gazette* to Steve, commenting, frowning and pouting with a puffed lower lip. He was happy the Raiders lost, sad that Joe Montana wasn't up to snuff.

"Joe probably still has a cold," Steve said. "He's such a pussy."

"Did you tell him?" He suddenly asked Sweets about me. "Does he know? Should we tell him?"

"Absolutely not."

I suddenly felt left out, rejected. I imagined the worst, that the NIS on board *Ranger* had intercepted my mailing of the editions of my book and questioned them about my affections. But maybe it was only some trivial knowledge about irrelevant gossip. Or something anywhere in between. But, I didn't press. If they didn't want to tell me something that was between them and made them feel closer, more special, I felt like getting the hell out of there. I'm competing with Steve and I'm no competition. He's younger, brighter, handsomer, more confident, and sees Sweets all the time. And they both know every cartoon ever put on TV. I'm out of my league.

I feel like retaliating by not being available the next time he calls me for chow. But, he'd only be less inclined to call me afterward. And I'd slip back into needing to see him. The best I can do is cry myself silently to sleep today, try and dream of someone else somewhere else--maybe that young dude who tried to pick me up at *Rage* in West Hollywood, when I went there with Amy. Why did she want to go there? She knew it was a gay bar. Is she a fag hag--is that all we had? Why couldn't I have just loved her when she came my way? Why did I have such a miserable past that I couldn't get over, that dragged into our relationship so that it scared her away?

The flight deck was open for jogging yesterday, and I went up after work. The sun was blinding. The Blue Shirts (flight deck Blue Shirts) and some of VF-1's Line rats and even a couple of AT's were scrubbing the nonskid. It definitely needed it.

I saw Rick, the other pretty baby boy out of 5,000 faces on *Ranger*, the one who was showing his belly I mentioned before. We talked a bit--an excuse for me to stare at him. I'm not sure what he gets out of me, flattery perhaps. A baldhead fag's affection. He could write home to Mom about me.

I walked up to an AT who was holding a broken scrub brush.

"Is that your last line of defense, spearchucker?"

"No. I'm a crossburner, not a spearchucker."

It took me a second to remember that the term spearchucker was a racist thing. I had used it literally, out of any racial context. It really cracked up some white dudes when I told them about it. I guess my black counterparts wouldn't think it very funny, but I'm sure they have their own stupid slang.

"Spoons, man." Steve said the other day. "The blue coveralls that just walked by? Spoon."

"He's kind of slow," Sweet Pea said.

"You can talk about them right while they're sitting beside you, man. You just pick up a spoon and say, 'I hate the spoons they have here.' And they don't know what the hell you're talkin' about."

"Well, I've been talked about behind my back in front of my face before," I said. I didn't tell them it was as an undercover narcotics agent in a pool hall where some locals were suspecting me.

Steve's a bad influence on Sweets. At least he's not a fag who lost a billionairess model girlfriend. Maybe we'll hit a mine and sink while I'm asleep.

Somebody once said religion keeps the poor from murdering the rich. The Gulf War is shooting holes in that theory. These people are supposedly poor, and extremely religious, and believe it's better to die (and see Allah) than to live long and prosper. We fight a war between haves and have nots. But I could take you around this ship and show you leaks, filthy urinals and shower stalls, disgusting food we have too frequently, imported milk designed to embalm you, and "bug juice" fruit drink mix that'll make your dick sting when you pee like a sexual disease.

Civilians cleaning up the great oil spill off the coast of Alaska, from the Exxon Valdez, walked off an $18 an hour job rather than live under the normal conditions of *Ranger*. My base pay is around $900 a month, and I'm nearly 35 years old. Tell me that Saddam Hussein has it worse than me in his bullet proof cars with his army and his bunkers. It's up to him to grow his grass and turn his desert into an oasis. He chooses war instead. Now we have to kick his ass.

0900 22 JAN 91. I was in Sweet Pea's shower room when the boatswain whistled to set MOP Level ONE. I couldn't remember for a moment if Level ONE was a step up or down in defensive posture, if it meant put your gas mask on, or you don't have to carry it.

I stepped out to the passageway where I could hear the loud speaker, and the Captain came on. He explained that since we were virtually unthreatened by SCUDs, and all of our intelligence showed us they didn't carry nerve gases, we could relax a little. "However, I won't hesitate to set us back to MOP Level TWO or higher, should the need arise."

I went back to the head and wiped my face with the Noxema Clear Ups that I use to stave off adult acne ever since I bought all those for Sweet Pea. (I guess you've got it straight that Sweet Pea and Sweets are the same guy. I'm not using his real name because I'm trying to protect him from the publicity this book could give him, negative or positive. I'm sure he'll be out of range of Naval regulations by the time this comes out, and thus immune to an investigation of moral turpitude. Unless he makes the mistake of staying in the Navy. As crystal pure as he is, the blame for any attraction for me that an imaginative reader might read into him, would come through my point of view, and lovely Sweet Pea doesn't know what I write. I won't dare show him until I publish it in full, when I imagine I'll have the guts to admit it, and we're both out of the range of people who would condemn the expression of love and affection in a military service.)

Steve called me in the Ready Room this morning. The SDO answered. "Petty Officer Graham, it's for you."

"Petty officer Graham, may I help you sir?" It went through my mind that it could be Sweet Pea--I had given him the number. But he never wrote it down, and had so much trouble learning my shop number that I had doubts.

"Is this Petty Officer Cracker?"

"Who's this?"

"This is Airman Steve."

"Oh, dude."

"Can you like, come meet us here at, where are we Sweets?" I heard the sweet muffled voice in the background. "Something called hangar control?" Steve drawled. I presume he was joking, because he works in the hangar. He and Sweets joke constantly--that seems to be the glue that holds them together. "Can you meet us here at five-twenty-five?"

"Let me check with the SDO. I have a recovery that's supposed to come in at six-thirty but everything has been a cluster fuck all night so I don't know. Hang on a second."

I looked at LT Zimberoff. I wanted to say, "sir," or "Lieutenant," but somehow just stuttered. "Hey, uh, is there anything coming back before six thirty that you know of? I'm thinking I'll go to chow."

"No, go ahead."

"Okay, I'll be there in ten minutes."

It was a complete clusterfuck on the phones tonight. I came on with an event at one o'clock this morning, and neither Air Ops nor Primary were on line. It's Air Ops responsibility to answer inquiries about the status of birds out on events, whether they have checked in coming back yet, whether they are overhead, and fuel status. They also normally request information from me such as the line-up (order of side numbers of the jets, like 110, 101, 100, etc.) for the next event, and the pilots' names.

Primary was the main man I needed. His job is to call out the side number of whatever jet traps (lands) or bolters (misses the wire with its tailhook and goes around again) or launches (goes airborne), so that I can log times on flight schedules for the Operations Yeoman who uses the data to verify total flight hours for the aircrew's official history of naval service.

Two aircraft launched on a strike mission with no word from Primary. I called repeatedly to both Primary and Air Ops, and after getting nothing back, began to question whether my phones were operative. The Ops YN happened to come through and I got him on the phone to Air Ops, who swore they had someone on the phones. Suddenly both Air Ops and Primary began communicating, as if by magic. "Primary, Ready Eight. Why haven't you been calling out the side numbers?"

"I've been calling 'em, Ready Eight. You got your underwear on too tight."

A professional response if I ever heard one.

Next, some other ready room missed Primary's announcement of a take-off, and requested a repeat call. "Primary, Ready Seven. Who just took off?"

"Listen up asshole, I'm only gonna call it once."

"Look, boy. If I didn't hear it and I ask for it again you better give it."

"Don't call me boy."

I flashed back to growing up. I was thirteen, sitting at the dining room table reading the comics. Dad was in the kitchen at another table reading another section of the paper. Sis was in the living room and poked her head through the saloon type doors. "Boy boy boy."

"You know you're not supposed to be calling me that."

Dad jumped out of his chair and chased ME down the hall to my bedroom, pulling out his belt along the way. I laid on the bed wailing that she started it. He got her in there, stood her by the door and, holding that menacing belt, asked her straight in the eye, "did you call him 'boy'?"

"No," she said fearfully between looks at his angry face and the belt and my whimpering lump on the bed. He turned on me and belted me to tears, and I suppose I never got over it for as long as I knew my sister. More than twenty years later we still don't speak. And for some reason I cannot explain, I have no affection for newspaper comics.

Between 0115 and 0130 I listened as Ready Room Nine placed nine unanswered calls to Air Ops on the 2JZ. I heard Air Ops talk to Primary and Martial. (Martial passes fuel status and radio frequency to Air Ops when the birds check in, returning from missions.) They could have said "stand by," "wait one," or "I'm too fuck' busy" instead of just ignoring Ready Nine.

"Ready Nine, Ready Eight. I suggest you write down the problem you're having with communication and forward it to their Division Officer."

"Roger."

"The complaint would come under 'improper watchstanding."

"Copy."

Suddenly things took on a professional tone for a while. Primary started calling out the side numbers of cat shots and traps, even told us who were backing the cats. I guess they overheard our conversation.

I know they're busy in Air Ops, probably in Primary as well. Although we have two TV's in our Ready Room, our skipper may be watching CNN on one of them, trying to catch up with the headlines he's been making, and a televised brief for the next event may be on the other monitor. So I don't know who's anywhere via TV. And it isn't up to me to tell the skipper to change to the PLATT. But it is my job to get the times right. And even if we have a TV on the PLATT, the cameraman doesn't always zoom in on the side number (human error or negligence), and when we're launching from both cat one on the bow and cat four aft at the same moment, I need information off the phones. CNN probably thinks they're doing a service to the nation and to us overseas when they air the stories of people close to the prisoners of war being held in Iraq. But when that came on tonight, the jet jocks started wandering out of the Ready Room. They are the ones who are helped the least, and in my opinion it does the most damage to the US side of this war effort, to see the ugly side of it all. The aircrew have no choice but to go up and fight. What are they gonna do, watch the broadcast of their friend's wife crying and see him reciting lousy Iraqi prose against US aggression, and tell the skipper they don't want to go?

LT Jones came in first, whining about a sore back, but doing it privately to the SDO to avoid spreading his own misery. "I was so uncomfortable in the cockpit, I couldn't sit still." LT Davis came in tired but laughing. He flew around up there eating pizza and drinking a coke. "I was wide awake for a while. I got up to Martial ... after about three, four, four-thirty," he trailed off, head drooping. Telling the SDO about it reminded him that it was now 0500, and he needed sleep. "I was so glad we didn't bolter." LCDR Neil (Cowboy) Zerbe came in around six. "Boy I tell ya," he said in the drawl that won him his call sign, "my days are gettin' so fucked up. Gettin' up at four."

On the Alert Schedule wipeboard over the SDO, on the wall above the little window into Maintenance Control, the offgoing SDO left a passdown:

0230 - 0630 Add On
0500 Hot Switch
0530 2 Alert 5
0535 1 Alert "A" / 1 Alert "B"
Air Plan ... What's an Air Plan?

Above that he drew our logo, a red profile silhouette of a wolf, called a "Wolfie," with a hammer labeled "CV-61" nailing its nose, a missile labeled "Air Ops" stuck in its throat, and a knife labeled "strike" in the back of its neck. Between it and the alert schedule he'd scrawled, "the wolfie won't die!!" It reflected not only the clusterfuck but the fact that we are all tired, especially the aircrew facing combat. At least we know, from constant vigil of CNN International, back home they have candles in windows, and ribbons on trees.

0400 23 JAN 91. "Four zero seven three quarter mile call the ball."

"Four oh seven's Intruder ball, three-five."

"Roger ball, Intruder, twenty-five knots, ten starboard."

"Wave off, three-five."

"Four zero seven Angel's one point two, cleared left downwind three-five."

"Roger." The Intruder made a three mile hook, came back and trapped.

Our Tomcats averaged 4-hour flights on CAP and Strike missions all night, all morning. Israel got hit. At least 2 civilians died; about 70 were wounded.

The President signed an executive order directing our pay to be tax free. I have yet to hear the exact story. I've heard bits and pieces on KRAN and someone said he heard it on CNN. When I see it in my check, I'll believe it.

I got mail today. A box from Bonnie and Ken from my church back in Walnut Creek, California. They sent me a book entitled *The Saudis (Inside the Desert Kingdom)*. I'm anxious to read it, but I'm too tired right now. And a tray of California dried fruits, oddly appropriate for this desert land of dates and figs. I got a letter from VISA. I wondered when that bill would come. I opened it and read, "this is a second reminder that your account remains past due." A second reminder and I haven't even got the bill yet! I guess it's in one of those sixty tri-walls of mail for the *Ranger* sitting in Cubi Point, Republic of the Philippines, along with the first past due notice. I wonder how many

Book-of-the-Month selections I've selected already.

LT Tom (Roobar, for being hit by a car bumper in Australia last cruise) Ferris came into Ready Eight, where LT Ross was playing harmonica at the SDO desk. "I can't sleep. I keep having this dream that I'm shot down. I'm running and running. Then I jump into this marsh and start swimming. And I come up on a raft and there's a dead guy on it, and I steal his radio."

The British have lost another Tornado.

AIDS protesters are starting to interrupt the major news broadcasters, reminding the world that the US has more problems than this war.

My college English professor once pointed out that, looking through history, whenever major world powers had serious economic troubles at home, they invariably got embroiled in a foreign war. That's what we've done, that's who we are. So I don't knock the protesters and I agree that, just as we grow weary of endless minute by minute updates and reports, the world has to try and get on with the rest of its life in spite of this trouble. That is the pressure to get it over with quickly, and to get us hurt by moving too fast, too soon, too far without starving the scuds.

0900 23 JAN 91. CNN reporters breezed through Ready Room Eight last night. I took my camcorder up like a newshound, to record them recording us. They interviewed LT Gary Smilowitz--but were done before I got there.

I advised a cameraman how to wrap his equipment to deflect our radar, and told him where to get RF shielding, which works better than aluminum foil and comes graded good, better, best. The best stuff is kept in the 09 level right under the main radars.

By the end of Westpac 89 I'd invented eight models of "radar raincoats" as I called them, found the best of the best, and made a glove that worked well enough that KRAN picked my shots above all others for a ninety second worldwide broadcast of *Ranger*'s August 2, 1989 rescue of 39 Vietnamese refugees 80 miles west of the Philippines. Several SAR (Surface Air Rescue) swimmers were recommended for the Medal of Heroism, with reference to obscure video footage released by *Navy News This Week*, who credited *USS Ranger*'s KRAN TV. I got top billing on a two-hour documentary.

CNN interviewed important guys, like the aircrew flying in the face of Iraq. It is largely their story, so far as *Ranger* is concerned. Enlisted men are here to help them fly so we don't die. Without BARCAP, the 150-mile envelope around *Ranger*, we'd be sitting ducks in the Persian Gulf. Maybe we are anyway. If this widens to an Arab thing, we will be.

I told them Charles Jaco had a fan in the Gulf, that he's a cool reporter I'd enjoy working a few jobs with, hanging out at bars, clubs and cocktail lounges. Maybe ducking grenades. And, if they weren't doing anything at night, since they're here for four days, I told them to stop by my shop.

"And interview you?"

"Yeah, sure. Why not?"

I gave succinct instructions how to navigate to my shop, but gradually realized that my Navy terminology was losing them, and they'd never find me. I was a fucking salty dog. "Just go through this passageway here and turn aft on the starboard side 'til you get to the elbow joint. Jog outboard and right--you're still going aft--until you come to another outboard passageway, with a green mat on the deck. That's the arresting gear shop. Turn outboard on the mat like you're heading to the flight deck, and you'll see a ladder just before the sponson. Go straight through the red door at the bottom of the ladder and you can't miss it." He had a pen and paper but didn't write anything. He looked like he was listening for English. Anyway, he was probably still trying to figure out where to get that RF shielding.

I'm sitting on my anti-smoking letter to the ship's XO (a former Blue Angel pilot). At this point I still have no one to blame but myself, for suffering without complaining.

I bought some plants at the North Island Navy Exchange just before we left, hoping to make things a little bit like home in the confines of our shop. But PNC had Scrapper put them in the passageway (in the foyer, as it were). We got some tiny flies now, that our kakhis are sure my plants are breeding.

PNC started complaining that I stink and that I never take a shower, calling me a scud, right as I went on a rampage about the cigarette smoke in our shop. The best defense is a good offense. But that seemed crazy. I take showers daily--looking forward to the day Sweet Pea and I may brush butts.

Today the big black guy was there again, but now instead of sweet soul music it was a muslim preacher haranguing blacks about blacks killing blacks in our nation's capitol, which he said is becoming the murder capitol of the world. If he finds out I love Sweet Pea (they work together), maybe he won't fag bash me like the Mexican shitheel who broke my tooth for wearing a hot pink hat on a Saturday at sunny Mission Beach.

We took on more bombs in a twin chopper vertrep two hours ago. I stuck my head up to see the sunlight like a groundhog on the sponson, saw choppers, ducked back in, grabbed my camcorder, cranial and floatcoat, and went on deck. I got some cool action shots, crates of explosives being lowered down, slick, sleek, and agile twin-rotor Sikorskis, ordnance jocks forklifting the cargo to Elevator Four (which Sweet Pea operated). And Beanpole, that tall, blond ordie with a tender tenor voice, no longer slaving on the mess decks but doing a real job now, a real dangerous job. He caught my camcorder eye, and mugged. "I can't wait to come visit you again at Mission Beach," he yelled through the din of choppers and the earcups of my cranial.

"I don't live there anymore," I yelled back.

"You mean you don't have that apartment? Oh, man. That was radical."

He lamented while I stared at his face and listened to his soothing voice, until the chopper dropped another load and he had to get back to the bombs. I taped until my battery died, and managed to get some shots of a wild looking helo that came from the desert with mail bags and looked like a car, with a wing on the back that made it look like it could be driven on a road.

I stood in the way of the ordies long enough to nearly get hit by a forklift, finally got my ass chewed by some wildly waving ordie chief. "Get the hell out of the way!" Hopefully he didn't read the big "WOLFPACK VIDEO" stencil on the back of my floatcoat.

"The following is a test of the general, chemical and collision alarms from the pilot house. The general alarm: beep bee- bee- beeee--. The chemical alarm: beeeeeeeeeeeeep. The collision alarm: b-b-bp b-b-bp b-b-bp. Test complete. Regard all further alarms."

Flight Ops. Turboprops of an E-2C Hawkeye vibrate overhead, rattling the steal deck. I let it go and drift to sleep, feeling good again about Sweet Pea and my place in the world, one eye open for the wacky Iraqi.

0900 24 JAN 91. Three boots checked in yesterday. And got sea sick. On an aircraft carrier (we don't rock much).

PNC called me "short" last night. He was talking about having me break in our new PNSN on the computer and how to handle the database. If he catches on quick, I'll get some leave when we pull in. "You know, you're getting short," PNC grinned. "And someday we're going to have your legacy with what you developed on the computer."

"Yeah. They'll say, 'what the hell did he do to it?'"

Funny how the concept is strange to me, as strange as when our old Command Master Chief first called me salty. You are a boot first, then salty, then short--or a lifer dog, in which case you still grow short in terms of a transfer date. For two years I have watched others come and go from VF-1. I'm a fixture. But I've done no better than one recommendation for Sailor Of the Month, the first month of this cruise. I have two things going against me. First, my chief dislikes me. Even when we have good moments, he's up against my second problem, of being a black shoe airedale, which is like being a bastard child. YN's and PN's are black shoe Navy--in other words, ship related. Airedales are aviation, which is elitist. This makes for a hell of a Wog Day, but we'll talk about that later. In the long run, it means I can forget about recognition. Wah, wah.

I love the Navy. It brought me Sweet Pea. There are plenty of jerks, but it's better than the street. The Navy has a chain of command that holds people accountable for their actions--or if not, at least promotes accountability, which will deter those who haven't learned to beat and abuse the system. Percentages are in your favor, when dealing with a cock, that you can make him toe the line. It's like a gang in that you can identify the membership of the person committing the crime. But in this case, theoretically and more often than not, once you identify the "gang" (command) you can notify them and expect disciplinary action to be taken.

Sweets called for breakfast. I was there in seconds flat. Up the ladder calling, "goin' to chow." Aft two knee-knockers, down three ladders swinging on chains, through the hangar bay to Hangar Control, up that ladder past the NIS into Sweet Pea's life in front of anyone who cared. Fortunately, the only ones who did care were friends of his, and he likes me so they like me so I'm safe with him and life is magic. You have to be brave.

He had hotcakes and syrup, bacon (not as good as yesterday), crackers and toast with salsa again, and his Frosted Flakes. He poured milk in the bowl, then added flakes as needed. He went from a taste of this to a bite of that, didn't finish anything first. A central processing unit, multiple end users. He is so animated. Dare I say, effervescent? He was hyper all morning, tapping the barber chair in Hangar Control like a drum, tapping his tray, tapping the counter in the serving line. "I'm happy this morning. But I don't know why." His voice rode just below the cracking line, terminally adolescent. When he got ahead of his diaphragm--crack--he sounded like a kid.

"You must have had a soda."

"Actually, I did have one. I've had two sodas since yesterday. And I'll have one more before I'm through."

"With your sugar rush?"

He brought another guy to chow. I'm used to his popularity so it didn't phase me not to have him alone. This guy was Rob, a logical dude so in touch with his feelings that he didn't get enraptured by Sweet's power of persuasion.

"You should do that, because you can," Sweet Pea urged. "Say it: 'because I can.'"

"No, that's your phrase."

"You'll have to think of your own saying then." Sweet Pea was clearly disappointed.

"Yeah, but it'll have to come natural."

Sweets and Steve have been doing the 'because I can do that' phrase all week. The talk got around to berthing, and I asked him where he got his baby blue sheets. I was impressed when I noticed them, loading his rack full of birthday balloons. "Last time I was home I bought them. I got my own sheets, and two of my very own pillows and pillow cases, not the *Ranger* crap that's older than the ship."

"You don't throw them in the ship's laundry, do you?"

"Are you crazy? They'd come back stinking and stained, and torn."

"How do you wash them?"

"I usually wash them every time we pull into port."

"Well, you're not gonna wait until the end of cruise?"

"I got two sets."

Poor Sweet Pea just realized, it's going to be months before we hit another port. I hope I can help him get them cleaned. I know some guys in laundry--and Scrapper worked there, too. If he'll take my help, I might be able to use my salty connections.

We left his pal and went looking for today's *Gazette*. We stopped by Wardroom Two and read the notes on the XO suggestion board, where he responds to comments and questions. Some geek hogged our view in front of the plexiglass. But I was glad, because when Sweets came around he compulsively put his hands on my shoulders, and gave me a subtle massage like a tickle. Brief, spontaneous, as if revealing something.

"Honey," I whispered. I couldn't tell if he heard.

As we went on down the passageway, he asked an odd question. "So, when are you gonna grow some hair?"

Who wants a bald headed lover? Well, Sean Connery is sexy.

I just read a quote from the *Penthouse* Forum article, "The Same Sex (when men want men)," about ancient Greece. They quote Plato:

> *Of his teacher, Socrates, Plato wrote, "Now I thought he was eager for my bloom of youth. And I believed that it was a windfall and my marvelous piece of good luck that it should fall to me to sexually gratify Socrates, in order to hear everything he knew."*

0900 25 JAN 91. The President signed an executive order last week declaring this theater of operations a combat zone. I am in a combat zone, which I find hard to believe. This is the stuff of books I read as a kid.

We had our first real General Quarters last night. What a fiasco. The man on the 1MC spoke too slow for his nervous hand on the alarm, and tried to speak and sound the gong at the same time. Men stumbled all over in a panic, the first nondrill of their lives. Mine, too, but I was already in the shop with my gear. I still got blinded with fear, enough that I couldn't find the flash hood and gloves in my survival bag, where I had labeled the compartments. I forgot that during the last drill I decided to keep them in the green canvas, government issue bag, with the mask and filter canisters. Finally I calmed down, looked in the green bag, found them, and put them on. If we'd been hit I would have been dead.

We had two new guys (our new PNSN and a YNSR) who stood with flash hoods and gloves, but had no other protective gear in case of CBR (chemical/biological/radiological) attack. This was an exocet missile threat, an antiship missile that we didn't think carried chemical, biological or radio-logical type warheads. The two guys just stood there looking at us pulling out our chemical masks. Welcome aboard, nice knowin' ya." And they were bootcamps.

One kid down in 24-Man (the Rain Locker) was popping out of the coop like a cork when a sailor above him decided to dog the scuttle without looking and swung the heavy piece of solid round iron down onto his skull. It knocked him back to the deck, blood squirting out. The guys found him with his flash hood pressed to his head, blood all over his clothing. He'll be okay in a week. Another dude walked onto the flight deck in the dark, right into a missile fin. He's now wearing stitches and a white gauze patch like a feather in his hair, nicknamed "little indian." No civilian job could give me this kind of heart pumping excitement.

0745 27 JAN 91. I set a record, being in the rack before Eight Bells. I had breakfast with Pea and Steve and Dean, briefed Scrapper, got the trash out to the fantail and over the side, and showered in the V3 head. All before zero eight. I had a feeling Sweet Pea would take an early shower. And I finally asked. I take a shower at all different times. Sometimes I run straight up there after muster, and sometimes I watch a movie and don't get in there until eleven. Yesterday I was in one shower as a dude came in, a skinny white form behind the translucent plastic curtain. He wore a white towel around his waist, stepped inside the stall opposite mine, opposite where my telltale trademark red plaid bathrobe hung on a hook, and made a high cracking sound in response to a guy leaving who said what sounded like Sweet Pea's name. But there was so much ambient noise, from pumps and all the other sounds of an aircraft carrier, I couldn't be sure. The form opposite me was using something, a wash cloth. I thought, Sweets has his own blue bedsheets, eats pizza with a fork, he probably showers with a washcloth. I bet his butt is always squeaky clean. He even brushes his tongue as he brushes his teeth. Just like I do. One beautiful cheek drew near the edge of the curtain as he bent over to wash his feet and chicken legs. Down boy, I said to my dick. I felt my temperature climb as I dried off and stepped into the sink room, passing his curtain. Ooo-wee, baby.

He came out as I was rubbing my face with cleansing pads.

"There she is," he announced with a smile.

If you want me to be a bitch, I thought, I'll be it for you. But I can't say anything that might come under the classification of soliciting a homosexual act onboard a Naval vessel. That must wait, maybe forever. For now, it's just an electricity shedding light on the human condition of extended deployment.

I'm reading T. S. Eliot's *The Waste Land and Other Poems*, fitting our proximity. Hussein has succeeded in dumping enough oil to ruin the Persian Gulf for the next forty years. It's so odd that such a major catastrophe would happen in a gulf named after Persians, Biblically attached to the wise men who visited Baby Jesus with gold, frankincense and myrrh. Allow me to share an ancient Persian proverb: "He who knows not and knows not that he knows not is a fool. Shun him. He who knows not and knows that he knows not is a child. Teach him. He who knows and knows not that he knows is asleep. Wake him. He who knows and knows that he knows is wise. Follow him."

Where does Hussein fit in?

YN3 Black Thing came in last night after running messages to CAG. A skinny black guy with a voracious appetite bottomless pit stomach, he has a rough no shave chit face and thick eye glasses. "You know something? I was just in the passageway, and I swear I smelled alcohol on two khakis. And believe me, I know alcohol. They were bustin' out about bullshit so I know they were drunk." Later, when the *Ranger* theme song The William Tell Overture played on the 1MC, and the Captain came on to tell us where the next strike would go, he sounded drunk. He spoke slowly, not noticeably slurred, kind of like I talked to the cops at Mission Beach the night I got arrested for calling 911 on acid. I'm sure his main objective, if he were inebriated, was to keep the crew from getting jealous. America, unlike most others countries, doesn't allow booze onboard naval vessels. Except, after 45 days at sea without hitting a port, we have a "beer day" and give each man two beers. We pulled out around January 4th, and have been at sea now 23 days.

The Navy has just made history, successfully firing a number of Tomahawk missiles from a sub to a real world target. So lifer dogs everywhere no doubt are celebrating. They must have had a drink behind those blue, two-star curtains on the blue-tile deck, where enlisted men can only pass through on "official business." The pilots came back excited about the international and patriotic flavor of their missions, tanking off Air Force jets with states like Illinois and Wisconsin painted on their sides. They've seen huge tankers stacked like stairways in the sky above the gulf, groups of various nations' fighters tanking three on a wing, six on a jet, twelve on another jet, with two more floating petrol stations above all that.

Last night in Ready Eight they talked about a pilot CAPping over an island known for anti-aircraft artillery (triple A, AAA). "Just to get shot at so he could come back and add two points toward a silver star."

"He's fuckin' crazy," the Pers-O exclaimed. "I'll never fly with him. I mean, of course I'll fly with him but we're not gonna pull that shit."

"I'm sure others have done it."

"Maybe so, but you could get killed that way. That's crazy."

I forgot I was enlisted again and chimed in about "Flight of the Intruder," the film that had not come out before we deployed. "They went out there in an A-6 and got a round of rifle fire through the window that killed the dude in the right seat."

They acknowledge me without remark. An enlisted puke is an enigma with a stigma in the Ready Room, doing the job on sound powered phones in a place to be seen, not heard. I forget since the pilots are my age or younger. Besides, I wore LT bars (railroad tracks) at age 16 in Army ROTC at the University of Missouri-Columbia campus. If only I'd stayed on track, I'd have been an Army Captain in this crazy war. But a little boy named Billy talked me out of it. Still, I'll never forget walking in uniform across the UMC campus near the tennis courts that doubled as a parade practice ground. My squad was strapping on leggings for a marching drill. "Hey, Rott-cee!" a voice hollered from a fraternity window across the street. "Bam-bam-bam-bam-bam-bam." Evidently, a blank gun.

LT Ed "Zimby" Zimberoff promised to take my camcorder out to the wasteland "any time I'm on the flight schedule." I just have to catch him in the daytime as I'm sleeping. But, the new First LT (janitorial division) petty officer, AMH2 Hensley just walked by, and offered to arrange it for me. He took my camcorder on the flight deck during Wog Day last cruise, while I got cleansed of my polywog slime. Now he's borrowing it to make a Valentine videogram for the wives back in the world.

"Flight Quarters flight Quarters." The mysterious voice on the 1MC interrupts our world onboard *Ranger* for a moment. *"All hands not actually involved in flight operations stand clear of all weatherdecks, flight deck, catapults, and flight Quarters stations."* He droned on with announcements about worship services now being held throughout the ship, then finished by announcing, *"The flight deck is open for jogging."*

"That's fucked up," I told the night checker pulling out his down sleeping bag in the rack beneath me. "He just called flight quarters, then said the flight deck is open for jogging."

"I wonder if hearing protection's required."

Pause.

"I thought sure he was gonna say, 'belay my last.'" That's the term used to tell people not to follow the last instruction.

"Usually somebody'll call and tell him he made a mistake."

"I guess it was so stupid nobody would do it, and he doesn't want to emphasize his stupidity." After so many daily repetitions, such incongruities on the 1MC give us something to talk about. At oh six thirty daily you should hear the exact same announcement, *"Check the setting of material condition yoke."* Except in the Gulf we set Material Condition Modified Zebra, with hatches secured but for the small scuttles you see in old war movies. "Make reports to *Damage Control Central."*

At zero nine thirty you always hear, *"Sweepers, sweepers, man your brooms. Give the ship a good clean sweepdown forward and aft. Take all sinkable, nonplastic trash to the fantail."* Or, *"The fantail is closed. Hold all trash and garbage on station. The fantail is closed."* And the tag, *"Now, sweepers."*

To break the monotony, the boatswain's mate will speed up the announcement, drag it out dramatically, make it fresh and stimulating, or attempt a quiet and unobtrusive delivery, as if thinking, why wake up night check and tell them the smoking lamp is out from frames 49 to 89 and 163 to 193, second deck and below while handling ordnance.

Chapter Nine

1800 27 JAN 91. God, another Sweets dream. We were home, safe, somewhere far from the Navy and the NIS. He seemed to be astral projecting from a bath, in there washing himself where the light came from, while at the same time his body, roughly scraped and scabbed over, as if he'd been thrown from a car as a child, stood in front of me. I had salved him, peeled his dead skin after the bath and covered it with cream, except he was still in the bath and yet standing before me. (Dreams are always a little chaotic.) Maybe someone else was in the room and we were being quiet. He was holding very still. There were no sounds. Not even breathing. His come hit the roof of my mouth, that thing hanging down like a bell--my epiglottis--like a BB gun shooting a star out of a card at the County Fair, like a softball knocking the doll off a carnival shelf. It woke me up.

I lay there thinking he must be awake a couple of berthings forward of me, at this instant playing with his penis and coming, concentrating on my lips, my mouth, my throat. I'll never ask.

0845 28 JAN 91. The weather has cleared, and CNN has caught clear SLAM shots slapping the sand. But our shop has pretty much burned out on the news. We didn't watch all night long. Instead there was "Like Father Like Son" with Dudley Moore and that young stud Kirk Cameron. And after that, some flick about a couple of sailboat racers after a rich girl. Rob Lowe vindicated himself as a true lover in the end, with multiple butt shots.

I missed the breakfast club. No phone call either. I think I'm getting thinner, eating with Sweets. Because if I don't eat with him I don't eat. I swung by Hangar Control the other night, went in and leaned against the CPO's barber chair.

"I don't think you want to sit in that," the CPO said as he came in behind me.

"Oh, I was just leaning on it," I said like a fool. I went over to the chair beside Sweet Pea as he read some sports pages sent from his grandpa.

"If you guys are gonna lounge around, why don't you go out in the lounge."

We moved to the room with a couch and TV.

"All right," a Yellow Shirt came in loud, "if you don't work here, please leave."

I was accompanied out by a dude who worked next door.

"Just go back and I'll call you," Sweets ordered quickly. But he canceled at 0045.

"That's okay, I can't make it now either. I have a recovery at oh one hundred."

Managing as a gay, bisexual, or sexually ambivalent member in the Navy is a chemistry of superiors having your number and giving a shit, as well as not liking any of the people involved. Like a fire triangle, take any one element and the fire goes out. Frankly, they probably don't give a damn, and like Sweet Pea too much to wrap him up in scandalous accusations.

But the NIS office is directly beneath them, and those guys already have a case file on me, just waiting for me to lick some sailor's ear on this boat.

I keep worrying that a Health and Comfort Inspection of my rack will turn up this diary. But they'd probably want to avoid a reaction of protest among the gay community which already has a militant constituency protesting this war and the President for ignoring gay issues. If they saw a sailor in the Persian Gulf receive a discharge for simply being gay in his literature, this little book might become the *Satanic Verses of the US Navy*. If they failed to suppress it somehow.

Last night in the wee hours our command received a call from COMM, to pick up a Top Secret message. It had to be picked up by the CO, XO, or the Security Manager, an LT. "I guess I'll go get it then," YN1 said. In other words, it was a joke you had to be an LT to get the message. YN1 has TS.

It's been a week since I mailed a dozen letters to the same address bearing excerpts of this diary, and I was paranoid that our government may have routinely opened one, and sent a message to our CO telling him what he already knows. "You've got a fag in your squadron." The thing is, he doesn't give a shit as long as I keep my hands to myself, which I do. He'd rather be strafing.

I wonder where they'd separate me. Probably Treasure Island since the last few guys went there. At least I'd have no Reserve time, no inactive obligated service.

As of 25 January, I completed three of four years of my four year contract, one of the requirements for receiving the GI Bill. Regardless when I get out now, so long as my character of service gets labeled, Honorable, I'll get the ten grand eight hundred for a master's degree.

Right now I could go tell my boss I like dudes, and I'd be out in five days. Out of General Quarters, out of DEFCON One, out of Modified Material Condition Zebra, out of the Combat Zone, out of the Persian Gulf and out of this war. All I would have to do is climb down out of this rack right now, and tell my bigoted chief I have sweet dreams of Sweet Pea. I have the power to waltz out of harm's way. And get a cat shot and a COD ride back to the world. And leave that doll-faced charming little lover-boy, Sweet Pea, suffering in the Gulf.

I haven't told him he's the beneficiary of my military life insurance policy (SGLI). I got the idea from the *USS Iowa* case, where two sailors put each other down as beneficiaries--then they called the one dude a suicidal homicidal homosexual fag, when the gun turret blew. Fifty thousand dollars go to Sweet Pea if I'm KIA. But if I am killed, since he's in the same boat, he'll be in deep water himself. His shit may not stink, but can he walk on water? This would be the part of the world to find out.

A V-3 kid got fired last night for crunching a bird, as a tractor driver in the hangar bay. One A-6 intruded on the nose of another on the aircraft elevator, and bent the nose cone. It was only down for ten minutes, and flew the strike. But his job was gone in sixty seconds. He's a lowly Blue Shirt again. Instead of towing jets around, he totes an air hose blowing pad eyes. Two birds did get scrubbed from a strike on the flight deck in similar fashion last night, however. That wasn't funny at all.

We're getting used to bombing runs, used to the William Tell Overture, tired, and complacent. We think we have it down so we can slide now, cut corners, and soon we'll have a major fuel leak on cat 1 just as it's burning a grease buildup, and ordnance will cook off and sailors will die. If we don't shape up.

This isn't the Captain speaking on the 1MC. I used to sleep under cat 1. And found out that once a month we have a fire on cat 1 as grease builds up inside it until the steam heat ignites it. And we're shooting birds off the cat with live ordnance over an extended period with no time for maintenance. And had a major fuel oil leak on cat 1 two nights ago. Now I can't sleep.

0830 29 JAN 91. I think it's Tuesday. I don't recall if, as we crossed the International Date Line and I reset my watch, I changed the day of the week along with the date. I want to throw it away and get a diver's watch. But first I have to get out of debt. My Visa bill came. I'm paid ahead but still owe $1200.

The war of words in the crisis in the gulf heats up like a missile cooking off. Hussein might use chemical weapons, which Israel says threatens his people and himself. I wonder about the eighty aircraft, sixty bombers, on the ground in Iran. Are they staging an attack against *Ranger*?

"Shouldn't we be at MOP level two, with those jets in Iran?"

"Nah, we know where they all are." A confident response from LT Neil "Waylon" Jennings in the Ready Room. "They can't move. If they did we'd probably go straight to MOP Level Four."

"How long would it take them to hit us if they did move?"

"It would take a day. There's a lot of logistics they'd have to do to get them all organized. I think Iran is planning to confiscate them after the war."

Plenty of time to get to MOP Level Two. I mean, Four.

I took my camcorder down on the hangar deck in the pre-dawn light of unrep. The hangar tungstens were burning (I guess they are tungsten--they're yellow). And the lights of the ship on our starboard side were yellow, just enough light for the grapes to pump fuel through lines across the calm gulf water into *Ranger*. It might have been the *Kansas City*. But several ships unrep us. This one gave the nice view of a helo perched on its afterdeck as I looked up through the wide open elevator doorway.

Sweet Pea and Steve were there. Sweets wore his Blue Shirt and floatcoat with a big EO (elevator operator) on the back, and his Mickey Mouse headset. Tossing the plastic, cup shaped mike across his chest like a pendulum from his earphones, he reminded me of a bored boy waiting to play ball, pitching into his glove. Meanwhile, the working party forklifted empty pallets of bomb containers onto his elevator to be airlifted off the flight deck.

Sweets looked so damn young it was incongruous that he could appear bored with his key role in such a major evolution. Steve danced around in his Yellow Shirt, mugging my lens.

People are making money off the patriotic war back home, selling flags. Here they've suspended the financial advisory messages that tell us how much we got paid, because Gulf message traffic is under Minimize. So if we're on Direct Deposit (DDS), we have no clue to our bank balance. And we're now in tax free status, supposedly getting Hostile Fire Pay on our next check. What the hell, banks are defaulting and the FDIC's going broke. What'll we come home to, bankruptcy?

What if the crooks exploit this terrorist threat against the US, and blow up transaction tracking companies so it takes years to reconstruct a history of American finance? I heard they tried to bomb Wall Street. Say they nix the NYSE, Mormon database and IRS. Could three strategic terrorist bombings throw us in chaos? When the smoke clears, regardless of how they arrived with money, will whoever has quantity be rich because we can't account for quality? Say, "nuke New York" three times fast.

"You are far across the ocean, in a war that's not your own. And while you're winning theirs you're gonna lose the one at home." Larry Norman, founder of Christian rock, warning us about the Vietnam war. Where did he go? Did they chap his lips with a wiretap?

1100 30 JAN 91. Nearly noon, I hit the rack. I spent all morning striking out for Scrapper, trying to find a way to hook him up for the advancement exam. In the shop most of the year, he still hasn't completed his Rate Training Manual. Ten lessons. Dry as it is there can be no excuse for not finishing it in three months. Much less eight, or ten. Promises, counseling sessions, more promises. Even bright moments. He brought the book to work and fessed up that he was not on lesson seven, but only on three. He got serious, and in three weeks got to nine. A month ago. Now he wants to take the exam that comes in March.

We'll have to cross rate him from Airman to Seaman. The Airedale community has no billet for a nondesignated Seaman. The closest is designated Seaman, as in PNSN (sometimes pronounced Penis-In, in a title like Penis-In Graham, as I once had), for Personnelman Seaman. In order for Scrapper, a nondesignated airman, to take an advancement exam in the path of a seaman, we have to make a special request to COMNAVMILPERSCOM (Commander, Naval Military Personnel Command). And that is supposed to be done no later than 90 days before the exam. So it's too late.

But exceptions are being made for Desert Storm participants. NMPC is granting liberal interpretations of requirements, maximum flexibility in administration of exams. "That means if you have to close up your books and go to GQ," PNC explained. "Where was he when I needed him, all last year, when we didn't have anybody, and he was looking out for himself?"

I finally wondered why I was fighting for the guy, since I even gave him a counseling chit advising him to finish the RTM "within five days of pulling out of P.I." He's twenty-five days late.

"I've been busting my ass," he swore.

"That doesn't hold any water with me," said YNCS. "I came into the YN rating out of Deck. I didn't have 'A' school either. My supervisor handed me the *Rate Training Manual* and told me to get it done as soon as possible. I assumed that meant at least within thirty days, or maybe forty-five days. But not whenever I felt like it, sometime next year."

"Why should we do all these things--it's hard," Chief added. "When he doesn't show me that he really wants to be a PN."

Scrapper just wants to walk off the brow with a crow on his shoulder. That's his real motivation. He told me how proud he would be, that he'd written to friends. He didn't really care to be a PN. But, neither do I. I got stuck in this rating by a DIS agent and a Classifier at Bootcamp. I failed a reliability test for the Intelligence Specialist rating, so it was the no security clearance needing PN way or the highway. I gave away my truck.

I stuck around the office and cut two hours out of my diary and sleep for nothing, drafting a message for a kid who's inner motivation could really be nothing more than keeping off a chock and chain gang--where he could be making flight deck pay.

They must be about to down the jet above me, because it's been turning at full burn on the cat for nearly a minute. If they turn for more than thirty seconds a Trouble Shooter usually wheels it off the cat. It finally stopped. It was just a high power turn. They're not even in a launch cycle. I don't know anything about the flight deck.

We have so many people coming that they're threatening to start "hot racking" us like they do in subs, where you have more guys than racks and you share your rack with a shipmate. Give me Sweet Pea, give me Ricky. Give me a baby or give me nobody. I'm a second class petty officer. E3 and below shall hotrack before they get to E4, much less E5. I hope.

Another dude is finally taking Buck's rack. Three weeks were long enough staring at that empty mattress. We still get ripples of his death, like what to do with his Leave and Earnings Statement, and occasional junk mail. Today Doc Robson called for PNC with some questions about Buck. "His medical and dental records came back from Subic and we have to reconstruct an overseas death certificate. So I just need to know his religious preference, marital status and his next of kin address."

"Well, I can tell you that he's Presbyterian. And his mother's from South Carolina."

"Are you sure?"

"Robby, he was born November 23. I was born November 25. His mother lives in Anderson, South Carolina. I was born in Anderson, South Carolina.

He's Presbyterian. I'm Presbyterian. And his rack was opposite mine."

"Jeez."

I looked on the outgoing message board for the letter from the skipper to all hands. He had invited letters, to express ourselves, or to comfort Buck's mom. I read Robby the address.

"Presbyterian," he said. "Is that Protestant?"

0330 31 JAN 91. The nicest thing about war is they start sending enough people to do the job. I moved Scrapper to the noon to midnight shift, and scheduled this PNSN fresh out of "A" school here through the wee hours.

I thought I'd refresh the PNSN on Standard Transfer Orders, since they probably glossed over them at the school in Meridian, Mississippi. It kills me they have Navy schools so far inland.

"I've never seen that form before in my life."

"What was your class standing?"

"Three."

The way I learned STO's was PNC stuck a few photocopied pages in my box, with the headers and footers trimmed off, and told me to find out where he got them as I finished the job. It took all night but I have it down now. I hadn't touched STO's in two weeks, and still did one tonight in thirty minutes.

A kid came up to me--now I know we've been at sea. He asked me to edit his letter to Miss January from an Operation Desert Shield calendar. "I just don't want to look stupid, ya know?" They call him Opey from Mayberry. He has bright red hair and a Texas drawl.

Superman is addressing the General Assembly of the United Nations. Just what we need on board *Ranger*. He's going to rid the planet of all nuclear weapons. This must be Superman I. He hurls them all in a net toward the sun.

"That would make a big enough explosion to take out the sun," says my new PNSN. He sounds frighteningly serious.

Meanwhile, *Ranger* continues running bombing missions on port facilities, coastal silkworm missile sites and patrol boats, dropping precision laser and cluster bombs. The William Tell Overture reigns over the 1MC, followed by our Captain's voice: "On *Ranger*, once again leaping out into the air. We've got a strike that's on its way out right now, with the XO of VA 155 going after a couple of silkworm sites out in the southwestern portion of Kuwait.

"After they finish nailing those two with laser guided bombs, they're gonna go up to an area that we've sighted with patrol boats. We're gonna go after them based on the imagery that we saw there this afternoon.

"There's been a significant damage done to the Iraqi Navy today, to start off with a couple of large landing craft, a couple of patrol boats, all of it sortied out of Iraq." He went on listing them in Naval jargon that officers and technicians, and maybe a few lifer dogs would understand, as if by make and model, TNC45, OSA and other odd words. "We're not sure where they were going and for what purpose, perhaps to a degree going over to Iran for refuge. But they were caught out in open waters today by aircraft from *Rosy* (*USS*

Theodore Roosevelt), *Midway*, and our own *Ranger*. And we've taken out a significant amount of the Iraqi Navy that existed before today.

"So, as it stands now, we're gonna go after the last couple of boats that we've found in imagery, and probably within the next two or three days we can say that there's little if any left of the Iraqi Navy. That's all."

PNSN reads what you should do if you're a prisoner of war.

"You're supposed to try to escape. It's a written law. I want to be a prisoner of war."

"Be careful what you pray for. They'd probably beat the shit out of you and slam you down into a target."

Sweet Pea went to day check. Gone as of last night (tonight if you consider 0440 night). Day check starts at 0715 muster, and I'm sure there's a phone in his berthing. Maybe I'll find out if he really wants to catch me for breakfast. I wouldn't blame him for sleeping to the last minute. He's so refined--raised by his mother. I spent our last leisure together watching him play a baseball video. He couldn't win but gave a good try. Then went to another game, a couple of fighters. "I've got to take out my frustration." I wondered if he were frustrated about losing contact as the system split us up.

He seemed to lean into me once or twice, but I kept hearing his echo from that day walking in the passageway, "stop rubbing up against me--I'll beat your ass." So I didn't melt into him. I can't imagine him dotting my eye, but why kid yourself about confusion. So he was confused a little about his affection; he needed to touch and be touched. Doesn't make him homosexual.

0800 31 JAN 91. Have I given the impression that so far this is a pleasure cruise? Having grown up in a family with seven kids, I've always had a fascination with the germination and mysterious course of argument. I was in the middle, number five, and had the most objective viewpoint toward the struggles of growing up. We had one girl, six boys. Had she been the youngest it might have been right to spoil her. But there was Mike, the littlest, and my sister seemed to regret him from birth. He seemed to become her chief scapegoat, which I resented. And I became her constant challenge. In my opinion, one can never quite recover from one's family. Same with this ship. I have trouble writing about arguments that thrive here in the cramped quarters of *Ranger*--the actual, painful yelling matches I get into with PNC, and his turn the Personnel Department into a smoking lounge partners, and the fuck flick fiend, two-inch cigarette ash hanging, close-up TV watching masturbator of the Command Master Chief who spends his work hours cataloging a pornographic film library for those who call nightly to borrow them. "They don't do anything for me," he said in a dry, tired voice. "I need a nice, warm living room with a fire in the fireplace, and a bottle of wine."

Parting is such sweet sorrow. I keep going over how to get Sweet Pea to stick with me but it will never happen. He gets out this September. What would he do between then and when I get out (January 92) if he moved in with me? Work at a gas station, or a paint store? Do clean-up in a detailing garage? How about going to San Diego State University? To major in Drama? "You should go to college and study acting," I told him at our last supper. "You have good memorization skills."

He didn't say anything back.

I didn't rave on about his baby blue looks or his Growing Pains voice. I haven't shown him any credibility. So what if some bald-headed Personnelman who claims to be a writer thinks he's gorgeous and enjoys his voice? Does that make him a movie star? I'm outa my mind.

The three of us--Sweet Pea, Steve and I--walked across the hangar bay, speaking of women. "With his face he can get anything he wants from girls."

"Yeah, but they can tell he doesn't want them."

I don't know where the topic came from, or went. In fact, it died after my remark. But Sweet Pea didn't dispute it. Dean told me Sweet Pea always tries to set him up with girls he should date himself. And Sweet Pea admitted he never had a girlfriend.

I think of photos I've seen of cherubs adorning the walls of Rock Hudson's home, bronzed nymph boys peeping eternally over his fence. Did he make love with James Dean? Is that why the young star fatally crashed in Mendocino, California? Did Jimmy spill his guts to a loud mouthed friend, fling out the truth and flop his career, then see no other exit than suicidal glory? Look at what happened to Jerry Lee Lewis for marrying a young girl in America. Who would keep the wolves away from our door? There may always be West Hollywood Invaders, Castro Street Killers, red neck fag bashers and God righteous murderer gangs who can't stand the sound of one sex kissing. Half of them will beat their meat to a lesbian video, a fourth will be homosexuals hiding in the cloak of homophobia, the rest are scared to death to slide a finger up their ass. Happily married heterosexuals? They'll just worry about their kids.

Many people still believe the big lie that homosexuality is unnatural. What is nature? It is Earth. Human inhabitants are controlled by forces of nature. If we grow where there is no food, water or shelter, if too many share finite resources, we'll die in droves like deer. Homosexuality will eventually save us.

Naturally, I'd be writing this from a combat zone. What if it comes to a split, one side or the other, either accept faggots as the cure for overpopulation, or accept war as how to trim the fat and shake the tree? Wouldn't you all just rather die than get buttfucked? As if that's what it's about. But truthfully, that age old primal lust for sacrificial bloodletting runs deep in human veins. Look at the percent of GNP that still goes into metals like the piece I'm riding.

0945 01FEB91. Entering our third month already. Gulf War: Day 15, as they say on CNN. A couple of strikes a night, still no lost planes since that first A-6. Rumors differ on that: some put the two pilot and the bombardier/navigator behind enemy lines, talking to *Ranger* on a hand-held radio, one at least in the custody of a SEAL team, trying to sneak back to

Kuwait. Others say that, since none of the three emergency beepers were on guard--in the plane, in the chair, and on the body--they both must have died when they got hit.

KRAN TV aired footage of the luckiest man in Iraq, crossing a bridge by car seconds before a laser guided bomb blew the hell out of it. In a movie it would have been hilarious.

"*The following is a test of the General, Chemical and Collision Alarms from the pilot house. The general alarm*: tone, tone, tone, beep. *The chemical alarm*: Beee-beee-beeep. *The collision alarm* d-d-d-p, d-d-d-p, d-d-d-p. *Test complete, regard all further alarms.*"

I finished chow and started walking back when who should I see by himself. I came up from behind and massaged his shoulders in front of who cares. "You're not eating alone," I said.

"Get something to eat."

"I already ate." I sat down on the opposite corner. He sounded tired. I couldn't rub elbows, but I stared at him. "I see you're having your syrup and salsa." Pancakes and syrup, dipped in salsa. This is what extended deployment will do to you.

"How do you like eating breakfast at breakfast time?"

"I like it. I really like getting a good night's sleep, and not having the lights turned on and people knocking around and watching the TV and laughing and yelling at each other all day."

"You're in the middle of the berthing at least. I have to contend with a door slamming all the time. And some dude coming through the berthing. I got woke up every two hours yesterday."

For once, Sweet Pea wasn't in a rush.

"Now you can call me whenever you wake up and go to chow, from your berthing, if you want to."

"If the phone is working."

I let it drop. The last time I prodded him to call me, he said he'd been busy. I flashed back to high school when I timed it out to call Billy just as he got off the bus, fifteen minutes after he passed my house, and how he always said he had to hang up to go to the bathroom, which was probably true, but I always took as a personal slight.

"How did you know I got switched to days?"

"Let's see, how many people told me? Steve, and Dean. And I knew you were gonna go." I enjoyed flattering him about his popularity.

He picked up his tray finally and nodded, and I followed him out like a loyal pup. A guy I knew vaguely had sat down beside us and tried to engage our conversation, directing a few lines to me. But I blew him off for the precious quiet time alone with my best buddy on the boat. He was still trying to talk to me as we left, as I was following Sweet Pea, and I craned my neck around to politely terminate the talk, but kept moving because I feared Sweets might ditch me if I didn't keep up.

I shadowed Sweets to the hangar deck, forward on an errand to the soda machines in the game room, back to the hangar deck to deliver seven-ups to a couple of his friends in silver crash crew uniforms, then back to the 03 level under the flight deck where he finally got rid of me at the V-3 coop. I'd have followed him in if invited, but felt certain relief in saying goodbye. With perhaps the exception of the night I did up his rack, there are no visitors allowed in his berthing. "Well, I'm gonna go hang out for a while." He turned at the door and offered a hand, with long, skinny fingers.

"It was fun being your shadow," I lied. I really felt like a dumb subordinate keeping two steps back, especially in narrow passageways, and sensed that even though he liked the attention, he was bothered. I walked away feeling the dull, familiar sting between my legs.

At sea it's not abnormal if guys couple up--not all of us but some--where one is a fetching bitch pup. That's why boys come home and sometimes introduce their shipmates with a grin, "he was my sea bitch."

"Here's something I want you to read." I shoved a poem into his hand, from T. S. Elliot's *The Wasteland and Other Poems*.

"What is it?"

"Oh, it's a classic."

The title wasn't on the page, and I didn't want to tell him it was "The Love Song of J. Alfred Prufrock." But it had those lines about a balding, fretting romantic who could never compete with a stud like Michelangelo. I was only pining for a sympathy fuck. It wouldn't be the first.

0745 2 FEB 91. Scrapper comes in noon to midnight, and the PNSN has it now until then with PNC, whenever he comes in. They had a 737 crash on CNN, at LAX, a US Air coming in that would go on to SFO, which is the leg I took all through my murder trial in 1984, back and forth from home and court. And still take, the same leg I was on when I started writing this book on a laptop, except I was returning to LAX from SFO. This isn't the first time PSA/US Air has gone down around LA. I should buy good highway cruiser when I catch up on my bills.

The newscasters haven't got around to speculating yet if it were sabotage or a political bombing, or a kamikaze crash by the other plane involved. It's odd how they hypothesize, like Larry King with the FBI director last night bracing for terrorist acts in the USA; then, with this LAX disaster, fail to mention the B (Bomb) or T (Terror) words.

Three new check-ins, Selected Reservists, not happy campers. "Yeah, I was at my job and the phone rang. My boss had been talking about it, what if they called. And like everybody else, I thought, 'it won't happen to me.' I thought he was jokin' at first but he was pretty bummed. I was a computer operator." Some of these guys seem to roll off a Kansas wheat field to the flight deck. They come from everywhere. "Welcome to the war zone," I hardly fathom it isn't a joke.

I found Steve's half of the breakfast club at 0600. He and some other dude were setting records of cereal servings again, as Sweets walked up with sleep in his eyes. "He will do anything you want sexually for a price. Right Sweet Pea?"

"Right."

"He didn't hear me. Sweets, do you know what you just admitted to?"

"What did I admit to?"

"I said you'd do anything sexually for the right price."

"Yep."

"Like let's see, tongue my asshole, give me a really good ream job."

Sweets didn't even blink, just grinned. It makes me wonder.

"If you were camping," I began. But everyone had heard it, and their laughter made it clear that the joke was told with only that much said, so I left it. The joke: if you went camping and woke up naked with an empty jar of vaseline beside you, would you tell anyone? No. Do you want to go camping?

"Bob, if you went to your rack and fell asleep, and someone came to your rack and woke you up and gave you a great blow job and swallowed your come and licked your ass and never said a word and went away, would you tell?"

"Hell no." It was great to say in front of Sweets. I knew he'd never come to my rack. But who knows if I may get that pad on the beach again, and have him over. It's just sailor talk.

"Well, come to my rack at eight-thirty."

Steve's joke was arousing and everyone agreed: why tell.

"If it works, don't fix it."

Sweet Pea led us to the scullery, where we exited against traffic. He gave me a slap on the biceps meaning "see ya later," a clean break that solved my problem, how I would part once I'd seen him this morning.

I could melt all over him at any time, like a shadow or like glue. But it's better in private. Besides, sitting at a table nearby was a dude from the Ship's Investigations office who took the report when I was called a fag and beaten by the *Ranger* thugs who broke my tooth. Was he keeping me under surveillance, and wasn't this the second or third time I've seen him nearby as we ate? And did this have anything to do with that top secret message for the skipper that came a week after I sent those excerpts through the mail? With the PN3 on our projected gains list to replace me, should I get planned for elimination? Does my heart have the courage for the changing of the guard?

My name didn't even come up in this month's discussion for SOM (Sailor Of the Month). Chief didn't even make the meeting. I knew it would be feast or famine, make it once in my career, last month, or never. That boat has passed. We're back to our family members, and Graham is getting out.

Our pay is so fucked up. They didn't stop our COMRATS ($180 per month "commuted rations" paid in cash instead of free food at the galley) when they were supposed to, so I've been overpaid and now they're pulling it out of my check beginning in March, sixty bucks a month. I don't think they've started our sea pay ($60 a month). I don't get flight deck pay, family separation allowance or BAQ with dependent or married VHA, so they didn't fuck that up on me. Hostile Fire Pay is supposedly retroactive to 1 January, depending on the Filipino interpretation of the US executive order. It hasn't kicked in. And there's that tax free status for being in the combat zone, effective back to 17 January, but it doesn't apply to FICA and may not apply to certain items such as Lump Sum Leave Sellback, once again subject to interpretation by the non-US citizen broken English branch of our American Navy. The DDS advisory message was wrong--people were told they got $80 vice $800. And that was gonna be suspended entirely because of worldwide "minimize" on message traffic, until too many service members raised hell. Last: taxes owed to the US government now are not due, nor is filing due, 'til 180 days after we return. Does that apply to state tax returns? Nobody knows.

Advancement exams come in March. I'm not up for E6 for the rest of my enlistment, and that's fine with me. If I were, I'd be taking it March 12, another year to the date Tony died. That would be seven years ago. Have I recovered? Was it worse than marines in the desert have now? Combat is combat, whether on LA streets or SA sand. What's that got to do with exams?

1600 2 FEB 91. Knock bang bump.

"Hey Countrytime," I leaned out of the rack. "Can't you clean the coop without slamming the racks? All that knockin' around is wakin' me up."

"Well I've gotta sweep."

"You want me to come down and show you how to sweep without hitting the racks?"

"You want to?"

"Man, it's 1600. I planned to sleep until 1830, and you just took two and a half hours from me. Now I've gotta try to get it back. You do it every fuckin' day. I can't take this every fuckin' day, man. Have a heart and think about the people sleeping."

"Arright."

2200 2 FEB 91. Chased out of the office by Preventive Medicine who came to spray for the fruity little flies that mysteriously arrived as we pulled into the Gulf. Of course, Chief was blaming it on my plants, retaliating for my complaints against his smoking--a way to hurt me back. I bought the plants at NAS North Island, for about twenty bucks. Chief made me move them to the space outside our shop a couple of weeks ago, then had Scrapper throw over the last plant a few days ago. But we still have flies. It was like that film, "Mister Roberts," when they got rid of the skipper's palm. I guess all the smokers got a laugh, heh heh.

When I came in tonight I had a bad feeling. I didn't even want to walk down the ladder. Chief's been trying to quit smoking--it makes him a worse asshole than he naturally is. My instinct was right--he started chewing me out.

"Did you have the PNSN type an STO (standard transfer order) for Lakers?" He had a way of asking a question so stupid that I couldn't tell if it was his language barrier or meanness. "Let me see the package."

I gave him the manila folder with the member's Transfer Information Sheet (TIS) filled out. "When I found the TIS in my basket with no explanation, I had to assume that I needed to type the STO. The Transman says to use PCS (Permanent Change of Station) accounting data from these." I pointed to the transfer orders stapled to the TIS.

"I understand," he began to soften his voice. "You were trying to help out. But whenever we receive one of these (NMPC order), we use a cover letter instead of an STO."

I'm a second class, I've been a Personnelman in the Navy for three years. I have done maybe two STO's in my tour, separations from overseas to CONUS. This is my first PCS transfer.

"Also, I want to talk to you."

Now what--a formal chat. An informal counseling session. I grabbed a pad of paper and pulled up a chair.

"Mister Malynn has heard some complaints about your customer service."

My jaw dropped as I recalled the grateful praise from AO3 White the night before, after I helped him figure out how much accrued leave (paid vacation) he could sell back to the Navy. "My customer service?"

"That's right. There have been some complaints that you have been telling people you will take care of things, and then you don't do anything."

"Nobody has said anything to me about it. Can you give me any specific example of what I might be doing wrong, so I can be more careful?"

"I don't know. It's just what he said."

I asked Hensley, who runs the First Lieutenant division.

"No, I haven't heard anything bad about you. And I work around everyone in the berthing."

I asked AO3 Wise.

"Well, you see. If I had a problem with somebody's service, I'm the type of guy, I'm a man, you see. I wouldn't go tellin' somebody else about a problem I had with you. I'd come talk to you about it straight up."

Later the PERS-O walked in to smoke a few cigarettes and play chess with the chief. "Hey, sir. What's the story?"

"Well, I've had a few times when I'd ask you to do something and your attitude has been kind of like, 'well, I'll try to get to it.' About like you were kidding around."

"Oh, then it's your own complaint?"

"Yeah, but then I heard it from a couple other people, and how you got pissed off because somebody took down your NO SMOKING sign. We all have to work together to make things operate smoothly around here. I don't have any problem about your performance. That's A-OK. I mean this isn't a counseling or anything. I just think maybe you've been a little too glib sometimes."

"Oh, okay. Well, I just don't want to under-react, but I don't want to overreact either, when I hear about my quality of service."

I was just told by a shipmate that our DK2 had three letters turned in to his Division Officer recommending an Executive Officer Inquiry for his inept handling of pay. I hoped they were confusing him with me, and thought if it wasn't that then perhaps it was a First Lieutenant guy lashing back at me for telling him to be quiet in the berthing. The whole thing reeked of vengeance.

Later, Scrapper told me the real story. "Oh, man. The whole thing was about smoking. They're all pissed of because they can't come down here and play chess and smoke."

The Navy and Congress will officially endorse my right to stop the smokers, no matter who they are and what their rank, just like the Surgeon General was able to force tobacco companies to write warnings on cigarette packs. So when the local chain of command tacitly endorses this health hazard, it becomes a very political item and they fuck you over and ignore your complaint with finesse, eloquence, dexterity and tenacity. It's becoming a battle of age and treachery, versus youth and skill.

Like the Command Master Chief glibly said last night, a cigarette burning off his bottom lip, "fuck you. If you don't like it, go TAD." (Temporary Additional Duty back to the mess decks, for instance).

And like the PNC told me, "since you don't want us to smoke, I want all those things out of here." He waved his hand at the VCR, portable tape recorder, and mikes I had set up to record off CNN and the 1MC for the book and plays and movies I might produce in the future--all my means of gathering our history of the war.

Chief backed off, lowered his voice and changed the subject to the shift turnover. Still, you could never know when he might snap again later, and yell, "I thought I told you get those things out of here!" I left it all in place, thus left him with ammunition, emotionally preparing myself for a future tantrum.

0800 3 FEB 91. Out of the mouth of a babe. I was lucky enough to catch the breakfast club, Sweet Pea and Dean hiding by the aft galley office. Dean had seen me as he came in past the scullery with Sweets. I was sitting with Ricky, the flight deck blue shirt. Dean made a dumb face. I had two empty seats at the table (Rick was at the next table), and wondered if I could hold it until they got there; then I saw Sweets get a carton of milk and go back aft, so evidently Dean didn't even tell him I was there. I guessed he wanted Sweet Pea to himself. I couldn't blame him, so I sat with Ricky and told him he should strike for PN or YN if he wanted a skate office job that would give him clean hands. "Do you type?"

"Oh, a little. I can type about forty words a minute."

I thought about my PNSN who can type 20, and Scrapper, maybe the same. And this little baby working 16 hours a day chocking F-14s could be sitting on his butt.

"Are you up for the exam?"

"Not 'til September. I could have been, but I didn't do my BMR."

"So you're still an E2?"

He nodded, weary. His face was clean and fresh but his jersey and greens looked like the Tin Man in need of an oil change. He would need nine months as an E3 before he could take the E4 exam, and couldn't be advanced to E3 until he turned in his Basic Military Requirements.

"After I hit the end of my enlistment, I'm gone."

"When's that?"

"June of '93."

"Ninety-three?" The way he talked I thought he'd say this summer. "Well then you might as well strike for something and get out of the blue hole."

I invited him to stop by my shop, to have a look at an Administrative office and talk to the PNSN and some of the YNs.

"I might stop by."

"You know where it is, just down that ladder off the green mat."

I left him to catch up with Sweets and Dean, and grabbed a glass of grapefruit juice without ice (there's never juice and ice on the same side of the galley together) just to keep the mess deck master-at-arms off my back for sitting at a table without being a diner.

They had Fruit Loops, a big box all their own. Fanatics about cereal, they run back and forth across the galley to the two salad bar stations where the cereal is put out, linger in the vicinity on watch for the food service attendant, then make mad dives for the Frosted Flakes, Frosted Mini-Wheats, and the Nut & Honey boxes. There are only six of each to a carton, and you'd better be quick to compete with the breakfast club. Now, however, they were perfectly contented carrying a large box of care package Fruit Loops under one arm from the second deck up four ladders to their coop. This morning Sweet Pea used the escalator. I followed him to the top where he turned left (forward), and I turned aft to cut through 81-Man and head back to my shop. We shook hands, and something made me grab his hand with both of mine. When we let go he held on a little and I held on a little and some of those other fucking shipmates walking around may have noticed that we really seemed to like each other a lot. I don't know what it means, because the Navy doesn't allow you to talk about it.

"You're just a split-tail with a dick," Dean called me. The feisty bastard. Maybe he's right.

"Hey, I never cut you down." I hoped Sweet Pea heard my nondenial.

"What, are you tryin' to make me feel guilty?"

"I'm just telling you how I feel."

The shock of this breakfast tryst was Sweets calling Dean a cockbiter. "This cockbiter...." I didn't even hear the rest of his sentence because I was so stunned by that word coming out of such a sheepish face. Is he a wolf? Why did he tell me not to rub against him in the passageway before? Is it make believe, as in make them believe what you want? Or is he still getting to know me, since only yesterday Steve brought out the sexual notions. Is he just hunkering down in the closet?

Hunkering down is what the Iraqi Republican Guard is doing right now. During the night we sent 20 airplanes on a bombing mission with a total of thirty thousand oversized grenades, to provide air interdiction for ground troops moving in. I heard we lost two Intruders and an A-10, which is a little bit larger and I think has more crewmen. None of the losses were from *Ranger*. Meanwhile, as if by surprise, trouble is brewing in Beirut. Hussein has kept stirring up the PLO until they're starting to make their back door move on Israel, creating another front. And they've created that other oil spill. And we're seeing wounded little boys on TV, begging the morality question. We, of course, have countered with news items of Hussein summarily executing children along with men. We're all dupes, but I wonder if the PLO will ever regret riding on the band wagon with Saddam.

I had the burn run last night, POIC (Petty Officer In Charge). A man without a security clearance, in charge of destroying the classified documents of a forward command. This points out the obvious--I didn't need a clearance to become a Journalist, and may as well have been an Intelligence Specialist as they guaranteed me in the first place.

They knew about the murder charge at the MEPS (Military Enlisted Processing Station) and let me in. But a DIS (Defense Investigative Service) agent, doing his fine job of probing me for my Privacy Act information about the arrest that led to my acquittal of murdering a gangster in 1985, noted "two homosexual encounters as an adult" and translated, he's a flamer we can't have onboard *Ranger* with 5,099 real men for six straight months. Legal hold, psych eval, investigation. I still got in.

Down the road the Skipper of world famous fighting Wolfpack decided to whine. He must have attempted to get me a clearance so I could stand PN/YN duty watches. He was probably rebuffed in Washington, since the DIS agent made it clear that his buddies in D.C. "think the same way." Like the KKK. "I'm concerned about the level of disclosure," my skipper said. His personal copy of the DIS report reflected that I hadn't claimed knowing forty or fifty other guys intimately prior to enlistment. But I had said I fucked two different males over the course of two years around age 25. Clearly not a young boy's virgin experimentation. Nor had I boasted of conquering females.

"Did you fuck a dog? Did you screw women in the ass? Did you suck a child's cock? Did you fuck sheep?" That interview convinced me I would never want to work for the DIS. Imagine filling a semester learning interview techniques of a groveling pervert.

None of his questions dealt with functioning for weeks and months in a gulf war combat zone at GQ with an exocet at 20 miles inbound.

"GET MBR TO DO TC AND SIGN 3057 SO WE CAN FWD HIS PFR TO DK2." This is a note I left for day check. It translates: *get the* (newly arrived) *service member to fill out a travel claim and certify that his family depends on his pay, so we can forward his personal financial record to the disbursing clerk.*

0915 4 FEB 91. We're alongside the *Kansas City*, somewhere in the gulf, taking on more bombs and components for building ordnance. The component cases, haze gray, have an eerie shape and coincidental size of a casket, dozens stacked between the number two and three arresting wires.

The view from the canopies of the two Alert Five fighters on Cat Four must be at once inspiring and foreboding to the aircrew, modeling new desert hats and sand-yellow flightsuits, as Helos hover over my rack on the sheet metal flight deck, which I hope some Intruder doesn't rupture like a can opener as my ass is in the rack and he's limping home, riddled by AAA and bleeding.

They've changed the configuration for the F-14's--at least our squadron. We're carrying four Sparrows and four Sidewinders, instead of three and two. I'd want a loaded clip out there, too.

We now have nine Selected Reservists, including that happy camper AO3 Stout, who used to be with us and thought he was out. He'll probably go home when we all do.

A PN3 reservist came aboard yesterday. He just made PN3 as he entered the Reserves, and it's been one weekend a month ever since. He admits he knows Jack Shit. He's another smoker, too. "I'm trying to quit." They always say. Fortunately, PNC put him on days. "Well, try quitting around six o'clock, so the last hour before I come on there'll be one less cigarette burning, okay?"

I even let the guy use my coffee cup, which will take on brown stains now and stink like an ashtray. I told him the cups are five bucks from the PAO, complete with red wolfie head and jet fighter silhouette on white. And spill-resistant lid. Why did he turn around and take me up on the offer of using my cup? Was he lazy or broke? Should I have asked if he needed any money for a couple of days? At least with him and the PNSN and Scrapper working under me, I can try to relax. Last night the boss and the PERS-O came down at midnight and set up the chess set. "I'm going to the gym. I'm gonna go work out."

Chief muttered something, but didn't really give a shit because he was so much more interested in the sudden pleasure of me not being there to rag on him for smoking. "You've got enough travel claims to last a while," I told the PNSN. "I'll be back in a couple of hours."

I went to my rack, and changed into a pair of black US Navy Diver sweatpants that I was issued at Consolidated Divers Unit, Naval Station 32nd Street, where I was a PNSN for a month before NMPC discovered CDU had no billet for PNs. I pulled off my white jersey and went to the gym in the white tee-shirt with the second class crow across the left tit, wolfie over the right tit. One of ten tee-shirts I ruined during a week that we were authorized to wear them in the Indian Ocean.

I popped in and out of Maintenance Control before anyone could say "get a job" or "what are your hours" or any other crap, as loving shipmates always do. But I had to get some ear plugs, the little yellow sponge types, because they were turning a jet in Hangar Bay Two. The gym is built over the aft end of that bay, like an open balcony.

I went straight to the sit-up board and raised it up so my feet were at maximum elevation, then did crunches. I used my arms as extra weight by stretching them over my head, bringing them together then apart, weaving them over and under each other across my chest, and winding them in horizontal circles. It seemed almost spiritual, zen like, reminiscent of Tai Chi. But it seemed to work. I could feel the edges of my belly hurting, hardening. I've got a skinny stomach for being 34, and I'm proud of it and intend to keep it that way. Not a fucking toothpick, 150 pounds at 68 inches. I have slender shoulders and a "gorgeous ass," or so Amy said back when I was "the one." Green Army pants have a nice cut around the butt, if you don't wear briefs.

That's one thing I like about the arduous life at sea--if you're not far out of shape, it tones you up just getting from one place to the other for six months. Up and down ladders, always going back two or three times to see the same fucker who blew you off the last time, hoping he'll get it straight this time, carrying shit that on the beach some service rep would come get from you, and just walking to the shower over seven sets of knee-knockers about the height of hurdles. You can get in shape without trying, if you don't pig out in the galley--like the fat shippies do.

I hit the thing you pull down, same effect as pull-ups only it comes down to you. I didn't have a macho weight lifting buff for a partner who could name all the terms. In fact, I was on a solo workout. I did several reps of 15, then hit the Lifecycle on a hill for 18 minutes at level three. My first workout since we left San Diego. At least I broke a sweat.

I walked back into PERS and "Twins" was on. "Danny DeVito Junior," said YN1. Another hapless, helpless crack at my need for a transplant.

I must be getting restless. How long have we been out here? We left 8 December, now it's February: two months. I wanted to blow some cash on a camera, to get some shots of this reality for my diary. Nothing incriminating, hopefully. What about pictures of Sweat Pea? I'll have to see. I want to put some in the middle of the book, like you check out a book in the store and it's more fun with photos if it's nonfiction (in this case, semi-fiction, depending on when it's incriminating). They don't have real 35mm cameras, just glorified snapshots for a hundred and fifty bucks.

I went to the Ship's Walk-In store this morning, after stopping by the Sales Office for check approval. They want your name, rate, division, ID card number, date of issue, EAOS, and phone extension on the check. You can't be on the bad check list, of course. As I got to the store the guy was just pulling the iron gate across, closing. My usual good timing. It turned out they were stocking the Oil of Oman perfume, three dollars a bottle, which they brought on board yesterday. They don't open until eleven, when I should be counting sheep.

A kid who worked with me on the forward mess deck as a night check red shirt walked up as I loitered around the store window looking at cameras. He just bought a used real camera. "Why spend a hundred bucks on something you don't want?" I guess he woke me up and saved me some dough.

Now I figure I'll hit up AZ3 Warner, the photo nut who by all rights should have come into the Navy as a JO, but for some stupid reason got classified Aviation Maintenance Administration clerk, a job he hates and for which he has no aptitude. And they don't like him in the shop. So guess where he is now? Forward mess decks, TAD, red shirt. He's in charge. And now he wants to hang his photos on the bulkheads.

I came to check number 251 and a renewal notice, where they offer the opportunity to change address. It gradually occurred to me, between getting that check approved and returning to my rack to put it away, I may not need another 250 with a Miramar address. What will I do? Where will I go? At the bottom again. Thirty-five and starting over. Middle age crisis. What about the economy? What are unemployment statistics? If I get out, I'll be too old to get back in.

GI Bill. Ten thousand eight hundred. Grad school, Film and script writing. UCLA. Get my application out. See if Dave needs a roommate. Is there a better neighborhood? Can I steer clear of Hollywood and still pursue show biz?

Chapter Ten

0900 6 FEB 91. Airman Caguiat lays in his bottom rack, with a chess game on the floor before him, playing another dude. Cag was the *USS Ranger* chess champion last cruise. He is shushed for loud laughter. YN3 Black Thing hangs his head in the TV lounge. Tired, stressed over the coming exam, afraid of turning forty as a YN3 with five mouths to feed. If he doesn't make second, high-year tenure will force him out of the Navy. "Who's gonna hire someone forty years old? I need some help, man. I got ten years and I'm lookin' at retirement. But I got to make second. If I can make second it's smooth sailin' from there on out. But I got to make it this test. And I'm still waitin' on the manual so I can study." His YN3&2, the rate training manual, is somewhere in the mail.

I thought about myself turning 34 last November. Fat chance of me staying in. In fact, when I came in this morning somebody had put a copy of the MILPERSMAN article on "separation: convenience of the government, personality disorder" in PNC's basket. Natural paranoia allowed thoughts of the NIS picking up a hardcopy of the diary I mailed to the states for safekeeping, to survive in case I don't, which would prove my undoing in the classic tragicomedy. Sifting mail for classified leaks, they'd find my sultry fantasies, and come screaming like a lumberjack.

The CMC milled around early this morning and stared at my application to the Library of Congress with check attached and a small envelope for the 3.5" disk. He leaned over, studied, then suddenly walked out. If he wants to backdoor me, he could be headed for the NIS office. I wanted to follow, but looked up the address to UCLA for grad students and drafted a letter instead.

I knew what was going down inside Western, when dearest Amy's daddy let me drown. So these guys--you guys who intercept these words--can have your saliva. Be slick and know that I don't respect you anymore than you respect me. And I don't wonder how you live with yourselves as you do your jobs of turning the Graham's of America over to the gatekeepers of the American way. Truth will out, and all of this will be shouted from some rooftop where the scud missiles and air raid sirens and Rock-Eye bomblets and laser guided warheads will compete for God's attention.

We passed an oil platform yesterday as I was videotaping Sweet Pea operating his elevator. We were close enough to see that it was exactly the shape that we have seen bombed on CNN. "Watch out for bullets. You're exposed here, you know."

"They can't get close to us."

"Well, don't say 'hi' to any passing boats."

One of the AT's has some kind of electronic world map, and they punched in our coordinates, latitude and longitude, then input the same of Kuwait City, and ZOOT! We are 278 miles from downtown.

They're mostly pretty smart in the AT shop. But to give you an exception,

I heard the following: "What day is it?"

"The first. It comes right after the thirty-first."

"I said day, not date."

"Oh, well it's Friday."

"Anyway, there are some months that have thirty-two days."

"There's no months that have thirty-two days."

"What about leap year?"

About every four hours we've run battlefield interdiction raids, for several days now, on field artillery positions in the Kuwaiti Killbox. Meanwhile, CNN says the President is considering future use of carrier based bombers for battlefield interdiction. They must be caulking the press pool. KRAN TV, in a nightly intelligence brief, presented a locally produced motion picture, recorded by the Bombardier/Navigator (BN) of an A-6 Intruder on a recent raid, that showed some men who were dubbed "the eight unluckiest men in Iraq." The BN watched them run from a truck and dive into a trench as he guided a Rock-Eye down through the heavens. He calmly adjusted the laser to follow them, and seconds later peppered the trench with nine hundred bomblets, each larger than a grenade.

I passed by an A-6 in the hangar bay last night that had eighteen camel stencils. And of course, they have their motto, "I'd fly 10,000 miles to smoke a camel." We still play the William Tell Overture for every strike, every raid, every mini-sortie. But we've narrowed the play-list to the CHR (Contemporary Hit Radio) version so guys off-duty can get some sleep.

It'd be a lie to say there's nothing funny about war, even if CNN considers classic their broadcast of a screaming Iraqi bitch in white, "these are human lives! Human lives!!!" As if she were telling us something we didn't know.

A card from home. They think I'm on a Mediterranean cruise. It's the Gulf--the other three carriers are in the Med. This is dated February 25, and they got the letter I sent from P.I. around the 8th of January. The church has a picture of me (and a star) on the bulletin board. And they are "looking forward to seeing (me) home soon." Heh, heh, heh! And they'll send coffee.

0830 7 FEB 91. Yesterday morning, or evening, depending on point of view, literally around 1800, or at least shortly after sunset, the Captain spoke on the 1MC and made us famous on the *Ranger*. Nobody in PERS flipped on my four-track so I'll have to summarize: Wichita 105 commanded by LT "ASH" Malynn, the PERS-O, led Wichita 103 commanded by the skipper of VF-1, CDR "BONGO" McElraft (but piloted by LT "MEAT" Broce, a wild man who wears his brown sideburns like Elvis, and whom Scrapper predicted would take the first VF-1 kill), up river into northern Kuwait where they were vectored to a bogie that turned out to be a Russian helicopter full of Iraqis. Spy was in the Ready Room leaking highlights of the skipper's debrief with the Admiral, like the various excuses they were giving for not having any video. "Uh, we had to pull out real quick anyway so it wouldn't have been any good," he mimicked the skipper.

LCDR Barnett was loading a pistol at the SDO's desk when the skipper came in and the room lit up. Somebody yelled, "Hey, helo killer," and they all cheered.

"Congratulations, Skipper," Mr. Barnett put the gun away and shook his hand.

"It was worth the trip." He went up front to his chair and pulled off his chaps and survival vest. "They turned and started haulin' ass the other way. We went on south, came back around and caught up with 'em, still haulin' ass, dropped to three or four thousand feet and woosh," he whistled. His arms made a broad arc, indicating the explosion. "A big fireball."

"But skipper," a junior pilot showed his colors. "Wasn't the limit thirty-five hundred?"

"Was it?" He flashed a sheepish grin, pulling off his spurs. "I said four or five thousand."

"Hey, helo killer," they cheered again as LT Broce (Meat) came out of Maintenance with a grin as broad as those sideburns are long.

"Boolah boolah, my first winder shot."

"How was it," LT Gram asked. Ready Eight was thick with envy and pride.

"It was ugly," Meat said. "I hit it and it was just like, almost blinding you know, rollin' in on the big fireball. I go 'woah, that's a helicopter. It wasn't supposed to blow up.' Next thing I know it goes right into the ground, and this helicopter blade went 'woosh woosh woosh' right past us. I guess you could call it a confirmed kill."

The skipper gave them a brief debrief with a hand on the chart.

"Here we go, and they said hey, we want you to go on up there. Well is there a tanker? No, well there will be a tanker. Well, is it area? No.

"So we go back to Puller (a flying fuel farm), top off. Then we go feet dry, go up here and start capping. About five minutes after we got there, got a bandit heading north. They came up with a bandit call thirty miles old. They clear us to fire an' we went 'oh shit! Here we go!

"The controller said eight thousand feet. We were at twenty-five. Nothin' on the radars. We get in there, ten, five. Merge plot. Soon as he said merge plot I looked down and there's the fuckin' helo, right there."

"So you didn't know it was a helo."

"No," Meat took it. "Except the close was real slow so we figured somethin' wasn't quite right."

"Arm 'em up." The skipper was still talking.

"Why didn't you shoot a sparrow? Couldn't you get a lock, skipper?"

"Why?" He was surprised. "Why should you waste a five hundred thousand dollar missile when you could do it with a nine thousand dollar missile?"

"I never been there," it was Waylon. "But I wouldn't really think about how much a missile cost."

Well, Bongo flew in Vietnam. And one difference between a skipper and even a seasoned, war tested pilot is that a skipper's mind is fully occupied with administration. You don't just fly. He's constantly dealing with all aspects of running two hundred enlisted and thirty-five commissioned personnel. And one detail that never escapes his mentality is squadron expenditures, with their constantly required reports to higher authority accounting for our use of funds. With a simple select switch, he saved Wolfpack four hundred and ninety-three thousand dollars worth of flying time later in the fiscal year, that we could use toward junior pilot training. This was a great, if simple lesson for the junior pilots about the modern warrior's proper mindframe in battle.

"How high was that helo?"

"It was prob'ly fifty to a hundred feet high. I started worryin' about pullin' out. I said, 'Meat, pull out.' Next thing I heard, 'woosh.' NOW pull. Boom." His arms rose and his voice dropped. "It was a big fireball. They all died. No question about it. They all died."

I wonder if it bothers him, the likelihood that the men he killed were on the run to Iran. They were probably attempting to flee the dictator, just trying to save themselves and get out of the war.

I wrote home and said morale is high. I guess that's true. And I hope what CNN reports about the moral support back there is also true. I want to include a letter that a cute dude gave me this morning, he got from his dad. I'm reading my copy for the first time as I type it.

> Dear Son, you don't really know how proud I am of you and you know I didn't really realize how much I love you. Yeah, that's me, dear old love struck Dad. Well, that's enough of all that shit. Anywho, how are you doing? Fine, I hope. Bet you don't get much sleep lately. Neither have I.
>
> So Mom and I are doing fine. (Some names) came out and spent the weekend with Mom and I. We made mixed drinks, had a beer, watched a couple of movies Saturday night. Got up Sunday, (names) went to church, then came home, fed and watered the horses. Then we went to Uncle Ben's house for turkey dinner. It was nice.
>
> I am putting that big deck on Uncle Ben's house. Gonna be nice when I get it finished. You know what, this is the most I have wrote, well, printed, in 20 years. So I guess that should tell you that I miss you very much. Hope this gets over quick.
>
> So I guess I better tell you something you already know, that is to take care of yourself. Be extra careful at everything you do. So that's all for now. With all my love, Dad, Old Fart, Skitch, Baldy.

I can see why he misses the kid, and I'm jealous of all the years he's had to play with him because the kid is really cute and he likes to be tickled. I mess with him every time he comes to PERS to check his mail, and he plays and laughs. I hope his father will appreciate that.

0830 8 FEB 91. I have to check my watch to see what day it is. Another big blow-out with the chief this morning. That was, last night. Over Scrapper coming to night check. PNSN has prior computer experience and just about has the shop down. And has had several hours a night of dead time so that he's finished his PN3&2 in two weeks. Scrapper took about eight months working day check. But they should change tomorrow night. The whole pretext is that Scrapper will get better PN training. But the reality is, he'll get better weight training. He wants to come to nights so he can skate off two or three hours a night--he has his RTM done and there is that dead time (barring flight ops). I'll pay for it, though, because I'll end up catching one or two launches or recoveries while he's down at the gym. Do I think he really gives a fuck about becoming a PN? No--not any more than I do. So I don't blame him for wanting to get that crow but wanting as much to fuck off and work out. It's just that, with PNSN on the night shift, I do the skating because I can trust him to crank out the workload I've assigned. With Scrapper, I'll be carrying the load and I know it. I'll make sure I get gym time.

I took two hours this shift. (Does that work better than "tonight/last night"?) The whole time concentrating on my waist. I laid on the sit-up board set on the top rung and did crunches, then added a five pound dumbbell in each hand, and later a twenty pounder each. To rest I got on the chair attached to it and did the thing where you pull your legs to your chest and stick them out straight, then back to your chest, then down is one. Fifteen sets, fifteen second break, fifteen more sets, then back to the board. My stomach was burning. I did a few sets of shoulder weight tiptoe stretches, whatever they're called, for defining your ass, and finished with 12 minutes on the Lifecycle, at level 3. The Bob Graham workout.

I started the cruise at 156 pounds. This morning I weight 149. And my tightest pair of dungarees doesn't have flab hanging over. I think I want to hit 145, but weight isn't a concern so much as tone. I want to walk off the boat with "a sixpack," as Scrapper put it. A set of stomach muscles that you can see at a glance. The kind that a baby like Sweets could rest his cheek on.

Talk about pissing me off. This fuckin' nigger came up real kind and sweet and tried to play me like a fiddle. "I just want to get some footage that you've got on your camcorder, that I could send home."

"I don't do it for everybody," I told him. "I haven't even taken the time yet to do it for myself."

When he finally came in with a blank VHS, it wasn't blank but had an hour of shit from half a dozen sources, already put to music. I had no desire to give away my outstanding footage to a former disk jockey, which he is, so he could exploit it and try to sell it on the street and use it in clubs without kicking me down. "I don't want to give you the wrong impression, but I thought you just wanted some video because you didn't have any. I didn't know you had all this stuff already. I'm only gonna give you that stuff in the hangar bay."

"Okay," he said with checked anger.

I gave him five minutes of himself in the hangar bay with the master-at-arms exercise class, that I had shot while taping Sweets at his elevator.

I had to visit the Top Gun Photo Lab to coordinate the request for a reenlistment photographer. I shot the shit with a PH as I gave him the form, then had a thought in passing. "You got any pictures I could get off you?"

"Naw, all we have is this one picture of *Ranger* pulling out of San Diego. But we're only printing a thousand, and they're for official use only." Then his eyes narrowed. "What do you do, where do you work?"

"You mean, what can I do for you?"

I traded him some of my video of the debrief from the Ready Room, dubbed "the Wolfpack Helo Shoot."

Maybe this'll make the cover, if they can shoot a good stat and cut a good interneg, or whatever those terms were that we used in the wonderful world of advertising, where I met Amy.

Jesus Christ! The general, chemical and biological alarms just went off, *followed by* the 1MC announcement, *"test complete--regard all further alarms."* But not *preceded by* the 1MC announcement, *"the following is a test of the general, chemical and collision alarms from the pilot house."* At the first tone my heart leaped. I'm totally nude in my rack with a laptop covering my dick up here in the 81-man berthing. How long would it take to get my ass to my shop and have GQ clothing on?

Then as it switched to the beeeep I wondered, "which is it?" And how many seconds were left to don the gasmask that's across the berthing, down the passageway, outboard and down the ladder in my shop? What about the Mark V that I stashed over my rack with the old fashioned canister, like they used in the certainly classic CNN interview? I was supposed to turn it in so they could send it back on another carrier last month. And if the bos'n's mate was too flustered at the pilot house to hit the right switch, how much time is already gone? Is the ship being showered with chemicals? Is a kamikaze jet about to crash through the flight deck?

As the third test came on, b-b-beep b-b-beep b-b-beep, I knew it was a drill. Meanwhile, I heard somebody jump out of a rack or slam into something. And with five thousand men hearing the alarm with no warning of a drill, in the northern section of the Persian Gulf, in a combat zone in the middle of a war, somebody is gonna want some butts!

I just figured out how the flip chief is trying to fuck over the striker. Since Scrapper finished his PN3&2 book, and his MRPO3 (Military Requirements for Petty Officer Third class), and his M/L E4 (Military Leadership exam for paygrade E4), and got all the PARS (Personnel Advancement Requirements, such as sound principals of customer service, filing and assorted bullshit tasks) signed off, and there is now no valid reason for not ordering him an exam, even though it requires a message to NMPC requesting authorization to allow his participation because he's an Airman striking for a seaman rating--this is the trick: The PNSN was a PG (Prospective Gain) who would be TIR (time in rate) eligible for PN3, so we already ordered a PN3 exam. Based on this, PNC declares "an exam has already been ordered" in response to the draft of a message I produced last night. I argued with PNC that he doesn't really give a fuck about the Airman advancing, whether he thinks he has some legitimate reason or not (such as the kid taking eight months to finish the RTM (PN3&2), to which I countered that he only made E3 January 16 and most people don't finish their book two weeks after making E3. I charged that he was trying to fuck Scrapper over by not ordering a supplementary exam.

I went to the skipper about it, carrying the NAVGRAM (like a message only it goes by mail, since we're in a state called MINIMIZE where only the most urgent message goes electronically and all else goes via envelope.

"These people (NMPC) don't give a fuck about when he takes the exam, they only authorize if he can take it," he explained. "Order him an exam, and if the message comes back too late authorizing him, he can take a late exam."

I went back to PERS, at about midnight, and drafted the request for a supplementary exam, and ran it past the PERS-O who was down there having a cigarette. Then PNC walked in and got pissed that I was drafting the NAVGRAM. "All exams have been ordered," PNC declared to the PERS-O. He pointed out to me that the striker and the new PNSN could split the test. And the message I had drafted went into the burn bag.

Now, presume that the authorization for Scrapper to participate comes too late. And the PNSN takes the exam, and the exam day passes. The exam would be compromised if Scrapper were allowed to take the same one on some future date, because theoretically the PNSN could tell him everything that was on it. It'll be shredded, or returned to the exam processing center.

I believe the NMP Manual says that requests for late exams will not normally be honored later than 90 days prior to the exam date. If they do in fact stipulate that supplementary exam requests cannot be honored after the Navywide advancement exam date, he'll be fucked out of his crow. I'll have to read the damned Advancement Manual again tonight. What if I can prove misconduct on the part of a PNC? I wish they'd get the fuckin' flips out of the Navy. Scrapper swears he's gonna go on a rampage just as soon as he gets out. "I'm gonna walk into a club and see some flips, and bam!" He smacks a fist into his open hand.

1830 8 FEB 91. I got off at zero eight, hit the sack at about eleven after the phony false alarm, enjoyed First LT knocking around cleaning at twelve, woke up again at 1500 for about 45 minutes to a special field day on the illegal makeshift mop closet they designed behind my rack, including moving out cruise boxes to put them back afterward, and again at 1710 as the line shackers arose. Now it's time to go to work. Oh--and here goes the second William Tell Overture of the day.

0745 9 FEB 91. I had a look at those manuals. There's a thing called a supplementary exam, which has to be ordered within thirty days prior to the exam. And another called a substitute exam, which can be ordered until 1 May, provided the member was absent from the exam through no fault of his own, and was fully qualified on the date of the regularly scheduled exam.

Scrapper will be absent the exam through the fault of the mail service if NMPC approval comes to late.

"Now launch one alert fifteen ASR, side number, five one five. Now launch one alert fifteen ASR, side number five one three. Now launch one alert ASR." What an idiot.

Where was I? Trying to prove my hunch that the chief is fucking Scrap over. Building that case file. Well, it's probably nothing more than a bullheaded egotism sending us the wrong message, because he's already signed the request chit acknowledging that the kid has completed all his requirements, and the typing test which he must pass at 30 wpm is one of those. Based on that note I don't see why the service record hasn't already been gundecked. What's he gonna do, turn around later and say, "sir, the Airman never passed his typing test--I thought he would make it, so I told you that he completed everything. I'm sorry, I took a chance on the guy, and he could not deliver. I wish that we could order him a substitute exam but you see he was not ready like it says here in the manual, on the date of the regularly scheduled exam."

Why wasn't he ready? He's only up to 19 wpm. And he's white. But a flip dude just passed the AK typing test, 15 wpm, and it's already entered in his service record. I happened to dig the test out of the burn bag and rescore it. I found one misspelling that the new selected reservist (SELRES) PN3 had missed. And I noticed four punctuation errors, since the flip only put one space after the period at the end of each sentence. And he didn't type it in double space format, another error. There were two errors checked already. Eight errors at 50 points each, from a total of 498 character, space or return keystrokes, is 98, divided by five to result in a gross character count of 19.6, divided by the five minutes of the test, comes out to a true score of 3.92 words per minute. Hardly qualifying. Oh, but he's a flip. Good to see that our chief isn't playing favorites within this office.

"Run it up the chain of command, and confront the chief with it," sayeth YN1. "That way you cover your ass and you don't cut your own dick off." He turned to me with the last of his statement.

The ramifications were predictable: Scrapper would miss the exam, and walk out of the desert storm and his naval career, still an airman. Chief might get his wrist slapped. But he certainly wouldn't lose his khakis. And flips would run the US Navy. His flip buddy would advance, too. Over the whites (and maybe blacks) who didn't get their typing quals from Chief.

Care for another? How about our DK2. A disbursing clerk who can barely speak English and has alienated (I kid you not) the entire squadron. Gets a 4.0 evaluation for both "speaking ability" and "writing ability."

Allow me to quote two of his latest notes to me:

Please attached the reporting endorsement to Detroit, MI. Have the plane ticket attach from Detroit Metro, to the procuring center.

I don't know what he means and I have a bachelor in English, a birth certificate from South Carolina and a California driver's license!

Please attached the reporting endorsement to Detroit, MI.

Am I being uncooperative to watch my made in USA shipmates losing out in the area of performance marks to foreigners with foreigner supervisors who overlook the lack of skill and disregard the value of reading and writing English? They want us off their fucking land in the P.I. Get them the fuck out of bootcamp. Of course, like anything else, there likely are Filipino's out there who despise this representation of their race and national origin who don't oppose American bases in Olongapo, Subic and Clark, and do speak perfect English and write even better than me. But so what? They're not the fucking boss I have to work for.

Rumor control. The *Midway* is pulling into the I.O. for two weeks' R&R. When she comes back to the fray, we're steaming over there and hitting a port. I guess they come in spurts. The other one is that 111 (Sticks) got hit by AAA. It's really cut up for corrosion control, but it looks a lot like some flak or something hit it. Some dude (not me) was videotaping it in the hangar bay and the green shirts were filling him in as if it was no bullshit. They took me aside and gave me the gouge, which was nice.

"All hands are reminded to stay clear of all weatherdecks, catwalks and sponsons, due to high winds and heavy seas." Maybe we *are* going somewhere else. On the other hand, reality check. My bunkmate says CNN reported that we cut down operations yesterday due to poor weather conditions.

0230 11 Feb 91. "And the mighty war dogs of CVW-2 are off again," said the Captain after William Tell played. "They're goin' up to Al Zibir railroad yards to destroy some armored personnel carriers and some tanks foolish enough to be positioned out in the open on the tracks. The airplanes are one E-2, six A- 6's, one EA-6B and two F-14s. Each A-6 is gonna have twelve Rock Eyes, for a total of seventy-two Rock Eyes. It's gonna be Saddam's worst nightmare. I hope he's got his Page Two filled out, 'cause he's prob'ly gonna need it."

The Page Two is up my alley, a service record item, the record of emergency data such as names and addresses of parents and wives and kids, and who we pay what if you croak.

1030 11 FEB 91. The XO called down sometime during the night. "We need emergency leave orders for (the guy), keep it close to your heart, this is secret." I knew that an AMCROSS had come in last night (American Red Cross message). Now I knew the secret. I don't have a clearance, of course. But I was the available PN. This was another brush with death. First Buck dies, who lived opposite my rack in 81 Man, aft. Now this guy who just got here and is going home to his father's funeral, lives in my old rack, 28T, in 39 Man, up forward. What's up with that? I keep hearing that vague phrase out of some Biblical chapter, "though a thousand fall at thy side, it shall not come nigh thee." Something like that. I keep reminding myself, this is not a holy war. It's a just war. I'm not Christ in judgment, I'm just a dude with a job on a ship with a mission for the government of the USA. This is not the millennium, the seven seals are not being opened with a B-52. And Saddam

Hussein isn't the anti-christ fooling thousands of believers.

I dug out the instructions, tried to get everything right and give the PNSN some OJT. I called YNCS at CAG, who explained that FLAG has a daily run out of Fujaira (Saudi Arabia) direct to Cubi (Cubi Point, Republic of the Philippines), so on the MTA (Military Transportation Authorization, a free airline ticket worldwide if I were criminal enough to type one for myself) I'd put Cubi to San Diego and return to VF-1 onboard *USS Ranger*. Well, it was probably an assumption that the guy had family in Sand Dog (San Diego) whom he'd need to pick up enroute to his midwestern destination. Ultimately, the MTA should have been written for LAX. But XO said the earliest COD would fly off no earlier than 1200, so there'd be plenty of time to complete the TAD orders and COD request when PNC came in this morning.

I did a 3067, an OCR document (computer scanned endorsement to orders) that would be a pain in the butt even if the typewriter were not giving us fits. I made arrangements to get his PFR (Personal Financial Record) from DK2, and prepared a special request chit for him to submit in the morning to be paid up to date. According to DK2 the member was on DDS and shouldn't need his PFR or the 3067, but we'd put him to bed and didn't know if it was his need or something the CO/XO had suggested to him, as a matter of course, without asking him if he were on Direct Deposit. If he got paid up to date and had DDS, he'd be overpaid and they'd fuck him over later getting it back in a single swipe, or at the very least his pay would be extremely confused for the next six months, even if he weren't losing Rats, BAQ and VHA and getting CSP, FSA and HFP tax free in a combat zone on a month by month basis.

PNC came in at 0945 with a headache and started bitching right away. He didn't like the MTA because it had NAVPTO Cubi Pt. RP on it like YNCS had instructed. I left it for the PNSN to X it out. "You can't make corrections on the MTA."

"Yes you can, chief. It says so right here." I showed him the fucking instructions and he seemed displeased.

"What if I said it's our standard?"

"Does the war ever stop?" YN3 Jackson, aka Mister Happy Go Lucky, was skating on out of the office, probably to go play a video game with Rod on the Ops computer.

"In here? Hell no."

Chief had the PNSN run the TAD orders to CAG, and I redirected him to also take the COD request by the skipper for signature, which seemed to piss off the chief even more.

I took the Military Leadership exam for Petty Officer First Class, just to get some kind of official growth notice into my record this year. I was sure I'd flunk and didn't want to go, but the PN3 came in and said he'd hold the fort, so I took a chance. It turned out easier than I expected. They had it at 0600 this morning in Ready Eight, proctored by Meat, the big helo killing hero with those Elvis sideburns. He reminded me that he'd give me a blank tape to record his grand entrance into the Ready Room with the skipper after the kill, as I got it on my camcorder.

"Well, I passed the Military Leadership exam." I figured that might make the son of a bitch crack a smile.

"Where's the list?" I guess he was calling me a liar.

"LT Broce hasn't brought it down yet."

He put his head into the shit on his desk and I fucking left.

I am going to stop letting him play my guitar. He has already killed my plants, and there's two new rips in my guitar case.

I worked off my anger in the gym. I hit the sit-up board and the stand-up thing, whatever the hell it's called. I pushed all of it a little more than last time, and hit the bike overlooking the hangar for 18 minutes on level six. Last summer I was up to level seven at Miramar. No, it was two summers ago. I AM getting short.

Sweet Pea wasn't at the elevator down below, where the deep blue water rolled by in white caps with a moderate swell. Somebody else was running a couple of jets to the flight deck, blowing that "a-ooh-ga" horn. Maybe the NIS COD'd him off, or something happened since I had Dean over to look at the video I took of Sweets working the El and not talking, just being there bumping his cherry bottom lip on the microphone cup under the mickey mouse earphones that centered his stern brows and serious, striving eyeballs. It seems like a week since I've seen him.

0845 12 FEB 91. I am not in the mood to write. But I already worked out so I might as well try to get my frustrations out here. I wanted to kick chief's ass this morning. I spent two hours figuring out a schedule, since we have five guys now, so that we could cut back to an eight hour day. I gave him two alternatives, and they got as far as the burn bag. The memo read, I recommend either of the following overlapping arrangements to reduce the crowd in Admin/Pers by scheduling a maximum of two PN's here at once, vice the current three on daycheck (PNC, PN3 and PNSN/AN), while allowing for optimum 24-hour service. I broke it down like this: *Primary schedule / Alternative schedule 0400-1200 / PNSN 0300-1100 PNSN 0800-1600 PNC 0700-1500 PN3 1200-2000 PN3 1100-1900 PNC 1600-2400 AN 1500-2300 AN 2000-0400 PN2 1900-0300 PN2*. I presented it as a way to decrease the crowd, then got to the point that it'd put us on an eight hour vice twelve hour shift.

"What's this? Are you crowded on night check?"

"No." I thought of all the gripes Scrapper had about traffic all day long, why he'd leave when he couldn't take it anymore. But I failed to argue the point. It would have been a lost cause, as usual.

"Do you want to work night check by yourself?"

"Chief, every time I come up with an idea it ends up in the shit can."

"That's right."

I have this list of all the fights I've been in throughout my 34 years, with where and how old I was at the time:

10 Greenville, IL - Mike Brown (next door neighbor, several between our two yards).

11 Greenville, IL - Brian someone, chopped him between the shoulder blades when he was beating up a friend.

14 West Jr. High, Columbia, MO - Jumped by Missouri Tigers Coach Norm Stewart's son, Jeff, coming off a bus. He and several of his friends took my wallet and played keep away.

16 University High School, Columbia, MO - Druggie didn't like the way I looked at him and pounded my head against the wall in front of my older brother, who didn't know who started it.

17 Mexico, MO - Drug dealer gave me six stitches over one eye trying to get me to confess to being a narcotics agent.

27 Hollywood, CA - Cholo went to bed with me, then decided to kill the faggot, and I killed him in self-defense and spent a year proving it in court.

28 Venice Beach, CA - Puerto Rican street bum who burgled my apartment found out that I knew he did it, so then he mugged me on the street and I didn't fight back because I was just coming off the murder charge.

29 Concord, CA - Drunk bum pissing in public at a drive-in hamburger joint didn't like the way I looked at him as he walked by the car I was in with my attorney, so walked up to the window and broke my tooth. We drove to a phone and brought the cops back, where I placed him under arrest and let him cry all the way to jail.

33 San Diego, CA - Four dudes off the *Ranger* came into my own apartment and mugged me, beating my ass and breaking that same tooth again, only worse, and called me a faggot although were I one, I'd never be interested in those ugly motherfuckers. I should have been a boxer. Or kept up karate and made love to Ralph Macchio. What a babe.

How about a list of fags who messed with me:

8, Greenville, IL - Red caught me taking the longest shortcut of my life, in the woods, pulled my pants down and had a look at my freaked out but fondled hardon. I promised not to tell and he let me go.

18, Denver, CO - Sales rep plopped a fuckbook on my lap on the freeway, then toward the back it got faggotty and kinky. He gave me a blowjob near some bridge.

18, Oklahoma City - Dude "out chasin' chicks" drove me around a while and finally confessed that he gave great blowjobs, took me to the abandoned house with rusty bedsprings stacked up on the porch, showed me a flick of two chicks and a double-ended inanimate male lead. That was the first tongue up my butt since my older brother licked my ass as a little boy, and now I was awakened to the great joy once again. Only this time I never forgot. Further, I have learned that 'tis better to give than receive.

20, Cape Cod - Some analyst tried to figure me out and fondle my cock.

I let him weasel me as far as showing it, then got out of his car.

20, Rochester, NY - Guy flipped a coin and turned left, then picked me up because I was there with my thumb out. I stayed at his house and the second night there I went into his room and let him have my youth under the blue moonlight where he said, "you're beautiful," and licked that ass.

21, San Francisco, CA - The dude who ran Polk Street Town Hall, a runaway youth shelter. One of the last times I made it with an older man.

22, San Francisco - Insurance salesman wanted to fistfuck me. I put him off until morning, then sneaked out in the wee hours. I thought of robbing or murdering the motherfucker, but just sneaked out, had eggs at the Hyatt and caught BART back to the suburbs at ten. That was the last older man.

28, Sherman Oaks, CA - A department head at Telepictures Corp., gave me a blowjob in the window seat of his plant rich house just a few days before I was let go.

As far as the DIS agent knew, there were only two besides the Hollywood story that opened the can (since it made police files). I coughed up one gorgeous actor I met at a cast party two blocks from my house in Concord, CA. He had a naked chest and loved my hairy chest. We were meant for each other and played around for hours before he coaxed me to fuck him, "so you won't ache." He was aching to be fucked. Then there was the young courier at the tax service in Walnut Creek, CA, a pothead rock guitarist bisexual with a jar of vaseline in his dresser. He had never done it before, and it hurt at first so he didn't think he could, but he wanted to try, then he went wild. I didn't go on about the sixteen or seventeen others on the list I guess I'll shred--but they were all young and lovely, cute and kind. They deserve better than to wind up on some file in Washington, alongside Martin Luther King and Larry Norman.

1015 13 FEB 91. Tomorrow's Valentine's Day. Somebody will probably write a card to Hussein, and put it on a bomb.

I got a nice letter from Mr. Ray, at J. C. Penney Company, Inc. He says they're pleased that I'm enjoying the convenience of both their regular charge and major purchase plans. But, they're concerned they haven't received payments of the amounts I owe on both plans. Hmm. He put his phone number on the letter. Maybe I should call and tell him the check is in the mail.

His letter was dated 24 January and got here 12 February. The bill was due 21 January and got here 27 January--it doesn't sound bad until you figure that one gets the bill well before it comes due. Well, the check *is* in the mail.

I got my copy of the *Graham Quacker*, a family newsletter that keeps all relatives of the Graham family current with each other. I found out, for instance, I have a cousin who's a Lieutenant Colonel in the Army, out here in Saudi Arabia. I sent him a letter asking if he has the time to pick up Khaled's screenplay diskettes from his downtown Kuwait City office, across the street from the social security administration building. My sister's new baby came out real easy, then got a medi-vac out to some specialist hospital with a heart attack. I didn't know she'd been pregnant. Maybelle wrote, from church. "I just realized how many years it's been since I've written to a sailor (his name was Howie, on the *De USS Canberra*, 1944!!). You're in our thoughts and prayers, Bob, you and all your shipmates and others in all of the services.

"Many of the houses in our neighborhood and all over the area have flags displayed, along with yellow ribbons. Our flag is going up tomorrow, in your honor.

"I'm not sure how many miles our love has to travel to reach you, but we hope somehow you can feel it." She wrote the letter on the front of the church bulletin. I put "NORELPREF" on my dogtags.

"Roman Catholic mass, for Ash Wednesday, will be held in the ship's chapel, at eleven hundred." I guess this is Wednesday.

Looking at the bulletin, I notice after the offering they have the Prayer of Dedication, preceded by an asterisk (*) meaning "all standing," followed by the Hymn of dedication (*), followed by the Benediction (*), followed by the Congregation Response (*) and the Postlude. After that it reads, "(*) Those who are able may stand." I guess if they're still able to stand after all that, they might as well go on home.

I've always wondered if I were one of those guys some high minded religious leader would say, "he was among us, but he was not of us." How does that jibe with a Messiah syndrome? I guess I'm well rounded. Speaking of which, what a workout from 0300 to 0500, tightening those stomach muscles. And that buttocks. Or is it those buttocks? Is it buttock? Do we have one buttock? We have buns, vice bun. I guess I could say my left bun got firmer than my right bun when I was commuting across the Bay Bridge in San Francisco riding a spring clutch in our '72 Chevy pick-up. I still weigh 149, and my health is excellent according to the fitness test on the lifecycle. (Is that a restricted trademark or a catchy name for a piece of metal?)

Maybelle sent a clipping, a picture from the paper where a class made a flag using children's handprints as the red stripes. What a great idea. They put the names of men and women from Concord serving in the Gulf war. My official home of record is Walnut Creek, so I probably didn't make it.

I still wonder about this whole thing, I have to tell you. What the fuck are we doing over here bombing the shit out of Saddam Hussein and his entire population? Well, I know, just the military. But they can't even surrender without being shot by that lunatic. Is there no way to get an elite Delta Force Navy Seal Rambo Karate Kid inside that bunker with a C4 surprise? I guess we can keep it up longer than he can, but now I hear he's crying toward Russia. We have got to bring that son of a bitch to his face losing knees, and make him beg the world for forgiveness and admit he'd gone mad. Or just kill him like a defect of nature.

Finally, some pictures from Christmas. Dad and Ruth got to show off their new $600,000 house. Modest by Amy's standards, if not downright lowbrow. But otherwise upper middle class. In the elite community of Walnut

Creek, California, a San Francisco suburb.

Dee Jr., my oldest brother, has a look on his face like he's overly conscious of his military reserve status. An AK1, aviation storekeeper first class, he's just been placed on "standby." If he goes to the gulf war, he's planning on requesting duty onboard *USS Ranger*. That'd be a nice treat, long as we don't see any silkworms.

Dad wasn't in any of the pictures. But all the guys and gals from church were there looking happy and thoughtful in the warm and cozy light of the foyer and the living room. In a sense they seem to be wondering what to make of the Christian mandate to glorify God and enjoy him forever. One guy has his hands in the pockets of his suit slacks, another has holds his hands in front of a Christmas red vest under a dark blue sport coat, fingers together. Are they all so worried in my dad's house with me out here? Nah, they know me well enough to know I'm having the time of my life. I'm writing this book, for Christ's sake. They probably all just had peanuts.

They had a picture of my niece Sarah, playing flute by the fireplace. A beautiful girl, nice, and polite, and blonde as the gold rimmed mirror on the mantle. Everyone laid around on the floor, or sat on couches listening.

"You don't got no hair," she said in San Lorenzo. What the hell, grass don't grow on a busy street. I've got to get a transplant.

I wanted to be there, it always seemed to be a natural thing as I played the guitar all those years over the garage. But not in most living rooms, and not in my dad's. It was good to see Sarah get some use out of that room. And last, but not least, Boots looking for goldfish in the bird bath in the back. My stepmother's cat has a grey fur with white paws. Hence, the name.

I guess I better get some letters off to these good friends of mine, if not to Mr. Ray. He'll get his check.

Oh yeah. I came in to work last night and found that Scrapper had been sent home early and told to come in at 1900. He's now on the night shift working with me. Nice of the boss to let me know what the hell he is up to. I guess my new schedule freaked him out enough to get some action on the previous suggestion, and he dealt with it in a face saving fashion after I left. How the hell could I know what goes on in his flipped out mind? I told him he had balls yesterday, when he complained that other chiefs might cry if we went to an eight hour shift. "Of course I have balls," he grabbed his meat. "You want touch them?"

I rolled over in my mind, to use the term of the prosecutor in my murder trial, the notion of how to respond to his question. But I only smiled and blushed and appended my case file.

Scrapper wasn't there. But he was when chief kept asking me, coming out of P.I., if I'd found a boyfriend. Whether or not I had, it's sexual harassment. And it was a bullshit thing to say about Ed, Edwin, Geoffrey and Totoy.

"Sweepers, sweepers, man your broom. Give the ship a clean sweepdown forward and aft. Take all sinkable nonplastic trash to the fantail. Now sweepers."

All those guys on one broom?

Disregarding that he asks me if I date guys, he repeatedly asks personal questions about his subordinate's sex life. And if he's a goddamn fag, he has a wife and family to cheat on and play off. What the hell do you think he was doing on this side of the International Forget Line? He's a real stud in P.I.

He's been giving me a great passdown lately. I get a request chit for an extension and a Post-It note attached reads, "do ext." So I dig out the book, fill in the blanks and this time, to really impress him, file the extension in the service record where it would go when finished, just for safekeeping and in memory of the time he chewed me out for putting incomplete pages on top.

"Just file them. I know where to find them," he scolded me months ago. Ever since, I've been implementing a routine of yellow stickies (first on the outside of the record, but he had enough of that so then on the top page inside).

"This is not done," he scolded last night. "Why did you file it?"

"Well, chief. A long time ago you told me you wanted pages to be refiled, where you could find them, and not to put them temporarily on top."

"Also, this block is not complete."

"Well, I did it by the book."

"What book?"

"The PAYPERSMAN." He started to go for the book but got distracted by DK2. In the book the block he referred to had instructions to put the reason for the extension. His reason was to accept orders from NMPC. With the great passdown, "do ext.," I thought I did a pretty good job. But I knew I'd get chewed out for something.

It's like the forty page nine entries I had the PNSN do his last night working for me. The passdown from chief was, "do a page 9." It was for evals ending 31 January. You have to put an entry on page nine, history of performance marks, and another entry that had not been made, if their evals had them recommended for advancement.

His passdown was to put in "recommended for advancement." So that's what we put, even though as I recalled all other times we'd put "recommended for advancement to (whatever their next rate was)." But in light of his instruction, and given that the member's rate is listed on the same line of the recommendation entry, it made no sense to add, "for (whatever rate). So I expected to be chewed out about that. I guess he forgot, or wanted to play my guitar today.

0530 14 FEB 91. Happy Valentine's Day. Since Rick came to my table and sat with me at breakfast, I wished it on him. He's the short, mousy looking blue shirt with a pre-teen tummy that works on the flight deck. I don't know if it's something about blue, little boy blue.

"Happy Valentine's Day."

"Is today Valentine's Day?"

"February fourteenth."

"Thanks, Bob."

Yesterday he rode the escalator up to his berthing, which is right next to 81 Man, and leaned on the door jam still talking to me for a minute. His soft, small face was sooty like a chimney sweep, and his blue floatcoat blackened, from riding the tow tractor by the JBD (jet blast deflector) and soaking up exhausted JP5. His green pants seemed to hold him up on dry cakes of grease. "I can't find it," he said with a tired Indiana drawl. "It ain't like I need to go shoppin'. I prob'ly won't even get it replaced 'til we get back t' San Diego. Then I'll go see the DK an' get a new ATM card an' find out how much money I've got."

This morning I finished an extra glass of OJ that gave me an excuse to hang around, then put a firm hand on his shoulder and said "I'll see ya later."

He knows I like him. I don't know how he feels about it. But I do recall talking to him late one night in the dim red light of a darkened passageway, as he leaned in a different doorway and some guy he knew interrupted us.

"Chester," the guy said. "Chester." And he laughed.

Rick didn't acknowledge his friend's derogatory remark. Neither did I.

That was the first night Rick pulled his shirt out of his pants and with a hand pulled it up showing his belly. Young guys know that's a turn on and they do it without projecting any knowledge of their actions.

This tough surfer AZAN comes down from Maintenance Control to make some photocopies, full of rage against our flipped out Navy.

"Did you ever wanna just go off on a Filipino and knock the hell out of him?"

"Why didn't you?" A hedging sort of answer.

"He was a First Class. I was down there eatin' chow, and he starts talkin' that ba-ling ba-ling crap in front of me. I told him to stop and he said why? So I said do you work in the American Navy? Do you abide by the rules of the American Navy? You're not supposed to do that in front of Americans. I'm an American. See? I'm white. He told me I had a problem."

"Take it up to Captain's Call."

He gave a nod as he pushed through the door and up the ladder. Fat chance of anything changing without a Congressional inquiry like they handled the cigarette problem. I only hope they'll stick with the freeze on enlisting them, since they don't want us in P.I.

I should've told him, "just ask the guy if he's Japanese." It seems that if you really want to piss off a Filipino, you ask him if he's Japanese, because during the second world war when the Japs occupied the Philippines, they reportedly humiliated the Flips by walking them around on leashes like dogs.

Or, "how deep *is* shit river?" Like I asked chief.

He said he didn't know.

Chapter Eleven

0730 15 FEB 91. "Hey chief, did we have this guy as a prospective gain long enough to order him an exam?"

"What makes you think I did not order him an exam?"

I think PNC is insecure. He feels threatened even when he's not being threatened. And of course, he shot back. "I need your brag sheet for your eval."

"What eval?" I had just signed my close-out eval for advancing to E5.

"March thirty-first."

Ah, yes. E5 evals are due March 31. I'm a PN2, I'm supposed to know these things.

The Navy has this form called Enlisted Performance Evaluation Report-Individual Input. Also known as a Smoke Sheet, it has eight sections and is defined as follows:

> The submission of this form is a means of ensuring that your personal accomplishments, achievements and creditable activity, during the current reporting period, are brought to the attention of your reporting senior, through the chain of command.

It's followed by a note at the bottom:

> The use of the information provided by the ratee is discretionary on the part of the reporting senior. Upon completion of the evaluation report, this form shall be returned to the ratee.

Like your Miranda rights, this is a hard fought and hard won procedure that you damn well better use. Let's see.

> SECTION 1. In-rate and normal duty qualifications achieved
>
> Leading Petty Officer, training three subordinates in service record maintenance, pay forms and correspondence, resulting in one hundred percent Navywide advancement exam participation within the work center.

Chief will say: You think you had anything to do with them getting ready for the exam? PN3 just got here--you teach him anything? He went to day check right away. I think you're trying to blow smoke up my ass. You still have a problem with pay forms yourself. Can you do a thirty-sixty with no mistake? I don't think you can. You submit one with the travel claim and every time it's coming back. What day is travel started, and when does it end when a member is comes from CONUS? Do you know if you charge travel on the date of detachment PCS?

> SECTION 2. Special qualifications achieved
>
> Completed Personnel Advancement Requirements for Personnelman First Class. Passed Military Leadership exam for Petty Officer First Class.

Chief will say: You haven't completed your PARS. When did you council the member on retirement and benefits for dependent? Have you done a recommendation for change in billet authorization?

SECTION 3. In-rate professional development

Dealt with special circumstances related to procurement of Selected Reservists due to the Gulf war and Operation Desert Storm. Handled casualty report as duty PN upon death of squadronmate on deployment to Western Pacific/Indian Oceans/ Persian Gulf, 1990-91, on board USS Ranger (CV-61).

Chief will say: Casualty reporting is one of your PARS. Do you think it's in-rate professional development, or PARS? You think you can use a member's death for advancement? I think you're blowing smoke up my ass.

SECTION 4. Other educational and training accomplishments

Self-educated via Writer's Digest book club, including Successful Scriptwriting and Reading For A Living. Maintained a physical fitness program while deployed this period.

Chief will say: You want credit for every book you read on your own time? And you take off and leave for the gym when you are supposed to be in here, you're supposed to stay in the office even if there is nothing to do, and you put it in your brag sheet?

SECTION 5. Voluntary Navy related civic and community support activity

Always available in berthing and passageway to advise personnel in matters related to official history of military service.

Chief will say: From what I hear, people in the squadron are not happy with your customer service. And anyway, the berthing and passageway are not the civilian community. You don't even know what it means, and you want credit. I don't know, sometimes.

SECTION 6. Other civic and community support activity

Responded with appreciation to various people/organizations who wrote the squadron/ship in relation to Operation Dear Abby/America Remembers USS Ranger.

Chief will say: What letter did you write? Let me see. You don't have a copy, you just write it down that you did this? What if I say I wrote somebody and I don't keep a copy? Are they going to believe me? Why should they?

SECTION 7. Commendatory correspondence received during this report period

Nominated once in this period for Sailor Of the Month (awarded runner-up for December) as noted on frocking eval.

Chief will say: I put this already. Did you not read the last eval? You signed it. You want credit again?

SECTION 8. Other achievements, accomplishments and significant events/actions

Trained PNSN and YNSR in proper watchstanding on 2JZ circuit in Ready Room Eight on board USS Ranger. Trained subordinates in operation of locally customized computer programs in areas of word processing and database management, for correspondence and statistical reporting.

Chief will say: PNSN can't even use the computer. He messed up the database and deleted two records. He can't even do a list of personnel by hometown. Does he know how to sort? And the striker, I don't want you to give him an access level so he can delete. I'm afraid he'll delete the records. How does it go? If you can't dazzle 'em with brilliance, baffle 'em with bullshit. At least the Navy does provide one form especially designed to blow smoke up your supervisor's ass. That's one good thing I'll remember about serving my time.

0900 16 FEB 91. I skipped the escalator and took a ladder to the hangar bay, just to see if Sweet Pea was there, running his elevator on day check now. He wasn't. But the water was like glass and the glare was blinding and hot.

I had not seen the sun since I videotaped Sweet Pea. And I couldn't see land now. But they said last night we were close enough to Kuwait that guys on the flightdeck could see missiles in flight on the horizon, and lights of battle striking brightly on the desert. The sea looked like a God could walk across it, smooth as a lake, and I had to remember we're not on the Mediterranean. It was so peaceful I thought of pre-war, maybe even pre-oil Kuwait. And it naturally led me to think of that foreign source of my Hollywood break, Khaled Siddik, internationally acclaimed documentary film maker of the transitional piece about Kuwait's oil boom. Where is he now, broke in New York City with his assets frozen, his disks scattered on the floor of his office in downtown Kuwait and the rest of his family murdered while trying to escape? His film is in the can, in a London vault, thank God. He's trying to get syndication now, and surely there's a market in the USA. I haven't had a chance to see it myself. Maybe, if we all come out alive, I'll get out of the Navy and collaborate with him on the sequal, post-oil boom Kuwait, the land that went from rags to riches and back to rags again, thanks to the raghead, Saddam Hussein.

Scrapper laid a good one on Chief. PNC had tried to pull a fast one, another power trip, and changed the combo on the top file drawer. It has a four digit combo lock that you can reset any time it's open. Since we've been out here, it's been set as the last four digits of the five position combo used at Miramar. Easier for the department to remember. But I went to back up the Personnel Database file and couldn't get in to where the disk was stored.

By some wild stroke of genius, Scrapper figured out that PNC had changed it to the first four digits of the old combo, and got it open. Then he changed it back to the previous setting, and we waited for the chief to go nuts. It happened on daycheck, while I was in the rack. When I came on, PNC went off on me. "Who changed the lock?"

"What do you mean, Chief? I thought you did."

"Someone changed it again."

"Well, I just tried to get into it yesterday and I couldn't get it open."

Scrapper went to nights shortly after that. And last night he told me the story. He watched PNC open the lock one day, and got the new combo. Then while chief was out, he opened it and changed the combo back to the old one. When chief eventually made the discovery, Scrap was sitting at the typewriter jamming along with some tunes on my headphones. "Did you change this?" Chief had to yell to get his attention.

"How could I change it?"

"I know you were fucking with it."

"I don't know what you're talkin' about."

"What is the number?"

He recited the old number.

"Someone changed it. Graham did it."

"Whatever," Scrapper threw up his hands. Then he left so he could bust out laughing in the head. Later on, he was there when chief went off on me and I reacted not only innocently but truthfully, and I gave chief a look like he was losing his mind. We never told him, by the way. And somebody is still fucking with him and the lock.

From the time I get off, at 0700, hit my rack at 0900 and try to sleep at 1100, shift change and First LT are slamming the berthing door thoughtlessly and turning on overhead lights. I feel the urge to smile at their complaints of cold showers, and see that I am beginning to hate them all.

The teeth marks on my tongue are so deep from this constant assault that I'm about to lose a chunk of it. Maybe I'll snap, hop out of the rack and attack the next poor SOB who slams that door. Instead, I cover my head with my pillow and rejoice that PNC was gone when I came to work last night and I got a break from that source of tension. Suddenly, the ship takes a roll and the door leaning in the gear locker awaiting a paint job leans away from the bulkhead and slams against my rack. Ka-BAM!! As if someone had hit it with a baseball bat.

1710 16 FEB 91. The 81 Man berthing door slams forty times in fifteen minutes, as night check goes to the head to shower, and another forty times as they return, and another dozen as First LT comes and goes turning on the light above my rack and banging garbage cans. They promised fifteen days ago to get a hydraulic doorstop, and finally traded a case of sodas to get one -- and I came to work to find it attached to that smoke filled Personnel Department/chess lounge, clamping the door tight to seal in the aromatic cancer that will surface in my lungs ten years from now.

0730 17 FEB 91. Got a couple of interesting messages lately. One was an intercepted Iraqi message dated 31 Jan 91:

FROM: SUPREME NAVAL FORCES, IR
TO: SUPREME ULTIMATE COMMANDER,IR
SECRET
Subject: NAVAL OPS SITSUM
1. THE MOTHER OF BATTLES GOES WELL.
2. OUR VICTORIOUS NAVAL DEBRIS WILL SOON BECOME A NAVIGATIONAL HAZARD TO U.S. AND COALITION FLEETS.
3. BY THE WAY, ARE WE TAX-FREE YET?

The other message came from Washington Center, Washington DC, subject line, IMPLEMENTATION PROCEDURES OF CZ TAX EXCLUSION FOR PERSIAN GULF AREA.

NARR/REF A IS AN EXECUTIVE ORDER EFFECTIVE 17 JAN 91 DESIGNATING THE ARABIAN PENINSULA AREAS, AIRSPACE AND ADJACENT WATERS AS A COMBAT ZONE.

RMKS/1. PURPOSE. THIS IS A DFAS-WC MSG WHICH PROVIDES COMBAT ZONE TAX EXCLUSION (EFFECTIVE DATE 17 JAN 91) FOR MEMBERS ASSIGNED TO OPERATION DESERT STORM. COMBAT ZONE TAX EXCLUSION ONLY APPLIES TO THE FOLLOWING AREAS; PERSIAN GULF AREA, RED SEA, GULF OF OMAN, THAT PORTION OF THE ARABIAN SEA THAT LIES NORTH OF 10 DEGREES NORTH LATITUDE AND WEST OF 68 DEGREES EAST LONGITUDE, GULF OF ADEN, THE TOTAL LAND AREAS OF IRAQ, KUWAIT, SAUDI ARABIA, OMAN, BAHRAIN, OUTAR, AND THE UNITED ARAB EMIRATES.

We finally got what everybody in the squadron has been bugging us about. The "Tax free" message. Now we can send DK2 the list of personnel onboard VF-1 eligible for the extra dough. Including me! It's retroactive to 17 Jan, so we've got some good backpay coming. And nowhere to spend it. Me, well I sent another check already to J C Penney, knocking them down to something like $500. The big check will probably come on March 15, and by then I won't owe those guys anything. Next I've got to start saving to have a car when we get back, so's I can live somewhere besides the BEQ at NAS Miramar. As long as we get out of this thing all right.

Somebody gave me a letter from an 11 year old boy last night. He was a twin, and my mom was a twin, so I took it and wrote back. I sent him a copy of the video I made of last Westpac, and hope his parents don't freak out about the occasionally harsh terminology implemented by some of the swarthier, saltier dogs on the *Ranger*. He's from Vermont, has two older brothers who are also twins and they are 13 years old. And a younger sister, age 10. His favorite sports are hockey, tennis and golf. Oh no, sounds like Billy. He also likes swimming, soccer and baseball. Now he sounds like The Terminator.

Another shade of Bill, this kid here has been to Old Cape Cod. Who was that bitch who sang, "you're sure to fall in love in old Cape Cod"? I could hate her for the circle in the sand I drew around Billy George and Cinda, that forlorn evening, after which I cried myself to sleep between some bush and the wall of a stranger's house up a silent road.

They were all sharing a peace pipe full of pot, high, romantic, lovesick, sensing mysterious impending doom, our unwelcomed destiny to split apart the following year, me writing songs for that small circle of friends, who never again would hear the sound of my voice. A little D/A/G ditty:

Come Clean

D A G

Rich soil in our shoes from behind the shed
We laid together in the back of my pickup bed
If I don't look back at the salt lick washing away
I can still feel my fingers on the back of your neck today

Come clean, you're the purest love I've seen
Come clean, in the clover where we're young and lean
Come clean, while there's nothing in between
Come clean, our love is so serene

All the songs I wrote for you I never could sing
About a faithful friend that you could never bring
Every step, every stroke, every heartbeat as you fly
I'll be rubbun' up against another stone in the fiery sky

Come clean, you're the purest love I've seen
Come clean, in the clover where we're young and clean
Come clean, while there's nothing in between
Come clean, our love is so serene

Someone on the news mentioned how this war would make people think of old friends they had not seen in ten years. And it, like this letter, reminded me of good old Bill, age 15, 14 years ago in Wellfleet, Massachusetts. They had come looking for me later that night, splashed around in George's 18 foot dingy until the dog, Shamus, pronounced "shame us," jumped out of the boat.

"When am I gonna see you again?" I still had hair.

"Prob'ly ten years." That sunsoaked afternoon on the Arlington beltway, still burning my brain cells in a painful memory that won't say die, I watched his brother David's car pull out, let my hand fall off his golden hair and hit my thigh, looked around at the millions of strangers passing by, and felt deserted for the very last time. I was finally free.

Crime of the Century

I never could have gone too far
If I never showed up again
I loved you like my shooting star
My lover, my friend

As the sun sank over Arlington
And a warm house in McLean
I was five hundred miles up the road to California
And you must have felt insane

The crime of the century
Was when you set me free

The crime of the century
You said goodbye to me

What an L.A. surprise
I thought I wouldn't care
But as the night lay dyin' and I looked in her eyes
I saw you lyin' there
Could you please try your call again later
I heard someone say somehow
Then she said this is your operator
All circuits are busy now

The crime of the century
Was when you set me free
The crime of the century
You said goodbye to me

Now here I am singin'
'bout a long, long time ago
And my memory keeps on bringin'
Up the tears that never show
In the evening, while I've got our golden glow
And when the stars are shinin' bright
Sometimes I flinch from the sting
Through my head to my toe
I felt as I left that night

The crime of the century
Was when you set me free
The crime of the century
You said goodbye to me

What the hell, I don't get much guitar playing in on this piece of metal. I hear they have a studio down at KRAN, but surprisingly I haven't checked it out.

I found an entry in Scrapper's service record, his Page Three, entered by the Military Enlistment Processing (MEPs) center, that says his typing speed is 35 words per minute. He says they tested him at the MEPs. Now I'm researching it with the Educational Services Officer, not the fucking PNC who says no to everything, to see if it would be legal to use that official entry as verifying a qualifying speed so he can get that requirement out of the way.

I can't wait to hear what they tell me tonight. Chief will say: "God damn God damn, ba-ling ba-ling, you don't follow chain of command! You should have asked me. I could tell you that we don't accept that. He doesn't have the required speed now. God damn, it has to be now. He has to pass the test. I don't know why you waste your time and you're trying to get yourself in trouble not following chain of command. You want to work nightcheck by yourself? Are you faggot? I don't know why you do so many things for this guy, and he only pulls the wool on your eyes. There must be something between you. I always thought there's something. How else are you taking care of him? Should I be down here at night and maybe get a blow job too?"

YN3 drew a caricature of PNC, and we reduced a copy and put it up on the bulkhead over Hussein's sketch, where the paper is titled, "Dickhead of the Decade." I wonder if he'll notice. I guess he could nail me for disrespect, and I'd have to come unglued about the smoking, and they'd send me back to the messdecks as a third again, and I'd finish the cruise section of this book like it started. At least maybe I'd see Sweets again.

YN3 to Hussein's troops: "Drop your drawers and walk home, 'cause you've been fucked."

0845 18 FEB 91. Everybody's getting to the horny point of sea bitch, it looks like. I'm hearing things like, "hey, sexy, come on over here and sit on this." And, "hey, Barney, Jimmy wants to fuck me." "He wants to fuck you? Well, that's between you and him. I got nothin' to do with that." And, "suck my dick." "Put it right here in my hand. Don't tease me."

I went up on deck and saw Marty doing a first class job, leading his team of electricians through some work on an oily as a gun F-14A. He seems all right, back on the job after losing his kid.

We had another guy return from emergency leave on last night's PERSTAT (the daily personnel status report I do for the Admiral), coming back from his sister's funeral. Hopefully he'll get right into the swing of things on that furious flightdeck.

The sky was mostly overcast, cumulus clouds in long, thick streaks, cooling off the guys. Fair winds and following seas. Rick was up there. He must have the dirtiest job on the flight deck, hooking up tow bars to the front wheels of jets. He had on his dungarees, no greens this time--but a green field jacket over his blue jersey. I can only assume he had his float coat on, and hope he isn't skipping that item. His face was clean, but those blue dungaree, bell bottom jeans were stained black from the shin up to his groin.

We had a plane guard out there, a guided missile cruiser between us and the coast. Just sitting patiently while we took a daytime break and got some maintenance done.

Scuttlebut on the mess deck has it that an LST, LSD, or some kind of amphibious landing craft, a troop carrier, took a mine last night and is taking on water now. We'll probably get the real scoop tonight on CNN. I figure the Iraqis must have all their eggs in the basket of a ground assault; so they'd naturally mine the hell out of the coastal perimeter.

An AT2 (Avionics Technician second class petty officer) told me a good one. He was carrying a wash bucket across the flight deck and passed in front of a turning F-14A. Suddenly the bucket flew out of his hand and got sucked right up the intake. He went crazy with hand signals to the pilot who, completely unaware of the mishap, had a hard time figuring out what he wanted and cranked the engine higher before shutting her down. Fortunately, and it would have cost a fortune, the bucket was just spinning around on the grating outside the motor and didn't hurt anything.

"The important question to ask," I teased, "is, does the bucket still work?"

It did.

PNC's sketch was off the wall--that is, taken down off the bulkhead, along with the paper saying "Dickhead of the Decade." Not a word said about it. Of course, he did grill me on my PARs. I got him to sign off most of them. And he assured me, "I'm not trying to be stingy with signing your PARs. You know, I just want you to study the things."

1700 18 FEB 91. Captain's update on the 1MC. Two, not one, ships hit a mine last night. Not only the *USS Tripoli*, but the *Princeton* as well. One serious injury, one damaged screw, both ships continuing 150 miles north of us, at least one of them with a fifteen foot by fifteen foot hole. One took it forward; the other, aft. A good reminder that we're in harm's way.

Bells. "*Major fuel oil leak, major fuel oil leak. On the flight deck. Aircraft number seven zero three. Port bow, catapult one. Away the flying squad, away. All hands stand clear of all decks, ladders and passageways.*" Five minutes later, a long two-tone whistle (meaning secure from): "*major fuel oil leak.*"

1830 18 FEB 91. Luck had it that I fell in line for chow three guys behind Sweets. I decided not to make a big thing out of it, and refrained from calling out. I thought I'd let him be. Still, luck would have none of that. I figured he would eat in his usual place, the first section aft of the main dining area; so I came back into the main room under the TV. There he was, all alone at a table with two strangers, head in his plate, with an empty seat right beside him five steps in front of me. Maybe I should have gone out of my way to get out of his way. But that little part inside of me whispered that I needed to sit by him and see what would happen. I sat down, and two guys at the next table beyond his right side noticed me, and said hello. I responded softly to both of them. Sweets never acknowledged me. He ate his spaghetti and meatballs with slices of cheese, and drank his cherry bug juice, taking over all perhaps ten minutes, not once acknowledging my presence. Nor did I speak to him. When he leaned back, I leaned back and opened so that I knew, he must have known I was right there beside him.

This whole scenario confirmed my suspicion that you guys, you men serving God and country and the NIS, are in fact intercepting my hard copy, and now you've shown some of this writing to Sweets. Or his shop has just teased him to death about the puppy dog baldhead wanna be boyfriend they perceived me to be, and gave him a bad name for putting up with me. Or, maybe he's just mad at me for videotaping him. I remember some of the shots he didn't like the way he looked.

"Let's get outa here. It's damn near your last night in the world, and you need to get fucked up."

"Where are we going?"

"Wherever you wanna go, bro."

I drove us to Johnny's. But on the way, Lou pulled the parking break up and headlights nearly crashed into my rear view mirror as I veered over to the curb. And, he shifted down and up for me when I was not in need. But at least he didn't drop the transmission out by, say, kicking it up to reverse.

"Fuck off and die, motherfucker."

He didn't know the three gentlemen at the next table. So I sort of moseyed to the middle of the bar near the pool table, and Greg walked over to face the problem. "I'm sorry, let's shake hands."

"That's okay but I don't want to shake, just go on your way."

"No, motherfucker. You shake my hand or I'll knock th' fuck out of you."

In the end he punched *me* in the nose. I guess he knew he could get satisfaction. Or it was his way of hating goodbyes. I left his ass at Johnny's after he bent the Toyota's antenna. He called just before I debarked on this piece of metal. We made up and I sold him the car for $300. He paid me two hundred, and left saying, "Bob who?"

I got a letter from Lucille. She was the court reporter on my trial in Los Angeles, the murder case. She still had the check I sent last year, $200 downpayment for the transcript. I sent her a check for the balance, another $600. I've a right to a copy of my first degree murder trial, but I have to pay for it at $2 a page. I guess it's a book in itself, at $800. That doesn't include the opening and closing arguments, which I already purchased for $250.

When that case ended and I got acquitted, I wanted to go back and sue for wrongful and malicious prosecution, bias, false testimony on the part of the LAPD, and negligent reporting on the part of the cops--like drawing the body sketch without eyes and letting the detectives think the kid was found face down. But that nagging element that the body was a kid pretty much took the fire out of any kind of fight I had left.

Here I sit in the middle of a war zone on a carrier sending jets loaded with ordnance that they're dropping all over, including on top of 500 civilians in a bunker. And I'm brooding over the seventeen-year old I killed with a baseball bat in 1984. I still see his pimpled face, and his smooth legs and ass on that bed that reeked with aerosol spray, whatever he'd been sniffing. And I still avoid vodka by the shot. And I still won't fight back, so far as I know.

Senior Chief Ross came down off the flight deck as I skated out of Personnel at ten 'til seven. I was just coming up the ladder as he came in through the hatch. "Hey, senior. How's the weather on the flight deck?"

"Actually it's real pretty out there right now." He's the maintenance master chief, the force behind getting the birds in the air, the backbone of the enlisted side of our squadron. He replaced Jaba the Hut, as they called the former master chief who stayed behind on some odd arrangement that I needn't go into. Some guys were glad to be rid of the old one. But mean as he was, at least he didn't seem to hold grudges, and you knew what he said would go since everyone--officers included--regarded him with fear. On the other hand, we seem to be getting the job done with up jets and a chief who doesn't rant and rave. I cut up there for a minute, just another scarce breath of fresh air. It was clear and cool. I guess we're standing alert 15's, because the two F-14A's set up at cat four had their canopies open and nobody in them. Our plane guard was there, off starboard.

I saw Rick again, over in the hell hole watching Fly 3 shoot some water on the nonskid. They had a couple of inch-and-a-half hoses of saltwater going. He didn't see me in the catwalk, and I didn't feel like getting up there and shooting the shit as if not soaking up his good looks.

I admit it. I was hurt all night and still feel sad about Sweets. I can't believe he just sat there beside me and didn't say a fucking word. I guess a little space made him realize I'm just a no good, dirty old man sniffing around lost. And going bald. Absence makes the heart grow fonder, when it doesn't clear the air. In this case, he broke through the smoke screen. Good on him. May I have the moral turpitude, the strength of character to leave him alone.

Suddenly I don't feel the need to walk to V3 to get a warm shower anymore, either. Like this morning, I discovered by trying that the ones across from 18 Man are working. I got in, got clean and got out without pleasure, without fantasy, just like a simple God dammed job, washing my body. No big thrill as it was at V3's head. No Sweets, no Dean, no Steve, no breakfast club. All that ended, last night, with the last supper. In silence. Now, if I just lay me down to sleep in this three by six rack and kill the racklight, and quietly rinse out my eyes, with secret tears like I learned growing up on twin beds, all will be forgotten when those human voices wake me up tonight.

0745 20 FEB 91. A short workout this morning. Their gods are their bellies, and I exercised my own. I put my legs up on a high bar with my ass on a sloping seat like a bitch in stirrups having a gynecology exam, then pushed like taking a crap and lifted over two hundred pounds fifteen times, letting each down slowly, resisting. It strains the knees, but firms inside your calves and tightens up that buttocks, those buttocks, your butt. Then I hit the thing where you lay on you belly with your heels hooked under a bar behind you, and you bend so your head is an inch above the deck, and you straighten out which raises your chest level with the rest of your body, and that strains your lower back (it hurts so good) and builds up your ass and flattens your stomach from behind. I used an iron bar across my shoulders and went level, twisted to look left then right, then down. About ten sets of ten.

I went up the ladder to the mezzanine next. It was about five thirty already, a late workout since I was busy with bullshit again, and chief had come in at midnight to light up with the Pers-O and play two games of chess.

"Chief, when you guys come in here at a quarter to one and light up, it really isn't fair."

"Point well taken," the Pers-O stated. They both doused their fags. "I understand." I knew then to prepare myself for an onslaught. Soon after, the Pers-O left and Chief went off. "You don't have anything to do?"

"Well, I've got to call this guy but he's on the roof right now, and I need to get ahold of this other guy but he's day check."

I was doing my Military Requirements for Petty Officer First Class, for no real reason because I'm getting out. Maybe I was doing it to fight chief when he tries to give me a fucked up eval on 31 March, saying I haven't done anything. I got one of the seven lessons done tonight.

"Where's (Scrapper)?"

"He's at chow."

Chief went through his box, looking to give me something back, and found the NAVGRAM I had done on Robles' travel claim. It was filed at Miramar on 5 November and normally takes ten days to liquidate. It's been three and a half months, and I gave chief a note earlier suggesting a message to the PSD at NAS inquiring. He returned it saying to make it a NAVGRAM, as if I wouldn't have known. Now it was done and he was looking at it. "Don't do the NAVGRAM yet. Call DK2. Ask him can we do it here."

"What, and just forget about PSD?"

"That's right."

I called. He was at chow. But he was there later, and chief was still playing chess with the Pers-O. "Hey, DK2. Robles' travel claim hasn't come back yet. Remember, I talked to you about it two weeks ago?"

"Yes, I remember."

"Well, chief wants to know if we can just do another one here and forget about the PSD."

"No, you have to send a message. What if you liquidate it here and they already paid it?"

Turned out, the guy owed eight hundred bucks. He'd been paid a dislocation allowance twice in the same fiscal year, which the Navy doesn't do, even if you need it. But the DK's at "A" school don't look to see if they've it coming, before giving it as they go, and now he's the second guy I've seen it happen to at this command.

Chapter Twelve

0830 22 FEB 91. We literally get the news faster from CNN than from our own chain of command. Last night I heard, via CNN, that we have been awarded the National Defense Medal--my first medal. This is the third time the award has been issued. First was World War II, I believe. Second was Vietnam. And now, whoopee! The Gulf War.

If I stayed in the Navy twenty years, I guess it would be nice to have a rack of ribbons that included this one. Maybe I should go have my cruisebook photograph taken again, with the ribbon or the medal on. (Medals come with corresponding ribbons and you wear the medal on the dress uniform, the ribbon on semi-formal occasions.)

Allow me to give you an example of the rhythm of last night: the Skipper called down from the Ready Room asking me to find some verification of a guy's VHA (Variable Housing Allowance). But the way he pronounced the name sounded like he either had a strange new accent or he wasn't sure of the name. Of course I was not about to question the skipper as he gave me an order. Even if I should have. Next, while I'm looking for evidence of this guy's VHA, the PERSO comes in looking to verify the VHA on some other dude. Two and two make four, right? Here's how I explained it to YN1.

"The Pers-O has me looking for a name I don't know, in a folder that doesn't exist, for a form he can't identify."

"Your chance for glory and immortality," came the wise response. Woody's been around. "I've got you the answer from nothing that you gave me." The Pers-O mumbled something about waking up the PNC. If only. Eventually he concluded, "we'll just handle it tomorrow."

The chief came in around midnight, just snooping around or having a cigarette or trying to catch us not working. In fact, I was working on a letter to the kids of Room 202, T. J. Kenny School, in Dorchester, Massachusetts. They're the ones who sent us a big banner at Christmas. I wrote back, and now a bag of valentines came specifically to me.

Scrapper, meanwhile, was studying the PAYPERSMAN. He'd just finished reviewing three travel claims and sorting out the correct distribution of endorsements and orders and receipts. He could have been doing some Page Four service record entries, but he said the PNSN had been bragging that there was little to do all day and he'd been studying for the exam coming up in two weeks, so I let Scrapper put the stuff in PNSN's box for now and hit the manuals. Plus, we had a major field day coming later for the zone inspection that was to include not just our cramped compartment, but the ladder and the space outside the door by the Shooter Shack as well. It was our turn to handle that, and guess who would handle that. Not me, dude. I was gonna work out. Actually, I did the office and he did the outside space and the ladder. And both of us worked out a couple of hours in there somehow. "What were all these Page Four entries doing in the PNSN's basket?" Not only was chief an asshole. He was a jerk. It was clear to me and Scrapper that he was bent on giving the PNSN every break possible to study for the exam, and to dog out the striker as if he didn't belong. I had the same notion, but I see too much of myself in the kid to let him go down without a fight. The PNSN already got an overall 4.0 eval after being here two weeks, and Scrapper, senior by a year, got a 3.8 going up for the same exam. Evals make about 30 percent of your chance to advance.

"I don't know if you wanna manage the nightcheck but I allowed my guy to put those Page Fours in the PNSN's basket."

"What do you mean, if I want to manage the nightcheck. Are you telling me you can't handle nightcheck? Maybe I should put you on days." He turned to the PN3. "PN3 do you want to go to nightcheck?"

I had already turned back to the computer and continued with my letter to the kids, ignoring that Flip flipping out. I didn't have to see or hear the response. First, I knew PN3 wouldn't say yes because he knew I liked nightcheck and he'd be stepping on me to go for it. He was friendly enough, and had enough respect for me that he wouldn't intentionally cross me. Second, chief was probably winking at him, since there's little chance that he'd really want me on daycheck with all my bitching about their smoking. He wouldn't get away with a single cigarette if he put me back on daycheck out of retaliation for my bitching at him for micromanaging my nights. I don't think he's heard from my letter to the SMO yet.

What did I say to the kids? Well, I thanked them for their sweet valentines. They were quite cute, and one struck me as indeed a piece of art. I think these kids are elevenish. I got one that folds out like a heart when you open it. Another, in pretty pink, has a constellation of glued stars, gold and silver and one white star. The most interesting came from a kid named Jeffrey, with a yellow haired cherub holding a bow and arrow, and another kid holding a heart in front of a sign, "I love you." I wondered if the kid were gay, since he was so creative. But I wasn't about to put that in the letter. It might subject him to ridicule from all the other kids. And what would it do to my heroic image? I did tell them that all of us out here love them. We love you back home. We fight for you, our friends, and our own families. We are honored to protect the interests of Kuwait, even though they are very different from us. They are much more formal in their religion and their dress, and they don't treat women the way I would want a country to treat them. But no country has the right to invade another and this is the reason we came to fight. I could eat my words if this is oversimplified. After all, we did invade Panama. Oops. Anyway, I said Iraq invaded Kuwait and we came to rescue the Kuwaitis and kick out the Iraqis even if it came to war, like it did because of Saddam Hussein, who I think is a poor excuse for a leader. there is a sayng, "pride comes before a fall." And Mr. Hussein got too proud for his own good, and too proud for his people. He won't let them tell each other how they really feel. As refugees come across the border, they are telling us that they hope we can kill him. Isn't that sad? I don't have to kill anyone directly. But everyone on the *USS Ranger* takes part in our job of killing the enemy, and sometimes by accident we kill innocent people. It bothers me. And when I hear about the protests that go on at home, I know they are thinking about the innocent people who suffer. I don't mind the protests against war, if they're clear about why they protest, and not just out there getting in the way.

Scrapper's mom is a loud protester back home, and he loves her but sometimes it embarrasses him, like when she made the front page of the city paper. He laughs about it but he's not laughing at her. He knows that she just doesn't believe people have to resort to fighting and wars in order to solve problems. People shouldn't, but they do. And we have to be ready for that, and able to win.

Hussein was on the radio again yesterday. Mentioning the word "martyrdom." How many of his people can he fool how much of the time? It's easy for him to make that call, from a bomb shelter. If his men are smart, they'll give up now. Some have. And the Army has been taking them in and feeding them. Man, how could their country get so fucked up to give that guy such a long rope to hang himself?

I got a letter from That Guy. Remember him? My old roommate. He calls himself my "old pal," and says he missed me that night I was "supposed to come over and spend some jacuzzi time." He neglects to apologize for never calling to confirm. What was I just supposed to appear?

His real intent, based on fifty percent of the letter being devoted to the subject, was procuring the VIN (Vehicle ID Number) of my old Toyota so he could sue the bitch who rear-ended him. I thought he would have gone to court by now. It seems he needs it all on 25 February. Let's see, maybe if I staple it to a sea gull?

He wonders why I didn't park the car in his extra space for the duration of this deployment. The car I sold to Louie. He's a real jerk, there's no doubt about it, and he's clueless. But I still like his enthusiasm, and he's probably no worse in his own right than any other dickhead out there. Aside from the constant theft of my toilet paper, and as far as roommates go, he was fun.

The funny part, including that it's too late to do anything for the guy, is that I don't have a clue about that car anymore. All the stuff I didn't give to him or Louie is either stored on the beach, stored in the void, or stored in the deep blue sea. One other part that fits in this paragraph--he didn't rave on about making second, so I guess he didn't. Yuk. What is it they say in the competitive world of show business: not only must I succeed, you must fail. Better luck next time, pal!

The total sorties since the war began 36 days ago is now over 88,000. The total number of Iraqi POWs so far is 1,355. As for *Ranger*, it's been overcast and rainy lately. But that hasn't prevented us from launching strikes against Iraqi targets. The Intruder, paraphrasing from the ship's paper, the *Top Gun Gazette*, has the advantage of being able to deliver its ordnance under low visibility such as severe cloud cover, rain or darkness. On Wednesday, for example, the day before yesterday, 25 Intruders, 10 F-14 Tomcats, five E-2C hawkeyes, and five EA-6b Prowlers participated in strikes. They dropped 102 Mark 83 1,000-pound bombs, 59 Mark 82 500-pound bombs, 20 Mark 20 rockeye cluster bombs and one Mark 82 laser-guided bomb. The first "package" was launched at 1700 and the last, recovered at 0145 (Thursday). Targets included airfields in northern Kuwait, patrol boats, armor and artillery positions in the Kuwaiti Theater of Operations. They encountered little opposition, and no planes were damaged.

We're no longer going after communications centers and oil storage facilities. Now it's troop concentrations, artillery pieces, tanks and bunkers. Like LTjg Mike Scheiber, VS-38's Intell Officer said, "every tank we take out with a bomb is one more Marine we bring home."

And a final piece of *Ranger* trivia: *Ranger* will be decommissioned in 1993. Reminds me of a song I haven't sung since Mission Beach.

Gun Turret Two

What really happened up in gun turret two
That killed forty-seven of the Iowa's crew
Was Gunner's Mate Hartwig a suicide fag
Or was somethin' wrong with a gunpowder bag
Certainly Hartwig is likely to blame
The Navy reported and tarnished his name
He could have had a reason with such a good friend
Who got his insurance when he met his end
The Iowa skipper, retiring in May
Said they're full of it if they're calling him gay
That crew wasn't trained. and the ship's undermanned
It's a helluva lot more likely the powder keg jammed
And I don't need the Navy defaming my crew
For whatever happened in gun turret two
They all knew the powder was dangerously old
And the budget for weapons had cut us out cold
For the plans had the Iowa scheduled to meet
The New Jersey enroute to the mothball fleet
So here's to the souls of the Iowa crew
It must have been hell up in gun turret two

The ship's POD says the Media Pool will be back onboard, 25 February. So we better keep a close watch for exocets or we'll be walking briskly to GQ.

0830 22 FEB 91. I come through the berthing compartment and pass the lounge as Louis Armstrong sings, "What A Wonderful World" to the video of Robin Williams in "Good Morning Vietnam," including the backdrops of burning villages and children crying. As it ends, the vibration of a real helicopter overhead grows louder until, ka-wham, it drops its load of bombs on deck. The vert rep lasts for hours.

We'll have a beer day on the 25, the day the Media Pool joins us. Unless the ground war starts today, or tomorrow. I bet it'll begin today. We're supposed to anchor at 0800, running late now with the underway replenishment. And do maintenance like fixing the flight deck, giving it a serious scrubdown.

Right now Steve says he can run and slide on the hangar deck, it's so slick from fuel spills that have had only cursory clean-ups in the past month. He's having a lot of fun racing motorized three-wheel carts through the hangar bay, fucking off like an immature E3 should.

It's a strange and charming mixture of boy and man that you find nowhere more abundant than the military. Well, except maybe in San Francisco where they separate the men from the boys with a crowbar. But I'm talking about the transformation acted out by teenage boys who grow up directing the movements of multi-million dollar missile platforms on a battle schedule, under a great deal of adult stress, heightened by the complicated psychological side effect of fringe fighting, being there but not "there," in the Gulf putting bombs on target but not in the desert fighting hand- to-hand, as this war makes heroes of us all.

They face, and must respond to a naive, but sincere and natural worship from those at home, friends and strangers. These boys cling to childhood antics and mystery thrills like the blue hole rumbles, where flight deck and hangar deck Blue Shirts invite Crash and Salvage crews (two to four at a time) into the Blue Hole (a lounge for blue shirts) and kill the lights then beat the shit out of them, actually just getting them down and giving red bellies, and doing a lot of wrestling and tickling, but making it into a huge rivalry to talk about day in and day out.

They look forward to wog day with whippings, and the punishing ritual of cleansing "special case" wogs, cracking them on the butt with a four-foot section of fire hose known as a sheleli, one in the hand of every self-respecting shellback, provided by the ship at the expense of older hoses; and "sea bats" in the hands of the vicious, made of the armpads stolen from lounge chairs, frighteningly similar to the blackjacks used by cops. They plan, chide and map out who'll get what kind of treatment when that day comes, and it'll come, whenever we can get this ship over the equator into the magic realm of Davey Jones' Locker. Pollywogs (wogs) are sailors who have not yet crossed the equatorial Latitude of 00 degrees in the company of shellbacks (who are little more than veteran wogs themselves) in the tradition of Shellback Initiation. This day holds promise that your ass will be sore for six fuckin' days straight.

This event is extremely sexual in nature, and harbors the only endorsement of homosexuality that I have ever heard of sanctioned by the military. It usually happens when you've been away from women for quite some time. If you're really lucky, you'll be ordered to climb up on a back and fuck another wog right in the ass. With clothes on, of course. One dude, whom I happen to know is a gay fag, got sandwiched on last Westpac. He had the time of his life, like riding a bronco between two other guys. He flashed a huge grin. And why not, after all the time going without, suddenly getting down and dirty and nasty and whipped and verbally abused and covered with food and peanut butter and grime and rubbing crotches among thousands of young men who are all too busy beating or getting beaten to have a square look at you getting off. I wonder how many sailors come in their pants. In the end, you throw off all your clothes and take a saltwater shower on the flight deck, butt naked in broad daylight. You throw your clothes on a pile to be dumped off the fantail, and parade nude through the ship to your berthing for a freshwater shower where you undoubtedly have to masturbate, if you haven't already. Trust me. I'm a shellback. These are your heroes, twisted and freaked out by what they have to do to serve America, land of the free. Going without beer for forty-five days, or until the war gives us a break.

An avionics tech got a message yesterday, his wife's ex-husband broke into their home and beat her up, then kidnapped their baby. So he launched a Ready Alert on the shop equipment. But the guy bought himself into it. Did he know she had already been married? Yes. Did he know she'd had a jealous husband? Yes, he did.

The shit is probably hitting the fan today about the smoking in my shop. The DAPA (Drug Alcohol Prevention Advisor, something like that) Officer, a Lieutenant, had the SDO last night when I called on some other deal, and mentioned my letter. "Were you trying to get ahold of me?"

"No sir, but I do expect you to take action on my letter."

"Is there any other place they can smoke that you know of?"

"I don't know." And, I thought, I don't care. "But maybe the Shooter Shack next door, they smoke a lot and YN3 has been going in there to light up lately.

"Well, I know where you're comin' from. I'm a nonsmoker, too." Hooray! The DAPA's a nonsmoker! I've got pull on my side.

"Well, if you can handle it at your level that's fine. But if you feel like you need to run it on up the chain, I'm all for it. I know that Cag is a nonsmoker, and he doesn't allow smoking in their Admin office. But I'm prepared to go a lot further than the Senior Medical Officer if necessary. I'll go all the way to Washington if I have to, because this is bullshit. And we've got four more months left of this cruise."

"Yeah, they've gotta go somewhere else."

I hope he doesn't just read it, feel impacted, and go flying.

Speaking of which, somebody found a razorblade in an engine, a day or two ago. The skipper probably overreacted, flipped out and put a note in the POD that it reeked of sabotage, he would get to the bottom of it and reward anyone who got him there, and let the punishment fit the crime. Come on. Razorblades are a weak link in squadron tool control, and every shop uses them. It probably fell out of some duct diver's pocket (where it shouldn't have been), and now the kid would be crazy to confess the error of his ways. What if they shot him? It's probably just another symptom of us being so close to the war, but with F-14's designed for air-to-air combat, the only chance we have against the Iraqis is chasing after helos. And the skipper got a taste of blood the other day, but all it did was whet his appetite. He probably feels embarrassed already about the note, after thinking it over and allowing the possibility of the conclusion I stated (which I confess was not my own but was put forth by the AMH2 running First LT). But he won't retract his blast in the POD any sooner than Hussein will lose face in Kuwait. Thus, like the weird arguments of the world, this will remain an unsolved mystery in the history of WOLFPACK at war.

0900 24 FEB 91. So much for beer day. We're making all preparations for getting underway, and expect to conduct flight ops again tonight by 2200. The Captain's boat went in the water last night, and came back up a few minutes ago. I'll bet he's pissed, because he didn't get to go fishin'. We were gonna have steal beach all day today, partying and eating and drinking beer and sleeping and lounging around.

Nobody really thought Saddam Hussein was gonna pull out. He's a fucking maniac, we all know that; and now he's on the verge of a massive mental orgasm, at the apex of satiation -- just about to come!

I wonder how he'll go, in the end. Do you suppose he'll stand there and toss up his hands, in some final surrender, expecting Noriega's treatment? Or perhaps blow his own brains out? I bet he's got a cyanide capsule, something quick and painless. He never struck me as having the guts to blow his own head off. But I'm sure he'll fair the same as Mussolini, if he lives. And I don't believe he wants to live. Isn't Mussolini the guy they hung upside down in Germany, at the end of World War II?

Sec Def put a lid on the Pentagon briefs a few hours after the ground war began. DESGRU SEVEN and *Paul F. Foster* were just gonged aboard. I guess they'll have a conference in the war room. Man, I just hope we keep the bombs on target and don't kill any of our own guys. I'm praying so hard for David Harris, five foot five and a buck oh five, cutest little Marine I've ever seen; his sergeants; and my cousin, and my uncle over there. I feel like their mother, over here supporting the boys (and girls now) with love and rockets, in the shit, but not in the thick of it.

Here's my famous note to the *Ranger*'s XO, if it gets pinned up on the bulletin board. Bear in mind I found out, after I wrote it, XO is a cigarette fiend. I was gonna take a new tack, but Scrapper convinced me not to compromise my writing--and that struck a cord with what I saw in "Biloxi Blues," which is why sometimes I feel like the NIS must be intercepting my mail. If I compromise anything I'm writing about, half-shut my mouth, there won't be anything worth prying open.

XO,

I'm doing my part putting bombs on target like the rest of us. But I am sick of putting up with a massive, passive smoke inhalation, from the burning oilfield that my shop has become. Sometimes in here it looks like Iraq from cigarette smoke: My supervisor, my LCPO, the Department Head, my CMC and our career counselor have all lit up at the same time and that's, a, drag.

Mine is one of the few remaining vestiges of mixed membership where non-smokers haven't rooted out smokers. There's the rub (and in my eyes). They gather here like some watering hole, and my eyes water. But I work with khakis, and since I wear the dungarees in the family, master chief puts it with an air of impunity: "f--- you. If you don't like it, TAD." Say the CO smoked, and his orderly didn't.

RANGERINST 5100.7B states "*there shall be no smoking in spaces shared by smokers and non-smokers, except in areas designated for smoking ... each designated area is to have ventilation sufficient to ensure non-smokers' breathing is not infringed upon.*" Are these instructions designed to blow smoke up my ass? Or were they written in the blood of guys who died with tar torn lungs? You don't have to remind me that we're cooped up in here--I'm the one who doesn't smoke. But push comes to shove. Are they gonna blow smoke up my ass? Or will you help me help them to help themselves, and ease the chain smoke off my chain of command?

You got the fat boys active. If they can sweat it out, can't you implement a program to clear the air and make the bulkheads white again? You control if, when and how many beers we have. How do you explain a smoker in khakis with an armload of cigarette cartons while the Secretary of the Navy proclaims, "nonsmoking is the norm"?

GRAHAM'S GAGGIN'

Tune in next week for the XO's response, if any. Scrap says plenty of heads will turn in the passageway. So maybe it will find a place on the board, who knows. But what the hell, man. I'm damn sick of the bullshit in my shop catering to the khakis. They can blow it out their own asses. No, I wouldn't want that, either.

0830 24 FEB 91. Over the deep end, out of control. Remind me to write myself a memo not to write anymore memos for the rest of my career. No matter what career. David O. Selznik I am not.

PNC gave me a punishment assignment to verify all service records. This has been done in the past, but now he wants it done again for not just the newly arrived. But once again for all. 200. If I don't gun deck the job, it should take about twenty minutes per service record. As he told Scrapper, "I don't want you and Graham working out on Navy time."

Oh, and another thing. He wanted to know who put the caricature of himself over the face of Hussein on the "Dick of the Decade" poster. He asked Scrapper four times. "Who did it? Did Graham do it? Who did it? I'm going to ask you again--who did it?" Man, he wanted blood. This was three days after the fact, at least two full days after it had been torn down. Suddenly he's all pissed off. I wonder if it has anything to do with me coming down on him for smoking....

Tonight when I come to work he's going to chew me out for doing only a couple of service records (and dealing with four customers, and organizing one reenlistment, filling out one 3068 without the Travel Claim, verifying one

Page Two and sitting two shifts on the 2JZ in Ready Eight as Scrapper saw the DK and went to chow) and spending the rest of the time researching, drafting and polishing a special request for time off during normal working hours to lift weights. Not that the fucking S/R's need to be done right away. I've been around long enough to know that they don't.

The dilemma is this. Coming fresh from the last inning, where I hit the senior chief for illegally smoking, this wasn't the best timing to swing at PNC's pitch about the workouts. I could have waited a day or two. In effect, it begins to look like I've gone mad with memos, a syndrome that didn't play well in the Western show with Amy. "Oh my god, not another memo," she'd say. And the trouble is, the khakis down in my shop have nothing else pressing but to fight this PN2 who complains about everything. He can't sleep for the noise in the berthing. He can't work for the smoke in his office. He doesn't get time off to go play in the gym. I can hear it now: FUCK THAT GUY.

Somebody told me that they had a nonsmoker speak up in Maintenance Control. A chief. Do you think they had to make that hard charging shop smoke free? The chief is now TAD to Flight Deck Control.

Somebody else mentioned that the berthings, which were not so designated last cruise, are now smoke free because one person put in a complaint to the command master chief. The dude said, "what's good for the goose is good for the gander."

Even the Shooters, next door to Pers, don't want me diverting my smokers to them. "Hey, I know how you feel," said TEE. "Even though I smoke, I don't want anymore smokers coming in here."

"Yeah," Hess said. "It's a lot different smelling somebody else's smoke than smelling your own." The point echoed between five guys in there, four of whom were in one stage or another of lighting up. Man, if the smokers can't hang with more, how in the hell am I supposed to hang? If it's by a Navy rope, they better get ready to swing with me.

"I go in there," I said, rubbing my face, "and thirty minutes later it's like I have an extra layer of skin."

This, my friends, is your battle I am fighting. You may have mixed feelings about me as I tell all. But I do fit the nonsmoking martyr box, and I am putting up a tremendous fight against enormous, and alas, perhaps insurmountable odds, on behalf of creating a smoke free, healthy environment aboard Naval vessels. What second class petty officer does anyone know who is crazy enough to take on his chain of command and put them at odds with the Secretary of the Navy on behalf of a policy that was tough getting through Congress in the first place, and many in the service take as so much rhetoric?

Am I a true blue professional abiding by the rules and seeking to enforce them in support of the Equal Opportunity program? Or am I just a hot headed, trouble minded fool?

I'm frocked to second, and if busted one paygrade (let's say for disrespect) I'd go from E4 to E3, meaning I'd lose both stripes off my crow.

From PO2 to NONPO. I wonder how thick is the case file, and who's holding it. No doubt it's PNC. But it could be YNCS. Master Chief would act the neutral, objective observer, coolly vouching for anything the rest of them say.

"He drew this picture of me and called me a dickhead. That's a second class talking to a chief. And he talks to me all the time with disrespect. I don't know, I know the guy has had some problems with his temper in the past -- it's in his record on his 1966, he was charged with a killing."

"Yeah, he scares me, too." Senior would sound genuine. "I remember when he went off on PNC in the XO's office back at Miramar. He had death in his eyes. I thought he was gonna jump out of that chair and strangle the chief." Meanwhile, I'd be standing there at attention before the XO, fuming at their bullshit or failing to restrain a maniacal smirk.

"What are we gonna do about you, Graham?" That would be the XO, pointed, cut and dry.

"Well sir, I was thinking I could solve the whole thing if I take up cigars. You got one?"

XO smokes. You know, it's like that dandelion from back in grade school--"she loves me, she loves me not." I go up the chain of command: YN1, the nightcheck LPO, is a nonsmoker, the Navy loves me. PNC, the office supervisor, is a smoker, the Navy loves me not. YNCS, the LCPO, is a smoker, the Navy still loves me not. CMC, the command master chief, is a smoker, the Navy hates me. LT Phillips, the DAPA, is a nonsmoker, the Navy loves me. XO is a smoker, the Navy loves me not. CO is a nonsmoker, I think, I think the Navy loves me. XO of the *Ranger* is a smoker, the Navy loves me not. CAG (Commander, Carrier Air Wing Two, our boss and at equal with the Captain of the *Ranger*) is a nonsmoker, the Navy loves me. Let me see, is the Commander in Chief a smoker?

How can I rave on about this trivial bullshit, while Marines are in the field? Look at it this way--Scrapper is ninety percent convinced he will reenlist to go SEALs. Who do you think he looks to in weighing his decision? I talked a friend into going SEALs when I was 16, and he became a SEAL and served in Nam and had a fantastic career. I could be responsible for one more feather in the Command's retention hat by encouraging this lad to get his PN3 crow and go SEALs. In the meantime, letting him have his nightly workout will help him pass the pre-qual for the program. That is a reasonable, common sense and supportive move for a responsible leading petty officer who sees things on the broad scale. Especially in my shop where there isn't any mission critical work at all, and the bullshit work is fairly slack.

I was almost too old when I came in, and was too young when I first wanted to join. And here's the pay-off, knowing what really matters, with a flip trying to fuck us over. That's the difference between those born and raised in the USA and these goddamn foreigners milking our Navy: A broader picture of American defense. When we have those budget cutbacks, and start phasing out the troopers, I hope to God that we get rid of the ones who want us out of their countries before we put American citizens in the breadline.

We stood up to MOPP level 2 last night when some of the ground pounders found chemical weapons enroute to Kuwait. So we carried the chemical weapons suits around all night. Just now, we stood back down to MOPP level 1, and in the words of the Captain, "latest intelligence shows that the threat to the ship of chemical weapons, is minimal, so keep 'em close by, but put those bad boys down and you don't have to carry 'em anymore."

0800 26 FEB 91. I feel like I've been beaten up. A few rounds with the heavy bag, you know?

At 1515 I heard the flip of a cigarette lighter outside my rack curtain. They can't get you this easily in civilian life.

"Graham. Mas' Chief wants to see you. So, dress up."

What the fuck did that mean, "dress up?" In English it would relate to the high school prom. Or Captain's Mast or at the very least, XOI. Did he mean for me to put on my dress whites? Naw, he's just a fucking flip who can't speak English, and he means "get dressed."

So, I got dressed in a clean jersey and dungaree uniform, went to the head and shaved, wetted down my worn out ragtop, and presented myself in Personnel.

The Command Master Chief pulled out a photocopy of my memo to the XO of *Ranger*. "Cag called the skipper about this and the (squadron) XO thinks you jumped the chain of command."

"I just wrote a letter to the XO board like anybody on the ship can. I didn't put the squadron in there."

"You didn't have to. The senior chief at XO Admin pulled it out of the XO's box, like he's supposed to do, and in the course of screening it apparently decided that it was improperly routed, and sent it up to Cag. Cag investigated, called around to a few squadrons, and eventually determined that it was from VF-1. I got this copy of it, and when the skipper read it he went off. Now the XO has ordered you to go find the original and bring it back.

"I know exactly where it is -- it's in XO Admin."

"Well, go get it."

I waited around half an hour and finally the senior chief came in. Meanwhile, two guys told me the famous *Ranger* scuttlebut, "if one person complains, the smoking lamp goes out."

"Can I help you?"

"Are you the senior chief?"

"Yes."

"I'm PN2 Graham from VF-1. I wrote a memo to the XO about the problem of smoking. Now I've been ordered by my squadron to come down and retrieve it."

He took my name and number.

"I know where it is." Back at Pers, the CMC had a worried tone. "The master chief of the boat has it. After the eight o'clocks, I'll go get it."

"Okay."

"We're gonna have a meeting tonight," he said. "We'll have a discussion and hash this whole thing out."

"I'm not trying to be unreasonable," I heard myself falling into an "ogre" mentality.

"Well, go get some chow, or go back to sleep if you wanna, and we'll work this out tonight."

"I'm going back to bed." I walked away thinking, who in the hell is my Congressman? I'm thirty-four and don't know the name and address of my Congressman. I never got back to sleep.

"How many service record verifications have you done?" Chief threw the first punch as I walked in. "I asked you last night at ten o'clock. And how many have you done until this morning?"

"Let's see. A couple."

"A couple."

Fortunately, a customer was waiting. So I took the liberty of breaking off the conversation--helping him for as long as possible, 'til the thought passed.

"And this request chit. You can run it if you want, but I'll write a note on it you might not like. You want to work out, you can work out if there's nothing to do. But do you have anything to do?"

"Well, there's always something to do."

"That's what I mean."

"But what I put in the memo is, as long as it doesn't significantly impact the work flow." Actually, I'd changed it to say "doesn't interfere with normal duties," which was a loser.

"Well, maybe I'll wait until the smoke clears." Finally, the master chief hauled me out of the frying pan into the fire.

"We're ready for a discussion," he said rather fairly.

I dragged in a chair and chief followed. I sat between YNCS and the master chief, PNC looking over my shoulder.

"I'm not your supervisor," CMC began. "But since I share this office, I'm part of this family here and I'm involved in working this out, and I'm the senior member present, I'll start it off."

I nodded agreement and wrote down everything he said on the back of my original memo to the ship's XO, which the CMC handed me.

"First of all, if I wanted to be a hard ass, at 0200 I got a call you were on the flight deck. You're not trained to be out there and you were wearing a floatcoat that you're not even supposed to have. And everybody out there knew who you were. I could have let that become a big problem, but I calmed the people down." I knew the son of a bitch he was talking about, the same chief who kept jumping in front of the camera as I was trying to videotape some night time cat shots, with glowing afterburners. He's the same chief who was counseled last cruise for beating on the line rats, and was almost written up on charges of assault a few weeks ago for the same behavior, only the shop

LPO went to First LT instead. And this guy is on my video roughs from Westpac 89, in a P.I. bar with a choke hold on a local flippette. I was up there with the very best petty officer the skipper has ever seen, of whom I quote from the recent evaluation which I typed, "the Navy must retain this superstar." All trainees are accompanied on the flight deck by such experienced hands, shortly after a spell on Vulture's Row behind the bridge overlooking the flight deck. And finally, the floatcoat was in the trash when I resurrected and refurbished it last cruise. My CMC was blowing smoke.

"Electrical safety checks," he went on. This is called retaliation, when something known to be ongoing is suddenly brought out as a problem, in the course of discussing unrelated events. "You have an illegal extension cord. All extension cords have to have a circuit breaker."

"Mine has one."

"No it doesn't."

"I'll show you." I got up and led him to the NC1's desk where my circuit breaker equipped extension cord was plugged in leading to my desk.

The CMC, however, pointed to the squadron extension cord, a homemade looking black piece of shit.

"Oh that. That's not even mine. It belongs to the squadron and we brought it from Miramar."

"It doesn't matter. It's illegal."

So he was blaming me for utilizing equipment provided by the command. Now I knew I was dealing with an unreasonable, pissed off and frightened type of guy. The best thing to do would be to be nice.

"And, your attitude has deteriorated since you made second. Other people have complained that you're, I don't wanna use the word 'cocky.' But arrogant. You and your Airman had it out the other night. I heard about it. He needs training and strokes, not you degrading him. Say you happen to be around when you make chief petty officer and he works for you. How do you want him to act as a second?"

"Can we get him in here? I'd like him to hear what you just said and get his response whether I've been degrading him. I had to break him of some problems with skating off. The other night, what you heard about, was I read him the riot act about coming in ten minutes late four nights in a row then going to chow on Navy time and coming back 90 minutes later and constantly taking off again."

"Well, there's no need for that. That's just what I heard. You've upset a lot of people. You've gotten a lot of visibility in the last week that you don't need. This isn't a master chief talking, this is just my personal observation."

"Who have I pissed off?"

"Well, let me put it this way. When I come in and a chief is leaving, and he mentions in passing that Graham must be having another bad day, that tells me there's a problem. Anyway, that's about all I have. Senior chief, do you want to add anything?"

"Well," he began to go off. "I don't see a lot of assholes in here. But I see you becoming one. And please put that pen away. I don't want you writing down every word I say."

"Why not?"

"Because I don't want it showing up in another memo out there," he waved an arm.

I put away the pen and let him wail on me a while.

"As a smoker," he said, "I feel pissed off. As a human being I feel like I have rights and I want to smoke. I've been smoking for twenty-five years and next month I'm going to quit on my birthday, and I've been planning this for ten years." He suddenly seemed to lighten up. "And I'm gonna be counting on you to stock me with gum and chips and candy, all right?"

PNC sat there behind me, plotting and planning and keeping his mouth shut. I better look out, because I figure when the smoke has cleared, he'll hit me with a counseling chit on some entirely unrelated incident, like the Dickhead of the Decade.

Finally CMC came around again with the pitch. "I don't want this to look like the joke I made about 'fuck you, go TAD.' But if you've reached the point where you don't want to work in here anymore because of the smoke, they really need a guy to go TAD to the Ship Master-At-Arms. And, if you still wanna fix that door, you could go to First Lieutenant. This is if you wanna."

Right, going to SMAA is like putting my disk on their desk. I don't need them getting to know me and snooping about my mannerisms. What if they think I have a lisp, or a slight effeminate swish, or if they remember the file and start poking around.... But the bottom line I woke up on is, you don't go TAD (especially as a second) unless you're somehow fucked up. So no matter how long or short I have in the Navy, fuck the TAD bullshit.

"Well, I wouldn't be too strongly opposed to going to the ship's master-at-arms billet. But I'd have to see how the chief feels about it."

I sensed him getting nervous behind me. Could his dream come true with me TAD? Or would that shatter his chance at slamdunking my periodic eval, 31 March?

"No, I don't want to go TAD. I want to stay here."

Chief suddenly got up and left.

"But I don't want my eval to suffer."

"Hey chief," senior called. But PNC was out the door already, gone to smoke I suppose. Why in the fuck did he walk out in the middle of this big discussion to resolve the smoking problem anyway?

"I wanted him to hear that. Anyway, your eval has already suffered. I've never seen the skipper so hot. When that memo came back he took it as if you had put him on report."

In the end (and I hope it's the end), we settled on a plan that recognizes the reality of serving our country, couped up in a Naval vessel where nobody in their right mind would spend six months if they didn't have to.

The 2300 to 0700 ban on smoking would prevail. And only those persons actually employed in the Admin/Personnel space would be authorized to smoke there. A memo that I would draft, subject to a reasonable chop, would be put in the POD forthwith stating something along those lines. I almost wrote it on a yellow pad, then thought better of covering my ass and put it in a memo.

Subj: REQUEST POD NOTE
Ref: (a) Conversation between YNCS, CMC, PNC and me

1. In accordance with reference (a), please include the following POD note at your earliest convenience: Smoking in VF-1 Administrative and Personnel Departments onboard Ranger is limited to Admin/Pers staff and NC1. Authorized hours, 0700 to 2300.

2. Thanks.

Later last night, YN1 brought me my memo about YNCS tearing down the sign -- which, by the way, he gleefully pointed out he had not thrown away but had moved to a position out of view above the shredder. Tricky, tricky.

The memo had green and red ink on it. The green read:

Pers O,
Have you been informed of this? Please investigate and pass to Admin O.
XO

To this minute, the Pers O has not said one word to me about this, other than "I'll smoke in the shooter shack" when it was after 2300.

The red read, *PN2 ... see me*. He didn't need to sign it. I tried to see him last night between his 0230 brief and 0400 combat air patrol. Doesn't this sound like small shit when you're fighting a war? But he was too busy, naturally, and left word with the SDO for me to try and catch him "tomorrow night." I guess I'll get my ass chewed, that's how it usually goes when you are told to see the CO. I'm sure I had a typo in my chain of command somewhere, like this memo bypassed the Pers O, who was one of my problems. And I didn't fully use the chain of command like it says in the Navy Rights and Responsibilities course, because when I read it my eyes fixated on the paragraph right below that sentence, giving the gouge about your rights to grieve and seek redress without fear of reprisal or retaliation. They could get off on a technicality.

Hopefully, the skipper will only cry about being made a fool in my memo to the *Ranger* XO, and I'll have the defense that I couched it in general terms. And I'll have corroborating statements from the CMC that Cag had to figure out where it came from. He'll have to blame himself for being preoccupied with the war to the point of neglecting the freedoms we're fighting for: Even if this is a war ship and not a democracy, there are instructions from higher authority that are meant to be followed aggressively and CO's will be held accountable. He'll bite the bullet and worry if this one aw shit ruins his attaboy for killing ragheads in a helo.

Off we go again with Billy Tell: Eight A-6's, 96 Rock Eye, battlefield interdiction, significant trucks, tanks and buses. Hits on buses, five tanks, armored personnel carriers, other vehicles. Looks like the guys are movin' out, and we're hittin' 'em hard until there's not much left of 'em. Joke 'em if they can't take a fuck.

0945 27 FEB 91. Did all that shit happen yesterday? I thought this book was gonna be four or five hundred pages. But if this war doesn't end soon, I'll have a fucking epic.

The Captain says we've averaged a hundred sorties a day over the past month and a half. I'm on fifty something in the PERSTAT daily, nearly two months since I started tracking whether anybody in VF-1 has been killed. So far so good, but we're still reporting ground fire. I'm not gonna say you can't hit an F-14A with a rifle.

Medals, medals, medals. Rumors abound. And reenlistments are up. After all, why get out when you're just about to get three rows of ribbons on your shirt? They won't do you any good on the mantle. We heard about the National Defense medal. Louie was asking me if we got that before I left. Now I have some idea what the hell he was talking about. Plus I heard they are granting the Joint Services Commendation Medal, which is good for three points on the beginning multiple of the Navywide advancement exam -- but won't come down in black-and-white until the test has passed. So it can't be figured in for the March exam.

It goes 9, 9, 6, 12, 36. You have to be an E1 nine months before you can advance to E2 (and have your request chit approved, in case your immediate supervisor (and thus, the chain of command, because they normally back him), wants to fuck you up. Or in the case of at least one asshole I know. This idiot got himself in trouble just before he was due to advance to E2, and got out of having his pay docked. But didn't dare run the chit to advance. Then a few months later, when things cooled down, he tried to run a chit for back pay. He had a couple of LT's going for it, but like I told them, the skipper wasn't about to forget that NJP (non-judicial punishment, where he got a suspended bust). So they advanced him on the 16th following the month he actually submitted his request.

Like me, you could come in as an E3. If you had some college. I had a fucking degree and supposedly could have been commissioned, but I believe you and I, we've been through that, and this is not my fate. So I skipped E2. In six months I was eligible for E4, and got "selectee" my first time up. That meant I didn't make "first, second, or third increment." You either got it, or made selectee. So I was advanced on the September exam, frocked 16 December if my memory serves, and started getting paid the following April 16th. I think E1 to E2 is about a $60 a month raise. E2 to E3 is maybe $50. But at E4 you get Career Sea Pay, an extra $60 a month, on top of your $40 or so a month regular pay raise.

They say E5 is your best tax bracket, where you make your most profit margin. Low tax bracket, relatively high income. You have to stay there three years before even testing for E6. Which means, you'll finish your first enlistment as an E5 at best. I got $850 on my last payday, but I've got all that wild shit happening now like no tax, back pay from half of January, imminent danger pay, and that career sea pay. I'm one of the few guys not sweating our DK, since I'm a PN and I hear it all, all the bitching. I feel sorry for him even if he can't communicate. Like, a couple of guys got $75 Beneficial Suggestion incentive awards and today the paperwork went out to DK2. So he comes up with this bullshit that it's taxable. The manual says incentives are. But it doesn't cover incentives given in a combat zone, evidently because nobody ever thought of it before. "Well, look at the foundation of the argument. Pay is taxable according to the manual, right?"

"No, there is a table." He showed me the DODPM (don't ask), and there was a column explaining the taxability for everything under the sun--except incentive awards given in a combat zone.

"Where's it say that you tax incentive awards given in a combat zone?"

"You have a good point, because it doesn't say that we have to tax it but it doesn't say that we don't have to either."

"So why make your decision against the interest of the member? I think you should run a bene-sug of your own, asking for a change to the publication to cover incentive awards given in a combat zone. Because you can't go either way without a decision from higher authority."

"I know, you have a good point there."

What the fuck. It wasn't gonna do me any good. But I'm like that, you see. I'm fighting for every penny that the government can give these guys. Look at it this way. I'm 34 living in L.A. as a reader, putting out a better script every three months. And getting those connections. Four years in the Navy, vice four in Hollywood? I would have made a fortune by now on something, some formulaic script with all the right pacing, angles, structure, tailored six different ways for potential principals. I figure it's an investment to be here, and I'm writing it all off to "bad debt." Hopefully, this fucking diary will settle the score.

Chapter Thirteen

1030 27 FEB 91. 1st LT has been working on that slamming berthing door for three days now. I finally got my door hinge, and it went out of adjustment so that every time it shut it slammed. It was 50% worse than before. But, the AMH2 running the show got pissed that a fucking door hinge was kicking his ass, and with a few adjustments he finally fixed it. For a day. Then last night the screw worked out and spilled fluid all down the door, and it started slamming even harder. Now, I think they've got it licked again.

"What did you do?" I asked the AMH2 running First LT.

"I took the one off Personnel."

What a sexy word at sea, licked. Take a licking. Or chew someone out. Let someone strike you as a gentleman. Or cold cock you. Tell someone to come on, come by, come here, come over. Drop on by and have a load of fun. Have a gay old time, fucking asshole. Say, "thanks for having me."

Like LT Davis (Ranch) said, "this cruise is like a sore dick. You just can't beat it."

Over my head I hear the acid trip whistle of a wave off, eeyoowwsh, gunning engines several feet above the flight deck. Another hooks the wire, plow, yank. It rewinds, zzzzzmmmmmnnn, kalakalakumpump; diddle iddle.

I heard another good one from Scrap, aka Dennis the Menace. Back in P.I., he ran into a couple of buddies in a bar. They had just banged a hooker, one in her ass, the other in her mouth.

"Hey, take your dick out of her mouth."

"Okay."

"Bitch, say fuck me fuck me I'm chief (name withheld)."

She did it as he pounded her doggie style.

"Where you guys goin' now," Scrapper asked.

"I'm off to fuck the skipper. Tomorrow's the XO."

Somebody published an open letter on the boat:

> My Dearest President Hussein:
>
> I hope this letter reaches you in the best of health. Think of you often, so I decided to write you this letter to let you know I am doing well and so is Babs. I understand we don't exactly see eye to eye on this Kuwait thing, but I am sure after I explain my feelings on the matter you will undoubtedly see my point.
>
> I guess I should just get straight to the meat of the matter and say....
>
> Read my lips, get the funk out of Kuwait you rag-head son-of-a-camel-humping-bitch before I turn loose my Air Force and make a multi-national parking lot out of your piece of camel shit country and then send the fuckin' Army and Marines to paint the fuckin' lines on it! I won't even need my Navy, because by that time your sorry ass will be sitting next to Allah and you won't be concerned about too much of anything any more! Now do you understand my meaning?
>
> Well, Babs is calling me to dinner so I'll close for now. Give my best to the other

little rag-heads. Keep in touch.

All My Love,

George.

P.S. I hear the old camel is pregnant again. I guess you still got it. CONGRATULATIONS!

Sweets came back to the pages of my book, lovely soul. He looked emaciated. I caught him on video as I stood on the flight deck over the edge of the elevator (and got my ass chewed for being over the guard wire). He was sitting on the round edge of the hole in the side of the ship, with his head between his knees and his mickey mouse ears and float coat on. Then I ran into him and Steve and we had a breakfast club reunion, as if he'd never sat beside me that day without speaking. Maybe he didn't see me that day and I'm a blooming idiot. Or maybe it's all far too deep.

He put a hand on my shoulder and squeezed, talking about the smoking bullshit. "Petty officer Graham," he announced.

"Like we knew him well," I said. But the touch was all I can remember. Oh yeah, he said he eats normally at 0630 or 0640. He said it like an invitation, so I've directed Scrapper that I'll be eating breakfast at 0630 daily. I'm two for two so far, and loving life again.

"Do you have a Lieutenant John Craig in your squadron?"

"We've got a Lieutenant Craig, and I think his first name's John. Why?"

"My grampa sent me a clipping," he's very close to his grandpa, beautiful boy that he is, you know. "It's about a pilot who flies F-14's on *Ranger*, who used to be a paperboy."

I checked it out. Yes, our LT Craig was the paperboy for none other than Paul Harvey, world renowned news commentator on Armed Forces Radio and paper syndications. He talked of little nine year old Johnny, and confessed that he took Johnny flying for the kid's first time. Years later LT John Craig graduated Annapolis, and is flying close air ground support, high value unit strike escort missions into the Kuwaiti Kill Box in the Persian Gulf.

I wonder what my own little paperboy Matt Gaunt is doing now, nephew of the fairly well known singer Jerry Van Dyke. I used to ride Matt around on paper deliveries in the ice and snow and rain back in the Midwest, just because I loved him. I think he was gonna be a lawyer or a rock star. And he loved Elton John.

Hey wait a minute. I, too, was a paper boy. In a long line of our family tradition, I might add. I was the fifth boy and it was handed down like a privilege, when the older boys outgrew it for gas station and restaurant jobs. I doubled the bags for taking bottles back to the store and made a killing. I remember coming home with eleven dollars when bottles were only worth a nickel. And down at Mission Beach it all came back to me, and I felt confident that like those homeless medal of honor winners I, too, could still make a living if I had to, off the first impressions that were sealed in my personality by age six.

I didn't dream and talk of flying, though. For me it was the railroad tracks of Greenville, wondering where they went after they passed my horizon. The train rolled through every night around nine, snagged the mail sack and rolled right on out, as if on some urgent business in a big city far away. Which it probably was. I lingered repeatedly at the railroad tracks, dreaming of one day becoming a vagabond. To me that was glory, in the sixties in America. There was no fear of a kid being ass-raped and thrown on the road-side bleeding with a torn rectum and getting used for target practice by a passing motorist. None of that happened until the late '70s. I was little when the memories were still fresh of Army soldiers hitchhiking from station to station as a way of life, when total strangers would see them at bus stops and haul them 400 miles and feed them without ever seeing them lift up their thumb.

Now on every military request chit that has an option for liberty, they print a reminder, "hitchhiking is prohibited." That is an era we lost. But it was also the time when those vagrants would appear on your couch.

What happened, really? I feel cheated, recalling my mother's childhood stories and hearing delight in her voice as she dwelt on her happier, trustier time. And memories of me at nine, hitchhiking 400 miles from Missouri to Kansas, running away from home on a lark. I wasn't kidnapped, raped, fondled or molested, and nobody used me for robbery or burglary. Something happened in the "me" generation that affected relations between American strangers. The divisions over Vietnam?

0815 28 FEB 92. We may have flown our last mission of the war. The President called a cease fire at 0500 this morning local time. I heard a rumor that at 0300 some planes dropped five 5,000 pound bombs on Saddam Hussein's bunker. I doubt if they killed him, since I heard the Germans helped him make a nuclear bomb shelter.

"On *Ranger* this is the Captain. As you know the cease fire went into effect 22 minutes ago. But of even more significance is beer day tomorrow. No fly tonight or tomorrow night, so prime yourselves, we'll put it down for Steal Beach picnic tomorrow afternoon."

I guess morale shot up about 80% with that brief speech. Yes, there were cheers in the berthing compartment. And some guys broke out in song, as happy as if pulling into port, almost as happy as if pulling into Sand Dog.

Even the guy two racks over who a minute ago was pissing and swearing, "what in God's name--in *God's* name" about something, started announcing, "beer day tomorrow, beer day. His problems seemed to pale in proportion to the beers he'd soon be guzzling.

I'm happy about the beer, and thrilled about the current state of this war. But I'm still paranoid about the USSR, Iran, and the men on the street burning US flags. I'm also disgusted with my chief. What did I tell YN1 last night? The reason Sweets put his hand on my shoulder comes back to me now. I told him the latest of the war in my office. All about smoke.

PN3 told me today that the Service Record Verification job that chief gave to the night check was bullshit, assigned because we had said we had nothing to do.

When my memos hit the fan, the skipper made the CMC and YNCS handle it with PNC and me, and it boiled down to the offer of me going TAD (temporary duty) to SMAA (Ship Master-At-Arms), ASDO (Assistant Squadron Duty Officer), First LT, or staying on the job and curtailing smoking to daycheck, 0700-2300, limited to persons who worked in the office.

I nearly took the SMAA job. But when I caught myself and said, "no, I want to work in my shop," PNC bolted out of the shop to go have a cigarette. "But I don't want my eval to suffer," I added.

"Hey PNC come back here," YNCS yelled. But the guy was gone, my supervisor who didn't give a fuck about listening to, or taking part in the resolution of his subordinate's problem.

"I'll come in tomorrow night," I said to YN1 a little later, "and find a counseling chit for poor performance." So I came in, and guess who was waiting for me.

"I want you sign this."

It was a "negative" counseling chit, for "job performance" and "responsibilities." Specific reason(s) for counseling:

> On two occasions you were told to purge S/R (25 & 26 Feb 91) btwn these two days you completed a total of 10 S/R. Your work performance (productivity) is not up to par."

Specific actions required to provide solution:

> Increase your productivity. Do your personal things after work. Also, utilize your subordinate if you got a lot to do.

I signed it, and could hardly write, I was so pissed off. "You were itching to do this, chief. You're just retaliating about the smoking."

> Counselee's comments: I do not gun deck the S/R verification job as was done in the past. My subordinate works the 2JZ at the most intensive hours of this war--we own the night. I am surprised at this counseling chit coming the day after a POD note that curtails my counselor's smoking.

I signed it, and turned around and pulled out a request chit and, barely able to write, printed out, "respectfully request CO mast."

"What's this?"

"I'm requesting mast."

"About what?"

"You're just retaliating about the smoking and you know it."

Chief took the chit, approved it--how could he not--and wrote his note:

> PN2 Graham submitted this request due to the counseling I gave him for his poor performance (see counseling form). I confront[ed] him on the first occasion (he does think it's spelled that way) but did it again. That's when I decided to formally counsel PN2.
>
> V/R
> PNC

Well, what do I have to say for myself? He's a no good racist egomaniacal SOB mo'fo' dickhead blah blah blah. Yeah yeah. I do want to say all that. But let's have the reasoned, even tempered rebuttal, couched in temperate and respectful language. *First*: I have photocopies of eleven, not ten, Enlisted Service Record Verification forms with PNC's signature. Eight are dated on or before the 26th. Eleven bore his signature before the counseling on the 27th: One on the 24th, one the 25th, six on the 26th, three on the 27th (between 0001 and 0700 the 27th, that is, while I was counseled at 1900 the 27th). *Second*: the smoking war was hot and heavy on the 24th and 25th, as I researched publications to determine the nonsmoker's rights in the face of a chain smoking chain of command. When else could I sit in the cramped and crowded "day check smoking authorized" shop and dig through the pubs to support of argument, and collect the facts to post *Ranger* instructions and ultimately file a written grievance against a senior chief petty officer, and a memo to the ship's XO, a Captain, which made the Commanding Officer of VF-1 feel as if he'd been put on report?

My Navy rights interfered with my Navy responsibilities. I guess that's why they teach both in the same course. I saw the First LT boss and asked him what he'd do in this situation. "I just stand there and tear 'em up. Right in front of 'em. And I look at 'em as I do it."

"What do they do?" I couldn't imagine.

"They don't do anything. Nobody's ever done that to them before. That's what's called gonads." Man, and I thought I had balls. I wonder what the fuck chief would have done.

Third: as I wonder why my productivity was down, I come to the Reenlistment he assigned. The passdown? "Do reenlistment." I did it by the book and it came back with his corrections. I completely redid it, then he came in at 0400 and argued it out with me, not to my satisfaction. The book says put the authorizing order number in to assure the member that all conditions of the agreement are met by the Navy. But he says put "benefits of rate." I wouldn't want to sign a reenlistment contract for orders somewhere, without putting the orders in the contract.

I could not find any instruction anywhere dealing with the bullshit he has me put on the back, like where does it say we're supposed to put the member's total active service? Although I remember doing it in "A" school, it would be nice to know I'm still doing it correctly, not just by looking at how the last one was done by someone else, and the one under that in the file was done differently.

I had used the PAYPERSMAN, done it by the book, but he went off on my striker making it sound like his supervisor was an idiot. If the member was born in the USA you're supposed to write, "US" in the citizenship block. The next block, citizenship country, is filled in "only if *other* appears in the citizenship block." So I left it blank. "What's this, U.S.? Us? Why he did not put USA in the block for citizenship country," he bitched to my striker behind my back. "I don't know about your supervisor, if he knows what he's doing."

When I showed Chief the book he couldn't argue anymore. "Well, it's already done. I only gave it as an exercise."

The next night he writes me up for low productivity.

Fourth: DK2 came by arguing beneficial suggestions and whether the $75 gifts were taxable. He said they were, I said they were not, he went away saying, "you have a good point," and planning to raise my questions to his chain of command. It was not a five minute chat.

Fifth: speaking of no passdown, I had a dude leaving on emergency leave. That much I got from the PN3. I still didn't know anything about where the chit was, and had to research it to find out. It was done by the YN2 and turned up in Admin, when it should have been done by a PN and left on the Pers side of the room.

Sixth: NC1 had a problem on his travel claim. He wasn't authorized COMRATS on his orders, but got to P.I. and his hours were impractical for eating in the mess. And the orders were so stamped, authorizing him a couple hundred bucks. Paying him back what he spent to survive on his mission. The DK wouldn't pay him unless we did the Pay Order. So the chief didn't catch it and now we have to do a 3060 after we retrieve his travel claim to get the inclusive dates from Cag, maybe a two week delay. I made this a training item but I doubt that PNC passed it on.

Seventh: a NAVET going up for AK1 had his worksheet all fucked up concerning his effective date of advancement to E5. It turned out it wasn't a problem, but I had to do a lot of explaining and actually had to correct a couple things. All this bullshit takes a lot of time.

Eighth: the last time the S/R rehab was done it was gundecked by PN2. Scrapper swears he was told (it was a Saturday at Miramar) to just "check all the boxes in this column, check yes here and no there and sign it. I did 20 in ten minutes." Where was the day check in all of this three day period? PN3 said he did one S/R the 24th, but didn't. He actually did two the 25th. But it's a night check job, eh. To keep 'em busy, then slam the supervisor for performance "not up to par."

If I haven't before, I may as well get into the real shit. The thing about P.I., he asked me if I'd found a boyfriend. Over and over. Back at the beach, installing the DD214 (separation discharge papers) form program in the computer, he insisted I use my own name for the prototype discharge. Repeatedly insisted, over Joe Blow. And what reason code for the discharge did he want me to use? Homosexuality. That mother fucker. Reenlistment code, of course, was RE4 (not recommended).

Finally: I dug out the facts on this son of a bitch. I'm just as guilty for not reporting him, but that gang mentality took me by the balls and I felt he'd only get a slap on the wrist and he was just making chief and they were dogging him anyway, which made him their pal, so I didn't write it out that he ordered me to falsify some official documents.

Tonight/last night, I sifted through the NO COST TAD 1990 file and found what I was looking for. A schedule of schools for the month of August, with an arrow beside each of two names. That's what clicked and made it all come back.

Two guys got hammered for disobeying orders by not going to fire fighting school. They protested that they were never given any orders to go. Well, an investigation ensued, performed by a nice and naive LT. He came to our office asking if we had a copy of the orders. Chief blew him off, then rousted through the orders to discover, voila!, we fucked up. On the schedule there were two columns, and two names in each column. One column had been typed up and those two guys went. But the other two names were missed, I'd guess because Scrapper was new and never pays attention to detail too well, even now. So he probably missed the second column all together.

"I want you to type up orders on these two guys," PNC said. "And backdate the orders to the eighth." I typed them up, wondering if I should walk over to see the skipper.

PNC took the orders and signed them, then shredded the original and all but one copy each. "This is how you cover your ass," he taught. "Now I can go to the master chief and tell him we did the orders."

I knew then he was a dangerous man, and that sooner or later it would come 'round that I'd be his target, and he'd probably try to fuck with me just as hard. Now it's time, and this confession is gnawing away inside. Joke 'em if they can't take a fuck.

The guy who got hammered about fire fighting school, was Gus.

0945 1 MAR 91. Trying to get my ducks in a row. PNC came down at 0230, for a spot inspection I guess.

Try to understand the following discourse:

"Go sleep pretty soon, so you can participate in the thing tomorrow."

"Okay. I sent (Scrapper) to bed already, for that same reason."

"When is he coming back?"

I didn't understand it either.

What I think, really, down deep, is this. His desk vibrates. There's a pump or something that makes his whole corner of the office jitter, and it makes him jittery. You can plop down in his chair and get a back massage, but you don't want to do any paperwork there.

He has it all day, and I think someday some medical officer is going to discover that sitting in that desk creates the same side effect as having a brain tumor the size of a grapefruit.

Anyway, here's the latest tact, and a good one for beer day:

From: PN2 Robert D. Graham, USN, Fighter Squadron ONE
To: Commanding Officer, Fighter Squadron ONE
Via: (1) Personnel Chief, Fighter Squadron ONE
(2) Admin Office Supervisor Chief, Fighter Squadron ONE
(3) Personnel Officer, Fighter Squadron ONE
(4) Admin Officer, Fighter Squadron ONE
(5) Executive Officer, Fighter Squadron ONE
Subj: GRIEVANCE AND REDRESS

Ref: (a) SECNAVINST 5100.13A
(b) COMNAVAIRPACINST 5100.13
(c) RANGERINST 5100.7
(d) FITRONONEINST 5100.13A
(e) NAVY REGULATIONS 1150
(f) UCMJ Article 138
(g) OPNAVINST 5354.1C

Encl: (1) My ltr of 21 Feb 91 to Senior Medical Officer, USS Ranger
(2) My ltr of 24 Feb 91 to Executive Officer, USS Ranger
(3) Counseling sheet to me from PNC dtd 27 Feb 91

1. On 8 December 1990, Fighter Squadron ONE (VF-1) embarked in USS Ranger (CV-61) for Operation Desert Storm (ODS). Embarked working conditions brought a severe stress to bear on VF-1 Administrative and Personnel staff in regard to references (a) through (d).

a. The compartment was of inadequate size and ventilation to support a mixed staff of smokers and nonsmokers totaling twelve.

b. The smoker to nonsmoker ratio was seven to five. Attempts were made to enforce smoking hours (0700-2300) and separate smokers and nonsmokers by shift (most of the smokers worked days; most of the nonsmokers, nights).

2. On or about 20 February, 1991, Ranger held a planned General Quarters drill. After two months of small but ongoing incidents, this brought the smoking problem to a head.

a. Smokers filled the Admin/Pers department with cigarette smoke in the few minutes anticipating execution of the alarm, as they sought to preserve their right to smoke, and to prepare for a two-hour hiatus during the drill.

b. Nonsmokers were equally required to report on station for the duration of the drill, and confronted an environment extremely polluted with cigarette smoke. They had to remain several hours.

c. I confronted the chain of command (Personnel Chief, Yeoman Senior Chief, Command Master Chief, and Personnel Officer), all of whom were smokers, and complained of their unfair handling of this situation and the resultant polluted environment. The Personnel Officer left. Whether or not the others continued to smoke, the damage was done.

d. In the next few moments preceding the drill, I phoned the SMO (Senior Medical Officer) and discussed the problem. He noted that compromise would be the key, and the conversation was interrupted by General Quarters.

3. On 21 February 1991, I forwarded enclosure (1) to the SMO via the DAPA, whom I had faith would support the referenced instructions. He said he would talk it over with the Executive Officer, and added, "they've gotta get out of there."

a. A compromise, setting smoking hours to 0700-2300, had already been agreed upon and hours had been visibly posted. This agreement was ignored by the Command Career Counselor, abused by the Personnel Chief, repulsed by the Yeoman Senior Chief (my leading chief petty officer), "unknown" by the Command Master Chief, and belabored by the Personnel Officer during the week leading up to the General Quarters incident.

b. Enclosure (1) was restrained at the DAPA/Executive Officer level, and no resolution appeared forthcoming.

4. On 25 February 1991, I followed up with enclosure (2), a letter to the Ranger XO bulletin board couched in round terms intended to elicit the XO's personal policy without pinpointing VF-1.

a. The Senior Chief Yeoman of Ranger XO Admin screened the memo and forwarded it to the Commander, Carrier Air Wing TWO as an item for the airwing to handle.

b. Commander, Carrier Air Wing TWO investigated, narrowed the problem down to VF-1, and called the Commanding Officer who, according to the Command Master Chief, "considered himself put on report."

c. The Executive Officer of VF-1, via the Command Master Chief, ordered me to find and retrieve the original of enclosure (2), which I was told was being routed by the Master Chief of USS Ranger to the Chief of Staff.

d. Our Command Master Chief eventually retrieved it himself and returned it to me at a 1900 meeting between him, me, PNC, and YNCS.

5. The following is the tone and substance of the meeting at 1900, 26 February 1991:

a. The CMC opened with various remarks, retaliatory in nature, dealing with unrelated items which, "if I wanted to be a hardass," he could hold against me as violations. Items included an untagged electrical plug which belonged to VF-1; a surplus float coat from Westpac '89 which I had salvaged and repaired; and my presence on the flightdeck at 0200, when I was accompanied by, paraphrasing the Commanding Officer, one of the Navy's most respected first class petty officers (a trouble shooter). He continued, warning that there was no formal, written counseling involved, "although maybe there should be, for not using the proper chain of command." He ended his remarks by stating, "you've gained a lot of publicity in the last week that you don't want."

b. YNCS followed with the opening comment, "I don't see a lot of assholes around here, but I see you becoming one." He insisted that I not write down his statements, "because I don't want to see them on another memo," and insisted (reasonably) that he had a right to smoke.

c. I was given a chance to speak, and focused on the abuses of the past agreement. The CMC pleaded ignorance. I also complained that other khakis used the department as a smoking lounge because it was a last vestige where nonsmokers were openly disregarded.

d. The PNC, my direct supervisor, sat behind my back throughout the half hour without speaking.

e. CMC offered four alternatives: I could accept an assignment for temporary additional duty with the Ship Master-at- Arms; accept an assignment to First Lieutenant; accept an assignment as permanent Assistant Squadron Duty Officer (ASDO)--a petty officer third class watch in Ready Room Eight; or remain in the department on night shift with smoking hours enforced 0700-2300.

6. The CMC, LCPO (YNCS) and I compromised to the following:

a. No smoking 2300-0700.

b. Authorized smoking limited to department staff.

c. This stated in the Plan Of the Day.

7. The minute I stated that I wanted to remain in the department, PNC got up and walked out.

a. I added, "but I don't want my evals to suffer." YNCS called out to PNC, but he was already gone. "I wanted him to hear that," he said.

b. YNCS added, "they already have, since the Commanding Officer saw your memo to the Ranger XO."

8. On 27 February 1991, our Plan Of the Day noted the following:

SMOKING: Smoking in the Admin/Pers Office is limited to office personnel only between the hours of 0700-2300. No smoking will be allowed at anytime between

2300-0700. In addition, the Admin/Pers office is not a lounge. Access will be limited to official business only. If you have a problem, question or need assistance, come on in for the best service around.

9. PNC refrained from active participation in the meeting and did not follow up to discuss or summarize, or to plan a course of action among ourselves, related to my decision to remain in the department and the setting of working hours and smoking hours. In fact, after walking out of the meeting, he did not speak to me again until I returned the following night for my shift. Then he gave me a written counseling.

a. The first words he said were, "I want you to sign this."

b. He produced enclosure (3), a completed counseling form that charged me with poor productivity related to service record verification, and inadequate use of my subordinate.

(1) Service record verification is a task normally performed when a member is received or transferred. According to the selected reservist PN3, who told me this at 0630 on 28 February 1991, the task was assigned on 24 February 1991 for the night shift to verify all service records, specifically due to a temporary lull in assignments, which allowed some well earned and much appreciated time off. In my judgment and authority as LPO, that down time was being used to work out at the gym, in support of the desire I share with the Navy for aggressive physical training, and my subordinate's irrepressible interest in converting to SEALs. But a complaint had been made from the day shift who were being kept in the office all day by PNC.

(2) My subordinate had a sound powered telephone watch in Ready Room Eight. This was the last week of the war against Iraq. Most of the flights were at night and I tasked him to support the Ready Room.

(3) I was interrupted from service record verification on the 25th when PNC tasked me to correct a reenlistment that I had done in accordance with the source manual (Military Pay and Personnel Manual), which I did a second time in accordance with the same manual. I later proved to him, by the book, that my performance was competent and his corrections were actually in error. I asked him whether he preferred my performance to be given by the book or by his personal method. He said, "PNC," then confessed the form was already completed, saying he had only given it as an exercise. Meanwhile, he told my subordinate that my performance was not up to par, and the following day counseled me for low productivity.

11. PNC has demonstrated an arrogant and selfish nature far beyond his relationship with me. But as his subordinate, I bear the brunt.

a. An enlisted chief, he uses a red pen. This embarrasses and offends me because in common sense it insults my Commanding Officer.

b. On a recent reenlistment document, he worded the member's initiation as a shellback in the possessive terms "my royal scribes" and "under my royal hand," drawing attention away from the tradition of Davey Jones and the mysteries of the deep, focusing on himself.

12. While the smoking issue has been satisfactorily resolved, this calculated reprisal demonstrates the need for references (e) through (g), and confirms the fear of many sailors who contemplate reporting abuses committed by higher authority.

a. After three years of service, I was nominated by this PNC as Sailor Of the Month (and awarded runner up).

b. PNC is an experienced player, using a "one-two punch" method of drumming up steps, in the form of written counseling, in order to drop the performance on my periodic evaluation 31 March 1991.

13. I can produce a list of embarrassing errors on the part of PNC, and will if necessary; but why should I? A preoccupation with self-defense is not how I like to get out of bed, and I'm tired of biting my tongue.

14. I request that PNC take a look at his motive for counseling me and reconsider whether I needed it.

a. If I didn't, I would like him to tear it up and leave it in the burn bag on 31 March.

b. If I did, I am sure to receive another written counseling session, even if I've got creases in my jerseys.

Very respectfully,

ROBERT D. GRAHAM

Wish me luck. Meanwhile, I'll go have a Heinekan. I have two free beer tickets, red like Monopoly money. Literally "beer money." I wonder where I'll drink mine. On the flight deck? In this rack? Up on Vulture's Row? And how much will those beers sell for, the hook-ups and extras from guys who believe it or not don't care about not having alcohol since January 5th? Fifty bucks? The most I've heard so far was ten. But some guy, just like those chiefs in the poker game, some guy somewhere on this bucket is gonna write home about the record setting price he paid for a beer onboard *Ranger* at the end of the war. The money he blew. And somebody else will say how many he drank. Six? A whole case? Some guy before we left was telling me he planned to take a beer on board every day for the last 24 days in Sand Dog, so on beer day he'd have a case.

Last night AMH2 was showing videos made of the wives back home. After a while of watching and laughing in the crowded Admin side of the room (using the CMC's VCR), a first class popped off, "so Graham, where's your wife?" The room got pregnant, so I had to bust out with it.

"Oh he couldn't make it."

Six people started rolling on the floor. It wasn't just what I said, it was the pause and the delivery. I'm a fucking comedian. I admit, I don't mind being the brunt of a good joke, and that one was worth it. All the guys you hear talking anyway about butt fucking each other and grabbing dicks, why should I cut that irascible and exuberant (where do I get these words) behavior out of my world?

Later, AMH2 caught me for a moment in the alcove to Pers. "Hey," he intoned ever quietly, "that joke you made? I would be careful, I mean I know you were just joking but some people might try to use that against you."

"You mean like if PNC had heard it?"

"Exactly."

"Oh yeah, he'd be looking up the article on homosexuality."

Later yet, I heard my Shooter hero going on about it, milking it for another laugh. So I spoke to him for a moment in the alcove.

"Oh, it stayed in there," he said.

0930 2 MAR 91. Four carrier Task Force Zulu photo exercise. The *Midway* lined up with us on her port side and *Roosevelt* behind. We led *America*. But don't take it out of context. (I thought for a moment, what if the Russians were coming. But when we broke and the sky slid away, it was more than reassuring. It was awesome.) We cranked up and there were 55 knots of wind across the deck. *America* split left and the *Rosey* banked to the right. They looked like they were going sixty, since we were all going away from each other at 25 knots or more. Fast moving metal.

The TAD guy they wanted me to replace at SMAA got an AMCROSS last night. His brother got his head crushed by a machine out in the bush. A bulldozer or something. I had to do the Emergency Leave package, which cut down my service record verifications. Oh dear.

PERS-O was the SDO today. Signing the emergency leave orders, he told me that he'd told PNC to throttle back.

"As far as I'm concerned, you are four-o. And if you keep up the work that you're doing, you'll get four-o's on your eval."

"Well, PNC could tear up that counseling chit."

"Yeah, and I could throw it away as department head. In fact, that's probably what'll happen. I know you didn't need it."

I sold my fucking Strat, and the amp, for a whopping $495, and one condition. "What's that," the dude asked me.

"Never let PNC play on it."

0130 3 MAR 91. ALL CONDITIONS NORMAL. I made the entry in the ASDO logbook. Yes, now I've got the ASDO watch. How did I find out?

"VF-1 Admin/Pers, petty officer Graham, may I help you?"

"Graham, do you have a copy of the watchbill?"

"I can check with Admin."

"I'm tryin' to find out who has the ASDO."

"No, Admin's copy isn't on the board."

A few minutes later it rings again.

"Graham, you have the watch. You're on the watchbill."

Twenty minutes Unauthorized Absent, late for a watch, an offense for which I could receive a counseling chit, even a report chit or Captain's Mast.

"YN1, is there something you didn't tell me about a change in policy?"

"Is there something I should have told you?"

"Well, normally PN's and YN's never stand the ASDO. And at sea we operate 24 hours and we don't stand watches. Now, I just found out I'm twenty minutes UA. I didn't read the watchbill but we're not supposed to be on it. So why should I? The thing is, who's supposed to give me the passdown? You're my LPO."

"I should think the PNC. I wouldn't expect PNC to tell YN2 about a change in policy affecting his work schedule."

"Hi Bob. What are you doin' standing this watch?" AN

"What are you doin' there?" AK1

"What's a PN2 doin' standing this watch? AME1

"What the hell are you doin' standing this watch?" AE1 (According to YN1 the maintenance guys were crying because they had all kinds of watches while Admin/Pers (translate, YN1 and YN2 and the PNC & PERSOFF) were playing chess. According to scuttlebutt, they ran out of PO3's because of a huge working party tomorrow. Time will tell.)

0545 3 MAR 91. PNC came halfway into the Ready Room, turned around and left. I looked up as he cleared his throat and thought it was him, and called down to YN1

"Did I just see PNC?"

"Of course you did."

A while later, he came in. "Bob, I'm sorry, I didn't know that you had this watch. I didn't tell you because you weren't there at seven."

"I was there. I was there before seven."

"The senior chief was trying to chew me out because you weren't there."

"I'll tell him to his face I was there."

I can't stand high enough on my tiptoes around this guy. As I walked down the passageway I was thinking about how important it was going to be that I show up on time or early, and whether Scrapper would be late. I looked at the clock, 6:53 pm. I got a passdown on all but the watch change from PNSN, who stayed until 7:04 pm. Just happened to look at the fucking clock as he left, because I was thinking about how dedicated he is. Scrapper came in at 7:20 as usual. Now I get this bullshit that I was late. That muthafucka. He goes on with a sympathetic diversion about what he should buy for his wife, a ring, something he and she both might like, he goes on about when he goes home he doesn't do anything, she's not that good looking but does everything for him, and I'm nice and helpful suggesting pearls from Singapore, jewels from Thailand. He isn't interested in my feedback, he's just covering his emotional tracks, betting that self-pity will cloak his hatred and elicit a lowering of my guard. Sure, pal.

Meanwhile, the wildest thing. An AME2 got orders and freaked out. His EAOS is July. He executed an extension "to complete deployment" on 28 November, *before we deployed*. The key is, you can't extend for that reason unless deployment has already commenced, or you obtain *prior approval* from Commander, Naval Military Personnel Command (NMPC). The files show no record of an attempt at receiving such approval. As a result, the member became available to detailers because of an *expired* PRD (Projected Rotation Date, December 1990). Now PNC is trying to fix it by covering and backdating. He gives the skipper a phony printout of a message dated 28 November requesting PRD adjustment. I find out the document was created 2 March, by looking at it with the computer DOS command to display directory, which shows the date of file creation. I do find a similar file created 30 November 1990, but again no indication it was ever sent.

Now the skipper is referencing a message with a Zulu date time group that will not exist on NMPC files (28 November), basing a new request (to keep the member) on receiving no response from NMPC to a message we can't prove was sent. I wonder why they never responded: PN2 was doing reenlistments and extensions. What would you suppose he was thinking about 28-30 November? He was absent on sailing 8 December, has not been heard from since. To cover his own ass, PNC is letting the skipper step on his dick. He backdated the message to the wrong date time group. What should I do? Help them flip out? Let the cookies crumble? Tell the skipper he's got an untrustworthy chief who happens to be my boss and has been using me for target practice? Where is my unbiased credibility? Will it make any difference, when you consider we're a Desert Storm unit and the skipper will probably get whatever he wants from NMPC anyway, especially when what he wants is to keep a topnotch guy around for a little longer, and the logistics nightmare of returning guys to the states is just about to begin? If this comes tumbling down, there will be some heavy hitters taking hard swings in every direction, and I may as well stay out of the fray. If nothing happens, should the PNC be allowed to continue this pattern of falsifying official documents to cover incompetence like he did with an AMH3 and this AME2? Who's next? Several guys did the "to complete deployment" extension prior to cruise, not "in accordance" with the MILPERSMAN as they claim. Spike Lee said, "do the right thing." Yo Spike. Put up or shut up?

I told the latest victim. He's got a flip in his shop. Will it cause a blood clot? Skin cancer? Will PNC find out everything? Is the best defense a good offense, or is well enough unsaid better left alone? To whom should I turn for help? The *Ranger* chaplain? The VF-1 legal officer? The CMC? XO? The Skipper privately? (How? Knock on the door to his stateroom?)

0930 3 MAR 91. If I'm lucky I may walk off this boat with the disk of this diary, sans computer, sans seabag, sans everything else. I turned to the PERSOFF. Now I hope that when they come to my rack I'm awake. It will be chief flipping that Bic. This time we'll be seeing the XO. And it will be about the Dickhead of the Decade. Sans second class.

The PERS-O put it that he's (chief has) set it aside -- not thrown it away or into the burn bag. Waiting for the opportune moment to prove disrespect. When it's most ripe. Say, any day now, or late March. "I don't think it was right, I talked to chief again and it was wrong what I told you, that you'd get four-o's. I mean, you've only been a second for a little while and a three-eight is not bad." (I should have mentioned right then about the PNSN's four-o's and that chief told him to hang onto his notes twenty-four hours a day, when he found out that the kid had offered to share them with Scrapper.) "I'm tired of you whining to me about every little problem." Two days ago he said I should come to him. Now he had led me to his stateroom to tell me he didn't want to hear it.

Since this now looked like my last stand, I went for it, to get the tension off my chest and bring it all to the table. "He's had me falsify documents." I explained all the crap about the fire fighting.

"Wow, what a can of worms."

"And now he's doing it again. He's got the skipper stepping on his own dick with a reference to a message that doesn't exist."

"Yeah, I saw that message."

I showed him the copies I'd made, and breathed a sigh of relief for a second. Maybe this was the right move, and I was glad he had bumped into me in the Ready Room, glad he had taken me to talk about my call to him last night. It was no longer important about the paper trail chief was creating on my incompetence. "I was walking through the hangar bay, and I almost went to the NIS." The door exits off the hangar bay.

"Don't do that," he squinched. "You're setting yourself up. Let's say the falsifications never happened. I mean, you've got your point of view on how it happened, but maybe there's some other reason that would make it more legitimate. Maybe it has to do with this Desert Shield, Desert Storm thing. Even if it's not, you're still gonna have to consider how to deal with chief."

"Yeah, could you imagine if they busted him down to a first, and I still had to work for him? I'd be lucky to walk off this boat with anything on my sleeve."

"He's got hard evidence of disrespect, you know that Dickhead of the Decade thing. He didn't like that very much. But he can show that he's been very patient with you, whether he has or not he can show that he has, and you've been disrespectful toward him with your attitude."

"This is intimidation. I'm setting myself up because I spoke up about the smoking and I'm being retaliated against and I'm the bad guy. We don't like the message so let's shoot the messenger. That's what this is."

"He's a criminal."

"I'll do the right thing. I'll talk to him about it."

"Do you realize how dangerous that will make me?"

"Oh yeah. I know." Flip flopping. "Even if everything is true, and it probably is, it's still not gonna be a big deal. It's not that bad. You've just got to solve the personal problems that you seem to have with everybody. You may think he's a criminal, but things like that happen all the time.

"Right." This was rich. "Late entries. Then forget it, forget everything I said about the documents." He chuckled and led me back to the Ready Room, where I left him to find a warm shower. I guess I should have cut my losses and gone for the TAD billet, say permanent ASDO. But then surely they'd put in my eval, "doesn't want to work in his rate."

0845 4 MAR 91. "Remember, only what you do for him will last." The great moral dilemma took a turn for the better. Not full circle or a hundred and eighty degrees. But a wider berth if nothing else.

I caught the PERS-O in the passageway, I was coming from the head and he, from the Ready Room, when we met by the outboard green mat of the arresting gear shop over the ladder to PERS. I started to whine that all the guys were pointing the finger at me for YNCS coming over to the senior section leader, AZ1, with the cute phrase, "hey, I got some names you can add to the watchbill." This directly after the "smoking" session. And how, for the first time since we deployed, I was standing ASDO (a third class watch).

"Hey listen, I'm in a hurry, I've gotta get to church," he said moving on down the passageway, away. Like a sign, a moment later on the 1MC I heard, "protestant worship services will be held in the foc'sle at twenty-hundred." An hour later I found myself sitting beside a Christian songbook on a folding chair. And two guys from VF-1 were in the band. AT2 Sloan played his trombone, and Petty Officer Martindale, soon to become an officer, was on sax. Not only, but sitting down beside me was the dude from VF-2, another PN. And there was the honest cop who got shot and took a furlough to the US Navy, a four-year hiding stint that reminded me of the way Frank Serpico had disappeared, only he didn't bring the dog. ADMIN MAA, on his yellow jersey. We sang and sang, then of all sermons this guy in khakis preached about "the trial of Jesus." How everyone in the system abused and covered and backdated and intimidated each other until the king ended up on a cross. "Now everybody shake five people's hands and say, 'God loves you, you're a wonderful person.'" I forgot about the offering, and took chocolate chip cookies back to my shop.

It didn't phase me but I noticed that PNC hasn't said another word about the service record verifications since the counseling chit. I guess it wasn't really such an important job, just a lame excuse for a chip off the old eval. I've thought about when you go up in rate you may not be expected to continue as a four-o sailor, because of the fact that you're taking on a new level of responsibility. Sort of like starting at the bottom of a higher step.

Word is, the bosses have given our Admiral (Zlatopher) the option to go wherever we want. That's a pretty good deal I guess. And the *Nimitz* is supposed to come replace us in late April. This means we'll make it home as originally scheduled, San Diego sometime in June. We might go to Australia --Perth or Matilda Bay. Or Sydney, (where uncle John lives. I could hook up with him and get out and head back, write another book: *The Matilda Bay Diary*, whatever the beach's name is.) If so, we'll go straight on to Hawaii, skipping P.I. I could wax melancholy about Totoy, chewing him out for an hour again. But the whole thing is soured by the want and need and rolling blackouts, coup attempts, armored cars and shotgun security guards all over town, and the memory of Gus and all the bad, dirty shit that flips me out.

Got a letter from Dad. Uncle Charles is "on the ground in Saudi Arabia." They have been flying the flag on the front of the house since I've been in the Gulf, and have one on the truck. And the church, YVPC, has a big blue star and my picture on the bulletin board. Sunday the preacher had a special prayer for me and all my mates.

The MARS phone system off Vulture's Row costs $3.50 for the satellite hookup, and about a buck-fifty a minute. A young country dude is bitching now about his girl, evidently cheating. She'll owe him five hundred dollars for "all my shit. Either she's gonna play me to the left and John to the right, or she's gonna play both of us and we're both gonna figure it out. I never broke one of my buddy's girlfriends. She goes through a miscarriage with one guy, man it hurts me." Ad infinitum.... "And another person I cannot stand is (so and so). One night he shit his pants, he was so scared up on the flight deck."

A card from some others at church. A kitty cat with flowers on the front. "You don't know me from a bale of hay, but my son was a Marine, and my grandson was just discharged from the Marines as he developed diabetes, so was unable to go to the Gulf. I never thought I'd be thankful that he had diabetes but I sure am now. Our hearts and prayers are with all of you wonderful brave men out there." I just hope we make it through these wars we make among ourselves.

"PN2's knowledge of EDVR was excellent. He answered my questions of prospective gains promptly & efficiently. He performs his duties in a courteous & professional manner." I don't know, I don't like asking someone to write it down, but it's time for some commendatory correspondence when you're up against a counseling chit and Dickhead of the Decade.

I tore up my special request for Captain's Mast, and stuck a Post-It Note to it to say, "chief, how about let's be friends?" An hour or two later I pulled the package from his basket and ran it through the shredder. There's no use doing something nice that I'd regret. And it would be nice and I would regret it, because this thing is circular. Like I said, touching God is giving him a wider berth. I hope that's good enough.

A couple of messages:

> BRAVO ZULU. Well the woodpile has been cleaned up and the copperhead turned out to be a garden snake. It has been a fast 43 days and we have all grown professionally and learned a lot of new tricks and relearned some valuable old ones. Again, the close relationship that our navies have established will stand us in good stead for many years to come. As always, sailors at sea share a strong and common bond. It has been an honor to serve with you and I congratulate each and every member of the force for a job extremely well done. VADM Arthur, U.S. Naval Forces Central Command - Sends.

Not to be outdone, a letter from SECNAV:

> To all the men and women of the Navy and Marine Corps, well done. With skill, with courage, and an awe-inspiring degree of dedication you have helped crush a maniacal aggressor and helped to make a safer, more peaceful world. You have earned many times over the utmost respect and gratitude of free peoples everywhere. Your performance has been simply superb.
>
> Our hearts go out to those who made the supreme sacrifice on behalf of freedom and justice. They gave their lives so that others may live a more hopeful future: They will not be forgotten.
>
> For those of you who remain on duty far from home, rest assured that you have the continued and unstinting support of your government and your Navy/Marine Corps leadership. On behalf of a grateful nation, I congratulate you and thank you all. May God bless each of you and your families... H. LAWRENCE GARRETT, III - SENDS.

Well, that and a dollar might get Lou a cup of coffee. But I hope this war, however short and relatively painless on the part of the many, will add weight to the needs of the few and put money in the fucking VA hospitals, and in the hands of the homeless war vets. No doubt--within a couple of years--we'll give billions to Iraq.

We're back to a regular Combat Air Patrol, focusing on the Iran side of the Gulf. The arresting wire snaps back into place over me, wind, rock-rock, click-click, stop. The whirs of turboprop engines rush by, eeeoowwwwhhrr. And wwoooooeeerrrhhh, of F-14A's. The pilots thankfully touch lightly. I guess that kid, John Craig, is up there.

0845 5 MAR 91. All over the Navy, ships and stations are holding Navywide Advancement Exams for E4 this morning. Scrapper had to have "prior approval" from NMPC to take an "out of the path" exam. He's an Airman and the PN3 exam is in the Seaman rating. But the request was forwarded during worldwide "Minimize," when all but mission critical electronic communications were (and still are) sent by mail. So it went three weeks ago as a NAVGRAM, a letter in an envelope through regular mail. Naturally, no response arrived by test time.

The PNC and ESO walked into the training room under the foc'sle where Scrapper was waiting with all the other Airmen. "By the way," said PNC in with a flippant accent. "You cannot take the test. We did not get approval from NMPC."

"Ar-right," the kid sighed, nodding, and walked out.

I had already had my argument with chief in Personnel, while the ESO stood flippergasted. "Why can't he take it?"

"Because I go by the book."

"You extend someone to complete a deployment before we deploy. Then you say you go by the book."

He just grabbed the pencils and split. I'd thrown another card on the table, betrayed my hand. So what. I went up to the Ready Room. "Skipper, can I bother you for a minute?"

"What's up, Graham?"

"Chief wouldn't let (Scrapper) take the test this morning."

"Why not?"

"He had to get prior approval from NMPC, and they didn't respond in time for the test. So chief let him think he was gonna take it right up until this morning, then walked in and told him he couldn't."

"Who's more upset about it? You or him?"

"I'm upset. But he doesn't even want to look at the chief, he's so mad. I guess it's my fault as much as anybody, for leading him on."

"Well, did you tell him he wouldn't be able to take it if the message didn't come in?"

"Yes sir. We told him three weeks ago, when we sent out the request by NAVGRAM. I knew it wouldn't come back in time."

"Well we can't let him take it without approval. What if he passes and they came back and say No?"

"Then we'd really look stupid." "Not just the command. It'd be a lot more embarrassing to him if he already had a crow on, and had to take it off."

"You're right about that." I was fading fast. "Thanks for your time."

"Wait and see what the message says, and if they approve him order a late exam. We've got 'til May, and he'll still be in the same cut off and if he makes it, he'll put on a crow in the same ceremony as everyone else."

"Thanks." I felt very stupid about yelling at chief all of the sudden, even if he was criminal in his handling of the extension. What was I asking, him to commit another crime while I'm narking on him for the last one? I know why Louie always called me a loaded cannon.

I discussed it with YN1 down in the shop. He went up to his rack and brought back a booklet he was reading on Bible verses, a thought on divine justice.

"There's gonna be some divine justice," I quipped. Well, in all divinity, this could be good for Scrapper. Say they order him a late exam (and chief doesn't fuck that away). He gets another month or two to study. He's got a better chance to pass, man. I can't complain about that.

I went to the classroom and got chief outside.

"I just want to apologize. I think you're right and I don't want you spend all day thinking I'm mad, or being mad at me. I shouldn't have got upset."

"Well, he came in the shop a year ago, and he had all that time to get ready. But his own personal things were more important than finishing the course. It's his own fault this happened. It's like paying someone for work they did not do." I had to agree. I had been drowning Scrapper in the waterhole as deep as I could, while still being friends. Meanwhile, he was late every fucking night (almost), gone forty-five minutes, back 20, gone another hour, back 45, gone to take a shit and showing up in the paraloft, back again with popcorn and sodas and just about to leave. What is truth?

Chapter Fourteen

0900 6 MAR 91. The tyrant and contrite subordinate must have been what PN3 saw when he checked in. His outside objectivity would have caught us between arguments, nice and professional, vague in our backbiting. Generously instructing him and the PNSN. That lasted half a week and our fangs came out.

I wonder what the watchbill will be like as we hit port in Abu Dabi, Oman; and in Pattaya Beach, Thailand; and Hawaii. Scuttlebutt has it that's our sked (schedule).

1830 6 MAR 91. I dreamed of Mission Beach. It had changed. You needed a permit to step on the sand. The permit cost money, and I was busted. "I'm a sailor and I can't walk on the beach?" I had addressed the cop, rather than the vendors I could have bribed.

"You have bare feet. Go back home.

"What do you mean, go home?" I threatened to take the cop to court --at which he suddenly pulled out his clipboard and wrote me a ticket. The charge, intimidating a police officer by threatening to sue.

"Darken ship, darken ship." In my slumber I thought that voice on the 1MC said, "duck and shoot, duck and shoot."

0800 7 MAR 91. Chief almost hit me this morning. He reminded me of my dad when my back was hurting so bad that, even though it meant money in my pocket, I couldn't get up to find work with the moving companies, or take it if I could get it. He was on his way to work (for $100,000 a year as an executive for Del Monte), came upstairs and charged across the room toward me with a raised fist.

PNC came in at 0330, another spot check. Last time I had talked to the Pers-O, he had assured me that he'd tell the chief to stop micro-managing that way. Well, he caught me doing something right, verifying a service record. He was immediately grumpy. He might have been pleased if he'd caught the TV on. "What's up, chief?" I didn't feel defensive, since I was doing what I should be doing. I think I was actually cheerful. "Have you got the 'can't sleeps' or do you have something you have to do?"

"How many service records have you done?"

Now I was dead. What the hell had I done all night? Let's see, came on at 1900, eight and a half hours ago. Give me one hour to do the verifications, in chief's time scheme of five an hour, and that leaves 7.5. Less 0.5 for Scrapper's typing test, 7. Less 2.5 more hours fixing Wolfe's travel claim, retrieving part two of the 3060 from the file, deleting the double line entry that erroneously started him for $900 a month variable housing allowance when all he really had provided us was (upon close scrutiny and discussion with DK2 which took a little more time), an application to rent rather than a bona fide rental agreement; entering three more sets of double line entries of his name, SSN, and a blank amount with inclusive dates of VHA for the zip code of Lemoore, CA (which I had to look up with assistance from Rod, a YN3), inclusive dates with $9999.00 (the indication of maximum VHA) for another set of inclusive dates at the zip code of Miramar, CA, and a third set with blank amounts using the zip code of Miramar; then disassembling his travel claim and three sets of copies of his orders to VF-1, retrieving all six parts of the 3068 receiving endorsements to orders, reassembling the 3068 and adding the code, 92145 C to initiate "temporary maximum VHA" that will last for sixty days, in order that, assuming he's not ripping off the tax payers with a phony rental agreement, he will provide us with a true and viable agreement within sixty days; then replacing all the copies of the 3068 with respective duplicates of the orders, and since the member went to school enroute, making another set of copies of every page of the orders and all four endorsements (our 3068 being number four), on the manually fed Savin photocopier, and correcting the placement of endorsements and receipts and copies of receipts in sandwich fashion, respectively, around the orders and sets of copies of orders, which the day shift (a selected reservist PN3 remember) hadn't figured out yet (even with a PNC on the shift)--all these things signed by the chief in error--then placing all these packages and the appropriate parts of the 3068 in the Personal Financial Record and our department retain files and sticking the PFR in the DK's box; then writing a memo to the member explaining that he'd given us an application to rent rather than a bona fide rental agreement, telling him that we'd started temporary maximum VHA based on his intentions, and warning him that it would all stop in sixty days if he didn't follow-up in the manner outlined in the memo; then putting the memo in a letter and sealing it and putting it in his shop's mailbox. That left me with 4.5 hours. Less 0.25 for the PERSTAT. Less 1.0 for midrats (chow). Less 0.25 for AO3 White coming down looking for a copy of his request for orders to Barber's Point, HI. I couldn't find a copy on our outgoing message board (where it should have been) but did find one in Admin, since it was a serialized NAVGRAM. Down to 3. Less 0.5 polishing a recommendation for a letter of appreciation for the guy who made our copier like new, since he kept us alive with special trips every other day last cruise and we never gave him any recognition, and here he's doing it again. 2.5. Less attending to President Bush's address on Crime on CNN, in my judgment a worthy 0.5 hours. 2. Less cumulatively 1 hour of distraction by the TV ("Days Of Thunder" was a 2-hour movie, regular CNN news updates on releases of prisoners and the Kuwait situation and the last Pentagon brief of the war). 1. Less 0.25 answering phone calls, 0.25 briefing Scrapper on the possible test questions based on a 0.25 debrief from the PNSN who took it this (that) morning, and 0.25 making head calls and coffee. Of course, I couldn't think of all this on the spot. "Four." I had to look at the list and count them. Since it had been a few days, I thought we weren't keeping track anymore. Look how wrong you can be.

"Four? What have you been doing all night?"

I backed away from PNC as his shoulder dipped and his fist wound up. He stopped himself, grimacing. It was like the ki-ai of a karate thrust, where you exhale sharply and pull the punch in mid-air. My first instinct was to kill him. I could imagine riveting his head against the in-baskets on the wall behind him, between Admin and Pers. But I was under control.

"I could put you on report for that, chief.

"Do my separation. Right now."

"What's the reason for separation?" You have to have that, ya know.

"Do it. You say you know everything." He walked off to have a cigarette. "Make it effective tomorrow."

I began to think, okay, maybe he hasn't snapped, maybe he isn't expecting me to separate him with a bad conduct discharge. Since he didn't give me the reason, maybe he wants me to cut an STO (Standard Transfer Order) for CONUS, temporary duty for separation back at San Diego. I spend an hour developing the facts as best I can, roughing it in pencil and typing it over. He takes a look.

"Separate me here, as if we were back at Miramar."

Okay, now the STO is out the window. Insufficient, inadequate communication has cost me an hour. Is this a language barrier, or is it a game? This is the reenlistment puzzle all over again. Does he enjoy sending me on wild goose chases? Am I gonna get another counseling chit for taking too long on his DD214 (discharge certificate)?

In the middle of all this, he comes to speak with me. "What are we going to do? We have to talk about this." The Master-At-Arms have come and gone, with YN1 ever peacefully talking me out of having the fucker arrested. I think you're just digging yourself a hole," he'd wisely counseled. "He didn't actually hit you. I know, it's in the Regs, he can be prosecuted for it. But they're not gonna do anything to him. It's all gonna come back down on you. They're gonna say, he was whining before, now he's really whining."

"Did somebody need a Master-At-Arms up here?"

"No, I don't think so," YN1 shooed them off. I didn't say anything either way, as chief stood there mum.

We had a nice chat, chief and I, about our mutual inability to communicate because of my loud voice that Scrapper can't hear. "The way you approach me, loud, gets like an argument, and you get it back from me." The error of my ways, from the lips of a CPO. "Why do you question everything I say?"

"Well, chief. I'm a PN2. I've been around you long enough to see you make a few mistakes. And maybe I've done something by the book and you're telling me it's wrong, and you're not saying why but your just criticizing and I have to show you in the book that it's not wrong."

Some of our conversation drifted into the advancement exam, and he'd bragged how his boy, the PNSN, had done so well on everything but they'd asked him questions on the Source Data System that squadrons never use.

"Yeah, while he was on my shift I showed him the only stuff we have on it, in the PAYPERSMAN."

"It's not in there."

"Sure it is, in the back."

"It's not in there."

"Chief, this is what I'm talking about. Right now, you're telling me there's nothing on SDS in the PAYPERSMAN. Either you don't believe me, or you're not listening to me. In the back there is very little, about three paragraphs. But there's also the SDS codes." I pulled the book off his desk right in front of us, opened it up and showed him.

"I take your point." Almost in the next breath, he turned the subject to my chit. "What did you do with your request for CO Mast?"

"I tore it up. I shredded it a couple of days ago."

"Because you know where I went when you gave it to me."

"Yeah, you probably went to talk to the skipper about it."

"That's right. He's been waiting. And you know you won't win."

I just looked at him, trying to figure out what in the hell was going through his mind.

"Because you know where I'm going now? To talk to the skipper again."

"Well, I'm not gonna fight the coalition."

"That's right, Saddam!"

Meanwhile, working on my Military Requirements for Petty Officer First Class (MRPO1), I study the following:

> As a good Navy leader, you will consider the trade-offs between job requirements and worker morale to maintain productivity and job satisfaction. Too much concern with job requirements may have an adverse effect on your people's job satisfaction.
>
> Poor morale shows up in widespread griping.
>
> If you are a poor leader who throws your wight around and uses constant threats, you may sometimes get what seems to be good discipline. For example, your sailors follow command rules to the letter and seem to be doing a good job without griping. However, this may be merely a cover-up, hiding a powder keg full of resentment and ill feelings waiting to go off.
>
> Obedience through fear should not be confused with good discipline. Threats and force may work for a time, but the hidden unrest that results from strict regimentation and the use of force alone may "explode in your face" at any time.

0900 12 MAR 91. I took a few days off the diary, exploding in another face. I've just about got all those God damned service records verified, old items removed, lacking initials noted, and hundreds of other discrepancies brought to the attention of PNC Hitler.

I just came back from the gym. Up to thirty leg lifts, up, out and back, and down on that funky chair. Several sets. But now I'm doing my workout on my own time, after 0700, since we're so busy at night. Dean was at the gym, and told me that Sweet Pea had gone to V3 "we like it tight" Supply, a little office right under the V4 head. I found myself taking a shower at the V4 head coincidentally. But I didn't run into my beautiful bud.

I did the new change to the MILPERSMAN last night (this morning on night check). No change to the chapter on homosexuality. The latest deal is that if you fuck some kid under 16, or make it with a shipmate on the ship, you get the Big Chicken Dinner (Bad Conduct Discharge or BCD). So stick with 17 offbase, for a General Discharge.

Everyone onboard *USS Ranger* during Operation Desert Storm will receive a Joint Services Commendation Medal, which characterizes our service as meritorious. By policy that elevates a General Discharge to Honorable. Therefore, were I to suck Sweet Pea in Abu Dabi, we'd both get no less than Honorable, with a GI Bill and a COD flight. And no reserve time. He could even remain in the Navy, if he swore it was a once in a lifetime experience (which it would be anyway), that would never happen again. Ah, the Coney Islands of my mind.

All the studs are talking of Thailand now. Fuck Abu Dhabi. You can't even stare at a woman (that's called paying undo attention to her), much less take her picture. And it's the month of Ramadan, so you can't smoke (they all knew I'd be happy to hear that), or eat or even drink in public. Bars (and restaurants) are only open after dark, and I hear that beers are about seven bucks. Thailand is the heart of that land across the mystical realm known as the International Forget Line. It's also the AIDS capitol of the world. Funny, the Navy always tests for AIDS shortly before deploying to this part of the world. And never tests its men upon return.

I fucked a whore at the massage parlor, Sabai Land, on last Westpac, around July 1989. Actually, we didn't fuck. I went in and found the girl I liked, number 121, on the bleachers behind a long glass window, summoned her through the waiter, bought her a beer and took her to the back. She stripped, I stripped, we got on the bed. She fucked up my fingernails with a bullshit manicure, coughed a few times as if dying from AIDS, then poured my bath. We washed each other. Then she whipped out an air mattress on the cement floor, poured hot soapy water on it, had me lay down there, and poured more water on me. Somehow she ended up underneath, and used her body as a sponge to wipe me down. I barely held back, and ended up in bed with her again. She offered to ride my cock, blow me, or stroke me off. I took an even greater pleasure in denying her the come shot somehow. I gave the dude 400 Bot, and gave her 200 more. I think it was 5 bucks to a 100 Bot. My AIDS test came in last fucking week. Negative, as Doc said, or I wouldn't be here.

I felt like writing Amy, letting her know I've tested negative again, in case wherever she is our social experiment still haunts her. But I got about a line, "if this letter finds you happy" or something emotionally self-destructive like that. I threw it in the burn bag.

I don't know but I doubt that I'll ever make it in the normal setup they called a family when I was young. You know, husband, wife, kids. I envy her brother the playboy, the alcoholic heir to a billion, Arthur Bach in the flesh, showing up in the party pages of New York and D.C. society rags. He'll die young, of AIDS or liver cancer. Judging from my shop, I doubt if his lungs will go first, even though he smokes like a fiend. He may just get bashed, in some alley, like the killing of Georgie in a Rod Stewart song.

Right now we're still hovering around in the Gulf, probably until George decides whether to resume air operations against that crazy motherfucker in Iraq. But so far we've been given a probable port schedule of this Abu Dabi bullshit any day now, then Thailand, Hong Kong and everloving P.I., followed by picking up the Tigers in Hawaii (I don't know why but they call male friends and relatives of crewmembers Tigers; and they have a traditional Tiger Cruise for them from Hawaii back to Sand Dog every Westpac)

I want to go scuba diving in Hawaii, like last time. I went down 90 feet in '89, saw a small shark and some sea turtles and swam around inside an artificial shipwreck. The water was unbelievably clear, and made me want to join Club Med. It was so blue, you could do circles and get vertigo. Plus, all that diving gear is cool. I guess my overall plan is: watch kickboxing, drink and relax in Pattaya Beach (Thailand); shop for electronics in Hong Kong with all my tax free income; chew ass in P.I. if I can't help myself, and dive around Hawaii. Oh yeah, and here in Abu Dabi, I want to see if I can find a magic genie. Or at least some dusty old bottle off an Arab shelf.

0830 15 MAR 91. We're at 26 North Latitude, 52 East Longitude, upgraded to Alert Fives again. Today, Iran is giving back to Iraq all the aircraft that flew there for refuge. This in the midst of a napalm campaign by Saddam against his people. Will he load them up with Exocets and launch them at *Ranger*? As I went up on the flight deck I could smell something besides JP5. It was tension. Then I noticed it as I came back inside.

We had a rumor of a 0600 mission, but I never heard any jets launch or even being turned. I expect the Captain will come on the 1MC sometime today, while I'm fast asleep, to give us the scoop. I hope the SELRES, PN3, will catch it on my four-track.

The PNSN went TAD. I think he's mess cranking at S-5, one of the wardrooms. They're working him sixteen hours a day. He never had it so good as in the shop. That's how they fool you in the Navy, they put you in the shop for a while, let you get used to the feeling of what it's like to do the actual job you signed up for, then throw you to the wolves in what's called Temporary Additional Duty (TAD) Support--for six goddamn months.

A guy came down two nights ago requesting CO Mast, to find out if he can work in his rate before the Expiration of his Active Obligated Service (EAOS). "When you comin' to nights, girlfriend? Before Abu Dabi?" This was a voice walking through the berthing. It was Gar, the man with the most Plane Captain of the Month and Junior Sailor Of the Month awards in VF-1.

"We're not goin' there." It was Dial, a kid who wants to be a lawyer. "Didn't you hear? We're startin' the war again. We're s'posed to start flyin'

CAPs again today."

Everybody's been bringing in their Atropine shots, in accordance with a note in the Plan Of the Day (POD). I haven't turned mine over. And I think I won't for a while. Earlier the Skipper came to Pers asking me to contact all of our SELRES guys, to find out when they want to go home. Two guys actually want to ride the boat back. Like one said, "hell, I'm makin' money." I guess he wasn't gainfully employed back in the states.

While he was sitting in Admin, some hot singer with a crewcut came over the television. "She makes herself look like a man in the audience," somebody said.

"I'd still go to bed with her," I said. "She's a hot number." As I spoke I realized the skipper was well within earshot, and I wondered how he took my remark. Was that confirmation, Graham's a bisexual? Anyway he's leaving, change of command on 1 April if it isn't a joke (April Fools' Day ya know). At this point I was glad I said it, and glad he heard it.

Speaking of the states -- news travels. I read an article in the Gulf News, a paper for Saudi Arabia, that covered a story out of Miami about cops burning the clothing, blankets and bibles of bums. And there was the fucked up story of the West LA beating, where they caught the cops trying to mutilate a suspect while he laid on the ground. It didn't make me want to hurry back to Mission Beach--where I hear they have banned alcohol, by the way. I hate to say I told you so. Louie will be out there pedaling acid out of my car, and sitting in it getting drunk on "the Beast" (Milwaukee's Best). Let's see if I remember that reeling rocking tune I wrote. I doubt if I can get it note for note (D///C///G///D///):

MISSING BEACH

D C
He spends the working hours of his day
G D
On the second deck of a hanger bay
and when the work is done he's on his way
out to Missing Beach where he can play
and not hear those jets
as soon as he forgets
how his country lets
another night go by on Missing Beach....
On Missing Beach

He's gonna be out of reach
hangin' over the wall
as the hippies preach
what the children teach
wearin' tye-dies and beads
and his oil from Egypt
this is all he needs

On Missing Beach it's a carnival there
sorta like a circus or the county fair
take a dose of the summer

and you won't care
you will just stop
--and stare--
at Missing Beach

Yeah, that's it. Everything you always wanted, and cops.

A little later on the Captain came on. We're heading back up there. He reminded the lookouts about the mines. And I thought of Sweet Pea. We'd shared a blue moon breakfast club again the other day, and he'd confessed about his sheets. His blue sheets. He'd changed the one set some time ago, and was hoping to hit Abu Dhabi and wash both. Now it looks like that's out.

0830 16 MAR 91. The Captain just came on with a word through the 1MC. It seems the director of "Hunt For Red October" is coming aboard today with a congressman from the L.A. area. I don't know if I should be happier that they're here, or that because they are the GQ scheduled to go down at 0900 just got rescheduled for 1900. That explains why GQ wasn't on the Eight O'Clocks. See, rumors always fly shortly before things like this, because certain people have to know about the drills, and they always have a few select friends who have select pals who have buddies and eventually the Captain has to come on the 1MC just to quell the rumors if nothing else. But the Eight O'Clock Report (also known as the Green Sheet) is a sound bet. If it ain't there, it usually ain't goin' down. Meanwhile, a dude whines in the berthing, "I came all the way up here (from the gym) expecting GQ to go down at nine o'clock and just as I got here the Captain comes on and cancels it." No doubt the gym will be packed by the time he gets back down three ladders and across the hangar bay.

Since that exciting day with CNN onboard (the first time), I haven't been too impressed with rubbing against the celebrities. What do they want, a look at our faces? Do they want to be able to direct that certain realism in future feature films, of how it looks on a man's face running down a corridor with chemical gear? Do they feel a camaraderie, since as heroes we're all celebrities, too? Do they just like flying around on helos and CODs? Are they really all military buffs? Does it give 'em a hard on to walk on a carrier? I could see a cheap thrill in visiting this place, the rush you'd get leaving at will. Visiting a deployed military unit as a civilian must be like being in the military without being under orders. You wouldn't have to say sir, but you'd enjoy saying it as a kind gesture. You wouldn't sweat the small stuff, like putting toilet paper on the toilet seats to fend off the scum, or hunting for a head that had any TP to begin with. Walking through a brown lake in the head would be another thing to overlook. You'd soon forget the stench. Pissing on a wad of chew and a cigarette filter in the urinal likely wouldn't bug you either. You wouldn't notice the no smoking sign. You might not be here long enough to hunt for showers that have hot water, or enjoy one that sprays intermittent hot and cold, or starts out unbearably cold and warms to scalding so that the only way to turn down the heat is hold the nozzle further from your nuts. You'd probably eat in the wardroom instead of the mess decks. So you'd miss the beef jerkey sausage the mess cranks use for hockey pucks after chow. Nobody would spill cream of wheat or bacon grease on your balding pate. You wouldn't traverse the mess on a scavenger hunt back and forth from the side with a glass to the side with ice and back for juice and forth again for silverware. I've learned to toast my bread while I'm doing this. You wouldn't likely pick up a tray with baked on peanut butter, or a cereal bowl with baked beans mashed and attached at last midrats. You might get the Singapore brand recombined milk (so much better than P.I.), but the odds of drinking JP5 (jet fuel in the water) are fifty fifty. So much for the Graham tour.

1830 16 MAR 91. Thirty minutes to GQ. The director probably has cameras set up somewhere by a passageway, to catch a knucklehead slamming a kneeknocker. Or a poor chap slapping a scuttle with his head. And in Personnel, they are probably lit up like fiends. Puff and puff. Like choochoo trains. Four or five simultaneous oilwell fires raging burnt nicotine throughout the office, where I'll have to sit for two hours. I think of the times I put oil of Oman in the vent shaft, just to sweeten up the stench of a sour mop somebody further back in the vent line placed by a hole. "This place smells like a french whorehouse," they'd say.

"What do you think your cigarette does," is what I should have answered back. But you don't answer back to khakis, boy. Or the chain of command will wrap around you like an attack of the killer tomatoes.

Lately, it seems the only recourse we have had is subversion. Scrapper dumps things in chief's coffee cup every night. Nothing is ever said. But one would have to think that it bothered the shit out of a guy. So what. Fight Back with David Horowitz against the Dickhead of the Decade. I offered him six packs of Juicy Fruit gum and after he thanked me left it in his basket. By the next day when he came to take some, it was down to three packs. I don't know what happened to the gum. How should I know? Somebody else must have wanted some, too. Ain't this a chickenshit way to live? This is what cruise does to you. You're in a place you hate with guys you barely tolerate when you have nothing to do except face them everyday and watch it get worse and worse, in spite of "The Chaplain's Evening Prayer" on the 1MC, reflecting the turmoil of the crybabies who saw him today.

At least we had a mail call.

0830 17 MAR 91. The Captain told us it was the director of "Red October." But I think it was also the producer of "Flight Of the Intruder." It was John Milius, for those who look up these things. He left us a late night presentation of "Intruder" on KRAN (with a blurb every few minutes to the effect that recording it was prohibited). And unlike the normal faire, it was not repeated 12 hours later for the daycheckers. Naturally the response from here was lackluster. I should have expected, after they tore up "Top Gun" in the Great Escape enlisted lounge at Miramar. Always critics, they didn't agree with the style of animation, or the hokey way the bombs came off. And the dialogue seemed phony and the acting frequently sucked and the relationships seemed contrived. Well. I agree that Rosanna Arquette was convenient. And I felt they spent too little time with the lead's motivating partner, too little development of their relationship even if it was more than one man's death driving him. William Dafoe was his captivating self. But not much else would impress any of us onboard *Ranger*.

The last couple of days filming were shot on *Ranger*. So it's likely that the director/producer came on his own. But I fancy that John Ferarro, Vice President for Acquisitions at Paramount Pictures, got my letter some weeks ago, and asked or authorized Mr. Milius to fly out here with a one-shot presentation for us. The thing is, Mr. Ferarro won't acknowledge my mail because I once enthusiastically (albeit naively) sent him an idea for a script. I got a letter back from the legal department certified, and thought it was a contract. What else comes from Paramount Pictures certified, return receipt requested? Well, an admonishment not to send him anymore pitches.

Rather than effusing over this pleasant surprise, I just took enough of a gamble to say "thanks," signed my name, and mailed the letter today. I didn't say "thanks for arranging for Mr. Milius to bring us a copy of the movie your company produced, and good luck writing off the potential loss of revenue from all the guys who thought it sucked and now won't book the rental when they hit home port." They have a right to snub the flick. I do to, but you don't look a gift horse in the mouth, man. Where did that phrase, gift horse, come from? And why do I picture an Alaskan sheep dog with a small keg of cognac.

Abu Dhabi is back on again. Who knows what's going on with the war? CNN grew boring, I had to finish my MRPO1, Scrapper went to days. Oh--that's a good one: Chief told me a couple days back, in front of ASH (the Pers O), that he was planning to move Scrapper to daycheck "because the PN3 (a SELRES) is leaving, and the PNSN is TAD." Now at GQ (last night at 1900), in front of the assembled staff of Admin/Pers, he announces the reason gleefully but professionally, "because I hear rumors that you two are always fighting and I'm afraid you're going to kill each other."

I give up. Scrap pleaded for night check. Chief leaned on me to get work out of him. Senior directed me to treat him with kid gloves. He skated off and the chief wrote me up for under utilizing my subordinate. I chewed him out for telling me he'd be in the Ready Room dutifully manning the phones, then having the SDO call me in Pers looking for a courier to pick up the latest Air Plan from Strike Ops. And turning up bullshitting in the paraloft. He always had an excuse for everything. It was only for a second, he'd cleared it with the SDO who forgot, it wasn't what I thought. But he'd give me that he was in the paraloft when I came looking for him, and he'd agree that I should not have to come looking for him.

Just as Scrapper warned me the night before, chief let it go around that there were problems in Personnel, but not that he was the source. That there were arguments, but not that chief had come charging across the room with his fist. Just the noise, the unwanted sound, without clarity. Everything pointed to Graham, and now chief can add that he pulled the striker off the night shift because of my inability, my failure to manage him. There goes another eval mark, 4.0 in directing dropping to 3.8, maybe 3.6. Not to mislead: 3.6 is average. 3.8 is exceptional, and 4.0 is an outstanding mark that must be specifically supported on the reverse of the enlisted performance evaluation report. But I live in that halo'd realm of perfection, where you have to remain if you want to survive. Like Dylan's philosophical lyric, "he not busy being born is busy dying." The system goes as low as 1.0, with 2.0 being the turn in the road for an E5. Hit that guardrail and you're in for a letter from the Navy's Petty Officer Quality Review Board.

PNC has ten months to fuck with me. Will he make it? You can do a special eval anytime to document exceptional or substandard performance. So it's extremely important that he begin now, as I enter the realm of the OCR eval. (E4 and below are non-OCR forms, meaning that they are not sent to Washington. It's when you hit the E5 level that headquarters begins to keep a record.)

Do I want to stay in? Imagine me working for another son of a bitch like this chief, ever again. I'd rather be dry-fucked by that black motherfucker who tried to have me in the New York City YMCA 15 years ago. My shore billet, should I decide to accept it, would put me in a PSD (Personnel Support Detachment) where I'd have a million Filipino fuckheads talking Tagalog, taking over the Navy. No thank you. Am I racist? Am I bigoted? Am I telling it like it is? Ask some other white boy--even a nigger for that matter. If a black dude hated me he'd still hate a Flip. I guarantee it. I never want to find myself in a position like this, with a contract that I can't nullify, in a job I can't walk off, for a racist tyrant I can't do a goddam thing about. FUCK!!! THE!!! NAVY!!! They promote this hell. On the other hand, my two months at Consolidated Divers Unit in San Diego were heaven. And my last PNC was a cool white dude.

The clearance thing, if you want to hear what really bugs the shit out of me besides racist pigs. This is it. I can't get any kind of a clearance because I "failed the reliability screening for the IS" (Intelligence Specialist) rating." But have I made it clear what kind of guys do get clearances and how they compare with me? Say I'm a buttfucking lowlife queer who likes it up the ass and sucks fine cock. What's that got to do with safeguarding classified information? I don't think Johnny Walker was a raging queen.

JR, my last PNC, told me all kinds of stories about busting into the local pharmacies and welding open the safes and making off with all kinds of drugs for sale. This guy's got Top Secret! And Scrapper, left his bride at the altar (!), joined the Navy to avoid a jail term, did all kinds of drugs and beat ass all over his hometown. He's twenty years old with a Secret clearance. And my new PNC is a naturalized citizen who brags about cheating his wife across the International Forget Line, stud king of PI. Who are these shady characters and what makes them better than me? Who in the goddam hell loves America more than I do? And who knows how to keep their mouth shut? I've been a goddam undercover narcotics agent for the DEA, for Christ's sake, and if I'm a goddam fag in the Navy and fags are "incompatible with Naval service," can I keep a secret? How the hell did I make it through Bootcamp and the legal hold the fucking DIS guy threw at me? How many times have I sucked cock since I've been in? Who wants to know? Fuck you.

"When the new skipper takes over in April," YN1 advised, "I think you ought to push real hard to get your clearance." We were discussing the upcoming inport watchbills. Somebody with a clearance has to pick up the messages. So on my duty days, Scrapper has to stick around. Or in some way the section has to get screwed by providing another person. That of course makes me Mister Popularity. They all wonder, too, why a decent white boy mysteriously can't get a clearance. Rumor has it I killed a man. My DD Form 1966, in my service record, confirms I was charged with first degree murder. Quite the red flag. It adds that my case was dismissed because I killed him in self-defense. It doesn't say he was a boy. I guess I'll haunt myself over that for the rest of my life, as this clearance bullshit and everything else pales by comparison. Give me a fucking court martial. It's a far enough journey to those pearly gates, not to have to think of rejection when you finally do meet your maker. Sometimes I still want to cry "mama, I just killed a man." I'm acquainted with grief.

0830 18 MAR 91. Had another blow out with the chain of command last night. This time with the Pers-O. His title is the Personnel Officer. He's an LT in the spot of an LCDR, a Division Officer who should have been a Department Head but was a junior jet jockey, a tired, balding no load who got fired from Ops and dumped on my shop, call sign Ash. But we low life enlisted pukes must call him Sir.

Ash was playing chess again, using the shop for a lounge, contrary to the POD note which constitutes an order from the Commanding Officer. He played AD1, the Safety Petty Officer who seemingly was forever associated with program problems immediately after he used our computer. Thus, AD1 is mentally and spiritually banned from our office, if not physically. We are cordial and cool, and we kick him out when he is not on official business. Except I had to steam and stew as he loitered with Ash.

"Wanna play again," Ash asked.

"Well, no, I have some other work I have to do." AD1 knew I was fuming as I walked around putting chairs on tables.

"Sir, I was going to field day here in a couple of minutes."

"Oh, that's okay," he frowned. "I need to talk privately to you for a minute, too." He led me out to the passageway at the foot of our ladder, right outside the Shooter shack. "That memo," he rolled his eyes. "I don't know where it came from but Lieutenant Commander Z gave it back to me and all he said was, 'what the fuck is this?'"

In reviewing my potential for a deathly eval this time, I had realized that the last time PNC and I fought toward the end of an evaluation period, I got unrelated 3.8s. In a moment of clarity I had noticed that the marks didn't jibe with the remarks on the reverse, i.e., an almost outstanding 3.8 in Rating Knowledge and Performance didn't equate to the phrase on the back, "displays sound judgment and takes independent action to resolve emergent problems."

"The thing is, your memo didn't even sound like a request." He was frustrated, talking in squelched bursts. "You drafted it in the tone of 'this is a mistake, correct it.' And you, again, you didn't use the proper chain of command. It seems like we keep having to tell you, this isn't the first time I've got on you about properly using the chain of command."

I took it and took it and began to explode on the officer. It was an odd privilege, somehow, that bordered on pleasure, to dump on the Lieutenant. It was a kind of thing enlisted men don't do. But I knew I had earned the privilege, and as much as he hated it, he had been there, too, and he allowed it through empathy. When it got through to me, I settled down and appreciated having him as my boss. Or, my boss's boss. "The chain of command is killing me, sir. Haven't you ever been in a position where somebody had you under his thumb and just kept stomping on your head and there was nothing you could do about it?"

"I have. That's what happened to me in Ops. I couldn't do anything right. But you're in a better position than I was. At least you have somebody you can talk to about it. I didn't have anybody. I was new in the squadron, and the only person I could talk to was my wife. Everyday I'd come home and try to explain to her what was happening and she couldn't understand any of it. I've been where you are and I feel bad that you have such a poor relation with your boss. But I think it would be better if you didn't go around creating so many enemies for yourself."

"Enemies? I know who my enemies are. I could name 'em off. But I have plenty of friends, too. And some of them are depending on my leadership and how my own conflict gets resolved in this office. Like the Line shack. Two guys have been physically abused in there, slapped in the head by their chief. And what happened to that guy? Not a fucking thing."

"I know. I know about that. But that's a different department and they've gotta handle it through their chain of command. We're talking about this chain of command. You can't keep slighting the chief like this and expect him to change his attitude toward you. You've gotta be more low key. And your memo to a former department head about an eval that happened nine months ago, that only draws attention to the fact that you've got a problem down here. He's not gonna go back and change it, just because he can. It should have been handled then." I sat on the shredder with a nauseous look. Man, this fucking Navy. Didn't I learn anything inside Western, with Amy and her dear old dad? Somehow, I finally calmed down enough to shake hands with Ash and let him go to sleep. I'm so tired of tracking every tidbit of thing chief did to me, way he distorted the reasons for things, and twisting points of view around various arguments. This thing has a characteristic of MacMurphy and Nurse Ratched, with YN1 serving in the role of Doctor Spivey. (I played Spivey in "Cuckoo's Nest" in northern California, and the play became the longest running show in the history of community theater in the East Bay. Spivey was torn by Mac's inspiration, versus the Nurse's drive to get his authority to use electroshock therapy.)

YN1 has decided to get the hell out of the Navy, after nearly twenty years of faithful service. He's had numerous awards. But he's reached the end of his tolerance for pain, for glory mongers who assign the work to him then take the credit. Not once or twice but day in and day out, month after month, year after year, as the endemic appendage to a Naval career. Who needs it? But over those long and painful years he learned the hard way to keep his mouth shut and his butthole waxed. He practically walks with a stoop from being ass fucked by so many bastards. And when I first got started, he assured me to keep quiet, not to worry, not to cry, not to raise the issues (and the stakes). Did I listen? *Moi*? Me? Hell no!

Over the past week he's been further demoralized by his own boss, that son of a bitch Yeoman Senior Chief. Meanwhile, he watched my PNC get a letter of appreciation for handling the car storage problems back at the beach as we prepared for deployment. He knew who sweated that load, and it was not my chief, not Scrapper, not the PN2 who deserted the Navy, and nobody else was left except me. And it was me, goddammit, me. But who got the glory at quarters, and stood beside his Filipino pal whose typing test was gundecked? That's right, folks: PNC. So YN1 started to encourage me a little. And when his encouragements backfired in my face, it only hurt him more, and further resolved him to get the fuck out. I think it's a shame. But I have no doubt he'll manage someone's office quite productively in a normal work environment. The pitfalls of civilian office politics are melted butter compared to the shit that goes on in Admin and Personnel in the United States Navy. (In case you haven't got it yet, let me clear things up. I'm the bad guy. I'm against everyone else. I'm the one guy all the others are talking about. I'm the guy referred to in the gossip about the problems in Admin and Pers. Now, is that clear? Let's hear no more about it. At least until 31 March, eh?

How many days left in this man's Navy do I have? Ten months on a thirty day basis. No, not three hundred days! That's too much! I always thought it was funny how sailors talked, even my brother Tim talked in terms of the number of days remaining to fulfill his contract. How could it be so bad, so miserable, that people would actually count the days, even mark them off the calendar like a young girl would the times she'd been laid? But they do. I've been a booter, a fucking new guy, newby to a new command, a wog, then salty, and a shellback, and now I'm getting short. My god, what a course in English grammar. A bachelor of arts in USN. Emphasis in Navy jargon. Minor in Mess Cranking.

I can tell this must be the 85 percent mark in my book, too. The war is supposedly over, except for this reflash watch. And the ports will comprise much of the remainder (if I don't spend that time in the brig). Like it's downhill from here, to the big parade on Grand Street, where the neon madmen lie. And when it's over, just like that dude in Memphis, like Dylan, I'll be: *Trying to find out what price / I have to pay to get out of / Going through all these things twice.*

"What's goin' on, Graham?" It was that old coop cleaner from 39 Man, Beave. Since early in the cruise he's been DCPO (Damage Control Petty Officer). "Have you turned in your Atropine injectors yet?"

"Naw, I was gonna bring 'em down after General Quarters. But the bag was gone. I guess you picked up all the others. I'll bring 'em down later."

"How's everything between you and chief?"

"Oh, the war? Snafu. Man, I don't know what to do."

"Well, I tell you. You know you can't win if you fight him. So the best thing you can do is not to argue with the man, because if you give him any kind of argument he's just gonna use that against you. So what I would do, and I've been in that situation before, when I was in the AO shop. I'd just do my job, and do it as professionally as you can, keep doin' everything right. And since you're on night check and he's on days, keep your distance between the two of you. And for that two or three hours when he's here and you have to deal with him, if you don't have anything of a professional nature to say to him, don't say anything at all. Because after a while as things lighten up, and you want to feel like you can be friends with him again, you know he's just gonna try and screw you again. So don't waste your time. Just keep up the silent treatment until you get through this cruise, and until you get out of the situation all together."

"Win by losing."

"That's right. Just take whatever he gives you and keep up your professionalism, and when he starts pingin' on you if you just keep acting professional and nice back at him, everybody around is gonna see that he's obviously fuckin' with you."

"Thanks a lot, Beave." That guy was a sage. Fuckin' Scrapper. Right now he's skating off with some dudes near Gus's old rack, stopping by on a message run, bragging about his fifteen thousand dollar final secret clearance. It goes twenty minutes, bullshitting about who's got what clearance. He's proud. I'm the one who told him they spent fifteen thousand on it. I only heard that from my old roommate, an AT with a final secret, who told me it was worth that to his potential employers (he was getting the fuck out, too). I wonder what cock and bull story he's planning to give PN3 as to why it took so long on the message run. And I wonder if he actually considers it part of his customer service to hang out in the berthing during his shift. Maybe he knows something I don't, and maybe Dean was wise in his decree that petty officers ain't shit and airmen rule the Navy. They've got nothing to lose.

0830 19 MAR 91. In the berthing passageway, a bunch of guys are playing push up poker. You deal out three cards, with the face cards ascending to fourteen for an ace. Each player takes a turn doing however many pushups his three cards total. (You don't want to get three aces.) It started out breezy. They're groaning over the rap music now, and dropping out. The only prize is toughness, and satisfaction. But you might be the talk of the squadron for the next shift.

Sweet Pea made the breakfast club. It was really only DJ and myself, when I called out to Sweets. He was dressed in a new, white, clean jersey. All right, I told him it was pretty. And he had greens on. He has this little mustache that looks so out of place, as if pasted on. It's black but almost pencil thin and the hairs are about a quarter inch long at the sides of his lip. He has a small vertical scar on his forehead over his right eyebrow, that makes him seem to scrunch his brow as if serious. He got a sports page from his grandpa, and a couple of letters. And he got Frosted Flakes when the FSA put them out, so he was happy.

He hasn't washed those blue sheets yet. Living on his second set, hoping to pull into Abu Dhabi--which was supposed to happen today--so he can do laundry.

At midrats I needed to take a dump so I went to the head by the forward galley. For two days I couldn't find a stall with a fucking roll of toilet paper. But this one had it. I took the last stall because it looked like they didn't have doors, and the only time I could ever shit in front of someone was in the L.A. County Jail. Those shitters didn't even have sides -- just aluminum bowls the size of an ashtray in front of the guard, God, and everybody. Even Amy had a hard time watching me shit. I could piss in front of her but when it came to number two, I had a thing about being alone.

They had doors that opened inward. But I was at the end by the time I figured that out, so I sat down. And on the inside of the door some dude had drawn a hard-on with balls, and written a note, "tap foot if you want it." On the sides someone had scrawled little notes about loving to suck cock. But they were mostly wiped off by the head cleaner or somebody who wanted him all to himself. I took a shit and looked at the drawing in front of my nose.

Somebody else came in and I heard the toilet paper rolling and tearing. Then it got quiet for a minute. I found my foot wanting to tap, if only from trying to avoid it. What if it was a set up? What if the dude knew me? What if he was ugly? I had a hard on before I knew it, and with a little spit from the back of my tongue, made love to myself. The thought was erotic and admittedly exciting. But fuck if I'd end my cruise in the head. I heard the other toilet flush, and I creamed in a wad of paper and zipped up, washed up like nothing happened, and made my way back up to Pers.

I stopped in the hangar bay and looked out at blackness, from the edge of the elevator. You couldn't see shit, and couldn't hear the waves. "You know," I opened up as we rode the escalator. "One morning I sat beside you, in the main section of the mess. And I didn't say anything because I wanted to see if you'd notice. I was right by you, right beside you. I even said hi to some of your friends on your other side. You never did see me."

"What was I, talking to all my friends?"

"No. You had your head down. I guess you were sleeping."

"When was that?"

"About two weeks ago."

"Oh. I can't remember that far back."

"You finished and got up and left."

"You should have said something, Graham."

We stopped in the elbow joint of the passageway at the top of the escalator outside Ready Room Eight. "Well, if you get into the groove where you can make six-thirty again, let me know and I'll arrange to eat with you." As always, we shook hands. It was a three position shake, like a white boy, like a brother, like a Mexican. At the last, we always hold on too long. We're like Billy and I, when I was 16 and he was 10. We didn't want to say goodbye in his driveway in my mother's Vega. It was my loss, God's history would paint the picture that way. He was looking to grow up, and I was already looking over my shoulder. That summer he went away to France and came back straight. I drove Mom's Vega through the Missouri river floodplain and ruined it. Years later I would find a negative and get it blown up to a 16" poster, Billy with his head half-cocked smiling into my camera from the shade of a tree in the green, green grass of his yard in Columbia, Missouri, wearing my T-shirt that was far too large and left a gape at the nape of his neck, half-way across his thin, soft shoulder. I would cry over that yellow haired boy's smile and the eternal flicker from his eyes. For I would hold him no more.

0800 20 MAR 91. Last night as I came in YN2 Jax called me aside. "Hey Bob," he motioned me close with a finger. "Do you know somebody name Sweet Pea?"

"Why?" I could feel the heat under my cheeks as I tried to hide my desperate attempt to hide my alarm.

"Do you know somebody name Sweet Pea, and is he on *Ranger*?"

"Yeah," I whispered. Unless I admitted it there would be no getting information out of Jax as to how he found out.

"Well I was cleanin' off the hard drive. And I come upon this Diary stuff. And I had to take a look to make sure what it was before I just deleted it. And of course I read it." He was fighting to keep the grin off his face. "That's some incriminatin' stuff on there. But don't worry. I don't think YN1's seen it and he's the only other person that operates this computer. I went ahead and deleted it."

"You've earned a place in my history, Jack. I'll never forget you."

I sent ten pages to the William Morris Agency, and printed them off with the Admin computer. And in that brief exercise I fucked up royally and left a copy on the hard drive. Instead of Jax talking to me, it might have been

Senior Chief Chainsmoker, or anybody else with an axe to grind or an urge to drum me out of the Navy before my time. The "f" word was in that passage, and I don't mean "fuck." I mean "f" like a black man talks about the "n" word. I guess I've been slipping all over lately. An eval I typed came back from XO, and PNC pointed it out.

"XO says, 'you wish'." I read the passage he'd notated:

> His excellent technical skills were major contributors to the unequaled operational achievements of this command in sex weeks of intense combat operations.

There was a little Post It note stuck to the word *sex*, with his two words in green ink. "We've been at sea too long."

When some guys walked by me today and one grumbled, "maybe we'll get some mail today," it made me wonder what a new guy might think if he heard that. It must be weird for a guy to check in on board a ship that's been fighting and steaming for several months without a port call. The sense of humor is twisted, and the urge to fight is extreme.

Like AE1 last night. He was going to eat and found the ladder tagged off right by the escalator. So he turned off the escalator and started down after letting some airman come up. However, the airman turned around. "Hey, you're not supposed to go down the escalator." Now, why in the hell should it matter to the dude? He was not a mess crank, not a messdeck master-at-arms, not a thing but an AZAN from another squadron. Not even ship's company!

"Look, I'm halfway down already."

"Well I'm turnin' it back on right now."

"If you turn it on I'm gonna beat your ass when I get back up there." AE1 got right to the point.

"Oh, now you're makin' threats. I oughta just write you up right now."

"Go ahead and write me up. I'm still gonna beat your ass."

By that time the AE1 was down, and the dude went around the corner. Not finished, however, he went straight into the Ready Room and whined to some officer. Naturally, the officer, being a college graduate and all, took the word of this airman that the AE1 was in the wrong, and a little later chewed out the first class petty officer. "You should have handled it differently. You didn't have to threaten him. What if he had turned it back on?"

"I'd have carried out my threat."

"Why didn't you use the ladder?"

"It was tagged out."

"Why didn't you go down another way?"

"I didn't want to. I was hungry."

"What if he'd been an officer? Would you have talked to him that way?"

"Yes sir. He was an asshole."

That didn't make the O any happier. But there were two sides. The O's unhappiness, and his insistence at driving such a piece of bullshit into the ground, just made the AE1, an avionics expert with sixteen years in the Navy, want to get out. Not to get out. To get the fuck out. He doesn't even want to give it four more years for a twenty-year pension plan. But he probably will. Like YN1 said, you get up to first class, then you're in a rut for fifteen years trying to make chief. There should be something between YN1 and YNC, between AE1 and AEC. Or at least after five years in the pay grade start giving more credence to a person's time in rate. AE1's been a first as many years as it took him to get to first. NC1's been at that pay grade since 1973. They have to watch some new guy with less brains waltz in and suck cock, and up he goes to a flag staff job at the pentagon, for Gene Hackman. Commissioned to Limited Duty Officer.

PNC--no, I'm not bitching and whining this time. The guy was trying to help a shipmate cut off his dependent dental payments back to the date of divorce. Why pay for her, right? Well, he told me to use an effective date on the 3060 of the date of divorce. I went by the book--did I tell you this already? The book said you have to put the date the member signs the disenrollment form. But common sense, the chief expected, would prevail. I actually agreed with him on this, and suggested he follow-up with a clarification or change request to the publishers. But guys in the field seldom do follow-up on these things. They work around them. Which is what PNC had been doing as a PN1 at the PSD. Unfortunately, DK2 kicked it back. The phone rang and chief started going off in Tagalog. But every few words or so I'd hear "dependent dental" in English. He got off the phone beaten, but not finished. "I have to talk to the DK chief."

"They kicked it back?" Had I not been on guard, I'd have shown some glee. But from here on out it's that intimidated environment where everything is professional, I'm behind him all the way, and it may weasel me a 3.8 overall. Joke 'em if they can't take a fuck.

"I would think, it's common sense that you're not going to pay for a service that you don't get any benefit."

"You should send that letter to request a clarification."

I knew he wasn't interested. I just wasn't sure why he'd fought for it in the first place. Was it just a bullheaded act refusing to lose face since he'd instructed me in front of Jax? (They were playing chess as I did the form.) Was it just flippant?

Even the movies have been weird on TV. That one about the twin brothers, one's a gynecologist and the other does something to make women more fertile, some bullshit like that. They get kinkier and kinkier until the one finally cuts the psychological siameseness out of the other and kills him. What the hell is that? And some horror flicks. "Nightmare On Elm Street Part Two." Last night was the first time I ever watched it, and frankly, I didn't give a damn. The only thing I liked about it was, I was working at the Completion Bond Company in Beverly Hills, when it was in production and part of my job included typing daily production summaries. Those were the days, coming off my case and starting to relax, word processing gigs in showbizland three days a week, Venice Beach the rest of the time. Doing the rewrite for Khalid. Driving around in flip flops. No Navy. No standing watches. No weekend musters. No legion of seniors fucking me on whims. No telephone recall. No counseling chits. No ship and no coffin rack. And no goddam war.

I think the cops are bad in San Diego. On the news Los Angeles cries out for Daryl Gates' throat. City of angels where they're all being killed. What the fuck did that crazy nigger do to get his ass beat by those pigs? Spout off? Rape a baby? What will it be like ten months from now, at my EAOS? Drive by race wars? Westwood under siege? Martial law? Am I safer in the goddam Navy?

I've entered the "window" for an incentive interview with NC1. I wouldn't mind staying in if I never had another bigoted racist Filipino favoritist pig as a boss. And if they give me a clearance to become a YN, or LN, or PH or IS or work at the Pentagon even as a PN. (Yeoman, Legalman, Photographer, Intelligence Specialist or the Personnelman I am now.) But if my book bites it's all moot. Like Jax said, "incriminatin' stuff." Like Dylan said, "in a guillotine."

Chapter Fifteen

0900 21 MAR 91. I received a letter last night from my dear friends at Internal Affairs, San Diego Police Department.

> Dear Mr. Graham:
>
> This to inform you that a thorough investigation into your complaint has been completed. It has been determined that the actions of the officer(s) were justified, legal and proper.
>
> A copy of your complaint and the subsequent investigation will remain in Department files for a minimum of five years.
>
> We appreciate your concern in bringing this matter to our attention. If you have any questions regarding your complaint, please feel free to contact me at 531- 2801.
>
> Sincerely,
>
> Bob Burgreen
> Chief of Police

Signed by a Lieutenant.

Well, I couldn't let that lie. Even if I was on acid, spaced out of my mind with goofball pupils, I still had a right to inquire who the fuck they thought they were hanging out at Mission Beach instead of turning in their equipment. And they did remind me of a death squad, scaring away the druggies and the skateboarding boys.

> Gentlemen:
>
> In the world of police business, perhaps it is proper to arrest persons for asking legitimate questions about utilization of personnel and equipment. It may also be justified to twist cuffs, choke hold and jam against cell walls, persons who are appalled at being arrested for asking such questions. And it may be legal to arrest a man for calling 911 to make the same inquiry, although the city attorney will decline to file the charge.
>
> However, in my book, this kind of behavior on behalf of a supervisor does not call for such a blanket endorsement from Internal Affairs or from Chief Bob Burgreen. It makes me wonder who is behind killing the prostitutes in San Diego, and who endorses the justified homicides that resulted in provocative benchmark ads all over America's Finest City. Perhaps I should live on base for my own protection against those paid to protect and serve me.
>
> From the Gulf, protecting you and your city.
>
> ROBERT D. GRAHAM

What the hell. I didn't mention Daryl Gates. But I felt like making the comparison. Half of Los Angeles was down at City Hall last week trying to oust him. I guess the camcorder is the next best thing to homeslice bread. What's going on with our traditional protectorate? Have we attained a police state that terrorists, who attempt to destabilize an economy, seek as a primary goal? Are the cops falling into the trap of not being able to distinguish random violence from subtle, calculated domestic terrorism like I saw those grad students reading up on at the Rand Corporation? At least being in the Navy I won't have to shoot students at Kent State in a crackdown by (or against) the Chief of Police. But in five years will the flight of the Intruder target Los Angeles or San Diego? What makes Daryl Gates (or Bob Burgreen or the county sheriff or any local law enforcement agent) less a threat to the populace than Saddam Hussein who brainwashed Iraq? Everybody loved him because his picture was up all over town, right? Who says the military won't someday mobilize in Los Angeles to root out a Chief of Police? City Hall is packed with outrage, and the guy refuses to step down. Where does that lead, what kind of storm does it bode? Will someone arm the homeless? Will cops drop like flies in major cities just for being in uniform, as citizens revolt against their unnecessary and arrogant, thus evil presence? Will some private militia of armed citizens conclude that cops are the problem vice the solution, and start picking them off like scabs in the failure of a political system to comprehend the removal of a police force whose purpose has passed? Can't we protect ourselves? Hoods do, as well as some neighborhoods. (In the description of some of my co-workers, the above speech is a Graham Slam.) Are we all missing the point? What about that destabilization? Would it have a purpose? Get the citizens up in arms against the cops and blur the lines between the good guys and bad guys, and come out slowly, carefully, with your prepositioned army, so that nobody knows there's an invasion taking place until all the cops are dead, some killed by that pissed off bunch of rednecks, the rest by that clandestine army of illegal aliens sponsored by Castro and mother fucker Russia. And martial law takes up the time of the National Guard, and replay the Persian Gulf with Iran this time. Finally we soak up the resources, finally we take over the country. Bye, bye Miss American Pie. We have all got to calm down or this will be it.

0830 22 MAR 91. I'll be getting bona fide E5 pay as of 16 April 1991. Adding BAQ and VHA, I will arrive at approximately the salary I made in 1985. $1400 a month. However, at that time I also took a second job, leaving the ad agency at five and making it over to the Century Plaza by six, wheeling around in the huge underground parking lot, and doing data entry for a scam cellular phone licensor from then to ten for six bucks an hour. There were two good things about that job. One, the head sales guy turned me on to jojoba oil, a natural hair tonic that never made my hair grow, but kind of made my skin feel nice. And it's great at the beachtowns, after a sunburn. The other great pleasure was up on the twentieth floor, at night, overlooking the Plaza Hotel where Ron Reagan was staying, standing behind the curtains overlooking Century City and jacking off. I felt young. Hell, I was under thirty. But I guess I was acting seventeen. I wonder how many janitors and late night workers have done themselves pleasure behind the curtains of a skyscraper.

Last night I came up with a Beneficial Suggestion, to use the Navy's terminology. A "Bennie Sugg." It's kind of like a Bennie Boy, only different. Either way I'll probably be the one to get fucked. A Bennie Boy is a transvestite across the International Forget Line. Usually a native from a far off land, and a complete surprise to the unwary tourist. A Bennie Sugg, on the other hand, is a way to save the Navy money by improving a job, a method, a system or some other device. Usually awards are given to the guys in Maintenance, where it really matters. I mean, you're not gonna be "Pro of the Week" in the base newspaper for saving a typewriter.

We have a thing in Personnel called SGLI. Servicemen's Group Life Insurance. Everybody gets it, with some lame exceptions. This is the thing I put Sweet Pea's name on. If I croak he gets fifty big ones from Uncle Sam, and I get the last laugh. They wanted to kick me out and I made them pay the boy I loved, hah! The problem arises with the disposition of the form. One goes in the service record, which remains in Personnel. Commands differ on the other two copies. Even our Admin guys differ with us, and I did it differently for the last chief than, for the Flip now. Admin sends a copy to NMPC (Naval Military Personnel Command) in Washington, DC. They handle officers' records (about 35 men). We give both copies to the member and let him do whatever he wants with them. We handle the enlisted side (some 200 guys).

Well, last night YN2 got smart on YN3 and enlisted me into an attempt at "training," which amounted to ridiculing YN3 for not being able to determine from the manuals where the copies go. "Jax, it ain't in there," I said.

His wide grin vanished. "What chu mean it's not in there?"

"That's what I'm sayin', homeslice." YN3 wasn't blind.

We referred the matter to the Captain's Office. The guy on the phone quite confidently assured us that a copy goes to NMPC.

"Could you show me the reference?"

A half hour later he called back. "Well, they must have taken it out with the changes."

"Are you still going to do it?"

"Oh yeah, that's how we've done it and we're going to continue."

Well my flipped out chief don't want it that way. So now what?

"Which way is the right way," YN3 turned back to me.

"That's it?"

"You mean send it, or don't send it?"

"That's right."

Now, for my motivation. Let's say a guy just came in, he's in the middle of a divorce. Soon as it's final he's getting married to the girl he truly fucks every night and he's wet dreaming of now. He wants the right girl to get the goods. So he fills out his SGLI and sticks her name there. Otherwise--if he doesn't designate her as the beneficiary--the $50,000 would go "by law" to his legally married widow. Fuck that bitch, right?

Thickening the plot, say Iran jumps into the action and follows my

Armageddon scenario on behalf of the Russians. Out of all those carriers overseas, they sink the *Ranger*. Well, bye bye dude, and bye bye service record. If he was serviced by Admin, his babe will get the dough. But if I helped him, under my fucked up chief's procedures, NMPC will have a hell of a time figuring out not to give his divorcee to be all the money. Now for the clincher: bitch gets the cash, honey hears about it from the family, and honey goes to Washington with a copy of the SGLI (that the dude gave her for safekeeping) and her hungry lawyer driving. While the attorney is at it, he files claims on behalf of 200 other members whose SGLI designated beneficiaries were neglected when NMPC paid off "by law" because they had no idea where those people were, or even where the filled out forms might be. That's 200 x $50,000. Plus punitive damages for negligence. Now, there hasn't been an aircraft carrier sunk yet, far as I know. But how about a submarine taking out a couple hundred guys and their service records? I'm not saying it's happened. But they are pretty exposed down there. How about a detachment to Beirut? Or say instead of a barracks, that scud had hit them in the daytime and landed where the service members worked, and had taken them out with their records? Not that it happens, but if it did happen it would be a big fucking nightmare for NMPC. So maybe they'll take it up the chain of command and throw me a hundred bucks for this suggestion: insert an article in each of the (three) relative manuals directing one copy be sent to NMPC. (Another Graham slam.)

0830 23 MAR 91. Uncle Bobby in Abu Dhabi. I had this dream that Sweets came to my rack at 1515 to wake me up. "Bob wake up. It's liberty call." I reached outside my curtain in the dark, felt his curly head of hair and ran my fingers through it down to the back of his neck.

"Come here." And I pulled him in on top of me.

Then I had another dream that I walked off the brow, got on a bus in Abu Dhabi and rode all the way to Kuwait, looked up Khaled's family through his business across from the Social Security Admin building in downtown Kuwait City, made films and published my book to the states from over here. No man can be a prophet in his own country, somebody said. And like Elvis echoed, "when a dream is callin' you, there's just one thing that you can do--you've gotta follow that dream wherever that dream may lead."

PN3 gets on the bus today. For Dubai. He and the rest of the SELRES dudes are going home. I guess they were here just long enough to fuck everything up and stir up the pot. Created extra paperwork for medical, disbursing, evaluation reporting seniors, and my shop most of all. We could have done fine without the reservists. Each eval, of course, will state unequivocally that the member significantly contributed to the squadron's 540 sorties in the six weeks of ODS. But think of the senior chief, principal of an Oklahoma high school. And the college student who had to withdraw. I wonder how many reservists lost their jobs, ruined their educations, and, if any, lost their lives in support of Desert Storm.

Phone calls are three bucks a minute. One if you hang up and have them call back. But that's its own gamble. I remember trying to call Khaled five years ago, listening to the international operator argue with the Kuwaiti operator. "Sir, you must dial oh-one first."

"Yes ma'am, I understand that. I dialed oh-one."

"No, it appears that you must have dialed one-zero. You must dial zero-one first."

He tried for twelve minutes, and never got through. And that was before the war. At least I didn't have to pay for the show.

They have a Burger Queen, not a Burger King, in Abu Dhabi. I suppose that means something. They have a Dairy Queen. I suddenly thirst for a chocolate shake, but wonder if they use camel's milk. It might not be so bad. The milk I had with cereal this morning had arabic writing. It was called Zane, which reminded me of Insane.

You had to have a request chit approved for "overnight liberty" in Abu Dhabi. I skipped PNC, and these things are always routed up the chain of command. I don't recall why I skipped him--I must have been out of my mind, striking a match like that in my powder keg shop. There's more ammunition waiting to go off in Personnel than the flight deck, boy.

My chit came back (approved) with a nastygram from the YNCS, "last warning. Don't jump the chain of command. My patience is gone."

All right, I skipped the Flip. But YNCS doesn't even fit in my chain. It goes PNC, PERS-O, XO, CO. Admin/Pers has two sides, two chains of command. YN2 Jax doesn't route his requests via PNC before YNCS, or PERS-O before AO (Admin-O). By now you must realize there is no justice in the Navy, it is not a democracy. It is run by the whims of senior personnel, and all of life is a popularity contest. Jax, for instance, got frocked the same day I did, to E5. His eval called him "number 3 of 40 outstanding PO2's." On the other hand, PNC tells the Pers-O that I should probably not be given 4.0 eval marks because "he hasn't been an E5 that long." Grumble, mumble, crush, kill, destroy.

I was set to type the transferring evals last night. However, the officers all went to bed. So now the PN3 and Scrapper, the little buttplug, will enjoy spending long hours smoothing out the documents while I'm dreaming of Sweet Pea and walking off the brow. Too damn bad, boys. Have a hell of a great day. Thank your kind and loving officers for fucking you over, hah-hah! And don't give the chief a heart attack. Say, got a collared shirt I can borrow?

2300 23 MAR 91. Considering deserting in the desert of Dubai. I haven't left the ship yet. Supposedly in Ramadan everything is open at night, so I'll still go soon. I've been laying in my rack since 1800 when nobody came by.

I don't have any real friends on board. Even if Sweets loved me he wouldn't allow himself to reveal it, to himself or to anybody else on board including me. "Stop rubbin' up against me or I'll beat your ass" could have been a cover for "please get me alone somewhere" which is covered by "everybody hang around me and keep me under the spotlights so I don't do anything I might later regret."

Road Runner hasn't seen me more than five times all cruise, and still hasn't lived down his blush from the night that we left.

Nobody in my shop, including Scrapper, really wants to go out there with me. Obviously none of those fucking superiors in khakis who, in YN2's words, "are tryin' to railroad you."

Jax has his wife to call. YN1 has his. Scrapper got alienated by PNC's successful antics, just enough to have me argue with the kid about towing the line. So now he looks at me as a supervisor and no friend. YN3 Black has duty, and he's broke anyway. Rod has his wife to call.

Dean talked to me after breakfast coming out of the mess. I took the hangar bay route with him instead of the escalator, and he semi-agreed, which was no agreement whatsoever, to come get me or send Sweets at six. Sweets was borrowing Dean's collared shirt to get off the boat. But they have their own world of twenty, and I'm in my prime of 34.

The Navy breached my contract when my chain of command endorsed the PNC's poor evaluation of my rating knowledge and performance and military bearing for questioning him whenever he issued me unlawful orders to backdate and falsify documents, which he did repeatedly. Is that enough to justify desertion? What do you do when the Navy breaches your contract? Why should one contract be anymore special or indisputable than another in America? Can I sue for breach of contract? Oh lord, can you sense a court martial coming?

0300 24 MAR 91. In the Navy, a "counseling chit" is a form used by supervisors to admonish their subordinates in a manner that, if the situation is corrected (i.e., behavior improves), the chit goes no further than the local command and is destroyed upon the member's transfer. The next level of punishment is a "report chit" which goes to the XO, and, if in his opinion meriting the skipper's attention, could result in "nonjudicial punishment" such as extra duties, or docking pay, reduction of rate, or worse. But the counseling chit is my focus here. Bear with me:

I went out for a bus ride through Abu Dhabi, watched the dark skinned driver drop off and pick up sailors, amused myself with the multi-lingual neon, and sat across from a country bumpkin eating his peanut butter and jelly on a spoon without bread at midrats. Then I stopped by Pers and found a fiasco.

One black racist pig loudmouth motherfucker drug addict who got popped for crack cocaine and sings/whistles through the berthing all the time keeping everyone awake and used to slam the door until they fixed it, ATAR Noload, in accordance with NMPCINST 1616.1C, had to have an extension letter attached to his last periodic enlisted performance evaluation report.

Well, on PNC's desk was a blast from the skipper that all they should do is rewrite his eval to include the period up to his date of detachment (later this a.m.). I found that the PN3 had done this, but nobody had provided a

Page 13 (Administrative Remarks) which is required of evaluations with adverse marks, like this dude had. So I stuck around in my civies and worked overtime on my day off--under nobody's direction but my own fucked up initiative--and covered the chief's ass once again. In the process, I made a trip to Ready Room Eight and checked for outstanding evals that needed to go with the other reservists. In that fine chore, I discovered my own eval. Finally, there it was. And as I predicted, the counseling chit was mentioned in the remarks. My motherfucking chief. You see, counseling chits don't go with you -- but your E5 and above evals go all the way to D.C. and follow your career. He had to mention "he has been counseled" for "at times lacking necessary judgment for good leadership" in the goddam eval. What a swine. He follows in the same breath with, "should become an expert in his field." Is that a slam or a dunk? It's just a conniving way of manipulating the XO to let the remark stand. Which I could see he has, since he's made other chops and it's in the basket for the Pers-O. Needless to say, my star performance of this early morning rapidly faded.

I took my music box and an old Jackson Browne tape--"Saturate Before Using"--to my rack with a cup of coffee and came here to cry, rant and rave.

The most satisfaction I got out of covering his ass was finding a note from the CO to the Pers-O, telling him that the PN's need to get more training in handling evals. Chief has been so pre-occupied slamming his subordinates that he hasn't been training. Like last night, prancing around like a flamer with a Shore Patrol brassard on his arm.

"It gives me a hard on," he said as he clutched his crotch. An embarrassment to the office, to his LPO, to his subordinate striker. "Boy, come here boy. What chu doing?"

"I'm over here fuckin' off, chief." Scrapper hangs out on the Admin side of the office and won't take his shit. "I always pick on him," chief let on to me, grinning proudly. He looked like he wanted to elbow me in confidence. "He's already used to it." They'll keep on joking until the boy explodes. But with him on daycheck now, as PN3 leaves and PNSN continues TAD, he'll wind up in the brig before cruise ends. I hope he makes it worthwhile.

1030 28 MAR 91. This is not one of my best days. Working on the disk for chapter thirteen, that unlucky number, I crashed the whole thing. The WHOLE thing. Chapters uno through dosi. But, a good boy scout when I was young, I had not one but two back-ups. So all I lost was Abu Dhabi, the 24th to 27th more or less. I shall attempt to reconstruct, but it's kind of weird reading a crashed disk. And I'm so geared to keep moving.

I guess life is like this. It feels like death, or like a phone call disconnected. You think you have something, then it's gone. Like if the NIS could get their hands on this, what a field day they would have fucking me over, cutting out my lights. Like putting a luger to the head of a jew. We took an all day bus tour from hell. The Al Ain (Inane?) City Tour. Starring me, Sweets and two guys from V-3, Stinky and Boog.

I was determined to spend at least one port in his company, unlike brooding all last Westpac. I woke him up in his baby blue blanket in the blue berthing behind his blue curtain snuggling his two blue pillows, in blue sweat pants. Little boy blue, okay?

We met the bus in the hot sun on the pier. Sweets dubbed our guide Armahn, but no one understood his name. "I em hippy to teel you, thot we shill see sim kimeels in thee deesirt."

"Oh boy," Sweet Pea shouted with glee. "I'm gonna ride a camel."

He took a million pictures--at least thirty-six--and I sat by him at the rear on the aisle, one foot on the unscrewed floorboard to keep the sand from blowing in. Finally Armahn pulled over and got a concrete block to hold it down. The air conditioner blew sunbaked air that was so hot we finally pulled over again, at a natural spring, and he and the driver unbolted the side rear door and tied it down in the luggage compartment. Now we had aircon!

We toured a meat market in Oman, just before lunch. Fortunately we started with the fish, then viewed the butchered goats, and got to the fruits and vegetables last before heading to the hotel restaurant. Had it been the other way, I don't think I'd have ate the chicken.

We laid out in back of the hotel and took pictures, pretending to be rich as water jets blew across, several feet over the pool. They had a bamboo cabana, but no bar today, because of Ramadan. One Arab had a special job of sweeping sand off the sidewalk.

"Eev'deeting ees fdee," Armahn explained. "Fdee house, fdee cah. Fdee gos. No tox. But, only eef you work." Just like America.

As we passed a compost plantation on down the road, a dude across from me--by the open door--decided to pull his camcorder down from the luggage rack and present the scene for his wife back home. I held it while he raved about the peculiar odor and his buddies pretended to be ragheads, with some of them wrapping bus curtains over their faces. He got up again to put the camera back, and turned pale. "Where's my wallet?" His lime green nylon velcro wallet with about $200, major credit cards, and all his identification, had fallen out of his pants and out of the bus.

We stopped in the middle of nowhere, turned the bus around, and rode back through the stinking kimeel dung plantation, searching for a wallet in the desert like a needle in a haystack. Then turned around again, to return through that endless dung heap.

We manned forward, aft and starboard wallet watches, thirty eyeballs craning, dizzily scanning the flitting flurries of furious desert haze in a brown vignette speeding by at eighty miles an hour, hoping to spot a fucking wallet before we all died of kimeel monoxide.

I spotted--not the wallet--but the lime green cassette cover of a famous Arabian pop singer. Armahn stopped, and I ran back to grab the box and brought it back, showed it to the dude, and threw it back to the roadside like a small fish. We went on, and finally found the fortunate fucker's wallet. A happy ending to his video.

The dude promised us a case of beer, but got off the bus in Abu Dhabi, never to be seen again. We rode back to the ship to put our Saudi Arabian desert roadside souvenir sand away and wash our faces. Then went souk shopping. I bought a 22 carat bright gold chain. For Sweet Pea. But, a good Sagittarius, he insisted I keep it. Sixty bucks gone in a landslide. Maybe I'll wear it, I don't know.

He honored me with the privilege of his company again the next day. At lunch on one beer--my first in seventy-four days, with the exception of beer day--I found his knee between my two knees under a small table. So in a seemingly innocent gesture, like a girl might grasp and squeeze her boyfriend's arm at a football game, my knees jerked together and caught his knee between, for a heartbeat. "Quit it." He looked me straight in the eye. Then we went on with lunch, Dean unaware, drinking lager. With desert he came back to me so nicely, affectionately scooping the whip cream out of my plate. Sharing food is one of the most intimate human acts. I always tried to share food with him. Now he made this intimate move, confusing me all the more. It hurt so good.

Back at the boat again we cleaned up, they ditched me for an hour, and I took a shower and laid butt naked in my rack wondering how to get out of another evening with them. How would I embarrass myself next, fawning over little boy blue?

We made a last trip to the souk. He wore my shirt, the beautiful purple and black one that highlights his glory. And would have looked perfect with gold. But he wore Dean's silver necklace.

Back to the future, we're alongside *Kansas City*, vertrepping, helos dropping supplies on our flightdeck. I wouldn't sleep even if Don Henley's "End Of the Innocence" weren't blaring in my headphones. This song reminds me of that little blue GEO I rolled, trying to get the gun back from Louie. And shifting gears all summer, gliding off the freeway to the beaches, down by the roller coaster where the hippies, silhouetted on the sea wall at the eight o'clock sunset, danced on acid and taunted tourists. I'd play it over and over in the Home Depot lot, considering all the arguments of our world and how I'll probably die, a gunfight with a child in a foreign land. At least I won't kill again. This is the end. Who knows how much longer this will last. Cruise is winding down. I may never kiss another living being. I will never kiss Sweet Pea. He would never imagine I felt this way. The tighter I held on, the more alienated he became. Each time I touched, he jumped. Then he cuddled back toward me out of a polite sense of apology that confused us all the more. While everyone jokes of each other as "bitch" and "girl" and "'ho'" I remain untouched by him. When it comes down to it this is the thing we'll live with. He came and went and let me down, and hurt my pride. I couldn't explain my yearning, couldn't hide my rage. But I sure let him know it was there. He didn't love me, so I shouldn't be confused.

I look up at my flightdeck boots on top of the light. Worn out leather. I'm old and bald, eh. Something about Bob Graham, if you joke with him he may get an idea. He's a camera, and he's heard the voice of Christopher Isherwood. The sailor said, "who?" Oh now, now.

We had pizza and made Sweets happy. We stopped for ice cream first and made him mad at me, because I was stupid to get off the bus at the Dairy Queen, which I had on my list of one place I wanted to see. And they didn't have any chocolate. So he was right. I was wrong and I failed and I was dumb. And I was old and bald and disgustingly ugly. And he was bright and young and quick and sharp and fast and fine. And I was always running to keep up, pathetic. I could use a good cry, all right? The tighter your grasp, the more flighty your beloved. "Quit it," I was scolded. I was rebuked and warned and chastened and told. Still I kept climbing up his leg. He was pure sugar.

0345 29 MAR 91. A shooter lies sleeping while YN3 Black burns photocopies off the message boards. I wait for the printer. Next project, continue printing names at the bottom of the service record Page 13 all 200 of us get for Operation Desert Storm:

CARRIER AIR WING TWO
SERVING ABOARD
U.S.S. RANGER CV-61

On 2 August 1990, without provocation, the Iraqi army invaded and overran its peaceful neighbor Kuwait, quickly positioning itself for further incursion into Saudi Arabia. On 17 January 1991, following six months of unsuccessful negotiations, a coalition of twenty-six countries, under auspices of the United Nations, launched Operation Desert Storm to liberate Kuwait.

Let all who read this be informed that

was an active participant in Operation Desert Storm and served with great honor in the greatest military victory in modern history. He was an integral part of the United Nations Coalition Forces that defeated Iraq in a swift forty-three day offensive that returned the country of Kuwait to its rightful leadership.

CONGRATULATIONS ON A JOB WELL DONE!

J. A. Campbell,
Captain, U.S. Navy
Air Wing Commander

0845 29 MAR 91. Shucks. I missed Senior Chief's birthday. I had a crepe paper roll left over from the night I did up Sweet Pea's rack. And maybe one or two balloons. Oh yeah, and the special gift, some nuts he could crack. And out pops a rubber. Maybe he'll need it next month, when we hit Thailand.

I wonder if Khalid (I can't remember if it's Khaled) has made it back to Kuwait City. If he's stuck in New York. I hear they're worse off than I'd be with all five cigarettes lit and the door shut tight in Personnel. At least I'd get off at 1900. They're breathing Havana cigars 24 hours a day, forever until the Hellfighters save them.

CNN had the *Kennedy*'s arrival home. And the *Saratoga*. All those people crying, hugging. Children and wives. "Man I wish they'd turn that crap off," somebody said on the mess deck. We figure the excitement will be over by the time we come home. But doubtless North Island will be packed. It was last cruise, and that was nothing scary. Few guys' wives fretted then, other than the normal fact that the flight deck is the most unforgiving work space in the world, maybe next to a ground war.

Here's a good one. Who's at fault? The YNCS from CVW-2 (Cag) a couple of nights ago called me up. Call him Chop, for lack of a better disguise. PNC and I just got done burning a copy of liquidated TAD orders for three guys who spent one day on the east coast, battle damage school for F-14s. I had them in the envelope, in the outbasket for the post office. Before they went out, Chop called. "Hey, I'm looking for TAD orders for those three guys VF-1 sent to aircraft battle damage school in Maryland."

"Woah, I was just about to mail them to COMFIT."

"Well get them out. COMFIT had nothing to do with those tango numbers. It's all AIRPAC money and we'll handle it from here. Hey, could you send them to me?"

"Do you need a copy or the real thing?"

"Well, send me the whole sheebang, because I'll have to make three sets of copies." So I sent him the originals. With a note telling him to be sure and return them as soon as he can.

The next morning chief gets my note and we talk about it. "Why did you send him the originals?"

"Well, because he wanted them. He has to make copies." In my mind, it was like a travel claim--you have to send at least the original and two copies.

"Hey, where are those TAD orders for those three guys?" It was Scrapper at my rack, pulling my curtains open. I was glad I wasn't having sex. "Chief wants them."

"Tell chief I sent them to Cag. Senior Chief should have them."

He went away. The chief came back. "What did you do with those TAD orders?"

"I sent them to Cag."

"Did you keep the originals?"

"No. I sent them all to him."

"You could have copied them."

"I asked him if I could send him copies. But he wanted the originals because he was going to copy them over."

"Who'd you give 'em to? 'cause Senior Chief came down lookin' for 'em."

My face went whoops. "Well, I put them in the box for Cag, and I believe YN1 or YN3 took them up. But I think it was YN1. Is he still there?"

"No, I don't think so."

"You want me to come down?"

"No, don't worry about it."

My dick was covered by my laptop and that was no fun talking to the chief. But maybe I'm at my best when I'm naked. Because I'm not intimidated and I'm vulnerable. Vulnerably undaunted.

Next item. End of Cruise Awards. This will be when those who do nothing are credited with all of the good their subordinates did in spite of them. I should be happy for seeing the NAM in the rough for my chief. NAM is Navy Achievement Medal--like YN1 said, it used to mean something.

They're putting YN1 in for an LOC (Letter of Commendation). "They wanna throw me that bone and say, 'here boy. Come on boy, we got somethin' for you.' I'd rather see them tear it up and burn it than stand next to that joker and see him get a NAM."

0900 30 MAR 91. On the hangar deck, a memorial service for the two flyers who didn't make it back. It'll be exactly like the scene in "Flight Of the Intruder," if you want to know go rent that movie. I know the place will be packed, and *Ranger* will be reminded of their ultimate sacrifice, our only losses of Desert Storm. But this is not a book about them. They have their books.

This is a book about backbiting and dogging on a trivial scale between enlisted chiefs and men in dungarees. How humiliating, after all, is it to a man of sensibility to dress him in bell bottoms for the express reason that such jeans are easier to pull off and use for floatation, when at the same time you put him in flight deck boots? This is a book about men tested for AIDS before cruise, then not tested again for 18 months after returning from places like Thailand, AIDS capital of the world. Does the Navy really care for her men? I think it's more important for diplomatic reasons to test her men prior to visiting, so that our heads of state can assure their heads of state that we're not bringing AIDS into their countries. But we don't really care about American sailors, or we'd be testing continuously as they return from far off lands, catching them as it first develops, and beginning treatment right away. Not bumping them from cruise, two months into cruise, two years after they caught it last cruise. This is why I hope Sweet Pea remains a virgin.

"Are you gonna get laid in Thailand?"

"I don't know."

"I wanna be there."

"What?" Sharply, of course. We were on that bus tour from hell.

"I said," I said with a laugh, "I want to be there."

Last night we had a major mail call, finally. The past few have been boxes, very little letter mail. I happened to be in line with a dude from V-3. "Anything for Sweet Pea?"

"Yeah, as a matter of fact I did see his name."

It was a box.

"Mind if I take it to him?"

I found the boy at his rack, topless, in his blue sweat pants, writing a letter. To a girl.

"Oh, thanks."

He climbed down and I watched his stomach muscles move, taut and velvet. He doesn't even work out. He's just extremely hyper. Three Dr. Peppers and he's a ping pong ball. I haven't seen any Dr. Peppers on the boat though. "I have to open this in front of a khaki or they'll have a fit."

He's so good. Or maybe that's just V-3, heavy with the hammer. I'm the guy at my shop who decides whether boxes have to be opened in front of me, or if I want to let 'em go with it--to prevent drug smuggling. Like as if Sweets would receive drugs in the mail, my God. But it wasn't for me to say.

I followed him up to the door of his coop, then let him see that I had to go the other way to get the bag of mail to my squadron.

"What time breakfast?"

"Seven-twenty is the best time. Because usually I don't eat before muster. So if I can I go right after muster." Seven-fifteen was the V-3 muster on the hangar deck.

Lady Luck didn't shine on me this morning. I grabbed four boxes of Frosted Flakes, two just in case I met him and he wanted them. He never showed. But I have faith that he was thinking of me, and just couldn't make it. "The Best of the Crusaders," in my ears this morning. "Keep That Same Old Feeling."

Ran into an Ordie in the chow line. A rough faced nice guy they call Dog, why I don't know. A black dude. "Just the man I needed to see."

"Wut sup?"

"Did you ever get those TAD orders to P.I. settled?"

"Yeah. I got fourteen dollars."

"Did we give the orders back to you when we purged service records a couple of weeks ago?"

"Naw, I was just lookin' at that stuff last night. And them orders wasn't in them. Why? Wha'd they fuck up now?"

He was short, trying to get orders the fuck out of VF-1. The NC1 had tried to get something cut from P.I., and Abu Dhabi. No luck.

In this case, PNC had fudged a logbook again. Three days ago, as I updated it, Dog's tango number was unresolved. A tango number is an accounting code, basically defining who put up the money. The logbook tracked when the liquidation was filed, completed, and for how much. Now it was resolved, only the number was the same for the guy next to it, which I had filled in using that guy's liquidated travel claim and original orders. So chief just copied the number and amount in case anybody who didn't know anything pulled an audit. Trouble is, the guys looking are the guys who do know what's going on, and have to account for this bullshit. It gets too fucking complicated. But the bottom line is, he falsely wrote in who paid how much money when for what member. And he was off by about three hundred bucks, and nobody can find the orders, and nobody can justify the lost three hundred. I ask myself, does he make a career out of this?

"Now muster the 20 man funeral service working party on the flight deck with the petty officer in charge." I guess it's over.

1215 31 MAR 91. Ice cream social tonight. Captain's call. And Sweets' laundry. He doesn't know that I will spend five bucks for the hook-up. I can't tell him that or he wouldn't let me do it. Like he wouldn't let me let him have the necklace. He only knows I have a hook-up to have his sheets, dirty socks and whatever else he wants cleaned. 1930 or thereabouts, I'll come to V-3 and pick them up from him, and take them to Dial's rack in 81-Man. Dial is TAD to ship's laundry, and like all the other sorry suckers who make the best of their time in hell, sells his services, five bucks a bag.

Four more weeks on station out here, in Camel Lot. Normal cycle flight operations. Hopefully no accidents. And no mines. Then we hit Pattaya Beach, Thighland. The heart of a dream come true, across that International Forget Line. Caligula Club, where the girl will dance on stage and pull a string of ten razorblades out of her cunt, and cut paper to show us reality. An artist in Bangkok will paint nude dancers with blacklight brushes and make them look like dragon flowers. A girl in the same bar will smoke cigarettes, two at a time, using her vaginal walls to toke and puff. Men will do the things here they can't even do in P.I. Things they will never forget, or speak of, back in the states. Some will carry the secret of AIDS to America, to their wives and children, to the women waiting on the pier. And thanks to the real policy of not giving a damn about her men, the US Navy will neglect to test them for at least a year. The political line is that service members in the fleet are tested annually for AIDS. But we came back from Westpac 89 in August, and our squadron wasn't tested until three weeks before we left on this cruise. We didn't get results back until we had visited P.I. But P.I. is not politically valued anymore. We've given up on them, and don't give a shit if we send infected sailors to see hookers over there. Thailand still likes us. So some men will have survived the gulf only to be killed in a sex game of Thailand roulette.

Fleetwood Mac sings "I'm not a child anymore" ("Beautiful Child") and I keep thinking. "Your eyes say yes, but you don't say yes; even if I never hold you...." Singing to a young one, no sex explicitly determined. How I have so much in common. But could I sing that to Billy? Not now, he'd be 28. Or what about this kid I protect with a made up name? Sweet Pea. Sweets, dare I say. Lovely man, prettiest boy on the *USS Ranger*, I wish you were mine, even if I never hold you. I get touched, I get stung, I keep looking over my shoulder from then on. Until I'm touched again.

1245 1 APR 91. It is common to mispronounce Change Of Command as Chain Of Command. I wonder how significant the chosen date of April Fool's Day will play in our forthcoming history, as I begin serving under my third skipper at FITRON ONE.

Fighter Squadron ONE History

Fighter Squadron ONE was originally established on 1 July 1922, and continued to operate as VF-1 until 1 July 1934, at which time the squadron was redesignated VB-2. One year later, 1 July 1935, the second VF-1 was commissioned and served for two years until it was again redesignated, this time as VF-6.

During these early years of Naval Aviation, the pilots of VF-1 flew biplane fighters such as the Curtis TS, Boeing F2B and F3B, Curtis F8C and BFC, and Boeing F4B. In January 1925 the decision was made to operate VF-1 from battleships. The Curtis TS land planes were overhauled, fitted with pontoons, and new engines installed. The squadron was assigned to 11 different battleships during the next few years. On 16 November 1927, the carrier USS SARATOGA was commissioned, with VF-1 assigned to her.

The third VF-1 was commissioned on 1 May 1943. During the 15 months that followed, VF-1 was both land based and carrier based, flying F6F Hellcats in day fighting, participating in some of the first Navy night fighting action in the Pacific, and conducting bombing and escort missions in such places as Tarawa, the Filbert, Marshall, Mariana, Bonin and Caroline Islands. After inflicting heavy damage upon the enemy throughout the course of World War II and aiding in the location and repatriation of American POW's, VF-1 was decommissioned on 25 October 1945.

On 14 October 1972, VF-1 was commissioned for the fourth time. After almost 30 years, this represented a significant change from the simple Navy fighters of World War II to the highly sophisticated, newest Navy fighter, the F-14A Tomcat, and marked the first two-man crew concept for VF-1, with the Radar Intercept Officer (RIO) operating the major weapons system in the rear cockpit. After aircrew transition training with VF-124 in the F-14A, and with the arrival of the first Tomcat assigned to VF-1, the Wolfpack of VF-1 separated from VF-124 on 1 July 1973 and began independent operations as a part of Attack Carrier Air Wing FOURTEEN (CVW-14).

By March 1974, VF-1 had received its full complement of 12 Tomcats, and the tempo of operations and workups accelerated in preparation for the first F-14 deployment with CVW-14 aboard the USS ENTERPRISE (CVN-65) in September 1974.

On 17 September 1974, the USS ENTERPRISE deployed with VF-1 aboard for the first operational cruise of the F-14A, giving the fleet a quantum increase in Maritime Air Superiority (MAS) capability. Flying the F-14A in the South China Sea, the Gulf of Tonkin, the Indian Ocean, and in support of the final evacuation of American personnel from South Vietnam (Operation Frequent Wind), VF-1 returned to NAS Miramar in May 1975.

During the next three years the Wolfpack completed two additional deployments to the Western Pacific and Indian Oceans onboard USS ENTERPRISE. Following an intensive turnaround training cycle, the squadron joined Carrier Air Wing TWO (CVW-2) and deployed onboard USS Ranger (CV-61) in the summer of 1980.

This deployment included over 130 days in support of the American units in the Indian Ocean and the Wolfpack was proud to be present in the Arabian Sea at the time the U. S. hostages were released by Iran.

At the completion of another highly successful deployment to the Pacific and Indian Oceans during the summer of 1982, VF-1 had amassed over five years and nearly eighteen thousand continuous accident free flight hours. For this as well as for their overall contribution to aviation safety throughout the entire fighter community, VF-1 was chosen by the Chief of Naval Operations as winner of the 1982 Aviation Safety Award for pacific fleet fighter squadrons.

In keeping with their reputation for operational excellence, and as a culmination to many months of dedicated efforts, Fighter Squadron ONE was presented the Admiral Joseph Clifton Award in July of 1983, officially recognized as the finest fighter squadron in the United States Navy. After completing an outstanding turnaround, which included winning the Fighter Derby as the best squadron on the west coast in Air Combat Maneuvering, the "Pack" deployed in January 1984 for seven months aboard the USS KITTY HAWK (CV- 63).

Upon return from deployment in August 1984, the Wolfpack commenced another highly successful turnaround, winning both the High Noon (Air-to-Air Gunnery) and ECCM (Electronic-counter-counter Measures) competitions. The wolfpack was awarded the 1984 F-14 Battle "E" given by COMNAVAIRPAC to the Pacific Fleet Fighter Squadron with the highest level of combat readiness. For these accomplishments, VF-1 was again awarded the Admiral Joseph Clifton Award as the Navy's best fighter squadron in 1984. As an additional measure of all-around excellence, COMFITAEWWINGPAC presented Fighter Squadron ONE the Golden Anchor Award for fiscal year 1985 for leading all Pacific Fleet fighter squadron in the retention of qualified personnel.

The Wolfpack entered 1986 committed to maintaining its operational excellence and it was not disappointed. On 1 April 1986, the Secretary of the Navy, the Honorable John Lehman, presented Fighter Squadron ONE the Meritorious Unit Commendation for sustained superior performance in every facet of naval aviation. Additionally, the "Pack" was recognized in July as the best fighter squadron on the west coast in Air Combat Maneuvering by winning the 1985-86 COMFITAEWWINGPAC Fighter Derby. Fighter Squadron ONE has set a precedent without equal through professionalism and operational excellence.

To further add to an already impressive list of accomplishments, the Wolfpack made several short deployments in 1986 and 1987. In July 1987 the "Pack" deployed again on a WESTPAC cruise to support the U. S. foreign policy of escorting reflagged Kuwaiti tankers in the Persian Gulf. In completing such a rigorous schedule, VF-1 accumulated more flight hours and sea time than any other Pacific Fleet Fighter Squadron in 1987. COMFITAEWWINGPAC presented the squadron with the Fighter Derby Trophy for an unprecedented third time. The remainder of 1988 proved to be a banner year for the Wolfpack. The squadron won the Electronic Counter Measures Trophy, placed second in the Fighter Derby and High Noon competitions, and capped the year by winning the Battle Efficiency "E" award as the most combat ready fighter squadron on the west coast.

1989 proved to be an even more successful year, with the adron winning a second consecutive Battle "E" and the Admiral Lifton Trophy as the best Fighter Squadron in the Navy. The current deployment aboard USS Ranger involving combat operations in the Arabian Gulf in support of Operation Desert Storm will be historic. VF-1 not only set records in terms of squadron sorties/flight hours and individual aircrew flight hours flown, it was the only F-14 squadron in the Arabian Gulf to have an air-o-air kill in the war. It is with this spirit of winning that Fighter Squadron One presses on with pride in its past and readiness for the future.

I dug this stuff out of the program for the change of command, and figured eventually you might want to know what the official lines of what we're supposed to be doing out here really are. So if that's the history, here's the mission:

Fighter Squadron ONE Mission

As a fighter squadron, the WOLFPACK is tasked with several aspects of fleet defense. These include Maritime Air Superiority (MAS), overland power projection and peacetime force presence.

Fighter Squadron ONE (VF-1) was the first squadron to receive the Gruman F-14A Tomcat, the U. S. Navy's most versatile fighter. After being officially established with the new Tomcat on 14 October 1972, VF-1 commenced its training and familiarization cycle to prepare for its mission of operating the F-14 from the deck of aircraft carriers. While much of this training is accomplished onboard the ship to which VF-1 is assigned, a great deal of the pre-deployment training is accomplished from the squadron's home base, NAS Miramar, in San Diego, California.

The WOLFPACK is composed of 34 officers, of which 28 are aircrew, and approximately 250 enlisted men. The normal aircraft complement is twelve. The Maintenance Department is composed of fifteen workcenters, each with its specialized group of trained personnel that work on the various aircraft systems. The remaining enlisted personnel comprise the force that handle the record keeping and administrative duties.

Aircraft markings consist of red wolf's heads on the vertical tails, and "VF-l" on the ventral fins. The WOLFPACK currently has all its aircraft painted in a red and gray, paint scheme with only the minimum required distinguishing marking, making the F-14 more difficult to recognize at great distances.

The Tomcat is powered by two Pratt and Whitney TF-30-P414 turbofan engines, with afterburner for thrust augmentation, and has a top speed of greater than Mach 2.0. Although normal training and combat scenarios usually need not be done at supersonic speeds, the Tomcat is able to accelerate smartly to supersonic speeds enabling it to travel great distances in minimal time, when required.

In addition to being a formidable air combat fighter, the F- 14 possesses a unique capability in the long-range AIM-54 Phoenix Missile which is controlled by the aircraft's AWG-9 radar and computer systems.

The Phoenix missile adds a long distance standoff capability. The security of a carrier task force is paramount, for it is one of the most effective means the United States has of wartime power projection as well as a powerful peace time presence. The Tomcat's computer controlled swing wing makes it an ideal fighter for Air Combat Maneuvering (ACM) in the demanding airborne dog-fight arena. The ability to employ, in addition to the Phoenix Missile, the AIM-7 Sparrow, AIM-9 Sidewinder and a rapid-fire 20MM vulcan cannon, makes the Tomcat extremely flexible in the rapidly changing environment of ACM. The AWG-9 radar system aids the crew by reducing its workload, and bringing the Tomcat's weapons to bear more quickly on its adversary. VF-l conducts extensive operations that includes simulated air combat against every possible aircraft that can simulate an enemy threat. Thus diversified training is needed to keep the aircrew honed to the sharpest edge possible.

The role of VF-1 and the F-14 reflects only one aspect of the Carrier Air Wing concept. This squadron is one of nine squadrons currently making up Carrier Air Wing TWO. VF-1 works closely with A-6E Intruder attack aircraft E-2C, early warning, S-3 anti-submarine and EA-6B electronic warfare squadrons to insure that Carrier Air Wing TWO is one of the most potent and powerful means of defense in the world.

Cooperation with the other squadrons in the Air Wing aboard the carrier is the way to success in the battle. Although the Carrier Air Wing Commander directs the wing squadrons according to the particular mission, the esprit de corps and enthusiasm that a fighter squadron shows in the delicate orchestration of fleet defense goes a long way in setting the tone for the entire wing. In this respect, the Wolfpack has set the pace in establishing a strong bond and respect for the other squadrons in Carrier Air Wing TWO (CVW-2).

Whether deployed onboard an aircraft carrier as the cutting edge of America's defense posture or ashore at NAS Miramar undergoing training, VF-1 is constantly striving for excellence. Presently assigned the Navy's best multipurpose fighter aircraft, the men of the Wolfpack are a proud collection of the finest personnel in the U. S. Navy. VF-1 has met those challenges of today and stands ready for the future.

What that all means is they dog the shit out of you, whip you and beat you, then throw you a twenty dollar bill. If you can make it through a tour at VF-1 without determining to get out, you're a good candidate for a lifer dog. Which is why I've been looking at ads for civilian jobs with the sealift command.

Chapter Sixteen

0930 2 APR 91. GQ this morning. And MOB. We upped the anchor and went to war games at 0730. In Pers, that consisted of toughing out another smokefest--cheerfully and without comment, of course--and wearing a flash hood. I did a diary message reporting the detachment of our corpsman, who left without a replacement, an AZ3 who gave me a good reference--thus, I lost an ally--and YN2 Jax. He will be a smart black man at YN "A" School in Meridian, Mississippi. And CDR McElraft, famous helo killing RIO, helo'd off *Ranger* to Fujaira, UAE, then Subic Bay, RP, then LAX, then US Space Command, Colorado Springs. He promised to watch us pull in on CNN.

I still haven't got my evaluation, due 31 March. I wonder what it is they don't want to tell me. Meanwhile, things are going awfully smooth with PNC. We're friends again, if you asked anybody around us. It should take a couple of months for us to blow again. But I quit sweating the eval, just planned to make a response if it's fucked up, and keep it all cool, calm and professional. That's the way to do it, right? Also, I responded to an ad in the *Navy Times*, "Former Navy E-5s And Above: Go to sea as a civilian!" The ad was from the Navy's Military Sealift Command, and they need admin types as well as hull technicians and boiler techs. I could sleep on this rack for $18 an hour.

I'm starting to think about California, going back there and getting a car, finding a house or apartment to rent, whether to live at the beach and worry about pigs (cops) or live in the suburbs by the base and hear the jets roaring over the entire desert basin at night.

Now Sweet Pea's getting dogged by his new supervisor, Stinky, who had him painting what didn't need painting, cleaning clean bulkheads and whatever busy work he thought of yesterday. "Aw," I seized the day to touch his shoulder in the passageway outside the V-3 supply room. Stinky showed me the autographed book of Garfield comics he got by writing to the author. And we talked about his handling of my baby, only we just called my baby Sweets.

"Please be friends and don't dog him out so much."

"I want him to do the work so when he supervises the Airman under him he'll make that guy work."

"I guess I can understand that," Sweets said to me later, still slaving away. But he didn't like not getting lunch.

I caught Sweet Pea at breakfast today, as he rushed to eat before GQ went down. He got off work at nine o'clock last night. I had two extra Frosted Flakes packages for him. Between my casual offer, "want 'em?" and his nodding reply, it's impossible to tell how either of us feel.

"Were you involved in any extracurricular activities in high school?"

"Nope."

"You didn't play sports, or anything?"

"None whatsoever."

"I guess you watched a lot of television."

He nodded up and down with a mouthful, breezing through the *Top Gun Gazette.*

"What about--did you go to a lot of movies?"

"Why are you asking me all this?"

I took this personally for bothering him, but he was just tired and I'm insecure. I wish I could have said that I just wondered how he got such a taut belly, and looked so goddam sexy. "Just curious. Just character development. Another paragraph in my book, I guess."

"I've gotta go muster." He picked up his tray and I followed him through the short scullery line, dumping the cereal boxes in a trash can and sliding the silverware through their respective slots in the stainless steel bulkhead where some guys took care of it all. By the time I got my tray delivered he was out the hatch and going to the hangar bay. I took a left up the tagged escalator, and hiked up the thing wondering if I'd worried him or pissed him off or intruded on his privacy by my interrogation, or if I was just mentally fagging off on him disgustingly. Shoot me and put me out of his misery. Like Louie would reprimand, "if I were, not if I was."

His duty section is four, with sections expected to rotate two, three, four, one, two during our five day visit to Thighland, where the new rumor is the whole country is under martial law. My duty day, as arranged by our more or less mutual agreement in our shop falls on the second day. I tried to get it changed to the third day, naturally. But since I didn't give Rod my popcorn, after he gave me half of his and I went down and got more and by the time I came back had eaten it all and threw away the empty bag in front of him, saying something smartass like, "oh, I was gonna bring you some more but I finished it before I got here," causing everyone to laugh at his expense, thus pissing him off, he wasn't sure if he wanted to trade. It depended on what the squadron would be doing, and when the parties would be. So, for now, Sweet Pea won't have to deal with me on his duty day, and I won't get to see him on mine. Plus two days in port we won't be together, and the way ports get you going, if you don't hook up with a plan from the beginning, you may as well kiss your buddy goodbye for the duration, which in my case would be some compromise, 'cause who knows where either one of you will be once they open the brow.

I kid myself that if I could just spend one night with him in the same hotel, in the same room separated from everyone else, in the same big brass bed arm in arm, he'd finally understand how I feel about him and we'd be lovers--but how to say it without sounding sex related. If I could glide my hands across his delicate face, touch his eyelids and not scratch him, tousle his wavy black hair and not tear it, lick his sculpted ears and kiss his soft, white neck and not make myself a total klutz--and pull his naked, hairless young heart to my furry chest. This'd be a fucking Harlequin, except he's a dude.

I could pretend it's my paternal instinct, except I've been too honest throughout the diary for anyone to buy that. I'd grab his ass and squeeze, and we all know it. But more likely it would be too hot and things would be in the way, other guys with us and we'd never be alone and I'd be pining over him and crying back to you, dear reader, lonely one in the world somewhere with the same wild love for someone else. What the hell? What the fucking hell.

The media is onboard again today. It's all quite low key, but we had a bit of difficulty with some stupid niggers calling themselves kidnapped muslims making a big issue of the war against Iraq. I mean, really. I guess they had a rap song of some kind, and wanted to make the big time with a hep hit record. One had a letter up on the XO suggestion board that I didn't note, but recall sounding lame. I suggested someone discuss the issue with him at the fantail. Maybe it's a real concern, and both young men should be excused from these hardships of cruise, returned to America and discharged to further a religious education. Absolutely.

1015 3 APR 91. Still waiting for my eval. Commander McElraft (MAK-l-RAFT) left yesterday, urging all of us, "call me if you need me." He promised he'd go have a beer with us.

I watched the AMH2's eval go back up where it belonged in Human Relations/Equal Opportunity, to 4.0, and simultaneously drop from the skipper's signature to the XO's, while a recommendation for selection to officer programs went away. The ADCS was sitting in there having a cigarette with PNC when I walked in. I said nothing, indicated no intense hatred, in fact enjoyed his company and joked around with PNC. All is well, eh.

At 2000 I was going to record the eight bells and the bos'n on the 1MC, but all I heard was the muffled jerk of the number three wire on the flight deck, someone landing at exactly 2000. At 2005 I called the bridge.

"Hey, man. You didn't call eight bells."

"Wait one." Then off, "Bos'n Mate of the Watch."

"Bos'n Mate of the Watch, may I help you sir?"

"Yeah, how come you didn't call eight bells?"

"Well, the reason I didn't call it is because we had an aircraft coming in with a lubrication problem, and I didn't know if I was gonna call an aircraft crash on the flight deck, or breathe again."

I appreciated that. And at 0500 or so, the CMC told YN1 and me about a similar occasion on another aircraft carrier. I guess it's a sea story: Two guys were on blue water ops doing ACM, when in the middle of their aileron roll, at the top of a circle pointing about 15 degrees upward, while inverted, the stick stuck and the pilot couldn't pull out. He had a foot on the dash of the cockpit, pulling like hell, and the stick broke off in his hand. Sparks started flying from the wires bouncing around. By now, both he and the RIO had been pulled by gravity up in their seats to where the ejection cords were halfway down behind their backs, and reaching back over their heads neither one could grab the cable.

Still struggling to eject, the pilot noticed the remains of the stick moving again. He grabbed what was left with both hands, damning the sparks, and guided the jet to an arrested landing on the flight deck. There wasn't a drop of hydraulic fluid in the reservoir. It drained out past a failed check valve.

They broke every blood vessel in their faces, and the pilot came back with silver eyeballs.

Someone found a story on the two black muslims off *Ranger* in the *Gulf News*. They face 10 years in Leavenworth, a big chicken dinner, forfeiture of all pay and allowances and a bust to E1. Another dude charged them with plotting to sabotage the boat and take the captain hostage. My buddy is a CO's orderly, too. I'll have to try to milk it out of him what really happened. If I do I'll let you know.

Meanwhile, a message came across my desk (unclassified) about an article for submission to a couple of Navy magazines. It's called, "We Own the Night." A six-page message. I wonder if Minimize was considered.

0800 4 APR 91. See no eval, hear no eval. NC1 did nothing at his desk all night but write to his wife and chain smoke until the 2300 curfew, then stuck around in the doorway puffing until 0400. And the CMC wandered in and lit up at 0515, two hours before the iron clad agreement said in the POD that he could. I suppose he figures it's all right or I'd say something. Or maybe, fuck you you're a second class petty officer. I'm a Master Chief, I've had to sweat and fight and do all kind of things you will never imagine and I've earned the right to blow smoke in your face, just like the smoke I blew up your ass in that meeting. If you don't like it, you can still go TAD.

I won't say anything while my enlisted performance evaluation is at stake. Maybe not after, either. Joke 'em if they can't take a fuck.

Speaking eval, I noticed mine on the hard drive and took a look for the hell of it. I started reading and thought, they've changed it all around. It's very positive, highly praising. Then I noticed the letters, DK2. No, he's not comparing me to DK2, he said he was only comparing me to PN2. How could it be then, that my eval was cloned off of DK2's eval? It must have been an accident. And that probably happened before the rough I saw or the smooth I heard about.

We're in Modlock, a sort of mysterious lala land where tension festers. Because we were supposed to pull out of the Gulf and make waves for the IO, in preparation for outchopping with *Nimitz*. Now that the pressure is building to fight the helos up in Iraq, we've been directed to remain on station, to outchop here. If we go after the helos, history shall reflect the world famous Fighting Wolfpack once again led the pack with that first helo kill. We showed that F-14A's can blow the shit out of Iraqi helos with relatively cheap missiles.

One of our Selected Reservists, who's gone home already, received a carton of 12 boxes of Girl Scout cookies. Imagine the dilemma. We could see the chocolate mints through the tape between the box flaps. opened the outer envelope, just to see if there were some indication that they were for the troops rather than for him to sell, and found instructions, basically, for him to inform "the woman who sponsored the cookies and the girl scout who sold them all" that he indeed received them. What does that mean? I figure they had a Desert Storm campaign to benefit the troops, and the cookies were sent to this guy who was on some local list of selected reserves. Ultimately, they must have been intended for the pure enjoyment of the troops on *Ranger*, right? Picture him fat, dumb and happy on the couch back home watching CNN, munching on 12 boxes of Girl Scout cookies that we sent back to him. I say we should eat the cookies and send them a thank you note, even request a bill that they'd probably waive. Or take a collection and make a donation to Girl Scouts, approximating whatever twelve boxes of cookies might cost. But there they go, back through the Saudi Arabian desert, enroute to the USA where the dude will undoubtedly laugh at the stupidity of the Navy and our lack of common sense.

I got another card, dated 21 March, from somebody I don't know at my hometown church. No hot love letters from half a dozen girls on my ass. This was a nice little note from a lady whose son is a high school senior looking forward to drinking and gambling on a Mexico cruise. "We're glad you came through the war safely and again, we look forward to seeing you when you get home. We'll keep you in our prayers."

Lucille got my $600 for the transcript of my L.A. nightmare, and has the other $200. Now she's very busy and it will be several months before she gets to work printing it.

I still haven't heard from my brother, or his wife, since I began mailing excerpts of this diary to their house for safe keeping. I put a hold on sending them until I get some indication they are not being intercepted by the NIS. Are you bastards really reading this?

I don't know if I mentioned this, I got a parking ticket from San Diego thanks to Louie, who assured me that he'd transferred the title to his name. Lyin' sombitch.

I ran across a nametag on the messdeck, on some guy's shirt, the name was DANG. I figure it was his first name. His last was probably SOMBITCH.

Chapter Seventeen

0800 5 APR 91. We still speak no eval. Yesterday afternoon as I lay sleeping, about 1430, a line rat slammed a coop cleaner up against the racks and the two of them argued at the top of their lungs.

Got a NAVGRAM (letter) from PSD Miramar about the travel claim of the shipmate who sleeps under my rack. It was filed last October, and after two messages to them we finally get the explanation, "the dependent travel address was wrong." Now what does that mean? This black bitch who made chief was the POC; she's always been a bit bitchy. Now she could have returned the thing, since it was rejected 4 December--four months ago. The dude tells me he was down at PSD and asked a guy sitting on his ass at Travel to give him a claim so he could bring it to *Ranger*.

"Somebody already picked it up."

Sure, buddy.

Suzanne Vega. I would have married her. Or lived with her for a while to suck her blood and learn how to loosen up on my formal rhyme schemes and write a little better lyric.

When Love Is Real

Let's go back to school again
You can be my long lost friend
Got you by the foot
On the Football field
So young
Young enough to know
When love is real

PNC made another stupid remark at 1930 last night. "I'll make money selling you in Thailand." Ha ha. Are you calling me a *puto*? Is this right, normal, expected of a Navy enlistment? Should my recruiter have warned me that I'd be assigned to a racist scum who would attack me every time he saw me, sometimes joking, sometimes not?

We're all warriors, and we're close to the warpath, in Modlock, spoiling, turning now on each other in the doldrums of uncertainty. We would love to go kill helos. We chafe at the bit. And all the same we can't wait to go to Thighland. In this meantime, we treat each other mean.

Old Bob Dylan looked a little round in the cheek on the Grammy Awards. They shipped us the tape a couple of days ago and put it on KRAN. I couldn't understand a word of the song he performed, except that made perfect sense as a statement about modern music, coming from a guy who's made a career of bitingly clear, upfront vocals.

"My dad once told me, he said, 'son.'" And he paused while the crowd held their breath, wondering what the motivating words might have been that started young Bob Dylan. "He said so many things."

He got his laughter and tickled me. Then, not to let himself down, he spoke his piece of wisdom. "He said you can become so defiled in this world. But God never loses faith in the ability to mend your own ways."

I'm wondering if I have any faith in my ability to mend my own ways now, with dear sweet Sweets. I was prying, bonding, leaning out over the abyss of assumption that we could become what obviously we are not, and blindly hoping I could wish it true. He is at weakest confused, half-closed eyelids and remarks like, "so, when are you gonna grow some hair." In his moments of great strength he is walking away from the table, having sat beside me without speaking, without acknowledging my presence; and later denying the incident from his subconscious memory.

He was among us, but he was not of us. Where does that come from? The Bible, the Navy. I was raised Presbyterian, hung up on the whole spectrum of Christian incompatibility with nature as I knew mine. Suicidal at 13, one bullet in a chamber playing Russian Roulette in the parents' bedroom, clinging to God and life tightly enough to allow one click, then decided it was destiny to live. "God, if what I'm gonna do in my life is wrong, I want to die right now." I looked in the bedroom mirror and squeezed, thoughts of Matthew--not from the Bible, from the neighborhood--dancing in my head, sitting on my lap in that recliner chair.

"I'm gay if you're gay."

I was sixteen, he was ten. My small circle of boyfriends, little brothers, hero worship that you lose when boys grow old.

Who was it, some professor, told me with my writing he was afraid they would know more about me than they cared to. Then some other scholar said you write what you dare not say. I think that was UCLA, Advanced Feature Film Writing. The guy who noted that in BATMAN it might have been nice to have a long take on the mask, as Bruce discovered himself.

Scrapper has a little bruise on his face. But the other guy got stitches on his head. They had to mop up the blood in the coop, that is, down in the 24-Man berthing compartment. One of the two last Selected Reservists started in again about the dudes in the regular Navy, then asked Scrapper if he felt froggy. So Scrap cleared the lounge, hustled the couches and chairs to the edge of the room and stood in his face. "Yeah. Yeah, I feel froggy."

The dude went on to get in his face, then made the final error. He pointed a finger at him, pushing it right up in front of his eyes. See, his father always did that as he abused him all his life until he finally beat his dad's ass. So pointing at him pushes his fun button. After that, all you have to do is touch him, like you'd touch maybe....

Jimmy Buffet. They sell this stuff in Abu Dhabi? "Creola in my soula." Why couldn't I have been this guy? Spend my career under the palm trees, hanging around with bamboo, a funny side of Hemmingway, in the Keys with the key. I wonder if he was ever in the Navy.

0900 10 APR 91. Missed a couple a days, eh. It's not for lack of bullshit. Back in the rack, Jimmy Buffett sings "Creola." In my soulah. We're having a

Steal Beach picnic today, 1000 to 1600 on the flightdeck. I'd like to sleep a bit, since I get no exemption from coming in at 1900, no comp time for staying up to party.

Oh, I got my eval. Yeah, buddy. Chief didn't get everything he wanted, less than 3.8. But he got in some slams. I typed a letter for the skipper the other day, just before the change of command, where he mentioned a second class petty officer who transferred and allegedly destroyed his service record copy of his eval because he didn't agree with it. The skipper wrote that his 3.8 in personal behavior and overall 3.8 reflected "less than optimum behavior."

Mine said that, although I was highly effective and would go out of my way to help everybody, I had been "counseled for a tendency at times to divert energy to personal interests and bypassing the chain of command." I asked the Pers-O what he was talking about. "Well, you spent a lot of time researching the instructions about smoking. And you sent that memo to the ship's XO."

I haven't signed the eval yet, although he's ordered me to at least twice. In the meantime, I've requested mast. What am I gonna do? I drafted a statement, which by proxy does not effect the marks even if it becomes a permanent part of the evaluation. If I don't sign, I'll get a page 13 to that effect. Knowing the chief, they've probably already mailed it with a letter explaining circumstances (from PNC's point of view), and will give me the page 13 (ready for signature) at Captain's Mast. For the benefit of the reader, here's the response that never was.

9 April, 1991

From: PN2 Robert D. Graham, USN, Fighter Squadron ONE
To: Commander, Naval Military Personnel Command
Via: Commanding Officer, Fighter Squadron ONE

Subj: ENLISTED PERFORMANCE EVALUATION, 90DEC26 TO 91MAR31

Ref: (a) NAVMILPERSCOMINST 1616.1A

1. Initially, this evaluation contains the following discrepancies:

a. Block 54 indicates service in Western/Arabian Gulf. Other E5 evaluations reported by this command this period read, "deployed 90DEC08-91MAR31 to Western Pacific/Arabian Gulf onboard USS Ranger (CV 61) in direct support of Operation Desert Storm including 43 days combat."

b. Block 55 neglected the fact that I received the Armed Forces Expeditionary Medal for Westpac '89, that I was awarded my (2nd) Sea Service Deployment Ribbon, and that I was awarded the Southwest Asia Service Medal per NAVNEWS 010/91.

2. The following pertinent facts, in rebuttal to less than optimum marks in military knowledge or performance; reliability; military bearing; personal behavior; and counseling, as reflected by remarks in block 56 about having been counseled for a tendency to divert energy to personal interests and at times bypassing the chain of command, and requiring proper supervision, are submitted in accordance with reference (a).

a. Military knowledge: Frocked to E5 for only three months, I successfully completed the military requirements for E6 and enrolled in the Enlisted Aviation Warfare Specialist (EAWS) course.

b. Military performance: I directly participated in Operation Desert Storm, including 43 days combat during which I stood a key military watch in Ready Room Eight, and trained four subordinates for this duty.

c. Reliability: VF-1 suffered the unplanned loss of the Personnel Department's Leading Petty Officer, who made PN1 on the September 1990 advancement exam, and then deserted the Navy leaving the PNC, myself and an Airman to meet department obligations through Operation Desert Storm, a period which required intensive transfer and receipt, customer service and training obligations. VF-1 also suffered an enlisted casualty in the Philippines, and this eval includes the fact that I was singularly responsible for preparing the casualty report, accurately and on time.

d. Military bearing: I am a nonsmoker, fit and trim at age 34 as noted in block 20, and a regular at the gym. Although not noted this evaluation, I ran the 1.5 mile in nine minutes, and passed all requirements of the Physical Readiness Test for the 19 year old age group on the last squadron PRT. I wear dungarees, as a courtesy to my supervisor, although "greens" are authorized.

e. Personal behavior:

(1) Off duty: This reporting period included liberty in Abu Dhabi, United Arab Emirates, during the holy month of Ramadan in which personal behavior was extremely important to the Navy and required best behavior on the part of all hands. I toured as far as Al Ain and Oman, and was considered an ambassador of the US Navy.

(2) On duty: As a nonsmoker I held up graciously under the most trying circumstances of an office filled with smokers who were all superior in rank, including an NC1, PNC, YNCS, CMC (AFCM), and the Personnel Officer. When repeated avenues of personal address failed, I researched the appropriate instructions to clarify Navy policy, and pursued its enforcement. This resulted in forcing my superiors to compromise by setting nonsmoking hours from 2300-0700 and limiting authorized smoking to department personnel. The 3.8 mark in this trait was directly attributed to this conflict by my department head.

f. Counseling:

(1) Emergency Leave--On March 2, 1991, AMS3 Langille wrote a thank you note to me "for speedily putting together an emergency leave package for me this morning. I could never show the appreciation I feel."

(2) EDVR--On March 4, 1991, AT2 Robles had several questions and by the end of my service decided to write, "he performs his duties in a courteous and professional manner." He added, "PN2's knowledge of the EDVR was excellent. He answered my questions of prospective gains promptly and efficiently."

(3) Transfer--On March 6, 1991, ADAN Wise wrote a note to the Personnel Officer specifically mentioning my service regarding his transfer as "great."

(4) Receipt--On March 7, 1991, AMEAR Marken, a new receipt to the squadron, felt that my counseling was so helpful that he put it in writing to the Admin Officer that I had "taken the time on the mess decks" and "led me in the right direction."

3. This eval infers less than optimum leadership and judgment by the frocked E5 LPO of an undermanned shop in an extremely demanding period. As such, given the facts, and in my consideration of the evals given to my peers that are beyond the scope of this rebuttal, I perceived my performance in keeping with the highest standards of Naval service, and accepted this report as unfair.

Very respectfully,

ROBERT D. GRAHAM

I made a couple of personally interesting discoveries in my diversion last night. Let me try to unwind this knot. Around 5 April that trouble shooter who had me on the flightdeck caught me in the office and raised an issue. His voluntary extension of his military service obligation had failed to show up on his Leave and Earnings Statement, and his Direct Deposit System was about to be terminated. I knew from the other dude's expired projected rotation date (PRD) in the enlisted Distribution and Verification Report that was flagged but missed, and drew a lot of attention, that there were some changes in policy slipping past the PNC. Like, when a guy's extension became operative in the past, you pulled the agreement out of the record and completed an additional block, then sent it to Washington. Now, though, that form is a single page and you don't send it in on the operative date of the extension. All you do, and you must not forget, is you send a message, via the Diary Message Reporting System (DMRS) to the Enlisted Personnel Management Activity Center (EPMAC) in New Orleans, on the date the extension becomes operative. Well, I looked through the DMRS manual and among all the copies of the diaries, found no entry on his date (3 February), no entry anywhere before or after his date, no entry in the DMRS notebook at all on this guy. Now, I have a BA in English, emphasis in writing, and I believe when I want to find something I'm pretty conscientious and capable. I wrote a note to the chief.

I came in the next night and guess what. "Hey Graham, it was in there. Chief found it and showed it to me."

Well well well. It was there. On 28 Feb there was a five-line NAVGRAM. Three lines were printed by the computer printer. Under them, two lines reporting the execution of this guy's, and another dude's extension, were listed like an addendum, with a different type font, from the typewriter. Being naive, too slow, I pointed out to the chief then and there, they were added after the others. "They were added after the skipper signed it," he volunteered. What else could he say? "You can do it, as long as you don't fraud waste or abuse."

I asked a commissioned officer about that, and his response was fairly curt. "Bullshit, you can't do that."

Then I had a wise inkling. Since it was a serialized letter (due to worldwide minimize impressed on message traffic), Admin would have two copies. Maybe, I thought, the fucking criminal had slipped up and overlooked covering his tracks in that office. I asked YN3 Black, whose job included serializing NAVGRAMs for our shop, to pull the serial file and the Standard Subject Identification Code (SSIC) file. The two extra typed in lines were there. Am I conquered? Is my theory blown? Well, don't forget I went through a first degree murder trial and beat five judges and every attorney the public defender discussed the case with. (On the murder trial, the first cop on the scene had drawn a sketch of the cholo laying on the floor, knife beside his hand and baseball bat in the crook of his arm. A year later, the public defender brought to light the fact that the cop's partner had done the write up several hours after the fact, at about 0400 in the station, and said he was face down, based on the sketch that had neglected to include the eyes. Two missing tiny marks in a piece of paper had given the detectives an impression that the guy was face down rather than face up, giving a strong sense of a murder that would not have been there if the eyes had. Also, the original notes to my statement had disappeared, and the public defender had brought to light the fact that a paper clip indentation on the detective's murder case file revealed that something had been clipped to the typed statement at some point. The detectives had questioned me with one writing, the other grilling, then testified that one did the writing and grilling while the other twiddled his thumbs. A week later under cross-examination it came to light that they had asked if I had intended to kill him, and I had replied, "no, I just wanted to stop him," and they had made a note, and conveniently the notes had disappeared. Except for the police department tape of my call, five minutes after the incident, there was no evidence that I had ever claimed self-defense. Of course, that tape mentioned that I was bleeding and had to do it. If that tape had disappeared I'd probably be in jail today.) So it's the little things. Like a scratch in the glass on the squadron's photocopier. I remembered the scratch. I was late to court my last day in San Diego in order to wait for the photocopier tech-rep to install the brand new (refurbished) copier, and I was extremely pissed off when I discovered that someone had evidently copied a paper with a staple in it and put weight on the cover and ruined the glass top that we'd be stuck with through cruise. After the piece of shit copier we'd put up with last cruise, I was livid. But now I was glad. If all three were created in the same act, the scratch would appear on all copies alike. If the old copy with two lines fresh off the typewriter were hastily shredded, and the culprit later realized he needed to cover his tracks in Admin, he would have had to use our copy to falsify those two copies. They would pick up the line on our copy, while the scratch--still in the glass-- created a second line in about the same spot on those two copies. Our copy has a small line to reflect the scratch two-thirds down the page on the right hand side. But Admin's SSIC file copy has two identical scratches there, about an eighth inch apart. As does their Serial file copy.

The Admin Officer was in, so YN3 laid them out on the desk and asked him for "a professional opinion." He concurred, advising me to discuss it with the department head--the only aircrew to smoke, who happens to believe in the 3.8 marks on my eval. Failing that, I should either come back to him or see the XO, I wasn't sure which. But I knew it made him somewhere between nervous and nauseous, and he asked YN1 right after that if this were a "grudge match."

"Well," YN1 said tactfully, "all he's showed me are facts."

A little later I went back to the No Cost TAD 1990 file to burn a copy of the fire fighting orders that Gus and the other dude were accused of accused of disobeying. Wouldn't you know, since I told the Pers-O about PNC ordering me to falsify those orders, the file has been quietly purged of August and before.

0835 12 APR 91. You've got to watch your ass. I'm not talkin' 'bout the whole ass. I'm talkin' 'bout the ass hole.

"No matter how or how far up the chain of command you take your complaint, it's gonna roll back down via the chain, with the most unpleasant repercussions at the bottom, on you." They may not have been his exact words, but that was basically the skipper's speech.

"Nothing would piss me off more," he added, "than having a letter or a phone call come to me from some higher authority over something I know nothing about. Don't jump the chain of command again. Because I've discussed it with you."

That was that for that. We held request mast in the Ready Room with the Skipper, Command Master Chief, PNC and myself. PNC was all slumped over in the chair (we got to sit, a major difference from Captain's Mast under orders). He's taking Valiums and several other muscle relaxers, dosing himself to oblivion for sleeping wrong about a week ago. Somehow I think it had to do with this mast, and have a feeling he'll be well soon. Back to his old son of a bitch self.

I died at request mast. Because I learned that the farther up the chain, the farther removed from the issue. Flight equals image minus substance. Somebody biased briefs an ally who in turn briefs a commissioned officer who trusts his khaki team and briefs the Skipper.

"Lieutenant, petty officer Graham had a problem using the chain to complain about the smoke."

"Skipper, PN2 Graham had a legitimate complaint that's been resolved but he mishandled the situation and that's what really needs to be addressed here, using the evaluation as a tool for demonstrating areas where improvement is needed."

"Graham, the profanity in that memo to CAG was immature."

I got slammed with smoke, then slammed for quoting the CMC saying "fuck you, if you don't like it go TAD."

At mast the CMC said, "you never once came to me like it was a problem." How in hell did he happen to provide me with the quote?

My complaint was minor to the khakis, like smoke in the face of a train engineer. I was glad to learn at request mast, rather than at mandatory Captain's Mast. The chain of command will tow the party line, just like a request chit. If you don't win your supervisor's blessing, you may as well tear up the chit. Except with Kelly flying off for the Apollo audition, one exception. And the leave chit I got approved over PNC's head after ATA. Second exception I've seen in my three Navy years.

"Bob, I'll tell you a story." The CMC confided outside Pers, in the passageway at the bottom of the ladder. "I knew a guy, he worked in a Navy Recruiting District. And he knew that they had a printing press in the back, and that they printed up high school diplomas on it. Well, he hated it. And he never used it. But what could he do, put the entire district on report? He just toughed it out and kept it to himself, and got out of there as early as he could. And after he left the place was investigated."

Maybe that was a hint, I don't know. It isn't like my PNC is breaking airplanes, or fodding engines, or instigating a mutiny on *Ranger*. He's just a new chief using immature methods of covering his trail of mistakes. And a mean, lowlife son of a bitch.

Now I know the meaning of that saying, about job interviews, "they want someone who walks on water and died twenty years ago." They want someone perfect who not only doesn't make waves, but has no history of wave abuse. It ain't me, babe. No no no, it ain't me they're lookin' for, babe.

CMC tried to convince me, I'd make a damn good PN if I stayed in the Navy. He'd give me his name to use as a reference, something he normally didn't mention until a guy transferred. Maybe he could see the death of my Naval interest in the course of request mast, and sought to encourage me to keep it alive. Or maybe he was just walking on water, smoothing out waves.

Where do I fit in? The job I had at West Coast, assistant director of videotape manufacturing, was about like a Lieutenant. Department head, or branch manager. I know it was more demanding than a second class petty officer. But at least I enjoyed it, and loved being involved with the business. Even so, it was a job for a jg, a twenty-three year old. I was over thirty. Now I'm knocking thirty-five, and thinking about the civilian world again. What will I do, type? What will I ask, $1500 a month? Will I get a third class petty officer gofer job in a private company? I started Army ROTC as a damn Lieutenant at age 16. I don't mean JROTC. I could have been, could have been, and could have been. But I'm a has been who never was.

Thanks to Lady Luck who shined on me, I spent some time with Sweets through this ordeal. The child who took my mind off of stress and let me tickle him a little, played Spades with me in his private office as the Supply Petty Officer Nonpetty Officer Senior Airman in V-3 We Like It Tight Division, *USS Ranger*. And yesterday, sweet God in heaven, I saw him brim with tears over losing a logbook. He was panicking, looking all around for that little red book, under the desk, behind the shelves, up in the pipes, inside lockers, through every drawer. No little red logbook. His ass, his heart shaped, beautiful ass in form fitted greens, my God my God it was right in my face *several* times as he stretched up to reach shelves. The tension of pretending to appear matter of fact, nonchalant, disinterested and disaffected, not staring, not grabbing him by the waist and caressing his smooth round buttcheeks and tight skinny torso with my tongue up his--quit it! This is not a porn book.

When he gave up looking he sat back in a brown padded chair and tried not to cry. His face was so expressive, his lower lip pouted, his chin scrunched up, his eyes grew big and brown, his forehead seemed to broaden and he looked helpless.

"It'll probably show up," I said. Then like a stupid fool I said something mean. "I thought you were gonna get new boots."

"No." He was pathetic, everybody's grandson who had just struck out.

I was only trying to change the subject, take his mind off the crisis. I had just pinged on him, kicked him while he was down. I wanted to kick myself.

"I can reconstruct it. All I have to do is get on the computer and call up the parts and I can get the part numbers and prices and write 'em in another book."

0815 13 APR 91. "Have I told you lately that I love you? Fill my life with gladness, take away my sadness, ease my troubles that's what you do." Van Morrison singing for me in the phones, so much better than hearing "one oh three on deck" or "triple stix airborne" in Ready Room Eight. I'm in rack forty-three. Thinking about Sweets night and day.

For a moment, though, this question takes me back to Missouri, a picnic lunch with Phillip Dudley, a kid I met at Lab School. He was getting some Cokes and I saw the note from his mom on the table. He moved to League City, Texas, and I never saw him again. His big sister was Queen of the Cotton Bowl, and when their mom wrote a few years back, said Justine had written her first screenplay.

If I ever make it in this world of entertainment, get my book sold and finally write movies, I have this recurring feeling I will find a bunch of my childhood chums in the business. Maybe I'm only picturing heaven.

Old Butch and Ted, in grade school making that pact with me to become cops. I was the only one, far as I knew, to ever come close. When I went undercover for the feds. Now I hate the cops of San Diego. And Los Angeles. And don't trust any of 'em.

Sweet Pea phones home. It's not confirmed yet, but his LT called yesterday. There's all kinds of media aboard, CBS, NBC, ABC and CNN. The LT called and asked if he wanted to call home. Of course he did. He thought the LT was talking about sending an "E" mail message until they told him to get a clean set of dungarees prepared. He'll be on national television talking to his loving mother. And he'll be swamped by Hollywood producers. He's the most charming, gorgeous, darling boy on this ship. Not to mention good looking, attractive, seductive, vulnerable, intelligent, bright and hyperactive, and has a voice like the kid on "Growing Pains" that cracks up high on a word every sentence or two. He thinks I'll be in that Beverly Hills mansion. But he's the baby they will offer Frank, and Cents, and myrrh. He's the doll of the V-3 division, a candidate for Wog Queen on Westpac '89.

The helos are at it again, chasing each other back and forth from the *Kansas City, Hasayampa* or whoever we have alongside. Whatever we're taking on, the Marines are back at the cages that go to the bomb rooms below. I never heard the hangar deck secured from photography--but I sleep days.

The last port schedule I wrote down reads like this: MAY 2-12 TRANSIT 13-17 PATTAYA BEACH, THAILAND 18-21 TRANSIT 22-24 REPUBLIC OF THE PHILIPPINES 25-26 TRANSIT 27-31 HONG KONG JUN 1-12 TRANSIT 13-14 PEARL HARBOR, HAWAII 15-20 TRANSIT 21 SAN DIEGO, CALIFORNIA.

Got a dude called Broke Dick limping around the berthing now. He's twenty-one, and got one of the few specialty surgeries they know how to do onboard *Ranger*. Circumcision. Sixteen stitches in his cock. A bulge of gauze in his crotch, wrapped around the head of his penis. Another dude last week had his cock cut. I guess its the new thing after shaving their heads. The other dude had his cut the night before we pulled a urinalysis. Since I could do that, I dropped his name from the list. Funny, by the way, how those whiz quizzes are legally random, to avoid a congressional prohibition, but every time ask for a social security number ending in two or seven. Two or seven. They must think somebody with a number ending in two or seven is doing drugs onboard. Trouble is, and I don't give a fuck I'll tell you now, the YNCS ends in a two or a seven. Is he pissed? You could say that again.

Ah, the women in my life. Three years since I spent three hours giving Amy carpet burns. "Don't come yet" and "don't pull out" were her favorite cries. No guts to get married, too many places to go, people to see. I doubt if she fucked them--she was prudish in the long run.

"We can't fuck tonight, wait until the night before my period."

I waited for that once a month penetration. Everything else was a lick suck trick and we never got it right.

"Get the foam. It's in the bathroom where I hid it when my parents visited."

I'd be soft again.

"Don't forget the rubber."

It slipped off in all the foam and the come and her juices. I couldn't even eat her after the foam. And she could never stroke.

It was passionate until she grew afraid of getting pregnant and suffering Daddy's wrath. Then it grew cool, cold, dead. And I went after Chris in the spa, thirteen and hard as a rock. He went on to TV fame in "Married ... With Children" although I'll never know for sure if that's him. What did we do? Jack off in the dark sauna at midnight. Big deal. I was suffering terminal adolescence. But it would never get me a clearance in this military world--never mind that dudes butt humped in foxholes in the Vietnam war, if I believe what the south of Market vets were telling me in Frisco, ten fucking years ago. I doubt if they hand out waivers for pre-service cock biting.

In the contract it's called "Character and Social Adjustment." The 1 AUG 75 version states, "a 'yes' answer will not necessarily disqualify you for enlistment. It will depend on the circumstances surrounding the situation involved." Like at boot camp, when the DIS agent sent me to legal for investigation of a fraudulent enlistment, the Legal folks told me to tell the JAG that it was done to me, not vice versa, and I regretted it, so it will never happen again. And it only happened twice in my life, regardless of the fact that what I copped to in the screening interview had been two incidents around 1984, at 28 years old. Not pre-teen experimentation, eh?

I can never figure out the hang up of security and society with this thing about anal sex. We cheer it in macho circles of men, and most dudes dig two chicks licking themselves. To buttfuck a girl is still the manly thing to watch on porno flicks in the Shooter Shack and on the CMC's TV. They watch, they enjoy, they stare, they go to their racks and jack off about it. But give a guy a clearance who is honest? Fuck NO! Kick him out of the Navy!

Have you ever engaged in homosexual activity (sexual relations with another person of the same sex)?

What business is that of an employee? What's it got to do with sharing a shower with a dude that you work with, berth with, eat with and put up with? If you ask me, I wouldn't fuck with a dude if I hated him, or even if I weren't attracted to him. I wonder how many guys became official liars for the first time when they entered the Navy, and how it affected them, if their entire contracts and careers became lies, if their lives became lies when they deceived the government for the sake of a job. I wonder how this foisted corruption affects enlistees subconsciously. And how many perfectly straight dudes at one time in their lives as kids, eight, nine or ten or eleven, sucked their best friend's cock and now at eighteen had to lie about it to the government. Will it turn them into scam artists at thirty? Why should they respect a country that, when it comes to giving their lives on the battlefield for her, holds it against them if they had played doctor in the bedroom with that long blonde haired boy of ten who was so affectionate and lovely that they gave in to their lust? They have to be pretty committed to laying their lives on the line when they walk into the recruiting station. If there's one sure thing, it's that military men have always died, no matter how the climate reeks of peace. Grenada, Noriega, Nicaragua, something or other will always take military lives. So whether or not they were gay, or women by the way, should have been X'd out of the deal a god damn long time ago. As it is, if and when this book comes out, it will be me getting out. All because for a while there I was hanging with a female, lovely beauty, arcing away from the men and the boys, convincing myself I was straight just like Jax wasn't bothered by cigarette smoke in our shop and got a NAM.

"If you only knew, what can happen to a man for tellin' the truth." Sing it Van. Once again, like a blurb across the screen, allow me to disclaim any criminal activity mentioned herein. It's purely fiction.

1045 14 APR 91. I was down in his shop again, loitering like a fool. Dean was sitting on the desk smoking, Sweets was holding a room deodorizer in front of the fan. Dean leaned back so his smoke went through the back of the fan. I took the little labelmaker gun and stenciled SWEET PEA. I wanted to stick it to his mirror but he scolded, he didn't want it there. Then I touched him one too many times in the chair beside me.

"Graham would you stop touching me? Every five minutes you're touching me, now stop it!" He was yelling at the top of his lungs.

I melted back in the vinyl sponge and felt face beginning to scrunch up so I suddenly felt like he looked the day he lost the logbook. I thought of the phrase he'd said so solemnly: Where did I go wrong...?

"Ooh, testy," Dean said as he tickled Sweet Pea's chinny chin chin.

I was quiet for a while, reading about Joan Rivers getting fucked over by Fox until her husband killed himself.

A moment later he was digging in the desk drawer and pulling things out, among them a "Forum" magazine. I remembered that I'd written a letter to them about Sweet Pea. I motioned to Dean and he threw it at me. In the table of contents I found a section, letters from men about men with men. I turned to it and read the letters as Sweets sat there invisible. Was he aware? Was it a plan? Why did he have it in there, why did he take it out? Did he want me to read about men with men? Or is my fucked up mind playing another sick joke that will trip me again and eventually put me in a room blowing a dude who comes and tries to kill me? I guess I'll stay away for a while, as long as I can. It's like those guys who I wish would quit smoking. They can't. I can't. We don't know why we should try. But I guess I will, as I listen to Van singing over and over, "have I told you lately that I love you, there's no one above you...." And cry myself to sleep once more on *Ranger*.

0700 15 APR 91. Well it was a good cry, one of those widely grinning silent types that stretch out your face and bare your gums until a tear bursts through the leather callous barrier and rolls down one side of your cheek into an ear, followed by inhalation so carefully controlled to avoid having a shipmate throw the curtains open, and ask you what's wrong.

Time to stay away again. Sadly, the best thing I can do is write off Pattaya Beach, plan to spend it far from him, and not see him between now and then. Otherwise I'm just going to keep staring at the beauty and wind up touching him again and getting scolded. Much as I would like, I cannot imagine that he feels strongly for me when he treats me like a dog. And I may as well die as continue to forfeit my self-respect. The whole goddam thing is too awkward and maybe it's good reason fags ought to be kept out of the Navy. They have a way of falling in love and throwing the emotional balance out of kilter in an extended situation like deployment.

I was loitering at the elevator in the hangar bay before daylight and thinking, would anybody see me step over? There's a thin cable at the edge to warn you. And there's a yellow and red checkered line well before that but it's commonly crossed so the hangar watches pay little attention to anyone over that line. Still, somebody would probably see me and they'd rescue me and then I'd really be fucked, with a fate worse than death. I thought about the fantail, down by the churning propellers if you drop in the wake where nobody would hear. But what a way to go, chopped liver. And the sharks came to mind, chasing our garbage. I'd be floating in it until hypothermia took me. If they got me before I passed out, that would be miserable. Joan's hubby just downed a lot of valiums and drank up Cognac, something like that. Now I'm working my way back to that gun beneath my mattress.

My cousin's brother was murdered last Wednesday night, in a drug deal

I suppose. He was living in my old bedroom upstairs in the house my dad sold to her when they built the new one. Five cops came to her house and searched the place, then questioned her and her husband for a couple of hours in separate rooms. I didn't find out if he were shot or knifed. But dead is dead. They're having him cremated.

My uncle, my dad's oldest brother, died last week, too. Death rain from home and local depression. My work is slipping to the 3.8 range now. That's all right.

What would happen to this book if I followed Sylvia Plath? She was a fine contemporary American poet who got in some books before dying off, at her own hands. I guess the characters I see on the screen or page before me would all end up in the sea, or buried in the files of the NIS. God knows they'd never see the light of publication, if I didn't survive to force it out there (to my own detriment). Living will be the death of me.

Do I really want the Sunday School kids reading this? Of course not. But when they grow up why not? They think I'm some hero because America says the boys in the Gulf are all heroes. And the brass and their brass bands all proclaim it to us, in televised briefs and parades on airport runways. At pierside. At the stadium sponsored by 101 KGB, the number one FM radio station in that Navy town of San Diego, with Russian call letters.

The hour when my ship rolls in I'll probably be stuck with flight deck parade again, and I'll stand up there in dress whites this time, and watch the throngs of probably fifty thousand mostly women and kids, hero worshipers, all, waving and cheering for the men of the *Ranger*. I'll watch the wife hug the husband, kids dangling on their tales. And lovers in long kisses.

Offload will be the best thing for me so I won't be faced with walking through it all to the white bus alone. I'll be happily required to remain until they taper down and fade away. Then me and a few lucky bastards will hump the cruise boxes onto the escalator down to the trucks, and in a few hours we'll miss the traffic back to the base, back to Fightertown USA, NAS Miramar, home of Top Gun school where That Guy is still fighting that girl who back ended his Mustang. You can bet he'll be getting laid, too. I won't.

What about Sweet Pea? "The Queen of the Slip Stream." He'll still be deep in the closet, running fast, hiding from his worst nightmares. Talking the talk without walking the walk. Skirting the issue. Looking for hair on his chest. Locking up the best days of his life, one at a time, like that day we'll walk over the brow and go separate ways.

In Abu Dhabi at a hotel counter he was trying to phone home and had his number out.

"Let me have your home phone number."

"No."

"I guess when you get out of the Navy, that's it, then."

"You don't need it now."

I guess that was true. He was right. I was wrong. He was protecting his mother. Or hiding me from her. Like Amy, fucking me for two years and never having me home for Christmas. Fitting so good, but never fitting in.

No doubt Dean's down there in his office, smoking and playing spades or reading a skin magazine. Sweets is wondering if I'm gonna come down. I'm in my rack, mourning.

"He prob'ly ain't gonna come down, after you shouted at him at the top of your lungs yesterday."

Oh well, I'm a fucked up individual.

0715 16 APR 91. "Sweepers, sweepers, man your brooms. Give the ship a good clean sweepdown, forward and aft. Clean all decks, ladders and passageways. Take all sinkable, nonplastic trash and garbage to the fantail. The fantail IS open. Now sweepers."

Sweeping is a collateral duty assigned to the boys in First Lieutenant who also handle swabs and foxtails, and collect and distribute the laundry. At various times throughout the day, the call "Sweepers" is given over the 1MC and they man their brooms en masse. Imagine the dust storm of a thousand brooms in action on this carrier. I'll have to write that in as a musical number in my play, "EL 4." If I enjoy life long enough to get to it.

For the second day in a row, after showing up there for about a week straight, I'm here instead of there at V-3 Supply. Topic of the day is I wonder if Bob's coming, or ever coming back. Then it's I wonder if he was a fag, always touching. Yeah, Dean would turn and add a thing about kicking my ass. Driving Sweet Pea deeper into the closet, where his destiny lies. At least, like Stinky said, he's young enough even at twenty, he can still be molded. So he'll get laid when he goes home a hero to Connecticut, and maybe let a girl there marry him. And he'll be better off than I would have been with Amy, because he's a good man who was raised true blue and delights in doing good and would never allow himself to think of cheating.

I've regressed at the office. Instead of applying my bachelor's in English, emphasis in writing, and assisting the skipper on the evals of a couple of chiefs who just transferred, I watched the errors pass through the chops and just typed them in as I saw them. A subtle change that I doubt they will notice. Things like, "strongest poss rec for advancement" scrawled in green. That's the XO's pen. The skipper writes in red. I would have, a week ago, spelled it out for the Executive Officer. I knew he expected me to fix it in the mix. But fuck him. Fuck the skipper and fuck the goddam Navy. They wanted me to be a 4.0 typist, not a 3.8 editor. So it went up "poss rec" and I got a call from the skipper, to come up to the Ready Room and speak with him.

"I missed a couple of things," he apologized. Ha fucking ha. In three hours, at 0500, they were catching a COD for the Philippines and heading home. And they were chiefs. And their evals were fucked away by the XO, and I didn't give a fuck. So they all had another half-hour of anxiety while I cheerfully retyped it. I didn't give a fuck how many times they wanted me to redo their mistakes. My joy is quiet, now. Maybe somebody will get the message, XO or CO, that something they had was taken away, and now they'll have to be more cautious in their grammar, and expect evals to take an extra chop and a little more time. That's one way to fit in.

The 4.0 Tagalog speaking DK had me on the phone this morning and gave an example of who represents VF-1 that allows me to describe the mentality of this group. He was trying to remember who it was that the Navy overpaid for several months because they were giving him Basic Allowance for Quarters with a Dependent, while he had been divorced several months. Maybe $150 per month he'd have to pay back out of the blue. Surprise, surprise. It happens all the time. Another guy just finished paying back $2000.

Even when they come forward right away and tell Pers they're getting a divorce, we can't stop their pay--because it's for their legal dependent--until the decree comes in. And if it's held up by the attorney or the wife or the mail or whatever, each month we just keep on paying what they'll have to repay. Then in January we get the judgment that was dated last August, and now we know we've overpaid him $750. Anyway, we couldn't think of the guy he was looking for. But I mentioned another dude and it triggered DK2.

"Now, that guy, he's a real VF-1 type of guy. You know what I mean?" The guy was the same guy who dogged my world when I arrived at this command. He was a second class, I was a PNSN. He was hanging around in the barracks as I came in with my seabag. Out of the blue he started fucking with me, him and five other guys, but especially him and his buddy, a third class. They wouldn't stop harassing me, saying they were going to fuck with me, literally fuck me, and keep fucking my world in any way they could to make me mad.

I was so pissed off I went back to 32nd Street until the No Later Than report date. When I did come back, they put me on Gate Guard at the flight line and that guy, with his bud, came out with the trash and paused to harass. I used the phone and put them on report, and he introduced me to the style of Navy that was so recently brought home in spades by the chain of command. "I'm a second class petty officer with a very high reputation, Bob. And he's a third class to back up my story. Who do you think they're gonna believe? Man, you haven't got a chance. You're just an Airman. They're not even gonna listen to you."

He's hotheaded, argues in a heartbeat, and turns a deaf ear in a blind rage. Nobody in his shop gets along with him, and the one guy who speaks up goes TAD to ship master-at-arms, then gets a write up on his eval that says he prefers not to work in his assigned billet, chooses to go TAD instead. And guess who had to type the victim's eval: PN2. That's Fighter Squadron ONE at its best, aka FUCKTRON ONE.

I just hope Scrapper doesn't come to my rack with any bullshit and catch me crying. It would be a definite problem, when you think about the fact I'm 34. Big boys don't cry. We had a message come in on suicide prevention last night, how ironic. Tendencies are evident through inappropriate behavior under stress. Sounds like a Rand Corporation study, you know, the guys who found that children of people who had dental plans tended to have healthier teeth than children of people without dental plans.

He worked four hours overtime, got six hours sleep and his boss chewed him out for not finishing the job he got two hours before he got off, and you wonder why the dude fell off the fantail. They say in most cases where a note is left behind, some particular person or thing is blamed. Well, unfortunately for them, I'm nasty enough to stick around and play. I just have to remember not to reenlist before the Diary debuts.

This is the end of the innocence. I put Don Henley back in my head and pretend I'm back on Mission Beach in the middle of a hot July day. Back when I was looking forward, Sweet Pea was a fantasy that had a hope. A grain of sand sparkled on the arm of a young boy fifteen feet away, lying in the sun with his best friend, mother and older sister along and distracted by books. Me walking over out of the blue summer sky, plopping down with a boogie box and blaring Don Henley just long enough for this song, looking at him, him looking back, then when it ended getting up and walking off.

Back to the wall with the retired senior chief who was the chief acid dealer on the beach, a Vietnam veteran SEAL with half a dozen bullet scars in his body, confirmed in his business like attitude toward our way of government. I watched him make a thousand bucks on the third of July. A thousand dollars in one day selling acid on the beach.

Fuck 'em all, just like Keasey said in "Cuckoo's Nest." Fuck 'em all. Nobody could catch him, they didn't even suspect him. What a helpless old man, talking through a throat vibrator, walking on crutches. I'd watch him hand out sheets to the coolest hippy, watch that go down the line and finally end in a square through the lips of a blond from the base, a dude who didn't want me to suspect he did acid. I guess he was afraid I would tell.

The old man gave me a couple. For nothing. Whenever I wanted since I was in the Navy. Then some kid about twelve came up wanting to buy a couple of hits. I told him to open his mouth and I stuck the blotter on his tongue and turned him on. We'll never forget it. But that's counter culture vice the status quo, and never happened.

0715 17 APR 91. Saw Dean at breakfast, walked by, paused, sat down for a while as he listened to the conversation of his yellow shirt hangar director buds. He clutched a box of Fruit Loops from home. I didn't bother asking, just waited for the veg prep guy to bring out Frosted Flakes, then got a bowl. He left as I started to eat. I didn't mention Sweets, neither did he. He's probably up there now, smoking against Sweets' wishes, milking out his tolerance better than I could.

I took a shower and jacked off to keep warm, rinsed my life force down the drainhole and came to my rack. I was tempted to go see him with a good excuse, to have a place to design my Shellback tee-shirt. His shop is where all the V-3 shirts are being made, and it's got the desk, the seclusion, even a trysting atmosphere. But I didn't want to accidently touch him again. I'm withdrawn, afraid to go in there again. Fear of rejection, thirty-four years old. An old man rejected by youth. What could be more natural?

I tried to read my book on reading for Hollywood, read about a paragraph and tossed it aside. I picked up this other book, ... *As One Mad With Wine*, a book of similes. I looked at trees, and then stumbled onto "thinness." Sweets is thin. I looked at the sayings, "thin as the edge of the moon," by Stephen Vincent Benet; "thin as the line between self-confidence and conceit" by Anonymous; and "thin as the skin seaming a scar," by Sylvia Plath. I stopped and read her name again, and wished I were back in the states where I could find a book of her poems.

I want to find that poem of hers we read in college, where she talked about putting on a jacket of a dead girlfriend, felt the form where her body had molded the leather, and found some item in one of the pockets. I want to remember what it was in the pocket, what it meant.

I remember the smell of dirt and grass from Billy's sweatshirt in Missouri, cuddled in my arms without him, since he left it at my house one day. I hated giving it back, but it was appropriate to do that. I sometimes wish I could climb inside the skins of these objects of my addictive affection. To see what impression I have, or how stupid and weak I must look.

"Men's thoughts are thin and flimsy like lace; they are themselves pitiable like the lacemakers." -- Soren Kierkegaard.

The smoking lamp is out throughout the ship while taking on fuel, and no doubt they're still smoking in Pers. I had a senior chief tell me this morning, a nice guy by the way, and a nonsmoker, that when they used busting the chain of command against me for sending that one dude to Cag, I should have mentioned the fact that I was in charge, so I couldn't have bypassed the chain of command. What the hell. I have resigned. In dramatic arts that's called "phoning it in," performing as if detached. Not putting your heart and soul into the presentation. An actor's balding, weathered body is what he brings to the party, and his intensity makes him. His striving for a goal. Like, as I might have been striving to do the best job two weeks ago. Now I'm like the show is going on and my mind is in the alley, backstage or somewhere craving wine.

I hitchhiked into New York City in 1977, got out of a car, walked up Canal Street, and found water from an open fire hydrant. I bent down and took my nourishment. My world was an open hydrant. And the YMCA at 38th street where the nigger fucked me just like the Navy, without Vaseline. At least I could fight him off. I tried to tell Sweets about it last week, sitting in his shop on Steal Beach day. I told him about walking out on the woman's directing class final, and the other dude's advanced acting class final, and selling my PA system for $25 and a ride to the freeway. I stumbled and stuttered through it, realizing I had never written that story, that it had grown vague and lost its meaning. I was almost trying to convince him God exists, but he needed salvation like Columbus needed maps. He already knows the world is round. I was rambling about clouds that looked like Jesus, a gypsy who called himself a wizard, the blackout in '77 and the nigger in New York. Right about then a friend came by to play Spades. So I left it with me fighting off a rapist. He already knows I killed a guy, in self-defense. But he doesn't know it was a seventeen year old boy in Hollywood who just got done fucking me and letting me tongue him in the ass. Now he probably thinks it was the New York nigger. Was I trying to warn him that I'm a dangerous psychopath that he should keep away from? Was I trying to convince him to spur on the scene where he gets rid of me meanly or nicely or any way he can, just to ease the trouble of parting in the future? Because I'd milk the present for all it's worth, and I'd be the last guy to let go. Like I did Billy, I'd be writing letter after letter, like Bette in "Beaches" and never hearing back.

I was trying to get to the scene in Oklahoma, where I for once and for the last time held my lonely arms up to God and said, "I love you," then got struck in the face by a shooting star flying into the Big Dipper. August 18, 1977. Or sometime in August of that year. Like a vision planted in my brain, it still remains. But I keep it at bay, letting others have their barren futures by comparison. I've endured my second coming, they're still looking. Or like the Mormons or other religionists, they've got their own songs to sing.

It was such a big deal back then I could hardly stand it. So for the sake of balance, God gave me the first degree murder charge to make me human again. I mean, I was like Moses come down from the mountain top, couldn't even look at a human for the deterioration it would cause the Christ inside who'd inhabited me that split second. Of all the blessing, though, it never cured my sexual curiosity. In fact, in some great bestowance of wisdom, it occurred afterward that homosexuality was that unfounded answer to overpopulation. Why would God put a cross like that on me, just for holding out my arms to the heavens and saying, "can I just dwell here in this thick darkness and tell you, I love you."

Crack through the heavens like a thief in the night, in the wink of an eye, over the black horizon of Enid, Oklahoma, fourteen years before the pages in this book were cut from tar on a plastic disk. Didn't NASA see it? Didn't it blip some radar somewhere? Wasn't there a huge electronic pulse? What about the listening scopes the world has spent billions of dollars on through modern history? Nobody saw it but a twenty-year old man torn between New York City Jesus freaks and Los Angeles California superstars? Why did Johnny Carson and Tommy Smothers have to look at the TV and say, "we love you Saint Louis" that night I came in off the road to my cousin's house in Saint Louis and flipped on the TV a couple of days before this?

And now, after the fireworks and after the trauma, what have I got? A 3.8 evaluation in personal behavior and reliability and military bearing as an E5 in the US Navy making less than a thousand bucks a month, no car, no house, a borderline contract with the NIS over my shoulder and a Bad

Conduct Discharge a stone's throw to the right. Maybe I'M the Queen of the Slipstream. And what if it wasn't God? What if it was Satan in disguise, as an angel of light? If God is all powerful and has dominion over space, would God allow me to be deceived? Is it some galactic experiment, injecting the notion in my head that God came back like a thief in the night (because he only revealed himself to one guy and all the scribes and pharisees will reek with envy)? And finally, bottom line, if the tree falls in the forest and there's no one there to hear it, does it make a sound? Does anyone alive in the world care about the story I live for?

CAUTION: NOT TO BE USED FOR IDENTIFICATION PURPOSES

THIS IS AN IMPORTANT RECORD SAFEGUARD IT.

ANY ALTERATIONS IN SHA[illegible] AREAS RENDER FORM [illegible]

CERTIFICATE OF RELEASE OR DISCHARGE FROM ACTIVE DUTY

1. NAME (*Last, First, Middle*): GRAHAM, ROBERT DAVID
2. DEPARTMENT, COMPONENT AND BRANCH: NAVY-USN
3. SOCIAL SECURITY N[illegible]: 493 | 62 | 1[illegible]

4.a GRADE, RATE OR RANK: PN2
4.b PAY GRADE: E5
5. DATE OF BIRTH (*YYMMDD*): 561125
6. RESERVE OBLIG. TERM. DATE: Year 94 Month 01 Day [illegible]

7.a PLACE OF ENTRY INTO ACTIVE DUTY: OAKLAND, CA
7.b HOME OF RECORD AT TIME OF ENTRY (*City and state, or comp[lete] address if known*): 1776 UNIT C CAMINO VERDE [illegible] WALNUT CREEK [illegible]

8.a LAST DUTY ASSIGNMENT AND MAJOR COMMAND: FIGHTER SQUADRON ONE (VF-1)
8.b STATION WHERE SEPARATED: FIGHTER SQUADRON ONE (VF-1) NAS MIRAMAR, [illegible]

9. COMMAND TO WHICH TRANSFERRED: NRPC NEW ORLEANS, LA 70149-7300
10. SGLI COVERAGE ☐ Non[e] Amount: $ 100,000

11. PRIMARY SPECIALTY (*List number, title and years and months in specialty. List additional specialty numbers and titles involving periods of one or more years.*)

PN-0000 PERSONNELMAN
03 YRS AND 07 MOS

12. RECORD OF SERVICE	Year(s)	Month(s)	Day[s]
a. Date Entered AD This Period	88	JAN	25
b. Separation Date This Period	91	DEC	1[illegible]
c. Net Active Service This Period	03	10	22
d. Total Prior Active Service	00	00	0[illegible]
e. Total Prior Inactive Service	00	00	17
f. Foreign Service	00	00	00
g. Sea Service	01	04	12
h. Effective Date of Pay Grade	91	APR	16

13. DECORATIONS, MEDALS, BADGES, CITATIONS AND CAMPAIGN RIBBONS AWARDED OR AUTHORIZED (*All periods of service*)

NAVY UNIT COMMENDATION FPE 91FEB07, NAVY "E" (2ND) RIBBON FPE 89DEC31, ARMED FORCES EXPEDITIONARY MEDAL FPE 89JUN05, NATIONAL DEFENSE SERVICE MEDAL FPE 92JAN24, SOUTHWEST AS[IA] SERVICE MEDAL (2ND) FPE 91APR20, SEA SERVICE DEPLOYMENT (2ND) RIBBON FPE 91APR08. X

14. MILITARY EDUCATION (*Course title, number of weeks, and month and year completed*)

PN "A" SCHOOL, 7 WKS, MAY88. X X X X

15.a. MEMBER CONTRIBUTED TO POST-VIETNAM ERA VETERANS' EDUCATIONAL ASSISTANCE PROGRAM: Yes / No
15.b HIGH SCHOOL GRADUATE OR EQUIVALENT: Yes / No
16. DAYS ACCRUED LEAVE PAID: 51.5

17. MEMBER WAS PROVIDED COMPLETE DENTAL EXAMINATION AND ALL APPROPRIATE DENTAL SERVICES AND TREATMENT WITHIN 90 DAYS PRIOR TO SEPARATION: Yes

18. REMARKS

19.a. MAILING ADDRESS AFTER SEPARATION (*Include Zip Code*)
2747 HUTCHINSON CT
WALNUT CREEK, CONTRA COSTA, CA 94598

19.b. NEAREST RELATIVE (*Name and address - include Zip Code*)
DEE M GRAHAM (FATHER)
2747 HUTCHINSON CT, WALNUT CREEK, CA [illegible]

20. MEMBER REQUESTS COPY 6 BE SENT TO DIR. OF VET AFFAIRS: Yes / No

21. SIGNATURE OF MEMBER BEING SEPARATED: [signature]

22. OFFICIAL AUTHORIZED TO SIGN (*Typed name, grade, title and signature*): [signature] [illegible]

SPECIAL ADDITIONAL INFORMATION (*For use by authorized agencies only*)

23. TYPE OF SEPARATION: DISCHARGED
24. CHARACTER OF SERVICE (*Include upgrades*): HONORABLE

25. SEPARATION AUTHORITY: MILPERSMAN 3630400 AND BUPERS WASHINGTON MSG 111928ZDEC91
26. SEPARATION CODE: HRB
27. REENTRY CODE: RE-4

28. NARRATIVE REASON FOR SEPARATION: HOMOSEXUALITY - STATED HE IS A HOMOSEXUAL

29. DATES OF TIME LOST DURING THIS PERIOD: TL: NONE
30. MEMBER REQUESTS COPY 4: RDG Ini[tials]

DD Form 214, NOV 88 S/N 0102-LF-006-5500 *Previous editions are obsolete* MEMBER-4

Chapter Eighteen

0800 18 APR 91. East bound and down. *Ranger* pulled out of the Gulf at about 2230 last night, at 26 knots. I don't think we've slowed down since. At 0230 it became 0330, and we'll keep changing our clocks forward until we hit the International Forget Line again. It's time to party without rings.

I think I've counted three divorces so far, in VF-1. On a *Ranger* Videogram for ship's company, some little kid said "Hi" to Daddy and added, dropping his eyes, "Mommy's got a boyfriend."

The PNC is still fucking with me hard as ever, that lubeless SOB. But last night had a couple of good moments. First, he set me up. This is how. We have two guys getting out in June, so he gives me the guy who's difficult. He's got a contract in his service record that says he's joined the Navy for four years. That's it. Nothing about the Reserves for eight years, which is Navy policy. Nobody gets in for four years active and no reserve time. But he has it there in his contract. So I'm bound to do his separation wrong, right? I can hardly wait to get chewed out tonight. On the other hand, figuring out his SGLI (Servicemen's Group Life Insurance), I stumbled across the distribution I knew was in the MILPERSMAN. The original goes to NMPC (Washington microfiche) and the next copy goes in the service record. The last copy goes to the member. But PNC directs that the original goes to the S/R and both copies to the member. Spark! A falsified SGLI goes to NMPC with PNC's friends' names as beneficiaries. Multiplied by the number of years in his career as a PN (20) times the number of S/R's he's verified and SGLI's he's processed (such as: number of new Navy members he's seen)--say an arbitrary thousand. That's 20,000 SGLI's. Make it a quarter of that number just to be more conservative, you know, he probably didn't learn this trick until he hooked up with the Channel 19 gang in San Diego. So five thousand dudes have his cohorts listed as their beneficiaries, without knowing. What are the odds that one of them will die under contract? One in five thousand? Ten in five thousand? Each SGLI submitted is worth $100,000 now.

I wouldn't be so concerned if he hadn't ordered me to falsify the TAD orders in the past, or if he hadn't falsified the Diary Message to the Enlisted Personnel Management Activity Center after the skipper had signed it on that trouble shooter's operative extension of enlistment date, or if he hadn't backdated the message reference on that other guy's executed, inoperative extension which caused an expired projected rotation date and got him orders he hated out of the blue because it was illegal. Or, and this is a good one, if his favorite phrase in customer service wasn't, "I get ten percent."

I seem to think that it's okay to break the rules and be a fag inside the Navy, because the rules are patently discriminatory and unenforceable, as you see. But when it comes to embezzlement I want to jump on the band wagon and shout from the rooftops. That's the case, mother fuckers. And fuck you.

All right all right. I couldn't stay away. They were blowing out the vents in our berthing and I couldn't hit the rack. So I put on my dungarees and went to the V-3 Supply shack. He was there, and on TV was a movie about swinging wild sex, lesbian sex, sex with a bald man, and intimate passion in words by the women. It had a Gay Paris set and 30's style hairstyle and dress. This was on KRAN TV onboard *USS Ranger*, and the Navy wanted me to take out the scenes of simulated buttfucking with clothes on in my video of Westpac '89.

"Just your kind of place, eh Sweets? I can't stand it."

"There's the door."

It was hard digging through my emotions and fear of rejection but I realized, or at least finally believed, he was sticking up for this type of action. He's got to be wild at heart. He must be. Oh god someday if I am oh so lucky I'll find out, and I'll never tell you.

He wasn't booting me out.

"I'm going through a phase right now," I told him outside the supply shack. "Saying stupid things, like that being just your kind of place. And I got too touchy the other day and got my feelings hurt."

"You'll snap out of it."

He took me in his shack and let me sit on his desk a while, and I got to talk with him. He was bored out of his mind, but I told him a little about my book, and what I would do when my tour ends. "If I don't get an offer from the agency by the time my enlistment comes up, I'll probably reenlist for Hawaii or to become a JO. But then I'll have to re-edit my book. Because if it comes out they'll kick me out of the Navy. There's just too much in it about having real deep emotions."

He was looking deep into my eyes and I couldn't stand it. I wanted to stammer out, "I love you." But of course you don't say shit like that in scenes like these on ships like this. You'd end up getting caught with his cheek in your hand, tears rolling down your face. And if you didn't get caught there you'd be kissing and all the macho mother fuckers would be mauling and puking in their nurses' arms. So I broke and looked away. What a moment that was. Now I wonder, what if I had not turned my face. I hope I find out. No, I pray to the good Lord I find out. Please have a happy ending.

0830 20 APR 91. Somewhere on the ocean, hot as hell. I'm sweating in my rack, in nothing but a tee-shirt. A little Wolfie over the right tit, and a crow and two chevrons above the left. The Navy insignias for the Wolfpack, aka Fighter Squadron ONE, and the second class petty officer, my military rank. I've ruined about ten tee-shirts with stencils that are only good out here. If you ever see someone walking around in a tee-shirt with a crow and chevron over the left breast, you'll know he's been on Westpac.

Sweets is working on his 21-Day, a periodic report of consumable expenditures incurred over the past 21 days. Something like that. This is his first time as V-3 Supply Petty Officer, and given that he's not even a petty officer yet, it's a challenge. Somebody with experience is helping, and Stinky gave him a brief before leaving. It's good training if he wants to work in a warehouse after this.

They handed out prophylactics last night at 1900. PNC had to put in his remark, sexual harassment. "You don't need a rubber to suck dick."

He got a nice laugh from Scrapper, Rod, and YN3 Black. It's always fun making sexual slurs against me. What the hell, it's like the cops at Mission Beach abusing the homeless. Most of them are carrying drugs for sale to make a living, so they're only going to take the abuse and thank the officers. At least I don't thank this mother fucker.

I just looked at the letter I received in the mail last night. I was rereading it, wondering why it said to have a happy holiday, if my brother and his wife were talking about Easter, then wondering what they meant, "we'll see you in 1991." I looked at the postmark and it read, 7 Dec 1990. From California. Now I'm really wondering if the NIS has been following this book. They probably censored--or intercepted--all of my chapters until I stopped sending them home for safekeeping, in case the disks got ruined. And censoring my return mail. They probably steamed this letter open and perused it for hidden messages. Finding none, after four months, they sent it on.

They're showing another kinky movie on KRAN, about some boy who cross dresses for the sake of peeping into the girls' locker room. Right. I think he's doing it for the sake of cross dressing. What a titillating movie for the guys on this ship, with no women around, only those pretty boys here and there to dream of.

Like Sweets. I did it, by the way. I took the *Forum* down to his shop while he was out. The night check dude let me in and I sat the magazine on his desk under a copy of a newspaper supplement with an article on the comic, Jay Leno. And a new deck of cards with San Francisco pictures on the back. I guess he'll guess I brought them.

Maybe it'll enlighten the good man, make him feel less alone if he's a stray cat in a closet. How many years can you go with nobody telling you you are ok no matter if you like other boys? I hope it comforts him and eases his troubled mind. He's forever running, if you asked me; but you didn't ask me.

We're still the war carrier, until we outchop in the Bear Box, changing the guard at Guam. So we'll continue to drill, like with Operation Gold Leaf this morning that had the Marine Detachment all over the ship with shotguns. And General Quarters, that place where every swinging dick is manned and ready for battle, such as us in the Pers office trying to keep awake. What a bunch of helpless no loads.

We have $4,000 to blow in Pattaya, at the squadron party. Last time it cost $2300. Inflation.... LT Davis says he'll hop a bus to Bangkok then catch an airline to Phuket. I remember that town from Army ROTC, University of Missouri-Columbia, a map reading exercise. "What Southeast Asia town or city has a name that sounds like an American cursing slang?" ... fuck it.

He says the beaches are great and the women are Aussies. It went through my mind, what if I could take Sweets down there, away from the Navy and the watchful jealous cocks? *C'est la vie*, Bob.

We had Captain's Call in the Ready Room last night. For E5's. I was in the middle of training in Pers, YN3 Rod giving a lecture on CACO, Casualty Assistance Calls Officer, actually a rundown of what we had to do when Gus was killed. I guess it didn't hurt me to miss that session. The Admin Officer got my attention, told me I could go, and at that moment made me aware of it in the first place. It was mentioned on the Flight Schedule but not on the POD. SNAFU. What black shoe reads the Flight Schedule? It's an airdale thing. I wasn't ready to ask any piercing questions.

I still managed to open some worm cans. Like, I mentioned that the Maintenance Master Chief Petty Officer is still permanently assigned to VF-1, and would he be coming back if he didn't transfer by the time we returned? Yes, he would, even though he's lost about sixty pounds. He was overweight to transfer, and in the process of losing his weight he's probably gotten his reputation around as such a mean bastard. On the other hand, he always reminded me of Brian O'Dennehy, the actor. I think he used to be Brian Keith. You know who I'm talking about. A tough guy to live with, but the kind of guy you'd like in the middle of war. It was the ultimate joke of this squadron that he stayed and we fought.

0745 21 APR 91. Bully went to Mast. The same guy who threw the 81-Man coop cleaner up against the racks, now disrespected the Safety PO on the flight deck. Now they're riding his rail, took him to XOI yesterday, CO Mast this morning. He thinks it's too much this time. But it was nothing last time and should have been something. Like YN1 said, you can get by, but you can't get away.

Wog Day is fast approaching. I haven't done my shirt yet, but I'm not going down there until he's done his 21-Day. This is the 21st and it could be that a 21-Day in his department is a report due the 21st. I don't know for sure. Besides, I fucking admit, I want to give him time to read the article and get over it, let it sink in or pass, whichever, give him time to deal with the why of my giving him that *Forum*.

We got a message last night, which I will include in its full text for your reading pleasure. From King Neptune himself, about our imminent arrival in his realm. As you know from this book, the Navy has its own abbreviated language, and no more so than in a Naval message. But the body of it is spelled out. AMPN means Amplification, as in amplifying the information provided by the previous line Ref A, which means Reference A. It's addressed to everybody in the Battle Group, Info to Cag.

U N C L A S S I F I E D ROUTINE SMN 041530
R 191240Z APR 91 ZYB ADMINISTRATIVE MESSAGE FM NEPTUNE REX
TO COMCARGRU SEVEN
COMDESRON SEVEN
USS RANGER
USS VALLEY FORGE
USS KANSAS CITY
USS PAUL F FOSTER
USS FRANCIS HAMMOND
INFO COMCARAIRWING TWO
CARAIRWING TWO

UNCLAS //N0000//

SUBJ: DIPLOMATIC CLEARANCE TO ENTER THE DOMAIN OF NEPTUNUS REX MSGID/GENADMIN/NEPTUNE REX//
REF/A/DOC/KING NEPTUNE/ANCIENT ORDER OF THE DEEP//
AMPN/REF A IS ANCIENT DOCTRINE GOVERNING THE VALE OF PACIFICUS IN THE COUNTY OF EQUATUS IN THE REALM OF NEPTUNUS REX//
RMKS/1. MY MOST TRUSTED AND DEDICATED SCRIBE DAVY JONES, HAS INFORMED ME THAT CARRIER GROUP SEVEN WILL SOON BE ENTERING MY ROYAL DOMAIN AND THAT THE GOOD SHIPS, WINGS, SQUADRONS AND DETACHMENTS UNDER YOUR COMMAND CARRY A LARGE AND SLIMY CARGO OF LAND-LUBBERS, LOUNGE LIZARDS, AND LIBERTY HOUNDS FALSELY MASQUERADING AS SEAMAN AND MAN-O-WARSMEN. LET IT BE KNOWN THAT REF A REMAINS IN EFFECT AND NOTHING HAS CHANGED SINCE THE LAST TIME YOU VISITED MY KINGDOM ADMIRAL. ALL THOSE WHO ENTER THE DOMAIN OF NEPTUNUS REX WITHOUT PROPER CREDENTIALS SIGNED BY DAVY JONES HIMSELF ARE SUBJECT TO THE WRATH OF THE HIGH ROYAL COURT OF THE RAGING MAIN. LET IT ALSO BE KNOWN THAT IN MY KINGDOM TRADITION PREVAILS AND THE GOOD CAPTAINS AND OFFICERS IN CHARGE OF YOUR SHIPS, SQUADRONS AND DETACHMENTS WILL OFFER TO MY KINGDOM A SACRIFICE UPON ENTERING THE RAGING MAIN, OF THE CLOSEST THING THEY HAVE TO A MERMAID AND WILL PROBABLY BE FOUND DEEP IN THE BOWELS OF YOUR SHIPS. NOT LATER THAN THE EVENING OF THE DAY BEFORE ENTERING MY DOMAIN ALL SHIPS, SQUADRONS AND DETACHMENTS WILL CONDUCT A ROYAL BEAUTY CONTEST AND EACH DIVISION WILL EXHIBIT NOT LESS THAN ONE ENTRANT. AFTER REMOVING THE ENTRANTS FROM BERTHING COMPARTMENTS, HEADS, BILGES, VOIDS, AIRCRAFT ENGINE INTAKES, CHAIN LOCKERS AND PEAK TANKS: THEY WILL BE THOROUGHLY CLEANSED OF ALL SAND CRABS, LAND MITES, DUNG WORMS, URINAL GNATS, BED BUGS, HELO FLIES, BILGE RATS, RECTAL URCHINS AND HIGH-TECH TERMITES. THE ANTAGONISTS SELECTED AS THE WINNERS OF THE CONTEST MAY BE THE FIRST TO APPEAR BEFORE MY JUST AND DISMEMBERING ROYAL HIGH COURT OF DESTINY CHAIRED BY THE HORRIBLE AND TORTUROUS JUDGE OF THE NORTH WIND. DIPLOMATIC CLEARANCE IS GRANTED. THE DOLPHINS WELCOME YOUR VISIT.
2. RELEASED BY DAVY JONES.//
BT
U N C L A S S I F I E D

Talk about hot. We've gone tropical. The Arabian Gulf was nothing compared to wherever we are now. Yesterday I laid in bed and felt sweat pour off like tears until I became dehydrated, got up and got some water. It's early yet and I'm beginning to sweat after a cold shower. I just hope the compartment won't start stinking in the heat with dirty laundry.

0700 22 APR 91. "All hands muster on station. Submit reports to Personnel prior to zero eight-thirty. Now station the underway replenishment detail. Man all starboard replenishment stations. Now station the underway vertical replenishment detail."

Thunderstorm Condition I. That is, destructive winds accompanying the phenomena indicated are imminent or are occurring. Associated lightning/thunder, torrential rain, hail, severe downbursts (wind and rain falling straight down at over fifty miles per hour), and sudden windshifts are possible. Take immediate safety precautions and shelter. Vertrep in this. Helos in hover time, a high velocity wind from the rotor blades picking up debris and blowing it in all directions, and extremely unstable operation in the best conditions. Back to the unforgiving moments.

Sometime this morning, I guess it was about five a.m., the CMC came down, sleepless again. After a while he walked up to me at the PNC's desk. "Do you mind if I smoke?" He was squarely settled on the deck in a pose that reminded me of meeting a drunk Lee Marvin coming off PSA airlines at LAX. Towering solid, even offbase.

"Naw, go ahead." I'd already lost. "But is YN1 back there?"

"Yeah."

"He doesn't like it either, but he's never gonna say a word."

In a minute I heard him and YN1, then I smelled the foul odor. My night was going so well. I was caught up with every fucking thing. I was drafting a letter to Paramount Pictures, hoping to get a job as a reader when 24 January comes around. Dreaming of the good life, maybe buying Rock Hudson's mansion. And seeing Sweets on the weekends, paying his airfare from Connecticut. Jet setting to meet him in New York. Suddenly I'm back in the political US Navy and permitting my command master chief to take another shot at me on the firing line. Knock another pint of blood out of my future. I was suicidal anyway.

I can't go down to V-3 Supply. "Some guys have all the luck, some guys have all the pain, some guys get all the breaks, some guys do nothing but complain." Sing it Rod.

They say there's a great big ribbon and bow hanging down from the San Diego Bay bridge, a glorious yellow ribbon. Welcome home, all you swabbies who get back before it rips. We'll get ripped before we get back. I guess that's fair.

We're five degrees over the line. But we'll go on toward Pattaya before dipping under. We won't hit the beach; we'll have wog day, then sail in. Pattaya's about the same distance to the equator.

1000 23 APR 91. I braved it today, went down the ladder to V-3 Supply. He was at chow but his night check buddy, also my buddy, a Filipino who is gentle and kind and defies all the stereotypical crap I've been feeding you based on a fucked up chief, let me stick around and wait. When he arrived, he was glad to see me and I was greatly relieved. What if he'd said, "out fag."

He sat beside me and told me he got through the 21-Day fine, had been very busy, had to go to RANGERMART and a couple of other places this morning, including the CONFLAG (hangar conflagration) watch at eleven-thirty, and hoped to get to painting WOG tee-shirts before 1600. "And what have you been up to?" Everything in his world, all the pressing errands were on hold for me.

"Well," I showed him the high gloss on my flightdeck boots. "As you can see, it's been slow up in my shop."

While I was waiting I had planned out Pattaya on his desk calendar, and now went over it. "The first day is open. The second day is VF-2's party and I've got duty, and Dean has duty. The third day you've got duty, and VF-1 is having their party, probably at Grace's again."

"I saw that place last time."

"Oh, did you go to the Wolfpack party?"

"No, we went in after and saw all the signs that said VF-1 personnel only."

"Well, as far as I know they haven't said anything about whether we can take a guest. I'll see if Dean wants to go. Anyway, the fourth day is open, and the fifth day is open until we have to be onboard at midnight. I figure me and Dean can get a hotel on the third night, and we can pick you up and you can go in on the hotel with us on the fourth night."

"Yeah, that sounds real good. I can go with that."

"What about the first night?"

"I gotta do my laundry."

"I figured you might be getting to that stage again. Why don't you let me use my hook-up again for you, instead of spending your time on liberty?"

"No I gotta lot of laundry, not just a bag full. But I'll do that later. First I wanna go out and look around and try to remember where everything is."

"I think you go to the right, when you first step off the boat."

"Yeah, most people go to the right."

"I think the little bar huts are right up there a ways."

"I wanna take a tour one of those days." He pointed at the last two days on the calendar.

Dean walked in.

"There she is." I wasn't the only one he had gender problems with.

He strolled in and lit up.

"Oh, there he goes with a filthy cigarette."

Dean and I proceeded making our Shellback shirts. Sweets sat cramped between us, beginning to feel useless, wasteing his time. "Are you two guys gonna be here a while? I gotta go down to RANGERMART."

He left us drawing, magic markering our shirts. When he came back I proudly presented my "California attitude bright colored shellback shirt" as dubbed by him. Dean's was far less colorful, but witty with slogans about his favorite V-3 wogs. I have such a hard time with the details because the underlying emotion was killing me. I wouldn't even have noticed when he got his fifteen minute perpetual hard-on, except he got up. Even then it didn't distract me from what I was feeling. I was deep into something genuine, some understanding and comfort, some nurturing thing. I could just call it love but who would understand--maybe a deeper level of friendship. God, I don't know. It just felt great. And strong. Secure. Bound. Time will tell.

1045 25 APR 91. We were dicking the dog in Pers last night when one of the shooters came in and told us what the Captain would say a little later on the 1MC:

> At 2249 here on the 24th of April, I just wanted to pass on a couple of great BZ's to the world's finest crew of 5100 fine, fine men, who worked their way out of an emergency here tonight that had disastrous possible consequences.
>
> From an aircraft that slid into the catwalk with a total of twenty-one aircraft airborne, the turnaround launch of four tankers to tank up the aircraft that were going low state, the work by the Air Operations people to tank the aircraft, to stack 'em, to monitor the fuel and to provide great support and assistance to getting them down when we were able to get a green deck; to the Staff who was in contact with the Malaysians and the Thais to open up fields that were two hundred and seventy miles away if we were unable to get the deck clear; and to the Airwing people who were Johnny on the Spot there to support the Air Department; to the engineers who had the A Triple F available when it was needed, to push it up and have it at the catwalks when we needed to put A Triple F down; and certainly, finally, as importantly Bos'n Doesky and the world's greatest crash crew, the aircraft handler, the Boss and all the crash crew who got Tilley out there and lifted the Bullet aircraft Two Zero Seven clean as pickin' cherries off a cherry tree.
>
> We've got an aircraft that is, very little damage, we've got all the aircraft and the airwing back on deck without emergency low fuel states.
>
> So, certainly from the Cag and myself, and certainly as forded from the Admiral to each and every one of you, fifty-one hundred great carrier guys, congratulations. You took what could have been something that was an untoward and disasterous possibility and made it happen good, so my hat's off to ya. That's all I got for you.

"Six Eleven, Tower." A helo coming in.

"Roger, Six One One. Go ahead."

"Roger, the landing area is foul. Make your approach up the port side and land on Spot Four. The winds are down the angle at twenty-five knots. Cleared to land Spot Four."

"Six One One Roger."

...

"Six One One caution, Tilley is moving in the landing area."

"Six One One Roger."

"Don't pay any attention to the Wave-Off. If you just hold a port delta there we'll get ya aboard. Try and get ya half way between Spot Three and Spot Four."

"Six One One Roger."

The helo made it, the crane called Tilley hauled the F-14 out of the catwalk without blowing up, and we went back to work with a lot to talk about that never made the news.

We had a beauty queen on the hangar deck at zero seven thirty. It was the photocopier bitch from Maintenance, a third class AZ dude with a tight ass who always acts stuck up because he's so sure I'm staring from behind my desk at his butt, with greens that hike up the crack and accent his well rounded workout. He's a young surfer out of Florida. He looks good, a handsome, young and vibrant man. But a wog queen he ain't. A cross dresser maybe. He wore a midriff showing shirt over a nice flat bald belly and had oranges in canopy wipes tied to a string around his neck that just made me want to squeeze. And I did. Ooh, baby. He shook his ass and made like he could blow a tree trunk, posing for pictures. Tight red sequin underwear, too. I think my fellow shellbacks will make him shave his legs, although the hair's downy thin above the knees. I always knew he had it in him, and I'd take him to my rack--or maybe off of El Cajon Blvd., on a real mean drunk. Anyway, he made the world famous Wolfpack's official entry for the *USS Ranger*'s 1991 Wog Queen Beauty Contest.

0930 26 APR 91. Wog Day is tomorrow. I have Scrapper's charge sheet (his subpoena):

IMPERIUM NEPTUNI REGIS
IN THE HIGHEST COURT OF THE RAGIN MAIN.
THE DOMAIN OF IMPERIUM NEPTUNI REGIS
SEND GREETINGS TO:
YOU ARE COMMANDED TO APPEAR BEFORE THE ROYAL COURT ON 27 APR 1991.
A complaint has been filed with the government of THE DOMAIN OF IMPERIUM NEPTUNI REGIS, STATE OF THE RAGING MAIN, EQUATORIA, against you:

WHEREAS; YOU HAVE CONSPIRED TO ENTER THE ROYAL DOMAIN WITHOUT VISA, PASSPORT OR PROPER AUTHORIZATION.

WHEREAS: YOU HAVE FAILED TO MAINTAIN THE PERSONAL HYGIENIC PERFECTION REQUIRED TO ENTER THIS DOMAIN, TO WIT: YOU HAVE ALLOWED TO COVER YOUR BODY AND ENTER YOUR MIND A CERTAIN AMOUNT OF SLIME THAT IS USUALLY FOUND ON POLLYWOGS AND OTHER LOWER SPECIMEN OF THE REALM.

WHEREAS: YOU ARE FURTHER CHARGED WITH BROWN BAGGERY, MOPERY, DOPEING OFF,M CHIT REQUESTING, APPLE POLISHING, SYMPATHY SEEKING, GUN DECKING, PROCRASTINATION, GOLD BRICKING, LIBERTY HOUNDING AND REVEILLE NEGLECTING.

WHEREAS: YOU ARE SPECIFICALLY CHARGED WITH THE HEINOUS CRIMES OF: ______________________________

- -

____

WHEREFORE: THE PEOPLE OF THE DOMAIN OF IMPERIUM NEPTUNI REGIS, STATE OF THE RAGING MAIN, EQUATORIA, PRAY THAT THE DEFENDANT BE BROUGHT BEFORE THE ROYAL COURT FORTHWITH AND BE TRIED BEFORE THE BENEVOLENT JUDGES PRESIDING.
Subscribed and sworn to NEPTUNUS REX

before me this 18th day of April, 1991
Royal scribe in and for THE DOMAIN OF INPERIUM; NEPTUNI REGIS.
DAVY JONES, ROYAL SCRIBE

I shall fill in the specifics tonight, and he shall carry the charges in his mouth on the morrow.

The Captain was on TV last night, the old traditional Captain's Call program. He basically summarized: "I do have one thing that I wanted to bring up to each and every one of you. And I don't want you to forget the fact that, with one month and two weeks to go before we get home, I don't want you all to forget that you are true American heroes, that what you have done in the last four months is significant, and that as you begin to get ready to make that final dash, of one month and two weeks home, be proud of who you are, be proud of what you've done, as much so be very very proud of each one of your shipmates, each one of your squadronmates, for the jobs that they have done. Because they also are great American heroes." So, that all having been said, he went off with the XO into the Tiger Cruise particulars, the Air Show, the Steal Beach, the tours throughout the ship.

Somebody called in a question, "is there any truth to the rumor that we'll be going right back to the Persian Gulf after Pattaya Beach?"

"I hope not," Cag took the question. "Because we've got a pretty good liberty schedule set up back to back with Pattaya, four days underway up to Hong Kong, for a five day stay, then another two or three days back down to Subic Bay before our scheduled departure to head across the Pacific and back pick up our Tigers and go home.

"But it is important for everybody to remember that we are the extended arm of the United States. We're one of two carriers now forward deployed, and we're very much on cruise. I think the events of last night really helped verify that. It's still a very hazardous business and we're in the business of doing what we do out here as a full up round, clear up until that day that we do tie up in San Diego. So, if there were some flare-up, in the very remote chance, as always has been true, we might be called upon for any action. But as it stands now, Captain we've got a schedule."

"I do remember, the Captain responded, "I was out raging around the flightdeck, and someone stopped me, we were loading up ordnance for one of the events, and he said 'my god, are we at war again?' Not to worry, we are not at war again. You will see that we load up ordnance periodically. We do so because the airwing must maintain currency. And there are a lot of exercises which we run, the ship as well as the airwing, which are required to maintain that currency. So, never fear, I'll let you know if we, well as soon as somebody lets me know--I'll let you know if we have a war, if we have anything which is gonna change our schedule. But as the Cag said, we are the tip of the spear, we are the carrier on the bubble. So if anything happens we're gonna be the ones."

POLITICAL SITUATION IN PATTAYA: According to the given gouge, recently the Thailand government suffered a military coup, with the democratically elected civilian government being replaced by a coalition of high ranking military officers known as the National Peace Keeping Council (NPKC). Since that time, a widely respected civilian premier has been appointed in order to redraft the constitution and, eventually, lead to national elections and a return to civilian democratic rule. Key ministries are now controlled by the military or their close allies, and a large portion of the council is or will also be military or affiliated with the military. Martial law remains in effect (not intrusive -- no unusual troop presence is visible). However, law enforcement remains the responsibility of the normal police forces and court system, and no curfew has been imposed.

IMPACT ON LIBERTY: If not told one would be unaware that a coup had taken place. Normal day to day life in Thailand has not been affected in the slightest. However:

a. Simply avoid discussing the coup altogether, and avoid criticism of the Thai military.

b. Terrorism -- Pattaya contains the largest export Muslim/Arab community (including Iraqis) in the Northern part of the country. In addition, a significant number of hotels and other businesses, especially in South Pattaya, cater mainly to the Middle Eastern Tourist trade and have seen their businesses severely hurt by the drop off in tourist traffic. While it can be expected that some members of these groups will not warmly welcome Battle Group ECHO to Pattaya, there is no reason to expect significant overt hostility.

1000 28 APR 91. Time flies when you're heaving. And the wogs were definitely heaving and hating life on their knees yesterday. There were all sorts of faggot innuendos, complete with the wog beauty contest the evening before. The Admiral, Cag, and *Ranger*'s CO and XO voted by holding up numbered cards, from minus five to plus ten. Out of twenty transvestites they narrowed it to six, then chose the first and second runner up and the queen. The Weapons' bitch got first runner up. She happened to be a pal o' mine from the good old days on the forward mess. She wore white lace and a curly blonde wig.

"Randy, I didn't know." I told her I'd call.

Wolfpack had two queen candidates, one ugly officer and the AZ3 who didn't look too bad. As it were, we had training in Pers during the contest, and PNC refused to excuse me. "Get someone to take your camera down there." I did, and later found out that the battery had run down. By the time I got there the hangar bay was too packed to find the dude, so out of twenty some odd, only four horny bitches made my tape. I missed some great jack off material! The XO was voting with numbers like 69.

The Executive Officer of VF-1 decreed in our Plan Of the Day that nobody would begin "festivities" prior to zero six hundred on Wog Day. So naturally at zero two, shellbacks came through the coop to round up as many slimy wogs as they could bullshit out of their racks, and made them crawl over to the Ready Room. The deck in there was lined with RF Shielding, which is basically thick aluminum paper, so the whole room shined like some kind of space capsule. The brutes who broke the time rule naturally broke every other rule, like the impact rule that you don't take a Yogi Barra swing, and the rubber rule that you take the inner rubber out of the length of discarded firehose that made a shillelagh.

I watched this kid Joel get butt fucked so hard that with each dry hump his head slammed the against the gear locker. "I wanna hear that head slam! Fuck him, wog! Fuck 'm like you love 'm!" the dude yelled and crashed down on the 280 pound wog with a long hard shillelagh across the ass that made him fuck the boy harder. Then they abandoned him with his ass facing the door. Each "Trusty Shellback" who entered found that ass facing them and started whacking. They'd get tired and another shellback entered and began.

"Wog, every time I hit you, I want to hear you say THANK YOU SHELLBACK MAY I HAVE ANOTHER! You got that wog?"

WHACK!

"Thank you Shellback, may I have another?"

"Why yes, you may!" WHACK!

"Thank you Shellback, may I have another?"

"Yes you may!" WHACK!

"Thank you Shellback, may I have another?"

"No, I'm tired," the mighty man said finally.

I took this new kid Todd, arrived 22 April, whose face was twelve and taut with horror. As they got him out of his rack I gave him some gloves and some knee pads. Then I protected him for two or three hours. He'll love me forever. "He's my wog." I finally got overrun by a cockbiter at zero five thirty.

"Get outa the way, Graham. Get outa the way."

"Hell no. It's not six yet."

"If you don't move I'm gonna go get a bunch of other shellbacks and we're gonna take him from you and you'll never see him again. 'Cause I'll be damned if he's gonna sit there and watch all those other wogs get their asses beat. It ain't fair."

"Just 'cause you illegally beat them, you're not getting this one. Man, I got my ass beat a lot harder than they ever allowed, when I was a wog. Now this is my revenge. You guys wanna beat ass, I'm gonna save his ass. If you try to hit him I'll take you right to the skipper."

"Let's go then, 'cause he's in the Ready Room beatin' ass right now."

"That doesn't matter. This is a whole different issue. They're already playing and he doesn't have to and none of you are supposed to."

"It's just gonna make it worse," another punk chimed.

"Let's go ahead," little wog boy said. What the hell, it was five-thirty, and I figured I could get him through the hangar to the elevator pretty quickly now. I just didn't want him sitting there with his ass hanging in the fire zone for hours. Besides, this bastard and his buddies were AE's, and Todd's an AE.

We took him down to the AE shop, me following those bastards with my camcorder on. The shop supervisor introduced himself. "Oh, a new AE?" He bent low. "I'm AE1 Rocque. And I'm your worst fuckin' nightmare."

Todd was lucky. The shop was about to go down to the hangar bay for "chow," so he only got a few good whacks and I took him away.

"Take your fuckin' wog, Graham."

"Come on, wog." Wogs are allowed to stand and walk down ladders. Once back on the deck, it's back to all fours.

"Man down in the hangar bay" was called two different times over the 1MC. I never found out what happened. But a guy from V1 got hit in the eye with "blast off," a hazardous material used for stripping the flight deck. He said there were six other guys in Medical for eye injuries when he was there. And another VF-1 wog begged me to take him from another shellback who'd hooked him up with the brutes on the hangar bay until his ass was literally bleeding. I stood behind my two wogs for the rest of the show, sacrificing the chance to walk around and see Sweets, and all the chances to find wogs I might have beaten, like Scrapper.

I caught NC1 dancing with another wog singing "Oh My Darlin'," and found out later that he had to carry a jalapeno in his mouth. "But I eat 'em all the time so it didn't bother me."

What did was the "19 year wog" somebody wrote on the back of his shirt. It wasn't libelous. He got away with serving 19 years in this fuckin' Navy without crossing the line. Every shellback who read that hit him 19 times.

The hazing in the Ready Room had to be stopped 3 times by the senior chief petty officers in Maintenance, because it got so brutal. At least 5 guys I knew of were pulled physically out of their racks 4 hours before the "legal" start time as put out by the squadron XO. One of them spelled it out clearly.

"I had a good time--the only reason I'm sayin' that's 'cause I got another cruise left an' I'm gonna kill someone."

Like a never ending cycle of child abuse.

0400 29 APR 91. Hunkee Doree. The likelihood of incorrect spelling is a reflection of the ambivalence with which it leaps to mind. That's how it is when rage is deeply seated, well hidden. I don't give a fuck, so I'm happier. Since I'm happy, I take it a lot easier when I am fucked with. Because I can't help taking it easy, I'm more fun to be around. It's fun to fuck with me. Does that make me an easy lay, a slut? Maybe. Probably. But my chief is a man fond of sluts. He's even been rubbing his dick in front of me lately. Like anywhere else, you get bennies when you suck up to the boss. So when the YNCS suggested letting me off to get some sleep before liberty call, to adjust to the daytime activity that goes with port visitation, the flip didn't balk.

"Well, whatever YN1 says."

Woody let me off after the last recovery (we were flying up 'til one), and I wandered down to Hangar Control to shoot the shit with Dean. He was out at the sponson off the Blue Hole, slouched in a chair like a young fisherman without the pole. His feet stretched over the rails and his head dozed on one shoulder. The night air blew by cool, drying the humid sweat beneath my tee-shirt. You couldn't see our full moon, high over the flightdeck from the sponson. But it laid a glare over the crests of waves and lit the entire horizon. A beacon flashed rapidly far across the sea, and it took about thirty minutes to push it from one end of my view to the other. It was too loud for talk with the noise of the ventilation system working overtime somewhere nearby. We knew we'd have plenty of time for bullshitting later on, so I stood by in silence. In a few minutes two guys at the other end got up from their seats, and I walked over and sat down.

They live it up sometimes, those blue shirt hangar rats. The chairs they keep out on the sponson are vinyl covered, overstuffed, soft and comfortable. I sat there for three hours doing nothing but staring across the blue black sea, watching the glimmering waves, and sometimes letting Sweet Pea's sexual self creep into my dreams.

YN1 had charge of the money changing in the First Class lounge tonight, as President of the First Class Mess Association. He called me up and offered to hook me up, so I got a hundred dollars changed. I have two thousand four hundred and seventy baht now in my wallet.

My little wog buddy hooked me up, too. While I was at Midrats he came by Pers and loaded the CMC's refrigerator with Cokes and Arabic Mountain Dews, and wrote "BOB" on each one with a wipeboard marker. What a nice kid, what a beautiful face. Sweet Pea better let me know if he loves me or not.

It's like women. If you're so goddam lucky to ever win the heart of one, then you strive for some commitment, and on down the line you get lucky again: now what happens? I always try to hold onto options--with my future, a book or the Navy; my choices of orders, Diego Garcia or Hawaii or the Mainland; why not with beauty and youth?

One false move and I could lose him forever, is how I feel with Sweet Pea. "You're gonna lose your privileges," he warned me once in a high cracking voice, when I didn't please him. Which to me means the privilege of staring at his thin cherry lips, brown ruby eyes, wavy dark brown hair and milk soft ears, long skinny fingers and thumbs, slender back and taut tiny belly, perfect ass in form fitting military pants, chicken legs with the birthmark under the right thigh, and size ten wornout boots. If he ever dared to express commitment, give some clear indication of love, instead of leaving me to imagine what may be possible signals under the stress of maintaining lock and key.... He's only twenty. I was in bed with a famous TV actor at twenty. I can't put on blinders. Sweet Pea won't cut loose for years.

In the Navy, it's that old thing about I can't tell you how I'm feeling because you might tell some square who'd kick me out and I'd lose my whole career over the notion it might have been a beautiful world if I had come onto you with love. Fags are incompatible with military service because the (Navy) bible tells me so.

The Jim Jones effect. Remember the Jonestown massacre where a phony preacher brainwashed some nine hundred people to commit suicide and shoot women and kids who all ended up in an Oakland California cemetery?

Anyway, Dean is to Sweet Pea as Craig was to me. My best bud for ten fucking years, never accepted me as what I might have been, always had me digging the fag jokes, finally the one guy I didn't tell as I ran away to join the Navy three years ago. And haven't spoken to since. Imagine when this book comes out. I'll never see my church again, let alone Craig, Duane, Jay and all the others from my neighborhood; and let alone the heroes of our Navy.

1900 30 APR 91. I've been walking around all day with that comical face Bogie had in Casablanca, boarding his goddam train. When liberty was finally called yesterday at about 1900, they authorized it via Boat Pass, numbers one through six. I had been given number Two, Dean had Three, Sweets had Six. I could go in the Three line with a Two. So I took Sweets' pass and spent half a day negotiating and calling in favors. I got a straight trade-off to a Four, which meant that friend's subordinate got stuck with Sweet Pea's Six. I got it down to a Three because another supervisor was borrowing my camcorder.

The next problem was, being an Airman, Sweets had no pull to let a visitor hang out in the V-3 coop. So I waited in my berthing or my shop for them to pass the numbers over the 1MC. Finally they called away Two. And I called Sweets. "They just called Two."

"I know, I heard it."

"Well, what are we gonna do when they call Three?"

"I tell ya what, when they call away Three, you haul ass up here as soon as they call it." I agreed, and hauled ass when they called Three. Except neither he nor Dean was there. I went by his shop. Not there. I went down to the hangar and found pass Three lined up all the way to the fantail. It was nice of them to call it away after they had already started lining up. But where the hell were Sweets and Dean? I felt my jaw slack, and checked my eyes from welling. Enter that scene of Bogie on the step of a train leaving Paris. Rain smearing the dear John letter.

I stepped off a speedboat to Thailand, grabbed a Baccardi and Coke and started chain smoking Newports with Sweets' counterpart, the good flip Mark, V-3 Supply night check, who had found me in the hangar line. We searched all over the strip, asking everyone Mark knew if they'd seen Sweets and Dean. Some guys had, so at least I knew my love was having fun. We walked through club after club of naked women prancing and blowing out candles with pussy farts to the gaga-eyed, amazed gasping of bootcamp squids. I paid no attention to those, or to the female beggars tugging at my sleeve. I was straining through the darkness for Sweets, as the evening ran out.

Mark got a room at the Grand, same hotel I stayed at last time in Pattaya. It looked like the same Thai dudes hanging around out front that I played "2025 Argyle" for on some kid's acoustic warped six string. And there was a six-string as we rounded the corner into the hotel alley. But I wasn't up to performing for anybody last night. Except some bitch I picked up at Grace's. She had regular Marlboro's and Mark had Lights. So I bumbed her cigarette, bought her a drink and me another and another, and woke up wondering when the rubber fell off my dick. I suppose Mark had a good time.

"Give me dollars," she whined at the end. As stupid as I was, I thought I'd found one who wasn't a goddam whore.

It was five fifteen when I dropped a 500 baht note on her tits in her hotel and grabbed a cab for the speedboat; around six when I spread peanut butter on my toast on the mess deck.

I had a great duty day. Taking craps and drinking water. I guess the second day is a good day for duty in a foreign port where you're likely to be sick from the contaminated water and food and ice in your drinks, plus hungover. Nobody died so far. One guy lost his wallet on the counter of the Weekender hotel. He thought he dropped something in a cab or on the curb, and ran back outside but left his wallet on the counter. By the time the light bulb went off in his head and he ran back in, nobody had ever seen the wallet. He lost 7000 baht (nearly $300). And credit cards, and his military identification card--which prompted him to get me out of my rack.

Today's SDO is a mail freak. I happened to see the mail barge pull up as I was getting sunset air, aft on the flightdeck, and knew it would be hours before mail call if any tonight. But you pay your respects to an "O" whose every whim is your command. So I got a call from the ASDO telling me to grab some volunteers from somewhere and go to the post office and see if they were ready for us to pick up our mail. I tried to call first, to avoid the stupid useless walk. No answer. Figuring they were busy heaving it onto the ship, I followed the whim and grabbed some empty mailbags from Pers. One guy came along. Naturally, they were barely getting it to the deck below the sorting room, and that room was locked. They'd have to get it all to that deck, then up the ladder to the sorting room deck, then inside, then sorted, and it was already 1930 with only the duty section working. Would you sort the mail? I'd let the next day crew have at it. But I'm sitting around waiting in uniform now, just in case.

Meanwhile, coming back past the V-3 coop, I ran into Dean.

"What happened to you guys?"

"Man, soon as they started tryin' to call it away and the speaker was all fucked up? I got Sweets and said let's get down there. Three's was already in line. So was Fours and Fives."

"Well, I gave Sweets your two tickets, in case I don't make the tour." I had gone to his rack, found him asleep with his back to the aisle, and put my arms around his neck. I went through the motion of choking him, but really only massaged his neck and shoulders. I had whispered, in that short minute, 'I love you, you bitch.' He had not stirred. A little later I had come back and slipped the tickets into his rack drawer, inside an envelope that I had written on the outside, 'In case I get ditched.'

"You don't know if you're goin'?"

"I don't know. I don't want to go through that again, doing all that planning and not get it together." My jaw trembled and I knew by his look that he could see I wanted to cry. He'll probably never forget that look, like I'll never forget my mom's jaw trembling the day I got on the bus to my Hollywood murder trial, and she wondered aloud if they had done the right thing, as parents, kicking me out of the house when I drove off to Hollywood. I turned my back on Dean and told him over my shoulder that I'd talk to him later. I didn't dare look at him again, or I would have cried.

0645 1 MAY 91. May Day. I begin to sweat in the rack. Thai revenge subsides in my stomach, with a little Pepto Bismo. Plenty of orange juice with peanut butter on toast. The SDO had me wake up at 0400, get dressed and come to the Ready Room. It turned out to be an AMCROSS and I'm not on the message pick-up list because I have no security clearance so I couldn't pick it up. It also turned out that YN3 Black had got up at 0300 and was down in Pers. He picked it up. Now, awake, I contemplate confronting Sweets, who certainly is expecting me because he knows that I know that he's trapped on the ship with duty. If I don't go on the tour, will Sweets? He may have had second thoughts anyway. A two hour bus ride to Bangkok. Dean may have suggested an alternative already. Like getting a hotel in Pattaya, without Bob. I am just a bald, old, unattractive man, looking for a sympathy fuck. Why didn't I listen to the world when everybody kept telling me to play with kids my own age?

At least we had one good moment two days ago. I killed some time staring at him playing Solitaire.

"I've been playing this for two hours and haven't one a game yet."

"Why don't you let me cut the cards for you?"

"Why, do you have some magical powers that can make me win?"

"Maybe I do," I said as I knocked on the deck. I watched as he won.

"Damn, Graham, I don't believe it. I'm taking you gamblin' with me."

Sure, honey. Sure you are.

UNCLASS //N00000//

SUBJ: DESERT STORM MEDIA INTERVIEWS
RMKS/1. REQUEST THE FOLLOWING MESSAGE BE RETRANSMITTED TO ALL UNITS THAT PARTICIPATED IN OPERATION DESERT SHIELD/STORM.
2. AS MORE AND MORE TROOPS REDEPLOY TO HOME STATIONS, THERE WILL BE COUNTLESS MEDIA REQUESTS FOR INTERVIEWS OF PERSONNEL WHO PARTICIPATED IN DESERT SHIELD AND STORM. THESE INTERVIEWS PROVIDE AN EXCELLENT OPPORTUNITY FOR OUR PERSONNEL TO SHARE THEIR EXPERIENCES AND INCREASE THE UNDERSTANDING OF THE AMERICAN PUBLIC OF THE SACRIFICE AND PROFESSIONALISM OF THE U.S. MILITARY FORCES IN THE GULF. THE RESULT WILL BE INCREASED POTENTIAL FOR POSITIVE COVERAGE OF THE PERSONAL ASPECTS OF THE OPERATION.
3. HOWEVER, UNIT COMMANDERS SHOULD REMIND THEIR PERSONNEL THAT U.S. FORCES HAVE NOT ALL LEFT THE THEATER AND THERE CONTINUES TO BE A NEED FOR OPERATIONAL SECURITY. ANY DISCUSSION OF UNIT STRENGTHS OR TOTAL NUMBER OF TROOPS STILL IN DEFENSIVE POSITIONS IN SOUTHERN IRAQ ALSO WILL BE AVOIDED. OTHER TOPICS WHICH SHOULD NOT BE DISCUSSED:

POSSIBLE FUTURE OPERATIONS; ANY SPECIAL FORCES ACTIVITY, PAST, PRESENT, OR FUTURE; DETAILED DESCRIPTIONS OF OPERATIONAL TACTICS THAT HAVE BEEN DESIGNATED AS SENSITIVE OR COULD REVEAL CLASSIFIED OPERATIONAL CHARACTERISTICS OF WEAPON SYSTEMS; PERSONAL ANALYSIS OR BELIEFS CONCERNING POLITICAL DECISIONS THAT WERE MADE DURING THE OPERATION THAT ARE THE PURVIEW OF THE NATIONAL COMMAND AUTHORITIES OR SENIOR MILITARY LEADERS; AND ANY SPECULATIVE COMMENT ON ACCIDENTS OR INCIDENTS THAT ARE UNDER INVESTIGATION SUCH AS AIRCRAFT ACCIDENTS, "FRIENDLY FIRE" SITUATIONS OR ACCIDENTAL DEATHS.
4. REQUEST COMMANDERS BRIEF THEIR PERSONNEL THAT THE SAFEST APPROACH TO MEDIA INTERVIEWS IS TO STICK WITH RELATING PERSONAL EXPERIENCES, STAY AWAY FROM DISCUSSIONS OF POLICY,K AND TO CONTINUE TO PROTECT CLASSIFIED OR PRIVILEGED INFORMATION. PLEASE PASS THIS INFORMATION TO THE PERSONNEL WHO SERVED WITH SUCH HONOR THROUGHOUT THE ENTIRE CAMPAIGN TO ENSURE THAT THE EXTENSIVE MEDIA COVERAGE DOESN'T JEOPARDIZE THE CONTINUING OPERATION.//
BT

UNCLASS //N05720//

SUBJ: PUBLIC AFFAIRS PROPOSED NEWS RELEASE FOR USS RANGER BATTLE GROUP VISITING PATTAYA, THAILAND
RMKS/1. THE FOLLOWING NEWS RELEASE IS SUBMITTED FOR IMMEDIATE DISTRIBUTION FOR PUBLICATION:
THE AIRCRAFT CARRIER USS RANGER (CV 61) BATTLE GROUP, INCLUDING FIVE SHIPS AND 6,500 PERSONNEL, IS VISITING PATTAYA, THAILAND APRIL 29 AFTER RETURNING FROM A THREE-MONTH TOUR IN THE ARABIAN GULF SUPPORTING OPERATION DESERT STORM.
RANGER, THE LAST OF THE FOUR ORIGINAL AIRCRAFT CARRIERS ASSIGNED TO THE ARABIAN GULF DURING OPERATION DESERT STORM, LEFT THOSE WATERS RECENTLY TO BEGIN THE 12,000-MILE EASTERLY TRANSIT HOME TO SAN DIEGO.
THE 81,000-TON CONVENTIONALLY POWERED AIRCRAFT CARRIER ENTERED THE GULF AFTER A 39-DAY TRANSIT FROM THE WEST COAST. WHEN RANGER JOINED USS MIDWAY (CV 41) JANUARY 16, IT MARKED THE FIRST SIMULTANEOUS PRESENCE OF TWO AIRCRAFT CARRIERS IN THE ARABIAN GULF. LESS THAN 48 HOURS LATER, RANGER AND ITS EMBARKED AIRWING - CARRIER AIR WING TWO - LAUNCHED MASSIVE AIR STRIKES INTO IRAQ AND KUWAIT AS PART OF THE ALLIED OFFENSIVE WHICH BEGAN THE 43-DAY WAR. RANGER AND MIDWAY WERE LATER JOINED BY USS THEODORE ROOSEVELT (CVN 71) AND USS AMERICA (CV 66) FORMING A FOUR-CARRIER BATTLE FORCE. AS THE ONLY DESERT STORM CARRIER HOMEPORTED ON THE WEST COAST, RANGER HEADED EAST AND WILL CROSS THE INDIAN OCEAN BEFORE ENTERING PATTAYA.
DURING THE WAR WITH IRAQ, THE RANGER AND CARRIER AIR WING TWO TEAM COMPLETED OVER 4,200 SORTIES AND DROPPED MORE THAN 4.2 MILLION POUNDS OF ORDNANCE ON ENEMY TARGETS IN IRAQ AND KUWAIT. THE 5,100 MEN EMBARKED ABOARD THE CARRIER DEPARTED SAN DIEGO DECEMBER 8 TO BEGIN RANGER'S 20TH WESTERN PACIFIC DEPLOYMENT. THE RANGER BATTLE GROUP IS UNDER THE OPERATIONAL CONTROL OF COMMANDER CARRIER GROUP SEVEN, REAR ADM R. J. ZLATOPER. RANGER IS BEING ACCOMPANIED BY FOUR SHIPS, INCLUDING USS VALLEY FORGE (CG 50) A SAN DIEGO-BASED AEGIS CRUISER; USS FRANCIS HAMMOND (FF 1067) AND USS PAUL F. FOSTER (DD 964) - A LONG BEACH-BASED FRIGATE AND DESTROYER, RESPECTIVELY, AND USS KANSAS CITY (AOR 3) - AN OAKLAND-BASED OILER. RANGER IS COMMANDED BY CAPT. E. E.

CHRISTENSEN. COMMANDER CARRIER AIR WING TWO, CAPT. JAY A. CAMPBELL, AND COMMANDER DESTROYER SQUADRON SEVEN, CAPT. G. T. FORBES, ARE ALSO EMBARKED IN RANGER.
USS NIMITZ (CVN 68) RELIEVED RANGER ON STATION IN THE ARABIAN GULF.

Black Thing's wife wrote that we should expect around 30,000 people on the North Island pier. That's all the Navy says they'll allow inside the base. Why do I expect to walk off the brow into the hands of the NIS for this fucking book? Or, if not them, then the tow yard wanting more money than my undying Toyota was worth?

What am I going to do about Sweets? Suggest he marry Dean?

0245 2 MAY 91. Cruel hoax, cruel devil. I was lying in my rack contemplating suicide again. Thailand is the place, with all its pure heroin and our CO's warnings about how easily you could die if you took any drugs. What would they say at my church? Sweet Pea would get his $100,000 as beneficiary of my SGLI (Navy life insurance policy). You weigh the pros and cons. The ultimate irony would be that I would die in Thailand, and on the date of death receive an offer from William Morris saying they love the sample and want my book. Who could I give the disks to without arousing suspicion? Who would get them to the Agency, or to my brother, without coughing them up for the NIS or CO? I can't think of anyone I can trust.

Tomorrow (this morning) is the tour I was supposed to take with Sweet Pea and Dean. I wonder if they're going. I bought the tickets and stuck them in Sweets' drawer. He'll feel guilty going if I don't go. So when Dean told him I was likely backing out, they probably both decided to shitcan it themselves. Sweets never came to my rack to speak to me. I never went there, or to his shop all day as he had duty. Dean had a great time out on the town getting that virgin boy shitfaced on Vodka with OJ. They can have fun again this morning. I don't care. I'll go check into a hotel and overdose.

Actually, I went to Pers to check fate, since I'd heard a mail call earlier. If there were nothing at all, or a normal rejection letter, it might have made all the difference. But fate complied, I got a letter from the Agency. From a Vice President, no less.

> Thank you for thinking of the William Morris Agency as a possible home for your novel, Desert Storm: The Missing Beach Diary. Unfortunately, the Agency does not have software in the Wordstar 4.0 format. Please feel free to send us another query, outline and sample chapters of your novel in hard copy (paper). We will then review your query and promptly respond to your novel.

Up to the word *unfortunately*, I could have been reading in my sleep. I've seen so many of those. But this was a crazy carrot on the stick, just enough of a tease to make me want to die in Hong Kong or P.I. or any place but Thailand right now. My life may still matter to someone, to an Agency who could turn my world around so I feel back on top. Hope.

You can't blame the people to whom your life doesn't matter. But it sounds like placing blame when you cry about them not caring. Take Sweet Pea. I wanted to record a few songs for him to get across how I feel.

"Naw, if it's gonna be that acid rock Bob Dylan hippy type of music I don't want to hear it." From a kid who likes Metallica.

"Van Morrison."

"Naw, save your tape. I've heard Van Morrison. I wasn't too impressed."

How do you get anything across to a guy who doesn't even want to hear it? All the negatives come rushing by. "You don't need to be buyin' me gold necklaces" in Abu Dhabi. "You don't need my home phone number."

"So, when you get out of the Navy, that's it then?"

"No, you just don't need it yet." And now, "save your tape." Along with getting ditched at Pattaya Beach.

I can't see talking to the kid again. I can't see walking back into the little V-3 Supply shop with my tail between my legs. What would I do, apologize for getting ditched? Or apologize for being sad and upset because after half a day's planning and frantic negotiating to arrange for simultaneous departure they fucked it up and left me behind? He chose Dean over me, didn't bother to assert the fact that he was waiting on me, didn't bother to assert the need to have me wait in their coop that one time, didn't bother to call me when they went rushing to the hangar, decided it was more important to get off ahead of a dozen others than go with me at all. How can I ever face him again, knowing so clearly how I don't fit in his bracket? Where did I go wrong? Why don't I play with kids my own age?

I laid in bed all day and prayed to have a heart attack. And it occurred to me that I'd be dead until I stank and nobody would notice, no one would come by my rack wanting me. Unless they wanted some work out of me. To get in Pers and check the mail. To type up a liberty card or a new ID.

Now, like a rock, I won't be ready to go if Sweets and Dean do come in here looking for me. So I plan to be gone, to disappear at the time they would come. Maybe I'll go sit on the flight deck and watch the sun come up. Let Dean have Sweets all to himself. I know that's how he wants it. And I don't blame him. I hate it, but I don't blame him. And I hate Sweets for wanting to be with Dean more than me. But I love him just the same, and hate myself for that. I just need to figure out how to last the next five weeks back to San Diego without seeing either of them again in this God damned small metal town. It's a challenge, but it can be done. After that I'll be back at Miramar, off the boat, and they can forget about Bob.

Meanwhile, instead of the tour, I guess I'll go see if I can mail off the query letter, outline and sample chapters I printed tonight. If I can find a civilian post office somewhere in Pattaya. Then get fucked up at the squadron party at Grace's, on Beach Road from noon to six.

This will be the closest I ever came to spending the night in a hotel with Sweets. I guess it's lucky for him, but I'll never know. Anyway, Dean would have been in the middle, straight as an arrow.

Chapter Nineteen

2220 3 MAY 91. The Al Ain City Tour Bus Ride From Hell this was not. Pattaya Beach, Thailand. Famous home of hookers, even an old man and a young boy can be seen, without being mugged. First night on *Ranger*, scenes of heads in sinks, water thrown on faces, drunks shaking hands. Words heard in the berthing: "Man, I got so fuckin' trashed, it's incredible."

"You goin' back out there?"

"Yeah. Yeah, I'm goin' back out there."

Our new PNSN reported that he was butt naked in a live sex show being sucked, butt reamed and fucked until his dick went limp. "No good," the girls were slapping it. He got booed offstage. The *Ranger* photographer happened to be at that club, taking pictures for the *Cruisebook*.

A married sailor was in a room with a broken rubber, hoping he hadn't received the gift that keeps on giving. He was fucking a heroin addict bitch who did it up her nose, then bought Dristan to clean her sinuses.

I took a ride through an emotional galaxy with Sweets. He was on the Billy end of Sagittarius (remember Billy was the first cut), and me on the front, 14 December and 25 November, respectively. Two of us connecting has never amounted to less than asking for trouble, but it's always been beautiful trouble.

After pouting and praying to die, for the first night fiasco, laying in my rack one entire liberty day and night, vowing never to speak to him again, I broke down at 0500 and taped a note to the inside of his rack while he lay sleeping: *Get me if you go. I'll be in my shop. I Got up at 0530. Bob*.

He showed up.

"I believe I owe you an apology," he said. He tried to sort of explain, but knew it was late. "Did you go out yesterday?"

"I laid in my rack with a broken heart and cried all day and night."

"Ah, Jees. I'm sorry."

I appreciated it, but still had enough chest pain to kill a less healthy man. I have prayed to die before. And as I keep reverting to that solution, God takes me serious. So he's working on it. Watch me croak right after my book comes out. If so, let the epitaph read, "be careful what you pray for." Because for one thing, you don't get that wish on the spot. Secondly, if things work out and you change your mind, like Sweets coming around and us going out together after all, the chest pains still eventually arrive--possibly just as you're really having fun. And there's only so much wishy washiness your body can take when it comes to praying for death. I'm getting too old for these moments of passionate, unrequited adolescent love.

Toon was the tour guide's name.

"Looney Toon," Sweets said.

Singha Beer was still the rage, but didn't taste as good after Sweets told me he couldn't stand it. I had one on the bus. Funny how tastes change over two deployments. "Sweets, you rarely drink, and you don't smoke, but you claim no religious background. I find that hard to believe."

He just puffed out his bottom lip and nodded, looking ahead in the window seat.

This is summer. They have three seasons, *Hot, Hotter, Hottest*. Average afternoon temp was 101 Fahrenheit. Fifty-five million people in Thailand, ten million in Bangkok, all of whom were out driving as we took our bus there. They're raising coconut palms and mangoes now.

Sweets wore his hot pink HOT TUNA teezeshirt for me, with a black swimsuit that had a Morango logo in rainbow colors, and his white double-bill hat and Oakley shades on a burgundy rope. His shirt had a fish being eaten by another fish imprinted over the left breast, and Toon handed out yellow fish to pin on our shirts for the tour.

"There's something fishy about your shirt," I said.

We had won ton at the Windsor, steamed miniature corn on miniature corn cobs, live Thai tunes with too much echo, muddled and monotonous. I imagined the lyrics decrying the current political climate, praising renegades and lamenting AIDS statistics. However, I had no idea what she was singing.

"Poor Dean," Sweets raved. "He doesn't know what he's missing. Best meal all 'Pac, opposite of that bus ride from hell."

A Thai guy sings, "What A Wonderful World" and suddenly I know I'm sitting just off the borders of Laos and Cambodia, and Vietnam and the reality of twenty years ago.

Putt Putts are called Took Tooks. Thailand has a miniature version of the Philippine's Jeepney, a small foreign flatbed pickup with a low roof, bleacher seats and no tailgate. It, motorcycles, or anything else that sound like a 2-stroke engine is called a Took Took. But Sweets kept calling 'm Putt Putts.

We ended up in that hotel room after all, just me and my baby. We checked into a room on the fourth floor, same deck as the pool, and swam for a while as some fat Europeans looked on. We wrestled in the shallow water.

"You bald headed old man are you ready to give up?"

I pulled his legs out and pushed his chest under.

We had only brought swim suits and tee-shirts. It was so hot, the evening breeze dried them quickly. But I took mine to the sink and rinsed out the chlorine, and took a shower, then put them back on. He was still laying by the pool as I brought out a soda and sat down quietly beside him. I was there gazing for a while before he saw me.

"I thought you were gonna take a shower."

"I did."

Being with Sweets is like wearing a ring. There isn't much you can do besides admire him and watch others gaze at his beauty. It's rich, but you can't eat it.

The evening slipped away down the Lethe. The Lethe is a river of forgetfulness out of English literature, where the farther you go the more you forget. Much as I wanted it to last, my dream of how that night might have been stole away under his self-control.

"You've got your bed and I've got mine, right?"

"Right." My feet were sticking across the narrow void and I had them pinned under his mattress. I wanted to jump across and pull his sheets down, rip off his chlorinated swim trunks and lick, kiss, touch and rub every molecule of his body. But that was a "no no." So I laid in the blue velvet light of our one night in Bangkok and watched him sleeping, listened to him breathing, and wished that each moist breath could have blown from his nostrils onto my cheek.

In the morning I sat at the foot of his bed. "You're a king. You know that? The boy king. I'll call you King Tut in my book."

He smiled.

"I should have given you a back massage for an hour. I would have." I laid my hands on his feet for a moment. Then I got off the bed and left the boy alone.

We had watched a live sex show that night, and throughout the scene our knees had melted together. How I had tried to keep that heated feeling alive as our driver took us back to the Ariston. But it slipped away, elusive, until finally touching his body seemed inappropriately intrusive; the twist of a Sagittarian riddle. I didn't even want to stare, for fear that I might intimidate my king.

The thing to remember is that with Sweet Pea, everyone falls under his spell. At the hotel buffet lunch even the gay waiters were talking about his ass. I could see them pointing and making diving motions behind him, as he bent over the table in front of them. I never mentioned it. But I've never been with him in public where people didn't turn their heads. Old queens were blowing fuses on Beach Road last night.

We shopped at a floating market on the second day of our thirty dollar tour package, via some long skinny inboard, far up some river in Bangkok. A bus took us to the river, and as he nodded of in the window seat I pined about our culture to myself. In another time and place he could have leaned on my shoulder and slept. Nobody would have noticed. Here, now, in the Navy, from the USA, he got a stiff neck alone.

When we stopped at the River City floating market, I bartered for a folding wall fan, 500 baht. Naturally, I heard later that other guys got fans for 300 baht. But I got a $65 pure Thai silk shirt down to $50. That was a grand accomplishment.

"If you happy. I not happy but if you happy, fitty dollar."

"I'm happy." And I was until I walked back out to our boat, number eleven, and it was no longer there. Suddenly, I was the only American, the only English speaking person, in a crowd of short, slant-eyed people trying to figure out that I was left behind on a tour. Try missing a boat in Bangkok sometime, on some back river neighborhood pier.

Fortunately, some guy took me by an arm, led me to a building where another guy dialed a number and without hearing a word of English, within ten minutes I had Toon on the phone. "Just go with th' man there, he'll take you where you need to go. We be waiting for you here, only 17 minute up river."

The dude took my arm again and walked me to a water taxi, spoke Thai, and motioned me to get in. The driver spoke Thai and everyone looked at me and laughed with pity. So I laughed. Twenty minutes later I was sitting by Sweets in a snake pit watching a Cobra spit.

"You made it! God damn, Graham. It could only happen to you."

"Were you worried?"

"Nah. The guy said is anybody missing? Then he described this bald white man with a hat and a red shirt, and then he said no problem, you'd just get on the next water taxi and they'd bring you right here."

"Well, it was a cool opportunity to ride a gondola with a Harley motor."

I guess if this were a screenplay, the 80 percent mark would have been hit at that hotel. Separate beds, a heartbeat apart, keeping that way and breaking the cycle that I should have broken at his age, when I slept with the fag who had picked me up in Rochester New York. Somehow back then I couldn't sleep knowing that fellow wanted me. I got my ass licked and with his head down there he told me I was beautiful. I barely had a hairy chest then, and in my rock climbing prime I had the belly of a rock. And I had hair. But this was a one-eighty. I was the old man, Sweets was the boy and he wasn't going for me going down on him. I didn't offer, but that I would blame on the Navy. An outright solicitation of a fellow servicemember anywhere is worthy of a Big Chicken Dinner, or at least a General Discharge. You're out of a job.

We visited the Temple of Dawn (aka, Temple of Doom) after the snake show. Sweets hiked up some steps that were steep enough that you could have used some rope and pitons. He left his camera with me, and if I had not been self-conscious about balding I would not have dropped the thing. A breeze came up and ripped my hat away so that I lunged for it, only half wanting the hat but more immediately freaking out like a bitch losing a bikini in a big ocean wave. My bald sweaty head might glare and blind somebody. It might attract attention. I scrambled. The camera fell out of my hands and down my leg as I tried to break its fall with my foot. Just then, naturally, Sweets posed.

I got the camera back as people laughed and walked by. I took the shot and he climbed back down wearing some wry grin. "If that camera's broken...." I couldn't hear the rest of whatever he said. I was too busy subconsciously berating myself. But it was okay, barely scratched.

"You're lucky, Graham."

He kept ragging on me until I ragged back until he suddenly came out with, "you're just like a bitch."

The heat was getting us. "Well, I can see why you don't have a girlfriend."

"What's that supposed to mean?"

"Well, you rag, rag and then you yell real loud so everyone can hear." I sensed my reminder of the yelling in his shop, not to touch him every two minutes. He yelled so goddam loud I thought I might have been kicked out of the Navy then, if some chief or zero came in and said what's the trouble.

Somehow we both made it through all that, and it was not our fate to break apart. If I climbed up his back like a monkey it had the effect of repulsing him after so many minutes. But watching the dude stick his dick in the bitch's cunt, five feet in front of us on rum and coke, he'd melted knees with me. But on the hotel beds it was yours and mine. In the pool it was "don't fuck with me, Graham" but only in the deep water. In the shallow water we had fun. And on the bus again going back to Pattaya, I swore never to touch him again. I tried to not even look at him. My heart couldn't take such a fucking tease.

We grabbed a speedboat back to *Ranger* and he picked up his receipts, then got another back to the beach to get some film he'd had developed by a place next to SabaiLand Massage Parlor. Of course, he'd never gone in.

"Let me take you into SabaiLand. I want to get you sucked and fucked and licked and massaged."

"No, Graham. You go in. I'll wait."

There was no point. I wonder if he's asexual, doesn't really have a cock (I've never seen it but there seems to be some bulge down there he rubs from time to time). Or is afraid of sex because he never had a dad.

One more thing, what I bought. Two tee-shirts with "Pattaya Beach" lettering. The silk shirt. Another gold chain while we stopped at a gem manufacturing plant on the last leg of that tour. And a blue sapphire with real diamonds in 14 carat gold ring, for what I do not know. Because it was there, for $475. And a gold chain for $125. No, none of it's for Sweet Pea. I know better. But I did get him a pair of hot pink shorts, and he accepted them.

One major accomplishment in Bangkok. We took a taxi all the way to the central post office and I mailed out ninety pages of this fucking story to William Morris. The stamps took up half the top of the envelope. Soon as I got done licking, Sweets showed me a sponge.

"Thanks for coming with me."

"Well, I could just imagine you getting out here all by yourself and getting lost and forgetting the name of the hotel and never making your way back." I don't know. Maybe the kid does feel something for me.

0845 5 MAY 91. Cinco de Mayo, haulin' ass for Hong Kong. Chest pain all last night like a motherfucker. End of the novel, end of my life? I'm not really worried, but I updated my SGLI last night in case. Sweet Pea gets it all, $100,000 if I croak while I'm still in the fucking Navy.

Imagine him with a hundred kay. People wouldn't believe he was once a low elevator boy on *Ranger*, vicariously admired and loved by some baldhead old fag hiding out in the Navy, stumbling stunned upon his looks. Well, they might. Depending if it says more about him or that crazy old dude. Or if they stumble too.

SAILORS DENY THEY PLOTTED TO SABOTAGE SHIP
The Associated Press
OLONGAPO, Philippines - Two U.S. sailors accused of plotting to sabotage their ship to aid Iraq during the Persian Gulf war claimed yesterday that they were being unjustly court-martialed because they were Muslims.

Airman Apprentice Abdul H. Shaheed, 22, of St. George, S.C., and Seaman Apprentice James L. Moss, 21, of Columbus, Ohio, accused a fellow crewman on the USS Ranger of fabricating the story of the plot.

The two were ordered Friday to stand trial for alleged offenses committed Jan. 17 aboard the Ranger in the Persian Gulf. The trial date has not yet been set.

I remember one letter to the XO Suggestion Board around then, a self-proclaimed Muslim feeling trapped, asking to be transferred or separated because of his religion. I recall a distinct feeling that someone should debate him at the fantail. And XO's response, *Ranger* is a warship, vice a democracy. Which is ironic, when you consider, America requires a military dictatorship to ensure her democracy.

I have a towel between me and my pillow to soak up the sweat. It's hard keeping track of the days. The hours are fairly easy with the ship's bells, except you can lose track of whether it's four in the morning or afternoon.

I finally picked up Dylan's Greatest Hits, in Thailand. How could I leave Mission Beach and go all 'Pac without Dylan? I tried telling Sweets about the master.

"My English teacher tried to tell me the same thing."

He's lost in youth for a while yet, sublimating those feelings of a kid who breaks from his father. Since he had none. Immersing himself in the new music of the 1990's, forget the past vague traces of skipping reels of rhyme, a ragged clown behind, I wouldn't pay it any mind, it's just a shadow you're seeing that he's chasing. In the jingle jangle morning he'll come following. Calling me up at my Bel Aire mansion like I did Roscoe, (213) 825-LOVE, Mister Brown's Residence, no I'm sorry Mister Brown isn't home. Is busy. Is out now. Hey, Mister Tamborine Man, play a song for me!

I had to send Lisa a self addressed stamped envelope just to find out what the hell was going on back in the states, with her typing job and the first two hundred pages of *The Missing Beach Diary*.

(1) Did it get so weird you couldn't finish it? No.
(2) Did it get too boring? No.
(3) Are you too busy? Yes, but things are slowing down.
(4) More money? I don't know where we stand.
(5) Do you want to return it as is? No.
(6) Did ya lose it? No.
(7) Did the Naval Investigative Service visit? Shit! Not yet!
(8) Are you receiving my letters? (I stopped in case of #7.) Yes, but you have the wrong zip code.

She also mentioned that they got a copy "of something from someone that did a deposition for you." That must be Lucille and the transcript. A Hollywood story if ever. First degree murder, a dying gangster boy seven blocks from Hollywood and Vine. Seven men thanked me for killing him. He was seventeen, going on eighteen, in 18th Street gang, the largest in Los Angeles through that decade. And terrorized the apartment complex. I stood trial all year, '84 to '85. A stress that took my mother's life, ushered her into her grave on Mother's Day, curse on her boy's life.

Say I live another thirty years, on Mother's Day what would I think of, how would I feel? I got over December 21st's, Billy's birthday. And I think I'll be all right with December 14th's, after Sweets. That jury's still out. But Mother's Day will always include bitter vodka recollections of Tony's tough, young ass, naked, wasted on his drunken, no spring bed in a Hollywood sprayed aerosol night, taut cuffs, a preconceiving system, corrupt trustees, jail crappers and unforgettable county overalls promising this uniformed present.

I joined the Navy to get the stench of prison blues out of my system. And to get away from Amy, and to keep out of Hollywood for a couple of years. So God gave me this fucking war to get my mind off of everything. Am I healed? I had my chance. War on Saddam, war on PNC, war on all Navy dickheads, war on my chain of command.

0845 6 MAY 91. The aft mess suddenly had royal blue table cloths, men in brand new dungarees and pressed Supply Department tee-shirts serving ice by the scoop, plenty of Frosted Flakes and other delights handy, and a deck that shined like a mirror. You guessed it, they're being inspected today. They will make the inspectors believe this is a normal routine, like tour guides in a communist country.

Tonight by 2300 tours have to be purchased for Hong Kong. A few require passports. If less than 10 sign up, the tour will be canceled. I feel like something exotic. I have duty on day one, none after that for the entire stay. I think we're here five days.

I copied the ship's Plan Of the Day with tour information and took it to V-3 Supply.

"Don't come near me, I'm sick. Don't visit me today, please just go away."

"Oh no."

"I've already thrown up once."

I couldn't argue. I smelled it. He looked miserable there in his broiling shop, in a white cotton jersey and greens. I explained the cut-off as he nodded vaguely, then left the POD pages with him.

"If you get better and decide on any tour, just get two tickets and I'll go with you. Whichever one you pick."

He nodded again, weakly. I slid a hand down lightly on his shoulderblades, and slipped away, looking back. He was staring at nothing on his desktop as I closed the bulky metal door.

What if he were dying? All alone in that shop, nobody would know. It could be heat stroke, or heat exhaustion. He looked cold and clammy, which is that? I should have told him to be sure and drink lots of water. What if it's a build-up of stress from having me follow him around on the mess deck yesterday at breakfast? What if he's embarrassed about people seeing this old baldhead trailing two steps behind everywhere he goes like a loyal puppy? What if he dies before I do? That would ruin everything.

He's probably suffering from thermal contrast--going from a cool berthing to a hot passageway, back to the cool berthing and then to his sweat shop. Or maybe wind chill, from the vent by his bed, or the fans in his shop blowing in his face to keep him cool. Whatever it is, God grant me the power in that touch between his shoulders to seep into his nervy spine and create healing. Let him be healed now in the name of Jesus. Amen.

I go through two towels sleeping. One becomes soaked with my sweat until I have to change it out at about 1400. The pillow is nothing but a wet sponge I have to turn to find a dry spot. If I ever open a health spa or sauna, I'll call it the South China Sea.

0830 7 MAY 91. "*The smoking lamp is out between frames two nine and five nine second deck and below while handling ordnance.*"

Scrapper gave me the lowdown on his DEA Thailand adventure. He was screened out by the NIS to pose as a sailor and buy drugs from European locals. "He looks like a drug dealer," in the Ready Room the CO recommended him. A great reference.

"I told 'em I wasn't gonna bust any of my shipmates, or any of my friends. They said I wouldn't have to. I told 'em if it turned out that way I'd walk out."

He busted a couple of dealers, one for a quarter pound of Thai stick that was laced with a finger's worth of heroin. They offered him a job if he ever came back to Thailand. And while they were on the street, the DEA agent whispered, "just between you and me, you really seem to have this street lingo down--have you ever done any drugs?"

"Like I'm gonna help him get his quota."

The ship begins to vibrate as we pick up knots. We'll be into flight ops shortly. Probably catching a mail COD. Just had a major lube oil leak in the number one main machinery room, this was not a drill. They set security around the problem and evacuated nearby spaces to the hangar deck. I suppose it could have become a major fire and disaster. But they had it isolated and secured within fifteen minutes.

Somebody handed me a formal evaluation sheet. I had never seen this exact form before, so I gave it a quick read:

> Under the Freedom of Information Act, and the Federal Privacy Act of 1974, I understand that my work performance is being evaluated. I have the right to explain and copy any documentation. I have the right to review and discuss differences in order to resolve them and I have the right to request amendment to and/or modification of any documentation.
>
> Name: ______________________________ Date: __________
>
> KNOWLEDGE:
> __ The son-of-a-bitch really knows his shit!
> __ Knows just enough to be dangerous.
> __ Only half a brain and is dangerous.
> __ Fucking brain dead. Coffee cup has higher IQ.

ACCURACY:	_ Does excellent work if not preoccupied with pussy. _ Pretty good only occasionally blows it out his ass. _ Has to take off shoes to count higher than ten. _ Couldn't count his balls and get the same number twice.
ATTITUDE:	_ Extremely cooperative (kisses ass frequently). _ Brown noser in poor standing. _ Often pisses off co-workers, thinks it's his job. _ Doesn't give a shit, never did, never will.
RELIABILITY:	_ Really a dependable little cocksucker. _ Can rely on him at evaluation time. _ Can rely on him to be the first one out the fucking door. _ Totally, fucking worthless.
APPEARANCE:	_ Extremely neat, even combs pubic hair. _ Looks great at evaluation time. _ Dirty, filthy, smelly son-of-a-bitch. _ Flies leave fresh dog shit to follow him!
PERFORMANCE:	_ Goes like son-of-a-bitch, if there's money in it. _ Does okay around evaluation time. _ Works only if kicked in the ass every two minutes. _ Couldn't do less work if he was in a coma.
LEADERSHIP:	_ Carries a chain saw and gets good results. _ Occasionally gets told to get fucked. _ Mother Theresa tells him to get fucked. _ Couldn't lead a pack of hungry wolves to meat.

I understand that I have been evaluated and know my rights under the privacy act of 1974 and further acknowledge that I am as fucked up as a football bat and will attempt to correct the deficiencies.

Signature: ______________________ Date: __________

There's something about the fact that Sweets doesn't like Bob Dylan that made me put on "The End Of the Innocence" instead. Now I'm back, shifting gears in that Geo Metro with sailboats piercing a deep blue sky over Mission Beach, on acid with a gorgeous blinding sunset and the roller coaster and saloons, with Greg pouring a Brave Bull for me behind the bar at Johnny's Surf Club. I know I'll play this over and over this morning.

I burned him out in Thailand, hogged his attention, rubbed up against him once too often. On the bus all he had to do was graze my ribs with his long skinny fingers and in half a minute I had to hide a hard-on, a challenge in UDTs. He had tied the Buddha lucky charm around my wrist only after I had insisted and accused him of worrying what strangers might think, and he'd said he knew I would cry if he didn't. He had finally asked me who I would be hanging out with if not him. I'd said basically nobody. "I'm very choosy about who I spend time with," I'd said. But it didn't jibe with telling him nobody would have found me if I died in my rack on the *Ranger*.

I figured out a plan for Hong Kong. I have duty on day one, he has it day two. I would fuck away day two entertaining him, maybe taking a half-day tour. Then we'd go out the morning of day three, book a hotel for two nights (I'd pay the $66 per night), go on the Aberdeen At Night tour (I'd pay the $45 per ticket) with drinks on the harbor cruise, and spend day four in Kowloon, stopping at the China Fleet Club on the way back to CV by God 61.

I went by V-3 Supply and found it chained. I went to the mess deck and found him walking around half asleep, still looking weak, hunting a clean bowl and spoon for his Fruit Loops. He saw me, and gave some vague recognition that I interpreted as less than raging enthusiasm. I took a self-esteem nosedive and reasoned I was the last man he wanted to see, which he confirmed by sitting with three guys he didn't know, leaving no room for me. I had already eaten. I was planning to have a glass of juice and talk with him. That out the window, I sat nearby with my back turned until he got up and passed me. He glanced back with a look that didn't quite say "glad to see you." I followed at a distance, watched him dump his wares and head up the ladder instead of the escalator. The direction he took, and the fact that he never looked back again (much less waited for me), turned me back to my rack. Was it astrological, or was it personal? Is he wondering why, after seeing him, I didn't show up in his shop? I doubt it. This was the time to make plans if we would.

I planned to coax him for two more nights in a hotel, even with Dean if necessary, based on the theory of therapy. His kingly nature was teaching me, I could spend a night alone in a hotel with a beautiful boy, and not suck his dick. Not even embrace. Maybe he was healing me as a man. Oh, na na.

I called out to the coop cleaner and invited him on the trip instead. I guess I've accomplished ruling Sweets out of Hong Kong. It'll show him I'm mature, independent, have other friends, and can withstand letting go. It'll show me I'm a stupid fool who just blew the last best chance at being with him I may ever have, since I won't see him once we're home. This is the end. Westpac. Indian Ocean. Arabian Gulf. South China Sea. This is the end of the innocence.

1230 8 MAY 91. Day One duty, best kind if you gotta have it. Only I just got off night check and should have been in the rack at 0700. I'm in my what the hell mood again. Cashed a $300 check last night and $300 this morning--you can only cash $300 per day onboard CV by God 61, at least at my rank. I bought a duty day-off from YN3 Black Thing for the Philippines, for fifty bucks, so I'll be duty free there unless I'm fucked over somehow, and I'm duty free in Hawaii so far. Since I already gave him $50 for what would have been my second duty day in Hong Kong, today is my last duty day of my last deployment, hurrah! No wonder I'm celebrating. I turned $500 into Hong Kong dollars at a rate of HK $7.80 to US $1.00. I think I'll buy a suit. But right now I've got thousands of (Hong Kong) dollars in my wallet.

The Eaton Hotel in Kowloon, by the "Golden Mile" of fascinating street markets, has 21 stories with a four-story glass atrium lobby and a landscaped forecourt and glass bubble elevators. They have 358 rooms, each with a mini bar. And every bed comes covered with a cosy feather duvet and has a convenient bed-side control panel. I can't wait to find out what a duvet is. I wonder if you can use it to tickle the human body. They even have secretarial, fax and translation services. The brochure at the table in the hangar bay was enough in to sucker me. For a US Military discount (double occupancy) of $65 a night, I booked two. All I need now is a lover, I mean, a friend to spend the night with me. I would die for Sweets obviously, but I'll probably end up with Matt from First LT in whom I have no bizarre interest, but who's fun. He and I got tickets for the Aberdeen Night Cruise, with harbor view, floating restaurant and harbor cruise on a modernized Chinese junk with unlimited drinks. I will probably chainsmoke and drink and talk about Sweets and wonder where he went and what he did in Hong Kong. However, I didn't plan anything for tomorrow, his duty day, in case I have the balls to brainwash, cajole, flatter, arm twist, bribe, hound, plead, persuade or somehow convince that little darling doll-faced dude to catch a cab to Kowloon with yours truly, dear sweet bald-headed old Bob.

The lucky Buddha fell off my wrist this morning. I was in Maintenance Control printing messages, since all three of our printers in Admin and Pers were down (and doubtless will be for the remainder of cruise). My wrist caught something and it came untied. I still have it, the rainbow threads laying in front of me with the Buddha medallion. But there's no one to tie it on again.

I put it in my little treasure box from the floating market, a purple and gold flowered, black painted box made of bamboo with a lid that sits loosely on top. Inside are my Abu Dhabi 22 carat bright gold chain, the 18 carat Thai gold chain, the 14 carat gold ring with real diamonds and a Siam blue sapphire, and my collection from last cruise, six jewels bought off the beach from a Burmese boy who claimed he stole them from his father's jewelry shop as they fled from Burma. A giant "ruby," two smaller rubies around three carats each, a blue sapphire about the same weight, a light blue stone I don't know the name of, and a five carat zirconium diamond. All waiting to be appraised and set, if they're worth anything. Of these last loose rocks I paid $60, but the boy wanted to trade them originally for my camcorder. So I don't know who got the better deal. Something tells me not all of them are real. But until they get appraised, I guess they're priceless. Anyway they look like a treasure chest in my little black box, and that makes me happy. For right now, I'll put my Buddha charm in there beside them.

Check this out. I'm looking at a map of Hong Kong and a section of information. The word for the all-important dollar is man. Which is a corruption of the English word for "money." To ask how much something costs, you say gay daw cheen? or gay man? Just like the Tenderloin in San Francisco. I can imagine walking around the street scenes getting discounts by repeating, gay man? gay man? What friendly people!

Speaking of San Francisco, I also picked up my ticket, round trip unfortunately, from San Diego to go home on leave. I got fucked by my boss again, he's keeping me around to help set up the shop when we get back. So I can't leave until June 13. I'll stop in LA for a couple of days to see drummer Dave. Then go home to Concord and Walnut Creek, not actually San Francisco. (I just let the Navy believe I live in the city so they can fuck with me.) I'll see my cousin and see my church, try to catch Dwayne and see Mike and Lisa and pick up the first part of the *Missing Beach Diary*, hoping she's got it typed, and pick up my transcript from the murder trial, what a nightmare; then fly back on good old US Air and hope nothing falls off the plane and none of the luggage guys are upset. And have six months left in the US Navy, if you please buy my book.

"Do you think you'll really get published?" Sweets asked me in Bangkok. It was like that time he asked, "so, when are you gonna grow some hair?"

"I think I have a good chance," I said. About the book I mean.

2200 9 MAY 91. I went down to the sacred V-3 Supply store, where I'd heard the music years before.... Sweets was wiping down the bulkheads, about to paint. I thanked God that the door was open and walked in hoping he wouldn't be too busy to see me.

"Doing some painting to keep yourself busy, eh?"

"More like because the chief wants it done."

He was up on the desk and I had to stare past his round ass in tight new dungarees just to see his face. Helluv distracting.

"I got a hotel over in Kowloon for two nights, the tenth and eleventh. And I have a tour for the night of the eleventh, with Matthew, remember from the time in Abu Dhabi? I'm hoping you'll go with us on the tour and stay with me in the hotel. Do you still have that third tour ticket that Dean didn't use?"

"No, like an idiot I didn't keep it. I didn't think about it being refundable. I'll get you the thirty dollars back."

"That's all right. How about, give me the thirty dollars and I'll add fifteen and get you a ticket for the Aberdeen by night tour so you can come with me and Matt?"

"Well, okay. But it can't be for tomorrow because I'm going out with the guys from V-3. And I don't know what we're gonna do or how long we're gonna be out there, so I'll probably sleep in after I get back. I'll probably sleep in until noon. Where is this hotel, in Kowloon?"

"I'll just come get you. Sleep in until I come and wake you up. Then we'll go shopping and take the cruise and end up in the hotel. So, not tomorrow but the next night, you're mine."

"Yes."

I can't reconcile the love I feel coming from him in our handshakes and the fright I sense when it comes to other kinds of touching. How can so much warmth freeze off at the wrist?

I left him to paint and went out to the bars with YN3 Black Thing in downtown Hong Kong. Like last time, the Suzy Wong district was full of Filipinas. April was a beauty so I bought her a fucking drink for $120HK. I got the address of her agency, and her phone number. She was Sweet Pea's age.

"What time will you call me tomorrow?"

"I'm not promising. I'll have to think."

She was five days new on a contract with the Mamasan for six months, then back to study in Manila to become a secretary.

"You'll escort a lot of men by then," I said. I told YN3 it was too bad she was a bar-girl or I'd marry her and take her home.

I keep drawing some parallel as I think of how it is in the states, where a woman might come join you and you'd buy her a drink and eventually go fuck her in a fling over two or three days. Is somebody offering the Dale Carnegie school of sexual solicitation to these girls? A friend of YN3 in the bar told us a $3000HK escort (translate, bar fine) won't give you a blow job.

They don't use the term Bar Fine in Hong Kong. But if I haven't explained, or you haven't picked up on it, a bar fine is a sum paid to a mamasan or barkeep when you take the girl with you for the night. It's paid to cover money she might have otherwise made sitting with suckers. You'd pay that, plus a healthy tip, unless you were one of those cute studs the girls try to milk for a home run via the pen pal program. For those dudes, the girls might even buy them drinks. But beware, they're out to get a green card.

My chest pains have worked their way to my stomach. I've been chewing Pepto Bismo tabs all day. Maybe the pain will reach my ass right as Sweets fucks me. Just kidding; he prizes his virgin cock.

I blew money again today. The Amy syndrome: I had to spend it because I saved so much. I finally bought a 35mm still camera. I got a Nikon with a 35-300mm zoom. Auto-advance, manual rewind. The box itself shows a list price $800US, but I got it and the lens and the bounce-light strobe and ten rolls of 36 exposure Kodak color print film and a carrying case all for $450. And I bought jade. How can you go to Hong Kong and not by jade, anymore than going to Thailand and not buying a sapphire, or going to Abu Dhabi and not buying gold? I bought a beautiful jade pendant with real diamonds in gold for $500HK, or $64US. It looks extraordinary on the bright gold, 22 karat chain from Abu Dhabi. It would look gorgeous, but alas, effeminate, on Sweets' soft, slender shoulders. So perish that thought. I got another pearl drop jade pendant for $200HK. I bought a small redwood treasure chest with inlaid ivory from an antique dealer for $190HK. Divide all the HK's by 7.8 to get the US amount. Anyway, somehow I was broke before I knew it. I stashed $200US in the rack, but tomorrow I'll be in the check cashing line again, just to be sure I have plenty of money to blow on Sweets. If I can't blow him. Did I say that? I must have been joking.

As it turns out, I'm not the only one running to the crapper. Every stall with toilet paper was occupied on the port side. So I went to starboard and found every stall that wasn't occupied had a bowlful sitting in stew. Not a pretty sight. I took my time wandering back to port and found some guys smoking in the boys' room, discussing none other than *le shit*. "My asshole can only take so much, man. It hurts." He was a big guy talking. "I'm tellin' ya we need softer toilet paper on this ship. I don't know what it is, but everybody I know has been shittin' water since we pulled out of Pattaya."

Maybe it's our karma for abandoning the Kurds, who're dying of the shits in camps. Curse o' the Kurd turd. Word. Now I know why Sweets was sick.

1630 10 MAY 91. Eaton Hotel, Room 815, Kowloon. A shore patrolman gave me vague directions to the "subway," which I went on asking the Chinese people for until a woman explained it is really called MTR, for Mass Transit Rail, much like BART is Bay Area Rapid Transit in San Francisco. Nobody calls it a subway.

Why can't I remember her name? She told me twice. She wore a coarse, white knit sweater, a beige knee length skirt, and black low healed shoes. She led me from the China Fleet Club to the MTR and got off with me at Jordan Station instead of going to her own stop. She walked me out to the street and three blocks to the Eaton. She even gave me change to buy the ticket on MTR. A sales manager for a furniture store, with flexible hours, she might have had more time. But I told her I could find my own way to my room. I was determined to suffer because Sweets had stood me up.

His duty section was supposed to get off at zero seven hundred, but they decided to move the birds out of Bay Two for a reception, and held the entire section to work with the oncoming guys until 1400. That ruined his plans to go out with the boys all day, and in turn set us back for tomorrow. I have a nonrefundable Aberdeen by Night $45 tour ticket reserved for him. Oh well. I'll throw it away like the $30 Floating Market Bangkok tour. Seventy-five bucks pissed into the wind.

I went back to the landing about 1500 and waited until he arrived. He came off the ferry with a bunch of macho guys, and he wore conservative jeans and almost looked like a cowboy. I bring out his pinks. But today he was up for the blues. I asked him if I could hang out with them, even though I was lugging my overnight bag and needed to go drop it off instead.

"No, sorry." He didn't want me to mix with them. "But if we come over to Kowloon later, I'll come get you. What's the name of that hotel, Eaton?"

"Yeah, it's right on Nathan Road. Right across the street from a McDonald's, too. What about tomorrow?"

"Well, we're gonna try again tomorrow since we got screwed out of all day today."

"What about the tour?"

"I think that's gonna have to be skipped. Aren't you going with that guy Matthews from your squadron?"

"Matthew. Yeah, he's going."

"Anyway, there's always the last day."

"Or maybe in P.I.," I said, swallowing and turning. I must be driving him crazy, the bald-headed old faggot who keeps hitting on him to spend the night together.

I poured a hot bath and a Baccardi and Coke, took out a little jar of vaseline and had a wild sexual encounter with myself. After that I laid on one of the two empty beds and watched HKTV, an English language instructional show that gave me another idea for what to become when I get out. But I won't pursue it. Ever since college I've known you could take your bachelor's and go teach English in Hongkong. I didn't do it then, so why should I think about doing it now?

It's been cool and dreary around HK, but clearing up pretty good in the afternoons. Over in 81-Man, on the boat, they finally got the berthing cool, too. The minute they fixed the circulation vent, it started raining inside the berthing, I mean puddles of water in the middle of the cross passage (the aisle going across the berthing port to starboard). They stationed a guy with a mop bucket there for two days while everyone onboard passed the responsibility buck to another shop. But finally, they fixed it.

The worst problem on that piece of metal all week has been the shits, or a percolating coffee feeling in the stomach, ever since we pulled out of Pattaya. I guess the water and ice were contaminated after all.

0800 11 MAY 91. Let us go then, you and I, while the storm winds blow across the desert sky like an angrily shaken child who cried for love and met with stinging scorn. Let's wrap our tail between our legs and fix our eyes beneath the window panes where loved ones come and go talking of cartoons and card games, and the burning oil smog wraps around the houses once or twice and lightly cuddles them until they sleep.

In that sleep like death, one dream will probably come when they'll say, "my, didn't he have a bald spot in the middle of his hair, where his receding hairline fell quite off?"

Shall I dare descend the stair? Why not? They may be kind, and they may pity me. They'll say they've seen the boy in New York City encircled on the curb by an old drunk's arms.

He must have made his way back to the ship with all the guys. Now, this morning, I pray that all their plans fall through and he gets stuck alone, dumped, ditched, forgotten and suddenly lonely.

1230 11 MAY 91. Two knocks on the hotel door. In a second Sweets' bright smiling face appears in the hallway. See, he says, I told you I'd come get you.

"Oh, I got the wrong room." It was a tall black man with an arm full of McDonald's.

The Hongkong Standard features a nice photo of some aviation mechanic jogging on the flight deck of the USS *Ranger*.

The *Ranger* arrived in Hongkong on Wednesday for a five day shore recreation break. It is the last aircraft carrier to leave the Persian Gulf since war broke out on January 17.

Since its arrival, the *Ranger*'s 5,000 crew have not wasted any time sampling Hongkong's sights, shopping and nightlife, a welcome end to the tense moments of the 43 day Gulf War for the crew, who have been at sea for five months.

The *Ranger*, which was commissioned in 1957, put its impressive military might to the test in the Gulf. It was the launching base for 70 of the United State's most sophisticated aircraft, which dropped 9.4 million kilograms of bombs on Iraq and Kuwait during 2,400 sorties. Measuring about 365 meters long and 909 meters wide, the huge carrier's capabilities as a mobile war vessel leave little to the imagination. The carrier suffered its only loss on the second day of hostilities, when an A-6 Intruder and its two pilot crew went missing in action.

The *Ranger* will leave Hongkong on Monday and will have a short maintenance stop in the Philippines before returning to its San Diego base.

Hanging out alone is a thrill. George Michael begins to sound like muzak in the afternoon, never going to dance again because of the careless whisper of a good friend.

The Cannes Film Festival began yesterday. Amy has a villa there--or rather, Amy's daddy has, or had if he's died by now. I suck down a carafe of the house white wine, sweet as I imagine the nectar of Sweet Pea.

0005 12 MAY 91. There should only be a thousand natural shocks that flesh is heir to. Ain't that what Hamlet said? I am waiting in vain in Planters, the bar at the Eaton hotel. Saw my love at Fenwick Pier changing money, couldn't get him to go on the tour after all, told him I loved him and promised that if he came over he would never forget it. Did he hear me? What did it mean?

0930 13 MAY 91. East bound and down, loaded up and truckin'. Man overboard, for mustering purposes only. Helluva reason to jump ship. Here's a bad joke from Hongkong: if you put your lips together and blow to hail down a cab, and holler the Chinese name for taxi, you're literally whistlin' dik si.

1900 14 MAY 91.

Good evening, this is the Captain. It's the evening of the 14th. 175 miles East Southeast of Hongkong. Clear skies, calm seas. Preparing for the last launches and recoveries. All of us onboard. Payday tomorrow, to spend in Subic Bay.

Flag thought Battle Group ECHO did a good job representing the Navy in Hongkong. A couple of instances were a little bit ugly, and a couple of guys (from VF-1) are in the brig or on restriction. Nobody was UA, and no speedboats were chasing Ranger like we had in Pattaya. Dignitaries were duly impressed with CV 61 and gave a thumbs up, adding that we were no comparison to the MIDWAY.

Subic will be a working port, duty sections working until at least noon, with standby duty sections onboard until three. We'll tie up around zero nine hundred, brows up at Alava Pier by ten.

0805 17 MAY 91. "First call, first call to colors." They are about to raise the flag onboard *Ranger*, moored at the Alava Pier in Subic Bay, Republic of the Philippines. WHISTLE. Pause. Everyone in the vicinity, onboard or on the pier, will freeze and face the flagstaff as Old Glory rises. WHISTLE WHISTLE WHISTLE. Carry on. On the 15th we had quarters up on elevator one as we were pulling in. Whaleboats met us with brownskin girls in bathing suits flashing their tits, which made standing at attention difficult for everything but our dicks. Then came the bad news. The skipper put out that everyone would muster daily at zero seven hundred, unless they had an approved overnight liberty chit.

I went immediately to Pers and filled out my chit, the second chit related to liberty in P.I. I'd already run one for YN3 Black Thing to stand my duty on the 17th. I had no specific plans to see Ed or toy with Totoy or get a hotel or anything, but if I followed my usual MO I would end up there. But fuck if I'd pay fifty bucks to get out of duty and still have to come back to the ship each morning to muster.

"Let me see that chit the Master Chief signed," YNCS stormed in, slamming a blue vinyl award folder down on the desk.

"Why, is something wrong with it?" The last time I had run a chit for a duty swap, it had gone through the duty section leader who was in charge of the men on duty only for the day concerned; and the Command Master Chief. But now this weavehead had a burr up his ass. I guess he felt out of control of his department.

"I don't have any problem with it, but goddammit, all chits go through me." He gave it back after gathering Admin and Pers for a lecture. "I'm gonna say this once. All request chits go through me, because I have to know what's going on in here. I don't want to find out on Wednesday that Graham's on leave all week."

Naturally, PNC fucked around with my request chit for overnight liberty.

"I don't know, you may be a liberty risk." Then he went off to run an errand and left my chit unsigned. This is why people get out of the Navy. Superiors with superiority complexes, men who lord their positions over you. It amazes me how prevalent and rampant and blatant this goes on with impunity, in a volunteer service.

"Either approve it or disapprove it, but sign it," I finally went off.

"It's no good," he said. And he handed it back.

I hadn't signed it myself. So I signed it, handed it back, and the bastard finally approved it and the game was over. He was on to better things, cheating on his wife.

I walked down to the laundry truck on the pier with a buddy and dropped off a bag. A dollar a pound, they'll have it back Saturday. I haven't known what day of the week it is since I left San Diego, but I guess he means tomorrow, the 18th, since liberty expires onboard then at 2400.

We went over to a cafeteria for canadian bacon and eggs with stale toast, juice and a chocolate milk. Then out the gate after changing $100 into 2,750 pesos.

"Hey mister, I give you advice," some flip grabbed my hand. He insisted on shaking hands and took me by the arm as I tried to keep walking. My bud was across the street already. "You know, you have to be careful or you lose your wallet," so the story went about the sailor who wasn't careful and got his wallet stolen. Meanwhile, six other flips gathered around and pulled a chair up and tried to polish my tennis shoes and charge me five hundred and fifty pesos, about $20.

"Okay, we go to the police," I said. They let go.

I caught up with the AT in a shirt shack where a couple of girls were pulling his arm. They got me for two shirts.

"How much?"

"One fifty," a sweet little voice. I guess they do this until they get old enough to be bar girls.

"That's too much. How about eighty?" I'd already haggled for cheap sunglasses. Just out of the gate, a dude on shit river bridge wanted three-fifty pesos for a pair that I finally got for eighty (just over $3), which was probably still a rip.

"No, not eighty. You give me good price. Okay one hundred. Last price."

"That's still too much. How about eighty?"

"Well, since my boss is not here." She discussed it with another girl in Tagalog and finally gave in. I paid her. "How about my tip? Ten pesos."

The shirt that meant so much had a description across the front:

> WELL, HERE I AM DRUNK SICK, PISSED OFF, HUNGRY STUPID NAVY BASTARD. GOT A HANGOVER DAMN FLAT BROKE, MISSED MUSTER, NO PASS, NO PUSSY, NO FRIENDS AND FEW RELATIVES, NEED A HAIRCUT, GOT A COLD, HOMESICK AND NO FUCKING MAIL IN THREE WEEKS, INEFFICIENT POOR CHARACTER RATINGS OVERTIME IN GRADE DAMNED RATE FROZE, PAY FUCKED UP, LAUNDRY REJECTED CLOTHES, MISSED CHOW, LEAVE DISAPPROVED AND THE CHIEF WANTS TO SEE ME AFTER QUARTERS, GOT A HARD ON, GOT VD, ABOUT TO SHIT IN MY PANTS & THE HEADS ARE SECURED FOR INSPECTION & SOME SON-OF- A-BITCH SAYS SHIP OVER ... THE ADVANTAGES ... WELL KISS MY ASS.

My bud left me there to go see his virgin barfly. I took a few steps further away from the base and turned around. If I wanted to get laid it would be easy. If I wanted to have gay sex it would also be easy, probably Totoy or Edwin or what's his name, the short little skinny one who I gave my $90 sunglasses to last time. Or Eddie, who fucked me probably fifteen times all night long on last cruise, since I saw him briefly on New Years' Eve. He nearly bit off my nipples, a little too rough but it made me come like a teenager.

Sweet Pea was coming out of the pier gate as I came up. I was hoping to catch him onboard, but saw him and a couple of guys get into a taxi. That's it, I figured. But my luck changed and they got back out of the car. It was already waiting for someone else. Now they passed me and I asked if I could tag along.

"What are you doin'?"

"I was just out to breakfast and bought a couple of shirts. What are you guys up to?"

"We're goin' up to the bowling alley. There's some phones up there and these guys are gonna call home, then we'll do some bowling."

"Well, would you mind if I come with you?"

"No, I don't mind. Do you guys care if he tags along?"

Everyone was friendly. One guy teased, "no, you can't come." I whined and puffed my lip. "Oh well, I guess you can come."

"I'm happy, happy, happy," I told Sweets. "Because I got to see you."

They had one-armed bandits in the restaurant at the bowling alley and I played a little with Sweets while the other guys made their calls. He ran out of quarters pretty quickly, and I got five dollars' worth. After that I put the money in and he pulled the arm. Eventually we lost. But I turned around on my own and hit the jackpot on the quarter slot, 100 quarters. Yes! It was great hearing that bell ringing and watching that light lighting and those quarters dumping into that tray, filling it up.

"Here," I gave Sweets a handful.

"No, it's your money."

"So what, it's all winnings." I insisted and he took them. "I want you to have fun."

The other guys came back and we bowled for a while, drinking beer. Sweets had drunk two Dr. Peppers, his favorite soft drink, full of sugar that wired him up. Chasing that with beer knocked him for a loop. He would walk up with the ball and drop it at the line like some little kid. Funny thing, he was hitting strikes left and right.

He had to go back for Dean, who was on standby duty until three. We had two beers left and all of us were full.

"Just leave them," Sweets said.

"I've walked away from a lot more than that," I said. We stopped enroute to race go carts. Sweets had his camera, a gift from his grandpa, and I guess didn't want to leave it sitting while we raced. So he had it in his lap when I bumped him with my cart, which was an illegal maneuver. I didn't notice but his camera flew out of the cart, and when we finished he was extremely pissed off. The thing was broken. This was the second time I'd been involved in fucking up his camera.

We found Dean in the V-3 coop. He hadn't showered yet.

"That idiot took his camera in the go-cart and when I bumped his car it fell out and broke."

"Well, what are YOU gonna do about it?"

"I guess I'll buy him a new one."

"Just go to your coop and when we're ready we'll come get you."

"No, just forget it. You guys can go by yourself." I walked away from them, and ultimately our friendship.

Laying in my rack I smacked myself in the forehead with the butt of my fists and cried. When I finally calmed down, I took out a pen and paper and wrote Sweets a note. This was it, I couldn't take it anymore. I had to figure out a way to keep out the melodrama, and not make it mushy, but get the point across that it was over, whatever it was.

I put $110 in the envelope and said I knew a new camera wouldn't replace a Christmas gift from his grandpa, then went on about how each time I see him it seemed to cost him something. It was hard to get my meaning across without saying I was gay for him, which I was not going to put on a note on this ship. But I said if we see each other on the mess decks "let's pretend we don't know one another." And I said I had "had it with dropping by." He had a PRT this morning, so I added that when he ran, "run me out of your system. By then I won't be thinking of you anymore." The last was obviously a lie, but maybe he's young enough and naive enough and thinks I'm old enough to mean it. I'll wish he would have the need to come get me and tear it up and demand my friendship, ha hah. But I have that sick sad feeling that he's always just been nice and that he never wanted me, so I'll just keep my feelings to myself. And from now on, I'll avoid him.

Chapter Twenty

1530 19 MAY 91. Mother died on Mother's Day, 1986. This year I stayed busy dumping Sweets and getting fucked in Olongapo. "The smoking lamp is out from frames five nine to one five nine, second deck and b'low, while handling ordnance." We pulled out a couple of hours ago, headed for Hawaii to pick up the "tigers" and go home.

P.I. was our last stop across the International Dateline, the last chance at cheating on wives in time to clear the drip. But if they suck your neck you may still have the hickey. They sucked some blood out of my wallet, but I guess it wasn't too bad.

ED (nickname Jong)--tour guide to Olongapo, master of hook-ups whose slogan was, "just point and I'll get it for you." His problem was living at home too long. He needed two thousand five hundred pesos to get to Saudi Arabia, the processing fee (around $90). On top of that he wanted some kind of special gift, which he didn't get this time. But when it came time that I no longer needed pesos, he was there taking me to the gate, and I dumped my wallet on the table. "Just whatever you have left," he said. That was about ten one hundred peso notes and other bills. I pulled a US $20 out of the stack. "Yes, you can keep that."

"My tip," I said.

JOFFERY--my number one problem child. His dick was just the right size to slam without hurting, if that's a commodity across the line. His nickname was WADS, and I came to know why. Now he is 19 years old, no longer satisfied with the $90 sunglasses I gave him last cruise, although he still has them and the yellow jacket from Hong Kong. Since Jong got a promise, Wads laid in bed about to have sex with me, and grilled me on what promise had I made and wouldn't I promise to help him and his sick grandmother, too, only $100 US, if I would just promise to help him. Finally I broke the promise. I didn't have enough money left. "Okay, if you want trouble, if that's what you want," he repeated over and over in the alley by Jong's house, the last words he spoke to me.

DON DON--the dream boy this time. Let's say he was sixteen. But his balls hadn't yet descended to the sack, and he never really got hard. He was ticklish when I kissed his underarms and inner thighs. He sat in the cheap hotel and told me he hated himself, his family hated him, he raised all the pigs until they had piglets in the pigpen, and his parents never gave him any because they hated him and treated him like a maid. The owner of a gay bar in town is coaxing him to work there as a call boy, but Jong tells him no. I told him maybe work as a waiter and a teaser and a dancer. His big talent is go-go. He stood at the headboard and massaged my forehead over and over. In the night, he laid in my arms and cried silently for hours. It was wonderful to cuddle him and hold him, to feel his breath on my cheek, to tickle his ears softly and run my fingers through his thick black hair. Everyone agreed I should try to adopt him. But I knew he'd probably cost too much, one way or another, loving leather and hanging out in hotels with old men. In the end I gave him my Mission Beach black leather jacket, US$250 used, hoping he could use it in the disco, hoping his big brother wouldn't take it from him to use in Baguio when he goes to school, and hoping Wads wouldn't take it in a jealous rage.

TOTOY--Toy for short. He showed up again, has a job at a gas station now making forty cents an hour. At least its a job and it gives him prestige. Out of all the boys in Olongapo, he didn't ask me for a present this time. I guess he was too shy. But he gave me something in the short timer's room. I toyed with him and it hurt so good.

Ed set us up there to go in separately, in case any sailors in town for the last several hours might spot us. I got the room and waited, then came a knock. The boys behind the counter had come up and wanted to sell me some beer and cigarettes.

"You know you only have for short time?"

"I know. My friend is coming."

"Only 100 pesos more you can have until noon tomorrow."

"I have to leave at midnight, I have to be on the ship."

"What ship are you on?"

"*Ranger*."

"Oh, *Ranger*? Your friend, is girl, or guy?"

"It's a guy."

They ran off thrilled.

Toy showed up and we showered and toyed around, if you know what I mean. He wore two gold necklaces, and nothing more. But I refrained from chewing ass this time. In fact, I barely kissed any asshole at all this time.

After two hours another knock. I went to find the manager boy and a security cop. I thought, my god, they've called the Navy.

"You have a companion inside?"

"Yes."

"Can I talk to him first?"

Toy got dressed and told me to wait. When he came back he was relieved. "It's only Jong."

Ed Senior--drinking San Miguel on the front porch in the heat and the shade with the cat and nursing kittens, and his little girl who still wore the shirt, "GAY FREEDOM DAY 1985" which I realized must have been to benefit me. We had barbecued pork sticks and some fish they grilled, rice, several cases of beer, cousins and friends together for my farewell party.

Olongapo is going to grow in importance as Manila realizes the Navy bases are not going away, and the business community of Subic Bay is an economic force to be reckoned with throughout the Republic of the Philippines. The tourist world needs a MagSaySay Drive and Gordon Avenue with cheap sunglasses, wildly worded shirts, exotic foods, and one night stands in cheap hotels. And with its cleaner water than Pattaya Beach, you won't walk away with the runs.

Now is a good time to buy a bar. When I get out, and sell this book, I'll probably partner up with Jong and get a gay bar. You can find me in the Philippines kicking back with Ed senior, counting his wife's bowling trophies, riding around on motor trikes and jeepneys, booking worldwide escape from reality tropical tours with Jong, and helping his older brother Ronnie run for office, in support of Dick Gordon, who will likely be the mayor for a long time. And drinking mango juice in the mornings, and San Miguel beer in the hot tropical night.

0700 21 MAY 91. It's raining outside. Transitting through time zones. Zero two hundred became zero three hundred, as it will for the next six mornings. Scrapper moans. I begin to worry about my car, my sedan that will not die or leave me alone. And to hope I never hear from my liability, Louie, the Vietnam Vet who bought it without a driver license, drove it five months and let it be towed, stored, and all charges forwarded to me, The Registered Owner. And last but not least expensive, my lime green nylon swimwear sleepwear briefs bought in Hong Kong, bold move anyway, disappeared now off my rack not even in Iraq, strike reminding fear of Cruise End thieving sure to come as the curtains shipmates lost those first two nights. Time to start locking things up again.

You need to lock things up twice on cruise. When you first come aboard and nobody knows anyone, rack curtains and mattresses and pillows and anything loose of interest including the contents of your unlocked locker disappear. During cruise, with the occasional exception of a working port, nobody rips off too much and you can more or less leave things out over your rack and around your space. But as the ship steams back to the mainland, thieves know they only need stash stolen goods a short time before having the satisfaction of using them freely, or in my case wearing them proudly. Maybe if I'm lucky I'm all wrong and they'll show up, pure fucking magic. I once thought I was wrong but I was mistaken, eh.

Admin is handing out invitations, two per service member, each good for a carload admittance onto NAS North Island. Five thousand guys times two carloads. People will come from miles around to celebrate the *Ranger* heroes' homecoming. Mister President may show up. Even distant relatives and friends. One of the last poignant lines given to me by my friend Sweets, "I wouldn't be surprised if I were surprised."

1600 22 MAY 91. Living inside an old pinball machine. Two or three racks down, a shipmate's alarm clock beeps continuously. He is at the gym, I know, because a few minutes ago he woke me up with a yell from beside my rack to someone across the berthing, "Bart! Bart!! Meet ya at the gym!" Since that, it's been the constant snap and grate of the tailhook convention on the flightdeck five feet over my head, controlled crashes and last second wave-offs as afterburners roar. Not to mention the frightening vibrations of a highpower turn as they go through the launch cycle and fling birds off cats three and four, also right above me. What if one explodes?

I got a vivid picture of my brief Naval career in a dream. The *Ranger* steamed into a set of locks at twenty knots. The sides grew tight and the water dropped and we were in a dark place with yellow bulbs lighting only the industrial metal as we slid in, and the keel tracked onto some railroad that took us up, up, up. I was on the bridge as we slid into the angle toward dark sky. Now we were fully out of water, in the groove, the entire machine of our ship being pulled up over the grounds, then turning horizontally ninety degrees to transit whatever canal these locks were for. The detail of this scene enthralled me, even made my heartbeat ebb and flow, or skip. Men were operating the equipment that lifted the aircraft carrier, and the tracks moved like a bowling ball return sends the ball to one side as it comes back. Suddenly *Ranger* was high, hundreds of feet in the air, suspended on the narrowest railroad track, and I realized my life was a roller coaster in your Navy. In a moment she began to drop, dropped straight down fast, faster, and scooped into the bend where she caught gravity, then slid down a less fantastic slope where clearly men were working the braking systems all around outside, under the yellow lamps, like in a mine. The men inside all felt the G-forces, braced, and resumed when she slid into the water of her next course.

"Look at how blue that water is," PR2 said in the catwalk. I noticed but looked again. It was deep violet, almost purple. "I love the South Pacific." I love it, too. But there is something eternally unjust about transiting these waters in a war machine, restricted and confined to eking moments of sunlight like a groundhog searching for spring, a moment in the catwalk between launch cycles, then back down below to the Personnel shop for several days. Steal Beach tomorrow, I'll get a look at the water and sky. But it's not like an island without a care in the world.

This month is full of dread. Offload is the worst part of Navy life, reserved most frequently for Airedales, gypsy squadrons who live on land but work at sea. Packing everything from every shop into heavy grey, and some smaller red metal boxes called "cruise boxes." Carrying the boxes up narrow ladders with a high risk of pulling your back out or slipping on the oily steps, sweat running into your eyes and you can't wipe it away with greasy work gloves, all this at three in the morning, what's called "staging." Then will come the offload itself, June 8, precisely six months from deploying. While thousands of family members and friends greet the lucky young kids who sailed out of high school, and married men with loving wives and children greet each other, those of us who haven't got anybody meeting us get offload chores assigned, as the Navy reward system demands. Can you imagine missing your wife and kids for six months, then telling them they'll have to wait on the pier while you offload the squadron's cargo? But that's Navy life; they'll pick the single guys like me first.

All the stuff will have to be delivered to the hangar back at Miramar, and unloaded off the large white stakebed trucks, two or three of them easily. Just for VF-1. A crew of us, perhaps thirty, will take a bus up to the base and unload all of it and carry those boxes again, up the ladders to the second deck, through the spaces to their respective shops, a major pain in the ass. But, true, it will all be laced with a silver excitement, The Pack Is Back, the land is home, the day will be done and we'll be setting up rooms instead of racks, going to the store and filling individual barrack room refrigerators, walking across grass and dirt, arranging to move into apartments, going home on leave, figuring out how to drive a car safely after six months, having four or five days off even if we aren't on leave. Then getting ready to load it all back aboard in a month, for a month, for Refresher Training.

0745 23 MAY 91. What a way to end the day. We got an AMCROSS at about five thirty this morning and the guy had to catch the COD with an ATO (Air Transportation Office) showtime at six thirty. YN3 Rod woke up the skipper, picked up the message from the COMM Center and met him in the Ready Room, then went down to the first class petty officer berthing, woke up our shipmate and got him packing. He had to empty his rack since he won't be back before the Wolfpack debarks *Ranger*. What a way to wake up.

Meanwhile, I typed his funded emergency leave orders, a 3067 detaching endorsement so he could take his pay record since he's not on direct deposit and may be gone for a couple of pay days and need to be paid locally. I pulled a blank COD request and gave it to the skipper, and filled out an MTA--Military Airlift Command (MAC) Transportation Authorization. At disbursing they told me he had $29 in the ATM-At Sea, so he'd have to stop off and withdraw $25 (five dollar increments) enroute to the ATO, and DK2 (asleep already) will have to cut him a $4 check for the balance later, since the ATM will be closed out while the dude's gone. And I ran the orders up to CAG Admin for a tango (special funding) number. I broke our record--AMCROSS to showtime in sixty minutes (including 3067). The poor guy probably woke up on the catapult.

Steel Beach Picnic today. Me and my new Nikon, love to take a photograph. I might have taken Sweets' nude chest, but I wrote our epitaph instead. "Let's pretend we don't know one another." Why didn't I say, "each other?" Because "one another" is universally associated with the thought/phrase "love one another." That's why.

0730 24 MAY 91. I went up on the roof at four a.m. I stopped in the catwalk, blind in the black, moonless night. I was almost afraid to walk, afraid of missing a step or somehow, by chance or design, slipping over the side. But gradually, my pupils widened and the Milky Way evolved, and the Big Dipper appeared in the port side sky, across the looming shadow of an absolutely still flight deck. Two F-14A fighters sat on cats three and four, set at alert fifteen, the red glow faint from their cockpits. Far forward, on the deck by the island, the integrity watch patrolled with his green shrouded flashlight.

I began to pray, and felt my soul breath return from 1977. The ghosts even played as shooting stars, reminding me of that August in a cut Oklahoma field. Aunt Sissy's farm and the Second Coming. I didn't want to get involved, or cry this time, or look too close at my wretched life. But I thanked my lord for Don Don, Ed and Joffery and Toy. I asked God to watch over them in P.I., and thanked my lord for Ed senior and Jong's mother, and his brother and little sister with her Gay Freedom shirt. And asked forgiveness. And I thanked God for Sweets. "Whatever you do in your life, you'll have some joys and some disappointments," I told Don Don. "Just be proud, make sure that you can be proud of whatever you do." I got a great picture of him in his underwear, posing with a foot on the hotel toilet seat, head in a bandanna, inhaling a cigarette. Maybe the attorneys will let me put it in this book.

I saw Dean at breakfast. Just as I was lamenting my losses, he walked by. That was a test. It would've been easy to make amends with him in the middle. He either didn't see me, or read Sweets' letter. Bet on choice two. He sat down fifteen feet in front of me, but another body blocked our line of sight. As a couple of guys walked between us, I got up and exited with the flow, so unless he made a distinct effort, he wouldn't see me passing by over his shoulder. I didn't look back. Now I sit in my rack with Santana's "Spirits Dancing in The..." too loud in my ears, alone with my jade and my secrets, drowning out the roar of jets, the bos'n's whistle, and other pains.

0800 25 MAY 91. Two weeks and a wake up. Sailors have an amazing capacity for subtraction. Why count the fifteenth day to go, when all you're doing is waking up and being there? And why count today if you're off work? That's two less days than another perspective. "San Diego, hurry up goddammit." We've been steaming at around sixteen knots under our authorized SOA (speed of advancement) toward Hawaii. We cut to five knots for the steel beach picnic I slept in.

Scrapper comes by and tugs at my towel, pulls it half off my rack. "Quit fuckin' with my shit, man." I didn't see him but heard his loud, boisterous mouth blustering howdies to all his buds in the coop.

"Ooh, ahh, ooh--ahh, ooh," he walks out of the berthing. Maybe he thought I was playing with myself, but my dick's too sore.

One of the fucking officers borrowed my video of the morning of the war last night. "Huh, can I, can I huh, please, huh?" So I gave in.

"It's for the Tailhook Convention, we're trying to put together a show."

"Last cruise," I told him, "I got up on the flight deck and taped our rescue of the Vietnam refugees. And it got shown worldwide on CBS, ABC and CNN. And CNN credited Navy News This Week, and Navy News This Week credited the *Ranger*, and I didn't get any credit."

"Well, I'll make sure you get credit this time. At least, I'll make sure it goes out with your name on the credits." The refugee bit had gone out with my name attached, too.

And for the Tiger Cruise, I got a call. A Lieutenant Shaw from CVIC (basically a combat information center), who's putting together a Tiger Video, found out that I was the only member onboard who had the wherewithal and equipment to record the 1MC announcement when the CO of *Ranger* told us, Tomahawks were in the air, the execution order had been given, and at zero four hundred *Ranger* would commence air strikes on targets in Iraq and Kuwait. Whatever day that was, the sixteenth or seventeenth of January, 1991, somewhere back there in infamy. But again, my name won't be there. These things are always bigger than the enlisted man. Obviously, what is important is the drama with which the Commanding Officer enlightened his men. Not the fact that some second class petty officer recorded it for posterity. So I gave him the fucking audio tape and resigned myself to being the strong bitch behind the great man. I got some beautiful pictures of the clear blue water being polluted with splattering bags of garbage and trash, paper plates and soda cans, sinkable nonplastic, even some nonsinkable plastic. The fantail was open. I was on the flight deck snapping away, as the bags were landing and trailing away from *United States Ship Ranger.*

I had the greatest temptation last night. It would have been sweet. PNC had a stamped envelope laying on his desk. It already had the address of his wife in his handwriting. And right there in the basket was his prize photo, him and his woman from P.I. Like it was two plus two, I longed to complete the equation. Stick it in the envelope and drop it in the mail, and let the shit hit the fan when he got home. There'd have been hell to pay, probably a divorce since he's been talking about it anyway. Payback's a bitch, I thought. You son of a bitch, you fucked up my career with those 3.8 evals, you dirty rat. Now you'll get yours. But let's not and say we did. I'll save it for the movie, eh.

I've been staying at my end of the ship. Eating breakfast well before seven (Sweets always ate about seven fifteen or later), eating dinner no earlier than 1800 (he would eat no later than 1700); and using the showers down here on the ass end, enjoying the cold water as refreshment or just punishment depending on my mood, awareness or consciousness of what probably was my last chance at intimacy for my entire life. After Amy, after Sweets, all that's left is solitude or a sea of one night stands. Both of them were slow--Amy at least two years, Sweets since Westpac '89.

I could say that Amy and I had sex without intimacy, while Sweets and I had intimacy without sex. One the standard romantic level, Amy and I had intimacy and sex; it's just that I looked at boys over my shoulder and she put her hands over my eyes to keep me from looking at other girls. She couldn't fathom--and never found out--that I gave a blow job to Chris, the fifteen year old neighbor in the hot tub, while she washed the dinner dishes in her upstairs Concord apartment. Anyway, he never came; and Don Don was bored; and Joffery wanted $100 cash. All my bugle boys were flops somehow.

Amy was even with my best colossal failures. She was a virgin and I was popping her cherry on my bed upstairs directly above my mother's bed where Mom was dying on Mother's Day and I could have been sitting beside her instead reading the book of Ruth from the Old Testament about loyalty and love. I didn't even enjoy the sex, pants half on, or comprehend that Amy was giving me her virginity. She bled. I cried, "I'm so sinful." Loud enough that my brother knocked on the door.

If I could have left the boys alone, I'd have been Amy's husband today, heir apparent to a billion dollar business that deals in personnel of all things. But it would have been Amy's this, Amy's that, nothing I would call Bob's. My drama teacher advised, marry the money, it's easier than making it. Friends said, have your trips on the side. But I walked away, fended her away, gave her reasons to stop clinging to my leg. Now I'm walking away from the boys, too. Maybe I will be happier as an old, lonely man, with fewer complications. Is this anything like the life of Christopher Isherwood?

Fish out of water, fag in the Navy. Two Westpacs and a Desert Storm. Graduated college in 1981. Four years with a single job, after ten years with not a single job lasting a year. Did I get what I paid for, accomplish my goal? Six months and a wake up, once we pull in. Just enough time to strike the deal with Hollywood, eh. What would they call the movie, Man Overboard, from Sweets' point of view, have me the fag be thrown over by some tough guys in a raging storm. You know, tragic hero, gays aren't allowed to be perfect role models in American show biz. Show their good traits, but kill 'em off with a tragic flaw. Like what the hell was I doing in the Navy in the first place? Trying to prove a point? Fags should be allowed in the Navy?

I may have succeeded in proving that fags are rightly denied Naval service. I bothered Sweets. I'm pretty sure my boss resented my presence and knew my persuasion. I succeeded in showing a fag who was unhappy most of the time. Arguing, fighting, getting his ass beat, a tooth broke, fuckin' with cops, feeling awkward, hearing things behind my back like "fag alert" and "Chester." Not to mention, whatever happened to Road Runner. Remember him? He sees me occasionally on the decks but rarely says howdy, since the night we pulled out--and he didn't from my gagging throat. "It ain't right," he said, just before he came in that barracks room. Each time he sees me he probably thinks of my bald head bobbin' on his cock; it's hard to respect, easy to resent.

Look at my fucking Hollywood murder case, built around a young dude who begged a blow job. But that's another book. Give me a few years for it. I didn't keep a diary. Well, I did, but threw it in the trash at the bottom of ACME landfill in Martinez, California.

0745 26 MAY 91. Some guy pitched a bitch to the Executive Officer about the goddam shellback certificates. And you know how shit rolls, downhill. Night before last I finished all the wallet cards and told chief I'd start on the certificates the coming night.

"Don't bother," he said. They don't look good on the typewriter. Just give it to them blank. They can take it to a store outside, at Miramar. It has to be calligraphy, unless they want it to look terrible. Because it's such a nice certificate."

The last cruise we did on the computer and it still looked awful. But at least the print didn't rub off. Now all three printers are down and we're using the dot matrix from Ops. That would be nifty. Chief's an asshole, but even he isn't an idiot.

But the Pers O had to get it from XO, recall any certificates already done on the typewriter, and hold all until we (Personnel Dept) figure out how to make them perfect. Great. Is the CO gonna dip $300 out of the Optar funds, take it out of the aircraft gas, to hire a calligrapher? YN3 Black Thing did the officers' certificates for $3 apiece (I still don't know who paid him, but he got paid) and naturally, Pers O mused, thirty- five got it, what's another hundred?

"Ortiz, Graham," calling the Airframes shop.

"What is it now Graham?"

"That shellback certificate I kept hounding you to pick up, before I threw it in the trash? That you finally came and got a minute ago?"

"Yeah."

"I need it back now."

Later in the lounge, I came across the dude who bitched. We hashed it out and there was no fact I could do to confuse him with, he had his mind made up that I didn't want to do the extra work of typing them all.

"Now I've got a reputation," I told the kid who's TAD to the ice cream machine forward.

"No, you've already got a reputation," he said.

"I do? What do they say about me?" I knew my shipmates all talked about me behind my back, but what the hell, let's hear this version.

"They say you're kind of cute."

"Oh. Well, at least if they're gonna talk about me, I guess that's nice." At this point I was desperate for flattery, losing Sweets, and the P.I. fiasco. It was marvelous of 'em calling me fag, if they called me a cute fag. Especially at 34.

A farewell note in the POD:

As you depart the AOR (I don't even know what the AOR is, Area Of something) and continue your transit home let me express my sincere appreciation for the superb effort you have put forth during your deployment. Your dash across the Pacific and Indian Oceans was reminiscent of the cavalry as you arrived just in time to ensure the Arabian Gulf Battle Force was ready to perform its assigned tasks, and perform we did. You can be justifiably proud of the major role you played in crushing the forces of Iraq and liberating Kuwait. Your vigilance in ensuring the peace was maintained was a further demonstration of your commitment to the ideals we hold so dear. It was a pleasure to lead such a professional group in battle, I salute each and every one of you for your magnificent achievements - you indeed wrote history. Fair winds and following seas for your journey home. - RADM March, CTF (whatever that is) 70.

"A View From the Bridge (of USS *Ranger*)." Due to the unique circumstances of hostilities related to Operation Desert Storm, the bigoted Commanding Officer of an aircraft carrier on station in the Persian Gulf invokes the long dormant war clause penalty of death by firing squad, in a hushed up case of homosexual solicitation onboard USS *Ranger*. What high concept. Fish out of water lands on the flight deck. Show biz all over it. What a premise! All I would have needed was to lick Sweet Pea's ear. Maybe back there, in the hotel room of some foreign port, Pattaya, that night in Bangkok. He could have turned on me like that 17-year old Hollywood gangster, only instead of attacking me with a meat cleaver, butcher knife and a baseball bat, reported me to the NIS. Under the circumstances, it might have proved much cleaner, orchestrated, surgical, ultimately even more effective. MARDET could have shot me on the fantail. And buried me at sea. Dad could have ended up like Jack Lemmon in the movie "Missing" by Donald E. Stewart, whose Oscar I got to hold one day on Mulholland Drive, moving him into John Badham's old house in 1985 when I was so close, yet so far from the biz, moving furniture, breaking my back to make a living. Looking back at it this way, I should have goddamm licked his ear. It would have been worth it.

In the middle of the night I got the sudden urge to play guitar and go over "Gun Turret Two" for the talent show for the Tigers, a brilliant stunt that would be, or just to play something, maybe just the beginnings of some song for Sweets, in case I were still destined to make my mark in music, fading thought. "What kind of guitar do you want?"

"Well a few days ago you told me you didn't have any strings for your acoustic guitars. If you have strings, I would love to use an acoustic. But if you don't, and you have electrics, that would be fine."

"Well, I'll have to climb into the storeroom and see what we've got. Give me about five minutes."

"All right, I'll call you back."

Ten minutes later.

"We've got an electric."

"You have the cords?"

"Yeah everything's all set."

I walked down there, turned right at the V-3 coop and ignored the "We Like It Tight" slogan and the fact that Sweets was inside a few yards away dreaming.

"There's no cord here."

"We don't have a cord."

"I thought you told me you had everything. You said you had the cord."

"No, I mean the cord for the plug for the amplifier."

What amp wouldn't have that fucking cord, I wondered.

I carried the equipment to Pers, borrowed a cord from one of the shooters next door, set the amp on PNC's desk, found the guitar way out of tune with a B string where the high E should have been. All the strings were rusted and as I tried to bring it up a little in a half turn the B/E snapped. I put it back in the case, unplugged the amp, gave back the cord to the shooters, and took the gear back to *Ranger* Special Services. I sat it down as the three guys stopped fucking off long enough to wonder what was up.

"When you guys find time," I said in tempered breath, "you may want to clean the guitar, put some new strings on it, and take care of the fucking equipment." I didn't wait around for them to tell me I didn't have to curse at them, or give me some lame idiot excuse as to why they couldn't manage any semblance of maintenance. I just walked back to Pers and flipped on the TV with some movie about an old man and his kid, Dabney Coleman in "Short Timer." Maybe I'm just not meant to play guitar anymore. Anyway, like Matthew said, if I sang "Gun Turret Two" for the Tigers, it would be like throwing gravel down in front of myself, just before some khaki threw me to the ground.

0800 27 MAY 91. Hurry up Hawaii. I'll have seventy-five bucks in my wallet, enough for dining out with Stasny, a YN3 when he left Wolfpack two years ago for Barber's Point. I don't know what he is now, except when I called him from Hong Kong he said he was getting out in four months. Just like a YN or PN can transfer to anywhere and have a job in the Navy, administrative jobs can be found almost anywhere in the civilian world. He's got several options lined up and plans to stay in Hawaii. A lot of pretty girls there, he says. Gee. But I wonder if they're tourists, Japanese, or Samoan. The Japs bought Hawaii a long time ago, long before the Pacific Rim was a buzz word. I think Thai women are prettier in general. I never thought about comparing the boys. But the last boy I noticed in Waikiki was a blond white tourist (in a pink shirt).

I wonder if Sweets wore his hot pink Thai shorts at steel beach. I nearly ran into him last night at the Combined Federal Campaign table, where they're raffling a Harley 1200, and they were selling *Ranger* Bingo cards. He was there as I was getting Cokes from a nearby soda machine. I just looked at the vendor, stuck my money in, picked up three Cokes and split for the escalator. I doubt if he saw me and I didn't look back. I don't want to have to explain anything, compromise what I wrote to him, classify him or defy him. All I really wanna do is get on without him. Sooner or later we'd have to split anyway, and this break saves me from potential years of writing letters, persuading him to come west or move to San Francisco if I end up there, ultimately wasted efforts, unrequited. If I can get through 8 June 1991 without speaking to him again, I'll have accomplished my mission.

In fairness, I want to put down a little more about that night of my farewell. Sweets wasn't calling it quits. I was. I took the letter to his rack believing he'd gone already. But he was stowing laundry.

"You're still here. I was gonna leave you a note."

"What about?" He was either sharp or urgent, I couldn't tell. And it made a difference, but I had to give up interpreting.

"I was gonna pay you for the camera." That wasn't a complete lie, since I'd put $110 in the envelope.

"Well, I thought about it, after I cooled down a bit." His choice of words, his voice, I don't know what it was about him but I had to get out of there because I was melting and it wouldn't do. "Tomorrow we'll go to the ship's store and see what they have."

I just stood there looking at him. His naked chest. He'd put on just enough weight in the past five months, since I'd first told him he looked emaciated, so now he looked healthy. I wished I could have told him about his body. I would have explained that indeed I was fully aware of his defects, the little white scars that spotted his chest and stomach, the brown birthmark on his inner thigh, the notch in his left eyebrow that made him eternally serious, the wart or mole or bump here and there, his too long and narrow hands and feet and the poor condition of his toes that I'd noticed at the hotel. I wanted to tell him that all these things he thinks I don't notice, because he thinks I'm blindly somehow enraptured, I noticed from the beginning and loved him in spite, if not in fact because of them. He was so vulnerable, a sparkling gem shining out of those defects that couldn't be stopped. I wanted to explain that all the friends he had around him loved his looks as well as the humble attitude he'd developed around his flaws. But I kept it to myself, hardly the speech to lay out in a berthing on *Ranger*. And back at the lanes, bowling, old team against young team, I'd made a remark that he probably didn't even have hair on his balls.

"I've got hair on my balls," he defied me. "I'll show it to you."

He was just hyper enough from two Dr. Peppers, and just tipsy enough from a few Buds to be uninhibited, and at that moment I had wondered if down deep, under his iron bars, he'd wanted to be close to me. Overall, his fears may have been more of rejection than of breaking the Navy rules and "coming out" as someone coined it. And after all, my sad, fucked up letter may have confirmed his fears.

"I'd like to go out with you tonight, if you want me to come. But I don't want to be there if you don't really want me."

"I don't care if you come." He said something like that but I have too much pain blocking the view. We were standing by the door to his coop, ironically with me on the inside and him outside.

"You don't sound enthusiastic about it."

"No. Let's just start over again in the morning."

"Okay." Again I lied. Still holding the envelope, I walked back through his berthing and dropped it on his rack, shoving it slightly up under his pillow like a God damned tooth ferry. So the relationship was God damned. So what. You can't have a man and a boy together, I don't care what they say in San Francisco. You know, they joke, how do you separate the men from the boys in that city, well, with a crowbar. Heh, heh. But they do get the crowbar.

We had another AMCROSS last night, too. The guy's brother was shot in a drive by, possible brain damage. In home sweet San Diego. And there are no more CODs, so knowing he needs to be there, knowing the situation, he has to wander around the ship until he can get off at Hawaii, and hop on a jet. At least he doesn't work on the flight deck.

0500 28 MAY 91. The first one. This morning we turned the clock ahead another hour. At 2400 (tonight) clocks will retard 24 hours to conform with crossing the International Date Line, and all things past shall be forgot. 28

May is the second longest day in the cruise--the longest being 8 June. It is also probably the least hectic and most confusing, which means people have more time on their hands than any other day of the cruise, to think about what time and day it is and become more confused by the minute.

I've heard a guy, I wish I could have recorded it, last cruise, arguing up in 39-Man, he went through the entire scenario of how it was the day it was at the time it was and everybody agreed, it was crystal clear until he concluded the wrong day. Before they figure that out, ask real quick what time is it in California? That will blow their circuits.

Speaking of stunning. I was walking out of 81-Man back toward Pers, carrying three cold Cokes and a bag of popcorn. Suddenly aft coming down the passageway, no time to flinch, nowhere to run, duck and hide, it was Sweets. What the hell was he doing on the 03 level this far aft?

"Sweets."

He didn't do his old *surprise* look, cock his head or anything. For once we seemed outlaws at high noon, head to head, man to man. He kept coming, looking me over. Instantly I began to melt in some variation of methuselah's curse. I could forget if I just didn't see him. Now I was had. And with his ensuing humble vulnerability he had me good. He stopped in the light this side of a knee-knocker and leaned back against it, well grounded.

"You're growing a moustache."

"Yeah, I thought if you could do it I could do it. It looks like you shaved yours off."

"No, I haven't yet."

I had told him once before, his pencil moustache didn't make him look like a man. It made him look like a boy with a moustache. In the haze of awe, I don't remember asking him what he'd been up to, but it took that discourse.

"I've been having trouble with my 21-Day report. My chief isn't happy with me. And we had an inspection yesterday, he wasn't happy with any of us."

"Maybe he just doesn't want to be happy."

"I have to man the rails going in and out of Hawaii, and I have duty in Hawaii."

He held his arms up, stretching from some overhead pipes. If I looked in his eyes they mesmerized me. If I pulled away from his face, I could only glance as far as his baby chest beneath the white cotton jersey, or his skinny stomach under green fatigues. I wanted to seize him in my arms. And it wasn't me, goddam it. First the senior section leader walked by. He stopped and had to bullshit with me over one of the sodas, blackmailing me about the watchbill and whatever power he had. All the time he kept looking at Sweets.

"Well, let me talk with my friend. Time is precious," I said.

Soon as I got rid of that guy, another dude came passing by and had to stop and bullshit, on and on as I kept turning him off to get rid of him. Sweets doesn't realize his power to attract. We're not all faggots. He's just magnetic.

"Did you get your camera?"

"No, I, I'm just gonna get Dean's. They didn't have anything down there, and I'll get his after we pull in. He's getting a new one. I didn't need it for that much more anyway."

"I guess you got my letter."

"Yes."

"All lies. I just wanted to make a break. I didn't want to go through the next five years writing to you, begging you to come out to California. From past experience, I know how that would turn out."

"Well, who knows? When we pull in, this time, I may find some things about California that will make me change my mind and want to stay. It might not be that bad."

"I wouldn't want you to just stay in California, you know. I'd want you to stay with me."

"Well, your sodas are getting warm. And I've gotta go down and change some money. Are you gonna play at the casino?"

"Nah, I'm on nightcheck, so I've gotta get back to the shop. I could probably come down for a couple of hours, if you want to come get me after you make change. Or, that would probably be out of your way."

"No, I've gotta be in bed by eleven. You know, we lose another hour tonight. It's like almost every other night now, and these time changes are wearing me out. In the mornings I'm ragged. I'm really only going down there to get a soda and come back to my rack, because they're selling sodas for twenty-five cents."

"I wonder if you have to play, to get a soda for that price. Ev'dyting is cheap. But only if you play."

He started off, fading into the darkened ship.

"I'll probably come by, you know."

"Okay."

The slightest trace of enthusiasm leaked through those two syllables, persuading me that he really wants me to come back into his life. It's only been a week, but doors are doors. This one's kind of heavy, and I don't want to stub my toe.

Besides, he's busy with his 21-Day.

0830 28 MAY 91. "All hands are reminded to stand clear of all weatherdecks and sponsons due to high winds." The groggy OPS yeoman walked into Pers at zero two-thirty.

"Let me ask you a question," he stared at the clock. "Is it two o'clock in the morning, or afternoon?"

"Zero two thirty. We set the clocks back twenty-four hours, not twelve." At twenty-four hundred, all clocks were retarded twenty-four hours to conform with time zone Plus Twelve Yankee.

"Oh. Then, they've only flown once today?"

"They're gonna fly." AZ3 Surfbum chimed his tenor from the photocopier.

"You're right back where you started from," I said. "On the twenty-eighth."

"Thanks. I'm goin' back to bed."

Last night the Navy showed a flicker of hope, a moment of triumph, one of those rare occasions of victory that makes all the bullshit finally (if temporarily) worthwhile. One of the shooters had a Leave chit come through. All the way up his chain of command it had been disapproved. His supervisor, his branch officer, his division officer, even the Maintenance Officer. But it was approved by the XO.

"Hey Cuz, gimme five." I walked it next door to him.

"Okay," he said, bewildered. Then I showed him. "YES!!" He lit up like Sweets with a Doctor Pepper. "Thanks, Bob!" He was pumping his arm, jumping up and down with a grin you could dry fuck. (Did I say that? I know I've been at sea too long.)

"Everybody in your chain of command disapproved it," I pointed out all the X's in the "NO" boxes.

"Goddam, even the MO," he cheered. "The XO went over the MO. That NEVER happens!" Indeed, it was rare.

"Man, this gives me faith," I said. "Fuck the Navy." NC1 was sitting there and raised an eyebrow. "Fuck 'em all."

We had a whiz quiz yesterday. If your SSN ended in five or nine you got to walk down to the SMAA and pee in the bottle. I'd been sweating it since P.I., after Jong and company had me up in the cheap hotel. It wasn't worth getting out with a BCD. But whatever that was had worn off by now anyway. Still, I'd be sweating if I'd pissed for them last night.

AK3 came by to read his Leave chit. He's the emergency case waiting to get to Hawaii, a brother with brain damage from a drive by shooting.

"Can I do anything to make you feel better, a blow job maybe, or back massage?" He sat at PNC's desk. "I know, it wasn't funny." I rubbed his back. There was no one around. He's a good friend, as far as customers go in Fucktron ONE, playful and polite every time. He's Filipino, another good example. Bookish. He sat there for a time, and I buried myself in a book, *Writer's Guide to Contracts.*

As we approach Hawaii, the POD note comes out, get rid of your posters of women in less than a bikini. "Welcome back to reality," it says. And they'll probably remind us not to walk around the ship naked like some idiots do, coming and going from usually inoperative heads.

"Are you gonna hook me up, man?" Scrap was at my rack. I gave him a fuckin' counseling chit this morning at zero seven ten, late again as usual. Now he wanted me to pull it.

"I'll tell ya what, man. It's like a running joke. I chew your ass and you're on time for a day or two. By the third day, it's predictable. YN1 comes in every day right on time. Back at the beach, it ain't gonna matter if you come in at seven ten, and you can quote me on this if I start flippin' out. But here, it ain't that far to get to work."

"All right, man."

"Is PNC there yet?"

"Naw, he ain't gonna be in for another half an hour."

"Well, you better go pull that chit before he gets there. It's in his second basket." Pushed over again. The dude had the shits and I had to get him away from my rack, standing there doubling up and farting on the chair. Yuhhh.

Five minutes later he's back, flipping the curtain. Glad I wasn't about to splooge.

"Did you do this eval?"

"Yeah. What's wrong with it?" They don't ask you if you did something unless it's fucked up.

"It's a transfer, not a periodic. Can you come down and change it? The skipper's debriefing him right now and he's all pissed off and you're the expert at fixing these."

"Fuck. I'll call him." I climbed down in my other pair of plain brown swim shorts from Hongkong that haven't been stolen.

"Yeah, Graham."

"Sir, is it okay if I do that tonight?"

"What, he can't handle it?"

"Well, that's my area of expertise, otherwise he'd have to do the whole thing all over again."

"Well, the thing is, he hasn't got his copy yet. You won't forget about it will ya?"

"No sir, he's not leaving 'til Hawaii. I'll take care of it and give him his copy tonight or in the morning."

"Well, don't forget about it or I'll shoot ya, then bust ya."

"Sounds like a deal." I told Scrap to put it in my basket, and he went off smiling. Why didn't I have him do it over, just for something to do? Well, to answer my own question, the fucking printers are all down but the dot matrix, and OCR evals are enough of a nightmare already, even for me. Ugh, that fucking smell again. That boy needs to go to medical.

All right, even if I have "the persuasion" that dares not speak its name, I'm not turned on by a smelly ass. Imagine someone you love. You'd be happier changing your baby's diaper than sitting in a stall by a guy shitting *Ranger* chow. And I'm still nauseous from Scrapper's lingering ass odor. But it doesn't mean if Sweets washed himself really good I wouldn't slide my tongue in there. Does that get a point across? All great modern lovers brag, they eat butt--trade secret of Casanova, for the girl who's had everything. But, it better be clean. Given that, I can dream of my naked cock in there, tightly hugged. Every fiber embraced. Digest me.

Do you realize, if everyone were gay, there would be no earthly reason for AIDS? Think about that ironically. Red Fox said, "yuh got to wash yo' ass. Not de whole ass, the ass hole." He knew what he was joking about. Zero population growth. Abundant food for the wildlife. Established, nonfluctuating territorial boundaries. The closest thing to a military exercise would be live birth. But we'd rather put women in combat. What if in the garden, the butthole was what to fuck and the apple, a cunt? Even if it were a heterosexual thing. God created us until we fucked ourselves in the wrong hole. What a tirade, eh? What a word, tirade. A mad rampage full of wonder. Thought dreams seen. Where's the guillotine? Oh yeah, the lumberjacks are coming. I couldn't read James Joyce and here I am with stream of consciousness. All right, let me get to the thing I wanted to say today.

Sweets. I'm in love with you, you're not female. To pretend society will accept that is like proclaiming atheism, as the very proclamation presents a case for God's existence. Perhaps my pretense is agnostic--I don't know society is against me. That would be a state of grace. Or bliss, like ignorance is. Maybe they aren't against me. Maybe the reader here, you, that is, understand all this after all, have sympathy for this devil. Maybe one of you is like me. God help you. But, I still haven't said what I want to say.

"Nothing charms like hidden beauty." That's it. A quote, my own, something I never heard anybody say before, made up in the dark last night, thinking about Sweets, lovely man in a boy's body, faults and all, humble. As Dirty Harry would put it, "a man's got to know his limitations." Foxy bitches are always put down, "but she knows it." All right. Thank you. I got it off my hairy chest. Nothing charms like hidden beauty.

0130 31 MAY 91. Hawaiian Friday. Doubt if I get laid. Jimmy Buffet "Floridays" in the headphones. A note outside, "NX SECURED."

We got the ribbons for the Southwest Asia Service Medal and the National Defense Service Medal, an hour ago. I got mine. Rod got his. NC1 got his, too. But the squadron isn't handing them out yet. Benefits of rate. I work here. The SWA ribbon has a thin black vertical stripe on the each end, then a thick light "desert" brown, moving in from each end, then a thin blue, white and red set of stripes, another thick brown, then a medium thick, dark green, and another thin black stripe making the middle. The ribbon for the National Defense Service Medal is cute. Triple thick red, going a half inch in from each end, then very thin white, blue, white and red vertical stripes inside, then a quarter inch wide, bright yellow stripe in the center.

Next question, can those of us who participated in Operation Desert Shield and Operation Desert Storm wear a star in lieu of the second award? Rumor has, our skipper has it. I called ship's Pers.

"Unequivocally, no way." He deferred me to the Captain's Admin Office when I told him I wouldn't rest with that answer. "It's not that I don't believe you, or don't agree. But I need to see it in black and white."

"Yeah, the star is authorized for guys onboard when we chopped with CENTCOM." A-ha, different answer. But nobody has it in black and white. And in a few hours guys will be standing all over the flightdeck in a parade wearing the ribbon, wondering whether they are supposed to have the star. C'est Na-vie. I have to remember, this is the same military intelligence that calls taking a shit "making a head call."

Heard a guy on the messdecks cluing in a couple of newbies on a new acronym. PAPER CLIP. People Against People Ever Reenlisting, and Civilian Life Improvement Program. You wear the paper clip on your dungaree shirt collar to show your support.

"I'll tell ya another one we had on Guam," NC1 said. "You know what Guam stands for? Go U/A, man. (U/A means Unauthorized Absent, like they used to say AWOL.) Or Give Up And Masterbate."

On the head, a new scrawl. "If you need a jack off buddy, leave date/time/size of cock and how long it takes you to come. Whites only." I took out my pen and commented, "racist pig."

I never look back at *The* Missing Beach *Diary*. When I get done I'll sit down and read it, see what the editor's done, see what the cover looks like. And not believe half of what I said, not believe I could have said the other half of it.

I wonder if I resolved the issue of the *Forum* magazine which I finally took down to V-3 Supply. I set it on his desk with a deck of San Francisco playing cards and didn't see Sweets for several days. Did he get the implication?

"Oh, those were your cards? We wondered whose those were. I thought they were someone else's. I should have known, with the San Francisco pictures on them. That was your *Forum*? So, the secret is out."

I still wonder what he meant, 'the secret is out.'

Tigers come onboard today. The AMH2 in First LT says he has a scam planned. "One of the guys has a son coming. We're gonna hook him up in the berthing. After taps, when all the lights are out and he's in his rack, we're gonna all sit around in the lounge in the dark and pull our cheeks." He pulled his right cheek rapid fire, slapping it against his jaw with a slick, squishing sound quite like that of a hand sliding over the velvet head of a slick wet dick. "Then we'll say things like, 'hey, roll over.' And I'm gonna take some dirty socks and fill 'em with RTV (like Elmer's glue) and throw 'em on the floor, so he'll step on 'em."

When you don't know what to expect, Naval service members will always make it a point to have a lot of fun messing with you. Like the guy V-3 stuck on Mail Buoy watch at El four for two hours.

My plans. Get off the brow, find the nearest bar, call Bruce at Barber's Point (Naval Air Station), see if they'll let him off work (I hear he's working for some assholes, too--but he's out in four months). Then start drinking Hawaiian classics until he shows up and drags me out to dinner. I cashed another $100 check tonight dedicated to boozing, wining and dining. Pina Colladas, Mai Tais, whatever exotic fruit cocktail concoctions they can come up with. Why this sudden urge? Because it's my last touch with the tropics?

Spy comes in for his ribbons. He's about to record a brief to be aired on KRAN TV for the Tigers, sanitized out of his 167 secret intelligence briefs from the 167 missions and 167 times the *Ranger* played the William Tell

Overture in Desert Storm. "They got a tape off the 1MC of the Captain just as the storm began," he says. "And some really neat video of BDA and all the bombs in the hangar bay. Oh yeah, you're the one who recorded the 1MC aren't you?"

PNC walks in, eyelids half shut, at about 0330. "What happened, I thought you were going to secure." Rod's been gone a couple of hours.

"Yeah, I just haven't secured yet." Now I'm fucked, he'll start finding things for me to do.

"Be sure the daycheck has those plane tickets."

"Casablanca" starts in five minutes.

0745 3 JUN 91. Time to catch up. He went off on me for not copying the itineraries from the plane tickets. And for giving them their orders on the 31st. "When do they detach on their orders?"

"On the first."

"What if they get in an accident on the thirty-first, and we are responsible for processing the paperwork? We won't have anything."

This ain't P.I., I felt like saying. "Oh, yeah, gee, I fucked up." He was satisfied.

"You can start putting LCNs on the leave chits. But you have eight days," he said. Next night he came in, I hadn't done any. He didn't get mad. "A tiger sleeps in the rack above me, and his feet stink. I'm going to get lung cancer. It's worse than you hate the cigarette smoke."

I'm sure it is, chief, I felt like saying. "You should get some foot powder and spray his feet while he's sleeping."

"No, I'm going to find out who his sponsor is, and talk with him."

Tonight he came in. Or rather, found me at Ops.

"What are you doing?"

"Helping YN3 bring the printer down to Admin."

"What have you done in the office?" He led me down to Pers and started going off. "What is the purpose of all these boxes? What is the priority? And why do I have to come down and find all of your personal boxes in the shop? I want those out of here. And why did you not do what I told you, about putting the training manuals in the boxes? Instead I find all your stuff in boxes and those manuals still sitting there."

"Well, it's barely two a.m. I have all night to get them in the boxes, and we have plenty of boxes here. I don't know why you have to come down here in the middle of the night--.

"I'm a chief. This is my office. I can come down here any time I like!"

"And you start yelling at me. I'm not your whipping boy. I think you're just not happy unless you're pissed off and yelling at somebody."

"I am pissed off. I told you to pack these manuals. What have you done?"

"I've emptied all four drawers." I started slamming open the file drawers to show him. Suddenly I felt his hand coming down on my shoulder, throwing me off balance toward the metal cabinets. "Don't push me, man!" I went off.

"I didn't push you."

"Oh, yeah--and when you came at me that time I called the Ship Master-At-Arms you ran across the room and said 'what are you talking about'."

Black Thing was standing in the doorway to Admin and couldn't believe his eyes and ears. Meanwhile, the CMC was packing his shit in there and, according to YN3, keeping his head down. "Don't try to scare me," chief said.

"I'm not trying to scare you. Just don't ever push me again."

"I know that's what you think, but I wasn't trying to push you. I thought you were going to fall, the way you were pulling at the drawers you seemed off balance, and I put my hand on you to calm you down. Maybe you think that I was pushing you because that's what you have on your mind, or you're feeling guilty."

"Chief, you weren't here when Admin had their stuff all set out in here and there was no room to pack, or even breathe. Since I couldn't work in here, I went up to my rack and took care of the packing I had to do up there sooner or later anyway, and I can't leave it in the berthing so I brought those boxes down here. I'll get 'em out of the office, and I have all night to get those manuals off the cabinets."

"Well, you can imagine I was frustrated when I came in and saw those manuals that I told you to pack are not done, and I see you have five or six of your personal boxes packed. That's why I got mad, but I hate to keep having this head butting between us."

Yeah, yeah. We both calmed down and he went away. I packed up the manuals in five minutes and brought down another box of personal stuff. Then I put my six boxes in the alcove passageway coming into Pers, by the mail slots. He'll probably go off on me tonight for that, but it's all I can do for the next couple of days until we get the tri-walls that our smaller boxes are supposed to go inside.

Meanwhile, the tigers have blessed us with a sudden supply of Frosted Flakes and real bananas and fresh bread and plenty of ice and a nearly perfect world of a chow hall. Wonderful to have them aboard. NC1's son is a tiger, and naturally chief thought he had a new victim.

"That's okay, son, you can hit him. You're a civilian."

"Oh, I'm just messing around with you, you know that."

I got a big package back from William Morris, which was a bad omen. Obviously, sending material back would not accompany a letter of acceptance.

The Vice President may have read it himself, I don't know. He may have had the 90 page sample covered by a reader for fifty bucks. "The story beyond the war," he wrote, "seems strange and out of focus." He got the impression it was a story about the homosexual relationship between the narrator and Sweet Pea. I wrote back that it was the story of how the Navy prevented that. "This is not the *USS Iowa*'s story." I told him I'd give the William Morris Agency eight weeks before I call Don Stewart ("Hunt For Red October"), a friendly success story whose furniture I moved in when he bought John Badham's house up on Mulholland Drive, back in 1985 when I was working for United Van Lines as a fallback Hollywood job. Maybe my screenwriting friend will hook me up. For the next guy, I'll submit the complete manuscript so that Desert Storm (the easy story) doesn't steal attention from *The* Missing Beach *Diary* (the sensitive small story). No more nibbling.

"Well, I got a letter back from the agent in New York," I told Sweets. "They thought the story beyond the war was out of focus. I have the war story, and the deep story. But their feedback helped me understand what my story is about, and what it's not about. And I know what to write back to the agent, and I'm just gonna keep going with the story, and if they don't want it I'll try some other contacts I know in L.A."

He had tears in his eyes, I swear. In the last week they moved his desk to the main office but we were back in the supply storeroom alone, where I'd been showing him some pictures I had taken of the garbage being dumped off the fantail, beautiful clear blue water splattered and spoiled with gigantic bags of trash. I want to blow some of them up and put them in airports like another artist did with bums at LAX. Maybe sell some to Green Peace.

I wanted to stand beside him and tell him to just not move, not resist, not say or do anything. Then I'd reach around and hug him so tight, yet so gently and lovingly at once. For five seconds, like Julia Phillips and Liz Taylor in her Hollywood version of a story like this, "You'll Never Eat Lunch in This Town Again," which I picked up in Waikiki for $22. "Between five and thirty seconds," I believe she wrote. That's what I'd want from Sweets. And I swear, I think he sensed it, wanted it, hoped I would make a move. Nobody could see us. The tears welling in his eyes were begging for something. He knew I'd be off the boat on 8 June, perhaps never to see him again. This could be one of our very last moments, God damn it.

"Well, I better go get some sleep."

"Yeah, I've gotta go down to RANGERMART and get some supplies." And our love filtered down to a handshake that lingered just a bit. Embracing fingers, for godsake. It's a man's world, so be all you can be.

Chapter Twenty-One

0800 4 JUN 91. The *Top Gun Gazette* announced "four and a wake up." But us night checkers see it differently. When I go to work tonight, it will be 5 June before I get off. And I won't sleep on 7 June because, first of all, rumor has it Janet Jackson, Bob Hope and someone else, another star, are signed to appear that evening; and we'll stage all the gear from our shop in the hangar bay at 0500 on the 8th, man the rails at around 0700, and hit the pier by 0900. So for me and Black Thing it's more like two and a wake up.

The shop is a world of cruise boxes now, and what a wonderful world it is. Our long since kaput Primage printer lies in a state of bubble wrap (is Bubblewrap a trademark?) and Ordie tape. The CMC had the gall to pack his personal TV in a cruise box. Who do you suppose will carry it off the ship and load it on the truck and hike it up to his office back at Miramar? Not him. Not that or his fuck flicks, which he packed in the DK2's brand new cruisebox, which was just the size to hold military pay records for the command.

The DK2 had two boxes that were cut open, which normally doesn't but that time happened to ruin the latches, the night before we deployed, as we had to pull the pay records of the guys who missed the boat for one reason or another. So he ordered two new boxes, and I helped him lug them up to our void a few nights ago. Now the CMC has his shit in one, and the YNCS put his personal stuff in the other one at Hawaii, and flew home. Who do you think has to lug his belongings off the brow now? Not him. And now, where in the fuck are the squadron pay records gonna be during offload? This is the arrogance of hiding behind stars and khaki uniforms that kills the sense of joy for junior sailors, and makes them want to get out. Not out, the fuck out.

I went up to the head, and Rick walked in. Remember him, that other little boy who showed me his belly one time at the 03 level store where his friend whispered Chester and he ignored it. He was in civies tonight, ready for bed, tee-shirt and shorts and rubber flip flops. We talked until a moment after I realized his buddy was waiting for me to go the hell away so they could be alone, and by then they were heading back to the V-4 berthing, right by 81-Man. As we got to the door of the head, the deck was covered with water from a typical fucking leak. Without a word, Rick stretched his arms out and around my neck, and climbed up on my ass to be carried over the threshold to the passageway. Oh, what a feeling. He was so light.

"Thanks for the ride, Bob," he said in a slow, quiet drawl.

"Any time, Ricky." I turned back around. "Are you gonna live on the ship after we get back?"

"Hell no. I'll be out in El Cajon prob'ly."

"Well, I hope you'll keep in touch. You can reach me at VF-1, just call me at work at Miramar. I'll be out in six months after we get back, and I'll have an apartment, probably in San Diego or L.A., if I don't go back to San Francisco."

"I've got fire fighting school for six weeks, then I'm goin' home on leave for a month and taking HARP duty (recruiting at the local station near his home) for two weeks after that. I'm gonna stay off this pig as much as I can."

Sweets's competition. But I don't have him down as beneficiary of my SGLI. Speaking of which, I read in that *Gazette* the bold headline, "Former *Iowa* sailor sues Navy." He's suing them and NBC for libel. I love it. Ten million bucks worth. From each. For allegations of homosexual conduct involving him and the alleged perpetrator of the explosion that killed 47 sailors in April, 1989. The fucking Tiger Talent Show is tonight or tomorrow. I still wonder if I ought to sing "The Gun Turret Two," damn it to hell.

I called the Point Of Contact (POC), a Lieutenant Fudge (his real name according to their SDO), at VF-2. The coordinator of the talent show. Now he's supposed to call me back, the show is in a couple of days. Maybe on the same night with Janet and Bob, how about that of all wild dreams. Maybe I'll get discovered and this book will become the unauthorized autobiography. On the other hand, if I read him the lyrics, the POC might not let me play. The only good point in my favor is, from what I've heard anyway, they don't have many takers on the offer to perform. God, now I've got gas.

0945 6 JUN 91. The gas went away. Nobody had told me, and I found the message on my desk (the LT from VF-2 had called) sometime this morning--far too late to feel comfortable performing. Talent Show tonight, 1845. Besides, at Captain's Call last night they snuffed the rumors of Bob Hope and all that jazz. It's Monty Byron and the Do Tells, or somebody nobody's heard of. What the hell, the players wanted to come out here. The least we can do is appreciate the ones who did.

Breathe on my cheek
Tear on my arm
Wrap myself around
To bring you no harm.

I went down to that sacred store--V3 Supply. First I passed the door. He's in that other office now, and the hatch always has one dog. So I didn't know if he would be inside, but figured he was. Somehow I couldn't bust through that metal barrier. Was it the fact that he'd urged me not to visit him there, out of his fear that his chief might be in (it's the chief's office, too)? Was it Sagittarius at work? Saying what he thought he had to say knowing it was exactly the opposite from what he wanted? How do you spell Sagittarius anyway? I've been one thirty-four years and can't spell it. I've never been that superstitious. But I think I am a mystic. I just don't want to lose this one, this time, this friend, this young man's love. What do I have to sacrifice? I think I can be loyal. What about Ricky? How did I lose Amy? Wouldn't we start arguing and how long before I pissed him off or took his love for granted?

I took some magnificent photos of an unrep with the *Kansas City* from the hangar bay, which gave me an excuse to pass the door again. It was still closed. I clicked a picture of the bulkhead where Stinky had left his mark, the slogan he'd created, "We like it tight" that supposedly referred to the hangar team's pride in their ability to park a lot of jets in a little space. I went up to the V-3 coop and photographed the door sign. Reluctantly, I wandered back toward the 81-Man berthing, and stopped at Ready Room Eight to get a shot of the bulkhead paint job and the door with its slogan, "World Famous Fighting Wolfpack." Suddenly, I realized I had a strobe in my pouch, so I went back to photograph the V-3 Supply bulkhead painting one more time.

Mark was coming out.

"Is Sweets in there?"

"Yeah, he's in there." He left the door open, I went in.

He had on a green nylon foul weather jacket. Funny how it got so cold, coming home. I guess it's early summer yet, we got back just in time. But I'm pretty sure I'm going to rent in the burbs this time. I can visit the beach like the rest of the crowd.

Some guy was waiting on parts and he was helping the dude, logging out the goggles and taking the liberty card in exchange. You don't bring back the borrowed equipment, sooner or later you bring it back or you don't leave the ship after liberty call.

I finally got him to sit still long enough to steal a couple of fractions of a second of his spirit's fleshly presence on this earth and on this pig of a ship that gets raves by the San Diego press. I wanted a warm, clear day with the sun on his face, not a cold clammy morning using a strobe. But if I don't get that, at least I've got this.

I remember Billy. Years after I'd lost him, I found a color negative that I'd taken of him in his front yard wearing my shirt, his neck and half a shoulder naked. He was thirteen. White blond with mostly straight bangs that had a slight curl at the end. I took it in to a camera store and blew it up to 11" x 14". Then I framed it, stared at it, and finally tried to have sex with it. I hope it doesn't go that way with Sweets.

"What kind of job are you gonna get?" He's out in four months and now, I find, has fifty days of earned leave on the books, meaning he could disappear as soon as--the end of next month.

"I don't know. I don't have any idea."

"Work at a gas station?"

"Yeah, after I just fought a war over it."

"Maybe go back to school?"

"Yeah, definitely go back to school. But I gotta get a part time job in order to do that."

"You'll probably move back in with your parents, and they'll give you three months to get a car and an apartment. Then you won't have enough money to come back out here, you'll have your car and everything keeping you there."

"I'll come back out, if nothing else, next year to get Dean and bring his ass back. That is, if he doesn't reenlist."

Somebody called.

"I gotta go. I gotta open a sea bag locker."

We walked up the ladder to the 03 level passageway, where he would go his way and I'd go mine. "Maybe after I get my apartment, you can come over and we can talk," I said, searching deep into his eyes. He stared straight back into mine. I think I said it like you would say talk but you wouldn't mean just talk. You would clearly mean fuck if you were talking to a woman. Or if you were a woman talking to him. In our situation, it was open ended.

"So, what are you gonna do now?" He had never asked me that before. Or if he had, now I heard it for the first time.

"Why?"

"I was just wondering what you were doing next. Are you gonna go pound on the typewriter for a while?"

"I hadn't planned on it. I'll probably just go lie down. Or take a shower, then hit the rack." I knew at that moment, I wasn't "out of sight out of mind" with him. I knew it out loud, which is so different from feeling or thinking or hoping it or even knowing in your heart. For all the times I've walked away from him with a stinging in my loins, this time all was good. All was warm. The handshake was long and warm. Even the goddam shower was warm.

2300 7 JUN 91. The night before Christmas. Not exactly, but the same feeling. Little tiger kids running crazy in the hangar bay. A USO 50 year anniversary show in Bay One, featuring numerous unknowns. Who the hell is Monty Byron? A couple of singers, some jokes, a female star with big boobs. Grand finale singing "Voices That Care" with everybody they could fit on-stage. Sweets and me in the background, on the sidelines, cameras in hand (he had finally replaced the one I broke). Bay Two full of cruise boxes and gear, packed to the middle with a section for each remaining squadron. Half the air wing flew off yesterday, back to Whidby Island, Washington.

This morning at 0915 Wolfpack departed, along with VF-2 and the rest of the wing. All the tankers gave us a fly by. I was out there on the foul line in a float coat that would have killed me (a squadronmate was popping off CO_2 canisters on everybody for the hell of it, and my bladder leaked).

In the berthing all is packed, except a few procrastinates. We have reveille (how do you spell it?) at 0400, and turnover the coop at 0500. For the next five, maybe seven hours or so, we will loiter in the hangar bay in dress whites (the Crackerjack uniform), or if we're in civics, barred from the hangars, we'll loiter on the mess decks. Since I got out of offload and manning the rails, it was a toss-up. I was gonna wear civies but decided they might not let me on the bus to Miramar in them until several hours after we pull in. The word is all whites for the first two hours. Even the offload working party, if you can believe that (a fine example of fraud, waste and abuse, tax dollars at work, exploiting the public's enthusiasm and looking sharp at the expense of everyman's uniform).

The Admiral said to put in a claim if your uniform is ruined. But he didn't say to whom and when funds would reimburse the member who carries a heavy red cruise box using the strength of his thighs and gets bumped by a turned up box bottom off the greasy deck. "We'll look sharp," he said.

This evening, PNC had me carry a bag of EEBD's down to the fourth deck, that is, a thirty pound package up one deck to the 03 level to get to the down ladder, then down seven decks to Chemical Warfare Dept., only to be turned back because they "haven't been receiving those since 0700."

My feet are killing me. My right pinky is jammed at the first knuckle, right index jammed at the second knuckle. Right middle finger cut on the print. Hands dry from cleaning chemicals in the Personnel/Admin field day. I threatened to kick NC1's ass and did throw the ashtray on the deck the second time he left a smoldering cigarette in it.

"It's gonna take more than you to stop me from smokin'," he said.

"Why's that?"

He pointed to the first class crow on his uniform.

We shook hands later as I wrote it off to end of cruise tension. I apologized for going off on him. He had his son out here with him as a Tiger, and I'd survived this long with the smoke. It was just that when I was humping and huffing the smoke was more gagging than normal.

I was tired, too. I'd worked the entire night shift--not that Black Thing or I did anything, but we were up. And the fly- off this morning wasn't done before noon. I had just dropped my pants and started climbing to my rack when Black Thing walked up.

"Oh there you are. What are you doing?"

"I thought I was gonna take a nap." I was at chow with Sweet baby Sweets.

"A nap?" He was torn up laughing. "They need you in the shop now. We're startin' stagin' man."

The whole day went like that, and I damn near missed the USO show and the concurrent Ice Cream Social, since at the last minute I had to help Scrap take the TV up forward to VF-2's Ready Room. At least it's over. It's over, it's over. No more seven day weeks and twelve hour days (for at least a month). No more chiefs pulling open my rack curtains and bitching me out. No more night check with PNC dropping in unexpectedly, invariably bitching me out. No more *Ranger* chow that you can't shit for five days, then you shit twice a day for two days. No more smokey work space with no window. The end of the last extended deployment of my life, hopefully. I should never be so desperate as to hide in the Navy for that job security again. It will always be focused on young people, dogging them out for whatever they're worth, breaking them rather than bending, pleasuring the khakis and presenting them like kings. The real high khakis are gods. Enlisted are peons, serfs. Pukes. Like children to be seen and not heard. If you talk back to a tyrant in the Navy, you will suffer and lose. And tyrants are a dime a dozen. But alas, no more Sweet Pea, the most beautiful thing that has happened to me in fifteen years. A young man opened himself up enough to become confused, and to confuse me. I leave him tomorrow, take four days off, and go on leave ten days. Then he goes to sea two weeks, followed by terminal leave. We never kissed, I never told him straight forward that I loved him. I'm sad. But I never got so close as to really ruin it either, so maybe the mystery will live forever. We might have been an item, you know. That man and his sea bitch. That boy and his tagalong fag. The end of cruise is the crowbar which separated the man from the boy. And the cruise is what brought us together. If I had licked his ear, the NIS could have had a case. If I'd sucked his cock, we'd both be out of the Navy. We'll both be out within a year anyway, but now we'll be able to schmooze our way. Or at least he will--I'm bound to fuck up by January, with that son- of-a-bitch chief forever trying to bite my head off and shit down my neck. What will he do when I'm gone? God help him and the U.S. Navy.

In a few hours I'll be a hero. Thousands of women, children and men will line the pier and welcome *Ranger* back to its homeport, San Diego, America's Finest City. Sweet Pea will be, too. Nobody is waiting for me. Pea's meeting Dean's parents. What will he think of that hillbilly family? "I'd never seen a black man until I joined the Navy," Dean told me. And he explained that the Japanese were taking over West Virginia, the dying coal capitol of the USA, where seventy percent of the pupils in the state run college must now be Japanese. We beat Iraq, Japan bought us. And the world kept turning. But don't worry for me. I won't turn up missing in Mission Beach.

0830 10 JUN 91. We came around Point Loma to the shouts and whistles of thousands of women and children. The local owner of a string of topless bars had his yacht full of women out to escort *Ranger* through the channel. The pier looked like a carnival, with balloons and tents of all colors pressed among the people.

Sweets got himself assigned to operate elevator four, and stood immaculate in his dress white jumper with mickey mouse headphones, a special privilege to be out in front of the line of men who stood at parade rest lining the hangar deck. He studied that yacht through a pair of binoculars. His Filipino friend we call Rice Man brought me down from the V-3 Division office and escorted me across the line to stand near Sweets, with the privileged at the edge of the ship. I took some fine photos with my new Nikon. Maybe we'll include a few in this book.

Sweets lowered the elevator as we approached the pier, and the crowd started shouting. Finally a crane lowered the brow down onto the edge of the elevator, and I snuck down with the media. I walked up to the officer brow where the new fathers were allowed off first, and stuck my camera in the faces and caught the excitement right along with the TV cameras and press. Teenagers came home fathers. Babies got squashed between lovers, then held up and worshipped.

I ran out of film and went back aboard. It was overwhelming and hard to face the thousands held behind the chain-link fence when I knew nobody was there for me. I stumbled across Sweets who was in a slight panic, running around trying to find the binoculars which he had loaned to somebody else but belonged to a third party.

"Where are you gonna be?"

"I don't know."

That was the last time I saw him. I found my two sea bags and carried them down a stake bed truck beside the bus to Miramar. We left a minute after I got on, and twenty minutes later I was in the barracks, finding my room. I help the offload working party, even though I wasn't assigned, and drove my personal boxes down from hangar one in the duty truck. I didn't unpack. I have seven months and fifteen days left in the Navy. I'm going to Hollywood Wednesday and trying to pitch a fish out of water movie. Women are the water. I spent $150 developing my pictures, and the owner of the photolab told me I had some great shots. So I must have. I took some that rival flightdeck scenes from "Top Gun." But the ones of Sweet Pea are the best. I laid them out in piles on my real bed, and embarked on the mission of never forgetting him.